LBJ's Neglected Legacy

LBJ's Neglected Legacy

How Lyndon Johnson Reshaped
Domestic Policy and Government

EDITED BY ROBERT H. WILSON,
NORMAN J. GLICKMAN, AND
LAURENCE E. LYNN JR.

University of Texas Press ◆ *Austin*

The publication of this book was supported in part by a gift from
Lowell H. Lebermann, Jr.

Library of Congress Cataloging-in-Publication Data
LBJ's neglected legacy: how Lyndon Johnson reshaped domestic policy and
government / edited by Robert H. Wilson, Norman J. Glickman, and Laurence E.
Lynn Jr. — First edition.
    pages   cm
    Includes bibliographical references and index.
    ISBN 978-1-4773-0054-1 (cloth : alk. paper) — ISBN 978-1-4773-0253-8 (pbk. :
alk. paper) — ISBN 978-1-4773-0055-8 (library e-book) — ISBN 978-1-4773-
0056-5 (non-library e-book)
    1. United States—Politics and government—1963–1969. 2. Johnson, Lyndon B.
(Lyndon Baines), 1908–1973. 3. United States—Economic policy—1961–1971.
4. United States—Social policy. I. Wilson, Robert Hines, editor. II. Glickman,
Norman J., editor. III. Lynn, Laurence E., 1937–, editor.
    E846.H68 2015
    973.723092—dc23

        2014045432

doi:10.7560/300541

Contents

Tables

Figures

Preface

The centennial anniversary of the birth of Lyndon B. Johnson and the fiftieth anniversaries of his signal legislative achievements—the Civil Rights Act, Voting Rights Act, and Economic Opportunity Act—have combined to stimulate renewed interest in the legacies of his extraordinary and controversial presidency. During and following LBJ's years in office, significant literatures have explored the social, political, and economic consequences not only of those historic enactments but also of his strategies for the war in Vietnam. Because he was viewed as a larger-than-life political leader, much has been written as well about Lyndon Johnson the man and his consequential life and political career. But there is more to the story.

Johnson's legislative achievements reflected his ambition to transform the federal government into an institution that could fulfill the liberal promise of Franklin D. Roosevelt's New Deal, Harry S. Truman's Fair Deal, and John F. Kennedy's New Frontier. Johnson's Great Society encompassed a wide range of domestic policy initiatives, and many have been studied in depth—the Elementary and Secondary Education Act, Medicare and Medicaid, and the Community Action Program—but the longer-term impact of his presidency on American politics and governmental institutions has received less scholarly attention.

Perhaps appropriately for a president of bold political ambitions and consummate political skill, the polarized politics of the twenty-first century's second decade gave rise to the war cry of conservative critics: America's liberal government is LBJ's fault. The nation's conflicted politics coincided with scholarly interest in sober appraisals of what we term in this volume as Johnson's "neglected political and institutional legacy": the transformation of the American administrative state. The remarkable Civil Rights Symposium held at the Lyndon B. Johnson Presidential Library and Museum in

April 2014, with the participation of three former presidents and the then-sitting president, provided additional evidence of the renewed attention being given to LBJ's policies and their long-term effects.

The genesis of the present volume occurred in the fall of 2008 when the Lyndon B. Johnson School of Public Affairs at the University of Texas at Austin organized a commemoration of the centennial of LBJ's birth. That symposium assessed domestic policy legacies for contemporary public policy and administration and for the newly elected president, Barack Obama. The symposium attracted considerable attention, which inspired its organizers to identify a significant lacuna in the scholarship concerned with Lyndon Johnson's presidency and its consequences for America. Soon after LBJ left office, there appeared significant studies on many policy initiatives, a number of which have been subject to persistent analysis over the decades, such as civil rights, voting rights, and poverty. But rarely has analysis dealt with the still-unfolding consequences of the bulk of LBJ's original legislative initiatives. Moreover, no one has comprehensively analyzed the impacts of these initiatives on policy and the administrative state.

The intellectual excitement generated at the centennial symposium at the LBJ School led its organizers to enlarge the project to a volume of presidential scholarship. We commissioned thirteen papers covering some of the domestic policy areas that most concerned President Johnson, although not addressing the full range of his legislative achievement. The authors come from wide-ranging fields, including public policy and management, economics, political science, sociology, history, environmental engineering, and urban planning. We believe the result of the effort advances the understanding of an important but heretofore neglected legacy.

Norman J. Glickman, Princeton, New Jersey
Laurence E. Lynn Jr., Austin, Texas
Robert H. Wilson, Austin, Texas
May 2014

LBJ's Neglected Legacy

PART I

RECONSIDERING LBJ'S DOMESTIC POLICIES

CHAPTER 1

Understanding Lyndon Johnson's Neglected Legacies

NORMAN J. GLICKMAN, LAURENCE E. LYNN JR.,
AND ROBERT H. WILSON

As the most visible and arguably most consequential symbols of America's constitutional scheme of governance, presidents and presidencies are irresistibly attractive subjects for journalists, historians, and other students of politics. How did a president influence and shape his times? What are a president's legacies in public policies, in the institutions of governance, and in America's standing in the world? How were a president's legacies affected by presidential character, personality, and skill; by historical circumstances; by the institutions of governance themselves; and by luck?

Lyndon Johnson became president in unexpected and tragic circumstances. But he quickly took command and unveiled an extraordinarily ambitious agenda (Caro 2012; Peterson 2012). Initially, he carried forward John F. Kennedy's civil rights legislation and New Frontier initiatives, which included the Peace Corps, expanding the space program, pursuing substantial antipoverty initiatives, and increasing aid to cities (Caro 2012). After winning an overwhelming victory in the 1964 election, he used his mastery of legislative politics, revenues from a rapidly growing economy, and large Democratic majorities in both houses of Congress to win passage of a breathtaking array of domestic policies and programs.

Independent assessments of Johnson's influence on American life began to appear before he left office, in so-called first drafts of history (e.g., Amrine 1964). Over time, a growing body of research deepened and enriched the nation's understanding of Johnson's efforts to reshape America's public policy agenda. In addition, personal memoirs of administration insiders appeared (Califano 1991; Watson 2004), and other primary-source materials were discovered and evaluated as the passage of time revealed consequences that emerged only slowly. The flow of assessments included ones that were mainly synoptic,[1] and those, such as the present volume, that are more specialized and thematic.[2] In addition, assessments of Johnson's bad luck or bad judgment, especially failures that followed the 1968 Tet Offensive and, more broadly, the military consequences of the Vietnam War, began to obscure his domestic policy accomplishments (e.g., Goldman 1969; Schandler 1977; VanDeMark 1991).

The purposes, perspectives, and methods in this diverse literature vary. Early evaluations are likely to be descriptive accounts lacking the benefit of hindsight (e.g., Sidey 1968). Such snapshots might focus on results: the state of the economy, America's standing in international relations, specific legislative achievements, and domestic tranquility at the end of a presidential term. Or studies might focus on qualities of leadership and statecraft as well as skill in handling crises, the ability to shape rather than merely respond to political developments, success in defining and moving the country in new directions, and good judgment in policy making and administration.

The purpose of this volume is to reflect on the legacies of a set of domestic policies. Many of these policies represented successful efforts to build on the work of previous administrations, including some programs that had never been fully implemented or that had failed to gain political traction. Previous administrations had attempted to improve health care, build urban infrastructure, provide more housing for the poor, and improve water resources. But Johnson mobilized federal institutions and resources to an unprecedented degree in order to address what he viewed as important national priorities. Other parts of the Johnson agenda took the federal government in directions that previous administrations had pursued not at all or with only limited success, as in education and human capital development. Other policies were critical for nourishing the roots of American democracy, such as those involving voting rights, civil rights, and fair housing.

But the Johnson years were turbulent; the nation experienced urban riots and broad opposition to the Vietnam War. Pressure from minorities, especially African Americans, clashed with the views of conservatives (mostly southern Democrats), who generally opposed federal aid to minorities and the poor. Johnson had to marshal his considerable political skills in order to forge majorities in both houses of Congress for his legislative proposals. Not all his efforts succeeded. His congressional influence was diminished by the results of the 1966 midterm elections, and Johnson's power thus waned. By the end of his administration, a concerted effort to dismantle many elements of his policy agenda, especially elements of the Great Society, was already under way.

Despite the breadth of his initial legislative successes, few of his domestic policy initiatives, especially those of the Great Society, remain unchanged fifty years later. Policies and programs were modified or dropped by subsequent administrations. In some instances, rollbacks reflected the growing impact of the conservative counterrevolution that began in the 1970s and became full-blown in the Reagan era (Shulman 2007). In other arenas, the "New Federalism," which devolved federal power to the states, significantly transformed and reversed many of LBJ's initiatives that were premised on federal leadership. Still other policies have been largely sustained but remain controversial even today. Despite this mixed record and the methodological challenges of assessing legacies, the essays in this volume demonstrate how Johnson restructured the federal government in significant ways; reshaped intergovernmental relations by creating new mechanisms for coordinating and regulating policy implementation by federal, state, and local governments; extended the authority and role of the federal government into new policy arenas; and extended and redefined the federally protected rights of individuals to pursue the American dream. Analyzing these legacies is the purpose of this volume.

Analytic Approaches to Presidential Studies

Academic scholars tend to analyze presidencies by using formal analytical approaches,[3] seeking causal explanations that may focus on legal, political, psychological, or institutional aspects of a presidency. Following the example of Richard E. Neustadt's (1960) seminal treatise on presidential power, assessments of presidential success began to be defined by achievements (or failures) that were largely personal and intentional and that could be attributed to a president's individual characteristics, including personality, political skill, and leadership ability. Terry M. Moe (2009) claims that Neustadt's approach neglected the theoretically more important influence of institutions, formal structures, and power on a president's accomplishments and legacies. In presidential studies, institutionalism is concerned with the "administrative presidency" and its tools—that is, the use of appointment authority, expenditure control, oversight and review, reorganization, delegation, and advisory systems. Moe assigns credit for a subsequent transformation of the field of presidential studies to the application of rational choice theory, "which has become the dominant (but not the only) analytic approach among the cutting-edge works of greatest influence in the field" (702). Cognitive psychology is also credited with furthering the analytic and theoretical revolution.

Stephen Skowronek (2009, 801) offers another perspective on Neustadt and presidential studies: "Assessments of the president's capacity to get things done *within* the system had crowded out examination of the impact of presidential action *on* the system, that our 'system' perspectives were assuming the whole rather than examining the historical composite of institutions that make it up and considering their makeshift movements over time." "Why not," Skowronek asks, "formulate an agenda for *our* day? Why not a more fundamental reconceptualization aimed at problems and questions that no one in 1960 would have thought to ask?" (800). He cites Hugh Heclo's *On Thinking Institutionally* (2006), which "advances an entirely different thesis about how institutions matter" by highlighting "their importance in providing rules of appropriate behavior" (Skowronek 2009, 800). Thinking institutionally, in Heclo's conception, is about law and administration. It means not only knowing the rules of the game, that is, the rule of law as legality and constraint, but also respecting the game, the rule of law as a principle of responsible administration.

With regard to the above discussion as it relates to this book, decisions that might be regarded as epiphenomenal from a Neustadtian perspective (e.g., Lyndon Johnson's support for a government-wide planning and budgeting system and for program evaluation [see Seligman 1983]) might be evaluated as much more consequential from an institutional perspective (see chapters 13 and 14). The study of institutional change focuses on processes such as path dependence, incrementalism, and critical junctures in the flow of history. Presidential choices are evaluated more longitudinally, as reflecting, in effect, the inside story of institutional evolution and change.

Lyndon Johnson as Policy Maker

Identifying the legacies of Lyndon Johnson and his presidency presents numerous challenges to any analytic effort to evaluate them. The best, the worst; wisdom, foolishness; light, darkness; hope, despair: Dickensian dualities confront anyone who would assess Johnson's legacies. After a dramatic and remarkable beginning, his five-year presidency ended poorly, and many of the achievements of his domestic policy initiatives have been obscured by a preoccupation with his domineering leadership style and by the public's ultimate repudiation of "his" Vietnam War and, therefore, of him.

Rather than revisiting the familiar issues, controversies, successes, and failures of the Johnson presidency, this book focuses on an aspect that has been obscured, the "neglected legacy" of how Johnson used the unique opportunity of his presidency to reshape American governance. Some of Johnson's policies considered here, like those concerning education and health care, are well known. Others, like programs for water quality, immigration, and program evaluation, have received less attention. Through case studies of individual policies, this volume seeks to identify the enduring impacts of Johnson's policies and programs by analyzing how his choices influenced, both intentionally and otherwise, the structures, processes, and institutionalized values of American government in subsequent decades.

An institutional view of presidential legacies necessarily requires consideration of both what preceded and what followed a presidency. These elements are linked with the choices and actions of that administration, that is, with a consideration of path dependence encompassing the presidency being examined. Thus, assessments of Johnson's legacy must acknowledge the extent to which he was a legatee of Franklin D. Roosevelt and the liberal domestic policies of the New Deal (Katznelson 2013) as well as the policies of Harry S. Truman and John F. Kennedy. The Great Society, as Robert Dallek (1999) has noted, reflected Johnson's determination to finish and even to exceed the achievements of his predecessors and to become the nation's greatest progressive president. But Johnson, as will be seen in several chapters, even built on the efforts of Republican president Dwight Eisenhower in several policy areas.

Yet while Kennedy, too, might have had a noteworthy effect on domestic policy had he lived, the singular nature of Johnson's political vision and his consummate political skill created a unique legacy. Johnson changed the powers of the presidency, the priority accorded to the least advantaged, intergovernmental relations, and the management and competence of the administrative state—which, although subsequently attenuated in many ways, merits full and careful consideration. With Kennedy's predisposition for policy innovation as a model, Johnson drew policy making into the White House to a greater extent than ever before; members of the president's staff eclipsed career officials in the departments and the Bureau of the Budget (now the Office of Management and Budget) as architects of the president's legislative agenda (Milkis and Nelson 2007). Because Johnson quickly "grew impatient with the slow pace of congressional and bureaucratic politics, he used dozens of extra-governmental task forces to import new ideas into policy deliberations on his terms and schedule, override the bureaucracy, and move policymaking power inside the Executive Office of the President" (Ott and Hughes-Cromwick 1988, cited in Flanagan 2001, 604).

Composed of governmental officials and outside experts, these task forces were largely secret and thus insulated from partisan politics, the public, and Congress. This isolation ensured that the president had access to new ideas for his agenda, thus achieving a kind of balance between openness and secrecy. "In terms of political theory," wrote David Barrett (1992, 111), "Johnson had a conventional understanding of the role of the president in the 1960s: the occupant of the Oval Office had the special burden and opportunity to lead the American government toward fulfilling its missions in the world and at home."

This strategy had a downside, however. The use of sequestered task forces had the advantage of avoiding political conflict while the president deliberated on his options. One example involved the Community Action Program (CAP). Richard Flanagan (2001, 603), in studying the CAP, argues that "the Johnson White House practiced a strategy of avoidance" of entrenched interests by failing to institute a strong, well-defined administrative process at the Office of Economic Opportunity, thereby leaving it to Congress and others concerned more with the "how" than the "what" of the CAP to fill the vacuum according to their own priorities. Flanagan continues: "The lack of bargaining by the president with other actors and institutions with a stake in the process will . . . ultimately become an obstacle for the president's agenda" (604), which was the case with the many other executive office task forces.

Although he had been a public servant early in his career, Johnson approached governing not as a chief executive officer or an experienced administrator might but, rather, as a master legislator would. His political strategy was to get "laws on the books" that he hoped would ultimately, not immediately, achieve his goals. As legislator in chief, he instinctively left it to future Congresses to resolve any controversies arising from the initial authorizing legislation. Dallek (1996, 80) has written that Johnson "understood from past experience that, once a major government program had been put in place, it would be easier for supporters to modify its workings than for opponents to dismantle it" (Flanagan 2001, 605, quoting Dallek 1996, 80). Laws become a set of mandates, powers, and constraints that defined the path that subsequent legislative, regulatory, and administrative processes would tend to follow.

A president's legacy, then, may include unintended (although not always unwanted) consequences. Flanagan notes, for example, that CAP programs had the effect of drawing heretofore marginalized minority leaders into civic and political life, including into leadership roles, even though their innovative model of service provision was not successful (Flanagan 2001, 606). Gareth Davies (2002) analyzed the bilingual education program, a highly controversial initiative of uncertain pedagogical value. He argued that the creative, mutually reinforcing actions of officials at the Office for Civil Rights, Latino activists, other governmental lawyers, and federal judges, all unelected and often unobserved actors, were necessary to sustain the program. The actions of high-profile lawmakers were, he argued, relatively inconsequential, again justifying an on-the-books strategy (Davies 2002, 1426–1427). Great Society legislative mandates and structures initiated debates on a number of intergovernmental relations issues, including intergovernmental fiscal relations and social equity, the use of block grants and revenue sharing, modes of civic involvement in policy making, and the consequences of federal regulation and standard setting on federalism (Wright, Stenberg, and Cho n.d.).

The existing literature on policy making during and following the Johnson administration, as noted in these examples, informs the approach taken in this book. These analyses are largely framed by his presidency. The longer-term ramifications have been less well considered, at least by historians. Davies suggests that the period following the Johnson and Nixon presidencies is so persistently viewed as a conservative backlash against Johnson-era liberalism (and use of war powers) and Nixon-era abuses of power that one might reasonably conclude that the Johnson legacy was relatively short-lived: "With the prominent exception of Hugh Davis Graham, it is hard to think of a historian who has seriously considered the tenacity of the reform impulse during the 1970s" (Davies 2002, 1407). As this book will show, however, Johnson's "laws on the books" changed public policy agendas and administrative structures at every level of government, creating what Douglass North has termed new institutional scaffolds for subsequent developments of the American administrative state (North 1990, 10).

This book considers not only Johnson's role as a political leader and unparalleled political bargainer, but also his use of the administrative presidency as an institution through which to achieve his goals. The former emphasis is the more familiar one in the case of the Johnson presidency. The latter, however, is particularly important for gaining an accurate understanding of Johnson's longer-term legacies. Johnson's mastery of legislative politics; his singular role, based on his interpretation of the Gulf of Tonkin Resolution, as commander in chief during the Vietnam War; and his larger-than-life persona have obscured many significant institutional consequences of his presidency, particularly in domains other than foreign policy and civil rights. Relatively neglected domains of domestic policy and public management are given due attention here, illustrating the possibilities and the limits of presidential power.

Research Questions and Methods

LBJ's Neglected Legacy: Reshaping the Federal Government attempts to expand our understanding of federal domestic policy making by examining a set of strategies central to LBJ's administration. The case studies explore three sets of questions.

1. *What was the policy and institutional status quo at the time that the LBJ administration adopted a particular initiative?* What was the administration's agenda in a particular policy arena, and how was the policy problem defined and the administration's approach justified? What were the background and antecedents for the initiative? What was the political opportunity for passage of the legislation? Was passage aided by actively involved interest groups or other political forces? Did LBJ's policies represent an expansion of earlier approaches, alternatives to a previous failed policy, or an altogether new approach?

2. *What were the features of the "new status quo," that is, the changes brought about by legislation or executive action, by the conclusion of the Johnson administration?* What were the administrative or regulatory instruments adopted to implement the policy? What political compromises in policy design were needed to achieve passage, and what sorts of opposition emerged? What types of budgetary commitments and systems, including intergovernmental finance, were involved? Importantly, what were the outcomes of the policy initiative during the LBJ administration?

3. *Following the end of Johnson's administration, was the policy sustained, altered, or terminated?* Did Johnson's programs expand over time, or did they disappear or decline in importance? What sources of resistance and opposition to the policies emerged? What were the sources of support? What were the impacts of the programs? Were policy and programmatic goals achieved? In the end, what were the legacies and lessons from the LBJ policies? By tracing these policies through subsequent administrations, explanations for their institutionalization, reform, or abandonment can be determined.

Case Study Selection and Overview

The volume editors commissioned twelve case studies by distinguished scholars from several disciplines. The choice of policies provides variation along several dimensions, including the degree to which policies and implementation strategies departed from then-existing federal roles, governmental institutions, and management strategies. Several, such as civil rights, voting rights, health policy, and education policy, were chosen for their broad and well-recognized impacts on American society.

The twelve case studies, introduced below and organized in sections on defining citizenship and immigration; social policy; cities, the environment, and science; and public management, were affected by multiple pieces of federal legislation and executive actions. The chronology of these actions (see table 1.1) mirrors the earlier description of Johnson's legislative strategy: a very aggressive legislative agenda was taken in the early years of his administration, and a less substantial legislative record was evident toward the end of the administration in 1967 and 1968.

Readers may ask why an even broader range of significant LBJ domestic policies was not considered. For example, important Johnson policies addressing public safety and criminal justice, consumer rights, arts and culture, and research and development are not included in this volume. Moreover, the book addresses only a single element of the Johnson administration's environmental policy, that of water resource management.[4] Despite the extent of his agenda and the importance of these issues, resource limitations, not the least of which is the scope of material that can be addressed in a single volume, precluded the examination of additional policies. Thus, the present volume does not presume to address the entire domestic policy legacy of the Johnson administration. That said, the policies analyzed here provide sufficient breadth and variation to allow for comparing policy outcomes and the range of factors affecting them. In other words, these twelve case studies provide a rich empirical base for multi-disciplinary research questions.

In chapter 2, Robert Dallek, a prominent presidential historian, elaborates on the justification for this volume. Dallek asks: Despite an extraordinary list of accomplishments, why has Lyndon Johnson become an invisible president and faded into the background? The chapter argues that the principal answer is Vietnam. The widespread frustration and bitterness with the war during that era, including the marches in the streets and on the Pentagon, eclipsed the Great Society's many achievements. Following that period, the country passed through an extended period of conservative governance. Dallek argues that Lyndon Johnson believed that government could be the solution to social problems and that, in time, he will once again be remembered as a great president who helped humanize the American industrial system.

The three chapters in part II address a set of policies that redefined the

Table 1.1. Chronology of approved legislation and presidential actions examined in this volume

1964

Legislation
  Economic Opportunity Act
  Head Start
  Food Stamps
  Housing Act
  Civil Rights Act
  Urban Mass Transportation Act
Executive actions taken and new agencies formed
  Office of Economic Opportunity and Community Action Program
  Appointment of Special Assistant on Science in Technology
  Urban Mass Transit Authority

1965

Legislation
  Medicare and Medicaid
  Elementary and Secondary Education Act
  Immigration Reform Act
  Water Resource Planning Act
  Water Quality Act
  Voting Rights Act
  Public Works and Economic Development Act
Executive actions taken and new agencies formed
  Department of Housing and Urban Development
  Planning-Programming-Budgeting System (by executive order)
  Incorporation of formal evaluation of federal programs (1965 and 1966)

1966

Legislation
  Clean Water Restoration Act
  Model Cities

1967

Legislation
  Social Security Reform
Executive actions taken and new agencies created
  Department of Transportation (enacting legislation passed in 1966)

1968

Legislation
  Fair Housing (last element of civil rights agenda)

rights of citizens and reformed immigration. In chapter 3, Gary Orfield addresses landmark legislation on civil rights (passed in 1964) and fair housing (1968). The battle over civil rights is a long and well-studied one. Orfield analyzes the enormous political challenge of passing this legislation; public reaction to it; and the effectiveness of its implementation strategy, through the judicial system, to extend and protect rights of citizens. But Orfield finds that effectiveness in implementing and securing the end of racial discrimination in public accommodations and in housing markets differed dramatically. Social practices changed quickly in the area of public accommodations, whereas high levels of residential segregation remain in this country even though discrimination in housing markets has been illegal since the 1960s. In contrasting these outcomes, the author draws interesting observations about the strength of various legal strategies and actual social practice.

The Voting Rights Act of 1965 was one of Lyndon Johnson's most effective and far-reaching legislative accomplishments. Chapter 4, by Jorge Chapa, examines the historical precedents of the act, the circumstances under which it became law, and its successful implementation, which Johnson himself observed. Chapa writes that the law Johnson signed, with its focus on protecting the voting rights of African Americans, was broadly extended in 1975 to encompass Latinos, Asians, and Native Americans. The number of minority elected officials has increased substantially. Court decisions have expanded the scope of the law to cover all aspects of election systems, including voter qualifications, election procedures, and redistricting. The Civil Rights Division of the U.S. Department of Justice enforces the law providing a partisan advantage to the party occupying the White House. But since the early 1990s, a series of Supreme Court decisions have restricted the ways in which the law can be applied to increase the legislative representation of these minority groups.

In chapter 5, Frank D. Bean, Susan K. Brown, and Esther Castillo examine the rationale for, and the results of, immigration policy reforms adopted in 1965. Although this legislation drew relatively little attention at the time of its passage, it literally changed the complexion of the nation. It allowed substantial immigration from Asia, Latin America, and elsewhere, opening U.S. borders to immigrants previously barred. The authors assess the nature and intent of the abolition of national-origin quotas as the basis for immigrant admissions in favor of family reunification criteria, in relation to emphases and changes in foreign policy and civil rights. The unforeseen demographic and social consequences of the policy reforms transformed the United States far beyond its traditional black-white divide and created new kinds of ethno-racial diversity.

In part III, the contributors address a set of significant social policies. Elizabeth Rose's essay on Head Start (chapter 6) captures the essence of one of Johnson's most visible and lasting legacies. The research of psychologists in the 1950s and 1960s found that early intervention could improve the malleable mental abilities of young children, thus enhancing their cognitive abilities later in life. The administration regarded this program as a way to reduce poverty when the more prepared children reached adulthood. Head Start marked an innovation in the federal government's role: Washington provided funding for local school districts and became the impetus for additional programs in low-income and middle-class school districts. Although Head Start was not always successful, it has been sustained and remains popular with parents and local schools officials.

Gary Orfield's chapter 7 provides a sweeping overview of the changes set in motion by President Johnson's efforts in education. LBJ understood the importance of education in the lives of poor and minority children, and his accomplishments in this field were significant. The Elementary and Secondary School Act (1964) brought substantial funding to thousands of school districts. The Higher Education Act of 1965 (which included Pell grants for college-bound low-income students) and other important programs have had lasting effects, although succeeding presidents and the Supreme Court later tried to reverse them. Johnson's successes in civil rights significantly enhanced the scope of his education legislation. Most schools were segregated, particularly in the South, but the Civil Rights Act (1964) greatly furthered the pace of integration. Orfield also reflects on how the current trend toward resegregated public schools is undermining Johnson's goals.

The Medicare and Medicaid programs, adopted in 1965, exemplify the greatest and the worst aspects of Lyndon Johnson's leadership and legacy. Paul Starr shows in chapter 8 that Johnson was deeply involved in shaping the legislation, and his mastery of Congress was critical to its passage. There is no question that Medicare improved the lives of the elderly, particularly in their access to health care, financial security, and overall health, and that Medicaid brought medical services to many of the poor. But at the same time, these programs created severe and lasting structural problems in the delivery of health services. So eager was Johnson to gain the support of health care interest groups that the financing provisions, particularly for Medicare, sharply inflated medical costs for decades and sowed doubt that a universal program based on social-insurance principles was feasible. Because of the compromises made at its inception, Medicare did not follow Social Security's path and proved difficult to extend to other groups. Rather than becoming the foundation for a national health insurance system, Medicare has inhibited such a future and made reform extraordinarily difficult.

Cynthia Osborne (chapter 9) reflects on today's social welfare policies and the extent to which they have been influenced by LBJ's vision of a Great Society that helps "more Americans, especially young Americans, escape from squalor and misery, and unemployment rolls where other citizens help to carry them" (Johnson 1964). Johnson believed education and employment were the keys to self-sufficiency and favored a comprehensive, community-driven approach. One set of programs sought to teach job skills and provide work experience. LBJ introduced a new federal structure for fighting poverty premised on a comprehensive, coordinated approach that included efforts at the national, state, and local levels. But in subsequent reforms of the social welfare system, cash assistance became the primary form of income maintenance, or "welfare," and to an extent far greater than that anticipated in Johnson's War on Poverty. Nonetheless, as Osborne shows, subsequent policy changes have revived LBJ's emphasis on human capital investment.

In part IV, the policy focus shifts to cities, natural resources, and science and technology policy. First, Norman J. Glickman and Robert H. Wilson (chapter 10) discuss the substantial expansion of the federal government's role in urban affairs during Johnson's time in the White House. Johnson's domestic policies to reduce poverty and hunger, provide better housing, improve education and urban infrastructure, and create jobs implicitly focused on American cities. He gave the federal government a broader, more activist role in urban affairs than that of his predecessors and those who followed. His administration championed the role of community-based organizations and other nonprofit groups in designing and implementing many of his initiatives, a highly controversial strategy, although one still widely used in contemporary America. Despite the overarching successes of Johnson's legislative agenda, few of his urban initiatives were sustained after his administration. Urban policy itself disappeared from the national agenda after Ronald Reagan's election. In large measure, the nation has not valued a federal presence in urban affairs since Johnson's time.

In chapter 11, David J. Eaton argues that Lyndon Johnson believed that the United States had a "moral imperative" to clean and restore its rivers. LBJ created America's first set of national water-quality standards in 1965. The federal government chose to enforce these regulations without legal proceedings, instead providing funds to help cities build sewers and wastewater treatment plants to prevent, remove, and treat pollution; the government likewise helped the states develop water-planning and water-quality management programs. In addition, these efforts supported the training of new water-quality professionals and research on difficult water-quality problems. The national water-quality program established by the Johnson administration has thrived over the past forty-five years and improved surface-water quality. Relationships between federal agencies, states, and local governments, along with businesses, nonprofit organizations, and citizens, have remained stable over the past five decades.

Gary Chapman, in chapter 12, notes that President Lyndon Johnson is not commonly remembered for his contributions to U.S. science and technology policy. But LBJ's political career coincided with, and helped shape, the most productive era of science and technology in history. This period has become known as the "golden age" of U.S. science policy, when prominent scientists and engineers were highly regarded by the public, were supported by the government, and held policy positions of influence and prestige. Not only did LBJ preside over the development of U.S. space exploration, his administration launched the first environmental science programs, began the research that led to the Internet, and built a system of governmental cooperation and funding for research institutions that became the envy of the world. But cracks in the consensus about the prominent role of American science had already appeared midway through LBJ's presidency, largely because of the war in Vietnam, which many in the scientific community opposed. Those troubles continued after LBJ left the White House. U.S. science and technology policy has never fully recovered its former prestige.

Although President Johnson's legislative skills are the dominant focus of presidential scholars, he was very much concerned with the skill and performance of the federal government. The fifth section of the book addresses the management practices that Johnson introduced. In chapter 13, Laurence E. Lynn Jr. describes how, in August 1965, impressed by Robert S. McNamara's success with program budgeting at the Department of Defense, President Johnson mandated the adoption of a similar planning and budgeting system in all federal departments and agencies. With the costs of the Vietnam War and Great Society programs accelerating, the president's decision to maintain a firm grip on the federal budget in order to preclude tax increases was good politics. Nevertheless, LBJ's support for the Planning-Programming-Budgeting System (PPBS) as management reform was genuine. But the progress of PPBS began to falter because of what appears in retrospect to have been flawed implementation. In 1970, the Nixon administration quietly canceled the PPBS mandate. Johnson's PPBS initiative has had three positive legacies: establishing policy analysis as an important ingredient of policy making; helping institutionalize graduate education in public policy in many of the nation's leading universities; and providing significant impetus to the growth of social research and development in American universities, think tanks, and consultancies.

Peter Frumkin analyzes evaluation research, a second Johnson concern with the performance of government, in chapter 14. Today, evaluation research is a multibillion-dollar industry focused on answering some variation on a seemingly simple question: did the program work? Over the past four decades, this enormously complex question has led to the creation of a limited set of large and successful firms—and a massive array of smaller and specialized firms—that collectively employ significant numbers of trained experts who spend entire careers searching for evidence of impact and effectiveness. Frumkin sketches a brief interpretive history of the evaluation industry, tracking the emergence and expansion of the largest and most visible organizational manifestations of the drive to track effectiveness.

In the final chapter of the book, the volume editors, Glickman, Lynn, and Wilson, draw on the case studies to answer the three research questions posed above. The authors situate these findings in an institutionalist and comparative perspective in order to understand how federal programs under LBJ and the breadth of his policy agenda reshaped the federal government in ways that can be recognized today. But the elements of his agenda that have disappeared or been transformed beyond recognition bring into perspective the underlying interdependences and changes in values that have nurtured and sustained much of the LBJ agenda. To be sure, shifting national politics and the never-ending tensions between the national and state governments have narrowed the legacy. Still, as can be observed in the following chapters, LBJ's agenda, and thus his legacy, has become part of the fabric of American government.

Notes

1. See, for example, Bullion 2008; Califano 1991; Caro 1982, 1990, 2002, 2012; Dallek 1991, 1999; Dugger 1982; Goodwin 1976; Shulman 2007; Updegrove 2012; and Woods 2006.

2. See, for example, Andrew 1998; Cohen and Tucker 1994; Divine 1987; Foster 1985; Gelfand 1981; Grofman 2000; King 1993; Laney 2003; Lerner 2005; Loevy 1997; Milkis and Mileur 2005; Muslin 1991; Redford 1981, 1986; Schott 1983; Schwartz 2003; and Sowell 1984.

3. A number of works have classified and evaluated approaches to studying the presidency; see, for example, Bowles 1999; Edwards and Wayne 1983; and *Presidential Studies Quarterly* 2009.

4. Comprehensive reviews of environmental policy can be found elsewhere (Daynes and Sussman 2010; McNeill and Unger 2010).

References

Amrine, Michael. 1964. *The awesome challenge: The hundred days of Lyndon Johnson.* New York: Putnam.

Andrew, John A. 1998. *Lyndon Johnson and the Great Society.* Chicago: Dee.

Barrett, David M. 1992. Secrecy and openness in Lyndon Johnson's White House: Political style, pluralism, and the presidency. *Review of Politics* 54, no. 1: 72–111.

Bowles, Nigel. 1999. Studying the presidency. *Annual Review of Political Science* 2:1–23.

Bullion, John L. 2008. *Lyndon B. Johnson and the transformation of American politics.* New York: Pearson Longman.

Califano, Joseph A. 1991. *The triumph and tragedy of Lyndon Johnson: The White House years.* New York: Simon and Schuster.

Caro, Robert A. 1982. *The years of Lyndon Johnson: The path to power.* New York: Vintage.

———. 1990. *The Years of Lyndon Johnson: Means of ascent.* New York: Knopf.

———. 2002. *The years of Lyndon Johnson: Master of the Senate.* New York: Knopf.

———. 2012. *The years of Lyndon Johnson: The passage of power.* New York: Knopf.

Cohen, Warren L., and Nancy Bernkopf Tucker, eds. 1994. *Lyndon Johnson confronts the world: American foreign policy, 1963–1968.* Cambridge: Cambridge University Press.

Dallek, Robert. 1991. *Lone star rising: Lyndon Johnson and his times, 1908–1960.* Oxford: Oxford University Press.

———. 1996. *Hail to the chief: The making and unmaking of American presidents.* New York: Hyperion.

———. 1999. *Flawed giant: Lyndon Johnson and his times: 1961–1973.* Oxford: Oxford University Press.

Davies, Gareth. 2002. The Great Society after Johnson: The case of bilingual education. *Journal of American History* 88, no. 4: 1405–1429.

Daynes, Byron W., and Glen Sussman. 2010. *White House politics and the environment: Franklin D. Roosevelt to George W. Bush.* College Station: Texas A&M University Press.

Divine, Robert A., ed. 1981. *Exploring the Johnson years.* Austin: University of Texas Press.

———, ed. 1987. *The Johnson years.* Lawrence: University Press of Kansas.

Dugger, Ronnie. 1982. *The politician: The life and times of Lyndon Johnson.* La Vergne, Tenn.: Lightning Source.

Edwards, George C., and Stephen J. Wayne, eds. 1983. *Studying the presidency.* Knoxville: University of Tennessee Press.

Flanagan, Richard M. 2001. Lyndon Johnson, community action, and management of the administrative state. *Presidential Studies Quarterly* 31, no. 4: 585–608.

Foster, Lorn S., ed. 1985. *The Voting Rights Act: Consequences and implications.* New York: Praeger.

Gelfand, Mark I. 1981. The War on Poverty. In Divine, *Exploring the Johnson years,* 126–154.

Goldman, Eric. 1969. *The tragedy of Lyndon Johnson.* New York: Knopf.

Goodwin, Doris Kearns. 1976. *Lyndon Johnson and the American dream.* New York: Harper and Row.

Graham, Hugh Davis. 1981. The transformation of federal education policy. In Divine, *Exploring the Johnson years*, 155–184.

Grofman, Bernard, ed. 2000. *Legacies of the 1964 Civil Rights Act*. Charlottesville: University Press of Virginia.

Heclo, Hugh. 2006. *On thinking institutionally*. Oxford: Oxford University Press.

Johnson, Lyndon B. 1964. State of the Union address. Washington, D.C. January.

Katznelson, Ira. 2013. *Fear itself: The New Deal and the origins of our time*. New York: Liveright.

King, James D. 1993. Presidential leadership of congressional civil rights voting: The cases of Eisenhower and Johnson. *Policy Studies Journal* 21, no. 3 (Autumn): 544–555.

Laney, Garrine P. 2003. *The Voting Rights Act of 1965: Historical background and current issues*. New York: Novinka.

Lerner, Mitchell B., ed. 2005. *Looking back at LBJ: White House politics in a new light*. Lawrence: University Press of Kansas.

Loevy, Robert D., ed. 1997. *The Civil Rights Act of 1964: The passage of the law that ended racial segregation*. Albany: State University of New York Press.

McNeill, J. R., and Corinna R. Unger. 2010. *Environmental histories of the Cold War*. New York: Cambridge University Press.

Milkis, Sidney M., and Jerome M. Mileur, eds. 2005. *The Great Society and the high tide of liberalism*. Amherst: University of Massachusetts Press.

Milkis, Sidney M., and Michael Nelson. 2007. *The American presidency: Origins and development*. 5th ed. Washington, D.C.: CQ Press.

Moe, Terry M. 2009. The revolution in presidential studies. *Presidential Studies Quarterly* 39, no. 4: 702–725.

Muslin, Hyman L. 1991. *Lyndon Johnson: The tragic self; A psychohistorical portrait*. New York: Insight Books.

Neustadt, Richard E. 1960. *Presidential power: The politics of leadership*. New York: Wiley and Sons.

North, Douglass C. 1990. *Institutions, institutional change, and economic performance*. Cambridge: Cambridge University Press.

Ott, Attiat R., and Paul Hughes-Cromwick. 1988. The war on poverty: Two decades later. In Bernard J. Firestone and Robert C. Vogt, eds., *Lyndon Baines Johnson and the uses of power*, 51–62. New York: Greenwood.

Peterson, James T. 2012. *The eve of destruction: How 1965 transformed America*. New York: Basic Books.

Presidential Studies Quarterly. 2009, Dec. The future of presidential studies. Symposium.

Redford, Emmett S. 1981. *Organizing the executive branch: The Johnson presidency*. Chicago: University of Chicago Press.

———. 1986. *White House operations: The Johnson presidency*. Austin: University of Texas Press.

Schandler, Herbert Y. 1977. *The unmaking of a president: Lyndon Johnson and Vietnam*. Princeton, N.J.: Princeton University Press.

Schott, Richard L. 1983. *People, positions, and power: The political appointments of Lyndon Johnson*. Chicago: University of Chicago Press.

Schulman, Bruce J. 2007. *Lyndon B. Johnson and American liberalism: A brief biography with documents*. New York: Palgrave Macmillan.

Schwartz, Thomas Alan. 2003. *Lyndon Johnson and Europe: In the shadow of Vietnam*. Cambridge, Mass.: Harvard University Press.

Seligman, Lester G. 1983. The presidency and political change. *Annals of the American Academy of Political and Social Science* 466:179–192.

Sidey, Hugh. 1968. *A very personal presidency: Lyndon Johnson in the White House*. New York: Atheneum.

Skowronek, Stephen. 2009. Mission accomplished. *Political Studies Quarterly* 39, no. 4: 795–804.

Sowell, Thomas, ed. 1984. *Civil rights: Rhetoric or reality?* New York: Morrow.

Updegrove, Mark. 2012. *Indomitable will: LBJ in the presidency*. New York: Crown.

VanDeMark, Brian. 1991. *Into the quagmire: Lyndon Johnson and the escalation of the Vietnam War*. Oxford: Oxford University Press.

Watson, W. Marvin. 2004. *Chief of staff: Lyndon Johnson and his presidency*. New York: Dunne.

Woods, Randall B. 2006. *LBJ: Architect of American ambition*. New York: Free Press.

Other References for Presidential Studies

Dickinson, Matthew J. 2009. We all want a revolution: Neustadt, new institutionalism, and the future of presidency research. *Presidential Studies Quarterly* 39, no. 4: 736–770.

Gleiber, Dennis W., and Steven A. Shull. 1992. Presidential influence in the policymaking process. *Western Political Quarterly* 45, no. 2: 441–467.

Lammers, William W., and Michael E. Genovese. 2000. *The presidency and domestic policy: Comparing leadership styles, FDR to Clinton*. Washington, D.C.: CQ Press.

Leuchtenburg, William E. 2005. *The White House looks south: Franklin D. Roosevelt, Harry S. Truman, Lyndon B. Johnson*. Walter Lynwood Fleming Lectures in Southern History. Baton Rouge: Louisiana State University Press.

Light, Paul C. 1999. *The president's agenda: Domestic policy choice from Kennedy to Clinton*. 3rd ed. Baltimore: Johns Hopkins University Press.

Lynn, Laurence E., Jr. 2009. Restoring the rule of law to public administration: What Frank Goodnow got right and Leonard White didn't. *Public Administration Review* 69, no. 5: 803–813.

Moe, Terry M., and William G. Howell. 1999. Unilateral action and presidential power: A theory. *Presidential Studies Quarterly* 29, no. 4: 850–872.

Neustadt, Richard E. 1990. *Presidential power and the modern presidents: The politics of leadership from Roosevelt to Reagan*. New York: Free Press.

Strong, Robert. 2006. Review of *Looking back at LBJ: White House policies in a new light*, by Mitchell B. Lerner. *Presidential Studies Quarterly* 36, no. 2: 336–338.

Wright, Deil S., Carl W. Stenberg, and Chung-Lae Cho. n.d. American federalism, intergovernmental relations, and intergovernmental management. Foundations of Public Administration Series of the *Public Administration Review*. Available at: http://faculty.cbpp.uaa.alaska.edu/afgjp/PADM601%20Fall%202009/FPA-FEDIGR-Article.pdf.

CHAPTER 2

Remembering LBJ: One Historian's Thoughts on Johnson's Place in the Pantheon of Presidents

ROBERT DALLEK

Let me begin by quoting what I wrote at the end of my second Lyndon Johnson volume, *Flawed Giant*:

> In a not so distant future, when coming generations have no direct experience of the man and the passions of the sixties are muted, Johnson will probably be remembered as a President who faithfully reflected the country's greatness and limitations—a man notable for his successes and failures, for his triumphs and tragedy.
>
> Only one thing seems certain: Lyndon Johnson will not join the many obscure—almost nameless, faceless—Presidents whose terms of office register on most Americans as blank slates. (Dallek 1999, 628)

And I concluded by saying, after almost fourteen years of work on this man, "He will not be forgotten."

In the spring of 2008, there was a symposium in Washington for the hundredth anniversary of Lyndon Johnson's birth. On that occasion, Joe Califano, a former secretary of Health, Education and Welfare, said that Johnson had become the invisible president, and the statement haunted me. It troubled me.

Why should this be so? What has happened? It is not as if the many achievements of the Great Society have disappeared. It is not as if someone had come out and pronounced them a failure. But LBJ has disappeared, as Califano noted, and it puzzled me. I learned that a documentary had been made by the LBJ Foundation to commemorate, at the 2008 Democratic National Convention, the hundredth anniversary of Johnson's birth, on August 22, and the anniversary of his nomination to the vice presidency in 1960. There was not a word about this at the convention; nothing was said by any official. With the emergence of Barack Obama, the first African American to be nominated for the presidency, one would think there would have been some connection made to civil rights, to voting rights.

I was puzzled, but maybe it should not have been so surprising—after all, most of our presidents become invisible. Think of the following: if you went out on the street and tried to talk to the average person, would they know anything about Millard Fillmore, Franklin Pierce, James Buchanan, James Garfield, Grover Cleveland, William Howard Taft, or Warren G. Harding? They would remember the names of Gerald Ford and Jimmy Carter. But how long will it be before those men are largely forgotten—another twenty years? Fifty years?

It seems unfair, however, to include Lyndon Johnson in the group of presidents I just mentioned. When people look back on these men, what achievements come to mind—what might we point to? What did Fillmore do? What did William Howard Taft do? I appreciate that even if one asks people nowadays, "What did Theodore Roosevelt accomplish?" not many people would know that he was the architect of the Food and Drug Administration. Or of his commitments to conservation. How many people would know that Woodrow Wilson was the architect of the Federal Reserve, which was so much in the news and the focus of so much attention during the Great Recession of 2007–2009?

Johnson is recent enough in our collective memory that people can remember his extraordinary body of achievements: civil rights, voter rights, Medicare, federal aid to elementary/secondary and higher education, environmental protection, clean air, clean rivers, clean harbors, consumer protections, truth in lending, safe tires, safe roads, the National Endowment for the Arts, National Public Radio, national public television (and the Corporation for Public Broadcasting), the Freedom of Information Act, and the extraordinary immigration reform statute of 1965.

I know the record, having spent years studying the man's life and his presidency. I was nonetheless stunned, I must confess, listening to Califano's recounting of that extensive body of accomplishments. So the questions remain: Why the low profile? Why should Johnson have faded so much into the background?

I think the answer—the principal answer I would give—is Vietnam. I don't think that surprises any of us. The credibility gap—all the talk about light at the end of the tunnel. Somebody said that sometimes the light at the end of the tunnel is an on-rushing train. And there was so much frustration during that era—and even more than frustration, the recriminations, the marches in the streets, the march on the Pentagon, the bitterness over the war—that it eclipsed everything and pushed everything else into the background.

Here we are, approaching four decades after that war ended. Why does it still haunt the country and tarnish Johnson's reputation? Harry S. Truman left office with a 32 percent approval rating. No one had a lower approval rating in presidential history than Harry Truman. During the Korean War, in 1951, Truman's approval rating fell to 21 percent. President George W. Bush's approval rating was as low as 24 percent, but not as low as Harry Truman's during the Korean War. Yet Harry Truman is now seen as a near-great president and has a kind of command of the public's imagination that is rather stunning. It might have to do with the Pulitzer Prize–winning biography by David McCullough (McCullough 1992), but I think there's another dynamic at work. Truman, of course, is now remembered for having won the Cold War: the Truman Doctrine (containment), which he put into place, was central to the U.S. victory in that Cold War conflict. And Johnson might get credit for the fact that Vietnam, at the end of the day, did not deter us from winning the Cold War. So why does it continue to haunt his legacy and relegate him to the background among great presidents?

I think that what brought Vietnam so much back into play, serving to eclipse Johnson's reputation, is Iraq. The war in Iraq stirred up feelings of anguish and frustration about the sense of a war that we never should have fought. Indeed, to this day, something like 63 percent of the country continues to feel that the Iraq war was a mistake (Gallup 2008). Even if one asks only people old enough to remember the Vietnam War whether the Vietnam War was a mistake, I think you would get a very similar result—something like 63 percent, maybe more, would say it was mistake.—And 63 percent would have the same response about Iraq.

I think that Johnson's reputation is so tied to the failure in Vietnam that it relegates to the background the legacy of his Great Society achievements. But it isn't just that. It is the fact that we passed through a thirty-year period of conservative governance. We remember Ronald Reagan saying that government is not the solution—government is the problem. If there was anything that Lyndon Johnson believed in, it was that government could be the solution to society's problems. Remembering the lessons of the New Deal and of Kennedy's New Frontier, Johnson, through the Great Society, wanted to draw young people into government, taking inspiration from the idea that public activism, progressive federal activism, is an honorable and worthy enterprise.

How do we account for the fact that Johnson was able to put across such a huge body of progressive reform? Generally, this is a conservative country.

It is right of center. Occasionally, you get an upsurge of activism, of federal activism, of progressive sentiment. What lessons can be drawn about Johnson's Great Society?

The first lesson is that Johnson seized upon the fact that conservatism in 1964–1965 was discredited. His campaign against Barry Goldwater gave him a huge opportunity because Goldwater had sunk conservative ideology for the moment. Indeed, Johnson could think back to the experience of Franklin Roosevelt and remember the 1932 campaign. Roosevelt trounced Herbert Hoover because Hoover was devoid of solutions to the Great Depression. He was personally and politically depressed. The joke at the time was that a rose would wilt in his hand. He was morose. He was so inconsequential. He was someone who was utterly discounted. And Roosevelt was able to beat him. In defeating him, he opened the way for the possibility that became the New Deal.

Goldwater denounced Social Security. He wanted to privatize it. But it wasn't just Social Security. His ideas about foreign policy were alienating to the great majority of people in the country. This disconnection was revealed in bumper stickers of the time. Goldwater advocates put bumper stickers on their cars that said, "In your heart, you know he's right." And some Democrats—at least, I saw these in California—had bumper stickers that said, "Yes, in your heart, you know he's far right."

Of course, the other fear could be stated as, "In your hearts, you know he might." Which referred to the anxiety, the fear that Barry Goldwater might produce a nuclear war, that he was a hawk committed to the idea of destroying the Soviet Union. He joked, "Maybe we should consider lobbing one into the men's room at the Kremlin." And it sent a chill of fear through people.

Johnson came into office in 1965 in his own right, elected in his own right, with an extraordinary opportunity. As with Roosevelt, it was a repudiation of conservative ideology, a repudiation of the idea that government should not be active in behalf of those in need and those middle-class folks who have needs as well. So Johnson was able to seize upon this shift, this paradigm shift, this shift in mood.

The thing about domestic reform that I think any presidential administration can learn from the Johnson experience and the Roosevelt experience is that, above all, you need to build consensus. You need to create a body of support, of backing for what you are going to do. Civil rights, Johnson understood, was an idea whose time had come; but more so, what he understood was that civil rights in 1964 and 1965 was not some special program that was going to merely accommodate African Americans angry and frustrated after decades and decades of discrimination: It was something that would change the entire South and the life of the nation.

Johnson, to his credit, understood that racial segregation in the South segregated the nation as well. The people in the North and the Midwest looked upon the South as a sort of crazy aunt you kept in the attic because there was something bizarre about that region of the country. Here was the United States, locked in a cold war with the Soviet Union, preaching ideas about liberty, freedom, justice, social justice, and the quality of opportunity—and then in its own backyard, in the South, there was a system of racial segregation that defied these propositions.

Johnson understood that eliminating racial segregation would integrate not only the races in the South, but also the South into the rest of the nation. It was brilliantly foresightful. Consider the following: who have mainly been the candidates for the presidency since passage of the major civil rights legislation? For the first time since the Civil War, southerners were successful in running for and winning the White House. We have had both Bushes from Texas, Jimmy Carter, Bill Clinton, and Al Gore (though he lost, he was also a candidate from the border South). The consensus on civil rights and voter rights led to a large number of black officeholders. It has made a huge difference in the life of the nation.

This lesson about forming consensus was even more important for Medicare. Johnson understood that for Medicare to succeed, it had to be like Social Security in that it would be a program not just for the poor but for all Americans. It was a program that would reach across all class, regional, and racial lines and touch the lives of everyone. Today, a politician trying to reduce or eliminate Medicare is committing political suicide. It has entered the fabric of American social life the way Social Security has.

During the struggle to get education-funding legislation through Congress, Johnson was told by one of his aides that federal funds would go to wealthy school districts as well as to poor ones, and Johnson concurred. Johnson knew that in order to pass the legislation, it would be necessary to make it a nationally acceptable program that reached into all school districts across the country.

In domestic policy, it seems to me that the greatest lessons for Obama are about consensus, about taking advantage of the downturn in conservative fortunes and forging ahead with a new progressive agenda.

A second lesson from the Johnson experience, and from American history more generally, is that war kills reform. They are incompatible, and the history here is dramatic and striking.

In 1898 the United States entered the Spanish-American War. The mood of the time was receptive to a certain amount of federal activism in support of a populist agenda. True, William McKinley won the White House—he was president—but nevertheless there were powerful reform sentiments in the air. That Spanish-American War dampened this down, sidetracked it, would not allow it to happen.

World War I essentially put progressivism on the shelf. The Woodrow Wilson reforms, the Theodore Roosevelt and Wilson impulse to use federal authority to improve the lives of Americans, to humanize the American industrial system, were pushed to the background by World War I.

At the time of World War II, Franklin Roosevelt said, "Dr. New Deal has been replaced by Dr. Win the War," and indeed the New Deal went a-glimmering. It wasn't reversed, but further additions to New Deal initiatives were rendered impossible. I am not saying we should not have fought the war. I am not saying that we could have avoided involvement in that war—but the consequence, one consequence of it, was that we could not continue with the New Deal programs.

In January 1944, Roosevelt himself gave the most radical speech of his presidency when he called for a new phase of the New Deal. That year he was preparing to run for the presidency again, and he wanted to talk about a new phase of the New Deal. But as long as the war continued, this could not happen.

Harry Truman won the presidency in 1948, and he promised the country a fair deal. So much of what we saw in Lyndon Johnson's Great Society had initially been promised by Harry Truman: civil rights, a Medicare-type program, federal aid to education. These were on Harry Truman's agenda.

The Korean War, beginning in June 1950, ended reform. I am not judging him for going into that war, and I think it was probably necessary for him to have done so. But I think he made a huge mistake in the fall of 1950 when he met with Douglas MacArthur at Wake Island and the question of whether to cross the thirty-eighth parallel and overturn the North Korean regime was confronted. Truman was convinced he had to do it. Politically, perhaps he had no choice. Remember that this was a time of McCarthyism. This was a time when if Truman had stopped at the thirtieth-eighth parallel, the right wing of the country would have eaten him alive. He would have been perceived as someone who didn't understand the need for rollback or liberation—themes on which Eisenhower campaigned. It trapped Truman in the Korean War and drove down his approval rating, making it impossible for him to put across the Fair Deal.

Lyndon Johnson kept talking about guns and butter, and he was committed to both, but the war in Vietnam sucked all the energy from the air.

It did not leave energy, money, or support for the Great Society programs in place because increasingly the war consumed all energies, finances, and impulses in the country. Johnson thus lost, in a sense, the ability to go forward with the Great Society.

Richard Nixon too wanted certain domestic reforms, such as the Family Assistance Plan. He wanted to go forward with major national health care reform, but was drawn off constantly by the Vietnam War. My supposition is that Nixon could have gotten out of the war very early in his presidency and that it would not have made an iota of difference in the outcome in Vietnam. He was profoundly cynical about using the war to win reelection in 1972. In a famous conversation, Bob Haldeman said to Kissinger that the president wanted to get out of Vietnam by the end of "next year," meaning the end of 1971. And Kissinger said, "Bob, that would be a mistake, because if he leaves the war and South Vietnam is destabilized and looks like it's going down, it could undermine the president's chances of reelection in 1972." So, cynically—for political reasons—they stayed in Vietnam, and Nixon felt compelled to stay through the 1972 election. It was only in 1973 that he moved to get out of the war.

Franklin Roosevelt said it best in his first inaugural address: "First things first, we have to deal with the economic problems in this country." Today we have to deal with the environmental problems we have. We have to deal with the energy issues that confront us. We have to reinspire a young generation of Americans to be drawn into public affairs and public life. We have to hark back to those experiences of the New Deal and the Great Society.

And tied to this, I believe, incidentally—but tied to it nevertheless—is the future of Lyndon Johnson's historical representation and standing. I am confident that as the wars in Iraq and Afghanistan fade, as they recede into the background, Vietnam will be less on people's minds. Johnson will be perceived more favorably and will indeed be seen as standing in the line of presidents from Theodore Roosevelt to Woodrow Wilson to Franklin Delano Roosevelt to Lyndon Johnson, who used the power of the federal government to improve people's lives. As FDR said, "Better the occasional faults of a Government that lives in a spirit of charity than the consistent omissions of a Government frozen in the ice of its own indifference."

Johnson, in time, will once again be remembered as one of those great humane presidents who helped humanize the American industrial system. Such are the notable achievements of a Great Society. These are the things that should be remembered, and I guess I am the consummate optimist. They will be remembered, and Johnson will rise above the Vietnam experience and come back into focus.

Note

This chapter is based on "Policy Challenges for the New President and the LBJ Legacy," originally presented at the Lyndon B. Johnson Centennial Celebration symposium, Lyndon B. Johnson School of Public Affairs and Lyndon Baines Johnson Library and Museum, December 5, 2008.

References

Dallek, Robert. 1999. *Flawed giant: Lyndon Johnson and his times, 1961–1973*. New York: Oxford University Press.

Gallup.com. 2008. Opposition to Iraq war reaches new high: Sixty-three percent say U.S. made mistake in sending troops (Apr. 24). Available at www .gallup.com/poll/106783/opposition-iraq-war-reaches-new-high.aspx. Retrieved Aug. 15, 2011.

McCullough, David. 1992. *Truman*. New York: Simon and Schuster.

PART II

DEFINING CITIZENSHIP AND IMMIGRATION

CHAPTER 3

Ending Jim Crow, Attacking Ghetto Walls

GARY ORFIELD

More change happened in civil rights in America during the Johnson administration than at any time in the twentieth century. Most reforms were designed to change practices of public agencies, but there were also mandated changes in racist practices in the private sector, two of which are analyzed in this chapter. The Great Society brought enduring changes to the racial system of the South. A Congress that had been unable to pass a major piece of civil rights legislation in eight decades passed three laws in Johnson's five years, and then none in the next forty-five. In very important ways, the South was transformed, and the agenda of a great social movement against apartheid practices of businesses became law. Housing rights and opportunities were later extended to those living in segregated ghettos of the nation's cities, and there were ambitious programs for systemic urban change. Although no administration since 1969 has shared LBJ's vision, and many of the urban policy reforms were aborted in the following administrations, the landscape of American race relations has not been the same, and the intensity of housing exclusion gradually declined in the following decades.

Background

Mid-twentieth-century America had won a great world war, had recovered dramatically from its longest economic depression, was in the midst of a great baby boom and the creation of white suburbia, and seemed quite content with the social status quo. It was still a society with a vast white majority, and immigration laws excluding non-Europeans that ensured that it would remain that way. The percentage of immigrants in the country was at a historical low point. Activists and some intellectuals were disturbed by the racial system, as were the leaders of civil rights groups and community organizations in nonwhite communities, but there were no major movements. Small civil rights groups had been working for decades, making slow gains in the courts, but found themselves unable to ignite large changes even after the Supreme Court in its 1954 *Brown* decision declared southern school segregation unconstitutional (Kluger 1975). The nonwhite population, overwhelmingly black before the 1965 Immigration Act led to a huge number of nonwhite immigrants, was still concentrated in the South and in a few northern and western cities. It was remarkable that the greatest period of social change ever to occur in a time of peace and prosperity was only a decade away from the complacent fifties. Its leader was a southerner who rose to prominence in the Senate under the mentorship of Senator Richard Russell (D-GA), the powerful leader of the South, committed to blocking civil rights reform. What Lyndon Johnson did changed the South and restructured politics well into the twenty-first century. The work was left incomplete, particularly the drive to change the cities, but it had been well begun. Though much criticized at the time as inadequate, and admittedly incomplete, in comparison with the record of the next forty-five years it was truly remarkable.

When the Supreme Court struck down legally mandated segregation in southern schools in *Brown v. Board of Education*, it seemed a bold step against the apartheid system that prevailed in more than a third of the states, but of little consequence elsewhere. Fierce southern resistance, cautious leadership by the courts, and tepid enforcement efforts, however, brought only modest, gradual change. After President Eisenhower sent troops to Little Rock in 1957, southern resistance intensified and change slowed to a crawl (Sarratt 1966). The action phase in what became a huge civil rights movement began with private discrimination. The bus boycott in Montgomery, Alabama, led by a young preacher, Martin Luther King, attracted a great deal of publicity but no significant federal action. The sit-in movement came when college students confronted segregated lunch counters. The "freedom rides" were about the segregation of interstate busses and terminals. Those protests ignited a great social movement in the early 1960s, helping stimulate a period of remarkable change (Branch 1988). Protestors were asking government to force changes in the actions of private businesses in a country where the Supreme Court generations earlier had said the government had no such authority under the Constitution.

The reforms Johnson fostered and enforced became a frontal attack on the entire racial system of the South. There were many dimensions to those changes, and they included both civil rights laws and supportive administrative, social, and economic policies. The battle in the South was about extending to a huge region practices that were normal in the rest of the country. When Johnson's focus turned to the cities, it was a different situation. His reform agenda sought to change systematic discrimination in northern and western cities in a society that lacked consensus on those issues and showed little support for governmental action to change them.

Civil Rights Laws and Social Change

Civil rights laws, by their nature, aim to achieve important changes in areas of life deeply rooted in social beliefs and practices often strongly supported by state and local leaders, institutions, businesses, and governments. The most radical civil rights laws involved large structural changes in the power of the federal government—such as mandates to integrate all the schools and colleges in the South, which had always been segregated, and the massive expansion of federal power over election practices in states where minorities had been excluded. Others had sweeping goals but limited means and involved giving the federal government power to initiate action against individual violators, case by case. This chapter explores two of those with important objectives but limited means—public accommodations and fair housing—looking at the struggle to enact them and the degree to which they established stable new norms and ameliorated the problems they were designed to address.

This chapter focuses on two key aspects of the 1964 and 1968 Civil Rights Acts that extended civil rights reforms into the private business sector, especially the parts of it complicit in the daily racial humiliations of southern life, and that began to undermine the ghetto system that imprisoned millions of families of color in separate and dying neighborhoods in the cities of the North and West. These reforms began with public revulsion at the openly racist defense of southern segregation, and were fostered by Johnson's great triumph in the 1964 election. The tremendous power of a president who was a truly great legislator was invested in this cause. Surprisingly, the momentum for reform continued even as Johnson's political strength eroded and as he entered areas where there was both little enthusiasm for a reform struggle and public resistance to further change. The effort continued to the very end of Johnson's years. Johnson understood political capital and the ways in which presidential power dissolves, and he spent much of his capital on these battles. He confronted southern apartheid at the peak of his power; when his power was slipping away, he confronted the bitterly controversial issue of urban segregation across the country.

In thinking about impacts, it is important to consider the ways in which a reform can produce change. The most dramatic change occurs when a new legal standard produces rapid and widespread compliance. The legal change alters behavior and norms because the new policy is accepted as legitimate. This outcome is, of course, what happens with many noncontroversial changes in law. Sometimes it also changes racial practices, even those rooted in local norms for many generations. A second form of change comes when either strong sanctions or strong incentives, or a combination of both, force a change in practices despite local resistance. Such change may or may not take root and produce the kind of modified attitudes that would make external pressure unnecessary in the future. It may or may not persist when pressure ends. A third form of change is grudging and gradual; a few individual cases are prosecuted, but very little changes as the old pattern endures. Attitudes too may be refashioned gradually in these circumstances. A last situation occurs when there is limited enforcement and persistent resistance. In these cases there are theoretical rights that in fact mean very little.

The integration of public accommodations in the South represented the second kind of change, in which the law produced a different and persistent reality. Fair housing was more like the third kind: a law with limited powers, modest enforcement, and gradual and grudging change for a long period of time. In each case, however, the laws marked a substantial change from the status quo ante, particularly in the more conservative portions of the United States. It is hard to see how those changes would have happened if the ideas had not been brought to life by laws passed during the Johnson years, since nothing significant had been enacted for nearly eighty years before then and no major positive initiative in civil rights or urban policy has been made since the 1960s.

The civil rights reforms of the LBJ era wiped out most traditional parts of daily southern apartheid and profoundly changed society in the states where most African Americans have always lived. This was an astonishing contribution. The changes were so fast and in many ways irreversible that it is difficult for younger southerners, white or black, to imagine what their parents or grandparents experienced—a truly transformative change.

As for civil rights issues reaching beyond the South, Johnson's great breakthroughs concerned winning laws against employment and housing discrimination; both laws had to be deeply compromised, by eliminating most of their enforcement power, in order to win passage in the Senate. In both cases, however, the laws contained possibilities that could have been exploited to achieve a different form of urban development had the Johnson administration continued or either Robert Kennedy or Hubert Humphrey won the presidency in the very close 1968 election. But Richard Nixon won. On fair housing, where LBJ moved far past the political consensus of his time and controlled only limited levers of change, the impacts were slow to come and often became bogged down in the face of resistance and indifference by succeeding administrations. They did, however, expand the agenda and help show paths of change that, in the long run, made some important differences. A half century later, there is still much to do in these areas.

Though they have sometimes been ignored, the Great Society laws remain on the nation's books. At the point of maximum political resistance to them, in the 1980s, the Civil Rights Act was reinforced when Congress passed the Civil Rights Restoration Act, and the fair housing law was strengthened in 1988 when Congress enhanced the Department of Housing and Urban Development's enforcement authority. Johnson's legislative victories remain part of the law of the land.

Ending Segregation of Public Accommodations

Though the United States has always had a mixed racial population, accompanied by severe discrimination and inequality persisting over the generations, a serious national commitment to changing deep structures of racial inequality happened only after the Civil War and in the 1960s. The Johnson era was the only time when serious steps were taken to change racial patterns invisible the South. Despite a brutal civil war against racial oppression and major changes to the Constitution during Reconstruction, the tragedy of the late nineteenth and early twentieth centuries was the judicial reversal of Reconstruction-era laws and the creation of virtual serfdom in the form of permanent indebtedness through sharecropping, which was powerfully backed by state and local laws and accepted by the federal courts and U.S. national leaders. It imposed and legitimated a system of comprehensive apartheid on blacks in seventeen states where the great majority of African Americans have always lived. Beginning with World War I, the nation saw a vast exodus from the rural South to the industrial centers of the North as millions of people left sharecropping behind to seek better opportunities in the cities. Some were pulled to good jobs during the wartime labor crises in World Wars I and II; others were forced off the land by the agricultural depression resulting from the Dust Bowl. In southern cities, African Americans faced myriad segregation laws and policies imposed by state governments. In the North, they were soon contained within urban ghettos, whose boundaries were often enforced by racial violence and discrimination and backed implicitly or directly by the courts and local officials. African Americans could not go to the same schools as whites, participate in the same unions, or live in "good" neighborhoods. Employment in much of local government and business was intensely segregated. During the Great Depression, black men were the first fired and were often forced to depend on black women, who could still get jobs as servants (Lieberson 1981; Myrdal 1944). When intense suburbanization began after World War II, the suburbs were for whites only. Too often, the dreams of African American families who had been part of the exodus off the plantations dried up "like a raisin in the sun."[1]

Lyndon Johnson's greatest contribution to American society was to use his formidable skills to undo structures of racial inequality that had been passively accepted for most of the nation's history. He built on a long and powerful social movement that fought southern de jure segregation, and his successes marked a profound turning point in the history of the South. The civil rights movement and decades of litigation and organization across the country had set the stage for these changes, but Johnson carried them out with speed and force. On southern issues, the Johnson administration achieved major and irreversible changes.

A Historical Perspective

As the civil rights movement took shape in the mid-twentieth century there were two distinct systems of racial exclusion and subordination limiting opportunities for African Americans. In the South, justified by judicial dismantling of the Reconstruction amendments to the Constitution and the Supreme Court's "separate but equal" decision in *Plessy v. Ferguson*, a complex system of racial separation, enforced with the full authority of state and local governments, took hold. Known as Jim Crow, a name drawn from a popular racist song, it came to describe the comprehensive public and private subordination of blacks. This system, which was fully developed and operating almost without challenge by the end of the nineteenth century, would not be seriously confronted until the 1960s.

The first southern president since the Civil War, Lyndon Johnson fostered changes that ended apartheid laws and practices and spearheaded a multipronged attack on the ghetto system. Johnson could not draw on the emergency war powers of the president, as Lincoln did in ending slavery or as Franklin D. Roosevelt did when he implemented a temporary wartime policy against job discrimination. Johnson faced leaders of legally segregated southern states who were largely opposed to any serious change, but he was able to achieve genuine breakthroughs. His unique mastery of Congress made a huge difference in forging what had to be broad bipartisan coalitions and in securing the virtually unanimous support of Democrats outside the South, as well as most Republicans, in order to overcome the Senate filibuster and all the internal vetoes available within the congressional process.

While LBJ was pursuing civil rights, his legislative program was ending a racist immigration policy, adopting an ambitious program of social and economic reforms, and giving the first serious official attention to Hispanics, whose number would explode in the coming generations. All in all, it was a record without equal in the nation's history. Johnson was remarkably successful in the struggle against southern apartheid. He had to win his victories in a Congress where the states with legal segregation controlled more than a third of the votes in the Senate, and where southerners chaired two-thirds of the committees in the Senate and more than half of those in the House, including the House Rules Committee, which determined those bills that could come up for a vote. Since the proposed laws were attacking the very foundation of the southern social and political order, they were fiercely resisted. In the Senate, thanks to the filibuster system, it was impossible to cut off debate and vote on a bill without a two-thirds majority supporting a cloture motion. In these conditions, even the most modest civil rights measures could languish for generations. For example, an anti-lynching law proposed by President Harding in the 1920s did not become law until 1968.[2] Johnson's first great accomplishment was to obtain congressional action on the sweeping Civil Rights Act of 1964.

The Civil Rights Act of 1964

Desegregating public accommodations was a central and bitterly controversial part of the Civil Rights Act. In fact, public accommodations had been at the epicenter of the struggle for desegregation all along. *Plessy* was about railroad segregation. Many of the young civil rights leaders took part in the lunch counter sit-in protests that began among students from black colleges. The daily insults, inconveniences, and humiliations attendant on a million racial barriers and rejections mobilized a mighty movement (Martin Luther King and Rosa Parks became icons of the movement for transportation rights in their response to the policy of bus segregation in Montgomery, Alabama).

The 1964 Civil Rights Act was the culmination of a struggle begun a half century earlier by a small group of African Americans and white supporters. The civil rights movement, with roots in the early twentieth century and led by the NAACP and the lawyers in the NAACP Legal Defense Fund as well as by many local organizations, had framed the issues and challenged the status quo with limited success for many years (Kluger 1975). The legal strategy of developing facts and fighting key cases across the country had important effects on legal principles, especially after the more progressive judges appointed by Presidents Franklin Roosevelt, Harry Truman and Dwight Eisenhower took over key courts. During and after World War II, a great war fought by a thoroughly segregated U.S. Army and Navy against a racist dictatorship, political and intellectual leaders began to reopen the question of southern apartheid. During World War II, President Roosevelt had created a wartime fair employment policy, partially to head off threatened strikes. President Harry Truman's administration issued the first presidential civil rights report in the twentieth century that recommended major change, and his Justice Department asked the Supreme Court to outlaw school segregation (President's Committee on Civil Rights 2004). The Democratic Party adopted the first civil rights plank in its history at the 1948 national convention. President Dwight Eisenhower's Justice Department supported the Truman administration's request to the Supreme Court to outlaw mandated school segregation (Anderson 1964). Though Eisenhower never publicly endorsed the *Brown* decision, he sent paratroopers into Arkansas to prevent a southern governor from using force to defy the federal courts. Eisenhower asked Congress to enact a modest civil rights bill, the first since Reconstruction, and the effort was masterminded and pushed through a reluctant Senate in 1957 by the Senate Democratic leader, Lyndon Johnson (Caro 2002, chs. 39–40; Caro 2012, 9–11). One important accomplishment was the creation of the U.S. Commission on Civil Rights, whose work was critical in developing the agenda for later civil rights laws (Berry 2009). Although *Brown* found the de jure segregation of schools in seventeen states to be a violation of the Constitution, the court's weak and vague implementation decisions produced little change, and there was virtually no voluntary compliance with *Brown* in the vast majority of southern school districts. When President Kennedy sent his civil rights bill to Congress in June 1963, 99 percent of southern black students were still in completely segregated schools. The court by itself could not exercise sufficient force to overcome the political mobilization of southern leaders in support of segregation.

Real change was initiated by a large nonviolent protest movement stimulated in part by the promise of *Brown*, which destroyed the legitimacy of the southern system. The movement took matters out of the courts and into the evening news and the national press. Using the Gandhi-like tactics of confronting evil with peaceful hymn singing, protestors asked for things that seemed perfectly reasonable to most Americans and were already policy in most of the nation. The campaigns provoked violent repression and triggered massive national concern. As the struggle for civil rights erupted into a mass movement of peaceful civil disobedience that had the active support of students and many black churches, creating great symbolic confrontations (particularly in Birmingham and Montgomery, Alabama), it shocked and aroused the country against the brutality inflicted on peaceful protesters asking for rights long held by residents of the North and West. These movements, strongly supported by religious groups, labor, and intellectuals, changed politics.

Although the 1960s are seen as a liberal era, the Johnson administration's breakthroughs in 1964 on southern segregation, and on housing segregation in 1968, were pushed through Congresses that did not have anything close to a majority of liberals. In the Eighty-Ninth Congress (1965–1966), LBJ did get to work with the most liberal Congress of the twentieth century, and it dealt with much of his domestic agenda, including aid to schools, Medicare, and voting rights. In 1964 and 1968, however, Congress was closely divided, and strong southern factions controlled a number of the key decision points on Capitol Hill. The fair housing law was enacted after conservatives had staged a strong comeback in the 1966 midterm elections, after the president had been greatly weakened by division over the Vietnam War and urban riots, and in the midst of a divisive presidential campaign.

Each of these great victories was a legislative tour de force that required the president and his congressional allies to make hard, risky choices about how to spend his political capital. In each case, LBJ had to hold all the liberals and moderates of his party and to win over a substantial number of Republicans, including conservative ones, to pass the bills. After the urban riots, the rise of the militant black power movement, and the turn of the civil rights agenda from the segregationist South to segregated and polarized northern cities, the ranks of northern Democrats splintered. Members from working-class white ethnic neighborhoods were willing to impose change on the South, but sometimes not on their own communities. Public opinion was turning against both LBJ and further civil rights initiatives.

To achieve historic breakthroughs under these conditions, the bills had to be effectively presented to the country, guided through the tricky maneuverings of the committees, carefully monitored in order to head off or defeat members who might try to interject an unrelated issue or split the party at any point—all while carefully courting Republicans in two election years in which the GOP was moving to the right on civil rights policy. Just weeks after LBJ won passage of the 1964 Civil Rights Act in Congress, the GOP nominated Barry Goldwater, one of the only non-southern senators to vote against the Civil Rights Act, for president. The resulting campaign made the GOP the voice of the white South and set the stage for a great realignment on the race issue, one that Richard Nixon would consolidate with his "Southern Strategy" in 1968 (Carter 1996; Davidson 1990, 221–239; Kessel 1968). California in 1964 passed, by a 65 percent majority, a referendum against fair housing that would have prohibited the state from adding a fair housing law to the state constitution; the measure was later overturned by the California Supreme Court and the U.S. Supreme Court.[3] (Ronald Reagan opposed both fair housing and the 1964 Civil Rights Act when he entered politics in the mid-1960s [Cannon 2003].) On the fair housing law, LBJ got the bill passed just months before the Republican Party, under the leadership of its presidential nominee, Richard Nixon, took a very strong anti-civil-rights, pro-"law and order" position as part of its Southern Strategy, which aligned the GOP with the white South. Nixon said the courts had gone too far, attacked bureaucrats who enforced civil rights laws, and promised to change things (Dent 1978; Murphy and Gulliver 1971). In the midst of all this change, LBJ nonetheless managed to carry his bills to victory.

In the battle over the 1964 Civil Rights Act, President Johnson immediately used the national concern triggered by the assassination of JFK to help focus attention on the issue and create a sense of urgency. Rejecting the advice of cautious aides, Johnson proclaimed, "First, no memorial oration or eulogy could more eloquently honor President Kennedy's memory than the earliest possible passage of the civil rights bill for which he fought so long. We have talked long enough in this country about equal rights. We have talked for one hundred years and more. It is time now to write the next chapter, and to write it in the books of law" (Caro 2012, 430). Speaking to a huge national audience concerned about where the country was going after the terrible loss of a young leader, Johnson channeled those deep feelings into the civil rights fight and pledged to use his power to win it.

The civil rights bill as it developed was a comprehensive attack on the Jim Crow system of the South. By the standard of U.S. racial history, the bill was revolutionary. It proposed to bring the full force of federal power to bear on the entire racial system of the South and, for the first time since Reconstruction, to outlaw some forms of discrimination by private businesses, both in public accommodations in the South and in hiring decisions across the nation. In a country where the federal government had been a passive bystander on racial issues for eighty years and the U.S. Supreme Court had long since eviscerated the Reconstruction civil rights laws, the bill was a direct challenge to laws and public beliefs in a third of the states. It was designed to produce rapid and fundamental changes in the states that had always been home to the substantial majority of black people.

Provisions regarding public accommodations were the most controversial parts of the bill because they involved extending civil rights protections into the workings of private businesses. Many of the largest civil rights protest campaigns in the South were directed against daily forms of racial discrimination that treated African Americans as if they were subhuman: refusing them the right to ride like any other citizen on a bus or train; turning them away from hotels, restaurants, public bathrooms, and even telephone booths and libraries, where everyone else could freely go; creating separate entrances and locations in everything from hospitals to cemeteries; prohibiting their use of pools and beaches; and much else—constant small and large rejections and humiliations. The black students of the South triggered the protest movement with the sit-ins at lunch counters, where, after demanding the right to be served, they were arrested. When the freedom riders came south in 1962, they attracted national attention by demanding equal treatment on interstate buses and terminals, for which they were attacked and jailed—forcing the federal government to intervene in order to prevent violence. Rosa Parks refusing to sit in the back of the bus, young students at black colleges demanding the right to buy a hot dog and a Coke at a lunch counter, travelers on the highways unable to find a bathroom or a place to eat—these became symbols of a large social movement.

These protests caused legal problems because the U.S. Supreme Court had concluded in the 1880s that the Constitution prohibited discrimination by government only. The idea that the federal government would tell a restaurant or a hotel whom it could serve seemed to conservatives a radical change in settled law and a direct attack on the customs and beliefs of the white South.

The Kennedy administration was cautious on civil rights, acting only when the civil rights movement reached its crest in 1963. Kennedy was determined to take significant action on sensitive public accommodations issues despite precedents reaching back to the Supreme Court's decision in the *Civil Rights Cases*, 109 U.S. 3 (1883). The government's legal position was bolstered by the great expansion of federal power to regulate anything that could be considered interstate commerce, which occurred when the Supreme Court in the 1930s and 1940s upheld key parts of the New Deal.[4] The Constitution gives Congress clear and unambiguous power to regulate interstate commerce, including local actions that had aggregate, interstate effects. The administration argued that as a result, government could forbid discrimination even by small local businesses.

That theory, which was ultimately upheld by the Supreme Court, did not, however, soothe furious southern conservatives. Senator Richard Russell, the leader of the southern Democrats, argued: "The fact that every citizen has the same right to own and operate a swimming pool or dining hall constitutes equality. The use of federal power to force the owner of a dining hall or swimming pool to unwillingly accept those of a different race as guests creates a new and special right for Negroes in derogation of the property rights of all of our people to own and control the fruits of their labor and ingenuity" (Mann 1996, 354). One of the most powerful leaders in the House, Representative Howard (Judge) Smith (D-VA), chair of the Rules Committee which had great power in shaping House legislative action, offered the example of a foot doctor: "If I were cutting corns I would want to know whose feet I would have to be monkeying around with. I would want to know whether they smelled good or bad" (Whalen and Whalen 1985, 110). This was the world that LBJ was committed to change.

The Kennedy proposal was limited to establishments most clearly involved in interstate commerce, that is, those with a "substantial" impact on commerce across state lines (Sundquist 1968, 263). The idea was to address the larger, more visible, and more moderate businesses and to avoid local businesses in the hard-core racist Deep South towns and villages. Congressional leaders talked with the Kennedy White House about dropping the public accommodations provisions, and there were many rumors that the administration was thinking about adopting that strategy before Kennedy's assassination (Whalen and Whalen 1985, 6). Despite urgent appeals from civil rights groups and a quarter century of battles to pass a federal fair employment law, Kennedy did not include a job discrimination title in the proposed bill.

The civil rights bill went first to the House of Representatives, where the Judiciary Committee was controlled by Representative Emanuel Celler, an unabashed New York liberal, who sent the bill to a special subcommittee whose Democratic members were liberal civil rights supporters. In Congress, as controversial bills pass through the legislative maze, it is typical for them to be reduced in reach and force. Compromise is piled upon compromise, and what emerges is often a pale echo of the original proposal.

This is what was widely expected of the Kennedy bill. Though the public was largely opposed to some of the racist actions by Alabama officials, polls also showed concern that things were going too fast. The initial vote counts in both houses showed that necessary support for the bill was lacking.[5] The House committee, however, not only kept the public accommodations provision but also strengthened it greatly to include all accommodations. The job discrimination title also became part of the bill. Title VI, which forbade racial discrimination in all federal programs, was changed from the provision in the Kennedy proposal, which permitted cutting off federal money from discriminatory institutions, to one that required action. The attorney general was given sweeping authority to sue to prevent discrimination. The administration supported a bill considerably stronger than what it had originally asked for and promised that it would not bargain away key provisions of the House version in the Senate, as had happened previously (Whalen and Whalen 1985, 13).

With the Johnson administration strongly behind it and the national public supporting the new president, the bill was released by the Rules Committee and sent to the House floor. There were no successful attacks, and the bill passed 290–130, on February 10, 1964, going then to the Senate, where no major civil rights bill had been passed since Reconstruction (Mann 1996, 389). The Senate had never forestalled a filibuster on a civil rights matter, and southern leaders were fully mobilized, determined to defeat a measure they understood to be designed to change their society. Facing this situation in a body he knew as well as anyone in the world, President Johnson decided on a no-compromise strategy. The chips were on the table for an all-out confrontation, and the president made it clear that he was prepared to shut down all other business in Congress as long as necessary to break the filibuster and bring the bill to a vote. After many weeks of debate, an agreement was finally negotiated with the Senate GOP leader Everett Dirksen of Illinois, who was most concerned about limiting enforcement power in the public accommodations and job discrimination titles, which affected his state. The compromises needed to win his support and GOP votes limited the enforcement authority of the attorney general to systemic cases, among other relatively minor changes (Mann 1996, 420–421). After the longest debate in U.S. history, and the massive mobilization of religious, labor, and other institutions across the country, the bill passed 73–27 on June 19 (Mann 1996, 428). The president signed it into law on July 2, and the country passed into a new era. The next part of this chapter explores the impacts of Title II, the public accommodations section.

Change Far Faster and Deeper than Expected

Passage of the Civil Rights Act of 1964 made the long-established racial practices of thousands of restaurants, hotels, libraries, hospitals, and other institutions across the South illegal. Officials expected a long, difficult struggle to enforce the new rights. A decade after *Brown*, political resistance still blocked school desegregation, and a similar struggle over accommodations was expected. Officials would be dealing with vast numbers of private owners and yet would lack the authority to impose real sanctions for noncompliance. But this fear turned out to be unfounded. Passage of the law itself, along with a modest enforcement and compliance effort, produced wide-ranging, peaceful change.

A title added to the civil rights bill in the House of Representatives established the Community Relations Service, which was charged with handling the explosive situations expected to arise in many places in the South when federal desegregation efforts ran into local customs. The Community Relations Service, headed by a prominent former southern governor, Leroy Collins of Florida, geared up for a long and intense struggle. What happened instead was one of the most encouraging and little-discussed results of the civil rights revolution. By and large, the South complied, and there were few serious problems; the apartheid policies in the vast majority of institutions passed into the dustbin of history with little notice or regret. The law reached into the heart of Ku Klux Klan areas, where segregation had been defended with violence for generations and where crossing racial boundaries could easily unleash violence. The Community Relations Service was given no enforcement powers and was made part of the Commerce Department, in hopes that it could communicate with local businessmen to offset some of the expected resistance.

In fact, change had begun in some parts of the South even before the law was enacted, after President Kennedy asked business leaders to take voluntary steps. "Our last survey of such desegregation, made just before the bill's enactment," reported Attorney General Robert Kennedy, "showed that out of 566 communities in Southern and Border states, there had been at least some desegregation in public accommodations in 397 cities—fully 70 percent." Cities with at least some theater desegregation grew from "109 in May 1963, to 300." Gains in other sorts of public accommodations were as impressive: "The number of cities in which some restaurants were desegregated increased from 141 cities to 325"; for hotels and motels, the increase was from 163 to 284; for lunch counters, from 204 to 366. But, Kennedy noted, "hard core" resistance remained (Kennedy 1964). Though only a small fraction of the institutions in the seventeen states historically segregated by law were desegregated, it showed that some were adapting to the changes they saw coming.

After passage of the law, resistance was rare and compliance general. In its first year of operation, the Community Relations Service worked on reconciling disputes in 178 communities in thirty-one states, mostly in the South. Two-thirds of the work came in southern states, with the largest concentrations of problems in Mississippi, Louisiana, Florida, and Georgia. Over half the work came in towns with populations under 25,000. In 79 of the communities, the problems concerned public accommodations. There was only one public accommodations lawsuit case in the entire country outside the states with a history of segregation by law (U.S. Department of Commerce 1966, 19–23).

Southern officials had joined to delay or block school desegregation (Sarratt 1966), and there were some attempts to mobilize resistance to the integration of public accommodations, but only one protester rode the issue to political power for a time—Lester Maddox of Georgia. Maddox was an outspoken segregationist and owned a large, popular, whites-only restaurant in central Atlanta called the Pickrick. He had run unsuccessful campaigns for mayor of Atlanta and lieutenant governor on a segregationist platform. When blacks tried to integrate his restaurant, he and a group of followers armed with axe handles stopped them. When the Justice Department successfully sued him, he sold the restaurant rather than serve blacks. On the strength of this issue, Maddox was elected governor of Georgia in 1966, defeating future president Jimmy Carter (Rice 1988). His election, however, was the last gasp of a dying idea, not the beginning of a new resistance on racial matters. Although an anti-civil-rights GOP would arise in the South in the 1970s and 1980s, it was not concerned mainly about public accommodations but about the deeper issues of racial change.[6]

The Community Relations Service reported that in "downtown sections of larger communities and along the interstate highways," things had changed rapidly. "It has been observed that Negro residents of many of the smaller communities are prevented from eating in restaurants and going to theaters by threats and acts of violence, even though the owner or manager may be willing to provide service." The report concluded: "National motel and restaurant chains have provided the primary leadership for the changes which have taken place. The convention trade has also been influential. The passage of the Civil Rights Act gave local owners who wanted to observe the law an opportunity to do so as law-abiding citizens." Earlier experience showed the truth of this claim: "The case-by-case approach of eliminating discriminatory practices is not often practicable in the South. A single restaurant, motel or public facility is generally unwilling to serve all customers when other owners in the same area do not follow the same practice. . . . Accordingly, in many communities owners prefer to be ordered by a court or be the subject of governmental sanctions before changing discriminatory practices" (U.S. Department of Commerce 1966, 24–25). One of the things often apparent in civil rights enforcement is that discrimination was frequently practiced to conform to long-held values in order to retain local customers, but businesses were willing to change if they could shift the blame to some agency that forced them to do it. Once the new practice becomes the norm, the problem tends to disappear. So, in this policy arena, the Civil Rights Act created a sense of inevitability and shifted the blame for change from businesses to the law, thus, relatively quickly and peacefully creating a new status quo that actually helped businesses by expanding their clienteles.

This sort of blame shifting as a way to make the inevitable acceptable was seen also in the desegregation of many types of public institutions, including libraries, hospitals, and train stations. Discriminatory practices had, to a considerable extent, been maintained by the fear that whoever began the change would be singled out and socially, politically, and economically marginalized. Making these practices illegal and threatening prosecution by the U.S. Justice Department completely shifted the blame, creating a situation in which all institutions changed simultaneously. Only a very modest and symbolic level of enforcement was ever necessary.

Less than two years after the law was enacted, Attorney General Nicholas Katzenbach told Congress that the Community Relations Service was originally designed "largely, if not exclusively, to work with business" facing very difficult changes. He noted: "Hundreds of angry demonstrations, spreading from Birmingham across the South, concentrated public anxiety on the public accommodations section. Under the circumstances, we believed . . . that the business community of the South offered the best rallying point for an effective force in support of the law so it seemed eminent good sense to enlist the support of the Commerce Department, headed by a distinguished former Governor of North Carolina, to seek the spirit of compromise. In fact, however, voluntary compliance with the public accommodations section exceeded the most hopeful expectations" (Katzenbach 1966a, 22–23). When the service published its fiscal year 1967 report, public accommodations were not even mentioned, and the service was working in big cities on police-community relations, employment issues, and actual and developing crises (U.S. Department of Justice 1968).

Even the courts moved swiftly and decisively. The law was quickly upheld by the U.S. Supreme Court, meaning that legal appeals would be useless. The Supreme Court acted with rare speed in sweepingly upholding the public accommodations provisions of the law in *Heart of Atlanta Motel, Inc. v. United States*, 379 U.S. 241 (1964), decided less than six months after the law was signed. Normally, years would be required to litigate a case and appeal it eventually to the high court. The government initially brought the case to trial before an unusual three-judge court and then appealed directly to the Supreme Court, which heard it immediately and quickly handed down a unanimous decision. The law prohibited "discrimination or segregation of any kind on the ground of race, color, religion, or national origin." The court noted that thirty-two states already had laws against discrimination against clients and that "no case has been cited to us where the attack on a state statute has been successful, either in federal or state courts." The courts firmly supported the law.

The irony is that the change happened so fast that it was never seriously studied or documented—it just happened. It happened so much faster than anyone imagined that the organization set up to deal with expected conflicts—the Community Relations Service—was virtually out of that business within two years, working on northern urban problems instead.

There were other parts of the racial reforms of the 1960s that had this character. For example, court decisions and constitutional amendments ended the poll tax and overturned numerous state laws forbidding interracial marriage. And, of course, the 1965 immigration act, which changed an openly racist immigration policy and transformed much of the country in the next half century. All these things passed with a modest level of controversy and almost no serious political mobilization or violence, though they had substantial impacts. Journalists and many historians tend to focus their attention on conflicts. These were cases where the absence of conflict was in fact the big story.

President Johnson noted the surprising success of the law in his 1967 message to Congress on equal justice: "When the 1964 Civil Rights Act was passed," he noted, "fears were expressed that this sharp change in established customs would bring about serious economic loss and perhaps even violence. . . . Yet from the start there has been widespread voluntary compliance with the law. Thousands of restaurants, motels and hotels have been opened to Americans of all races and colors. What was thought to be laden with danger proved generally acceptable to both races." The law broke the logjam. "Because all businesses of a similar type are covered, each businessman is free, for the first time, to operate on a non-discriminatory basis without fear of suffering a competitive disadvantage" (Johnson 1967).

Sometimes the mere existence of a law solves a collective-action problem—the fear of being ostracized—and permits relatively easy progress on big questions.

Vice President Hubert Humphrey, who led the congressional battle for the act, noted: "The acceptance of the public accommodations provisions by businesses—even in those areas where they constituted a reversal of generations of custom and practice—exceeded our most optimistic predictions" (Humphrey 1965).

The quick and remarkable change in the operation of hospitals was similar to that in restaurants and hotels. After the U.S. Court of Appeals for the Fourth Circuit found the traditional "separate but equal" policy for federal aid to hospitals unconstitutional in 1963 (*Simkins v. Moses H. Cone Hospital*), the secretary of Health, Education and Welfare (HEW) in 1964 blocked all pending and future applications for federal construction money until nondiscrimination was assured (Celebrezze 1964). Hospitals are places of extremely personal events and problems, and they had been thoroughly segregated. The American Hospital Association, in the November 1964 issue of its journal, *Hospitals*, featured an article titled "The Civil Rights Act of 1964," which attacked the coming intervention in hospital operations. Following passage of the law, the administration held many sessions around the country on implementation. The HEW secretary told the White House, "In order to assure an effective and consistent department-wide effort in eliminating discrimination in programs for which we are responsible, we called in our top-level headquarters and regional program administrators for two and a half days of intensive discussion" (Celebrezze 1965).

The Johnson administration's success in enacting Medicare and Medicaid in 1965 meant that there would be a vast expansion in federal support for hospitalization of the elderly and the poor. When the administration informed the segregated hospitals that they would be ineligible to participate without strong civil rights compliance, there was a sudden transformation. The White House noted: "This year [1965], Negroes are being admitted to hospitals which barred them in the past. By January, 7,130 hospitals—more than 95 percent of the hospitals in the nation—had agreed to provide services without discrimination. More than 1,500 of those hospitals have had to change past policies to make that commitment." The administration noted: "Getting rid of discriminatory practices has benefitted the hospital system, as well as the people they serve," because segregation was costly. "Last year, for example, half the beds in an all-white hospital were unoccupied. Yet Negroes in the community were sent to a completely segregated and overcrowded hospital. The half-empty hospital changed its policies to admit Negroes, and it now operates at full capacity. The formerly Negro hospital will be converted into a nursing home serving both races. The effect of the change was to provide better medical care for the entire community" (White House 1967). Within the span of a single year, southerners of all races were being born and dying in formerly segregated hospitals.

Another part of life in the region changed, and no one paid much attention. The public accommodations success was the dream of civil rights reform—though difficult to enact, it quickly crystallized a new norm, took the blame for change off the offending institutions, and required very little enforcement or legal coercion. A new standard was peacefully accepted and would not be challenged during the next half century. Once the civil rights struggle moved to the North, the battle was much tougher.

The Fair Housing Battle as Part of LBJ's Struggle to Address the Urban Crisis

The Johnson administration had no sooner won passage of the second great civil rights reform to change the South than a deep urban crisis began to explode across the country. Just weeks after the enactment of the Voting Rights Act, a massive riot swept across huge areas of the Watts ghetto of Los Angeles, creating fear and anger across the country. This time, the dominant public image was not of peaceful, respectful protestors being attacked by racist local officials, but of mobs breaking into and looting stores and setting fire to large areas of a great city. There was intense publicity both for the black leaders using quasi-revolutionary rhetoric and for white leaders demanding harsh measures to restore "law and order." Black leaders warned that there were more "long, hot summers" coming, and they were right. For many outside the South, the issue of race was no longer about creating basic rights for oppressed southern blacks but about the fear of out-of-control violence committed by black mobs against whites and their property. By the time of the 1966 midterm elections, these themes had become central to a Republican Party trying to recover from its huge defeat in the 1964 presidential election. The politics of change became far more difficult than before.

The Johnson administration, deeply concerned about the social crises of American cities, was committed to action. The poverty program of 1964, the education reform of 1965, and the creation of Medicaid in the same year all directed funds to help the families, schools, and communities most affected by concentrated poverty, a great many of which were black or Latino. Johnson won passage of the bill creating the new federal Department of Housing and Urban Development and named the first African American cabinet member in U.S. history, Robert Weaver, to head it. The president appointed special commissions to propose solutions for urban decay, and in his historic speech at Howard University in June 1965, the president recognized the deep and persisting disadvantages of the ghetto and the need for extraordinary measures to create real equality (Johnson 1965). But expectations rose and frustration grew once these efforts did not quickly change the underlying realities of profound urban inequality. The riots cut deeply into the president's support for further action on racial issues. And Vietnam protests were dividing Democrats and taking energy away from civil rights efforts.

The Johnson Urban Agenda

Lyndon Johnson ran what was by far the most urban-oriented administration in American history, though he faced more urban upheaval than any other president. He succeeded in moving through Congress a visionary agenda of urban change, including major parts that were enacted after he declined to run for reelection. Johnson persuaded Congress to establish the Department of Housing and Urban Development and fundamentally transformed programs of subsidized housing, eliminating many of their worst features. His administration ended the virtual exclusion of nonwhite home buyers from the federally insured mortgage (FHA and VA) programs. His task forces and commissions called for a greatly expanded federal role in dealing with a deep social and economic crisis in the heart of U.S. metropolitan areas. LBJ won passage of the largest program of subsidized housing in American history, and of the Model Cities program, which was designed to coordinate federal programs for the comprehensive development of cities. The administration began a rent supplement system for poor families over bitter opposition in Congress and initiated a substantial program of leased housing, bypassing some of the local politics over site selection for public housing projects (Solomon 1974, 168–169).

These victories were not easy and were far from complete. Congress almost wiped out the rent supplement program before it could get started. The Model Cities program was enacted, but vital elements were rejected as the bill worked its way through Congress. An initial proposal to focus on a small number of cities, to take a metropolitan-wide focus, to have an explicit commitment to integrated housing opportunities, and to appoint a federal coordinator ended up with all these goals deleted; the number and type of locations to be helped were expanded broadly, only modest funds were allocated for planning, and none were designated for operations (Haar 1975). The administration won passage of the first federal law banning housing discrimination, as discussed in this chapter. In a number of federal programs, the Johnson administration bypassed the traditional state control of federal grants in order to provide substantial direct funding to cities, since many states had historically been unresponsive to the needs of their big cities and to civil rights concerns. The administration put in place significant elements of an urban policy that could have profoundly redirected the development of metropolitan America over the next half century had it been funded and seriously implemented.

In 1965, President Johnson asked Congress to create a commission to study "slums, urban growth, sprawl and blight, and to insure decent and durable housing" (U.S. National Commission on Urban Problems [U.S. NCUP] 1968, vii). What ensued was a massive examination of urban realities; hearings were held across the country, and more than forty studies were commissioned (iii). The investigations showed widespread unmet housing needs and documented profound racial inequities in the housing and urban renewal programs, which had destroyed housing in what had been large black and Latino neighborhoods. The work had a strong impact on developing ideas about federal policy, and the commission's unanimous report filed in the last days of the Johnson administration provided a sweeping set of recommendations for addressing the urban crisis. Concerning housing, the commission concluded that 16 percent of all housing units, more than eleven million of them, were substandard or overcrowded and that the "critical aspect" was "the *concentration* of substandard housing and of poor people" (9).

A fundamental problem was how to acquire building sites in good areas, since many city neighborhoods and suburban communities systematically excluded subsidized and affordable housing. One of the innovative ideas of the 1960s urban policy agenda was the development of "New Towns," freestanding comprehensive communities that would provide housing for all income levels and a job base and would be situated on large sites outside the suburban rings of major cities. The idea was to create an alternative to vast, unplanned, segregated sprawl, which required long-distance commuting that entailed an enormous loss of time (Clapp 1971, 152–155). HUD underwrote funding for thirteen New Towns that could serve as possible models.

Housing segregation was seen as a major threat by several presidential task forces and commissions. Projected over a quarter century, existing trends meant that the white population of central cities was likely to decline while the nonwhite population grew 94 percent, and that the white suburban population would double in size (and remain 94 percent of the total). According to the National Commission on Urban Problems, "Slums in our big cities, which are now in the midst of social decay, may well become social and economic disaster areas" (U.S. NCUP 1968, 5). Its report added: "We must build decent housing in the slums, and we must provide freedom of residence for all Americans" (26). It called for building "low-rent housing in the suburbs as well as in the cities . . . [and on] sites in outlying areas"; states were to be given "incentives to act where localities do not," and the government would tie "a locality's eligibility for Federal grants such as for highways, sewers, and water to that community's effort to house its share of the poor" (26). Title VIII of the Fair Housing Act would provide a possible tool for such sanctions.

To change cities and metropolitan areas, the federal government needed leverage, which the Johnson administration created. Major funding for housing, community development, and urban infrastructure gave weight to its priorities. The 1968 goal of creating six million new subsidized units for families through new programs promoting ownership and nonprofit rental housing, for example, called for an unprecedented expansion of the federal role.

Although LBJ's administration launched a multidimensional urban strategy, there was significant resistance even at the height of liberal influence in Congress. Given the growing fiscal pressures of the Vietnam War, much of the housing program was launched in a way that spurred rapid action but postponed large costs. New policies were enacted, but the funds provided were modest and there was not enough time to produce results and build a constituency during the Johnson administration.

The Civil Rights Struggle for Housing Rights in the Cities

To change race relations in a society with profound racial divisions and deep and persisting inequality is so difficult politically that most leaders do their best to ignore the issue, though its effects are all around them. The worst use it as a way to gain power by exploiting the division and fear that has always accompanied racial issues. Very few choose to spend their political power in a struggle to change strongly defended practices of neighborhood segregation.

Less than a year after Johnson's landslide election, the Watts riots stunned and angered the country. The War on Poverty, begun the year before, had not settled rapidly rising urban tension and racial polarization. The White House was in the midst of the most consequential period of social reform since the New Deal, and the cities cried out for action. Black leaders warned that there were more riots coming. Liberals, fearing that the cities were coming apart, searched for answers. Many local political leaders, including the California GOP gubernatorial candidate Ronald Reagan, called for stronger police action. Fear of black mobs threatening whites and their property stirred conservative demands for "law and order."

When the president called for a fair housing law, he moved far ahead of public opinion. Fair housing groups, never a major political force, were continually asking President Johnson, like President Kennedy, to issue executive orders to rein in housing discrimination, at least in federal programs. Given the political climate and the situation in the Congress, even the most fervent fair housing supporters saw little or no chance of passing a federal law. Yet in his state of the union address in January 1966, Johnson promised "legislation, resting on the fullest constitutional authority of the Federal Government to prohibit racial discrimination in housing" (Johnson 1966, 5). Even the President's Committee on Equal Opportunity in Housing was reluctant to endorse the measure, which some dismissed as a strategy to evade an executive order (Giesey 1969). The National Committee against Discrimination in Housing (1966), the leading lobby for open housing, claimed that the law would be little more effective than an executive order.

When Johnson announced his commitment, no bill had been prepared. As the bill was drafted, it called for broad coverage of the housing market but little enforcement authority. It was a parallel in some ways to the employment discrimination provisions of the 1964 Civil Rights Act, which had given the Equal Employment Opportunity Commission the power only to investigate and try to conciliate. The draft was discouraging to fair housing advocates, who had seen too many state and local laws that made sweeping promises but had few teeth and left housing discrimination virtually untouched.

When Johnson sent the bill to Congress, he noted: "The day has long since passed when problems of race in America could be identified with only one section of the country." He called it a way to ensure that blacks would have "the right to live in freedom among . . . fellow Americans" (Johnson 1966). Clarence Mitchell, the deeply respected lobbyist for the NAACP, called the bill a "giant step," but others were doubtful (*Washing-*

ton Post, April 29, 1966). The Congress of Racial Equality (CORE), a major civil rights group moving toward the black power idea, was also bitterly critical of LBJ, reflecting the increasingly fragmented turf the administration had to work on.

The U.S. Commission on Civil Rights, an influential independent bipartisan agency (until it was politicized by President Reagan's successful challenge of its independence), testified that the bill was far too weak to make much difference, arguing that the bill needed to give HUD "cease and desist" authority to compel change.[7] The president's own White House Conference on Civil Rights (1966, 4, 26–27) echoed the call for serious enforcement tools and argued that all federal aid should require "submission of a metropolitan-wide plan providing for desegregation of housing and promotion of communities inclusive of all races and incomes."

The bill went to the most liberal Congress of the century, the Congress that had given Johnson victory after victory on great and difficult issues in 1965. By 1966, however, it was clear that the peak of the liberal coalition was fading and that public opinion was shifting as news footage of race riots and the Vietnam War, as well as of the militant black power movement, were replacing images of dignified hymn-singing protesters seeking basic rights in the Deep South. After passage of the Civil Rights Act and the Voting Rights Act, and all the sweeping changes in racial policies since 1963, a majority of Americans thought that racial change was going too fast (Pettigrew 2003, 25–26). President Johnson, who had seemed invulnerable a year earlier, now faced declining popularity, as he had predicted to his staff earlier.

What the Public Thought

Attitudes about race are complex. In some areas there has been long-term and apparently irreversible change. In others, change has been halting and sometimes reversed. There have also been major gaps between the share of people who believe that there is a problem of discrimination and the proportion supporting governmental action to solve the problem. In fact, there has rarely been any lasting public commitment to the expansion of civil rights laws and enforcement, and there has often been a perception, particularly by whites, that change came too fast or went too far.

As segregation became consolidated at very high levels in the nation's cities from the 1940s to the 1960s, some attitudes gradually improved. In 1942, 62 percent of whites said that they would be concerned if a black person with the same income and education moved into their block, but that figure had declined to 36 percent by 1964 and 21 percent by 1968, according to national surveys. Yet in 1966, the year when LBJ asked for the fair housing law, 34 percent of whites admitted that they would move if a black person moved next door, and 71 percent said they would go if "great numbers" moved in. Fifty-one percent of whites said they would object to "having a Negro family as [their] next door neighbor" (Pettigrew 2003, 25–26). In April 1968, the month the fair housing law passed, 54 percent of whites agreed with the statement "White people have a right to keep Negroes out of their neighborhoods if they want to and Negroes should respect that right" (26). Two years after the fair housing law was enacted, 43 percent of whites still took that position (26). When asked in 1967 whether they would "favor a federal law forbidding discrimination in housing against Negroes," 63 percent of whites said no. A 1968 survey of whites in fifteen cities found that although only 40 percent opposed a law against job discrimination, 51 percent were against prohibiting housing discrimination (26–27). When asked in 1968 whether the worst conditions facing blacks in housing and other areas were products mainly of discrimination or "something about Negroes themselves," 19 percent of whites said discrimination, 56 percent blamed it on something about blacks themselves, and another 19 percent said "both" (26–27). The ambivalence of white opinion was deeply rooted, as summarized by Thomas Pettigrew (2003, 30): "Most white Americans are well aware that racial discrimination in housing exists . . . And in a list of 14 white institutions . . . 'real estate companies' comprise the only institution rated by whites in 1966 as 'keeping Negroes down' . . . Yet only a minority of whites favored laws against housing discrimination."

Because of the multiple vetoes built into the workings of Congress, a substantial and persistent majority is usually required to enact a highly controversial and visible change. In the fair housing battle, the odds were heavily stacked against the law. At the time of the fair housing debate in Congress there were still few stably interracial neighborhoods in the country, so many whites saw the first entry of black households into an area as the beginning of irreversible neighborhood change. The urban riots only intensified the problem. Johnson was asking for an unpopular and unproven change that was opposed by many urban white Democrats.

Congressional Democrats outside the South had been virtually unanimous in backing civil rights legislation affecting the South, but were much more divided about laws affecting the cities. The coalition of civil rights groups, labor, and churches, so powerful in 1964, was no longer in place; whites feared urban violence; and the Supreme Court would not act on school segregation outside the South for another seven years. Martin Luther King's 1966 fair housing marches in Chicago did not evoke the kind of national response that the great southern marches had engendered (Ralph 1993). The great challenges and increasingly negative political situation made many doubt the wisdom of the president's request to Congress to enact a national fair housing law in 1966, in marked contrast to the standing ovation for the president's voting rights proposal in 1965.

Before the president sent his proposal, the attorney general sounded out leading congressmen and senators and reported back: "Our principal difficulty in both Houses is apathy. There is no great push for civil rights legislation this year, save as we give it. Important congressmen like McCulloch [a moderate Ohio GOP Representative who had played a critical role in the earlier civil rights bills] are very cool. This means that we will have to push hard for hearings and for Committee action, and I have impressed this upon the civil rights leadership as well. Those who are knowledgeable about Congress agree" (Katzenbach 1966b). The president craved information on pending legislation. Califano (1966) reported an early count on the relevant House committee. There were nine favoring fair housing legislation, eighteen opposed, and six doubtful.

Though it seemed possible to eventually win in the House committee, the situation in the Senate seemed so negative that "House members are reluctant to vote on housing if it is not going to pass the other body" (Califano 1966). The only chance to overcome a southern filibuster and enact a civil rights law in the Senate was to win broad Republican support. With the GOP Senate leader Everett Dirksen (R-IL) opposed, there was no chance. Even a number of the strongest civil rights supporters in the Senate were skeptical. The attorney general thought it possible that the bill could pass in committee, but saw no prospect of breaking a filibuster and getting a vote on it in the full Senate (Califano 1966).

A White House congressional liaison, Larry O'Brien, thought that chances were "remote, if not impossible." Though he thought that the president should ask for action, he noted, "There is no great enthusiasm for Civil Rights legislation this year" (O'Brien 1966). The president's own worries about the impact of the ongoing upheavals in the black community were evident in the message, as reflected in a memorandum, dated April 2, 1966, to LBJ from his aide Jack Valenti: "In line with your suggestion, several paragraphs were added at the end . . . to get across the idea that Negroes must make use of the opportunities now available to them. The Federal Government cannot do it alone." But in spite of the grim prospects, the president asked Congress to act.

When the legislation went to the House Judiciary Committee, there was pessimism. In the Senate, the reaction of Senator Dirksen, the Republican leader, was toxic. He was actively hostile, describing the bill as "absolutely unconstitutional."[8] Unlike the earlier civil rights bills, which had not confronted any major hostile lobby, the president's bill was strongly opposed by the powerful real estate lobby, representing a group present and politically active in all parts of the country. Realtors mobilized opposition across the country (Emlen 1966). With supporters in disarray and the civil rights movement visibly coming apart in the Mississippi march at which the rising black power movement leaders' dismissal of nonviolence dominated the news (Muse 1968, ch. 16), the Republicans were happy to rain on the president's parade in June. Dirksen was joined in strong opposition by Congressman Gerald Ford of Michigan, the House GOP leader.[9]

Even a weakened bill with little coverage was threatened with death by referral to the hostile Rules Committee, a tactic narrowly defeated (*Congressional Record* [*CR*], July 25, 1966, 16058). The frightening reality of urban riots permeated the discussion. While the House was debating the measure, there were serious riots in Cleveland and Brooklyn, and violence on Chicago's West Side, stirring the pot of racial polarization.[10] Public support for LBJ's civil rights efforts fell sharply.[11] Ford, the House minority leader, pointed to the "riots, the looting, and the tumult and the shouting" (*CR*, July 25, 1966, 16318). For the first time in the civil rights movement, GOP leaders were actively opposing a civil rights measure. One congressional opponent blasted the fair housing bill by claiming that if homeowners' right to discriminate were prohibited, it would amount to a threat to "the whole fabric of our social environment, our economic structure, and our basic theory of private ownership" (*CR*, August 1, 1966, 16969).

To prevent outright defeat of the measure, Representative Charles Mathias (R-MD), a GOP moderate, moved to create a giant exemption, allowing homeowners to tell their real estate agents to discriminate (*CR*, July 27, 1966, 16378, 16380). Liberals countered with a stronger bill covering all types of housing, which was defeated by a margin of more than 2–1. Even the eviscerated Mathias amendment was carried by only a single vote (*CR*, August 3, 1966, 17328, 17337). The bill was further amended by the addition of sweeping "anti-riot" provisions aimed at those agitating for violence (*CR*, August 8, 1966, 17651–17670). Thus, anti-civil-rights language was written into a civil rights bill. Seeing no chance to salvage the president's bill, the House committee pared it down to a nearly empty shell, exempting individual homeowners from the bill's coverage and leaving out most of the nation's housing units. Even the faithful mainstream NAACP civil rights leader Roy Wilkins said that the bill would leave suburbia "lily-white." He saw little value in a law full of loopholes.[12]

Eventually the tattered remnants of the bill passed the House, 259–157. Martin Luther King was deeply skeptical, saying it would "increase despair and discontent," and Wilkins said that the antiriot provisions (likely to be used against civil rights groups) would "set the civil rights clock back 150 years."[13] Even that remnant of the president's proposal was much too much for the Senate. When the bill reached that chamber, it hit a stone wall as the GOP decisively shifted sides in a major civil rights battle; tension in the cities imperiled any hope of passage. Martin Luther King, whose great marches in Birmingham and Selma had powered national movements that helped enact the 1964 Civil Rights Act and the 1965 Voting Rights Act, was marching again, but in the North and against a different enemy—and what would be his last major movement produced searing images of angry confrontations but no outpouring of support for another civil rights law. He said that the fury of the mobs he faced in Chicago were worse than anything he had encountered in the South (M. King 1967).

President Johnson acknowledged the limited House bill as a "symbolic" victory and called for prompt Senate passage.[14] Getting anything at all through the House without any real support, and over active opposition from the powerful Realtors' lobby and GOP leaders, had been an accomplishment.

The bill arrived at the Senate with Dirksen firmly opposed and civil rights support dropping. King's successful strategy in the South had been to focus on an urgent moral issue and create a peaceful, dignified protest, displaying the anger and racism of his opponents and arousing sympathy and support for change from across the country. Invited to Chicago by a coalition of civil rights groups, King identified housing segregation as a central dimension of inequality for the city's blacks, one creating persistent intergenerational poverty.[15] Chicago was notorious for the violence waged against African American families moving into white areas. As King's marchers entered bitterly resistant southwest Chicago and inner-suburban neighborhoods, they were attacked, racist signs were waved, jeers rang out, and King was hit by a brick. He said, "I've seen many demonstrations in the South but I've never seen anything so hostile and hateful as I've seen here today."[16]

Unlike the southern demonstrations, the marches produced no wave of sympathy, positive publicity, or mobilization for fair housing legislation. *Newsweek* (August, 15, 1966) reported that Chicago "verged on racial war." By fall, a Gallup poll showed that most Americans thought integration was being pushed "too fast."[17] Civil rights supporters who had carried more than two-thirds of the Senate on the earlier bills could not get even a majority of senators to come to the floor for quorum calls necessary to keep debate going in the face of a filibuster. When the bill came up on a vote to end the filibuster, the GOP attacked it, saying that white resistance was due to bad behavior by black neighbors (*CR*, September 14, 1966, 21691).

Dirksen told the attorney general that he was opposed to the housing section and had promised another GOP leader to oppose the provisions against segregated juries as well (Katzenbach 1966c). Without Republican support, the bill was dead. Dirksen predicted GOP electoral gains from the defeat of the bill, which quickly died when supporters fell 11 votes short of cutting off the filibuster.

The 1966 midterm election returns seemed to underline the country's turn in a more conservative direction. There was a major GOP comeback in the House, with a loss of 47 Democratic seats. Although the Democrats maintained a substantial majority, this was a huge loss, and the liberal Eighty-Ninth Congress was gone. Now the old "conservative coalition" of southern Democrats and Republicans was back in business, and the Republicans sensed the wind of public opinion at their back. With dismaying speed, new members of Congress were demanding sweeping antiriot laws and ever harsher criminal sanctions.

Under these conditions, it seemed chimerical to many to even try to enact the legislation. In his 1967 state of the union address, however, the president renewed his call for legislation on fair housing and a number of other civil rights measures, including the protection of civil rights workers.

Unhappily for the Johnson program, the election had restored conservatives' power on the House Rules Committee, which permitted consideration of only a limited bill protecting civil rights workers, and even that only in exchange for an agreement to accept sweeping antiriot legislation that conservatives saw as a way to prosecute "outside agitators" who, they believed, were stirring up racial violence. This modest and, to many liberals, threatening bill passed the House by a large margin, but in the Senate was sent to the conservative Judiciary Committee, headed by the segregationist James Eastland (D-MS), where it was reported out on the last day of the session, preventing any Senate action on it in 1967.

The administration kept pushing. The attorney general wrote to President Johnson in September: "I have visited several times with Senator Dirksen without success. Yesterday he told me unequivocally that he would not help us to get cloture on the bill with or without the Housing Title. . . . We met today and Senator Dirksen repeated his position." Dirksen sent the message that his caucus was so negative about the bill that "even if he would change his position it would not be possible for him to secure the votes necessary for cloture" (Katzenbach 1966c).

The legislation was given new life by a parliamentary stratagem that turned the committee's stall at the end of the 1967 session into an opportunity for Senate action in early 1968. Senate Democratic leader Mike Mansfield (D-MT) held the bill over to the beginning of the next session, hoping to work out a compromise with southerners on a modest bill and avoid a major floor fight. Mansfield created an advantage for civil rights groups when he called up the bill as the first order of business for the Senate in 1968.

President Johnson, greatly distracted by what was becoming the enormous battle over Vietnam that eventually led him to renounce his reelection bid, paid little attention to the fair housing issue in his 1968 state of the union address. In the words of a leading advisor, he thought that pushing for fair housing under these conditions was "unwise" (McPherson 1971). The debate on the minor bill from the House had little urgency. Though there was talk of a compromise with southern leaders to further weaken the bill, thirty-six liberal senators protested. They showed surprising strength on the successful motion to table the southern substitute, winning 54–29 with considerable GOP support.

Following this surprising victory on the first skirmish, Senators Walter Mondale (D-MN) and Edward Brooke (R-MA) promptly introduced a fair housing amendment, vastly raising the stakes.[18] This move, early in a presidential election year, challenged the GOP, which had been greatly hurt four years earlier when its nominee, Barry Goldwater, opposed the 1964 Civil Rights Act, lost moderates, and totally polarized the black vote. Senator Mondale, with very little seniority, had been given charge of the issue at hearings in 1967, in good measure because colleagues thought they were "going through a ritual" on an issue that was going nowhere (U.S. Senate 1967, 213, 232). His cosponsor, Senator Brooke, the Senate's only African American member, had even less seniority. Mondale hoped that "most Americans are now asking for the first time what is going on in these rotten ghettos and what can we do as decent Americans to help deal with this problem" (U.S. Senate 1967).

Although the proponents of the amendment expected to lose, they were determined to put up a good fight. Senate leader Mansfield said that supporters did not have the votes and were likely to risk losing the limited House bill (U.S. Senate 1967, 329–331, 365–366, 420–421). The Mondale-Brooke amendment went far beyond the limited 1966 House version, covering nine-tenths of the housing market, forbidding biased advertising, and granting HUD broad enforcement authority (*CR*, February 6, 1968, 990, 994). In a national capital where Democrats were worried about the political fallout from Martin Luther King's "poor people's campaign," which set up camps on the National Mall, there was little enthusiasm for a civil rights fight. Because of the limited attention paid to the amendment, which seemed certain to fail, the real estate lobby did not even seriously mobilize (Mondale 1971). Conservatives excoriated the amendment. The low-key debate went on for a month, and then Mansfield called a cloture vote to test the strength of the amendment's supporters. Since there had been only two successful votes to cut off civil rights filibusters in U.S. history, and those had happened in vastly more favorable political circumstances, it seemed wildly improbable that the effort would succeed. Mansfield, concerned about getting back to the Senate's other business, said, "The issue must be met in its present posture" (Weisberger 1968, 111). The present posture included strong opposition from Republican leader Dirksen (111–112). It seemed like the end of the road.

The cloture vote, however, showed surprising strength, falling just seven votes short of the necessary two-thirds majority, carrying virtually all non-southern Democrats and winning support of half the GOP senators. The Senate still had a significant number of moderate Republicans who identified with their party's antislavery origins. The key was to win the support of other, more conservative Republicans who had voted for the earlier civil rights measures. When Mansfield moved to table the amendment, supporters defeated the motion by a large 58–34 margin, keeping the proposal alive for another day (Weisberger 1968, 112–113).

The only real chance for the legislation was to win over Senator Dirksen, the key to support from more conservative Republicans. Dirksen had been critical to passage of both the 1964 Civil Rights Act and the Voting Rights Act. In spite of his earlier hostility, Dirksen hinted, in conversations with the attorney general, that he might support a proposal that would exclude homeowners selling their own homes. While discussions were underway, supporters came within six votes of ending debate. Then Dirksen announced he was for some kind of bill. Conservatives began to generate apocalyptic descriptions of the bill. John Sparkman (D-AL) called it a "federal police state bill," and Eastland said it was a plot to force the creation of racially balanced neighborhoods (*CR*, February 27, 1968, S1780, S1788).

Negotiations were undertaken with GOP leaders, including Dirksen, who had lost control of the GOP moderates supporting Mondale and Brooke. Dirksen was more interested in the politics than the details, but wanted something that conservatives in the GOP could be convinced to vote for (Waters 1969). The debate focused on how much of the housing market would be covered by the new law. The liberals were surprised and happy that Dirksen was agreeable to broad coverage and to a bill, in Mondale's words, "far stronger than we believed possible just a week ago" (*Wall Street Journal*, February 27, 1968).

What was lost in the negotiations was any real enforcement power for HUD. The arrangement was much like the employment discrimination provisions of Title VII of the 1964 Civil Rights Act—broad coverage but limited enforcement. Granting the housing agency power to issue "cease and desist" orders, as in the 1966 House bill, gave way to a process modeled on the employment title of the 1964 Civil Rights Act, in which the agency could only investigate and conciliate; change could happen only through Justice Department litigation in federal court. The negotiators felt that they had to accept these limitations (Weisberger 1968, 115–116; Segal 1969; Frye 1969). After frenetic negotiations, Mondale and Brooke withdrew their amendment, and a compromise Dirksen bill was substituted. Dirksen told the Senate that he had changed his mind and bargained hard. He expected that his support would get the other five GOP votes needed to end the filibuster and permit the Senate to enact the bill. Two days later, however, after an onslaught of telegrams from concerned Realtors, Dirksen decided that he didn't have the votes. He proposed a further change, one greatly narrowing coverage and weakening access to the courts for victims of discrimination.[19] Dirksen, however, could not get more than two more votes, one of which was his own.

As the last chance for the measure approached, the White House sent out planes to bring in vacationing and campaigning senators and to keep one supporter sober. It all came down to the last three votes, and President Johnson, who had been following the battle very closely, weighed in with calls from Air Force One to Senators Bob Bartlett (D-AK) and Howard Cannon (D-NV), both small-state senators and defenders of the filibuster system, after Mondale told Johnson that it was the last chance to save the bill (Mondale 1971). In the end, Bartlett and Cannon voted for cloture. Cannon said that it was to protect the rights of the many minority soldiers fighting in Vietnam, an argument that President Johnson had repeatedly emphasized (Ferris 1969). The final vote was won when, during the roll call, Brooke appealed to the conservative Jack Miller (R-IA), promising to support Miller's amendment limiting coverage to veterans if he voted to cut off debate (Weisberger 1968, 118; Frye 1966; Ferris 1969; Mondale 1971). The filibuster was defeated in a great and unexpected liberal victory.

The bill, however, still faced eighty proposed amendments. Most were defeated, but the administrative enforcement process was further weakened by requiring federal officials to send all complaints to "substantially equivalent" state agencies before taking any action (*CR*, March 4, 1968, S2062). The complex political setting was apparent when the Senate added to the bill a sweeping "anti-riot" measure authored by a leading segregationist, Senator Strom Thurmond (D-SC), as well as other amendments increasing police power and infringing on free speech rights—especially of the "outside agitators" whom conservatives blamed for the riots.[20] The Senate narrowly defeated an amendment authorizing homeowners to sell their homes through brokers who discriminated (*CR*, March 5, 1968, S2239). Senator Miller's amendment to limit coverage to veterans and their families went down 13–73 (*CR*, March 8, 1968, 2454).[21] After all the skirmishes, the final tally was anticlimactic, a 71–20 vote to enact a law no one had expected to pass.[22] All but three GOP senators ended up voting for the bill.

The compromises with Senator Dirksen focused on how complaints were to be handled and how enforcement was to occur. The administration and other supporters focused on coverage. No significant attention was paid to key language in Title VIII. Potentially the most important part of the 1968 law was a sweeping but little-noticed provision in Title VIII that directed "all executive departments and agencies [to] administer their programs and activities . . . in a manner affirmatively to further the purposes of this title." In addition, since Title VI of the 1964 Civil Rights Act required all recipients of federal funds to take positive action to undo the effects of past discrimination, there was a substantial legal basis for making serious changes to many federal policies affecting cities and housing (24 *CFR* Sec. 570.601 [1982]). The sweeping language of Title VIII would produce many policy debates in the future.

Senate passage of a confusing and somewhat incoherent bill sent the measure back to the House of Representatives, a House that the midterm elections had made far less liberal than the one that had passed a much more limited bill two years earlier. President Johnson hailed the "overwhelming vote" in the Senate and called on the House to enact the Senate version, pointing to the popular antiriot provisions (Johnson 1968–1969, 374). The House Democratic leadership directly challenged the GOP in a presidential election year, recalling the Goldwater debacle after the GOP nominated a leading opponent of the 1964 Civil Rights Act. Alabama's segregationist governor George Wallace was running a major third-party campaign for president, threatening to siphon off conservative votes, and the GOP had to compete for mainstream support. Democrats rejected the Republican effort to send the bill to a conference committee, where it might have been buried or hopelessly delayed, and challenged the Republicans on the Rules Committee to let the House vote directly on the Senate bill.[23] The campaigns of two leading GOP presidential candidates, Richard Nixon and Nelson Rockefeller, asked House leaders to pass it (*CR*, April 26, 1968, 933). In the Rules Committee, however, all Republicans and three Democrats initially agreed to delay the measure, which would allow the Realtors' lobby to mount a serious campaign to block it. The bill's supporters were on the defensive about the poor drafting, the lack of committee hearings in either house of Congress, and the extraneous measures, including a long Indian bill of rights, which had received no serious attention before being included in the legislation (U.S. House 1968, 6). President Johnson demanded that Congress "quit fiddlin' and piddlin' and take action on the civil rights bill."[24] He again underlined the need to provide fair housing choices to wartime servicemen facing segregated housing even near military bases.[25]

The country's attention was soon focused on the stunning report of the president's riot commission, known as the Kerner Commission, which concluded that the U.S. was moving toward two separate, unequal societies. Days later, the nation was deeply shocked by the assassination of the century's most important black leader, Martin Luther King.

The day after King's assassination, the president wrote to the Speaker, asking for immediate action on the fair housing legislation, which had been blocked in the House Rules Committee (Johnson 1968–1969, 496–497). A key shift in the Rules Committee brought the bill to the House floor five days later, where it passed by a solid majority. The decisive vote that allowed the House to act on the bill came from Representative John Anderson, a conservative Republican from Rockford, Illinois. Anderson had been openly skeptical about the legislation and had voted against a much more limited bill in 1966. Mail from his district was "very, very heavily opposed" to the measure, and his party leaders urged him to hold fast. His change of heart was influenced by clergy and by the dire warnings of the Kerner Commission, which had investigated the riots, and then by the assassination of King and the subsequent riots that sprang up across the country, including two very visible riot corridors just a few minutes from Capitol Hill (Anderson 1981). The climate in Washington was very sober as troops set up machine-gun positions to protect the White House and the Capitol from potential violence. On the Tuesday following the assassination, Anderson cast the decisive vote to bring the bill to the House floor. The mood of the country had changed as the brutal racial crisis became manifest across the nation, and in spite of opposition from the GOP leader (and future president) Gerald Ford, Republican support grew. The key motion to send the bill to conference failed 229–195. The final vote was 250–171.

An accident of congressional timing meant that within days of the King assassination, Congress surprisingly enacted a much broader fair housing measure than anyone had expected. President Johnson, who had shocked the nation with the announcement that he would not run for reelection, signed the bill the next day, recalling how pessimistic the response had been to his proposal two years earlier and adding, "The proudest moments of my Presidency have been times such as this when I have signed into law the promises of a century" (Johnson 1968–1969, 509–510).

President Johnson's role in the final stage of this important late victory in his presidency was muted. The key leadership came from within the Senate, where Democrats were surprised by their own victory, and the House, where put Republicans were put on the spot in an election year. Johnson and his legislative staff followed the process and provided support, and the president pushed hard for the final votes. His Justice Department was at the center of the negotiations with Senator Dirksen. But fair housing never would have become a serious legislative possibility if Johnson had not raised the issue in 1966. There would have been no Kerner Commission report had not the president named the commission and set the stage for a broader view of the nation's racial situation in his historic Howard University speech. As the country clearly began to turn away from federal action for racial justice, Johnson continually pressed for more, even though his power was declining and his time running out. The president was proud to sign the third of his great civil rights laws in the tragic aftermath of the assassination of the greatest black leader of the twentieth century.

A Law Hardly Enforced: The Evolution of Fair Housing Policy in the Courts and in Successive Administrations

In the American system, the president proposes and advocates; Congress creates the binding policy, usually in general and unspecific terms; the executive branch develops regulations and enforces the law; Congress allocates resources; and the courts make the ultimate decisions about the law's reach, its relationship to the Constitution, and the range of issues to which it can be applied. In the policy stream, court decisions and administrative regulations, which have the force of law, carry considerable weight. This is especially true in civil rights, an area governed by a set of broad laws and basic constitutional provisions and subject to ongoing legal battles.

In the early history of fair housing law, the Supreme Court handed down strongly supportive decisions. As the courts and administrations changed, the outcomes became far less positive. In contrast to the striking limits of the fair housing law, the Supreme Court handed down a historic decision in a 1968 housing case, *Jones v. Mayer*, 392 U.S. 409, in which it brought back to life an 1866 civil rights law that had been interpreted away to nothing by the Supreme Court in the late-nineteenth century. The Warren Court in *Jones v. Mayer* held that the law, 42 U.S.C. 1982, adopted a year after the end of the Civil War, was still valid and that it permitted anyone experiencing housing discrimination by race to sue for a remedy in federal court. The court ruled that the Thirteenth Amendment, the amendment that abolished slavery and the "badges of slavery," provided a legal basis for a law prohibiting private discrimination. Although the high cost and severe delays of federal litigation were huge obstacles, this decision meant that the high court had restored a right covering all housing and had created a forum where plaintiffs could recover far larger remedies than those possible under the federal fair housing law. This distinction would prove important for developing the law and creating real risk for violators.

Another Supreme Court decision, *Hills v. Gautreaux*, 525 U.S. 284 (1976), was important in creating a basis for suing local and federal housing authorities for fostering housing segregation, and even more importantly, it legitimated a remedy that could actually work—a remedy whose success would trigger serious federal interest in the 1990s. The Supreme Court held that the long experience of local and federal officials in building and operating segregated, substandard public housing was a constitutional violation and required a serious remedy. The decision approved the kind of metropolitan remedy that it had forbidden in *Milliken v. Bradley*, 418 U.S. 717 (1974), a school desegregation decision that denied illegally segregated Detroit black students access to suburban schools. In *Gautreaux*, the court recognized that the metropolitan-area housing market—in this case, the Chicago market—was the appropriate target for implementing a housing remedy, since housing is basically provided through metropolitan markets. The remedy was a rent subsidy (section 8) certificate that would allow a household to pay for standard housing wherever landlords accepted the certificates, including the suburbs. New subsidized housing was being built by private companies, and so renting it did not require court orders against suburban governments.

This decision led to an extremely important experiment run by the nation's largest fair housing organization in one of the most resistant, most segregated housing markets. It proved that many low-income black families were willing to move to virtually all-white distant suburbs. The experimental program further showed that these moves could be done at a modest cost and would meet with little resistance, and that the families' educational and other opportunities were greatly improved by such moves (Rubinowitz and Rosenbaum 2000). This evidence triggered strong interest in the Clinton administration, which initiated a related but different experiment, an effort to implement policy on a substantial scale along the same lines in the "Moving to Opportunity" proposal, which was shot down in the U.S. Senate.

The Supreme Court was to take one other important step for fair housing. In *Havens Realty Corp. v. Coleman*, 455 U.S. 363 (1982), the court upheld the right of fair housing organizations using matched testers of different races or ethnicities to file cases to enforce the law. This was a vital tool for fair housing organizations, since testing was usually the only way to obtain proof of discriminatory intent—people in the housing business no longer expressed their prejudices outright. By sending testers of different races with the same desires and qualifications to the same firm at the same time, compelling evidence could be produced.

The *Jones v. Mayer* decision provided an opportunity for litigators and reinforced the message of the federal fair housing law, but its implementation depended on litigating individual cases, which represented never more than a tiny proportion of the millions of estimated annual violations. The *Gautreaux* precedent was important because many U.S. cities had a history of intentionally segregating public housing, but its remedies could work only if there was money to bring costly court cases and if there were federal housing resources in the budget that could be channeled by the courts. Only a small number of these cases were brought, and the resources were dramatically diminished by the cuts in housing programs beginning in 1981 with the Reagan administration. Using the authority granted under *Havens*, re- quired resources for testing and for prosecuting cases. Those resources were always limited, and some of the major private fair housing organizations went out of existence, including the nation's largest, in Chicago.

Unlike segregation by school districts or violations by prisons or other major institutions, discrimination by housing authorities could not be fixed by a court ordering the reassignment of residents. Often, courts did not even have the resources to help those being discriminated against find any alternative. What could be done within the small but important sector of subsidized housing was strongly linked with the resources that successive administrations made available for housing and related policies. Those resources, as discussed below, increasingly diminished over time.

Some hoped that the federal courts would sustain a frontal attack on the suburban exclusion of subsidized and affordable family housing, which had strongly negative effects on the housing and school opportunities for minority families. Their earlier exclusion from home ownership meant that even those with good incomes tended to have far less wealth in the form of home equity and, thus, fewer resources with which to buy in an exclusive area. By the 1970s, civil rights litigators were trying to win legal victories against suburban land-use and building policies known as "exclusionary zoning," in order to bring down barriers that prevented the development of affordable, subsidized housing in areas with rapid job growth and strong public schools. In practice, these communities typically blocked the construction of affordable rental housing, especially for low-income subsidized tenants, and there were often racial overtones in local decisions. There was a dramatic breakthrough on this issue in New Jersey beginning in 1975 with the *Mt. Laurel* decisions by the state supreme court.[26] But in *Arlington Heights v. Metropolitan Housing Corp.*, 429 U.S 352 (1977), a five-member majority of the U.S. Supreme Court created massive obstacles to bringing such cases in the future by requiring that lawyers not only demonstrate the effect of such decisions or the context in which they were made, but also prove that local officials had a racially discriminatory *intent* when passing restrictive zoning laws. Proving an intent to discriminate is extremely difficult, since local officials almost never openly express racial bias on the public record and always justify their decisions on other grounds like traffic problems, school capacity, or myriad others. There were no major changes in suburban exclusionary practices as the suburbs expanded exponentially in the decades after *Arlington Heights*. The combination of reduced resources and judicial unwillingness to change the built-in barriers of local control of housing in intensely segregated metropolitan areas was devastating.

The Evolution of Policy against Housing Discrimination after LBJ

The Johnson administration had no time to begin enforcing the new law or to do much about the gigantic housing programs enacted in 1968. As the country recovered from the assassination of Martin Luther King, worked through primary battles in both parties for the presidential nomination, witnessed the assassination of Senator Robert Kennedy and the rioting at the Democratic National Convention, LBJ's power rapidly disappeared. A new era was also signaled when Chief Justice Earl Warren announced his retirement. Six months after the new fair housing law was enacted, the country had a president-elect, Richard Nixon, who had campaigned in part by promising to roll back civil rights laws. What would happen to the law and all the urban programs and policies that might interact with it, as well as the future of the courts, was now in the hands of succeeding administrations. There would be nothing even close to the civil rights and urban policy breakthroughs of the 1960s in the next twelve presidential terms. Those years would see brief periods of interest in expanding executive-branch fair housing enforcement and developing new strategies, but they were dominated by declining interest and resources for urban policy and housing programs, shrinking public resources for domestic programs other than health and Social Security, and periods of rollback and inaction on civil rights. In the seven terms of Republican presidents in the period 1969 to 2009, the key civil rights agencies and the Justice Department were often headed by officials who took a very narrow view of their responsibilities and were opposed to any broad initiatives in the area of housing. Often there was nothing but a modest network of private fair housing groups and lawyers trying to create significant progress on the issues. Although there was a limited grant of enforcement authority from a Democratic Congress at the end of the Reagan administration, there was never more than a modest enforcement effort. Yet there was a significant reduction in the level of black-white residential segregation in many cities, though it was modest in areas that had been most intensely segregated at the time the law was passed.

Consolidation of the GOP View of Housing and Urban Policy, the Nixon Moratorium, and a Radically New Housing and Urban Policy

Housing and urban policy have always been partisan issues. Conservatives are deeply skeptical of any governmental intervention to change local practices and markets, and are heavily influenced by the real estate and home construction industries as well as by local governments. Liberals have been much more sensitive (though far less than in most other industrialized societies) to the need to take up matters such as housing for the poor, urban planning, and environmental issues. They have seen the hostility of many local and state governments toward equity in housing. For many years there were moderate urban Republicans from industrial states and suburban communities who straddled these lines. As the GOP after 1968 became more dominated by southern and antigovernment conservatives, the numbers of moderate Republicans and southern Democrats declined, producing even more abrupt changes of policy and ideology. During the Nixon and Ford administrations, the positions advocated by GOP moderate-progressives gave way to far more negative positions that tended to ignore market flaws (such as discrimination) and were extremely skeptical about making positive changes at the federal level. In housing, Nixon's second term was oriented toward thinking about subsidies not as a way to create homes and neighborhoods but as an issue of cash-for-housing cost, of thinking about housing as a market (ignoring the obvious racial separation in local markets), of assuming that people were restrained only by price when making choices, and of not worrying about either the supply of affordable housing or the quality of the residential neighborhoods in which poor people lived. In urban policy, the conservative assumption is that the market should decide within the parameters set by local zoning and land-use laws. In practice, this means that the political leaders in a jurisdiction can use zoning and building regulations to screen out lower-income and subsidized families, whatever the impact on the larger market and society might be. Officials in middle- and upper-class suburbs typically decide to exclude poor and working-class people and affordable rental housing for families, and to adopt zoning and building code requirements that provide housing only for affluent people.

The Nixon administration came to office committed to paring back federal civil rights policy. It began, however, as a combination of conservatives and moderate Republicans. George Romney, a former Michigan governor and a civil rights supporter, became the secretary of HUD. The responsibility for implementing LBJ's revolutionary agenda in housing, urban development, and housing discrimination shifted only months after enactment from an administration deeply committed to social change to one committed to controlling costs and transferring more resources and responsibilities to the states. The new administration promised to cut back on what candidate Nixon had characterized as excessive enforcement of civil rights laws by federal agencies and the courts. Urban policy became a special target. By Nixon's second term, a sudden and drastic change in policy had been imposed.

On fair housing, the Nixon administration ended strong support of housing for the poor and of housing integration, and instead stirred up public opposition by denouncing a modest effort to create housing for low-income families in the industrial suburbs of Detroit. Detroit, home to one of the largest black communities in the North because of its massive industries, had one of the two most segregated metropolitan areas in the nation (Darden 1967, 129–160). Suburban communities, including those where many black families worked, refused to accept any share of the region's subsidized housing for families, even while receiving large federal grants for their infrastructure and other needs. If there were to be leverage to incentivize suburban change under the Civil Rights Act or Title VIII of the fair housing law, Detroit would be an important test. Secretary Romney wanted to condition urban aid on participation in "fair share" housing plans. When an angry mob confronted Romney in the Detroit suburb of Warren, the event was reported in the newspaper and caught the president's attention. Nixon put out a statement denouncing what he called "forced integration of the suburbs" (Lamb 2005, 9; Nixon 1971). The Romney initiative was dead, and the issue wouldn't arise again until the Carter administration. The idea that all federal programs had to be administered in a way that would foster fair housing was largely forgotten.

After Nixon won his landslide 1972 reelection victory over George Mc-Govern, the president believed he had a sweeping popular mandate to reverse many of the commitments of the New Deal and the Great Society. His goal was to foster what he called the "New American Revolution" (Nixon 1978, 761). "Armed with [a] landslide mandate" (he carried forty-nine states), he wanted to drastically reverse domestic policy (762). He planned to "reorganize, reduce, or abolish the remaining behemoths of the Great Society that had done little to aid the poor" (766). He proposed budget cuts and the consolidation of many programs into "block grants" to be administered by the states with little federal control. With 68 percent public support as his second term began (770, citing a Gallup poll), Nixon asserted the power to cancel federal programs that had been funded by Congress (770). Presidents had long exercised a limited authority to withhold federal funds, called "impoundment." Nixon decided, particularly in the field of housing policy, to use the power in an unprecedented way to unilaterally terminate virtually all federal programs to provide new subsidized housing, throwing housing policy and housing developers into chaos and provoking intense legal battles across the country. He proclaimed "a moratorium on all of HUD's major housing assistance programs," including the huge new programs enacted in LBJ's last year (Struyk and Bendick 1981, 32). This extraordinary action was later ruled illegal, but it fundamentally changed housing policy.

The future of subsidized housing, especially for families, turned toward vouchers and dramatically reduced public efforts to build new housing for poor families. Nixon rejected the policies of the historic 1968 fair housing act and the whole idea of the federal government as the creator or funder of new housing units for poor families. He launched a massive experiment that relied simply on subsidizing the cost of housing units, conceptualizing the problem of housing affordability as not involving either increasing the supply of housing or focusing on giving poor households access to better communities. The development of subsidized housing in outlying white areas was largely abandoned. Since the recipients of the subsidy certificates had to find units where the landlord would rent to them, minority families were less likely to be able to use their certificates, and the more desirable subsidized housing in white areas was rented to lower-income whites (Gray and Tursky 1986, 235–252).

After the Watergate scandal drove Nixon from the White House, Congress enacted the Housing and Community Development Act of 1974, which relied heavily on section 8 certificates permitting low-income families to move into private housing that was available under cost ceilings and whose owners were willing to accept subsidized renters (Gray and Tursky 1986, 33).

A fundamental problem in fair housing or any urban reform was the radical reduction in resources to implement remedial measures. In the four decades after the Nixon moratorium, federally overseen housing construction for poor families did not resume.

Model cities and the New Town effort were also victims of the Nixon cuts. Nixon blocked funding for the Model Cities plans that had been funded under Johnson.

President Ford presided over the initiation of the Community Development Block Grant program, which combined funds for urban measures into a smaller lump sum for local governments. Although it did include language regarding the "spatial deconcentration of the poor," a kind of housing integration policy as a goal for housing programs, there was no serious implementation. The act authorizing the program included these goals: reducing the isolation of income groups within communities and geographic areas, increasing the diversity and vitality of neighborhoods through the spatial deconcentration of housing opportunities for persons of lower income, and revitalizing of deteriorating or deteriorated neighborhoods.[27] The law was, in practice, largely just rhetoric.

The *National Growth and Development Report* (1974, 4–5) issued under Ford reflects the conservative perspective: "For the most part, the matching up of individual needs and directions of growth is accomplished through operations of the private market. . . . In the United States, the fundamental posture toward growth is that the private decisions of people operating through open markets allocate goals, resources, and the people themselves more efficiently and with more satisfaction for all than does any alternative method." The report noted that the amount of urbanized land in the United States had tripled from 1950 to 1970 and that 70 percent of the nation's population growth in the 1960–1970 period was suburban (29). Further, the report claimed that the federal policies that most deeply affected cities were those usually undertaken with little or no concern for urban (or racial) impacts, such as interstate highways, sewer systems, and federal housing credit systems (44–52), although it admitted that "federal influences on the quality of life, on growth and on development at regional and local levels [are] more pervasive than generally realized" (62). But only one solution to urban ills was offered: "Perhaps the states should solve these problems" (63). There was no priority for fair housing.

The Carter Presidency

President Jimmy Carter brought the Democrats back to power after Nixon's resignation. Many Democrats hoped for a revival of urban initiatives. Carter, a former peanut farmer in the tiny rural community of Plains, Georgia, was a business-oriented southern moderate who promised to bring efficiency to the White House. After the radical cuts made under the previous two administrations, city leaders pressed for a major recommitment to the cities. But during the 1976 presidential campaign, little had been said by the contenders about urban policy or civil rights (Farrell 1976).

Fair housing issues, however, generated a major uproar. President Nixon's position on suburban integration had injected the issue into national politics. In a 1976 interview with the *New York Daily News*, Carter responded to a question about scattered-site public housing for the suburbs: "I see nothing wrong with ethnic purity being maintained, I would not force a racial integration of a neighborhood by government action. But I would not permit discrimination" (Schram 1977, 122). When questioned later, he said ethnic purity was "a natural inclination on the part of people," adding, "I don't think government ought to deliberately break down an ethnically oriented community deliberately by injecting into it a member of another race" (122). One of Carter's most important black supporters, the Atlanta congressman Andrew Young, who had been a top aide to Martin Luther King, called it an "awful phrase," saying, "I don't think he understood how loaded it is with Hitlerian connotations" (123). Although Carter apologized after several days for using the word "purity" (but not for the policy he expressed [Stroud 1977, 280]), and although it did not become an issue after he was nominated, it seriously worried civil rights advocates.

Carter had promised to review and consolidate the maze of federal programs affecting state and local governments, but announced no major changes, though congressional advocates and Democratic mayors were determined to expand and revive programs (S. King 1977). Urban leaders were disappointed by the lack of new programs and substantial funding increases. A report by the U.S. Conference of Mayors said that the budget for urban programs was far short of what was needed. The report noted that "in many budget areas, important urban programs have been cut below 1977 levels or their growth restrained to rates well below inflation rates." Worse, "the Carter budget does not include any significant deviations from the earlier Ford program" (quoted in Cannon 1977).

A series of task forces worked for months to devise an urban policy. A draft version of the plan to be presented to Carter included about $5 billion in new spending and was largely based on the expansion of existing programs, financial subsidies for development, and jobs programs (Ottenad 1977; Coursar and Close 1977, 3). Carter, in late 1977, torpedoed the whole thing, publicly repudiating the effort, sending the planners back to the drawing board, and making clear that there would be little new money (Reinhold 1977). He insisted that tax cuts be a priority (*New York Times* 1978a). In March 1978, Carter finally announced his urban strategy, which relied on promises of increased efficiency, flexibility, and coordination as well as on modest incentives for private investment. In his message, Carter called for "a New Partnership involving all levels of government, the private sector, and neighborhood and voluntary organizations" (*New York Times* 1978b). It was a kind of Model Cities strategy with virtually no funding, delivered to cities with an urgent need for funds and to state governments with little interest in cities. There was no significant housing element in the plan. Urban leaders were greatly disappointed by the limited resources, lack of attention to housing issues, and absence of policies to encourage metropolitan-wide plans for urban areas (Hunter 1978). The Carter administration ultimately had little impact on urban or housing policy. Carter wanted proposals that did not incur significant new expenditures, expand traditional programs, or require seriously facing issues of poverty and race.

Civil rights policy might have gone in a different direction if Carter had been reelected. Over time, Carter's HUD and Justice Departments included civil rights experts and developed some initiatives that could have been important in a second Carter term. The most important innovations were a HUD effort to produce voluntary metropolitan plans about the location and development of subsidized housing in return for modest extra funds, and the idea of combining strategies for school and housing integration. HUD-commissioned research showed that a substantial portion of unconstitutional school segregation in urban areas was caused by the segregation of subsidized housing (Cummings and Zatopek 1980; Orfield and Fischer 1981). Federal courts and the U.S. Civil Rights Commission had reached similar conclusions. Under Carter, HUD tried to leverage the language in the Community Development Block Grant program and federal regional planning requirements, along with supplemental housing and planning funds in the small Regional Housing Mobility Program, to reward jurisdictions that were willing to cooperate in the location of subsidized housing.

It turned out, however, that in some metropolitan areas where local officials were willing to cooperate, the program was criticized for drawing off scarce monies from the cities in order to fund suburban housing (Goering 1986, 200–201). In the coordinating of housing and school integration strategies, HUD deputy secretary Robert Embry, who coordinated the urban policy group, and assistant attorney general for civil rights Drew Days understood that much school segregation was the product of misguided housing policy and that many existing housing developments did not link poor, usually nonwhite children with decent school opportunities. On the Justice Department side, the Civil Rights Division combined its housing and education sections and brought pioneering litigation seeking coordinated remedies on both dimensions while pressing for more integration across urban-suburban boundaries.[28] The first case seeking a combined remedy was brought in Yonkers, New York. While there were only a few such cases, important ones in Phoenix and Houston could have established significant precedents. In Phoenix, the city government was prepared to settle a school desegregation lawsuit brought by the Justice Department by adding an extensive housing desegregation remedy to the city's development strategy, but the idea was quickly abandoned after Carter was defeated for reelection.[29] At the end of the Carter administration, HUD had finally written a regulation for the implementation of Title VIII, twelve years after the enactment of the fair housing law.

Though modest, both these efforts represented a large share of the most creative thinking about housing and school desegregation issues between the 1960s and the present. Unfortunately, their potential was never developed, and the tools and strategies as well as the goals were quickly abandoned by the Reagan administration. There were many local experts and officials who recognized that something better should and could be done.

The Reagan Counterrevolution

Ronald Reagan's administration was the counterrevolution to the Great Society and its laws. Although the Nixon and Ford administrations had turned policy away from LBJ's transformative urban and housing vision, there were divided voices within these GOP administrations, and their appointees to federal courts were often not rigid conservatives. The Reagan administration was something very different—a genuinely ideological movement that viewed government as a consistently negative force. It was committed to rolling back the affirmative aspects of civil rights policy that went beyond simply outlawing individual cases of overt discrimination. Such policies were responsible for breakthroughs on school desegregation, voting rights, and diversifying the labor force. Great Society programs were based on an understanding of the deep and multiple roots of inequality in American society, and particularly the central role of race. The Reagan administration, committed to radical individualism, saw this emphasis as both unnecessary and wrong. The administration believed that society had overcome its history of discrimination and that overreaching federal policies were hurting whites. It was strongly committed to dismantling social programs and urban policy, devolving power from Washington to the states, protecting whites from what it saw as excessive favoritism to minorities, shutting down judicial interventions as rapidly as possible, and transforming the courts. By the time of Reagan's first election, moderate GOP voices had been greatly diminished; southern conservatives were taking over the party. That branch of the party had ceased making any significant effort to win the votes of minorities, who, not surprisingly, tended to perceive the Reagan coalition as actively hostile to their interests.

Very important for the long run was the intense and focused effort to transform the federal courts through the rigid ideological screening of appointments, a focus on young candidates, and the systematic creation of new constitutional theories, which ultimately became the law of the land after conservative control of the Supreme Court was consolidated in the early 1990s (Savage 1992; Sunstein 2005). The administration turned civil rights agencies into active opponents of civil rights groups, and the president was successful in instituting political control of the previously independent and critical U.S. Commission on Civil Rights. That was the beginning of a period of consistent rollback of minority rights. But the Reagan coalition never succeeded in repealing Johnson's sweeping civil rights laws.

Norman Amaker's assessment of fair housing in his book *Civil Rights and the Reagan Administration* (1988) was that the administration decimated an already weak enforcement program and quickly abandoned some important gains achieved in the courts and in major pending litigation strategies from the Carter administration. Its first action was to rescind the Carter regulation on federal agencies' responsibility to consider the racial impacts of decisions affecting housing. It replaced the effects standard with an "intent" standard that was extremely difficult to prove. It forbade testing, which was often the only way to prove a violation or to assess a housing market or major housing providers. The net effect was to make a very weak law vastly weaker. The administration decided that despite court decisions defining exclusionary zoning as a civil rights violation, it would not pursue that issue (Amaker 1988, 88–101). The administration attacked race-conscious plans for stable integration. In cases involving both the gigantic Starrett City complex in New York City and a church-related integrated development, the Atrium Village project in Chicago, the administration demanded an end to policies that actively pursued stable integration by giving preference to tenants who would help maintain lasting integration.[30] This issue was bitterly divisive, and the administration prevailed despite civil rights leaders' support for the policies, which were more like the policies applied in school desegregation plans than in traditional fair housing cases. In the Reagan administration's philosophy, a race-conscious plan for integration was just as bad as a race-conscious plan for segregation.

Concerning substantive housing and urban development issues, the administration cut back on urban aid and subsidized housing construction and moved sharply toward voucher policies that had lower levels of subsidies. The Reagan policies virtually ended the role of the federal government in the construction of subsidized housing for families except through the tax system, which gave private developers large tax subsidies through the Low Income Housing Tax Credit, which is administered by state governments and is still the only significant source of low-income family housing construction. The credit, created as part of the Tax Reform Act of 1986, had a modest impact in the early years. Unfortunately, since the credit was administered by state agencies under Treasury Department supervision, and since neither the Treasury Department nor the state agencies had developed any significant civil rights enforcement programs or expertise, the building and tenanting of the housing were left overwhelmingly in the hands of corporations. The result, of course, was the construction of housing mainly in segregated, high-poverty areas that offered poor opportunities to residents, and the leasing of housing was done without significant antidiscrimination requirements.

The Reagan administration never enjoyed the overall control of Congress that George W. Bush would experience, since the House of Representatives remained under Democratic control throughout his presidency. Though the Senate had a small GOP majority for the first six years, the Democrats took back the Senate in the 1986 midterm elections and began to press the administration on housing and civil rights issues. Nonetheless, Reagan was able to use budget policy and appointment power, as well as internal divisions among Democrats, to achieve major changes.

Truly decisive changes came in the first months of the Reagan administration with the sweeping budget and tax cuts included in the Omnibus Reconciliation Act and the Economic Recovery Tax Act of 1981. These massive bills eliminated or transformed many programs and dramatically shrank federal revenue. Reagan had a decisive advantage, and the parliamentary tool of the reconciliation legislation, which was immune to normal filibusters in the Senate, allowed him to force a vote on a vast set of simultaneous changes in policy (Schick 1981, 267–268).

Conservatives in Congress and in some Washington think tanks saw the large 1980 victory as an opportunity to quickly implement radical reforms. The reforms rushed through Congress in the giant reconciliation bill ended the growth of urban programs, consolidating or eliminating a number of them, changing policies, and rolling back future budgetary authority (Schick 1982, 174–193). Urban programs were specifically targeted. The budget cut community development funds, eliminated a variety of urban programs, radically reduced planning funds, and virtually eliminated new budgetary authority for building subsidized housing for families (U.S. Department of Housing and Urban Development 1982, 1983). It increased to 30 percent the share of its income that a low-income family had to pay for rent. The Reagan administration substantially lowered funding for urban programs (in constant-value dollars), eliminated the war on poverty (Office of Economic Opportunity), deregulated federal programs (ending any significant tie they had with civil rights reforms), and virtually eliminated funding for construction of housing for low-income families.

In broader terms, the Reagan era marked the end of significant federal policy discussions on urban policy and of the launching of substantive policies to address urban issues. It was part of the general reduction of the share of gross national product devoted to the public sector, which was more than offset by the substantial increase in the proportion that went to defense and to interest payments on a rapidly increasing national debt attributable to the tax cuts. Although the president was unable to change Social Security or Medicare, everything else in domestic policy was subject to serious cuts.

Changes in federal budgets and resources, and in the courts, made it virtually useless to sue HUD, even if there was evidence of a history of clearly illegal racial segregation in subsidized housing. Without funds to construct new housing in other areas or to counsel tenants trying to escape illegally segregated housing, groups who won a victory and established an affirmative right to better housing had no resources to support a remedy. This circumstance—together with the creation of increasingly conservative courts—created a huge disincentive to pursue litigation.

The Reagan Justice Department rendered those few civil rights cases it filed as insignificant as possible by seeking remedies only for individual home buyers. Since the department maintained only a tiny caseload despite millions of violations, it was relatively safe for violators to engage in systemic practices of unequal treatment; the risk of being caught in an overt individual act was infinitesimal.

Reagan appointed Samuel R. Pierce Jr., an African American Wall Street lawyer, as his secretary of HUD. Pierce loyally defended the cuts to HUD, which were the deepest made to any department. In Reagan's first six years, during a period of severe inflation, HUD's budget authority declined by more than two-thirds, and the staff by almost a fourth (McAllister 1987). The basic idea was to lower costs, cut commitments, reduce the federal role, and rely more on the private market and local decisions. Civil rights was nowhere on the list, and there was no desire to create any federal urban policy.

Ironically, it was under a Democratic Congress near the end of the Reagan administration that HUD was finally given modest enforcement power under the fair housing law. All HUD secretaries of both parties had spoken of the department's feeble enforcement authority. The National Association of Realtors, long opposed to the fair housing law, eventually accepted changes made in 1988. The amendments gave HUD the power to order a violator to "cease and desist" discriminatory practices and raised the maximum penalty for violations. Nonetheless, most complaints were referred to state and local fair housing agencies, where there were long delays in processing complaints, followed by a lengthy, quasi-judicial process in HUD if a sanction was warranted. It turned out that this authority was rarely used.

Clinton: Moving to Opportunity's Rise and Fall

President Clinton made no significant changes in urban policy, though he appointed a widely admired secretary of HUD, Henry Cisneros, who was strongly committed to dealing with homelessness and rescuing failing subsidized housing projects. Cisneros, who had a deep commitment to fair housing, launched the most significant initiative in decades in the Moving to Opportunity program. Unfortunately, Cisneros's personal problems, spurred by blackmail by a former lover and a cover-up of the case that involved lying to the FBI, gravely diminished his effectiveness, as did the failure of his proposal in Congress and the 1994 takeover of the House of Representatives by conservative Republicans led by Newt Gingrich. Neither the George W. Bush White House nor the Barak Obama administration in its first term developed any significant urban policies or positive civil rights initiatives on urban housing issues, though the Obama administration, like those of other post-LBJ Democratic presidents, appointed officials committed to civil rights.

In the four decades after the Johnson administration, there were no significant federal urban policy proposals and no significant policies for constructing a substantial amount of subsidized housing, or for ensuring that units constructed by private builders with large tax subsidies would provide integrated housing opportunities in areas with good schools. Instead, the federal government continued to invest in segregated housing in areas with inferior, segregated schools (Pfeiffer 2009).

Both the Clinton and George W. Bush administrations gave a high priority to encouraging minority home ownership, to deregulating banks and lending institutions, and to extending federal home mortgage guarantees on a vast scale while providing little oversight of the quality and equity of the mortgage finance process.[31] These policies fostered historically high levels of home ownership by Latinos and African Americans, which both presidents hailed, but also created conditions that ultimately led to the collapse of the housing industry, the largest financial crisis in eighty years, and foreclosure and a massive loss of home equity for thousands of minority families.

The Obama administration has created no significant initiatives in housing and urban policy. Obama arrived in the midst of a massive worldwide financial disaster caused by speculation and fraudulent activity by banks and the mortgage industry in trying to generate massive fees by issuing predatory mortgages to families who could not afford them. Often, homes were sold with virtually no down payment, no honest appraisal of the value of the home purchased, and an impossible escalation of mortgage costs unless home buyers could refinance within a few years. The system was viable only if home values continued to soar for many years, mortgage money continued to be easily available, and home buyers who were overextended held onto their jobs and raised their incomes. In the fiscal collapse in 2007, the housing bubble burst, mortgage money froze as banks faced disaster, many families lost their jobs, and foreclosures began on a massive scale. Many foreclosed homes were owned by black and Latino buyers who had been encouraged by the Clinton and George W. Bush administrations to rush into the market as the federal government deregulated the banks and encouraged the Federal Housing Administration and the federal home finance agencies to underwrite risky loans to buyers with poor credit. The resulting high levels of minority home ownership were built on financial quicksand. The result was a vast loss of family wealth by minority families—by one estimate, $350 billion by 2010—whose wealth was typically little more than the equity in their home (Sperry 2011; White House 2002). There was no new urban vision. The Obama administration was faced with cleaning up an enormous housing disaster, saving the institutions whose deregulated greed produced it, and dealing with incredible budget deficits that made it impossible to launch significant new programs.

At the end of eleven presidential terms since Lyndon Johnson, the United States faced a bleak picture of continuing segregation, conservative courts, far smaller resources for new affordable family housing, and a government facing a virtual shutdown of the housing market in the Great Recession. It was a market flooded with foreclosures and plummeting home values, and few banks were willing to write mortgages. The federal government was locked in battles to save at least some parts of domestic policies. There had never been a period of active enforcement of fair housing, and there were now few sources of significant federal leverage remaining. During the 2008 presidential campaign, two former HUD secretaries, Henry Cisneros and Jack Kemp, headed the bipartisan National Commission on Fair Housing and Equal Opportunity, which held hearings across the country and submitted a report, *The Future of Fair Housing*, in December 2008. The report concluded that "discrimination is endemic" and that there were "at least 4 million fair housing violations in our country every year." It described the administrative enforcement powers granted by Congress in 1988 as a "farce" characterized by virtually no administrative proceedings and no "administrative law judges with fair housing knowledge and experience assigned at HUD." It also found that federal housing programs still did not comply with the requirements of Title VIII of the 1968 law (National Commission on Fair Housing and Equal Opportunity 2008).

Housing segregation greatly contributed to and compounded the true catastrophe that hit black and Latino homeowners in the Great Recession. When the leading independent source of housing research, Harvard's Joint Center for Housing Studies, released its report *State of the Nation's Housing 2012*, the news was terrible for the country as a whole, but particularly devastating for the households the Johnson reforms had aimed to help. Families who could not afford decent housing represented a large and growing share of households. Many young people were not forming households because they could not afford to do so. The foreclosure crisis and the dramatic declines in housing values had wiped out, in a few years, a very large share of the wealth of families of color, greatly increasing what had already been huge differences between minorities and whites. The flow of mortgage money to hard-hit neighborhoods had virtually dried up. Even as the crisis deepened there was a failure to make provision for the growing needs of the displaced, and existing housing programs were being cut back. Since rates of foreclosure and the loss of housing wealth were most severe in non-white neighborhoods, the tragedy could be blamed in part on the failure to seriously enforce fair housing laws regarding access both to desirable and economically stable neighborhoods and to mortgage finance. To make matters worse, as home ownership levels fell (much more rapidly for non-white households than white ones), the rental market tightened, rents went up much faster than family income, and the federal rent-subsidy programs were not expanded significantly.

It was a perfect storm of housing inequality (Joint Center for Housing Studies [Joint Center] 2012, 2). Nearly a fifth of all U.S. households (20.2 million) were paying more than half their total income for housing, which meant that, on average, they were spending 40 percent less on food, 50 percent less on clothes, and 40 percent less on health care than similar families living in affordable housing (5). Only about a fourth of very-low-income families were receiving housing assistance (5). Foreclosures were concentrated in about a tenth of U.S. neighborhoods (census tracts), and the future of those communities was grim: "the flow of mortgage credit to these deteriorating neighborhoods has all but dried up," as lending there fell by 74 percent (13, 30). These communities were on a continuous downward path without an exit. The lack of any coordinated housing and transportation planning meant that the growth of households was concentrated at the very outer exurban area of the nation's metropolitan areas, creating housing and transportation patterns that maximized energy costs and pollution potential (31). In this situation, the supply of affordable rental housing in the market shrank, and HUD rent vouchers barely increased as the need for them soared; the president's budget called for cutbacks in housing aid (32). The need for aid was highest and was increasing most rapidly among black and Latino households, and was especially severe in the central cities (28).

The racial impacts were dramatic in other ways. Because the loss of housing equity was much greater proportionally for African Americans and Latinos, and because minority families had much more of their wealth tied up in housing rather than other investments, black wealth after the Great Recession plummeted to one-twentieth of the wealth of white families, on average, and Latino wealth to one-eighteenth—both figures were far worse than the already large inequalities recorded in 2000 (Joint Center 2012, 166).[32] Looking at this portrait of disaster for the nation's African American and Latino households and many of their neighborhoods, it is clear that all the major issues that the Johnson administration tried to address are still alive today and still linked with segregation and discrimination within the housing and mortgage finance industries—and that the country now has few tools to address them, in part because of the staggering costs of bailing out the banks facing collapse.

In an interesting development, shortly after President Obama won re-election in 2012, HUD finally issued binding federal regulations on the sweeping provisions of Title VIII of the 1968 fair housing law, more than forty-four years after its enactment. The new regulation adopted a standard that called for evaluating the impact of urban policies on housing segregation, rather than the intent of the policy makers—a very important change. Though the regulation had been delayed for generations, it was praised by civil rights organizations; however, its long-term consequences will depend on decisions in the coming years. There were also some notable enforcement activities undertaken by the Obama administration (Whelan 2012).

Did the Fair Housing Law Work Anyway?

Start with a weak fair housing law and continually fail to enforce it vigorously or to develop the potential of Title VIII. After adding in the failure of the courts on the exclusion issue, and the dismantling of many of the urban and housing programs that gave the federal government leverage over the supply and location of affordable housing, it is hard to see how Johnson's initiative in enacting the fair housing law could have made much of a difference. But before reaching this conclusion, we need to look at the degree to which segregation has changed and to think about the ways in which civil rights laws can work. In fact, segregation declined significantly in many places despite all the weaknesses of the fair housing law, though it did not in others—and it increased for Latinos, now the nation's largest minority group. In some ways, the most critical outcome of the civil rights revolution that LBJ strongly embraced and so greatly strengthened was a widespread belief that the country had changed, and that overt segregation could not and should not be enforced, whether or not the law was being enforced by federal officials.

Before fair housing legislation, there was extreme black-white urban segregation in much of the country. The level of segregation in the nation's large cities in 1960 was staggeringly high. On an index in which 0 indicated equal distribution by race among all blocks in a city and 100 represented total apartheid, each block being either all-white or all-nonwhite, the segregation level for Boston was 83.9, for Chicago 92.6, for Cleveland 91.3, for Kansas City 90.8, for Philadelphia, 87.1, for Atlanta 93.6, for Baltimore 89.6, for Houston 93.7, for Miami, 97.9, and for Washington, the nation's capital, 79.9. Many of the nation's largest black communities were only a few percentage points from total racial separation in housing. As measured in 1960, these patterns had not changed significantly since before the Second World War (Massey and Denton 1993, 47).

The 1980 census offered the first real opportunity to examine the possible impact of the fair housing law. Though the data showed that residential segregation of blacks had remained high through the 1970s, there were signs of change. The pattern of wide areas of total exclusion of any black families was less prevalent than before, individual neighborhoods and suburbs could no longer totally exclude black families willing to fight for their rights, and real estate and rental agents knew that what many were still doing was illegal and involved some possible risk. Those changes, plus the economic pressure of a serious decline in the housing market, all contributed to changes in the nature of housing segregation. It became less absolute and less fixed in space, more dynamic and more open to change. Though families could and often were "steered" in ways that reflected and spread segregation, and although information and financing could differ greatly by race, a family who knew where it wanted to live, and had sufficient resources and a willingness to assert its rights, could move into an area that would have been absolutely off-limits before.

The changes were most apparent in areas that were newer and rapidly growing, that were outside areas with large established black populations, or that were near military bases and universities, where attitudes were more accepting or policies clearer. Two leading demographers—Reynolds Farley and Robert Wilger of the University of Michigan—observed these trends in their analysis of the 1980 census for the National Academy of Sciences. They pointed out that racial attitudes were improving and that black families had more money to invest in housing. The analysis concluded, "Between 1970 and 1980, the residential segregation of blacks from whites decreased in all regions, in metropolises of all sizes and in both rapidly and slow-growing locations" (Farley and Wilger 1987, 1). But black segregation remained high, especially in the historic centers of black urban settlement, and whites continued to experience very little residential contact with blacks. The 1980 data showed a number of small to moderately sized metropolitan areas with low segregation of blacks, many of them where the leading employer was the "Armed Forces or a major university" (2). The researchers found that by 1980 there was a significantly lower, though still serious, level of segregation in areas where a substantial portion of the housing had been built since fair housing had become law (7). One of the discouraging findings was that blacks with higher incomes and educational levels were just as segregated from their white counterparts as were those at lower levels, strongly indicating that segregation was not primarily a class issue. In metropolises with at least a quarter million black residents, "blacks were thoroughly segregated from whites regardless of how much income they obtained or how many years they spent in school" (11). At high-income levels, it was as severe as at poverty levels (11).

Traditional migration destinations with large ghettos retained very high levels of segregation, and segregation had increased in some parts of Florida (Farley and Wilger 1987, 11). About half the nation's black population lived in just twenty-five large metro areas, and segregation was higher there than in the areas with smaller black populations. Cities with extreme segregation included Chicago, Detroit, and Cleveland, the first two of which had been consistently among the nation's worst (5). Douglas Massey and Nancy Denton's classic book *American Apartheid* (1993) documented the devastating impact of segregation on the lives and opportunities of African Americans. It concluded that "despite the passage of the Fair Housing Act in 1968, this situation had not changed much in the nation's largest black communities by 1980" (195). Segregation was still strong, but it was gradually diminishing in some places.

By 1980, the immigration reforms enacted in 1965 and mass migration from Mexico had led to a significant increase in the U.S. Hispanic population, and the census conducted its first national study of Latino residence. Comparing patterns for sixteen areas with the largest black populations in 1980, the study found that the average segregation index for blacks was 79, but 48 for Hispanics and only 43 for Asians (Farley and Wilger 1987, table H). The assumption at the time, however, was that Hispanic segregation of residence would not become a serious national issue. That hope turned out to be premature as the vast population changes continued.

Another major analysis of the 1980 census, this one by Karl Taeuber of the University of Wisconsin, focused on central cities only. Its analysis of the twenty-eight cities with more than 100,000 black residents reached a more negative conclusion. More than a third of blacks lived in those cities, which were home to the most infamous black communities. The average dissimilarity index was 81. Chicago's level was worst, 92 (Taeuber

1983, 1). Some of the cities, such as Gary, Indiana, had lower scores because black residents were moving outward rapidly as whites left, creating transitional neighborhoods that looked integrated at the time the census was taken. Segregation was even higher in these cities in 1970, with an average segregation index of 87. Taeuber concluded that this was a "slow downward drift" (4) that at the current rate would take a half century to lower the figure to 50. Another study showed that black access to areas with a fifth or fewer black residents had grown from 13 percent of the black population in 1960 to 17 percent by 1980 (Harris and Wilkins 1988, 107).

Many things changed in the decades after 1980. Black suburbanization that had begun in earnest in some areas in the 1970s continued to grow. The country changed from what had been basically a black-white society to a four-race society, and in the western half of the country, Hispanics became far more populous than blacks. Many neighborhoods included more than two races. The expansion of the black population in many cities slowed because of falling birth rates and a substantial net migration of blacks from the Northeast and Midwest to the South. The suburbs grew exponentially, and the percentage of nonwhites in suburban rings multiplied. Gentrification spread to more central cities, and attitudes changed. Fair housing laws meant that families of color who knew their rights, and had down payments and financing in hand, could buy a home in an area that had stayed all-white for many years. It meant that discrimination was illegal, and though the risk of sanction was very small, it did exist. It also meant that Realtors who sold across racial lines could blame the law and not face the same sanctions from their colleagues or customers as in the past.

By the 2010 census there were more signs of real declines in black-white segregation in some places. The declines were most notable in rapidly growing cities in parts of the South and the West and in areas with smaller proportions of blacks, and were least impressive in what has been called the "ghetto belt" of the older industrial cities of the Northeast and Midwest. Looking at the fifty most segregated large metropolitan areas in the United States between 1990 and 2010, segregation between blacks and whites declined in all but one. In most, the declines were modest—a few points on a 100-point scale. In six metropolises, the segregation index dropped by more than ten points in this twenty-year period (Population Studies Center 2010). None of the areas were near the extremes of the most segregated metro areas of the 1960s.

The demographer John Logan (2010) of Brown University concluded: "Declines in segregation between blacks and whites since 2000 continued at about the same pace as in the 1990s. Segregation peaked around 1960 or 1970. Between 1980 and 2000 it declined at a very slow pace. . . . The new data shows another decade of steady but slow decline." Another of the nation's leading demographers, William Frey of the Brookings Institution, reached a similar conclusion: "The data shows us that there's still a lot of segregation in the country," he said, "but it is going down slightly." He explained the change this way: "It's taken a civil rights movement and several generations to yield noticeable segregation declines for blacks" (quoted in Jonsson 2010). Although segregation remained high in traditional areas of black concentration, better possibilities were reflected in rapidly growing metropolitan areas and in the West, where black-white segregation was considerably lower; in the fact that the number and percentage of virtually all-white neighborhoods had declined substantially; and in the fact that over two-fifths of African Americans were living in the suburbs, though many of those suburbs were segregated or in racial transition.

In 2013, HUD published its fourth national audit of the housing market, using trained housing searchers of various racial and ethnic backgrounds to systematically report their treatment in housing markets across the United States. In that report, the Urban Institute found that there had been a major decline in some forms of relatively overt discrimination in housing markets since the first national audit study, conducted in 1979 (Turner et al. 2013). In some important respects, the values of the Fair Housing Act were, at long last, becoming part of mainstream real estate practices. In contrast to the almost immediate acceptance of the public accommodations law, the change in the housing market came very slowly and was far from complete even forty-five years later.

No one can answer with any precision, of course, the question of to what degree the fair housing law and the new racial perspectives and norms that arose from other civil rights laws accounted for a significant movement away from a level of black-white segregation that was only a few percentage points away from total racial apartheid. In a massive, complex, and changing society, many things happen over the course of more than four decades. Communities are created and grow where there had been only farms or desert, cities change or wither, great immigrant streams flow into the society, generations are replaced, values change—no one will ever know how much difference the law made. But it seems reasonable to assume that it mattered, and it contributed to the change of an extremely difficult problem that is at the root of inequality in metropolitan society in an era that was, in many ways, inhospitable to racial change or active government.

Conclusion

What is a reasonable standard for judging the civil rights contributions of the Johnson administration? On one hand, by the standards of history before and since the Great Society era, it was unprecedented and astonishing. It was a masterful use of the power of a determined president to push large changes through Congress and into law. Nothing of real substance on civil rights had been accomplished in Congress since shortly after the Civil War, and nothing even vaguely so groundbreaking has been accomplished in the nearly half century since Johnson left office.

On the other hand, it is reasonable to think about whether the reforms solved the problems, though this is more than a bit unfair in a political system designed to create great obstacles to major, lasting reforms of any sort. The answer is mixed. In some ways, the changes of the Great Society period solved serious problems so effectively that they simply disappeared as issues after the reform was implemented. On other fronts, of course, the problems remain serious. The policies may have helped significantly, but there is still much unresolved. Johnson's reforms were meant to be part of an ongoing struggle for racial justice, but that struggle stalled for decades.

Outcomes were shaped by the strength of resistance to the laws, the strength of the laws and supporting court decisions, and the political and social climate of the time. On the issues of public accommodations and some of the other reforms, it turned out that resistance was not as serious as feared, that the law crystallized a change that institutions were willing to make, and that some had a vested interest in being forced to change. The success of the president and his congressional allies in decisively defeating southern maneuvers in Congress, along with seriousness in enforcing the law, produced a sense of inevitability. Passing the law and showing firmness about it solved the problem, but passing the law took the president's skill and determination.

In areas in which there was no consensus, laws were weak, and political and institutional opposition arose, things were different. In the areas of both job discrimination and housing, the president and the administration were far ahead of any serious social movement. They tried to change things in parts of the country that believed things were already fair. When it came to outlawing housing and job discrimination, things that hit close to home for Republicans and some urban Democrats, the laws were weak, the administrative enforcement powers almost nonexistent, and the resources to enforce the changes minimal. For many who voted for them, the votes came without real conviction or continuing support. The reforms, important as symbols, were weak in many respects.

They were, in fact, like the first modest civil rights bills, on voting rights, that Johnson had helped enact in 1957 and 1960, complex laws that required proving how discrimination had taken place voter by voter, community by community—laws that failed, but set the stage for something better. There were plenty of violations when those first laws went into effect, but the enforcement process, despite strong efforts by the Justice Department, was unworkable. It would have been hundreds of years before a truly open electoral process could be achieved. The frustration of trying to correct obvious wrongs in that way led to the inclusion of dramatic powers in the Voting Rights Act, which simply suspended local control over key parts of the election process in communities where minorities had been excluded.

Johnson got only to the first stage in housing and employment. In fact, it could be said that we have been stuck at that stage or worse ever since. One study of state fair housing laws concluded:

Existing fair housing legislation has proved to be incapable of *systematic* enforcement. . . . Equally clearly, if fair-housing legislation is to do more than give relief to scattered individual Negro professionals and reinforce the contemporary Zeitgeist, new types of fair-housing legislation need to be developed. The basic reliance on coercive sanctions and the handling of individual complaints can only give piecemeal relief, barring sharp shifts in the whites' attitudes and in the nature of the housing market. . . . Additional and different sorts of fair-housing legislation must be invented and adopted if the promise of the civil-rights revolution is to be fulfilled. (Bloy and Casstevens 1968, 389)

The enactment of the federal fair housing law in the final months of the Johnson administration was an astonishing breakthrough in expanding federal civil rights law into a highly controversial area that had very little public support. When the president first asked Congress to act on this issue, in 1966, it seemed a quixotic quest against overwhelming odds. Yet his administration ended with the law on the books, together with an array of urban reforms and policies that has never been equaled before or since. The laws created tools of great potential power. It turned out that a president who was most comfortable at his ranch in the Texas Hill Country was the great urban reformer, the only president who seriously took on the issues of race and poverty and urban decay—though his accomplishments in this arena are little remembered. The administration was not able to institution-alize these reforms enacted late in Johnson's tenure, and they were followed within months by the election of a new president who did his best to turn the country in a very different direction. After the Great Society, no pres-ident to date has put forward major reforms addressing urban inequality, and most administrations were committed to shrinking the federal role. The worst proposals played on the "wedge issue" of white fear of racial change.

Looking back at the stream of policy development and urban change nearly a half century later, it is disappointing that the issues of concentrated urban poverty and racial discrimination have virtually disappeared from the national conversation as both parties aim their appeals at the suburban mid-dle class—one playing on fears and praising private markets and local gov-ernments, receiving almost no votes from the nation's minorities, and the other determined to avoid issues of race and class, but offering a more posi-tive view of public schools, civil rights, and other basic government services. Since the 1960s, many millions of new homes have been built, new commu-nities have been created across the country, the typical home has changed hands many times, the population has grown by more than 100 million, and there has been a massive increase in the share of the population that is nonwhite. Although the Great Society experts a half century ago correctly predicted that the trends would create massive social and economic prob-lems, we have discarded most of the tools that were created to address them. It is interesting that one of the few that has survived and been modestly strengthened is the fair housing law enacted against heavy odds in 1968 and modestly strengthened two decades later—and that housing has become modestly less segregated over the years, beginning in the 1970s, in many American metropolitan areas. The law may well have been a significant con-tributor to changed attitudes and practices despite its nonenforcement.

The Johnson's administration's combination of urban policy, housing policy, and urban civil rights policies was truly remarkable in its range and vision, but the effort rested on a fragile public support. There was never any strong public support for outlawing discrimination in housing or for ma-jor investments in poor urban communities. President Johnson acted on the fair housing issue against the advice of his own advisors and experts, who thought it was impossible, and he persisted in very difficult circumstances, eventually achieving an improbable victory.

The LBJ administration persuaded Congress to create a framework of law and policy that could have been levers for deep change had they not been largely abandoned by the Republican presidents who came after him, presidents who won five of the next six presidential elections with strategies based on mobilizing the white South, the working-class and lower-middle-class white electorate, and forsaking any real effort to win minority votes under a strategy of racial polarization. Many of the issues the Johnson administration raised have not been seriously addressed since, and we are living with consequences of that failure, consequences that the administration predicted. Effectively implementing these tools might have produced a significantly different society. The political history of the half century following Johnson shows that no president dealt with urban racial issues positively, but some significant progress on the housing front continued. Housing segregation has declined substantially in a fair number of American cities. The absolute segregation of many white neighborhoods gradually declined, the number of stably integrated communities grew, and the racial line between cities and suburbs was broken, though black housing segregation remained serious, especially in the older industrial cities. The Johnson reforms were imperfect, enacted in a great rush by a political genius who was willing to spend a great deal of capital to accomplish them. In the best of circumstances, the changes would have been challenging, and the coordination of the policies politically perilous. Johnson could create the tools, but he could not control the political reality that came after him. Those who look at the severe problems and profound inequalities in our metropolitan areas today could only wish they had such tools. Those who live in the integrated neighborhoods of today should understand that civil rights reforms created possibilities that were virtually nonexistent before the Great Society, and that some of those changes trace back to the man from the Texas hills.

Notes

1. Lorraine Hansberry's classic play *A Raisin in the Sun* was a triumph on Broadway and on film, telling the story of a black family in Chicago, like hers, that faced violence after moving into a white community. Hansberry's family, ordered by a Chicago court to leave its home in a white area, fought the issue to the Supreme Court.

2. Address of the president of the United States, "Celebration of the Semicentennial of the Founding of the City of Birmingham, Alabama," October 26, 1921, reprinted by Government Printing Office. The law against racial violence finally became part of the 1968 Civil Rights Act, best known for its fair housing provisions.

3. *Reitman v. Mulkey*, 387 U.S. 369 (1967).

4. *Wickard v. Filburn*, 317 U.S. 111 (1942).

5. Senate Democratic staffers reported that there were only forty-seven of the sixty-seven votes needed to break any proposed filibuster (Whalen and Whalen 1985, 11).

6. Interestingly enough, President Nixon would put on the U.S. Supreme Court a young Justice Department official, William Rehnquist, who had opposed a public accommodations law in Phoenix that was supported by the conservative leader Senator Barry Goldwater. President Reagan would later make him chief justice.

7. *Chicago Sun-Times*, May 24, 1966.

8. *Washington Post*, May 3, 1966.

9. *Washington Post*, June 17, 1966.

10. *Washington Post*, July 21, 1966; *Chicago Daily News*, July 23, 1966.

11. *Chicago Daily News*, July 18, 1966.

12. Ibid.

13. *Washington Post*, Aug. 10, 1966.

14. *Chicago Sun-Times*, Aug. 22, 1966.

15. *Chicago Sun-Times*, May 3, 1966.

16. *Washington Post*, Aug. 6, 1966; *Chicago Tribune*, Aug. 5, 1968.

17. *Washington Post*, Sept. 12 and Sept. 29, 1966.

18. *New York Times*, Feb. 7, 1968; see also the minority report on the bill (S. Rep. 721, 90th Cong., 1st sess, 1967).

19. *Wall Street Journal*, March 1, 1968; *Washington Post*, March 1, 1968.

20. *Washington Post*, March 6, 1968.

21. See also Department of Justice Legislative History files, "Technical Amendments Introduced in Senate Just prior to Final Passage," March 8, 1968.

22. *Chicago Tribune*, March 12, 1968.

23. *Washington Post*, March 14, 1968.

24. *Washington Post*, Mar. 28, 1968.

25. *Chicago Tribune*, Mar. 28, 1968.

26. *Southern Burlington County NAACP v. Township of Mount Laurel* [Mt. Laurel I], 67 N.J. 151, 336 A.2d 713, *cert. denied and appeal dismissed*, 423 U.S. 808 (1975); *Southern Burlington County NAACP v. Township of Mount Laurel* (Mount Laurel II), 92 N.J. 158, 456 A.2d 390 (1983), decided.

27. Housing and Community Development Act of 1974, Title I, Public Law 93–383; 88 Stat. 633; 42 U.S.C. 5301.

28. For a discussion of the background of this issue, see Orfield and Taylor (1979).

29. I worked as a consultant to the Phoenix Human Relations Commission on these negotiations, which won the support of the city's business, religious, and elected leaders, but were immediately abandoned after Reagan's election.

30. *U.S. v. Starrett City Associates*, 840 F. 2d, 1096 (2d Cir., 1988); *U.S. v. Atrium Village Associates*.

31. Clinton signed the Financial Services Modernization Act of 1999 and the Commodity Futures Modernization Act of 2000, which abandoned many of the regulations on banking institutions that had been set up to stop the kind of speculation that produced the Great Depression. George W. Bush, who was aggressively opposed to regulation, appointed officials who allowed banks to speculate. Both the Federal Reserve and the Securities and Exchange Commission failed to regulate abuses in the mortgage markets, much of it underwritten by the Federal Housing Administration (Ritholtz 2009, chs. 11–21).

32. U.S. Department of Housing and Urban Development, 24 CFR Part 100

(Docket No. FR-5508-F-02) RIN 2529-AA96, *Implementation of the Fair Housing Act's Discriminatory Effects Standard.*

References

Amaker, Norman C. 1988. *Civil rights and the Reagan administration.* Washington, D.C.: Urban Institute Press.

Anderson, John. 1981. Interview with author. Jan. 28.

Anderson, John Weir. 1964. *Eisenhower, Brownell, and the Congress: The tangled origins of the Civil Rights Bill of 1956–1957.* University: University of Alabama Press.

Berry, Mary Frances. 2009. *And justice for all: The United States Commission on Civil Rights and the continuing struggle for freedom in America.* New York: Knopf.

Branch, Taylor. 1988. *Parting the waters: America in the King years, 1954–1963.* New York: Simon and Schuster.

Califano, Joseph. 1966. Memorandum to President Lyndon Johnson. Mar. 15.

Cannon, Lou. 1977. Mayors say Carter's first budget inflates the military, slights cities. *Washington Post* (Feb. 27).

———. 2003. *Governor Reagan: His rise to power.* New York: Public Affairs Press.

Caro, Robert. 2002. *The years of Lyndon Johnson: Master of the Senate.* New York: Knopf.

———. 2012. *The years of Lyndon Johnson: The passage of power.* New York: Knopf.

Carter, Dan T. 1996. *George Wallace to Newt Gingrich: Race in the conservative counterrevolution, 1963–1994.* Baton Rouge: Louisiana State University Press.

Celebrezze, Anthony. 1964. Memorandum to Lee C. White. Mar. 4. LBJ Library files.

———. Memorandum to Jack J. Valenti. Mar. 16.

Clapp, James A. 1971. *New towns and urban policy.* New York: Dunellen.

Cousar, Gloria, and Ellis Close. 1977. Towards a national urban policy. *Focus* (Nov.–Dec.): 3.

Cummings, Scott, and Wayne Zatopek. 1980. Federal housing policy and racial isolation in public schools: The case of Dallas. In Scott Cummings, ed., *Racial isolation in public schools: The impact of public and private housing policies.* Arlington: Institute of Urban Studies, University of Texas at Arlington. Report to the U.S. Department of Housing and Urban Development.

Darden, Joe T. 1967. Residential segregation of blacks in metropolitan areas of Michigan, 1960–1990. In Joe T. Darden, Curtis Stokes, and Richard W. Thomas, eds., *The state of black Michigan, 1967–2007.* East Lansing: Michigan State University Press.

Davidson, Chandler. 1990. *Race and class in Texas politics.* Princeton, N.J.: Princeton University Press.

Dent, Harry S. 1978. *The prodigal South returns to power.* New York: Wiley.

Eley, Lynn W., and Thomas W. Casstevens. 1968. *The politics of fair-housing legislation: State and local case studies.* San Francisco: Chandler.

Emlen, Alan. 1966. Letter to state association presidents and executive officers [of the National Association of Realtors]. May 12.

Farley, Reynolds, and Robert Wilger. 1987. *Recent changes in residential segregation of blacks from whites: An analysis of 203 metropolises.* National Academy of Sciences Report 15. Population Studies Center, University of Michigan, Ann Arbor.

Farrell, William. 1976. Older cities' plight muted as an issue by candidate. *New York Times* (Apr. 1).

Ferris, Charles. 1969. Interview with author. June 12.

Frye, Alton. 1969. Interview with author. May 8.

Giesey, Walter. 1969. Interview with author. Aug. 12.

Goering, John, ed. 1986. *Housing desegregation and federal policy.* Chapel Hill: University of North Carolina Press.

Gray, Robert, and Steven Tursky. 1986. Local and racial/ethnic occupancy patterns for HUD-subsidized family housing in ten metropolitan areas. In John Goering, ed., *Housing desegregation and federal policy.* Chapel Hill: University of North Carolina Press.

Haar, Charles M. 1975. *Between the idea and the reality: A study in the origin, fate and legacy of the Model Cities program.* Boston: Little, Brown.

Harris, Fred R., and Roger W. Wilkins, eds. 1988. *Quiet riots: Race and poverty in the United States.* New York: Pantheon.

Humphrey, Hubert. 1965. Recommended reassignment of civil rights functions. Memorandum from vice president to president. Sept. 24.

Hunter, Marjorie. 1978. Urban leaders call plan a start but say financing is inadequate. *New York Times* (Mar. 28).

Johnson, Lyndon B. 1965. To fulfill these rights. Commencement address at Howard University. June 4.

———. 1966. *Public papers of the presidents.* Special message to Congress. Apr. 28.

———. 1967. Special message to the Congress on equal justice. Feb. 15.

———. 1968–1969. *Public papers of the presidents.*

Joint Center for Housing Studies. 2012. *State of the nation's housing 2012.* Cambridge, Mass.: Joint Center for Housing Studies, Harvard University.

Jonsson, Patrik. 2010. Census: Segregation hits 100-year lows in most American metro areas. *Christian Science Monitor* (Dec. 14).

Katzenbach, Nicholas. 1966a. Testimony before the Committee on Government Operations, Subcommittee on Executive Reorganization, Hearings, reorganization plan no. 1 of 1966. Community Relations Service, 89th Congress, 2d Session. Mar. 3.

———. 1966b. Memorandum to Joseph Califano. Mar. 12.

———. 1966c. Memorandum to President Lyndon Johnson. Sept. 9.

Kennedy, Robert F. 1964. Remarks to the National Citizen's Committee for Community Relations (Aug. 18). LBJ Library and Museum, Austin, Texas.

Kessel, John H. 1968. *The Goldwater coalition: Republican strategies in 1964.* Indianapolis: Bobbs-Merrill.

King, Martin Luther, Jr. 1967. *Where do we go from here? Chaos or community.* New York: Harper and Row.

King, Seth S. 1977. Nation's mayors urge Carter to establish an urban policy to aid cities and ask access to the White House. *New York Times* (Nov. 9).

Kluger, Richard. 1975. *Simple justice: The history of "Brown v. Board of Education" and black America's struggle for equality.* New York: Vintage.

Lamb, Charles M. 2005. *Housing segregation in suburban America since 1960: Presidential and judicial politics.* New York: Cambridge University Press.

Lieberson, Stanley. 1981. *A piece of the pie: Black and white immigrants since 1880.* Berkeley: University of California Press.

Logan, John R. 2010. The persistence of segregation in the metropolis: New findings from the 2010 Census. Census Brief prepared for Project US2010. Available at: www.s4.brown.edu/us2010.

Mann, Robert. 1996. *The walls of Jericho: Lyndon Johnson, Hubert Humphrey, Richard Russell and the struggle for civil rights.* New York: Harcourt, Brace.

Massey, Douglas S., and Nancy A. Denton. 1993. *American apartheid: Segregation and the making of the underclass.* Cambridge, Mass.: Harvard University Press.

McAllister, Bill. 1987. HUD's "stealth secretary," Pierce has reputation as least visible, least effective member of cabinet. *Washington Post* (Jan. 24).

McPherson, Harry. 1971. Interview with author. Jan. 29.

Mondale, Walter. 1971. Interview with author. Feb. 10.

Murphy, Reg, and Hal Gulliver. 1971. *The southern strategy.* New York: Scribner.

Muse, Benjamin. 1968. *The American Negro revolution: From nonviolence to black power.* Bloomington: Indiana University Press.

Myrdal, Gunnar. 1944. *An American dilemma: The Negro problem and modern democracy.* New York: Pantheon.

National Commission on Fair Housing and Equal Opportunity. 2008. *The future of fair housing.* Washington, D.C.: National Commission.

National Committee against Discrimination in Housing. 1966. Press release. Jan. 19.

National Growth and Development Report to Congress. 1974. Dec.

New York Daily News. 1976. Interview with Jimmy Carter (Apr. 2).

New York Times. 1978a. Carter's tax program: Some skepticism in the cities (Feb. 6).

———. 1978b. Excerpts from the president's message to Congress outlining his urban policy (Mar. 28).

Nixon, Richard. 1971. Statement by the president on federal policies relative to equal housing opportunity. June 11.

———. 1978. *RN: The memoirs of Richard Nixon.* New York: Grosset and Dunlap.

O'Brien, Larry. 1966. Memorandum to Joseph Califano. Mar. 14.

Orfield, Gary, and Paul Fischer. 1981. *Housing and school integration in three metropolitan areas: A policy analysis of Denver, Columbus and Phoenix.* Report to the U.S. Department of Housing and Urban Development, Washington, D.C. Order No. 5007–80.

Orfield, Gary, and William L. Taylor. 1979. *Racial segregation: Two policy views.* New York: Ford Foundation.

Ottenad, Thomas W. 1977. $12 billion program for aid to cities to go to Carter. *St. Louis Post-Dispatch* (Nov. 13).

Pettigrew, Thomas F. 2003. Attitudes on race and housing: A social psychological view. In Amos H. Hawley and Vincent P. Rock, eds., *Segregation in residential areas: Papers on racial and socioeconomic factors in choice of housing.* Washington, D.C.: National Academy of Sciences.

Pfeiffer, Deirdre. 2009. *The opportunity illusion: Subsidized housing and failing schools in California.* Los Angeles: Civil Rights Project. Foreword by Gary Orfield.

Population Studies Center. 2010. New racial segregation measures for large metropolitan areas: Analysis of the 1990–2010 decennial censuses. Ann Arbor: Population Studies Center, University of Michigan. Available at: www.psc.isr.umich .edu/dis/census/segregation2010.html.

President's Committee on Civil Rights. 2004. To secure these rights: The report of Harry S. Truman's Committee on Civil Rights. Boston: St. Martin's.

Ralph, James R. Jr. 1993. *Northern protest: Martin Luther King, Jr., Chicago, and the civil rights movement.* Cambridge, Mass.: Harvard University Press.

Reinhold, Robert. 1977. Cities uneasy about Carter plans. *New York Times* (Sept. 12).

Rice, Brad, 1988. Lester Maddox and the politics of populism. In Harold P. Henderson and Gary L. Roberts, eds., Georgia governors in an age of change: From Ellis Arnall to George Busbee. Athens: University of Georgia Press.

Ritholtz, Barry. 2009. *Bailout nation.* New York: Wiley and Sons.

Rubinowitz, Leonard S., and James E. Rosenbaum. 2000. *Crossing the class and color lines: From public housing to white suburbia.* Chicago: University of Chicago Press.

Sarratt, Reed. 1966. *The ordeal of desegregation: The first decade.* New York: Harper and Row.

Savage, David G. 1992. *Turning right: The making of the Rehnquist Supreme Court.* New York: Wiley.

Schick, Allen. 1981. How the budget was won and lost. In Norman J. Ornstein, ed., *President and Congress: Assessing Reagan's first year.* Washington, D.C.: American Enterprise Institute.

Schram, Martin. 1977. *Running for president 1976: The Carter campaign.* New York: Stein and Day.

Segal, Terry. 1969. Interview with author. May 8.

Solomon, Arthur P. 1974. *Housing the urban poor: A critical evaluation of federal housing policy.* Cambridge, Mass.: MIT Press.

Sperry, Paul. 2011. Fed housing policies backfire: Good government gone bad; Black ownership back to what it was when subprime push began. *Investor's Business Daily* (Apr. 1).

Stroud, Kathy. 1977. *How Jimmy won: The victory campaign from Plains to the White House.* New York: Morrow.

Struyk, Raymond J., and Marc Bendick Jr., eds. 1981. *Housing vouchers for the poor: Lessons from a national experiment.* Washington, D.C.: Urban Institute Press.

Sundquist, James L. 1968. *Politics and policy: The Eisenhower, Kennedy, and Johnson years.* Washington, D.C.: Brookings Institution.

Sunstein, Cass R. 2005. *Radicals in robes: Why extreme right-wing courts are wrong for America.* New York: Basic Books.

Taeuber, Karl. 1983. *Racial residential segregation, 1980.* Madison: Center for Demography and Ecology, University of Wisconsin.

Turner, Margery Austin, Rob Santos, Diane K. Levy, Doug Wissoker, Claudia Aranda, and Rob Pitingolo. 2013. Housing discrimination against racial and ethnic minorities, 2012. Prepared for the U.S. Department of Housing and Urban Development. Washington, D.C.: Urban Institute.

U.S. Department of Commerce. 1966. *Annual report of the Community Relations Service, fiscal year 1965.* Washington, D.C.: Government Printing Office.

U.S. Department of Housing and Urban Development. 1982. Fiscal year 1982 budget: Summary, H1.

———. 1983. Fiscal year 1983 budget: Summary, H6.

U.S. Department of Justice. 1968. Community Relations Service. *Annual report for fiscal year 1967.* Washington, D.C.: Government Printing Office.

U.S. House. 1968. Committee on Rules. *Hearings, Civil Rights Act.* 90th Cong., 2nd sess.

U.S. National Commission on Urban Problems [U.S. NCUP]. 1968. *Building the American city.* 91st Cong., 1st Sess.

U.S. Senate. 1967. Committee on Banking and Currency. Subcommittee on Housing and Urban Affairs. *Hearings, Fair Housing Act of 1967.* 90th Cong., 1st sess.

Waters, Bernard. 1969. Interview with author. June 16.

Weisberger, Bernard A. 1968. *The District of Columbia.* New York: Time-Life Books.

Whalen, Charles, and Barbara Whalen. 1985. *The longest debate: A legislative history of the 1964 Civil Rights Act.* Cabin John, Md.: Seven Locks Press.

Whelan, Robbie. 2012. A Texas-size housing fight: U.S. threatens to cut aid after Galveston rejects rebuilding low-income units. *Wall Street Journal* (Aug. 2).

White House. 1967. Background Briefing on the Message on Equal Justice. Feb. 15.

White House. 2002. Press release: President focuses on home-ownership in radio address. June 15.

White House Conference on Civil Rights. 1966. To fulfill these rights, housing section report.

CHAPTER 4

Expansion and Contraction
in LBJ's Voting Rights Legacy

JORGE CHAPA

The Voting Rights Act of 1965 was one of Lyndon Johnson's most effective, enduring, and consequential legislative accomplishments. At his final press conference as president, when asked what he regarded as his greatest accomplishment, he indicated that it was congressional passage of the Voting Rights Act (VRA). LBJ elaborated by saying, "I have felt very deeply most of my adult life, that . . . we did not have a real democracy as long as a substantial percentage of our population was disenfranchised" (Johnson 1969). Before the act was passed, African Americans in the southern states were generally barred from voting in many ways, among them literacy tests, poll taxes, discriminatory malfeasance by election officials, economic sanctions, and physical violence.

The number of African American voters and elected officials has increased tremendously since this law went into effect. The 1965 act did much to improve voting conditions across the country, and the temporary provisions of the law have been extended, and the scope of the law expanded, several times since 1965. Presenting an accurate portrayal of the legacy of the VRA must include a consideration of these post-1965 addenda. Notably, Congress extended the scope of the law to include Latinos, Asians, and Native Americans in 1975. The temporary provisions of the act have been extended through 2032. The scope of the law has been expanded to cover all aspects of elections, including voter qualifications, election procedures, and redistricting. The law is administered by the Civil Rights Division of the U.S. Department of Justice (DOJ). It should be noted that the office has taken different enforcement approaches over time and has been accused of interpreting and applying the law in a way that provides a partisan advantage to the party occupying the White House. These decisions have further shaped and constrained the VRA. Moreover, some Supreme Court decisions since the early 1990s have restricted the ways in which the act can be used to increase the representation of ethnic or racial minority groups. While this chapter was being written, the Supreme Court declared that a major component of the VRA was unconstitutional. The *Shelby County v. Holder* decision in June 2013 has resulted in a major reduction in the scope and effectiveness of the VRA. This chapter discusses the impact of that decision after first examining the following topics in order to assess the legacy of the VRA:

1. LBJ's experience with the historical precedents of the VRA; the Civil Rights Act of 1957; and the historical context in which the VRA became law in 1965
2. A description of the major aspects of the original VRA
3. Congressional expansions and renewal of the VRA from 1970 through 1992
4. The two major dimensions for evaluating the impact and effectiveness of the VRA in expanding voting rights for African Americans and other minorities: preventing discrimination that blocks an eligible voter from casting a vote, and providing minorities protected by the VRA the opportunity to cast an effective vote, that is, one that allows them to elect the candidate of their choice
5. The VRA's impact on the ability to draw effective minority districts
6. The 2006 revision to the VRA; the VRA and the 2012 presidential election; and the VRA after *Shelby County v. Holder*

The Voting Rights Act of 1965 in Historical Context

The expansion of the VRA described above is wholly consistent with the beliefs that LBJ expressed to support, encourage, cajole, and engineer the passage of a very weak law to improve African Americans' access to the vote. The passage of the Civil Rights Act of 1957 was Johnson's greatest achievement as Senate majority leader. It was the first civil rights act passed by Congress since 1875 (Caro 2002, 29). Robert Caro titled the third volume of his LBJ biography *Master of the Senate*, in recognition of this legislative triumph. Even though this act was "toothless" (1030), LBJ made great compromises and put tremendous effort into its passage. The extent of these compromises can be seen in the law's title and the fact that the proposed legislation was originally a broad-based civil rights bill that addressed access to public accommodations, transportation, employment, education, and voting. To win the bill's passage in the Senate, LBJ agreed to eliminate all provisions of the bill except voting rights. He also agreed to make the law so weak that any voting rights violation would very likely go unpunished (1029–1033). Perhaps the only consequential aspect of this law was the creation of the U.S. Commission on Civil Rights (USCCR). Most of the compromises that LBJ made were necessary in order to get an agreement from southern Democratic senators not to use a filibuster to kill the law. As Caro points out: "Lyndon Johnson saw, why the passage of *any* civil rights bill, no matter how weak, would be a crucial gain for civil rights. Once a bill was passed, it could later be amended: altering something was a lot easier than creating it" (932). Moreover, Johnson believed that voting was the civil right that mattered most. With the right to vote, a group could then start fighting for other rights (Caro 2012, 8–10). The history of the expanding scope of the Voting Rights Act of 1965 is completely consistent with the vision that LBJ articulated while shepherding the 1957 act through the Senate.

The civil rights movement, which had the goal of granting full citizenship rights to African Americans, provides the general context for the passage of the VRA. The movement's tactics included boycotts, sit-ins, demonstrations, marches, freedom rides, voter registration drives, and other activities, all of which were often violently repressed by jailings, beatings, teargassings, attacks with fire hoses, and murders. Taylor Branch's three-volume history of the movement provides a compelling and detailed narrative of the civil rights movement and Martin Luther King's leadership (Branch 1989, 1998, 2006). The third volume, *At Canaan's Edge: America in the King Years, 1965–1968* (Branch 2006), presents the immediate historical and political context in which the VRA became law. One major precipitating event was the brutal repression of the nonviolent march from Selma to Montgomery, Alabama, to advocate for African American voting rights and to protest the fatal police shooting of a civil rights marcher.

On March 7, 1965, now known as "Bloody Sunday," about 600 civil rights marchers were brutally and violently attacked by 175 state troopers, sheriff's deputies, and mounted posse members after they crossed the Edmund Pettus Bridge in Selma. The troopers pursued and attacked the marchers for more than a mile. About 100 marchers needed medical attention, and 58 required hospitalization. Images of the Bloody Sunday brutality were broadcast on national television that evening during the widely watched television premiere of *Judgment at Nuremberg*, a movie about the trial of Nazi war criminals. It was uncomfortably easy to make the association between Nazi storm troopers and the Alabama troopers. According to Branch, "The Nuremberg interruption struck with the force of instant historical icon" (2006, 44–57; see also Tuck 2005, 83–84). There were protests against the Bloody Sunday brutality across the country.

A week later, LBJ gave one of his most effective and moving speeches,

"The American Promise," to a joint session of Congress. In this speech, he called for the passing of the Voting Rights Act. While he acknowledged that the events at Selma had outraged the conscience of the nation, and that his speech was a response to the attack on the Selma marchers, it is nonetheless important to note that Johnson's attention to voting rights was not solely a response to Selma. After being elected president, in November 1964, Johnson ordered Attorney General Nicholas Katzenbach to draft the "toughest voting rights act that you can devise" (Fisher n.d.). Katzenbach responded in December with a memorandum to LBJ outlining possible legal approaches to ensuring voting rights and a draft of the VRA a few days *before* Bloody Sunday. The timing of LBJ's address was a response to Bloody Sunday, but the goal and the general components of the VRA had been well established before then. Thus, LBJ's speech could argue for the necessity of a VRA and outline the major components of the 1965 law. The speech (Johnson 1965) can be read as a précis of the proposed law and as a sincere, personal appeal for its passage.

This speech addressed the following issues raised or addressed by the VRA: states' rights versus federal control of elections; the use of "literacy" tests, grandfather clauses, and other devices and restrictions used to keep African Americans from voting; the creation of federal registrars to step in when local officials discriminated; making the federal government the active enforcer of the law rather than requiring the typically poor and vulnerable victims of voting discrimination to pursue their rights through lawsuits. LBJ closed the speech by saying, "And we shall overcome." Many who heard him say these words were moved to tears. Moreover, the words signified that LBJ was allying himself and the federal government with the voter registration and voter participation efforts of the civil rights movement (Branch 2006, 44–57).

The Voting Rights Act of 1965

One of the enduring tensions in voting rights law pits states against Congress in determining the procedures used in elections. The Fifteenth Amendment of the U.S. Constitution, quoted below in its entirety, clearly shows that voting rights law does not raise constitutional issues.

Amendment XV (ratified February 3, 1870)
Section 1. The right of citizens of the United States to vote shall not be denied or abridged by the United States or by any State on account of race, color, or previous condition of servitude.

Section 2. The Congress shall have the power to enforce this article by appropriate legislation.

Despite the clearly indicated role of Congress in regulating elections, states have largely regulated their own elections for most of the nation's history and have generally resisted federal control (McDonald 2005, 161–162).

The VRA became law less than six months after Bloody Sunday. It begins with the phrase, "AN ACT to enforce the fifteenth amendment of the Constitution of the United States." The two most important functions of the act were to prevent disenfranchisement and vote dilution. Disenfranchisement was effected by literacy tests, poll taxes, whites-only primaries, intimidation through threats of (and actual) violence, economic sanctions, and a long list of other ways of preventing minority voting. Vote dilution was achieved through electoral boundaries, schemes, and procedures that prevented minorities from electing their candidates of choice when they did vote. Examples of these schemes include at-large elections; "cracking" the minority vote among several districts so that minority voters are not a majority in any single district; "packing" many more than a majority of minorities in a few districts so as to minimize the number of candidates they could elect (National Commission on the Voting Rights Act 2006, ch. 2).

The VRA had both temporary and permanent provisions. The major permanent provision is section 2. It applies to the entire country, and it prohibits any practice or procedure that denies the right to vote to any U.S. citizen on the basis of race or color. It is essentially a restatement of the Fifteenth Amendment with the major addition of authorizing the attorney general to take action to stop discriminatory practices and procedures. Before the VRA, private citizens could sue to redress violations of the Fifteenth Amendment, but such suits were complicated and expensive, and the plaintiffs were subject to harassment and intimidation; additionally, the suits were typically brought in hostile courts. Section 2 made the intentions of the Fifteenth Amendment a reality.

For most of the history of the VRA, section 3 was largely unknown and rarely used. Section 3 permits federal courts to place preclearance (section 5) requirements on political jurisdictions found to have violated minority voting rights. After such a finding is made, the jurisdiction must get prior approval before making any changes to its voting procedures. In this, section 3 is similar to section 4 (discussed below) in its consequence, but section 3 can be triggered by litigation brought by the DOJ or by civil rights and legal advocacy groups (Crum 2010; Wiley 2014). The Supreme Court's recent *Shelby County* decision has already made section 3 much better known and more widely used.

The temporary provisions of the VRA, presented in sections 4–9 and 13, have been more controversial. They were initially authorized for a period of five years. Section 4 specified the criteria for identifying jurisdictions that would be subject to these temporary provisions. If a jurisdiction used a test or device that limited voting in a discriminatory manner and if less than 50 percent of the voting-age residents were registered to vote, or if less than 50 percent voted in the previous presidential election, it would be subject to very close monitoring by the Justice Department.

Most notable and controversial among these temporary provisions was section 5. For areas that met the criteria outlined in section 4, section 5 required that they seek approval for, or preclear, any changes in their voting procedures, either through judicial review by a three-judge panel of the U.S. District Court of the District of Columbia or by administrative review by the Office of the Attorney General. This formula identified the following states as "covered jurisdictions": Alabama, Georgia, Louisiana, Mississippi, South Carolina, and Virginia. It also covered many counties in North Carolina (USCCR 2005, 2). Section 5 thus put the burden of proving that any proposed changes in voting and election procedures were not discriminatory on the state and local governments that wanted to enact these changes (Tuck 2005, 89–93). There is a procedure by which covered jurisdiction could "bail out" of section 5 coverage. Section 5 is different from most laws, which generally presume that governmental actions are legitimate and legal. In contrast, section 5 required the covered jurisdictions to prove that any proposed changes in electoral procedures were not discriminatory before they could be implemented. Congress believed that obstacles to African American voting in the South were to extend that their intrusion into the decisions of state and local government should be done only as a temporary, emergency measure. Section 5 has been the most controversial and most harshly criticized aspect of the VRA. No other federal law applies only to parts of the United States and requires the specified jurisdictions to get prior approval from the federal government before enacting state or local laws and ordinances (Persily 2007, 178). The Supreme Court affirmed the constitutionality of the VRA in its 1966 decision in *South Carolina v. Katzenbach*, 383 U.S. 301 (Valelly 2005, 271–280; McDonald 1999, 209–212).[1]

The other temporary provisions of the VRA enabled the attorney general to deploy federal election examiners, observers, and monitors who could register voters and monitor elections to ensure that all eligible citizens were allowed to register regardless of their race and that these newly registered voters were allowed to vote (Tuck 2005, 89–93). These provisions were very important in the period following passage of the VRA. Within months of the VRA's becoming law, 250,000 new black voters were registered in the

South, many of them by federal examiners. Selma is the county seat of Dallas County, Alabama, where the number of registered black voters increased from 383 before the VRA was passed to around 8,000—or about half of Dallas County's voting-age population—in November 1965. In Mississippi, black voter registration jumped from 6.7 percent to 59.8 percent in 1967. In 1968, nine African Americans were elected to Congress. There had not been that many since 1875 (ACLU 2005).

Congressional Expansions and Renewal of the VRA from 1970 to 1992

The 1970 Extension of the Voting Right Act

The temporary provisions of the VRA, particularly section 5, were due to expire in 1970, during Richard Nixon's first term as president. In contrast to LBJ, who recognized support for voting rights and civil rights as a political liability but who nonetheless was their leading proponent, Nixon took a cynically pragmatic attitude toward voting rights. Nixon was vice president when Johnson led the effort to pass the Civil Rights Act of 1957, the toothless voting rights law mentioned above. As president of the Senate, Nixon closely followed Johnson's maneuvers to get the bill passed. At that time, support among Republicans for African American civil rights was about as prevalent as it was among some northern liberal Democrats. The most vehement opponents of civil rights for African Americans were southern Democrats. In the 1950s, black voters in northern cities were starting to be seen as a growing and influential swing group. Under a different set of historical circumstances, Republicans might have become the party of African American civil rights. Nixon was furious that LBJ and the Democrats were able to garner the reputation, credit, and black votes for advancing civil rights without doing anything substantive. If Nixon could have gained a political advantage by supporting voting rights for blacks—if it would have helped him and other Republicans win elections—he would have been a proponent of them (Caro 2002, 870–1028).

On the day that he signed the 1965 VRA into law, LBJ is reported to have said, "We just delivered the South to the Republican Party for a long time to come."[2] Nixon was the first presidential candidate elected by capitalizing on this partisan realignment, which became known as the "Southern Strategy," that is, counting on the growth in black enfranchisement to increase and polarize white voter participation, especially in the South. (See Boyd 1970 for an early exposition of the Southern Strategy.) Kevin Phillips, an advisor to Nixon's presidential campaign and a well-known Republican strategist, urged the GOP to support the VRA because it would increase white backlash (Davidson 1990, 232–234). John Ehrlichman, Nixon's special counsel, described an aspect of Nixon's 1968 presidential campaign strategy to increase votes by saying, "We'll go after the racists." Ehrlichman also thought that a "subliminal appeal to anti-black voters was always present in Nixon's statements and speeches," even in the absence of overtly racist appeals (Alexander 2012, 47).

By the time that Nixon became president, Democrats were strongly and clearly established as the party of civil rights for African Americans because of LBJ's Great Society legislative legacy. Nixon's presidential campaign took advantage of this fact by maximizing his appeal to conservative white southerners (Kotlowski 2001, ch. 3; Moore 2005). In a further effort to attract the support of this group, Nixon proposed "nationalizing" section 5 of the VRA so that it applied to the entire country instead of just to the areas that met the triggering criteria. Nixon also proposed changing the law so that the Justice Department would have the burden of proving that changes in voting were racially discriminatory. In 1969, there was strong public and political support for civil rights, a crescendo in the protests against Vietnam, and strong tensions in the black community. The politics of renewing the VRA was mixed up with the movement to lower the voting age to eighteen and many other issues. Section 5 and the other temporary provisions were extended for another five years. The only change in the law was that the section 5 preclearance trigger was now based on registration and turnout calculations from the presidential election of 1968 rather than 1964 (Kotlowski 2001, ch.3; Moore 2005). While the triggering criteria were based on calculations of registration and turnout as before, the new data now included four counties with significant Latino populations: Apache County, Arizona; Monterey County, California; and Kings and New York Counties, New York (de la Garza and DeSipio, 1992–1993, 1481).

Mexicans/Hispanics/Latinos and the 1975 Extension of the Voting Rights Act

There were many ironies to LBJ's support of the VRA. In his special message to Congress quoted above, he referred to his experience teaching impoverished Mexican American children of Cotulla, Texas, as a major motivation for his support for the VRA:

> My students were poor and they often came to class without breakfast, hungry. They knew even in their youth the pain of prejudice . . .
> It never even occurred to me in my fondest dreams that I might have the

chance to help the sons and daughters of those students and to help people like them all over this country. But now I do have that chance—and I'll let you in on a secret—I mean to use it. And I hope that you will use it with me. (Johnson 1965)[3]

One irony can be seen in the fact that the 1965 VRA did little to protect the voting rights of Mexican Americans.[4] The historical record makes clear that almost all congressional debates and discussions regarding the VRA were focused on protecting the voting rights of African Americans. Another irony can be found in the fact that LBJ's career was based in part on buying, falsifying, or otherwise misappropriating the votes of Mexican Americans. Caro gives many detailed examples in the four volumes of his biography of LBJ published to date. Manipulating the Mexican vote was commonplace in Texas elections from the 1920s through the 1950s and seems to have been a factor in every election in which LBJ was a candidate.[5] Caro makes it clear that LBJ was directly involved in these massive efforts to control the Mexican vote.[6] Also note that Texas was not covered by section 5 and the other temporary provisions of the 1965 VRA.

After the first renewal in 1970, the temporary provisions of the VRA were due to expire in 1975. Barbara Jordan, then a member of Congress from Houston, proposed a bill expanding the preclearance coverage of VRA to include the following language-minority groups: Latinos, Native Americans, Alaska Natives, and Asians. She explained her reasons as follows:

My bill would extend the provisions of the Voting Rights Act to Texas, New Mexico, Arizona and parts of California. H.R. 3247 would guarantee to Mexican Americans and *blacks* residing in these jurisdictions the same special attention to their voting rights now afforded blacks in the South . . .

In its simplest form my bill amends the definition of the phrase "test or device" to make explicit the rulings of federal courts that the failure to provide bilingual registration forms and ballots constitutes the use of a literacy test. (U.S. House 1975, 76; emphasis added)

Her proposal to protect the specified language-minority groups became law as section 203 of the VRA as amended in 1975. Areas with populations that met these criteria were now covered by section 5 of the VRA. While many considerations motivated Jordan's legislative proposal, covering all Texans and all Texas jurisdictions under section 5 must have been one of them. (See Barbara Jordan Archives 2011 for more on the context of her decision to propose this expansion of the VRA.) In addition to extending coverage of the VRA to Texas, New Mexico, Arizona, and California, the VRA now covered jurisdictions in twenty-six other states (National Commission on the Voting Rights Act 2006, 33). Also, areas with high concentrations of U.S. citizens with a limited proficiency in English were required to provide language-appropriate ballots and election materials (Tucker 2006).

Section 2 was amended to make it clear that discrimination against language minorities was now prohibited, just as the original act prohibited discrimination on the basis of race (National Commission on the Voting Rights Act 2006, 32–33). The calculations of the triggering thresholds for section 5 coverage were updated so that they were based on statistics from the 1972 presidential election. It is important to point out that the 1975 revision was the last time that the coverage formula has been updated.

Preserving the Effectiveness of Section 2: The 1982 and 1992 Extensions of the VRA

Throughout its history, the VRA has been the subject of numerous court decisions that have determined how parts of the law would be implemented and what their ultimate impact would be. An extensive literature analyzes and critiques the implications of these cases. While informed by a reading of these cases, this chapter mentions them only when necessary. Discussion of the renewal of the VRA in 1982 necessitates mentioning the Supreme Court's decision in *City of Mobile v. Bolden*, 446 U.S. 55 (1980). This decision required that suits filed under section 2 of the VRA had to prove that there was a discriminatory *intent* behind the voting law that the suit addressed. It is generally difficult to prove intent in such cases. In the 1982 renewal of the VRA, Congress addressed this problem by changing section 2 to make it clear that a discriminatory *effect or result* would be sufficient to support a successful VRA suit. The 1982 amendments to the VRA also extended until 2007 the preclearance provisions of section 5 for the states and counties identified by the data and analyses specified in the 1975 VRA amendments. Also, the requirement that specified areas provide bilingual election materials was extended until 1992 (Moore 2005, 105–108).

There was one more major change to the law in 1982, which can be seen as creating the basis for future limitations or contractions of the VRA. A clause known as the "Dole Compromise," after Senator Bob Dole (R-KS), was added to section 2. This clause stipulated that section 2 does not establish "a right to have members of a protected class elected in numbers equal to their proportion in the population" (McDonald 1989, 1273).

Parts of the VRA had expiration dates and extensions of different lengths. In 1992, the criteria for coverage under the section 203 language-minority provisions were extended until 2007. This section's specific coverage formulas were revised so that smaller population concentrations were covered than before. This change resulted in covering more Asian American populations under the act (Tucker 2006, 223–228).

The Effectiveness of VRA in Preventing Disenfranchisement

The VRA has been extremely effective in removing barriers to voting by racial minorities. These devices included poll taxes, literacy tests, white-only primaries, intentional loss or destruction of registration records, threats of physical harm, economic reprisals, and the like. One of the compelling reasons for requiring the preclearance of changes in voting laws in areas with a history of discriminatory barriers to voting was that voting officials in those jurisdictions readily came up with new ways to block protected groups from voting (Klarman 2005).

Before the passage of the VRA, voting barriers minimized the vote of African Americans. At that time, African Americans constituted a majority of the Dallas County, Alabama, voting-age population, but only 1 percent of registered voters (Tuck 2005, 80–81). In the first election held in Selma after the VRA became law, the number of votes cast in a local election increased from 6,500 to 17,440 (Doar 1997, 17). By 1972, 67 percent of eligible voting-age African Americans were registered, and black candidates won half of the ten seats on the Selma city council (Lewis and Allen 1972–1973, 118).

One need not hark back to the days of Jim Crow to find examples of racially biased disenfranchisement. The 2000 presidential election will likely be best remembered for the Supreme Court's still controversial decision in *Bush v. Gore*, 531 U.S. 98 (2000). But most of the discussion of the decision has overlooked the racial disparities in Florida's voting procedures (Overton 2001). Underlying the issues raised before the Supreme Court was racially discriminatory voter disenfranchisement on a mass scale. For example, there were 180,000 spoiled ballots—that is, ballots cast but not counted. Most of these, 54 percent, were cast by African Americans, who made up 11 percent of the electorate. This is attributed to the fact that many of Florida's African Americans live in poorer counties with technology more likely to produce spoiled ballots. A report by the U.S. Commission on Civil Rights cites evidence that there was a huge disparity between the "countless" number of black voters and the nonblack voters who were "wrongfully turned away from the polls": "The Commission found that the problems Florida had during the 2000 presidential election were serious and not isolated. In many cases, they were foreseeable and should have been prevented. The failure to do so resulted in an extraordinarily high and inexcusable level of disenfranchisement, with a significantly disproportionate impact on African American voters" (USCCR 2001, executive summary). The circumstances of the 2000 Florida election show what can happen when the protection of voting rights is not given high priority.

The general effectiveness of the VRA in minimizing discriminatory barriers to voting came about through the vigorous actions of the DOJ. Between 1966 and 2000, more than 23,000 federal employees were assigned to observe polling procedures (Weinberg and Utrecht 2001). For the areas covered by section 5, DOJ reviewed almost 360,000 proposed changes in voting procedure between 1982 and 2004. DOJ objected to less than 1 percent of them (USCCR 2001, 29–30). Instead, the DOJ much more frequently responded to section 5 submissions by requiring additional information. These requests often deterred the implementation of proposed discriminatory changes in voting procedures (Perales, Figueroa, and Rivas 2007, 714; also see Fraga and Ocampo 2007). Finally, 321 lawsuits addressing section 2 of the VRA were filed between 1982 and 2004, resulting in 748 decisions (Katz et al. 2006, 6). An important detail regarding the suits filed under section 2 is that 81 percent of the ones that had outcomes favorable for minority voters occurred in areas covered by section 5, even though these areas were home to only 25 percent of the U.S. population (McCrary 2010, 12–14).

The VRA, Redistricting, and Effective Minority Representation: The Effectiveness of VRA in Increasing Minority Representation

Initial Success

In 1965, there were fewer than 100 African American elected officials in eleven southern states. By 1972, there were 873 (Lewis and Allen 1972–1973, 114). For all elected offices across the United States, the figure increased from 1,469 in 1970 to more than 9,000 in 2001 (U.S. Census Bureau 2006, table 403). The number of Latino elected officials across the United States grew from 3,147 in 1985 to 4,651 in 2004 (table 404). So there has been a huge increase in the number of minority elected officials, and there can be no doubt that the VRA was an important factor in this increase. But it is in this area of minority representation that the interpretation and implementation of the law have undergone the greatest change—the greatest expansion and contraction. In *Allen v. State Board of Elections*, 393 U.S. 544 (1969), the Supreme Court decided that the VRA extended beyond preventing disenfranchisement to include a review of all state actions concerning the voting process. The interpretation of the VRA that is faithful to LBJ's vision means giving minorities the right to elect their candidate of choice as well as ensuring that they are not disenfranchised. Many, perhaps most, of the elections since the VRA became law have been characterized by racially polarized voting, that is, people tend to vote for candidates who belong to their own racial group (Crayton 2012, 985–989). Most African American and Latino legislators represent areas with a majority of minority constituents (National Commission on the Voting Rights Act 2006, tables 3 and 4).

There is a large literature on the preferences for benefits of minority representation for minority constituents. Electoral districts with Latino majorities are more likely to elect Latino representatives, and a related literature shows that Latino representatives are more likely to substantively represent their Latino constituents than non-Latino representatives (Casellas 2007, 2009). The opportunity to vote for a Latino candidate increases Latino voter turnout (Barreto 2007). Other research looking at specific aspects of representation by examining votes, bill sponsorships, committee service, and so on has found that African Americans are better represented and better served by African American congressional representatives. Moreover, the symbolism of being represented by an African American was very important to African American voters (Tate 2003). While there are many good reasons for minority voters to prefer to elect minority representatives, there are also many instances in which minority voters have voted for majority candidates. Regardless, as a general rule, if minorities are to be able to elect candidates of their choosing, they must vote in electoral districts where they are the majority. Furthermore, where voting is racially polarized, if minorities are to be able to elect minority candidates, they must also vote in elections were they are the majority. In the eyes of critics, this logic changes the VRA from a guarantee that an individual has the right to vote into a group right (Thernstrom 1997).

The VRA prevents electoral schemes that discriminate against minorities. A key question about vote dilution is whether districts can be drawn in a way to provide an opportunity for voters to elect their candidate of choice. This, in turn, depends on the population concentrations in a potential district. One scheme to dilute minority voting strength occurs when district boundaries are drawn to divide a minority population between districts and

Fig. 4.1. African American and Latino members of the U.S. House of Representatives, 1964–2014

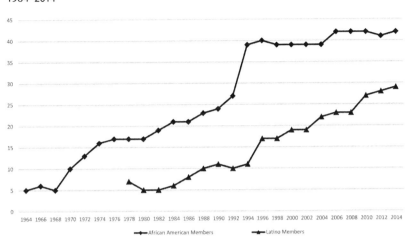

Sources: Amer 2005; U.S. Census Bureau 2010; U.S. Census Bureau 2011; and U.S. House of Representatives 2013.

reduce its vote to less than a majority. Another scheme packs the minority electorate into a few districts instead of allocating it so that it could have constituted a majority in additional districts. The major challenges to the use of VRA to increase minority representation originate from redistricting efforts to draw districts with a majority-minority population.

Figure 4.1 shows the number of African American and Latino members of the U.S. House of Representatives since 1964. After this initial period of very rapid growth, the line showing the number of African American representatives leveled off in the early 1990s. The line showing Latino representatives has a parallel rapid increase, but is lower because the VRA did not do much for Latino voters' representation until 1975. Just as a point of comparison, if African Americans were represented in proportion to their share of the U.S. population, there would be 40 percent more African American representatives than at present. If Latinos were represented at parity, there would be 140 percent more Latinos in the House.

There are a number of reasons that there are proportionately far fewer Latinos in Congress than African Americans. One reason is Latinos are more widely dispersed, or less segregated, within many jurisdictions. This affects the districting of local and state legislative bodies and of the U.S House of Representatives. This makes it harder to create Latino-majority districts or other types of "opportunity to elect" districts. Another major impediment to creating more Latino-majority districts is that in several appellate jurisdictions, Latinos have to make up a majority of the *citizen* voting-age population (CVAP). Since about one out of every three voting-age Latinos is a noncitizen immigrant, a CVAP majority is even harder to include in a district. In contrast, the reason that the number of black representatives leveled off in the early 1990s is tied to several Supreme Court decisions that undermined the ability to create majority-minority districts under the VRA.

Majority-Minority Districts: Empowerment or Odious Racial Classification?

Starting with the Supreme Court's 1993 *Shaw v. Reno* decision, efforts to increase minority representation by creating majority–minority districts have faced judicially imposed barriers. North Carolina submitted a congressional redistricting plan that created a majority-black district that followed 160 miles of Interstate 85 and was, in parts, no wider than the I-85 corridor. Five North Carolina residents claimed that this district's boundaries were so "bizarre on its face that it is unexplainable on grounds other than race"—and that this was an unconstitutional racial gerrymander that violated the Fourteenth Amendment. Justice O'Connor wrote:

> Racial classifications of any sort pose the risk of lasting harm to our society. They reinforce the belief, held by too many for too much of our history, that individuals should be judged by the color of their skin. Racial classifications with respect to voting carry particular dangers. Racial gerrymandering, even for remedial purposes, may balkanize us into competing racial factions; it threatens to carry us further from the goal of a political system in which race no longer matters—a goal that the Fourteenth and Fifteenth Amendments embody, and to which the Nation continues to aspire. It is for these reasons that race-based districting by our state legislatures demands close judicial scrutiny. (*Shaw v. Reno*, 509 U.S. 630, at 657)

Moreover, she asserted that since this bizarrely shaped district was designed only to create a congressional district along racial lines to ensure the election of a black representative, it disregarded traditional redistricting considerations such as compactness, contiguousness, geographic boundaries, and political subdivisions. A. Leon Higginbotham, Gregory A. Clarick, and Marcella David (1994) show that North Carolina had a long history of political discrimination against African Americans that deserved remediation, yet the Supreme Court decided that oddly shaped districts that increased the opportunity to elect African Americans posed a greater risk to democratic principles.

Following similar logic, the Supreme Court found in *Miller v. Johnson*, 515 U.S. 900 (1995), that a Georgia congressional district was a geographic "monstrosity" that linked "metropolitan black neighborhoods together with the poor black populace of coastal areas 260 miles away." The district was declared unconstitutional also because race was the "predominant factor" used to determine its boundaries.

These decisions raise two issues that must be addressed here. The first concerns the sanctity of the shape, that is, the importance of the appearance of district boundaries and traditional redistricting considerations. The second is the issue of individual versus group rights. With respect to the shape of these districts, they were, indeed, irregular and noncompact. But as critics have pointed out, other congressional districts have similarly bizarre shapes (Kouser 1999 is one of the most compelling of these critiques). But these other bizarrely shaped districts had white majorities and drew no judicial notice. The other objection to these cases of "racial gerrymandering" was that they transformed the right of an individual to cast a ballot into the group right guaranteeing African Americans the right to elect the candidate of their choice, often another African American. Still, there are many examples of redistricting giving favorable consideration to group membership in deference to white ethnic and religious groups. I must agree with Kouser. In their effort to minimize the consideration of race in redistricting, these decisions have weakened an important way in which the VRA could mitigate past racial discrimination. Furthermore, the data presented in figure 4.1, and many other considerations, show that these decisions have stunted the growth of minority representation in Congress.

The Supreme Court further weakened the ability to create majority–minority voting districts with its decision in *Georgia v. Ashcroft*, 539 U.S. 461 (2003), ruling that a minority "influence" district could be created instead of a majority-minority district. An influence district is one with a substantial number, but not a majority, of minority voters. The court assumed that this group could not be ignored by the elected representative and would thus be able to influence his or her political actions (Engstrom 2012). Richard L. Engstrom discusses many examples, particularly Texas Congressional District 23, created in 2003. Although 46 percent of the eligible voters were Latino, the district was created to protect a Republican incumbent, Henry Bonilla. While only 8 percent of the district's Latinos voted for Bonilla, he was elected six times (94–96). The influence that an electoral minority has in a district very much depends on the composition and characteristics of the rest of the district's population. By ignoring this issue, the judicial decision authorizing the creation of influence districts instead of majority-minority districts has undermined the ability of the members of the groups protected by the VRA to have an effective vote.

The 2012 Election and Suppressing the Minority Vote

One surprising aspect of the history of the VRA is the strong bipartisan support that the VRA has received in Congress, both for extensions of its temporary provisions and for the amendments meant to contradict some of the Supreme Court rulings that limited the VRA's scope. Five different Congresses have voted on VRA revisions and extensions. All but one was supported by a majority of Democrats and Republicans. The only exception was the 1992 extension of the bilingual ballot provisions, which was opposed by a majority of House Republicans. Along the same lines, the only Democratic president to sign a version of the VRA was LBJ. Republicans signed all the other revisions: Nixon, Ford, Reagan, George H. W. Bush, and George W. Bush (Laney 2008; Moore 2005; Tucker 2006–2007).

The current version of the VRA, known as the Fannie Lou Hamer, Rosa Parks, and Coretta Scott King Voting Rights Act Reauthorization and Amendments Act (VRARA), became law in 2006. The law extended section 5 of the Voting Rights Act for an additional twenty-five years. It also addressed two Supreme Court decisions that had undermined the act, including *Georgia v. Ashcroft*. The VRARA asserted that section 5 was intended to protect the ability of minorities "to elect their preferred candidates of choice."

In the 2012 presidential election, for the first time in history, African Americans voted at a higher rate than whites. African Americans made up 12 percent of the eligible electorate yet cast 13 percent of all votes. Before that election, African Americans had accounted for a smaller percentage of votes than their percentage of eligible voters (Taylor 2012). If proportionally more African Americans are voting than whites, it is reasonable to conclude that racially discriminatory disenfranchisement is not prevalent at the national level.

Likewise, the number of Latinos and Asian Americans who voted in 2012 was at a record high. The protection and assistance offered to these groups under the VRA seem to be working. It worthwhile to note that while the voter turnout rates for these groups are increasing, these rates are substantially lower than those for whites and African Americans. The growing electoral impact of African Americans is due to increased turnout rates. In contrast, the growing electoral impact of Latinos and Asian Americans is due to their rapid population growth (Taylor 2012). Another factor driving the rapid growth of the Latino electorate is that Latinos are a young population, and most Latinos younger than eighteen are U.S. citizens. The number of Latinos who turned eighteen years old between 2008 and 2012 increased the number of potential Latino voters by about three million (Chapa et al. 2011).

Despite the tremendous effectiveness of the VRA and its enforcement by the DOJ in reducing discriminatory disenfranchisement, this does not mean that the VRA is no longer needed. When the VRA was last renewed, in 2006, the House Subcommittee on Civil and Constitutional Rights compiled a report of more than four thousand pages that provided evidence of the continued need for the VRA (U.S. House 2006). Much of the material provided as evidence at the hearing was eventually published as scholarly peer-reviewed publications.

Further evidence of the continued need for the VRA can be seen in the efforts by many states to pass laws to restrict access to the ballot. The 2008 presidential election was the previous high-water mark for minority electoral participation. In anticipation of President Obama's reelection bid in 2012, many states passed laws to restrict access to the ballot. The report *Defending Democracy* (NAACP Legal Defense and Educational Fund, Inc./NAACP 2011) lists the following means by which electoral access has been reduced:

- Photo identification requirements
- Restrictions on access to voter registration
- Limitations on when and where voters can register
- Enhanced registration eligibility requirements
- Increased disenfranchisement of people with felony convictions
- Voter roll purges
- Shortening early/absentee voting periods
- Other restrictions on early/absentee voting

These laws had both a partisan and a racial bias. Generally, they were passed by Republican-controlled state governments and were apparently intended to diminish the electoral participation of African American and Latino voters, who tend to vote Democratic (Weiser and Norden 2011). In particular, new laws institutionalizing stringent voter ID requirements generated much controversy. Indiana's voter ID law, one of the strictest in the country, was found to be constitutional by the U.S. Supreme Court in *Crawford v. Marion County*, 553 U.S. 181 (2008) (Stout 2008). A lower court judge said, "Let's not beat around the bush: The Indiana voter photo ID law is a not-too-thinly-veiled attempt to discourage election-day turnout by certain folks believed to skew Democratic."[7] Texas passed a similar law in 2012, but because Texas was covered by section 5 of the VRA, this change in voting could not go into effect immediately. Attorney General Eric Holder said that the Texas voter ID requirements amounted to a poll tax, and the DOJ ruled that Texas had failed to show that this new requirement would not discriminate against minority voters (Savage 2012).

Shelby County v. Holder and the End of Preclearance

The contrast between the Supreme Court's decision in sustaining Indiana's voter ID law and the DOJ's opposite finding in the Texas voter ID law highlights the significance of the case heard by the Supreme Court in the spring of 2013 and decided in June. The central issue in *Shelby County v. Holder*, was stated in Shelby County's Petition for a Writ of Certiorari: "Whether Congress' decision in 2006 to reauthorize Section 5 of the Voting Rights Act under the pre-existing coverage formula of Section 4(b) of the Voting Rights Act exceeded its authority under the Fifteenth Amendment and thus violated the Tenth Amendment and Article IV of the United States Constitution." Alabama and the other jurisdictions identified by section 4 and covered by section 5 felt that the preclearance requirements were unjust and unreasonable. Chief Justice Roberts and a majority of the Supreme Court agreed. As previously noted, section 4 has not been updated since the 1975 version of the VRA was revised according to voter turnout data from the 1972 presidential election. Legal scholars indicated that a majority of the Supreme Court justices had warned Congress of their concern about the out-of-date content of section 4 in an earlier decision, *Northwest Austin Municipal Utility District No. 1 v. Holder*, 557 U.S. 193 (2009) (Block 2012; Crum 2010). Chief Justice Roberts argued that many things have changed since 1975, including the ability of minorities to vote. Writing for the dissenting minority, Justice Ginsburg observed tartly, "Throwing out preclearance when it has worked and is continuing to work to stop discriminatory changes is like throwing away your umbrella in a rainstorm because you are not getting wet." This well-turned phrase succinctly expressed the thinking of many voting rights advocates (Katz 2014).

This chapter was completed within months of the *Shelby County* decision, but many developments have already occurred. Within a few weeks of the decision, many southern states previously covered by section 5 "rushed" to pass voter ID laws that seem intended to restrict access to the ballot (Cooper 2013). Within a few more weeks, the DOJ moved to have Texas covered by section 3 of the VRA, with the specific goal of stopping the implementation of the voter ID law (Liptak and Savage 2013). Within a few months, a bipartisan group in Congress introduced an updated version of the VRA (*New York Times* 2014). But congressional polarization and gridlock mean that this bill has very little chance of ever becoming law. The most recent development is an effort by nine swing states with Republican governors and legislative majorities to pass laws to restrict voting by using all the means listed above (Yaccino and Alvarez 2014). Many of these states were not covered by section 5. This highlights a major problem with relying on old criteria for proactive enforcement efforts: old data do not identify new violators of voting rights. As Michael LaVigne (2014) and many others argue, we need comprehensive electoral reform.

Conclusions

The Voting Rights Act of 1965 must be seen as one of the most successful and influential components of Lyndon Johnson's legislative legacy. The status of African Americans and other minorities in U.S. society, as well as the quality of the relationships between all racial groups, has gone through tremendous, irrevocable change and improvement. Young people today cannot imagine or comprehend the Jim Crow conditions that persisted into the 1960s, just as a youth of that period would have difficulty imagining that an African American would be president of the United States. The success and enduring impact of the VRA is due to its positive feedback mechanism. In a democratic society, what could be more important than the right to vote? Enfranchising minority voters empowers them to pursue and achieve other rights and other goals. LBJ was prophetic in asserting that voting was the civil right that mattered most. But as we have seen in this chapter, other things matter, too. The VRA worked because it transformed and extended the federal government's role, making the DOJ proactively involved in defending minority voting rights. The VRA worked because section 5 requires (or required) state and local governments to get federal preapproval before enacting any changes in voting procedures. All these factors worked together to expand the scope and effectiveness of the VRA.

LBJ was also prophetic in seeing that the VRA would help Republicans win elections for a generation. But there is no indication that he foresaw how the success of the Southern Strategy would change the composition of the Supreme Court and its jurisprudence from the liberal Warren Court to the conservative Roberts Court. As argued in this chapter, the obstacles that stymied the continued effectiveness of the VRA can be traced directly to conservative Supreme Court decisions. While it seems unlikely that the

United States will ever return to the overtly racist disenfranchisement that was prevalent under Jim Crow, it is evident that a Supreme Court with a conservative majority will find constitutional voting laws and procedures that clearly have a racially disparate impact. Many elections in the twenty-first century have been subject to attempts to disenfranchise large groups of people. Even if we assume that these attempts sought to manipulate voting procedures for partisan advantage rather than from a racist animus, these efforts clearly had a disparate racial impact on the groups protected by the VRA, who generally vote Democratic. Voter ID laws, limitations on early voting, and felon disenfranchisement are among the many examples of these tactics. Applying the prohibition against racial gerrymandering for minorities but not for whites is another example of an obstacle to minority political empowerment created by conservatives on the Supreme Court.

Further undermining the court's credibility as an impartial arbiter is that decisions limiting the VRA also had a strong partisan impact. Most of the justices that have written decisions limiting the VRA were appointed by Republican presidents. Moreover, Adam Cox and Thomas Miles (2008) find that judges appointed by Democrats are much more likely than Republican appointees to vote in support of minority voting rights in suits filed under section 2 of the VRA.

Perhaps we can find hope for future electoral fairness in the example set by LBJ. While he was an active participant in, and beneficiary of, fraudulent voting, he eventually became the most effective advocate for minority enfranchisement in American history. All involved in voting must aspire to the standards for democracy set forth in our highest national ideals and rise above our often disgraceful history of voting abuse, disenfranchisement, and partisan bias in election administration.

Notes

The author thanks Allen Fisher, archivist at the LBJ Library, for his assistance.

1. Here is a key paragraph from the Supreme Court's decision: "[Section 5] may have been an uncommon exercise of congressional power . . . but the Court has recognized that exceptional conditions can justify legislative measures not otherwise appropriate. Congress knew that some of the States covered by [the section 4 coverage formula] had resorted to the extraordinary stratagem of contriving new rules of various kinds for the sole purpose of perpetrating voting discrimination in the face of adverse federal court decrees. Congress had reason to suppose that these States might try similar maneuvers in the future in order to evade the remedies for voting discrimination contained in the Act itself. Under the compulsion of these unique circumstances, Congress responded in a permissibly decisive manner" (quoted in USCCR 2005, 11).

2. According to Germany (2010, n. 4), Bill Moyers claims that LBJ said this on the day that he signed the Civil Rights Act of 1964 and that "Lady Bird Johnson and Harry McPherson trace the statement to a conversation after the signing of the Voting Rights Act in 1965." LBJ may have repeated the statement on both occasions. Caro's biographies of LBJ indicate many instances of LBJ repeating a good phrase. Both laws clearly did drive southern Democrats to change their party registration and to vote for Republicans.

3. See Caro (1982, ch. 10) for an account of LBJ's time in Cotulla.

4. For most of this country's history there was not an agreed-upon federal label or "identifier" for the group known variously as Mexican Americans, Latinos, or Hispanics. In 1976, the term "Hispanic" was adopted; see Chapa (2000) for a discussion. See Cartagena (2004–2005) for an analysis of how section 4(e) of the 1965 VRA did protect Puerto Ricans in New York City from disenfranchisement through English-language literacy tests. Cartagena argues that this provision and favorable judicial decisions laid the basis for expanding the VRA to concentrations of language minorities across the nation.

5. In the references listed under the heading "Kilday's brother running the West Side" (a neighborhood in San Antonio), Caro quotes John Connally as saying, "They [low-income Mexican Americans] went [to the polls] because the Sheriff told them to go." Caro adds, "Connally was talking at the time about the 1948 election but then said that situation had existed in the 1956 election and in 1960" (Caro 2012, 648). Regarding LBJ's victory over Coke Stevenson for the U.S. Senate in 1948, in a chapter titled "The Stealing," Caro draws the following conclusion: "In Duval County . . . the voting pattern was dramatically out of keeping with the normal patterns of democracy. How much of that 35,000-vote edge can be said to have been 'bought,' either by payments to *jefes* and other political bosses who wrote down voting totals with little or no reference to the actual votes that had been cast, . . . But from the descriptions given by men familiar with the voting in the Valley and on the West Side that Election Day in 1948, it is apparent that the overwhelming majority of those votes—not merely thousands of votes but tens of thousands—fall into that category" (Caro 1990, 310–311). Caro also indicates that the votes of African Americans who lived in areas controlled by these corrupt county officials were manipulated in the same manner (310–311).

6. Caro shows LBJ's personal involvement with vote buying in the following passage: "Lyndon Johnson had been using money as a lever to move the political world for a long time—ever since, as a young worker in a congressional campaign, he had sat in a San Antonio hotel room behind a table covered with five dollar bills, handing them to Mexican American men at the rate of five dollars a vote for each vote in the family" (Caro 2002, 429–430).

7. Judge Terence Evans quoted in Hasen (2012, 5).

References

ACLU [American Civil Liberties Union]. 2005. Voting Rights Act timeline. www
.aclu.org/files/assets/voting_rights_act_timeline20111222.pdf; accessed Oct. 29,
2012.

Alexander, Michele. 2012. *The new Jim Crow: Mass incarceration in the age of color-blindness.* New York: New Press.

Amer, Mildred L. 2005. *Black members of the United States Congress: 1870–2005.* CRS Report for Congress, Order Code RL30378. Washington, D.C.: Congressional Research Service.

Barbara Jordan Archives. 2011. Voting Rights Act of 1975 exhibit. Texas Southern University. Available at: www.flickr.com/photos/barbarajordanarchives/sets/72157626645873842/detail.

Barreto, Matt A. 2007. ¡Si se puede! Latino candidates and the mobilization of Latino voters. *American Political Science Review* 101, no. 3: 425–441.

Block, Melissa. 2012. ID laws bring new attention to Voting Rights Act. National Public Radio (Sept. 10). www.npr.org/2012/09/10/160899032/id-laws-bring-new-attention-to-voting-rights-act.

Boyd, James. 1970. Nixon's Southern Strategy: "It's all in the charts." *New York Times Magazine*, May 17, 25, 105–112.

Branch, Taylor. 1989. *Parting the waters: America in the King years, 1954–1963.* New York: Simon and Schuster.

———. 1998. *Pillar of fire: America in the King years, 1963–1965.* New York: Simon and Schuster.

———. 2006. *At Canaan's edge: America in the King years, 1965–1968.* New York: Simon and Schuster.

Caro, Robert A. 1982. *The years of Lyndon Johnson: The path to power.* New York: Knopf.

———. 1990. *The years of Lyndon Johnson: Means of ascent.* New York: Knopf.

———. 2002. *The years of Lyndon Johnson: Master of the Senate.* New York: Knopf.

———. 2012. *The years of Lyndon Johnson: The passage of power.* New York: Knopf.

Cartagena, Juan. 2004–2005. Latinos and Section 5 of the Voting Rights Act: Beyond black and white. *National Black Law Journal* 18.

Casellas, Jason P. 2007. The elections of Latinos to the California legislature pre- and post-2000 redistricting. *California Politics and Policy* 11, no. 1: 43–61.

———. 2009. The institutional and demographic determinants of Latino representation. *Legislative Studies Quarterly* 34, no. 3: 399–426.

Chapa, Jorge. 2000. Hispanic/Latino ethnicity and identifiers. In Margo J. Anderson, ed., *Encyclopedia of the U.S. Census.* Washington, D.C.: CQ Press.

Chapa, Jorge, Ana Henderson, Aggie Jooyoon Noah, Werner Schink, and Robert Kengle. 2011. *Redistricting: Estimating citizen voting age population.* Chief Justice Earl Warren Institute on Law and Social Policy Research Brief. University of California, Berkeley Law School.

Cooper, Michael. 2013. After ruling, states rush to enact voting laws. *New York Times* (July 5).

Cox, Adam, and Thomas Miles. 2008. Judging the Voting Rights Act. *Columbia Law Review* 108.

Crayton, Kareem. 2012. Sword, shield, and compass: The uses and misuses of racially polarized voting studies in voting rights enforcement. *Rutgers Law Review* 64.

Crum, Travis. 2010. The Voting Rights Act's secret weapon: Pocket trigger litigation and dynamic preclearance. *Yale Law Journal* 119.

Davidson, Chandler. 1990. *Race and class in Texas politics*. Princeton, N.J.: Princeton University Press.

de la Garza, Rodolfo O., and Louis DeSipio. 1992–1993. Save the baby, change the bathwater, and scrub the tub: Latino electoral participation after seventeen years of Voting Rights Act coverage. *Texas Law Review* 71.

Doar, John. 1997. Work of the Civil Rights Division in enforcing voting rights under the Civil Rights Acts of 1957 and 1960. *Florida State University Law Review* 25, no. 1.

Engstrom, Richard L. 2012. Influence districts and the courts. In Daniel McCool, ed., *The most fundamental right: Contrasting perspectives on the Voting Rights Act*. Bloomington: Indiana University Press.

Fisher, Allen. n.d. I'm going to get them the vote power: Lyndon B. Johnson and the fundamental importance of voting rights. LBJ Presidential Library, Austin, Texas.

Fraga, Luis Ricardo, and Maria Lizet Ocampo. 2007. More information requests and the deterrent effect of section 5 of the Voting Rights Act. In Ana Henderson, ed., *Voting Rights Act reauthorization of 2006: Perspectives on democracy, participation, and power*. Berkeley: University of California, Berkeley Public Policy Press.

Germany, Kent B. 2010. Lyndon B. Johnson and civil rights: Introduction to the digital edition. Available at the website Presidential Recordings of Lyndon B. Johnson, http://presidentialrecordings.rotunda.upress.virginia.edu/essays?series =CivilRights#; accessed Oct. 24, 2012.

Hasen, Richard L. 2012. *The voting wars: From Florida 2000 to the next election meltdown*. New Haven, Conn.: Yale University Press.

Higginbotham, A. Leon, Jr., Gregory A. Clarick, and Marcella David. 1994. *Shaw v. Reno*: A mirage of good intentions with devastating racial consequences. *Fordham Law Review* 62. Available at http://ir.lawnet.fordham.edu/flr/vol62 /iss6/2.

Johnson, Lyndon B. 1965. Special message to the Congress: The American promise. Mar. 15. Available on the website of the LBJ Presidential Library, www .lbjlibrary.net/collections/selected-speeches/1965/03-15-1965.html.

———. 1969. President's news conference, National Press Club. Jan. 17.

Katz, Ellen D. 2014. Justice Ginsburg's umbrella. University of Michigan Public Law Research Paper 389. Available at SSRN: http://ssrn.com/abstract=2402868. Forthcoming in Samuel R. Bagenstos and Ellen D. Katz, eds., *A Nation of widening opportunities? The Civil Rights Act at fifty*. Ann Arbor: University of Michigan Press.

Katz, E., M. Aisenbrey, A. Baldwin, E. Cheuse, and A. Weisbrodt. 2006. Documenting discrimination in voting: Judicial findings under section 2 of the Voting Rights Act since 1982. *University of Michigan Journal of Law Reform* 39, no. 4.

Klarman, Michael J. 2005. The Supreme Court and black disenfranchisement. In Valelly 2005.

Kotlowski, Dean J. 2001. *Nixon's civil rights: Politics, principle, and policy*. Cambridge, Mass.: Harvard University Press.

Kouser, J. Morgan. 1999. *Colorblind injustice: Minority voting rights and the second reconstruction*. Chapel Hill: University of North Carolina Press.

Laney, Garrine P. 2008. *The Voting Rights Act of 1965, as amended: Its history and current issues*. CRS Report for Congress, Order Code 95-896. Washington, D.C.: Congressional Research Service.

LaVigne, Michael. 2014. Swing state rulings on restrictive voting laws highlight the need for comprehensive electoral reform. *University of Colorado Law Review* 85, no. 2.

Lewis, John, and Archie E. Allen. 1972–1973. Black voter registration efforts in the South. *Notre Dame Lawyer* 48.

Liptak, Adam, and Charlie Savage. 2013. U.S. asks court to limit Texas on ballot rule. *New York Times*, July 25.

McCrary, Peyton. 2010. Declaration of Dr. Peyton McCrary. In the United States District Court for the District of Columbia. Shelby County, Alabama v. Eric H. Holder, Jr. Civil Action 1:10-cv-00651-JDB. Available on the website of the Moritz College of Law, Ohio State University: http://moritzlaw.osu.edu/electionlaw/litigation/documents/Shelby-Dec1-11-15-10.pdf.

McDonald, Laughlin. 1989. The quiet revolution in minority voting rights. *Vanderbilt Law Review* 42:1249–1297.

———. 1999. Whatever happened to the Voting Rights Act? Or, restoring the white privilege. *Journal of Southern Legal History* 7.

———. 2005. Federal oversight in elections and partisan realignment. In Valelly 2005.

Moore, Colin D. 2005. Renewals and extensions of the Voting Rights Act. In Valelly 2005.

National Commission on the Voting Rights Act. 2006. *Protecting minority voters: The Voting Rights Act at work, 1982–2005*. Washington, D.C.: Lawyers' Committee for Civil Rights under Law.

NAACP Legal Defense and Educational Fund, Inc./NAACP. 2011. *Defending democracy: Confronting modern barriers to voting rights in America*. New York: NAACP Legal Defense and Educational Fund, Inc.; Baltimore: NAACP. http://naacp.3cdn.net/67065c25be9ae43367_mlbrsy48b.pdf.

New York Times. 2014. A step toward restoring voting rights. Jan. 18.

Overton, Spencer. 2001. Place at the table: *Bush v. Gore* through the lens of race. *Florida State University Law Review* 29.

Perales, Nina, Luis Figueroa, and Griselda Rivas. 2007. Voting rights in Texas: 1982–2006. *Southern California Review of Law and Social Justice* 17.

Persily, Nathan. 2007. Promise and pitfalls of the new Voting Rights Act. *Yale Law Journal* 117.

Savage, Charlie. 2012. Justice Dept. blocks Texas on photo ID for voting. *New York Times*, Mar. 12.

Stout, Davis. 2008. Supreme Court upholds voter identification. *New York Times*, Apr. 29.

Tate, Katherine. 2003. *Black faces in the mirror*. Princeton, N.J.: Princeton University Press.

Taylor, Paul. 2012. *The growing electoral clout of blacks is driven by turnout, not demographics*. Pew Research: Social and Demographic Trends. www.pewsocialtrends.org/files/2013/01/2012_Black_Voter_Project_revised_1-9.pdf.

Thernstrom, Abigail M. 1997. More notes from a political thicket. In Anthony Peacock, ed., *Affirmative action and representation*. Durham, N.C.: Carolina Academic Press.

Tuck, Stephen. 2005. Making the Voting Rights Act. In Vallely 2005.

Tucker, James Thomas. 2006. Enfranchising language minority citizens: The bilingual provisions of the Voting Rights Act. *Legislation and Public Policy* 10: 195–260.

———. 2006–2007. Politics of persuasion: Passage of the Voting Rights Act Reauthorization Act of 2006. *Journal of Legislation* 33.

U.S. Census Bureau. 2006. *Statistical abstract of the United States*. Washington, D.C.: Government Printing Office.

———. 2010. Table 395. Members of Congress—Selected Characteristics: 1993 to 2007. www.census.gov/compendia/statab/2010/tables/10s0395.xls; accessed Jan. 26, 2013.

———. 2011. Table 413. Members of Congress—Selected Characteristics: 1995 to 2009. https://www.census.gov/compendia/statab/2012/tables/12s0413.pdf; accessed Jan. 26, 2013.

United States Commission on Civil Rights [USCCR]. 2001. Voting irregularities in Florida during the 2000 presidential election. www.usccr.gov/pubs/vote2000/report/main.htm.

———. 2005. Reauthorization of the temporary provisions of the Voting Rights Act: An examination of the act's section 5 preclearance provision. Briefing Report. Washington, D.C.: United States Commission on Civil Rights.

U.S. House. 1975. *Hearings before the Subcommittee on Civil and Constitutional Rights of the Committee on the Judiciary: Extension of the Voting Rights Act*. 94th Cong., 1st sess. Feb. 25 and 26; Mar. 3, 4, 5, 6, 13, 14, 17, 20, 21, 24, and 25. Serial no. 1, part 1. Available at the Digital Repository of the University of Texas Libraries, http://repositories.lib.utexas.edu/bitstream/handle/2152/13050/_Jordan_VRA_House.pdf?sequence=2.

———. 2006. *Voting Rights Act: Evidence of continued need: Hearing before the Subcommittee on the Constitution of the Committee on the Judiciary, March 8*, 109th Cong., 2nd. sess. Serial no. 109–103, vols. 1–4. Vol. 1 available at the Hathi Trust Digital Library, http://hdl.handle.net/2027/pst.000058845998.

———. 2013. http://pressgallery.house.gov/member-data/demographics, accessed March 9, 2013.

Vallely, Richard M., ed. 2005. *The Voting Rights Act: Securing the ballot*. Washington, D.C.: CQ Press.

Weinberg, B. H., and L. Utrecht. 2001. Problems in America's polling places: How they can be stopped. *Temple Political and Civil Rights Law Review* 11.

Weiser, W. R., and L. Norden. 2011. *Voting law changes in 2012*. New York: Brennan Center for Justice, New York University School of Law.

Wiley, Paul M. 2014. Shelby and Section 3: Pulling the Voting Rights Act's pocket trigger to protect voting rights after Shelby County v. Holder. *Washington and Lee Law Review* 71. Available at SSRN: http://ssrn.com/abstract=2421605.

Yaccino, Steven, and Lizette Alvarez. 2014. New GOP bid to limit voting in swing states. *New York Times*, Mar. 29.

CHAPTER 5

An Unexpected Legacy: The Positive Consequences of LBJ's Immigration Policy Reforms

FRANK D. BEAN, SUSAN K. BROWN,
AND ESTHER CASTILLO

The presidency of Lyndon Baines Johnson presents the historical observer with intriguing contradictions. As noted by Robert Dallek (1998, 3), Johnson was a man of outsized ambition, one who "needed to win higher standing, hold greater power, earn more money than anyone else." In short, he played to win, and he sought to achieve large objectives. But at times his goals overreached his and his country's ability to attain them, dooming his efforts to failure. His presidency thus shows more paradoxes than most. The most pronounced undoubtedly was derived from his uncertain handling of the Vietnam War, where his drive to succeed prevented him from cutting his losses when he arguably had opportunities to do so (Dallek 1998). In multiple domestic policy initiatives, especially his historic civil rights achievements, he was generally more successful. Here we focus on one of his minor domestic efforts, that of immigration policy reform, which offers a different kind of paradox—not one of contradiction between means and ends, but rather one of discrepancy between perceived and actual long-term consequences. The immigration legislation passed in 1965 was viewed at the time as relatively insignificant. Its stated rationale was often a secondary consideration (that is, supporters stressed that not passing it could undermine other, more important foreign and domestic policy initiatives), and it was not expected to lead to much in the way of changes in the nature and extent of immigration.

Its legacy, however, has turned out to be profound. Because the changes it ushered in were largely unanticipated, it would not have seemed at the time to provide an example of a Johnson-era inconsistency. But in fact, the elimination of discriminatory national-origins quotas and adoption of family-based criteria for immigrant entry led to rises in both the volume and diversity of immigration to the country (Bean and Stevens 2003; Reimers 1983). By shifting the national origins of newcomers from European to Asian and Latin American countries, the legislation facilitated the entry of groups that were neither black nor white, thus eventually helping promote the breakdown and dissolution of racial and ethnic barriers among U.S. ethnoracial groups. The civil rights reforms adopted during the Johnson era sought primarily to cope with the nation's long-lasting and severe black-white divides by dismantling the legal foundations of Jim Crow discrimination against African Americans. Some of the policy shifts generated backlashes, especially against affirmative action and busing as tools to combat job discrimination and school desegregation (Lukas 1985; Skrentny 2001). But even as the drama of resistance to changes in black-white relations unfolded, Asian and Latino immigrants were unobtrusively arriving in the United States and spreading a new diversity throughout many of its states and cities (Bean et al. 2004). The irony today of LBJ's immigration reforms is that legislation thought to be inconsequential at the time has unexpectedly led to trends that seem to be exerting beneficial effects on white-nonwhite relations, changes that have helped offset some of the negative reactions to the early civil rights legislation. This illustrates why it is important to examine the ramifications of Johnson's immigration reforms within the context of the country's ever-changing race relations.

This chapter assesses the implications of the 1965 immigration reforms, not only for immigration itself, but also for shifts in the ethnoracial makeup of the United States and for modifications in the country's race relations. We focus on three topics. The first concerns the historical dynamics surrounding immigration and race in the United States, as well as those impinging on the politics of U.S. immigration policy. The second concerns the 1965 legislation itself, including the political and international contexts leading up to its passage as well as the evolution of Johnson's own positions on immigration reform issues. The third involves presenting a demographic portrait of the country's ethnoracial makeup nearly four decades after the 1965 law was passed and plumbing the social science literature to assess how immigration-related diversity seems to be affecting ethnoracial relations. A final section summarizes Johnson's immigration-policy legacy, noting that it consists of positive but incomplete social consequences for relations among U.S. ethnoracial groups.

The Historical and Immigration Policy Contexts
Preceding the 1965 Reforms

W. E. B. Du Bois famously drew the nation's attention to its black-white fault lines at the beginning of the twentieth century. At the time, the United

States was becoming the world's leading industrial power. Du Bois ([1903] 1997) recognized that U.S. economic development would expose the social fissures stemming from a rigid black-white divide, make them increasingly hard to ignore, especially as the country's growing economic prosperity spread to a wider swath of whites than blacks. In a poignant statement in 1903, he said, "The problem of the twentieth-century will be the problem of the color line." In referring to the color line and the country's history of black-white relations, he foresaw that slavery's contradictions would become ever more conspicuous and that its legacy—still painfully apparent in the lingering stains of Jim Crow racial discrimination, rationalizations, and continuing stereotypes put forth to justify resulting inequities—would long plague the country (Berlin 2003; Du Bois 1935).

Although remarkably penetrating and prescient, his insights focused on but one of two often emphasized defining themes in American history and culture. One was the stain of slavery; the other was the opportunity and prosperity promised by immigration, symbolized in nineteenth-century America by the Statue of Liberty and Ellis Island (Handlin 1973). If slavery represented the scar of race on America and the new nation's most visible failure, immigration exemplified hope and the prospect of national success. Such dreams turned into reality for many nineteenth-century immigrant settlers, who fueled the expansion of the westward frontier. In this they were aided by the Land Act of 1820 and the Morrill Act of 1862, which provided land and technical assistance for America's new arrivals, though not for ex-slaves and their descendants (Nevins 1962).

Even as the western frontier began to close at the end of the nineteenth century (Turner 1893, 1920; Klein 1997), and as the United States increasingly became an industrial society, it nonetheless remained a country in need of newcomers. But now the need was for workers to labor in the burgeoning factories of its mushrooming cities. Immigrants once again provided a solution. The new arrivals, like their predecessors in earlier immigration waves, seized the opportunity to construct, or reconstruct, themselves anew through their transatlantic journeys, eagerly participating in the American tradition of seeking opportunity and identity by starting over rather than remaining in Europe, where they and their governments faced the challenge of trying to knit together peoples torn apart by internecine conflict (Zolberg 2006). Nation building in America, at least outside the South, rested on the foundation of new immigrant settlements and expanding urban immigrant workforces; the newcomers were energized by their own dreams and by the idea that they were part of a "nation of immigrants." By World War I, American immigration had thus served multiple purposes: the eighteenth-century waves provided the country with largely agrarian settlers eager to begin new lives in a land of opportunity; the early twentieth-century wave, the one coterminous with Du Bois's statement, furnished industrial laborers seeking an urban version of the American Dream.

If immigration represented the optimistic side of the country's past and future, slavery and its aftermath tainted the fabric of national memory—a blot many sought to eradicate through denial and romanticization (Blight 2001). Indeed, the desire to overlook the lingering contradictions of slavery's legacy often constituted a reason to emphasize the country's immigrant origins. Immigration and race thus played strangely symbiotic roles in shaping the founding mythology of America, a relationship evident in the fact that the two phenomena were often divorced from each other in treatments of the country's history (Glazer 1997). Well after the end of the Civil War, the country struggled to cope with the inconsistent and seemingly irreconcilable motifs arising from immigration and slavery (and, by extension, race). Efforts to compartmentalize depictions of the immigrant and slave experiences, especially at an intellectual level, were the rule. Many historians embedded discussions of immigration in narratives about the frontier and industrialization, and others confined treatments of slavery only to the history of the South (D. Davis 1998). Although race might have been acknowledged as a historical problem, scholars tended to view the issue as a regional matter limited to the southern states, not one that afflicted the country as a whole.

The Conflation of Immigration and Race

But early in the twentieth century, a number of trends began to undermine such convenient compartmentalizations. From 1900 to 1920, the arrival from eastern and southern Europe of America's third wave of newcomers agitated some natives to advocate for the "Americanization" of groups they viewed as non-Nordic and feared might be unassimilable (Gerstle 1999; Ignatiev 1995; Jacobson 1998; Roediger 1991). The new arrivals scarcely resembled the western and northern European immigrants of the country's past. Moreover, they were Catholic, not Protestant, and they largely settled in industrial cities outside the South. Thus, many at the time viewed foreigners in reductionist terms that conflated national origin and race (Zolberg 2006; Nightingale 2008). For those living outside the South, this meant they had to confront and accommodate persons of different "races" (that is, national origins) on a scale theretofore not experienced, although to a lesser degree Irish immigrants of the 1850s and 1860s had engendered the same response. Whatever success may have come from Americans' contacts with foreigners during this time, improved relations with blacks, almost all of whom still lived in the South, remained elusive. Denials that racism existed, or that black-white race relations were strained, continued as national problems throughout the Great Depression, World War II, and even afterward (Bean and Bell-Rose 1999; Fredrickson 2002; D. Massey and Denton 1993).

This substantial new wave of immigration began roughly at the end of the nineteenth century. The wave, which peaked roughly in the decade before World War I, represented the culmination of immigration as an integral part of the country's nation building. The United States embraced an identity as a "nation of immigrants," its population made up of European settlers and industrial workers and their descendants. It would be a substantial exaggeration to characterize the 100-year period from 1820, when national immigration statistics first began to be kept, to 1920, as a time when laissez-faire immigration policies held sway (Zolberg 2006; Neumann 1993). Nonetheless, major policy efforts to limit immigration at the national level were largely absent during those years (Tichenor 2002). To be sure, restrictive flare-ups—based on fears of labor market competition and justified in racist terms—occasionally occurred (principally, the Chinese Exclusion Acts of 1882 and 1888) (Zolberg 2006), but for the most part, immigration from Europe remained unfettered.

But restrictive pressures based on nativism had gradually been building since the Civil War, and became especially pronounced early in the twentieth century (Higham 1963). U.S. entry into World War I, in 1916, served initially as a temporary distraction from restrictionist concerns, but the conflict's human and financial cost and its spawning of a new emphasis on "internationalism" quickly renewed fears of foreigners and fostered further isolationism (Tichenor 2002). When combined with worries about the spread of Russian revolutionary ideas, the result was the first broadly implemented, racially and ethnically restrictive U.S. immigration policies, the National Quota Law of 1921 and the National Origins Act of 1924. Written to take effect in 1927, the latter legislation limited the number of immigrant admissions each year to only 2 percent of a given national origin's population living in the United States, as indicated by figures to be taken from the 1890 census; until 1927, the limitation was to be based on the percentage of a given country's foreign-born population in that same census (Tichenor 2002). The discriminatory effect of the national-origins quotas was to bar from immigrant entry into the United States almost all persons from any country outside northern or western Europe. With the advent of the Great Depression in 1929, and then the beginning of hostilities in Europe in the late 1930s, followed by the U.S. entry into World War II in 1941, immigration issues mostly disappeared from the national policy agenda. As things ultimately turned out, it was not until 1965 that major national immigration policy reforms were again undertaken.

The immediate post–WWII era brought new immigration policy concerns and anxieties, even if no major reforms. Most importantly, the Berlin blockade and airlift of 1948 dramatized the reality of the Cold War and the ever-present possibility of, and danger from, the accidental or deliberate use of nuclear weapons. The introduction and deployment of such weapons by President Truman at the end of World War II had greatly expanded the powers of the presidency (Tichenor 2002). As commander in chief, the president bore full and final responsibility for decisions to deploy. Accordingly, considerable latitude was extended to the White House for the execution of foreign policy. As the executive branch sought to use such powers to cope with the flood of refugees from World War II and subsequently from the Cold War, it found its hands often tied by restrictive and discriminatory U.S. immigration laws. The need to admit refugees for humanitarian and foreign policy reasons was repeatedly stymied by national-origins quotas.

Temporary relief for World War II refugees came from the Displaced Persons Act of 1948, and for persons fleeing communist regimes from the Refugee Relief Act of 1953, the Refugee-Escapee Act of 1957, and the Cuban Refugee Act of 1960, all the product of ad hoc, piecemeal legislative endeavors not intended to address the fundamental need for immigration reform. To make things worse, the passage in 1952 of the Immigration and Nationality Act (better known as the McCarran-Walter Act), done in part because of the anticommunist insecurities during the McCarthy era, reaffirmed the national-origins quota system with only slight changes. The Truman and Eisenhower administrations found themselves trying to reconcile the inconsistency between legislative proposals meant to ameliorate injustices faced by returning black veterans, on the one hand, and, on the other, exclusionary immigration policies that discriminated against immigrants from friendly countries. This created national and political embarrassment and made it difficult to build Cold War alliances with Third World countries whose denizens were not allowed to immigrate to the United States. Such contradictions underscored the need to eliminate national-origins quotas in immigration laws.

The 1965 Immigration Policy Reforms

To understand both the significance of the 1965 immigration reforms and their subsequent, unanticipated effects, it is instructive to examine the McCarran-Walter Act of 1952 in more detail. This legislation set the stage for the 1965 act in a number of ways. It reaffirmed the 1924 quotas, dramatizing in the process their discriminatory nature. That is, despite growing dissatisfaction with national-origins quotas after World War II, primarily because of the difficulties they created for the effective implementation of Cold War foreign policies emphasizing anticommunist alliances, the law underscored Congress's willingness to perpetuate discriminatory practices and place such alliances at risk. When McCarran-Walter first was passed, President Truman vetoed the legislation, noting in particular that it undermined the NATO alliance, particularly our relations with Italy, Greece and Turkey. He said: "The countries of Eastern Europe have fallen under the Communist yoke; they are silenced, fenced off by barbed wire and mine fields; no one passes their borders but at the risk of his life. We do not need to be protected against immigrants from these countries; on the contrary, we want . . . to save those who have managed to flee into Western Europe, to succor those who are brave enough to escape from barbarism" (Truman 1966).

At the height of the McCarthy era, however, congressional support for continuing the quotas ran strong, reflecting both the isolationist views of lawmakers who presumably believed domestic security concerns ought to trump Cold War foreign policy needs, as well as the xenophobic fear that foreigners might be troublemakers. In the words of one, "Criminals, Communists, and subversives of all descriptions are even now gaining admission into this country like water through a sieve" (quoted in Tichenor 2002, 192). In fact, Congress overrode Truman's veto by votes of 278 to 113 in the House and 57 to 26 in the Senate, with then-senator Lyndon B. Johnson siding with the majority (Martin 2011).

But subsequently, and as an indication of just how important for foreign policy Truman considered immigration reform, he unflinchingly responded by establishing a presidential commission to address the need for national-origins quotas. The report of the commission, entitled *Whom We Shall Welcome*, blistered the 1952 legislation: "The Immigration and Naturalization Act of 1952 injured our people at home, caused much resentment against us abroad, and impairs our position among free nations, great and small, whose friendship and understanding is necessary if we are to meet and overcome the totalitarian menace" (Commission on Immigration and Naturalization 1953). Certainly in the minds of internationalists, the contrast be-tween the restrictive legislation and the realities of the Cold War, including its risk of nuclear disaster, could never have been clearer.

Ironically, McCarran-Walter, while maintaining the discriminatory sta-tus quo on national-origins quotas, ushered in other minor, little-noticed changes that paved the way for increased Asian migration. One, based on appeals from American missionaries, was to allow a small amount of im-migration from the so-called Asia-Pacific Triangle (covering most nations in Southeast Asia) (Reimers 1983). A second was to grant all Asians the right of naturalization, which had previously been denied. A third was to increase somewhat the numbers of immigrants who could come by dint of possessing high skills, particularly those helping meet shortages of doctors, nurses, scientists, and engineers in the United States. None of these were set up to generate large numbers of entrants, but two of them provided bases for mostly college-educated Asians to be admitted, and the naturalization provision allowed those entering to transition to a status that brought the possibility of adding immediate relatives without restriction. The overall re-sult was the beginning of a small but significant, largely college-educated Asian flow. Later, when family reunification provisions were adopted as the primary basis for entry in 1965, Asians naturalized quickly in order to bring in family members (Martin 2011; Reimers 1983).

After the McCarran-Walter Act was passed, major immigration reforms in the 1950s were thwarted by political deadlock over the issue (Tichenor 2002). Although the Eisenhower administration frequently expressed its frustration with the negative foreign policy implications of national-origins quotas, the political stalemate offered little prospect of changing them. To take immigration-related action, Eisenhower relied on executive powers to deal with crisis situations, primarily involving refugees. Thus, he invoked the "parole powers" established by McCarran-Walter to permit his attor-ney general to admit more than thirty thousand Hungarian refugees after Soviet suppression of the uprising there in 1956. But in general, immigra-tion reform remained on the back burner until John F. Kennedy was elected president in 1960. It was assumed that immigration reform under Kennedy would enjoy a much higher priority than it had under Eisenhower, and ad-vocates of eliminating the national-origins quotas thought legislation for their abolishment would stand a much higher chance of being passed. But little action took place, and no mention of immigration occurred in Ken-nedy's 1961 state of the union address (Tichenor 2002). It was not until Francis Walter (D-PA), one of the staunchest supporters of national-origins quotas and the cosponsor of the 1952 bill, died, in May 1963, that there appeared any break in the political logjam. At that point, the Kennedy administration drafted and submitted to Congress reform legislation sponsored by Representative Emanuel Celler (D-NY) and Senator Philip Hart (D-MI).

But Kennedy's assassination in November 1963 cut short the reform process. When Lyndon Johnson became president, those hoping for change were dismayed. Not only had Johnson supported McCarran-Walter, but as Senate majority leader he had often opposed efforts by Kennedy and others to modify immigration law. As president, Johnson's priorities were to pass Kennedy's New Frontier proposals, even in fact to exceed them with his own Great Society initiatives. More significantly, he initially worried that immigration reform might hurt the chances of civil rights reforms and that he would lose political clout by endorsing something that did not enjoy broad public support, particularly since he had unhesitatingly voted for the McCarran-Walter Act in 1952. But Kennedy advisors and Johnson's own close advisor Bill Moyers persuaded him that immigration reform was important and indeed consistent with his own major civil rights efforts (Tichenor 2002). In his 1964 state of the union address, Johnson outlined his proposals for pathbreaking civil rights legislation, noting as well, "We must also lift by legislation the bars of discrimination against those who seek entry into our country" (Johnson 1965). After the president persuaded Senator James Eastland (D-MS) not to stand in the way of the legislation, the Immigration Reform Act of 1965 passed both houses of Congress with strong bipartisan support.

"This bill is not a revolutionary bill. It does not affect the lives of millions," said Johnson in 1965 when he signed the Hart-Celler Act, or more formally, the Amendments to the Immigration and Nationality Act (Johnson 1965). Rather, he saw the bill as an overdue correction of an unjust system of national-origins quotas that for more than forty years had discriminated against southern and eastern Europeans and non-Westerners. Nor was Johnson alone in his assessment of the bill as symbolically but not materially significant. A two-paragraph editorial in the *Washington Post* (1965) praised the bill as a "reaffirmation of an American tradition." The *New York Times* did not see the signing of the bill as warranting a story in its own right; its article on the signing led with news on the admission of Cuban refugees (Semple 1965). As late as 1973, a four-page feature in the *New York Times* on the Johnson presidency devoted only one line to immigration (Krebs 1973).

Of course, Johnson also had political reason to downplay any potential effect of the bill, because public opinion was scarcely on his side. In 1965, polls showed 2–1 opposition to any change in immigration laws to allow more people to enter the country, with the strongest opposition coming from rural areas, Protestants, southerners, those on the lower end of the socioeconomic scale, and those of English or German background. While more people favored skill-based immigration than country quotas, the margin was a relatively slim 36 percent to 29 percent (L. Harris 1965). A Gallup poll sought by the administration found that about half of the public favored abolishing the national-origins quotas (Zolberg 2006). Public support for the bill came from such ethnic and religious groups as the Anti-Defamation League of B'nai Brith (Martin 2011; Zolberg 2006). The perception that the legislation was limited in scope probably helped secure its passage.

Although the Hart-Celler Act abolished national-origins quotas, it retained many of the restrictions from the McCarran-Walter Act of 1952 (Martin 2011). In addition, Hart-Celler imposed overall hemispheric caps on visas—initially, 170,000 for the Eastern Hemisphere and 120,000 for the Western Hemisphere—and a per-country limit of 20,000 visas for nations of the Eastern Hemisphere. This was the first time that any caps had been placed on the Americas. Although the Johnson administration had opposed the Western Hemisphere cap, members of the House and Senate Judiciary Committees argued for it on the grounds of fairness in the application of the laws and out of fear of unregulated spillover from rapid non-white population growth in Latin America (Bartlett 1965; United Press International 1965; Zolberg 2006). The Western Hemisphere cap represented 10,000 fewer people than the average annual migration from the region. But that count excluded countries in the West Indies, whose independence had led to the lifting of immigration limits in place while its countries were under colonial quotas (Martin 2011).

Most importantly, besides replacing national-origins quotas with hemispheric caps, the Hart-Celler Act emphasized family reunification. In particular, it set up a series of preference categories for immigrants from the Eastern Hemisphere. While broad preferences had existed under the McCarran-Walter Act, they had privileged highly skilled immigrants. Under the Hart-Celler Act, four of the top five preference categories gave priority to the reunification of families, amounting to nearly three-fourths of the slots (Zolberg 2006). In addition, the law added parents of adult U.S. citizens to the list of immigrants not subject to numerical limitations (Keely 1971). Beyond that, up to 10 percent of slots were allotted to professionals, scientists, and artists; another 10 percent would go to skilled or unskilled workers in occupations with a short supply of workers. Refugees and a "nonpreference" residual classification rounded out the preference categories. In all these categories, minimal provision existed for unskilled migrant labor, despite the termination during the previous year of the Bracero program, the treaty-based contract labor agreement under which tens of thousands of agricultural and other manual Mexican workers were admitted to the United States starting in 1942 (Calavita 1992; Zolberg 2006).

The ramifications of the Hart-Celler Act cannot be understood without considering the fact that actions taken in the 1960s to limit or change legal admission to the country through its "front door" also carried implications for "back door" migration. While the members of the restrictionist coalition that had held sway for four decades were influenced by the need to do away with discriminatory immigration, particularly because of Cold War imperatives, the fears of southern Democrats and western Republicans about non-white immigration led them to insist on unprecedented limitations of Western Hemisphere immigration as their price for going along with the new reforms. Thus, for the first time, a ceiling was imposed on the number of such legal immigration approvals, including those involving migrants from Mexico, of 120,000 visas a year. Moreover, applicants without immediate relatives who were citizens or legal permanent residents now needed a job offer from an employer, who had to obtain certification from the Department of Labor that native workers were not available to do the work and that local wages would not be affected. Legislation passed in 1976 expressly limited the number of legal entrants from Mexico to 20,000 a year (Cerruti and Massey 2004; Fragomen and Del Rey Jr. 1979). In short, a political compromise between conservatives and liberals within both parties, one that would prove difficult to resurrect in subsequent years, was instrumental in the passage of the legislation. Restrictionists were willing to support front-door modifications in exchange for ostensibly tightening at least legal back-door migration (Zolberg 2006).

But the unanticipated consequence was to increase unauthorized Mexican migration, something the southern and western senators had not been much worried about, believing such migration to be mostly temporary. Particularly significant were the labor certification changes in the new legislation that required employment clearances for those seeking to fill jobs in short supply. According to Charles Keely (1971), the McCarran-Walter Act barred such workers if the secretary of labor certified that the United States had enough qualified workers to do the jobs or that the immigrants would depress U.S. wages. Since this certification had seldom occurred, applicants were mostly free to enter. Under Hart-Celler, the burden of proof was shifted, in an effort to protect U.S. labor. Immigrant workers were barred unless the secretary of labor had certified that the United States lacked enough suitable workers. Now, without Labor Department certification, the default condition was that the country *did* have enough suitable workers. In effect, the applicant now had to show that that assumption was false. As the inevitable regulatory backlog grew, the change in certification requirements fell particularly hard on applicants from the Western Hemisphere, who were not part of the preference system. In particular, Canadians were crowded out (Zolberg 2006). For many Mexicans, not all of whom considered themselves circulatory migrants, entering the country illegally rather than as contract laborers under the defunct Bracero program became almost their only option. As a result, unauthorized migration grew substantially (Zolberg 2006).

The 1965 legislation held few direct implications for changes in the structure or responsibilities of the federal agencies responsible for implementation and administration. Because of emerging wartime security considerations, in 1940 the Immigration and Naturalization Service (INS), including the Border Patrol, had been transferred from the Department of Labor to the Department of Justice; legal immigration visas continued to be granted by the State Department. But no comparable major shifts in governmental responsibility occurred as a consequence of the 1965 legislation, and indeed none of any substantial import arose until the aftermath of September 11, 2011, when many immigration functions were merged into the new Department of Homeland Security.

But there were unintended consequences that can be traced to the 1965 law, principally the growth in influence of the Border Patrol, which bore responsibility for "controlling" the southwestern border with Mexico. Hart-Celler was not the sole cause of unleashing the unauthorized Mexican immigration that began to rise shortly after its passage, but its limitations on legal entry certainly indirectly contributed to the influx. With the rise of unauthorized migration, and its eventual spread outside the border states to much of the rest of the country (Leach and Bean 2008), the size and power of the Border Patrol within the INS has continued to increase (Bean, Vernez, and Keely 1989). In addition, policy makers have repeatedly turned to border enforcement strategies as a first line of defense in attempting to deal with such migration and to "control" the country's borders (Bean and Lowell 2004), a tendency resulting in part from the Border Patrol's own efforts during this period to expand its role and influence (Calavita 1992).

The effects of the Hart-Celler Act on legal migrant streams, however, were immediate and direct. Immigration from Europe shifted to southern countries such as Greece, Italy, and Portugal. Immigration from the West Indies and Asia rose dramatically. In fiscal year 1964, all of Asia had a quota of 2,290. By 1969, the first year after the transitioning period of the law, 54,176 Asians entered under the quota for the Eastern Hemisphere. Within ten years of that, India, South Korea, and the Philippines were closing in on the annual country quota of 20,000; but far more family reunification entrants, who were not subject to limits, came as well (Keely 1971; Martin 2011). Among those coming under the occupation categories, the number of professionals rose, but so did the number of laborers and live-in maids, evidence for the first time of a strong class distinction in immigration to the United States (Keely 1971; Ueda 1998). The family reunification procedures also allowed for gradual growth in Latin American, mostly Mexican, legal immigration. The latter had averaged nearly 30,000 a year during the 1950s, and after the 1965 law, legal permanent residents could more easily bring in immediate family members.

The New Ethnoracial Diversity and Its Consequences

The Johnson reforms, passed after nearly four decades of relatively low immigration, thus provided mechanisms for both larger immigrant flows and greater national-origin diversity among those arriving (Bean and Stevens 2003). Most of these provisions did not directly create major changes. But given that some Asians, Mexicans, and West Indians had already started to come in greater (although relatively small) numbers, sometimes through refugee programs, indirect increases through family reunification were easier. Now, almost four decades after the law's enactment, what can we discern about the legislation's effects on the nativity and ethnoracial composition of the U.S. population? What are the consequences of the increases in ethnoracial diversity that have taken place? How do these new realities interact with the legal changes resulting from Johnson's civil rights reforms?

The Changes in Ethnoracial Population Composition

By 2010, 39 million foreign-born people were living in the United States, up from 9.6 million in 1970. Moreover, the population share that was foreign-born rose from 4.7 percent to 12.5 percent (Gryn and Larsen 2010). And the number of foreign-born residents exceeded the country's 34 million native-born African Americans (U.S. Bureau of the Census 2010). To be sure, not all foreign-born persons in census data are immigrants. Some are students or visitors, but the vast majority are immigrants of one kind or another, including unauthorized immigrants (Bean and Lowell 2007). And if we include the children of the foreign-born in the total, the number of immigrants and their children now surpasses 68 million, more than twice the number of native blacks. Moreover, about two-thirds of those arriving since 1965 have come from Asian, African, or Latin American countries (U.S. Department of Homeland Security 2010). Altogether, about 43 million first- or second-generation nonwhite persons (that is, nonwhite, non-black foreign-born persons and their children) are now living in the country (U.S. Bureau of the Census 2010). In short, immigration trends since the passage of the 1965 legislation have led to a recent nonwhite minority living in the United States that is larger than the native black minority.

Within this minority, Mexican immigrants and their descendants are by far the most numerous, because of both high immigration and relatively high fertility (Smith, Brown, and Bean 2011). In 2009 alone, almost 165,000 persons from Mexico became "legal permanent residents" (14.5 percent of the total for that year) (U.S. Department of Homeland Security 2010). In 2006, about 250,000 unauthorized Mexicans also established de facto residency, bringing the total number of unauthorized Mexicans to over 6 million, or 56 percent of all unauthorized persons (Passel 2010). The second-largest number of legal entrants in 2009 came from China (almost 61,000 persons, or 5.4 percent of all legal permanent residents), while the second-largest number of unauthorized persons living in the country originated in Latin American countries other than Mexico (2.5 million, or 22 percent of the total unauthorized).

At the same time, the relative size of America's white population, while still quite large, has diminished somewhat. About 73 percent of the U.S. population reported only a white identification in 2010 (Ruggles et al. 2010). If we exclude from this figure whites who also reported that they were Latino (about 8.8 percent of the population), non-Latino whites make up about two-thirds of the population. This proportion may appear sizeable, but it comes at the end of a steady decline over the past three decades. In 1970, 83 percent of Americans were non-Latino whites; by 1980, this figure had shrunk to 80 percent; by 1990, to 75 percent; and by 2010, to 66 percent (Ruggles et al. 2010), a 17-percentage-point decline since 1970. If whites were as relatively numerous today as in 1970 (that is, if they exhibited the same population share), there would be about 50 million more of them in the country. This perhaps helps explain the anxiety on the part of some Americans that whites may soon become a minority in the United States.

While the proportion of non-Latino whites in the country has steadily declined, the shares of Asians and Latinos have grown considerably. The

Asian percentage has increased by about four percentage points and the Latino by about ten percentage points since 1970. The share of non-Latino
blacks has increased by a modest two percentage points (J. Lee and Bean
2010). Thus, the major gains in shares of the U.S. population since 1970 are
accounted for by Asians and Latinos, the groups that have made up most
of the shift in the composition of immigrants coming to the country since
1965, when the Hart-Celler Act replaced the national origins quotas that
had first been adopted in 1921 and then reenacted in only slightly modified form by the McCarran-Walter Act in 1952. Most importantly, the rise
of Asian and Latino groups has increased the racial and ethnic diversity of
the whole country. The United States is now no longer primarily a black-
white nation. Because the new immigration has been geographically concentrated and unevenly distributed, some states and metropolitan areas are
much more reflective of Asian and Latino immigration than others. But the
new diversity deriving from immigration has recently (since 1990) become a
national phenomenon, primarily because of Mexican immigration, which is
now much more spatially dispersed than previously (D. Massey 2008).

Not counting Hawaii, California is the most diverse state in the country, reflecting not only its relatively large nonwhite population, but also the
fact that it contains several ethnoracial groups that are all relatively large. In
actuality, many other states and cities also show considerable diversity because they contain substantial numbers of at least three ethnoracial groups.
Such places exhibit higher ethnoracial intermarriage rates than other parts
of the country, and higher percentages of persons who report that they have
multiracial backgrounds (J. Lee and Bean 2010). In particular, states in the
western region of the country show high levels of both diversity and intermarriage, something that reflects the generally lower levels of sociocultural
conservatism there. States and cities with very low intermarriage rates tend
to be either in the South, such as Mississippi, or overwhelmingly white,
such as Vermont. Generally, higher-immigration states show higher levels
of racial and ethnic diversity, as reflected in the percentage of their populations that are neither non-Hispanic white nor non-Hispanic black. They
also boast larger multiracial populations than states that are less racially and
ethnically diverse. This reveals why states like West Virginia and Kentucky
exhibit very low rates of multiraciality; there simply are scarcely any racial
and ethnic minorities in these states, and thus little racial and ethnic diversity as well as few opportunities for intermarriage. Levels of multiraciality
(having a multiracial background) and multiracial reporting (reporting this
background in surveys) are quite lower in such places. In general, the higher
immigration rates since 1965 have led to much greater racial and ethnic di-

versity, more intermarriage, and more multiracial identification across both states and cities throughout the country than was previously the case.

Also, this pattern of greater intermingling of different ethnoracial groups is not seen in black-white states. For example, Mississippi, Alabama, South Carolina, and Louisiana have relatively large black populations, yet the racial and ethnic diversity in these states takes the form of the traditional binary black-white model. Unlike the new diversity brought about by contemporary immigration, high levels of black-white diversity do not lead to high rates of multiracial reporting. Even though Mississippi, Alabama, and Louisiana have relatively large white and black populations, they have low levels of multiracial reporting. Despite the long history of racial mixing between whites and blacks in the South, the strongly constraining nature of the dividing line between these groups limits multiracial identification, leading persons to identify as either black or white rather than as black and white (Bean et al. 2004; F. Davis 2001; Farley 2002; D. Harris and Sim 2002). In short, black-white diversity differs starkly from the ethnoracial diversity brought about by contemporary immigration. And most importantly, higher levels of black-white diversity do not seem to be related to high levels of intermarriage and multiracial reporting, which provide indications of dissolution among ethnoracial groups, as does diversity resulting from contemporary immigration flows.

The Effects of Ethnoracial Diversity

What other trends are related to these new diversity increases? Are they associated with changes that imply greater tension and conflict among ethnoracial groups? Do they seem connected with shifts that suggest growing tolerance and more harmonious intergroup relations? These are hard questions to answer, particularly when many other factors are changing at the same time. Nonetheless, the social science research literature yields numerous reasons to think that increased racial and ethnic diversity may in fact be contributing to the breakdown of barriers among ethnoracial groups and to increased tolerance among groups. One finding is that as minority groups grow relatively larger, the probabilities of contact between the members of such groups and majority natives increase, thus promoting familiarity, respect, and greater liking across the groups. These are the processes that Gordon Allport (1954) noted in his long-standing contact hypothesis, which predicts that greater interaction between members of different groups fosters familiarity and increases affect and liking. A second finding is that the presence of a larger number of different groups may tend to diminish the negative significance of any single group, since multiple minority groups may diffuse the intensity of negative affect and stigmatization associated with a given group (J. Lee and Bean 2010). In addition, greater diversity may yield other positive psychological and social dividends. These include improved creativity, problem-solving capacities, social resilience, and interpersonal skills—all tendencies that result from learning to cope with the differences, challenges and opportunities presented by diversity. Such factors have been found to strengthen workplace productivity and societal communication, cohesion, and effectiveness, especially in technology- and knowledge-based economies (Benkler 2006; Chua 2007; Grewal 2008; Herring 2009; Page 2007). Adaptive advantages have also been found among second-generation persons growing up in diverse environments (Kasinitz et al. 2008).

Additional reasons suggest that diversity per se may foster boundary dissolution (that is, the breaking down of color lines). Ethnoracial diversity entails both the presence of multiple ethnoracial groups and the absence of the relative predominance of any single group. Thus, the more a single ethnoracial group makes up a large percentage of the population of a social, political, economic, or geographic group or area, the less the diversity of that entity. Similarly, the greater the number of groups and the more equally they are distributed within an area, the greater the diversity. In essence, this idea of diversity is akin to the idea of heterogeneity as it is often more broadly invoked in sociology (Blau 1977; Blau and Schwartz 1984; Laumann 1973). Increased diversity in its most profound sense involves multigroup, not just bi-group, heterogeneity. This sort of diversity especially facilitates contact and promotes tolerance, as has often been noted by proponents of the contact hypothesis and others (Allport 1954; Blalock 1967; Blau 1977; G. Massey, Hodson, and Sekulic 1999). Diversity thus may contribute to increases in the likelihood of phenomena that reflect boundary dissolution, such as exogamy and multiracial identification, because it fosters interaction and the loosening of ethnoracial barriers as well as facilitates flexibility in marriage and identity options for members of ethnoracial minorities and their offspring.

At the same time, other social processes may strengthen divides among social groups. For example, "group threat" theoretical perspectives posit that larger ethnoracial minority groups increase the likelihood of negative consequences of diversity because they boost fear of minorities on the part of majority whites, who may perceive that some ethnoracial groups—specifically, blacks—are more threatening than others. Interestingly, this is most likely to occur when there is only one minority group or when one minority group of several is treated distinctly differently from the others. American whites have often seen blacks as threatening, in part because of worries about economic competition and in part because the harsh discriminatory tactics employed for decades after slavery against blacks have engendered fears among whites of black reprisal (Blalock 1967; Fossett 2005; Fossett and Siebert 1997). Because newly arrived, largely nonwhite immigrant groups have not experienced similarly crushing discrimination on such a widespread scale for so long (Zolberg 2006), whites are not as likely to perceive them to be as threatening as blacks.

Another reason that whites may see blacks as more threatening than other groups is that African Americans often constitute a less preferred source of less skilled labor than immigrants (Kasinitz and Rosenberg 1996; Kirschenman and Neckerman 1991; J. Lee 2002; Waldinger and Lichter 2003; Waters 1999). Asian immigrants, by contrast, are not as numerous as blacks or Latinos and are much more highly selected for higher levels of education than most Latino immigrants. They may thus be viewed more favorably and be more likely to occupy higher positions in the American stratification system than Latinos, and therefore may be unlikely to generate comparable group-threat effects. Such a hierarchy of group-threat differences is in accord with the tenets of queuing theory (Lieberson 1980; Sakamoto, Liu, and Tzeng 1998) and group-position theory (Bobo 1999, 2004; Bobo and Hutchings 1996; Bobo and Tuan 2005), both of which state that social-status ordering among groups characterizes the extent to which they face discrimination in the labor market and other kinds of negative reactions in the United States (Dixon 2006; Link and Oldendick 1996).

The possibility of negative white reactions to minority-group threats seems partly to lie behind some of the recent expressions of doubt about possible benefits that might be associated with greater ethnoracial diversity (Schlesinger 1992; Schuck 2003; Smelser and Alexander 1999; Wood 2003). Skepticism about diversity's positive implications may also reflect distaste for the romantic and simplistic terms in which appeals for "greater diversity" are often expressed. Indeed, one research study seemed to produce results that appear consistent with the idea that diversity strengthens the barriers separating groups (Putnam 2007). It should be noted that the results of Robert Putnam's work may reflect the influence of black-white but not Latino-Asian-white diversity, since the former is interspersed with the latter in the data. Moreover, it is not appropriate to assume that whites will treat new nonwhite groups as more like blacks than whites, or that nonwhite groups will come to see themselves that way, thus engendering negative diversity effects. Other recent research indicates that diversity derived from growing numbers of nonwhites, larger numbers of new ethnoracial groups, and more equally sized ethnoracial groups seems to foster boundary loosening, especially when black-white diversity is factored out of the equation (Lee and Bean 2010). Also, numerous studies in Europe show generally similar results (Portes and Vickstrom 2011), as has recent research in Canada (Reitz et al. 2009), although this latter work indicates that economic inequality weakens any positive effects of diversity.

Conclusions

When John F. Kennedy was elected president, in 1960, the prospects for immigration reform seemed bright, especially given that Kennedy was a politician who, as a senator, had published a book entitled *A Nation of Immigrants* ([1958] 1964). Because Senator Lyndon Johnson did not have a history of supporting immigration inclusiveness, many observers thought that Kennedy's assassination would cut short any impetus for reform. But the Johnson administration, after initial skepticism and hesitation, resumed a push for immigration policy reform in 1964, along with major civil rights reforms. By the end of 1965, Congress had passed several landmark pieces of legislation: the Civil Rights Act of 1964 and the Voting Rights Act of 1965, making discrimination against blacks illegal; and the Hart-Celler Act in 1965, which abolished national-origins quotas as the basis for immigrant admissions (Reimers 1992; Skrentny 2002). Scholars such as Nathan Glazer (1997) thought the civil rights and voting rights acts would quickly lead to the full incorporation of blacks into American society. Supporters of the Hart-Celler Act generally did not expect it to generate much new immigration; rather, they thought it would remove the embarrassment of the country's prior discriminatory admissions policies (Reimers 1998). The two kinds of legislation thus both contributed to the prospect of improved racial and ethnic relations in the United States. But neither turned out as anticipated. Blacks did not quickly become economically incorporated, and thousands of new Asian and Latino immigrants gradually but unexpectedly began to arrive in the country (Alba and Nee 2003; Bean et al. 2009; Foner 2000; J. Lee 2002; Skrentny 2001). These immigrants have fostered more diversity and changed a once black-white country into one of multiple nonwhite ethnoracial groups.

Rates of intermarriage and multiracial identification have increased along with rates of immigration (Bean and Stevens 2003; Jacoby 2001; S. Lee and

Edmonston 2005). In 2010, about 11 percent of marriages among young Americans were ethnoracially mixed, a significant increase that cannot be attributed to population growth alone (Bean, Lee, and Bachmeier 2013). The rise in intermarriage has resulted in a growing multiracial population. These rates vary by ethnoracial group. Asians and Latinos are far more likely than blacks to intermarry with whites and to identify themselves as multiracial (J. Lee and Bean 2004, 2007). Such findings suggest that legal and structural changes alone—while of considerable importance—are insufficient to explain group differences in intermarriage and multiracial identification. It seems that although the black-white color line has faded, its legacy is still etched in long-standing cultural and institutional frameworks.

Overall, the country now seems characterized by a black-nonblack color line more than a black-white one (J. Lee and Bean 2010; Bobo 2011). On the nonblack side of the line, rising ethnoracial diversity appears to be fostering intermarriage and thereby increasing the number of persons from multiracial backgrounds, leading in turn to increases in multiracial identification. All these dynamics signal the dissolution of boundaries among ethnoracial groups. But this is much more the case for Asians and Latinos, whose ranks have swelled from immigration since 1965, than for blacks. The legacy of Lyndon Johnson's immigration reforms, evident in the nation's growing diversity due to immigration, is thus arguably positive. Waves of Latino and Asian immigrants, rather than creating societal fissures and fomenting intergroup tensions, instead appear to have increased rates of white-nonwhite intermarriage and multiracial identification, outcomes consistent with more harmonious relations. These tendencies are also true for blacks, but on a vastly reduced scale.

The civil rights reforms of the 1960s, while removing legal obstacles to blacks' incorporation into American society, appear to have been less successful than expected in eroding sociocultural and institutional barriers to full black integration. The immigration changes of 1965, which were not expected to be of much consequence, have in certain respects led to greater change than the civil rights laws, at least relative to expectations. But ironically, Johnson's civil rights reforms, which were expressly intended to redress black grievances but were in subsequent years extended to other nonwhite groups, may have helped facilitate nonblack immigrant incorporation (Foner and Alba 2010; Kasinitz et al. 2008). (This phenomenon is not discussed in this chapter.) Returning to the earlier discussion of the disjunction of race and immigration as prominent leitmotifs in American cultural history, we note that the full story of their evolving relationship is still unfolding. Johnson's immigration and civil rights reforms are helping to move certain social trends in the right direction, although maybe at different speeds for particular groups. The challenge going forward, given rising economic inequality, will be to keep them heading that way (Hacker and Pierson 2010; Blow 2014).

Even though rising diversity resulting from immigration appears to be a growing strength of the country, opposition to immigration continues. But according to a recent Gallup poll, only a minority of the population (about 27 percent) is dissatisfied enough with current levels of immigration to think they should be decreased (Morales 2012). Nearly three-fourths of the population thinks it should be increased or kept at the same level. Despite being relatively limited, opposition to additional immigration nonetheless has stymied recent efforts at immigration reform. This resistance will probably weaken further in future years because anti-immigrant attitudes are more concentrated among the elderly (those over sixty-five) than among those who are younger. Thus, the prospect of immigration reform, which has gone nowhere in recent sessions of Congress, is likely to grow over time, all else being equal. The political compromises necessary for such reforms remain difficult today, just as they were nearly fifty years ago, but do not seem insurmountable. In 1986, such compromises emerged between restrictionists and nonrestrictionists (who were represented in each party) because the former supported employer sanctions and the latter supported legalization. Enough members of each group felt strongly enough about their group's issue that they were willing to support the other's position in order to get what they wanted. With evidence growing that the country's changing demography means that not enough less skilled natives will be available to do all the work that needs doing (Bean, Brown, and Bachmeier 2012), it suggests that the political compromises necessary to generate new immigration legislation will soon transcend the failures of recent years.

References

Alba, Richard, and Victor Nee. 2003. *Remaking the American mainstream: Assimilation and contemporary immigration.* Cambridge, Mass.: Harvard University Press.

Allport, Gordon W. 1954. *The nature of prejudice.* Reading, Mass.: Addison-Wesley.

Bartlett, Charles. 1965. House balky on immigration issue. *Los Angeles Times* (Aug. 24).

Bean, Frank D., and Stephanie Bell-Rose. 1999. *Immigration and opportunity: Race, ethnicity and employment in the United States.* New York: Sage Foundation.

Bean, Frank D., Susan K. Brown, and James D. Bachmeier. 2012. Luxury, necessity and anachronistic workers: Does the United States need unskilled immigrant labor? *American Behavioral Scientist* 56, no. 8: 1008–1028.

Bean, Frank D., Cynthia Feliciano, Jennifer Lee, and Jennifer Van Hook. 2009. The new U.S. immigrants: How do they affect our understanding of the African American experience? *Annals of the American Academy of Political and Social Science* 621 (Jan.): 202–220.

Bean, Frank D., Jennifer Lee, and James D. Bachmeier. 2013. Immigration and the color line at the beginning of the 21st century. *Daedalus* 142, no. 3 (Summer): 123–140.

Bean, Frank D., Jennifer Lee, Jeanne Batalova, and Mark Leach. 2004. *Immigration and fading color lines in America.* New York and Washington, D.C.: Sage Foundation and Population Reference Bureau.

Bean, Frank D., and B. Lindsay Lowell. 2004. NAFTA and Mexican migration to the United States. In Sidney Weintraub, ed., *NAFTA'S impact on North America: The first decade,* 263–284. Washington, D.C.: Center for Strategic and International Studies.

———. 2007. Unauthorized migration. In M. Waters and R. Ueda, eds., *The new Americans: A guide to immigration since 1965,* 70–82. Cambridge, Mass.: Harvard University Press.

Bean, Frank D., and Gillian Stevens. 2003. *America's newcomers and the dynamics of diversity.* New York: Sage Foundation.

Bean, Frank D., Georges Vernez, and Charles B. Keely. 1989. *Opening and closing the doors: Evaluating immigration reform and control.* Santa Monica, Calif., Washington, D.C., and Lanham, Md.: RAND Corporation and Urban Institute Press.

Benkler, Yochai. 2006. *The wealth of networks: How social production transforms markets and freedom.* New Haven, Conn.: Yale University Press.

Berlin, Ira. 2003. *Generations of captivity: A history of African-American slaves.* Cambridge, Mass.: Harvard University Press.

Blalock, Hubert M. 1967. *Toward a theory of minority-group relations.* New York: Wiley.

Blau, Peter M. 1977. *Inequality and heterogeneity.* New York: Free Press.

Blau, Peter M., and Joseph E. Schwartz. 1984. *Crosscutting social circles: Testing a macrostructural theory of intergroup relations.* Orlando, Fla.: Academic Press.

Blight, David W. 2001. *Race and reunion: The Civil War in American memory.* Cambridge, Mass.: Harvard University Press.

Blow, Charles M. 2014. The self-sort. *New York Times,* Apr. 12.

Bobo, Lawrence. 1999. Prejudice as group position: Microfoundations of a sociological approach to racism and race relations. *Journal of Social Issues* 55, no. 3: 445–472.

———. 2004. Inequalities that endure? Racial ideology, American politics, and the peculiar role of the social sciences. In Maria Krysan and Amanda E. Lewis, eds., *The changing terrain of race and ethnicity,* 13–42. New York: Sage Foundation.

———. 2011. Somewhere between Jim Crow and post-racialism: Reflections on the racial divide in America today. *Daedalus* 140, no. 2 (Spring): 11–36.

Bobo, Lawrence, and Vincent L. Hutchings. 1996. Perceptions of racial group competition: Extending Blumer's theory of group position to a multiracial social context. *American Sociological Review* 61, no. 6: 951–972.

Bobo, Lawrence D., and Mia Tuan. 2005. *Prejudice in politics: Group position, pub-*

lic opinion, and the Wisconsin Treaty rights controversy. Cambridge, Mass.: Harvard University Press.

Calavita, Kitty. 1992. *Inside the State: the Bracero program, immigration, and the I.N.S.* New York: Routledge.

Cerrutti, Marcela, and Douglas S. Massey. 2004. Trends in Mexican migration to the United States, 1965–1995. In J. Duran and D. S. Massey, eds., *Crossing the border: Research from the Mexican Migration Project*, 17–44. New York: Sage Foundation.

Chua, Amy. 2007. *Day of empire: How hyperpowers rise to global dominance—and why they fall*. New York: Doubleday.

Commission on Immigration and Naturalization. 1953. *Whom we shall welcome*. Washington, D.C.: Government Printing Office.

Dallek, Robert. 1998. *Flawed giant: Lyndon Johnson and his times, 1961–1973*. New York: Oxford University Press.

Davis, David B. 1998. A big business. *New York Review of Books* 45, no. 10: 50–53.

Davis, F. James. 2001. *Who is black? One nation's definition*. Tenth-Anniversary Edition. University Park: Pennsylvania State University Press. Originally published in 1991.

Dixon, Jeffrey C. 2006. The ties that bind and those that don't: Toward reconciling group threat and contact theories of prejudice. *Social Forces* 84, no. 4: 2179–2202.

Du Bois, W. E. B. (1903) 1997. *The souls of black folk*. Edited by D. W. Blight and R. Gooding Williams. Boston: Bedford.

———. 1935. *Black reconstruction in America*. New York: Harcourt, Brace.

Farley, Reynolds. 2002. Racial identities in 2000: The response to the multiple-race response option. In Joel Perlmann and Mary C. Waters, eds., *The new race question: How the census counts multiracial individuals*, 33–61. New York: Sage Foundation.

Foner, Nancy. 2000. *From Ellis Island to JFK: New York's two great waves of immigration*. New Haven, Conn., and New York: Yale University Press and Sage Foundation.

Foner, Nancy, and Richard Alba. 2010. Immigration and the legacies of the past: The impact of slavery and the Holocaust on contemporary immigrants in the United States and Western Europe. *Comparative Studies in Society and History* 52, no. 4: 798–819.

Fossett, Mark A. 2005. Urban and spatial demography. In Dudley L. Poston and Michael Micklin, eds., *Handbook of population*, 479–524. New York: Kluwer Academic/Plenum.

Fossett, Mark A., and Therese Seibert. 1997. *Long time coming: Trends in racial inequality in the nonmetropolitan South since 1940*. Boulder, Colo.: Westview.

Fragomen, Austin T., Jr., and Alfred J. Del Rey Jr. 1979. The immigration selection system: A proposal for reform. *San Diego Law Review* 17:1–36.

Fredrickson, George M. 2002. *Racism: A short history*. Princeton, N.J.: Princeton University Press.

Gerstle, Gary. 1999. Liberty, coercion, and the making of Americans. In Charles Hirschman, Josh DeWind, and Philip Kasinitz, eds., *The handbook of international migration*, 275–293. New York: Sage Foundation.

Glazer, Nathan. 1997. *We are all multiculturalists now.* Cambridge, Mass.: Harvard University Press.

Grewal, David Singh. 2008. *Network power: The social dynamics of globalization.* New Haven, Conn.: Yale University Press.

Gryn, Thomas, and Luke J. Larsen. 2010. Nativity status and citizenship in the United States: 2009. American Community Survey Briefs. Washington, D.C.: U.S. Bureau of the Census.

Hacker, Jacob S., and Paul Pierson. 2010. *Winner-take-all politics: How Washington made the rich richer—and turned its back on the middle class.* New York: Simon and Schuster.

Handlin, Oscar. 1973. *The uprooted: The epic story of the great migrations that made the American people.* Boston, Mass.: Little, Brown. Originally published in 1951.

Harris, David R, and Jeremiah J. Sim. 2002. Who is multiracial? Assessing the complexity of lived race. *American Sociological Review* 67, no. 4: 614–627.

Harris, Louis. 1965. More than 50% hit immigrant increase. *Los Angeles Times,* June 1.

Herring, Cedric. 2009. Does diversity pay? Race, gender, and the business case for diversity. *American Sociological Review* 74, no. 2: 208–224.

Higham, John. 1963. *Strangers in the land: Patterns of American nativism, 1860–1925.* New York: Atheneum.

Ignatiev, Noel. 1995. *How the Irish became white.* New York: Routledge.

Jacobson, Matthew Frye. 1998. *Whiteness of a different color: European immigrants and the alchemy of race.* Cambridge, Mass.: Harvard University Press.

Jacoby, Tamar. 2001. An end to counting race? *Commentary* 111, no. 6: 37–40.

Johnson, Lyndon B. 1965. Remarks at the signing of the immigration bill, Liberty Island, New York (Oct. 3). Reprinted in *International Migration Review* 45, no. 1 (2011): 200–204.

Kasinitz, Philip, John H. Mollenkopf, Mary C. Waters, and Jennifer Holdaway. 2008. *Inheriting the city: The children of immigrants come of age.* New York and Cambridge, Mass.: Sage Foundation and Harvard University Press.

Kasinitz, Philip, and Jan Rosenberg. 1996. Missing the connection: Social isolation and employment on the Brooklyn waterfront. *Social Problems* 43, 2: 180–96.

Keely, Charles B. 1971. Effects of the Immigration Act of 1965 on selected population characteristics of immigrants to the United States. *Demography* 8:157–169.

Kennedy, John F. (1958) 1964. *A nation of immigrants.* New York: Harper and Row.

Kirschenman, Joleen, and Kathryn M. Neckerman. 1991. "We'd love to hire them, but . . .": The meaning of race for employers. In Christopher Jencks and Paul E. Peterson, eds., *The urban underclass,* 203–232. Washington, D.C.: Brookings Institution.

Klein, Kerwin L. 1997. *Frontiers of historical imagination: Narrating the European conquest of Native America, 1890–1990.* Berkeley: University of California Press.

Krebs, Albin. 1973. Lyndon Johnson: Controversial president. *New York Times,* Jan. 23.

Laumann, Edward O. 1973. *Bonds of pluralism: The form and substance of urban social networks.* New York: Wiley.

Leach, Mark A., and Frank D. Bean. 2008. The structure and dynamics of Mexican migration to new destinations in the United States. In D. S. Massey, ed.,

New faces in new places: The changing geography of American immigration, 51–74. New York: Sage Foundation.

Lee, Jennifer. 2002. *Civility in the city: Blacks, Jews, and Koreans in urban America.* Cambridge, Mass.: Harvard University Press.

Lee, Jennifer, and Frank D. Bean. 2004. America's changing color lines: Immigration, race/ethnicity, and multiracial identification. *Annual Review of Sociology* 30 (Aug.): 221–242.

———. 2007. Reinventing the color line: Immigration and America's new racial/ethnic divide. *Social Forces* 86, no. 2: 561–586.

———. 2010. *The diversity paradox: Immigration and the color line in 21st century America.* New York: Sage Foundation.

Lee, Sharon M., and Barry Edmonston. 2005. New marriages, new families: U.S. racial and Hispanic intermarriage. *Population Bulletin* 60, no. 2: 1–36.

Lieberson, Stanley. 1980. *A piece of the pie: Blacks and white immigrants since 1880.* Berkeley: University of California Press.

Link, Michael W., and Robert W. Oldendick. 1996. Social construction and white attitudes toward equal opportunity and multiculturalism. *Journal of Politics* 58, no. 1: 149–168.

Lukas, J. Anthony. 1985. *Common ground: A turbulent decade in the lives of three American families.* New York: Vintage.

Martin, Susan F. 2011. *A nation of immigrants.* New York: Cambridge University Press.

Massey, Douglas S., ed. 2008. *New faces in new places: The changing geography of American immigration.* New York: Sage Foundation.

Massey, Douglas S., and Nancy A. Denton. 1993. *American apartheid: Segregation and the making of the underclass.* Cambridge, Mass.: Harvard University Press.

Massey, Garth, Randy Hodson, and Dusko Sekulic. 1999. Ethnic enclaves and intolerance: The case of Yugoslavia. *Social Forces* 78, no. 2: 669–693.

Morales, Lymari. 2012. Americans' immigration concerns linger. *Gallup Politics,* Jan. 17. www.gallup.com/poll/152072/Americans-Immigration-Concerns -Linger.aspx.

Neumann, Gerald. 1993. The lost century of American immigration law (1776–1875). *Columbia Law Review* 93, no. 8: 1833–1901.

Nevins, Allan. 1962. *The origins of the land-grant colleges and universities.* Washington, D.C.: Civil War Centennial Commission.

Nightingale, Carl H. 2008. Before race mattered: Geographies of the color line in early colonial Madras and New York. *American Historical Review* 113, no. 1: 48–71.

Page, Scott E. 2007. *The difference: How the power of diversity creates better groups, firms, schools, and societies.* Princeton, N.J.: Princeton University Press.

Passel, Jeffrey S. 2010. *The size and characteristics of the unauthorized migrant population in the U.S.* Washington, D.C.: Pew Hispanic Center.

Portes, Alejandro, and E. Vickstrom. 2011. Diversity, social capital, and cohesion. *Annual Review of Sociology* 37:461–479.

Putnam, Robert D. 2007. *E pluribus unum:* Diversity and community in the twenty-first century. The 2006 Johan Skytte Prize Lecture. *Scandinavian Political Studies* 30, no. 2: 137–174.

Reimers, David M. 1983. An unintended reform: The 1965 Immigration Act and third world migration to the United States. *Journal of American Ethnic History* 2 (Fall): 9–28.

———. 1992. *Still the golden door: The third world comes to America*. 2nd ed. New York: Columbia University Press.

———. 1998. *Unwelcome strangers: American identity and the turn against immigration*. New York: Columbia University Press.

Reitz, Jeffrey G., Raymond Breton, Karen Kisiel Dion, and Kenneth L. Dion. 2009. *Multiculturalism and social cohesion: Potentials and challenges of diversity*. New York: Springer.

Roediger, David. 1991. *The wages of whiteness: Race and the making of the American working class*. New York: Verso.

Ruggles, Steven, J., Trent Alexander, Katie Genadek, Ronald Goeken, Matthew B. Schroeder, and Matthew Sobek. 2010. Integrated public use microdata series: Version 5.0 [machine-readable database]. Minneapolis: University of Minnesota.

Sakamoto, Arthur, Jeng Liu, and Jessie M. Tzeng. 1998. The declining significance of race among Chinese and Japanese American men. *Research in Social Stratification and Mobility* 16:225–246.

Schlesinger, Arthur M., Jr. 1992. *The disuniting of America: Reflections on a multicultural society*. New York: Norton.

Schuck, Peter H. 2003. *Diversity in America: Keeping government at a safe distance*. Cambridge, Mass.: Harvard University Press.

Semple, Robert B., Jr. 1965. U.S. to admit Cubans Castro frees; Johnson signs new immigration bill. *New York Times* (Oct. 4).

Skrentny, John. 2001. *Color lines: Affirmative action, immigration, and civil rights options for America*. Chicago: University of Chicago Press.

———. 2002. *The minority rights revolution*. Cambridge, Mass.: Harvard University Press.

Smelser, Neil J., and Jeffrey C. Alexander, eds. 1999. *Diversity and its discontents: Cultural conflict and common ground in contemporary American society*. Princeton, N.J.: Princeton University Press.

Smith, Christopher D., Susan K. Brown, and Frank D. Bean. 2011. Not so big after all, but maybe getting bigger? Generational differences in fertility between Mexican-American and Anglo women. Paper presented at annual meeting of the American Sociological Association, Las Vegas, Nevada, Aug. 19–21.

Tichenor, Daniel J. 2002. *Dividing lines: The politics of immigration control in America*. Princeton, N.J.: Princeton University Press.

Truman, Harry S. 1966. Veto of bill to revise the laws relating to immigration, June 25, 1952. *Public papers of the presidents of the United States: Harry S. Truman, 1952–1953*, 441–447. Washington, D.C.: Government Printing Office.

Turner, Frederick Jackson. 1893. The significance of the frontier in American history. Annual report of the American Historical Association. Washington, D.C.: American Historical Association.

———. 1920. *The frontier in American history*. New York: Holt, Rinehart and Winston.

Ueda, Reed. 1998. The changing face of post-1965 immigration. In D. Jacobson, ed., *The immigration reader*, 72–91. Malden, Mass.: Blackwell.

United Press International. 1965. Johnson stays silent on hemisphere immigrants. *Los Angeles Times* (Sept. 13).

U.S. Bureau of the Census. 2010. *Current population survey: Annual demographic files.* Washington, D.C.: U.S. Government Printing Office.

U.S. Department of Homeland Security. 2010. Office of Immigration Statistics. *2009 yearbook of immigration statistics.* Washington D.C.: U.S. Department of Homeland Security.

Waldinger, Roger, and Michael I. Lichter. 2003. *How the other half works: Immigration and the social organization of labor.* Berkeley: University of California Press.

Washington Post. 1965. Nation of strangers. Oct. 5.

Waters, Mary C. 1999. West Indians and African Americans at work: Structural differences and cultural stereotypes. In Frank D. Bean and Stephanie Bell-Rose, eds., *Immigration and opportunity: Race, ethnicity, and employment in the United States,* 194–227. New York: Sage Foundation.

Wood, Peter B. 2003. *Diversity: The invention of a concept.* San Francisco: Encounter Books.

Zolberg, Aristide R. 2006. *A nation by design: Immigration policy in the fashioning of America.* New York: Sage Foundation.

PART III

EDUCATION, HEALTH, AND SOCIAL WELFARE POLICY

CHAPTER 6

Head Start: Growing beyond the War on Poverty

ELIZABETH ROSE

Head Start was born in a time of enormous optimism, both about the possible impact of early intervention on children's development and life trajectories, and about the ability of the federal government to solve deep-seated problems of poverty and inequality. It has long outlived its original parent, the War on Poverty, and has established a role in programs for young children as part of the federal government's role of promoting equity and equal opportunity.

With the creation of the Head Start program in 1965, the Johnson administration staked out a new role for the federal government in child development, linked to the larger goal of guaranteeing equal opportunity through education. Head Start represented an innovation in the federal role in education, bundled within the policy innovations of the War on Poverty: experimentation with different strategies for attacking poverty, direct federal relationships with local community agencies, and an emphasis on empowering the poor to press for change. Sargent Shriver's immediate goal for Head Start—to create an appealing image of the War on Poverty by focusing on children—succeeded quickly. Head Start also turned a national spotlight on the promise of addressing the needs of young, disadvantaged children through a combination of federal funds and community involvement. In the long term, Head Start set the stage for continuing federal involvement with issues of young children's care and education. While its fortunes have risen and fallen with the political tides over the past five decades, and its promise has been only partially fulfilled, Head Start has remained significant as a symbol of the federal government's commitment to poor children, and as an expression of optimism about early intervention and the efficacy of governmental action to reduce the effects of poverty. Its survival and success over five decades have been nurtured by ideas about the power of early intervention combined, crucially, with political support rooted in the program's broad constituency.

Creating Head Start

Head Start was created when an activist federal government picked up ideas being explored by psychologists about the malleable nature of intelligence in young children and then launched them into policy, on a much larger scale than most thought possible (or even advisable). Head Start was shaped by ideas about children's development and by political calculations: the promise of early intervention to improve the lives of the poor inspired federal action, and political considerations shaped decisions about the size, structure, and goals of the program. The intellectual foundations of the program were called into question within four years of the program's beginning, but the political judgment that led to launching Head Start quickly and on a large scale was dead-on. The idea struck a responsive chord in communities across the country and quickly produced strong grassroots support for the program, which would ensure its survival over the course of decades.

Head Start echoed earlier federal efforts to provide nursery schools for the poor during the 1930s, as well as the philanthropic efforts of earlier generations of reformers who sponsored charitable kindergartens and day nurseries in order to help families rise out of poverty (Rose 1999). But Head Start's creators did not spend much time assessing the results of these earlier efforts. Rather, they cobbled the program together quickly out of different approaches, relying on an emerging body of research about what could make a difference for children.

Intellectually, Head Start was inspired by dramatic changes in how psychologists thought about intelligence. The mainstream view had long been that intelligence was fixed, determined largely through heredity, but researchers in the 1950s and early 1960s started to argue that it could be modified through experience. The work of J. McVicker Hunt (1964) and Benjamin Bloom promoted the idea that intelligence was plastic and that a child's environment was a critical factor in development. "With improved understanding of early experience," Bloom wrote, "we might counteract some of the worst effects of cultural deprivation and raise substantially the average level of intellectual capacity" (1964, 83). Several researchers launched small-scale experimental projects to explore the promise of preschool for helping poor children. In Tennessee, Susan Gray found that an intensive summer preschool program for poor African American children, followed by a series of home visits, produced a modest increase in the children's IQ and verbal abilities (Gray, Ramsey, and Klaus 1982). In New York, Martin and Cynthia Deutsch created carefully structured preschool activities designed to help poor children develop language skills and key concepts, emphasizing the labeling of common items and using puppets and other objects to teach key concepts (Deutsch 1964). In Ypsilanti, Michigan, the school psychologist David Weikart was frustrated with his school district's acceptance of African American students' dismal academic achievement. He turned to the idea of creating an enriched environment for poor children, ultimately finding that his Perry Preschool program had a striking short-term impact on children's IQ and a long-term impact on their school achievement (Buder 1962, 1; Deutsch 1964, 252–262; Gray et al. 1982; Weikart 2004).

This emerging research entered federal policy as a way of bolstering political support for the Johnson administration's antipoverty efforts. In 1964, Sargent Shriver, newly appointed director of the federal Office of Economic Opportunity (OEO), was looking for a way to spend money on children. Not only had he recently learned that half the nation's poor were children, but his political instincts also told him that programs for children would be much more popular than other parts of the War on Poverty. Much of the money that Congress had allocated for the OEO was not being spent because city and local government leaders were wary of initiating community action projects that might result in riots, protests, and threats to their political base. The OEO was under attack by some members of Congress, and Shriver wanted to offer a program that would build support for the War on Poverty both in Congress and in local communities. He later recalled thinking, "In our society there is a bias against helping adults . . . but there is a contrary bias in favor of helping children. Even in the black belt of the deepest South, there's always been a prejudice in favor of little black children. . . . I hoped that we could overcome a lot of hostility in our society against the poor in general, and specifically against black people who are poor, by aiming for the children" (Shriver 1979).

Preschool, increasingly seen as an innovative response to the challenges of poverty and schooling, was part of antipoverty discussions within the Kennedy and Johnson administrations. In the Senate, a committee report on the 1964 antipoverty legislation specifically mentioned the importance of preschools that could provide "an opportunity for a head start by canceling out deficiencies associated with poverty that are instrumental in school failure." The commissioner of education, Francis Keppel, starting talking about the importance of early childhood education in mid-1964; one of his advisers called the expansion of such programs "inevitable." Vice President Hubert Humphrey noted the importance of early childhood education in breaking the cycle of poverty in his 1964 book *War on Poverty*, and Johnson's Education Task Force included recommendations for preschool education in its report. Shriver may have worried that other federal agencies would seize the issue if the OEO did not (Vinovskis 2005, 42–52; Shriver 1979, 52).

Shriver remembered, from his earlier involvement with the Kennedy Foundation on mental retardation, visiting Susan Gray's research project in Tennessee and being "dumbfounded" at Gray's success in raising poor children's IQs. He also recalled, from his time serving on the Chicago school board, the barriers that poor children faced in adjusting to school. He envisioned a program that would get poor children ready for school and accustomed to the school environment. He recalled his goals: "Let's get these youngsters *ahead* of time, bring them into school and culturally prepare them for school: for the buildings and teachers, desks, pencils and chalk, discipline, food, etc. . . . We'll find out where they stand in reading, and find out if they need 'shots.' . . . We'll help IQ problems and the malnutrition problem; we'll get these kids ready for school and into the environment of a school" (Shriver 1979, 52).

Believing that an antipoverty project for young children would be "smart policy, and also smart politics," Shriver started asking doctors and psychologists in his circle for their opinions (Stossel 2004). In the late fall of 1964, he asked his friend and family pediatrician Robert Cooke of Johns Hopkins University to organize a committee of experts to plan the program. Cooke's committee shifted the program away from Shriver's idea of getting poor children accustomed to the school environment toward a much more holistic child development effort that was to include health care, nutrition, and family involvement. The intention was to create a comprehensive program of health, social, and education services directed at children, families, and communities. Head Start would cover not only what happened within the preschool classroom but also medical and dental care, nutritious meals, home visits, parental participation, and community organizing.

Thinking like scientists but not realizing the scale that the administration had in mind, the planning committee focused on designing a workable program for field trials. Shriver had rejected the respected psychologist Jerome Bruner's opinion that only a small pilot program serving about 2,500 children was possible, since there were not enough trained teachers to do more. Such a small program could not begin to address the fact that there were a million children living in poverty, nor would it do much to shore up the administration's antipoverty efforts. Instead, Shriver insisted on a big program with big publicity and big numbers. Urie Bronfenbrenner, a committee member, remembered Shriver declaring, "We're going to write Head Start across the face of this nation so that no Congress and no president can ever destroy it." In fact, before the planning committee made any recommendations, the Johnson administration had already decided to launch a preschool initiative that would be based in the OEO's Community Action Program and serve 100,000 children (Bronfenbrenner 1979, 82; Vinovskis 2005, 25). Ultimately, despite the reservations they shared about such rapid expansion of an untested program, the committee went along with this plan, recommending launching 300 programs to serve 100,000 children that summer. Shriver was thrilled; he was eager to launch a program that would bolster the OEO's efforts to fight poverty and appeal to a wide public audience. Indeed, the OEO needed Head Start more than Head Start needed the OEO. According to Shriver's biographer Scott Stossel: "Bruised by the mounting assaults on Community Action and the Job Corps, Shriver was desperate for the OEO to have a political triumph. Head Start seemed to fit the bill" (2004, 422). Within a day of receiving the committee's report, Shriver presented it to Johnson, who shared his enthusiasm and upped the ante, saying the program should be tripled to serve 300,000 children.

The kickoff event for the program—a White House tea for 250 women, hosted by Lady Bird Johnson—signaled that Head Start would have a very different reception from some of the administration's more controversial antipoverty efforts. As word of the social event spread, senators and representatives started to call, asking for invitations; even the wives of governors who were most resistant to LBJ's civil rights initiatives were eager to attend. A *New York Times* article described the tea as including "some of the most glamorous women in America today," including the actress Donna Reed (who subsequently made television spots to promote Head Start). The First Lady, serving as honorary chair of Head Start, asked her guests to help recruit thousands of women volunteers for the new program. Coverage of the event in the society pages cast the program in a very favorable light and spurred an outpouring of volunteers to aid the program. For instance, in covering the White House tea, the *Charleston (WV) Gazette* emphasized the need for citizen support: "Every West Virginia woman will be given an opportunity this summer to work for a just cause" (Zigler and Muenchow 1992, 24; *New York Times* 1965; *Charleston (WV) Gazette* 1965).

The work of many volunteers, as well as creative thinking by program administrators, made it possible to get the program off the ground only twelve weeks from when it was announced—an administrative miracle that earned it the nickname "Project Rush-Rush." Wives of cabinet members and members of Congress spent hours on the telephone finding people in the country's 300 poorest counties who would be willing to sponsor Head Start programs, and 125 interns from different federal agencies spent their weekends traveling to these communities to help them fill out applications. A flood of other applications soon filled the bathtubs at Head Start headquarters. A colleague of Shriver's who saw the application-processing line said he hadn't seen anything like it since his days as a marine during World War II: the only sound was a repetitious thumping of rubber stamps as the reviewers (substitute teachers from the D.C. public schools) scanned each application, checked five boxes, and sent it on for funding. The goal was not to find the highest-quality proposals, but to fund as many programs as possible, especially in the poorest communities (Zigler and Muenchow, 34, 40). Shriver was eager to spend money from his OEO budget, so as more applications for Head Start programs came in, they were approved. Shriver recalled: "It was like wildcatting for oil in your own backyard and suddenly hitting a gusher. . . . I pumped in the money as fast as we could intelligently use it. It was really quite spectacular" (Shriver 1979, 56). The budget for that first summer eventually mushroomed from $10 million to $70 million. The program began that summer in over 3,000 communities and eventually served 560,000 children, thereby surpassing even President Johnson's ambitious target.

In the rush to launch programs, elements of Head Start that had seemed important to its planners were often set aside. The OEO staffer Polly Greenberg was concerned that only a few of the hundreds of proposals she was getting from southern communities "bore close resemblance to Head Start as it had originally been conceived," with meaningful participation by the poor and creative teaching techniques geared to young children. Nevertheless, proposals were accepted, "because the President wanted thousands of Head Starts to announce in the Rose Garden on Thursday" (Greenberg 1969, 40). Similarly, project leaders were not daunted by the fact that there were not nearly enough trained nursery educators in the country to provide teachers for a half million children. David Weikart remembered attending a meeting in Michigan in the spring of 1965 with more than three hundred teachers and administrators who would be involved in operating Head Start programs. "They asked how many of us worked with or had experience with preschool children. About 15 people raised their hands. A very slender reed for a national program, indeed" (Weikart 1979, 144). In late March, the government contracted with 140 universities to provide six-day training programs for about 42,000 Head Start teachers (many of them elementary school teachers who were willing to staff Head Start during the summer). Some of the program's planners had worried that teachers accustomed to teaching older children in public schools would not be ideal for Head Start's more holistic and creative classrooms, but staffing the programs took precedence over such concerns.

Committed to getting the program off the ground quickly, Shriver and other administrators made important decisions somewhat haphazardly. Before announcing the program, Shriver needed a quick estimate of the cost per student; he gave Jule Sugarman, an administrator, an hour to provide the answer. Over lunch at the Madison Hotel, Sugarman came up with a figure of $180 per child, based on assumptions about using inexpensive teachers with little specialized training (Vinovskis 2005, 33). Martin Deutsch, whose model preschool program for poor children in New York City was one of the few operating in the country before Head Start was created, thought the expenditure should be much higher—at least $1,000 per child. He had opposed plans for a summer Head Start program in 1965 on the grounds that there was not enough time or funding to provide a quality program. Others with experience in running preschools, such as Frances Degen Horowitz at the University of Kansas, found the government's figure inadequate. She submitted an application to establish a Head Start program in 1965, creating a budget based on her years of experience in running quality preschool programs. Horowitz later recalled the response from Head Start officials: "This is not supposed to be a quality preschool program; this is Head Start" (quoted in Zigler and Muenchow 1992, 44).

The official launching of the program took place in the White House Rose Garden; President Johnson had been encouraged by his aides to take part, for they saw it as "a whopping big announcement and a terrific story" that would gain plenty of positive media coverage, especially since it was coming close to Mother's Day (Shriver 1965; Valenti 1965). At that ceremony, Johnson made some big promises for the fledgling program: "All this means that nearly half the preschoolers now stagnating in poverty will be given head starts on their future. . . . It means that thirty million man-years —the combined life spans of these youngsters—may be spent productively and rewardingly rather than wasted in tax-supported institutions or in welfare-supported lethargy." He declared, "Five- and six-year-old children are inheritors of poverty's curse and not its creators. Unless we act, these children will pass it on to the next generation like a family birthmark" (Johnson 1965a, 67–69; see also Johnson 1965b).

Organizing Head Start's Structure and Approach

When the experts on the Cooke planning committee recommended the program to Sargent Shriver in 1965, they listed seven general goals for the program. These included improving poor children's physical, cognitive, and social-emotional development; strengthening the bonds between the child and the family; increasing a sense of dignity and self-worth within the child and the family; and developing in both child and family "a responsible attitude toward society." At the same time, they said the program should provide "opportunities for society to work together with the poor in solving their problems" (Schrag, Styfco, and Zigler 2004, 20). These relatively vague goals left open many possibilities for programs, making clear only that Head Start was to take a comprehensive approach to the challenges faced by poor children and that families were part of the equation.

Organizing the poorly shaped Head Start structure and approach was left up to antipoverty staff members in the OEO, who were committed to local autonomy. Believing that only grassroots efforts could mobilize poor people and create change, the OEO channeled federal aid directly to local community action agencies, bypassing the usual structures of state and local government. These community agencies were meant to be run with "maximum feasible participation" by the poor themselves. For the OEO, then, empowering poor parents and transforming communities was an important part of Head Start's promise. OEO staffers such as Polly Greenberg hoped that parents, empowered and brought together within Head Start, would start to demand changes in the public schools and from health care providers, welfare agencies, and local government. Greenberg explained later that she saw Head Start affecting poverty not by changing individual children, but by changing "the political equation," maximizing the involvement of poor parents and poor communities in the decisions that affected their lives (Greenberg 1998; Harmon 1979, 89).

To involve parents and create opportunities for them, Head Start policy emphasized employing parents and community residents as teachers, aides, cooks, and drivers. An explanation of Head Start's hiring policy in 1970 reiterated that along with quality programs, "employment opportunity and career development of economically disadvantaged persons (particularly the parents of enrolled children) are major purposes of Head Start programs" (*Head Start Newsletter* 1970). Teachers did not need to have college degrees or certification; Head Start training courses, lasting from six days to eight weeks in the 1960s, taught both new and experienced teachers about the goals of the program and techniques for working with young children. Additionally, staff members could take college courses leading to a degree through the Supplementary Training Program, a particularly welcome opportunity for poor parents with children in Head Start.

Hiring poor parents and community residents helped Head Start programs provide opportunities and link the preschool program to the community, but did not always result in the provision of well-trained teachers. In some communities, the desire to provide jobs outweighed the desire to operate a high-quality educational program; some community action agencies dictated the choice of Head Start staffers and drove away teachers with experience in early childhood education. By 1967, the early childhood educator Eveline Omwake worried that "the employment function of the project was taking precedence over the educative function," leading to a program that had better outcomes for parents than for their children (Omwake 1979). The Head Start planner James Hymes reflected later, "We never did face up to the disadvantaged young child's need for skilled and trained teachers; we never did face up to the need for top-flight educational leadership in what was to be a massive educational program." Operating from the mistaken assumption that "anyone can teach young kids," he argued, "Head Start was never staffed to produce consistently good educational programs" (Hymes 1979). Tension between the program's goals for children (promoting physical, cognitive, and socio-emotional development) and its goals for adults (creating new job opportunities, empowerment, and community action) was thus built into the way the program was implemented.

In accordance with the OEO's emphasis on grassroots change, control over Head Start resided largely outside the structures of public schools. Jule Sugarman recalled that the Head Start planning committee was "deeply skeptical about the public schools," an attitude "perfectly compatible with the prevailing view of OEO staff that existing educational institutions had failed" (Shriver and Sugarman 1979). Planners hoped that in the more nurturing soil of community agencies, the holistic child development and parental involvement program they envisioned would grow, and in turn inspire local schools to change. Similarly, OEO staffers, fearing that minority parents and staff members would have no voice in a Head Start program run by white-dominated school systems, believed that setting up a parallel structure outside the schools was the only way to compel change. (In fact, during Head Start's initial "Project Rush-Rush" start-up phase, school districts played a large role, sponsoring more than 80 percent of the first summer Head Start programs and providing most of the teachers. Once the structure shifted to yearlong programs, however, two-thirds of programs shifted to community agencies, and school districts operated about one-third, often as subcontractors of community agencies) (U.S. Department of Health, Education and Welfare 1972; Zigler and Muenchow 1972, 174).

Poor parents and their advocates often had good reasons for mistrusting local schools, and Head Start's independent structure enabled it to offer a federally sponsored alternative. In many places there would have been no Head Start program if it had been up to local school authorities. In other places, school-sponsored programs would have been less likely to focus on poor children or to provide the range of health and social services that Head Start did. (This was true, for instance, of Title I–funded preschool programs during this period) (U.S. Senate 1967). In Lee County, Alabama, in the early 1970s, Head Start parents requested permission from the county to use a school building that was being shut down (largely because white parents refused to send their children to the formerly all-black school). The school board not only rejected the parents' request but also announced that instead it would sell the building for a dollar to a man who was starting a segregated white academy. Only under threat of a lawsuit by the local Head Start director did the board reverse itself and allow Head Start to have the building (Zigler and Muenchow 1992, 182). In an era of struggle over school segregation across the country, OEO officials were proud that federal Head Start programs were required to open their programs to families of all backgrounds. In a 1966 memorandum (marked "for the president's night reading"), the OEO aide Bill Crook wrote, "When I left the Nacogdoches area in 1960, school officials were pledging to 'die on the door step' before they would permit the integration of the races. The President might be interested in seeing the attached pictures," which showed black and white children and teachers playing together at the Head Start site in Chireno, Texas. Crook noted, "Deep East Texas will never be the same again thanks to the Head Start Program" (Crook 1966).

Indeed, Head Start's location outside the structure of the public schools gave it freedom to innovate in many of the ways its planners had hoped. Programs combined preschool education with health care, social services, and parental involvement in new ways; benefited from an enormous outpouring of volunteer labor and donations; hired and trained poor parents to serve as teachers and aides; gave parents a role in governing programs; and adapted Head Start ideas to local conditions, producing a wide variety of program approaches. It is difficult to imagine any of this happening within the ordinary structures of state departments of education and local school districts at the time.

Yet the decision to separate Head Start from the public schools also carried a serious risk: the lack of ongoing institutional support in a politically charged environment. Jacqueline Wexler, one of the original Head Start planners, feared the rigidity of public school bureaucracies, but also feared that unless Head Start programs "became first-class citizens of the established school systems, they were doomed to an ephemeral success" (Wexler 1979, 113). James Hymes observed in 1979, "I found it hard in the planning days to visualize a continuing, growing service to young children cut off from the public schools. . . . I find it hard to visualize this today. I am afraid that Head Start did not help us find a proper and permanent place for early-childhood education in our governmental array" (Hymes 1979, 97).

Head Start's structure of making direct federal grants to community agencies made it possible for local communities to shape their Head Start programs as they wished, resulting in a rich diversity of approaches. Individual Head Start programs had enormous flexibility about how to shape their programs, leaving room for struggle over which of the programs' many goals was paramount. Local programs took different approaches to helping young children prepare to enter school. Some focused on teaching pre-academic skills, such as letter and number recognition; some depended on children's exploration and discovery of materials to enhance their overall development; and others followed no specific curriculum at all. June Solnit Sale described the eleven agencies running Head Start programs in Los Angeles County in 1966 as a mix of grassroots organizations, community action groups, religious organizations, school districts, and philanthropic agencies. None of them had much previous experience operating early-childhood education programs, and each interpreted the programs' educational goals differently. Programs offered a range of approaches, including "'warmed-over' kindergarten" and a "summer camp" approach with lots of field trips to programs based on ideas about creative play, Montessori philosophy, or behavior modification. At one site, where a reading lesson was taught via television monitor, children spent thirty minutes repeating the words "I see Sam"; they were also taught colors, shapes, and forms by rote repetition. At another site, children were busy playing in different areas with blocks, housekeeping toys, paint, and dough; there was a great deal of peer interaction and warmth shown between teachers and children. Some programs were exemplary, and a few, Sale believed, should have been closed down (Sale 1979, 184–189).

Some programs saw their mission as primarily about community building rather than the education of preschoolers. In answering the question "What is Head Start?" the director of the program in a rural Indiana community wrote about linking Mexican migrant working families with the public school; giving a local girl employment in the kitchen and encouraging her to pursue more education; training a teenage mother to be a classroom aide; and educating parents about the need for preventive medicine, dental care, and vaccinations. This director also described Head Start as an outpouring of volunteer effort from all sectors of the community: a teacher taking care of a hospitalized child, a dentist spending his day off treating

Head Start children, a group of young men creating a wonderful playground from discarded equipment, sorority members volunteering in the classroom, and civic clubs and churches providing a graduation party, a Santa Claus visit, shoes, tricycles, and a trip to the zoo or farm (Iliff 1968).

Indeed, Head Start attracted thousands of volunteers from doctors' offices, churches, boys and girls' clubs, YMCAs, and local businesses. The award for the most unusual contribution to a Head Start program might have gone to Pacific Southwest Airlines, which in 1968 flew fifteen Head Start children from San Diego to Los Angeles and back again every Saturday. After the twenty-minute flight, the children toured the Los Angeles airport and were given a snack while they watched planes land and take off. This adventure "was arranged as one way of providing new experiences for the Head Start children" (*Head Start Newsletter* 1968, 2). The OEO reported that 250,000 people—half of them Head Start parents—volunteered in classrooms that first summer. Recognizing the public support generated by volunteers as well as their contributions to the program, the OEO used every opportunity to recruit volunteers for Head Start, producing TV spots featuring the First Lady in 1968 and a poster entitled "Head Start Wants YOU," which was plastered on 68,300 U.S. mail trucks in June 1969.[1]

The importance of Head Start's local, grassroots approach—and the context of larger political struggles within which Head Start operated—is best seen through the Child Development Group of Mississippi (CDGM), a highly effective network of Head Start programs that placed a premium on empowering poor parents. The CDGM, which received the largest Head Start grant in the country in 1965, grew directly out of the civil rights organizing of the 1964 Freedom Summer in Mississippi. Polly Greenberg, who left the OEO in order to work for the CDGM in the spring of 1965, described the effort to create "Freedom Schools at the nursery level," programs planned, staffed, and controlled by the poor. Asking directions to one hard-to-find rural Head Start site, Greenberg had no luck until she asked for "the school Negroes are making for themselves" (Greenberg 1969, 105). Each of the eighty-four communities in the CDGM ran its own program, found its own building, hired its own staff, and decided what it wanted Head Start to be; the central staff provided resources, ideas, and training. CDGM staff saw their work as part of the broader civil rights struggle: they strongly emphasized empowering poor communities and individuals to make their own decisions, even at the risk of creating administrative chaos and uneven programs for children. Indeed, Greenberg reported great variety among the local CDGM programs, ranging from one where children spent their time "creating, pretending, playing, singing, looking, listening, and wondering" in a playground in the woods, to those that stressed rote learning and etiquette, punishing children if they did not address adults with correct manners. Parents were involved in nearly every aspect of CDGM programs, working to construct and repair buildings, cook meals, find classroom supplies, recruit and transport children, staff classrooms, and other tasks that in most other Head Start programs were done for pay or by outside volunteers. After visiting the CDGM, Head Start's national training director said "that now he really understood for the first time what participation of the poor really means" (Greenberg 1969, 163; Kagan 2002, 531).

Not everyone was so enthusiastic about empowering poor black parents, however. Both whites and blacks in Mississippi recognized that the CDGM represented a new phase of the civil rights movement in the state, one that was pouring millions of federal dollars into black communities.[2] Local segregationists harassed CDGM workers and burned some Head Start sites, and Senator John Stennis of Mississippi sought to cut off its funding, claiming the group was misusing Head Start funds for civil rights activities. Following several rounds of investigations, protests, and negotiations, Shriver decided in October 1966 to cut off funding to the CDGM and to grant the funds instead to a group less threatening to Mississippi's power structure. This decision came right in the midst of an uncertain congressional vote on OEO appropriations, and was influenced by the fear that Stennis, who was chair of the Appropriations Committee, would eliminate funding for the OEO altogether (Shriver and Sugarman 1969, 61–64). The CDGM became a cause célèbre among northern liberals and others who saw Shriver's move as a betrayal, sacrificing Head Start and civil rights to appease a powerful segregationist. Protests came from liberal senators, the National Council of Churches, and other respected sources. Martin Luther King met with Shriver, and Vice President Hubert Humphrey offered to mediate. Shriver was crushed when a group of 160 religious, educational, labor, and civil rights leaders signed a full-page ad in the *New York Times* denouncing his capitulation to political pressure; in large, bold type the headline read, "Say It Isn't So, Sargent Shriver."[3] Within the OEO, debate raged and morale sank; employees circulated a petition of support and crowded a large in-house meeting to protest the decision (*New Republic* 1967, 10). Ultimately, a reorganized, much smaller, and somewhat subdued CDGM was refunded. It operated Head Start programs in the state alongside the group that had been created to replace it.

Head Start programs besides the CDGM encouraged parents to become community activists. A 1970 report commissioned by the U.S. Department of Health, Education and Welfare (HEW) found examples of Head

Start parents organizing to desegregate health facilities, establish a community food cooperative or a visiting-nurse program, or pressure the public schools to provide tutoring, after-school programs, social workers, and a multicultural curriculum. In one (unnamed) western city, Head Start parents "allied themselves with local black activist groups to bring about specific changes they wanted in the school system." Organized and encouraged by Head Start staffers, the parents sought "changes such as hiring Negro teacher aides and providing free hot lunches for needy children" (Kirschner Associates 1970, 7, 9). In the mountains of central Pennsylvania, Head Start parents worked together to get television service for their community; they "got excited when they began to see that they could make an impact on their environment." In New York City, Head Start fathers studied together to pass the employment examination to get public jobs as apartment building custodians (Valentine and Stark 1979, 298). In Clark County, Washington, Head Start sponsored a Public Assistance Club, whose members studied public assistance laws, raised money to hire a bus, and traveled to the capital to talk with legislators, the state public assistance director, and the state attorney general about their proposals for improving welfare and child support ("Parents Get to Work" 1967).

Like everything in Head Start, parental involvement varied substantially from program to program, and many local programs struggled to offer a meaningful role to parents. They took the politically safer route of encouraging parents to volunteer in classrooms, hiring some of them as staff members, and offering "parent education" classes that focused mostly on becoming better parents and household managers. Such classes featured topics such as child development, speech, health education, purchasing nutritious food at low cost, discipline, weight reduction, home beautification, and money management. The tone of reports on these programs was sometimes condescending, as in the description of a Phoenix Head Start program called "Mothers Learn to Cook": "300 mothers . . . accustomed to a traditional diet, were shown ways to prepare balanced meals from canned meat, dry milk, flour, cornmeal, split peas. . . . The women, whose cultural differences have made it difficult to prepare dishes using some of the staples, have been eager to learn ways to improve their families' diets" (*Head Start Newsletter* 1966). Surveys of local Head Start programs conducted in the 1960s suggest that parents found such instructional programs of limited value. In New Haven, Connecticut, only half the Head Start parents reported attending parent education seminars, and in Los Angeles they were rated the least helpful aspect of the program (Kagan 2002, 538).

Fostering meaningful parental involvement in Head Start programs meant doing more than offering cooking classes. In 1967, the OEO reported that half the programs were lacking in parent involvement, in part because of the attitudes of directors like one in Massachusetts who thought "too many cooks spoil the brew," or the head nun in a Louisiana program who called parent participation "touching but irrelevant" (Gonzales 1967). Furthermore, empowering parents risked alienating school boards and other local officials. When the OEO's initial guidelines gave parents veto power over Head Start hiring decisions and urged their involvement in budgetary decisions, some local school boards immediately protested. Fights ensued in several large cities where school boards were already facing increasing demands for "community control" of public schools. The OEO backed off, but remained committed to parental empowerment and involvement in governing local Head Start programs. Head Start's 1967 manual cautioned that real parental involvement meant that staff "must learn to ask parents for their ideas" and "take care to avoid dominating meetings" (Project Head Start 1967, 11). A staff position of parent coordinator was created to encourage and organize parental involvement in local programs, and many programs established parent rooms to encourage both involvement in the classroom and networking among parents.

In the first four to five years of Head Start's existence, the program tried to fulfill its promises to provide education and services to poor children as well as jobs and political empowerment to poor parents. Programs varied widely in how they combined these goals and in what priority they assigned to each. The "glorious goalfulness" of Head Start—produced by the planning committee, OEO staffers, and others—left room for many different understandings of the program's purpose, and its emphasis on local, community control of programs meant that Head Start would look quite different from one community to another. As time went on, however, Head Start supporters were pressed to choose which of its goals was most important, and to eliminate some of the local activism that had marked its early years.

Surviving the Nixon Years

In the late 1960s and early 1970s, both the political context and the intellectual foundations that had given rise to Head Start were shaken up. Head Start, which had emerged from the War on Poverty and had been shaped by the culture and priorities of the OEO, started a new chapter as a sort of orphan in the post-Johnson years. Its broad-based political and public support helped ensure its survival as a program, but it would now stand alone, vulnerable to the winds of political change. At the same time, its impact on national discussions about the needs of young children and the responsibility of government became evident in debates over federal child care policy. While the Nixon administration was deciding what to do with Head Start, evaluation studies were released that cast doubt on the program's effectiveness at improving children's performance in school, and psychologists again debated whether early education programs could affect children's intelligence and school performance. The promises of researchers—that children's IQs, school careers, and life chances could be improved through brief preschool interventions—were questioned. But the political judgment that Shriver and Johnson had made in 1965 paid off. Creating Head Start on a massive scale had helped produce a broad base of political support, overriding questions about whether its intellectual foundations or principal assumptions were strong enough.

The national evaluation of Head Start, conducted by the Westinghouse Learning Corporation and Ohio State University, was released at a time of political transition in 1969, gaining much attention in Washington circles and sparking controversy among researchers. To determine whether Head Start had long-term positive effects on children's academic achievement, the Westinghouse researchers compared cognitive test scores of first-, second-, and third-grade children who had attended Head Start with those of children who had not. (The study contained no information on the characteristics of the Head Start programs that the children attended or of the public schools that they went to afterward.) They found no effect for the six-week summer program, but a limited effect for the full-year program among both first- and second-grade children, with greater effects among certain subgroups, such as black children in large southeastern cities. These relatively negative findings were not surprising to those who had seen smaller evaluation reports showing that cognitive gains in Head Start tended to "fade" (or more accurately, that non–Head Start children tended to "catch up") as children progressed through elementary school. But the conclusions that the Westinghouse researchers drew were damning: "Head Start as it is presently constituted has not provided widespread cognitive and affective gains," and "its benefits cannot be described as satisfactory" (Cicirelli 1969, 11; also quoted in Zigler and Muenchow 1992, 70). This assessment, of course, was ammunition to those in the Nixon administration who were eager to criticize Johnson-era social programs.

This first large, national evaluation of Head Start aroused considerable controversy among researchers, who critiqued its methodology and reanalyzed the data, producing different results. Of particular concern was the fact that the control-group children came from higher socioeconomic-status families than the Head Start children; researchers disagreed about whether any statistical corrections could adjust for this. Others raised questions about the sample size and whether it was representative. The Stanford statistician William Madow, who had been a consultant to the study, resigned and asked to have his name stricken from the report. Sheldon White of Harvard, who also served as a consultant, defended the study, as did its authors and sponsors in the OEO's Planning and Evaluation office.

Beyond these methodological issues lay broader questions about what grounds could be used to judge the program's effectiveness. Both Head Start's grassroots structure and its multiple goals made it particularly difficult to assess. There was never really one "Head Start program" that could be evaluated, but thousands of variations, shaped by local community needs and dynamics. Researchers had to decide which of the program's multiple goals—improving children's health, empowering parents, providing employment, promoting cognitive development—to focus on. Years later, Edward Zigler identified the main problem: "We did not know what to measure. Public health researchers might have assessed the number of measles cases prevented, or the reduction in hearing or speech problems. Sociologists might have looked at the number of low-income parents who obtained jobs through Head Start. But the only people evaluating Head Start were psychologists, and, for a time, that greatly limited the focus of the research. . . . Head Start had been designed to de-emphasize cognitive development, yet it was being evaluated primarily on the most cognitive measure of all" (Zigler and Muenchow 1992, 51–53). Indeed, one unintended consequence of the Westinghouse report was to define for the public Head Start's primary goal: to raise children's scores on cognitive tests. "To the public," Zigler noted, "Head Start appeared to be a quick, two-month program to make poor children smart, while to the planners, and those in the program, it was but the beginning of a long cooperative effort of teachers, health-care professionals, and parents to make children physically healthy and socially competent" (Zigler and Muenchow 1992, 25–26).

Although the program's planners and administrators saw Head Start as a "comprehensive child development program" tied to community action, those concepts were not easy to communicate. Johnson, Shriver, and others charged with "selling" Head Start found it easier and more effective to simply talk about IQ scores, even though expecting significant change in IQ (a very stable measure) created unrealistic expectations. For example, during Shriver's testimony before Congress on the Equal Opportunity Act amendments of 1966, he was asked to identify the War on Poverty's greatest measurable success, and he named Head Start, pointing to initial research indicating that the summer program produced an IQ gain of ten points. This also fit in with Shriver and Johnson's initial conception of Head Start as primarily an effort to improve children's academic success in school. This academic emphasis made sense to the OEO's evaluation director, Robert Levine, who wrote in 1970, "Head Start may be a fine Community Action program, and the indicators are that it is. It may improve the health of kids. But it is *primarily* a program to improve children's learning abilities, and on this criterion it must finally stand or fall. If the program does not bring about educational improvement, then the other favorable effects may be brought in much more cheaply" (quoted in Vinovskis 2005, 105). Indeed, it is not surprising that public discussion of the program focused on modifying IQ. Head Start had been inspired by experimental studies that showed improvement in IQ scores, and by the work of J. McVicker Hunt and Benjamin Bloom, which suggested that manipulating the environment of young children could make them "smarter" (Hunt 1961; Bloom 1964). Furthermore, IQ and achievement measures were available, and their validity was widely accepted, while there was nothing comparable for assessing children's social and emotional growth. Promoting children's success in school was the most popular of Head Start's objectives, and the Westinghouse evaluation seemed to show that it was not succeeding.

The Westinghouse study was part of a string of evaluations that cast doubt on the effectiveness of educational interventions to change poor children's school performance. The 1966 Coleman Report had called into question the utility of compensatory programs other than Head Start. Evaluations of the Title I program of aid to schools serving disadvantaged children also found little effect. Around the time when the Westinghouse study was released, the *Harvard Education Review* published an article by the psychologist Arthur Jensen on the nature of intelligence, which opened by saying, "Compensatory education has been tried and it apparently has failed," and went on to argue for a genetically deterministic explanation of IQ and achievement (Jensen 1969). Taken together, these reports had a strong effect. Lois-ellin Datta characterizes this period as a long "winter of disillusion and some despair about education and the Great Society in general" among researchers (Datta 1979, 405). As one put it, "Sooner or later since Head Start was oversold, the balloon would have had to deflate. But the Westinghouse Report was like a pinprick to the balloon. It exploded" (Datta 1976, 160).

While these negative evaluations had a large impact on researchers, they seem to have made only a small dent in Head Start's political support. Head

Start's appeal to legislators and its broad base of political support continued to be at least as important as any research findings. Almost no mention was made of the Westinghouse study in the *Congressional Record* either when it was released or in the following year. The researcher Jeanne Ellsworth notes, "I am astonished that the 1970s Westinghouse study, generally cited as central in Head Start's history, was not covered by the newsmagazines at all, and was dismissed by some in congressional hearings, where increasing amount of time were given over to testimonials from parents or graduates, which show the gratitude of program recipients" (Ellsworth 1998, 328). During hearings on a bill that Senator Walter Mondale introduced shortly after the Westinghouse report was released, he commented, "One of the things that always strikes me about Westinghouse-type studies is that their results so often conflict with the judgment of people experienced in the program. I have rarely talked to educators or Head Start teachers or parents of children in Head Start who weren't delighted. They think it is working, they think it is helpful. . . . Wherever you go you get the same reaction except from reports like Westinghouse" (U.S. Senate 1969, 357).

The Westinghouse report did not lead Nixon to cancel Head Start. Calculating that the political costs of eliminating the popular program were too high, his administration continued it with level funding. The report did, however, help justify moving Head Start out of the OEO and shifting funding from summer programs to full-year programs, which was politically difficult because it meant cutting the size of the program by about half. It also provided a reason not to expand the program. In notes from a meeting with Nixon in May 1969, the president's domestic advisor, John Ehrlichman, noted that it "may be too late to abolish" Head Start, which was supported by powerful members of Congress, but that no increases should be considered (Datta 1983, 271–280; Zigler and Muenchow 1992, 70, 75). Since Head Start was serving only about 10 percent of eligible children, this was a serious problem. Jude Wanniski wrote in his newspaper column, "Educators and social scientists who had envisioned Head Start doubling in size and ultimately solving all the preschool deficiencies of the poor will now have to wait until HEW finds a formula that it believes will work" (Wanniski 1969). Head Start would remain an "experimental" program, albeit a very large one.

In drawing attention to the promise of preschool for the nation's poorest children, Head Start raised questions about whether early education might benefit all children. The spotlight that Head Start focused on young children's learning led to an increase in other early-childhood programs, particularly public school kindergartens, which grew dramatically in states that had not previously offered it, through the use of federal Title I dollars as well as eventual state funding. Enrollment in private nursery schools likewise increased substantially in the late 1960s, which some attributed to publicity about Head Start. The chief of day care for the New York City Department of Health explained to *Newsweek*, "The middle-class parents read about Head Start, and figure 'if it's good for children from the other side of the tracks, it must be good for my children too.'" Following this trend, the article continued, "Many educators feel it is only a matter of time— and a considerable amount of money—before every 3-, 4-, and 5-year-old can toddle off to preschool" (*Newsweek* 1966). To provide exposure to early learning for all children, the television show *Sesame Street* was launched in 1969, financed by a combination of federal and other funding, including some from Head Start. The show, which was aimed particularly at poor, inner-city children, tested television's promise to teach young children skills that would help prepare them for school.

At this time, Congress was also considering a child care bill that was inspired by the successes and promise of the Head Start program. For supporters of Head Start, this growing momentum for child care seemed like an ideal opportunity to protect the vulnerable program by linking it with the broader demand for publicly supported child care. Marian Wright Edelman, a veteran of civil rights organizing in Mississippi and an advocate for poor children, explained later this rationale: "Head Start's survival depended on broadening the base of its constituency. This meant identifying the need for child care services in the larger population" (Edelman 1974). Although her main concern was for poor children, she thought that addressing the needs of all children was the best approach. She led the Ad Hoc Coalition for Child Development, a broad alliance of more than twenty labor, civil rights, education, welfare, and women's organizations in pushing for a child care initiative that would continue Head Start's emphasis on parental and community involvement but go beyond its focus on the poorest children. Indeed, the coalition urged Congress to create a system of publicly funded child care centers that ultimately would be available to all families. Labor unions and feminist groups supported the idea of child care centers that would be available to all families, and education and children's experts saw a promise for expanding Head Start's focus on child development and comprehensive services (including health, nutrition, and social services). In introducing hearings on his child care bill in 1969, Representative John Brademas noted, "If we hadn't had Project Head Start, I dare say we wouldn't be having these hearings this morning, and nobody would give a tinker's damn about preschool programs anyway." Head Start provided a crucial precedent for the idea of broadly based child development programs and for the idea that the federal government should be involved in running them. At another point in the hearings, Brademas added, "Middle-class America has seen the advantages of Head Start to poor children. They want these opportunities for their children" (U.S. House 1969, 825).

The child care bill passed both houses of Congress but was vetoed by President Nixon in 1971 after it became clear that his welfare reform plan would not be advancing, and in the face of growing Republican concerns about administrative aspects of the child care plan. Head Start had spurred national awareness of the needs of young children, especially in disadvantaged communities, and of the possible ways that government could help meet those needs. But rather than becoming the foundation for a new system of federally funded children's centers, Head Start would continue to stand alone.

Head Start's future did not look very bright when Ed Zigler took over as administrator of the program in 1970. The influential Office of Management and Budget proposed cutting the program's budget that year and developed a plan to phase it out in three years. A staff member in the office of HEW secretary Elliot Richardson recalled a "'great deal of talk about Head Start being dead, cut out of the budget, over'" (quoted in Datta 1976, 150; Zigler and Muenchow 1992, 92). The president himself seemed uninterested, refusing to discuss the pledge he had made to address the needs of children during the "first five years of life." Zigler and Richardson were frequently confronted with demonstrations by Head Start parents worried about funding cuts. Richardson fought for the program, but its long-term future did not seem secure. Zigler described the period this way. "We were at best in a holding pattern." He undertook a "whistle-stop tour" to publicize Head Start, stressing that the Westinghouse report was flawed, and that the program should not be expected to perform miracles, especially with IQ scores. He wanted to show the public all the possibilities of Head Start and related programs: "I tried to dazzle people with all types of new demonstration projects. . . . I wanted Congress and the public to associate both Head Start and OCD [the Office of Child Development] with such a blur of useful activity that the administration would not dare close them down" (Zigler and Muenchow 1992, 150). To this end, and to put a Nixon stamp on a Johnson-era program, Zigler introduced new formats for delivering Head Start services, such as Home Start, Health Start, and the Child and Family Resource Program.

Improving the program's quality and administration was also a high priority, since Head Start needed to stand on its own feet. Like the rest of the OEO's Community Action Programs, Head Start had been designed to circumvent state and local government in favor of grassroots community agencies, but it had never really implemented an alternative system of managing and supporting local programs. Thus, Zigler later recalled, at the end of almost five years of operation, "Head Start administrators really had no accurate data as to how many children were served, or even what services were *actually* provided at what cost or benefit to those reported as enrolled" (quoted in Harmon and Hanley 1979, 390). To answer the need for a system of accountability and management control, Zigler's office worked to develop performance standards and procedures for assessing and monitoring programs as well as offering technical assistance. Head Start would continue to be an intensely local program, but it would function within a federal infrastructure that would standardize its operations.

Zigler moved to protect Head Start by eliminating anything that raised hackles in Congress, notably the emphasis on community action. Coming on the heels of the negative conclusions drawn from the Westinghouse report about the program's effectiveness, "any notion in Congress that Head Start money was being spent on inappropriate forms of activism was simply a perception the program could not afford" (Zigler and Muenchow 1992, 110). Of course, Zigler's own ideas about the program—based on his expertise as a psychologist and his experience in planning Head Start— shaped his commitment to stress services to children rather than community action for adults. He worked to develop a clearer policy about parental involvement, giving parents a significant role in setting policy for Head Start programs but limiting the program's involvement in broader community-change efforts. Activists who wanted to make Head Start a catalyst for community organizing objected to this move. At a meeting with a group of local community action leaders who were upset by his decision to prohibit the use of parental-involvement funds for "disruptive tactics" such as sit-ins, Zigler recounts, one frustrated man said, "Dr. Zigler, you don't understand. We are interested in systemic change. We are willing to give up a whole generation of our children in order to get it." "I stood up at the other end of the table," recounts Zigler, "and said that he might be willing to give up a generation of children, but that I was not, and that was not my mission in OCD" (111).

Zigler's leadership through the early 1970s made this a period of consolidating and institutionalizing the program, separating it from Johnson's OEO and the War on Poverty, and making improvements in program quality and administration that would help it weather a period of uncertainty. Since Head Start's intellectual underpinnings had been questioned and its political support in the Nixon administration was shaky, it seemed wise to focus the program in ways that would help it survive. Through most of the 1970s, Head Start remained an embattled and inadequately funded program, divorced from its original context in the War on Poverty and without an influential administrative home. The promise that Lyndon Johnson made at the end of Head Start's first summer—that soon all poor children would be getting two years of Head Start—remained far from realization.

Head Start's Revival

From the late 1970s through the 1990s, a combination of new research and coordinated, grassroots advocacy reversed Head Start's fortunes, leading to the program's expansion. Again, research findings and political mobilization were equally important in reshaping the attitudes of policy makers toward the program. During this period, Head Start shifted from being a survivor of the War on Poverty to a program with broad-based support.

Research was an important source of Head Start's revival during this period. Lois-ellin Datta observed that while it is not unusual for a social program to fall "from favor to the abyss" relatively quickly, Head Start may be a rare example of the reverse, its climb back into political favor supported by a new body of research (Datta 1983, 271). In the 1970s, in the wake of the Westinghouse report, researchers and Head Start officials continued to look for answers to the pressing question whether early-childhood programs like Head Start could be expected to have a long-term impact on children's success in school. The Office of Child Development s research director recalled: "A case had to be made for or against the long-term benefits of preschool programs for children in poverty, even though no other program in the history of education, health, or welfare had ever been required before to justify its existence by long-term benefits" (Grotberg 1983, xii). In 1976, the agency funded a group of researchers to create the Consortium for Longitudinal Studies (CLS), pooling data from eleven early-intervention projects dating back to the early 1960s. Each of the CLS projects was a well-planned and carefully researched preschool intervention that aimed to enhance low-income African American children's cognitive and social development. Each of the studies used experimental or quasi-experimental designs and tracked children's progress over time, although they differed in the ages of children served, the curriculum used, the duration of the program, and other variables.

This research, which was first published in 1977 (and, after additional follow-up, again in 1983), found that while differences on cognitive measures like IQ disappeared after a few years, the children who had participated in early-intervention programs continued to do better in school and later in life than the children who had not. The children who went through the early-intervention programs were less likely to be put into special education classes or have to repeat a grade and also differed from their peers somewhat in high school completion rates, occupational aspirations, and employment rates. The consortium director, Irving Lazar, wrote of the findings, "The independence of the separate studies makes these findings highly reliable. Indeed, few examples of this kind of multiple and independent replication exist anywhere in the social sciences" (Consortium for Longitudinal Studies 1983, 463).

Reports about the positive effects that the CLS researchers discovered had a powerful impact, establishing the need to look beyond IQ scores in order to discover the long-term impact of early-childhood programs. By asking how these programs affected long-term outcomes like high school completion and employment, the study revisited the most ambitious promises that Lyndon Johnson and Sargent Shriver ever made for Head Start. Head Start advocates had distanced themselves from some of these promises in the early 1970s, seeing them as leading to inevitable disappointment. But the CLS findings suggested that even some of Johnson's most extravagant claims for Head Start—that it would lead to success not only in school but also over the whole life span—might be true (Consortium for Longitudinal Studies 1983, 468; Datta 1983, 271–280).[4] "Research, which almost killed Head Start," wrote Ed Zigler and Susan Muenchow (1992, 170), "would finally help save it."

Reporters linked the CLS research directly to Head Start, with headlines such as "Head Start Efforts Prove Their Value," "A Head Start Pays Off in the End," "Head Start Saves Children and Money," and "Head Start Gets a High Grade" (Michalak 1978; Rubin 1980; Woodhead 1988). In fact, these connections were exaggerated; the CLS research was based mostly on experimental, model programs whose funding, expert supervision, and professionally trained staff were far superior to those of most Head Start programs. For example, the Perry Preschool, which would become the best known when researchers later estimated that it had a cost-benefit ratio of 1:7, was not a typical program. For instance, it spent about $5,000 per child per year and its teachers had postgraduate degrees in early-childhood education. Head Start was spending less than half that amount and often hiring teachers with little formal education. Additionally, the carefully controlled nature of the experimental programs could not be replicated in Head Start's 1,200 sites. Researchers were careful to note that their results showed more about the validity of the early-intervention *concept* underlying Head Start than about how this large federal program was implemented: "what Head Start could be rather than what it has been" (Consortium for Longitudinal Studies 1983, 17). Nevertheless, the study validated the promise of Head Start for improving outcomes for poor children, and eager listeners often glossed over the details.

Advocates pushed to translate these research findings into increased funding for Head Start. Harley Frankel, a lobbyist for the Children's Defense Fund, began blanketing congressional offices with research summaries of the CLS findings (packaged with a George Washington University study that favorably synthesized some 150 other Head Start research studies) concluding that Head Start had a positive impact on children's cognitive development and health, the family, and the community. The new National Head Start Association, made up of teachers, parents, and supporters of the program, fought hard for funding increases, visited legislative aides, sent out copies of newspaper articles about the consortium's findings, and generated thousands of letters from all over the country. Ultimately, Head Start received an extra $150 million in 1978, the program's first significant funding increase since Johnson was in the White House. In 1980, the White House hosted a fifteenth-anniversary celebration for Head Start, at which President Carter spoke of his commitment to Head Start's future. To help guide that future, he appointed Ed Zigler to head a committee of sympathetic experts charged with examining the program.

In addition, Head Start supporters had mobilized to resist Carter's attempt to move Head Start into the new Department of Education in 1977. Since federal education programs were typically run through state departments of education, moving Head Start to the new department threatened its unique, federal-to-local-community structure, and advocates feared this would be a harmful move. Marian Wright Edelman of the Children's Defense Fund was adamant that Head Start remain a social welfare and community action program and not be joined to the education bureaucracy, which she believed had not served poor and minority children well in the past (Vinovskis 2002). A group of prominent civil rights leaders wrote a telegram calling the move a threat to Head Start's integrity. Edelman wrote to her former ally, Vice President Walter Mondale, "If you do this, I and those thousands of poor people in the 1,200 Head Start communities . . . will view your action as a betrayal. We will fight you in every way we can" (quoted in Vinovskis 2002, 56). The National Head Start Association joined the protest, helping coordinate a massive letter-writing campaign that sent thousands of personal letters a day to members of Congress. While visiting legislative aides in their congressional offices, the Mississippi civil rights activist Aaron Henry would ask, "What is going to happen to black children if Head Start is put into the schools?" (Zigler and Muenchow 1992, 185; Zigler and Styfco 2010, 209). Head Start mothers from Hartford and New Haven rode a bus all night to Washington to ask Senator Abraham Ribicoff (D-CT) to remove Head Start from the bill creating the new education department. The next morning, Ribicoff—who had previously pledged to support the president on this issue—joined the rest of his committee in voting to delete Head Start from the legislation.

The combination of new research findings and the growing political muscle that Head Start supporters exercised helped protect the program in the early days of the Reagan administration, when funding for many social service programs was slashed. The day after Reagan's inauguration, the former lobbyist and White House staffer Harley Frankel placed a call to the Office of Management and Budget, where by luck a high-level official picked up the phone (no secretary had yet been hired). "I know you'll be cutting a lot of programs," Frankel said. "But to avoid bad press, you'll need to save a few, and let me tell you about Head Start: everybody likes it, and it doesn't cost very much." A week later, at the cabinet meeting, the administration's budget director, David Stockman, proposed that Head Start be placed in a "safety net" of social programs that would not be cut. The new secretary of education, Terrel Bell, and the secretary of defense, Caspar Weinberger, both agreed. Not coincidentally, Bell was among the education leaders with whom the CLS researchers had met in the late 1970s to explain their findings, conducting what was "in effect, a small seminar on the study from researchers skilled in presenting results and their implications, confident of the sturdiness of the findings, and assured that they should be put into practice in expansion of quality early childhood programs" (Datta 1983, 276). At that cabinet meeting, Bell voiced the view that Head Start was effective in preventing later school failure and therefore deserved continuing support.

This support for Head Start in the early days of the Reagan administration presaged a growing support for the program during the 1980s, when policy makers across the nation paid increasing attention to the promise of early-childhood programs such as Head Start for improving children's school achievement. A national movement for K–12 education reform embraced early-childhood education as an important tool for improving the educational outcomes of poor children. As "school readiness" became an important part of the education reform agenda, governors and business leaders looked favorably on Head Start and other programs that promised to help prepare young children to succeed in school. The education reform movement, catalyzed by Terrel Bell's *Nation at Risk* report in 1983, culminated in a national "education summit" of the nation's governors in 1989. Governors agreed on six national education goals that would become the focal point of reform efforts for the next decade. First on the list was that "all children in America will start school ready to learn" (Rose 2010, 90–91; Vinovskis 1999). State legislators launched a range of new initiatives to improve educational standards and resources, including funding new prekindergarten programs and providing state funds to expand Head Start services. The movement for K–12 reform, backed by the widely circulated findings of research studies showing positive long-term effects of early-childhood programs, helped reframe Head Start as an important tool for a twenty-first-century education system.

By the end of the 1980s, it seemed that, as writers for *Newsweek* put it, "Everybody likes Head Start" (Leslie 1989, 49–50). The National Head Start Association played a crucial role in cultivating support for the program in Congress, even among conservative legislators, who saw it as a self-help, family-strengthening program rather than a federal "handout." Republicans and Democrats almost competed to see who could provide the greatest boost for Head Start, and governors and business leaders lent their strong support as well. For instance, in 1990, the George H. W. Bush administration sought to add $500 million to Head Start's budget, while Democrats in the Senate pledged a $6 billion increase in order to "fully fund" the program, which would mean serving three- as well as four-year-olds and increasing the operating period in order to achieve higher quality outcomes (Cooper 1990; Rovner 1990, 1191–1195; Zigler and Muenchow 1992, 202, 209–210). The 1990 reauthorization of Head Start provided the largest budget increase in the program's history; authorized funding levels would have allowed all eligible three- and four-year-olds to be served, but not enough was appropriated to meet this goal. The reauthorization also set aside funds for quality improvements and increased qualification requirements for teachers. Vice President Al Gore referred to the program's next reauthorization, which passed by huge margins in both houses of Congress, as a "lovefest" (Dewar and Vobejda 1994).

Despite this support, however, Head Start remained vulnerable to shifting political forces. The George W. Bush administration raised fundamental questions about Head Start's structure and goals, pushing to shift authority over the program to the states in order to refocus its purpose more narrowly on preparing children academically for school. The administration and its allies in Congress sought to shift control to the states through a block grant, with the idea that this would help increase Head Start's academic effectiveness; supporters of the program feared this would mean the program's dissolution. The National Head Start Association went into high gear to defend the program, launching a national campaign, "Save Head Start," by mobilizing grassroots support. Congressional offices were flooded with e-mails and faxes, and public demonstrations highlighted opposition to the move. This effective mobilization, building on Head Start's widespread popularity, helped convinced lawmakers in both parties to oppose the bill. Republican leaders in the House pulled the Head Start bill from the floor schedule in mid-July, fearing that with several members absent, they would not have the votes to pass it. One leadership aide said, "A lot of the local Head Start [advocates] are so ginned up. Their grass roots are just gunning" for the bill, and GOP lawmakers were worried that they would come across as "voting against 5-year-olds learning" (Schuler and Allen 2003). The House did pass the bill a week later (by one vote), but it did not survive in the Senate.

A different effort to reshape Head Start came in 2003, when the George W. Bush administration introduced a standardized assessment of letter, number, and word recognition, which was to be given to all Head Start students twice a year. This effort followed on the heels of the No Child Left Behind Act and reflected its effort to use federally mandated standardized testing to hold schools accountable for student achievement. This program, the most widespread standardized testing of such young children ever conducted in the United States, aroused criticism from early-childhood experts, who contended that the test was not an appropriate tool and that the difficulties of assessing preschoolers would make the data of limited usefulness. The test violated what professional early educators considered to be important guidelines for assessing the development of young children, such as developmental appropriateness, use of multiple measures based on observation of daily activities, and ability to capture preschool children's rapid and uneven growth (Epstein et al. 2004; NAEYC and NAECS/SDE 2003). After some public outcry, Congress ultimately halted the test in 2007 and asked the National Research Council to provide guidance on appropriate assessments for early-childhood programs (Committee on Developmental Outcomes and Assessments for Young Children 2008; Strauss 2007).

The Bush administration's 2003 proposals to change Head Start's structure were striking in part because the program was thought to be secure, even untouchable. The broad bipartisan support Head Start has enjoyed since the late 1970s, along with the effective political organizing of its constituents and supporters, gave the program a special status. For instance, amid partisan bickering surrounding the 1998 reauthorization, Helen Blank of the Children's Defense Fund said, "If you can't reach agreement on Head Start, then what can you agree on?" (Lowy 1998). And columnist Andrew Ferguson wrote in the business journal *Bloomberg News*, "Reform Head Start? You might as well patch the crack in the Liberty Bell" (Ferguson 2003). This special status, of course, helps protect the program, but means also that there is little political will to make adjustments suggested by new scientific research or changes in the worlds of education and social services. Head Start gradually became an icon in American social policy, representing an important symbol of federal commitment to poor children and families. The psychologist Jerome Kagan commented that the program gives poor minority families a "sign that the U.S. government cares about your children" (quoted in Holden 1990, 1400–1402).

Despite the program's iconic status, however, Head Start's challenges were far from over. It had not been able to reach more than about 40 percent of eligible children, leaving a large number of poor and low-income children unserved. Continued questions about its quality and long-term effects have continued to keep researchers and administrators busy. Advocates for expanding preschool education have increasingly looked for models other than Head Start to serve as the basis for a system of universally available, high-quality programs. Recognizing the limitations of Head Start's structure as a special federal program for the disadvantaged, they have sought instead to attach preschool to public education by expanding state-funded prekindergarten programs, with the goal of making them available to all children (Barnett and Hustedt 2003, 54–57; Committee for Economic Development 2002; Rose 2010, chs. 4, 5).

At times, the debates over Head Start have seemed like referenda on the effectiveness of the federal government itself, which is fitting for a program that emerged from an expansive vision of what the federal government could accomplish. Recent debates over Head Start show that the federal government, although much less trusted today than in the 1960s, is still seen as the best guarantor of the rights of the underprivileged. Americans may be skeptical about the federal government's effectiveness in managing social programs in general, but they opposed the Bush administration's move to give up federal protection of a popular program for disadvantaged children and families. In an era marked by mistrust of large federal programs, Head Start continues to attract broad-based support. Opinion research suggests that some of this support is based on the perception of Head Start—with its direct grants to community agencies and emphasis on local control—as a neighborhood and community program rather than a federal initiative (Sparks 2003).

From its creation, in 1965, Head Start was shaped by the Johnson administration's expansive vision of an active federal government that could afford to experiment in order to find the best ways to provide equal opportunity for all children. Reflecting the War on Poverty's commitment to poor people's participation in their own empowerment, Head Start's openness to local variation gave rise to creative, community-controlled approaches to programs, but also made it difficult to ensure quality or standardization— and therefore difficult to evaluate its impact. Federally supported autonomy from local schools and governmental agencies was important in ensuring the program's reach in the 1960s and has helped build its reputation as a community-run program rather than one imposed by Washington. As one of the few direct survivors of the War on Poverty, Head Start has struggled to find a secure base and to gain adequate funding to meet its aims. Because of its separation from the infrastructure of local governments and schools, it has had to build its own administrative systems from the ground up. Partly as a result, recent advocates for expanding early education have looked to plant current efforts in secure political and administrative ground. Nevertheless, in their blueprints for a new system of early education, they depend upon Head Start as a touchstone for the federal government's commitment to ensuring equal opportunity for young, disadvantaged children. They also draw upon Head Start's striking legacy of mobilizing both research-based knowledge and political constituencies in order to sustain a promising approach to learning.

Notes

Some material in this essay appears in Rose 2010, and is used with permission of Oxford University Press.

1. The TV spots are described in *Head Start Newsletter* 3, no. 4 (July 1968), and the poster is featured in *Head Start Newsletter* 4, no. 4 (June 1969).

2. Christopher Jencks (1966, 20) wrote that the CDGM was seen as the "residual legatee of 'the movement'" in Mississippi and was large enough to have a substantial impact.

3. "Group Acts to Aid Head Start Fund," *New York Times*, Sept. 14, 1966. The ad appeared in the *New York Times*, Oct. 19, 1966.

4. Some earlier studies of Head Start had suggested that there had been impacts on special education placement and grade retention, but had not proved these conclusively.

References

Barnett, W. Steven, and J. Hustedt. 2003. Preschool: The most important grade. *Educational Leadership* 60, no. 7: 54–57.

Bloom, Benjamin. 1964. *Stability and change in human characteristics.* New York: Wiley and Sons.

Bronfenbrenner, Urie. 1979. Head Start, a retrospective view: The founders. In Zigler and Valentine 1979.

Buder, Leonard. 1962. Preschool help planned in slums. *New York Times,* June 16.

Charleston (WV) Gazette. 1965. "Project Head Start" due in summer. Feb. 23.

Cicirelli, V.G. 1969. *The impact of Head Start: An evaluation of the effects of Head Start on children's cognitive and affective development.* Report presented to the Office of Economic Opportunity (Washington, D.C.) by the Westinghouse Learning Corporation.

Committee for Economic Development. 2002. *Preschool for all: Investing in a productive and just society.* New York: Committee for Economic Development.

Committee on Developmental Outcomes and Assessments for Young Children. 2008. *Early childhood assessment: Why, what, and how.* Washington, D.C.: National Academies. Available at the website of the Administration for Children and Families, www.acf.hhs.gov/sites/default/files/opre/early_child_assess.pdf.

Consortium for Longitudinal Studies. 1983. *As the twig is bent: Lasting effects of preschool programs.* Hillsdale, N.J.: Erlbaum Associates.

Cooper, Kenneth. 1990. Head Start endures, making a difference. *Washington Post,* Apr. 22.

Crook, Bill. 1966. Memorandum to Bill Moyers. Aug. 22. *The War on Poverty, 1964–1968; Part I: The White House central files* (reel 7, frame 304). Frederick, Md.: University Publications of America.

Datta, Lois-ellin. 1976. The impact of the Westinghouse/Ohio evaluation on the development of Project Head Start. In Clark Abt, ed., *The evaluation of social programs.* Beverly Hills, Calif.: SAGE.

———. 1979. Another spring and other hopes: Some findings from national evaluations of Project Head Start. In Zigler and Valentine 1979.

———. 1983. A tale of two studies: The Westinghouse-Ohio evaluation of Project Head Start and the Consortium for Longitudinal Studies report. *Studies in Educational Evaluation* 8, no. 3: 271–280.

Deutsch, Martin. 1964. Facilitating development in the pre-school child: Social and psychological perspectives. *Merrill-Palmer Quarterly* 10, no. 3: 252–262.

Dewar, Helen, and Barbara Vobejda. 1994. Clinton signs Head Start expansion; president's $700 million promise on crash course with budget caps. *Washington Post,* May 19.

Edelman, Marian Wright. 1974. An interview with Marian Wright Edelman, by Rochelle Beck and John Butler. *Harvard Educational Review* 44:53–73.

Ellsworth, Jeanne. 1998. Inspiring delusions: Reflections on Head Start's enduring popularity. In Jeanne Ellsworth and Lynda Ames, eds., *Critical perspectives on Head Start.* Albany: State University of New York Press.

Epstein, Ann, Lawrence J. Schweinhart, Andrea DeBruin-Parecki, and Kenneth

B. Robin. 2004. Preschool assessment: A guide to developing a balanced approach. NIEER *Preschool policy matters* 7 (July).

Ferguson, Andrew. 2003. Can Bush touch an untouchable federal program? *Bloomberg News* (July 1). www.bloomberg.com/apps/news?pid=newsarchive&sid=aXZ Nu93ADdXM.

Gonzales, Jack. 1967. Too many cooks? *Head Start Newsletter* 2, no. 1.

Gray, Susan, Barbara Ramsey, and Rupert Klaus. 1982. *From 3 to 20: The early training project.* Baltimore: University Park Press.

Greenberg, Polly. 1969. *The devil has slippery shoes: A biased biography of the Child Development Group of Mississippi.* London: Macmillan.

———. 1998. The origins of Head Start and the two versions of parent involvement. In Jeanne Ellsworth and Lynda Ames, eds., *Critical perspectives on Head Start.* Albany: State University of New York Press.

Grotberg, Edith. 1983. A tribute to the consortium. In Consortium for Longitudinal Studies 1983.

Harmon, Carolyn. 1979. Was Head Start a community action program? Another look at an old debate. In Zigler and Valentine 1979.

Harmon, Carolyn, and Edward Hanley. 1979. Administrative aspects of the Head Start program. In Zigler and Valentine 1979.

Head Start Newsletter. 1966. Mothers learn to cook. Vol. 1, no. 7 (Nov.).

———. 1968. A flying adventure. Vol. 3. (June).

———. 1970. Head Start policy change. Vol. 5 (July).

Holden, Constance. 1990. Head Start enters adulthood. *Science* 247, no. 4949: 1400–1402.

Hunt, J. McVicker. 1961. *Intelligence and experience.* New York: Ronald.

———. 1964. The implications of changing ideas on how children develop intellectually. *Children* 11, no. 3 (May–June).

Hymes, James. 1979. Head Start, a retrospective view: The founders. In Zigler and Valentine 1979.

Iliff, Nedra. 1968. What is Head Start? *Head Start Newsletter* 3 (Nov.): 1–2.

Jencks, Christopher. 1966. Accommodating whites. *Nation* 154, Apr. 16.

Jensen, Arthur. 1969. How much can we boost IQ and scholastic achievement? *Harvard Educational Review* 39:1–123.

Johnson, Lyndon B. 1965a. Remarks on Project Head Start (May 18). In Zigler and Valentine 1979.

———. 1965b. Suggested remarks of the president at announcement of 2,000 Head Start centers. *The War on Poverty, 1964–1968; Part I: The White House central files* (reel 7, frame 348). Frederick, Md.: University Publications of America.

Kagan, Josh. 2002. Empowerment and education: Civil rights, expert advocates, and parent politics in Head Start, 1965–1980. *Teachers College Record* 104, no. 3: 516–562.

Kirschner Associates. 1970. *A national survey of the impacts of Head Start centers on community institutions.* Report prepared for the U.S. Department of Health, Education and Welfare. Washington, D.C.: Government Printing Office.

Leslie, Connie. 1989. Everybody likes Head Start. *Newsweek*, Feb. 20, 49–50.

Lowy, Joan. 1998. Head Start program loses status as sacred cow. Scripps Howard News Service. Aug. 29.

Michalak, Joseph. 1978. Head Start-type programs get a second look. *New York Times*, Apr. 30.

NAEYC and NAECS/SDE [National Association for the Education of Young Children and National Association of Early Childhood Specialists in State Departments of Education]. 2003. Early childhood curriculum, assessment, and program evaluation. https://www.naeyc.org/files/naeyc/file/positions/pscape .pdf.

New Republic. 1967. Shriver comes across. Jan. 7, 10.

New York Times. 1965. Mrs. Johnson urges help for children. Feb. 20.

Newsweek. 1966. Preschool boom: Its pressures and rewards. May 16, 109.

Omwake, Eveline. 1979. Assessment of the Head Start preschool education effort. In Zigler and Valentine 1979.

"Parents Get to Work." 1967. *Head Start Newsletter*, Vol. 2, no. 7 (July).

Project Head Start. 1967. *Head Start: Manual of policies and instructions.* Office of Child Development, Department of Health, Education and Welfare. Washington, D.C.: Government Printing Office.

Rose, Elizabeth. 1999. *A mother's job: The history of day care, 1890–1960.* New York: Oxford University Press.

———. 2010. *The promise of preschool: From Head Start to universal pre-kindergarten.* New York: Oxford University Press.

Rovner, Julie. 1990. Head Start is one program everyone wants to help. *Congressional Quarterly Weekly*, Apr. 21, 1191–1195.

Rubin, Nancy. 1980. Head Start efforts prove their value. *New York Times*, Jan. 6.

Sale, June Solnit. 1979. Implementation of a Head Start preschool education program: Los Angeles, 1965–1967. In Zigler and Valentine 1979.

Schrag, Rebecca, Sally Styfco, and Edward Zigler. 2004. Familiar concept, new name: social competence/school readiness as the goal of Head Start. In Zigler and Valentine 1979.

Schuler, K., and J. Allen. 2003. Head Start vote pulled from Friday's House floor schedule. *Congressional Quarterly Today* (July 16, online version). Available at the website of the Democratic whip of the U.S. House of Representatives: www.democraticwhip.gov/content/head-start-vote-pulled-fridays-house-floor-schedule.

Shriver, Sargent. 1965. Memorandum to Jack Valenti. May 6. In *The War on Poverty, 1964–1968; Part I: The White House central files* (reel 7, frame 356). Frederick, Md.: University Publications of America.

———. 1979. Head Start, a retrospective view: The founders. In Zigler and Valentine 1979.

Shriver, Sargent, and Jule Sugarman. 1979. Head Start, a retrospective view. In Zigler and Valentine 1979.

Sparks, Phil. 2003. What the public thinks about early care and education. Paper presented at the Yale Center in Child Development Social Policy Luncheon Series, Yale University, New Haven, Connecticut, Jan. 24.

Stossel, Scott. 2004. *Sarge: The life and times of Sargent Shriver.* Washington, D.C.: Smithsonian Books.

Strauss, Valerie. 2007. Preschoolers' test may be suspended. *Washington Post*, Mar. 18.

U.S. Department of Health, Education and Welfare. 1972. Office of Child Development. *Project Head Start 1969–79: A descriptive report of programs and participants.* Washington, D.C.: Government Printing Office.

U.S. House. 1969. Committee on Education and Labor. *Comprehensive preschool education and child day-care act of 1969.*

U.S. Senate. 1967. Committee on Labor and Public Welfare. *Examination of the War on Poverty, Part 9.* Washington, D.C.: Government Printing Office.

———. 1969. *Headstart Child Development Act: Hearings before the Subcommittee on Employment, Manpower, and Poverty on S. 2060.* Washington, D.C.: Government Printing Office.

Valenti, Jack. 1965. Memorandum to Lyndon Johnson. Apr. 30. In *The War on Poverty, 1964–1968; Part I: The White House central files* (reel 7, frame 356). Frederick, Md.: University Publications of America.

Valentine, Jeannette, and Evan Stark. 1970. The social context of parent involvement in Head Start. In Zigler and Valentine 1979, 291–313.

Vinovskis, Maris. 1999. *The road to Charlottesville: The 1989 Education Summit.* Washington, D.C.: National Education Goals Panel.

———. 2002. The Carter administration's attempt to transfer Head Start into the U.S. Department of Education in the late 1970s. Unpublished paper, University of Michigan Institute for Social Research.

———. 2005. *The birth of Head Start: The growth of preschool education policies in the Kennedy and Johnson administrations.* Chicago: University of Chicago Press.

Wanniski, Jude. 1969. This week in Washington: A lagging Headstart. *Congressional Record* 115, part 9 (May 12).

Weikart, David. 1979. Head Start and evidence-based educational models. In Zigler and Valentine 1979.

———. 2004. *How High/Scope grew: A memoir.* Ypsilanti, Mich.: High/Scope Educational Research Foundation.

Wexler, Jacqueline. 1979. Head Start: A retrospective view. In Zigler and Valentine 1979.

Woodhead, Martin. 1988. When psychology informs public policy: The case of early childhood intervention. *American Psychologist* 43, no. 6 (June): 445–446.

Zigler, Edward, and Susan Muenchow. 1992. *Head Start: The inside story of America's most successful educational experiment.* New York: Basic Books.

Zigler, Edward, and Sally Styfco. 2010. *The hidden history of Head Start.* New York: Oxford University Press.

Zigler, Edward, and Jeanette Valentine, eds. 1979. *Project Head Start: A legacy of the War on Poverty.* New York: Free Press.

CHAPTER 7

Lyndon Johnson and American Education

GARY ORFIELD

Lyndon Johnson wanted to change American education, and he did. Education was central to his vision and to the program of the Great Society, and American education has never been the same since the laws that were pushed through Congress in 1964 and 1965. Johnson loved education, believing it had truly transformative powers, but he was deeply concerned as well about poverty and racial discrimination—they were all part of the same broad vision. Although he wanted to change them all as quickly as possible, he was acutely aware that once the barriers of race came down, those who were freed from discrimination but whose lives had not prepared them to take advantage of new opportunities would need extra help and support. He wanted to do all that. He wanted to finish the work of Lincoln, to carry further the economic vision of Franklin Roosevelt, and to be to federal education policy what Horace Mann and the great reformers of the nineteenth century had been to the creation of state systems of education. Unconcerned with ideology, he wanted to hear the advice of experts and leaders about what would work. He wanted to improve the many shamefully weak schools. He knew that access for black, Latino, and poor children was unequal, and he wanted to open the doors of opportunity for them.

None of Johnson's education policies solved all the related problems. They were the products of a political process loaded with barriers and lubricated by compromises. They were designed in a huge rush and became law just as quickly. While launching great enterprises, his agencies initiated research that would show that the barriers were more deeply entrenched than he thought, and that the tools he forged were less powerful than reformers wished. In retrospect, observers tend to look at the variety of reforms aimed at increasing opportunity for the young one by one. But they were all part of a larger vision of equal opportunity.

Since LBJ served just one full term before being replaced by Richard Nixon—whose Southern Strategy made the South Republican, reversed civil rights progress, and tried to turn education funds back to the states as block grants to be used as states wished—and a succession of GOP presidents with views fundamentally alien to Johnson's, it is amazing that anything remains from these brief years of reform. But there is much. If one looks today at preschool education, at a time when the importance of preschool is more compelling than ever, the discussion revolves largely around changes to Head Start, created as part of LBJ's War on Poverty in 1964. In the world of higher education, by far the important federal policies are the Pell Grant and guaranteed student loans, both of which evolved from provisions of the 1965 Higher Education Act. In elementary and secondary education, Congress is still debating Title I, the basic mechanism of federal aid for nearly a half century—whereas the only other major legislative reform, No Child Left Behind (NCLB), failed spectacularly, as did the more modest Clinton–George H. W. Bush Goals 2000 legislation. The NCLB ended with most American schools being branded as failures and with states willing to do almost anything to escape the senseless and destructive process of absurd demands and damaging sanctions. Goals 2000 ended with none of the goals achieved and backward movement on some of the most important. The Johnson reforms, however, are still very much alive and central to educational, political, and legal debates nearly a half century later. If one searches the landscape of federal policies affecting American schools positively from the first Congress to today, what Johnson and Congress accomplished in 1964 and 1965 stands like a mountain above the plain. The vision was all-encompassing. According to Johnson, "Every American child will have all the education that he can take, that he can absorb. He will have it from the best teachers that any enlightened nation can train. He will have it with the best facilities that a rich nation can afford. That commitment begins with the kindergarten. It extends through the university and even beyond" (Johnson 1966).

Background: Historic Obstacles to Federal Aid

The reasons why major education legislation and federal initiatives were virtually absent in American history before LBJ relate to the particularly sensitive dimensions of educational policy making. U.S. public school systems were formed at the state rather than the federal level, drawing nearly all their resources from state and local taxes. There has been a consensus that the federal government should not control the content of education. Education is not mentioned in the Constitution, and before the mid-1960s the federal government was not a major force in it. There are complex racial and religious issues involved in making educational policy. Southern members of Congress for a century after the Civil War were strongly opposed to a major federal role in education for fear that the federal government would force changes to the region's segregated schools. About a sixth of U.S. children attended nonpublic, mostly Catholic schools in the 1960s, often in large cities. Those Catholic parents, a key part of the Democratic Party's coalition, believed that their children's schools should receive part of any available federal aid. On the other side of that question were liberals committed to the separation of church and state, and Protestants, including the powerful Southern Baptists, who were opposed to public funding for Catholic schools. Then there was the complex problem of devising a formula to divide the federal dollars. Any formula would help some states and districts more than others and thereby create possible political divisions. Pleasing one side on one of these divisive issues could trigger a veto from the other.

To win, the president had to create and hold a supermajority in order to overcome the internal obstacles in Congress and also to hold in check all these volatile divisions within the coalition. These conditions had proved insuperable before Johnson (Price 1962, 1–71). Presidents in their campaigns promise changes, but, after the glow of election wears off, their policy successes are dependent on Congress. Congress enacts all laws and allocates all appropriations. Often there is divided government (that is, the presidency and Congress are under the control of different parties), and it is difficult to move any controversial policy through the congressional maze in even the best of circumstances (Brady and Volden 1998). Education faced an especially fearsome set of barriers, and President Kennedy's ambitious efforts had gone nowhere. Writing shortly before the Johnson presidency, Richard Fenno (1963, 195–235), one of the leading twentieth-century students of Congress, concluded that experience since World War II showed that enacting a major federal-aid-to-schools program was virtually impossible.

There had been federal land grants and small, targeted programs before LBJ's reforms. State vocational education programs began to receive a modest amount of federal funds under a 1917 law. There were dollars for areas "impacted" by federal activities. In 1957, the National Defense Education Act provided money to encourage the development of science and foreign-language programs to help the United States compete in the Cold War. Despite many efforts, however, Congress could not enact a program to alleviate the enormous problems created by the rapid, massive expansion of suburbia and the baby boom after World War II. President Kennedy's effort to break the logjam failed. In all of U.S. history, no general program of aid to public schools had ever been enacted.

In higher education, the Land Grant College Act of the Civil War era (the first Morrill Act) and the second Morrill Act (1890) provided some funds to help create what eventually became the flagship state universities and to support agricultural research. The Servicemen's Readjustment Act of 1944 (commonly known at the GI Bill) was the first effort to extend assistance for college on a mass basis, but it was available only to wartime veterans (Bennett 1996). Universities were dramatically affected by the growth of military, nuclear, space, and other research efforts, but there had been very little effort to develop general policies to expand access to college for the great majority of potential students even as higher education became far more important to a person's success in the U.S. economy. Federal higher-education policy was a history of miniature steps and long-term frustration. The baby boomers were entering college, and the states lacked the resources to meet the need or the policies to bring down barriers of race and class in higher education.

The Political Situation

LBJ's basic idea was to move everything he could through Congress as quickly as possible before the 1966 midterm elections; he knew that the huge congressional majority was likely to decline after the elections, greatly increasing the barriers to legislative accomplishments. Getting a major national education program through Congress for the first time in U.S. history was his initial objective after his landslide 1964 election. Before Congress turned its attention to the next election, he wanted to reshape the federal role at all levels of education and to address the related social issues that hampered children's opportunity to learn.

Though Johnson carefully avoided any effort to control teaching and learning or to regulate curriculum or assessment, his program had a very strong central goal of expanding opportunity and ending exclusion and discrimination.[1] This was achieved not only through policy directly aimed at the schools but also through the strongest expansion and enforcement of civil rights policy in American history and through War on Poverty efforts intended to expand social and economic mobility, especially for poor and minority people and communities. The comprehensive program was based on an intensely optimistic vision of a country rich enough and good enough to extend real opportunity to all and to help those hobbled by inequality to compensate for what they had not been given, affording them the chance to compete fairly in the struggle for the American dream.

Most histories of education policy focus on the important education laws of the Johnson era, particularly the Elementary and Secondary Education Act (ESEA) and the Higher Education Act, both of which became law at the peak of Johnson's presidency in 1965. These are, indeed, landmarks in American educational history, but some of the greatest enduring educational impacts of the Great Society were not the products of education bills but of the laws establishing the War on Poverty and of the Civil Rights Act of 1964, the first major civil rights law in nearly ninety years and the most powerful civil rights legislation in American history.[2]

Schools and the War on Poverty

There were no major laws explicitly about education passed in the first year of the Johnson administration, but the War on Poverty legislation (the Economic Opportunity Act) quickly gave birth to a number of education programs of lasting significance. The most important (and the first national initiative) was the Head Start program, launching public support for preschool education, something that had simply not been part of educational policy at any level of government (Heckman 2011, 31–36). (The Head Start experience is analyzed by Elizabeth Rose in chapter 6 of this book.) Given the educational inequality that children bring with them to kindergarten and that public schools do not overcome, even a half century later, this is an issue of fundamental importance. There have been no other major preschool initiatives in the succeeding generations.

Before Johnson there was no significant federal effort to deal with college costs, but the poverty program began a transformation of the federal role. Since higher education played an increasingly important role in determining lifetime success, these were important beginnings. The new work-study program, subsidizing colleges to pay students for on-campus work, became an enduring pillar of college access. Johnson strongly identified with student aid, remembering his own struggle to pay for college. "As a student," he commented, "I worked at a dozen different jobs, from sweeping the floors to selling real silk socks. Sometimes I wondered what the next day would bring that could exceed the hardship of the day before. But with all of that, I was one of the lucky ones" (Johnson 1965, 1105). Financial aid would greatly expand with the Higher Education Act of 1965. In addition to money, a central barrier to college has long been poor students' lack of knowledge and connections with colleges and their lack of basic pre-collegiate skills. Another innovation of the War on Poverty was access programs, including Upward Bound, designed to connect disadvantaged students from weak high schools with college through counseling, summer programs at colleges, and other strategies. The Job Corps was also a product of the War on Poverty, sending jobless young people to disciplined camps for work and education. The Job Corps has now been sustained for nearly a half century. All these programs still exist.

The 1964 Civil Rights Act and American Education

Johnson, a former teacher, knew that blacks and Latinos had never had a fair chance at education, and his administration implemented civil rights change at what he knew would be a huge political cost in the South.[3] The 1964 Civil Rights Act had an immense impact on American education, in some ways much deeper than his education legislation.[4] It played a central role in expanding access to educational opportunities and in ending virtually totally segregated education in the South. The act provided a model for future reforms addressing the rights of girls and the handicapped, and for building major civil rights responsibilities into American education. Histories of education policy tend to focus only on education grant programs. This oversight may stem from the end of the civil rights era and the dramatic conservative turn that American politics has taken since that time.

The 1964 Civil Rights Act was the most bitterly fought legislative victory ever achieved for civil rights, and the most consequential. The longest debate in the history of the Senate virtually stopped all other activity in Congress for weeks on end in the middle of 1964; progressive senators slept in the Capitol to beat the endless southern filibuster (Whalen and Whalen 1985). Johnson, who intensely courted the Republicans, eventually won a massive bipartisan victory without compromising any significant provisions of the historic law. In fact, it became stronger as it moved through Congress. It included a broad prohibition against discrimination in federally funded institutions, which had been strongly advocated by the NAACP and Congressman Adam Clayton Powell (D-NY), and mandated sanctions for violators.

The Civil Rights Act, as enforced by the Johnson administration and supported by the Warren Court, transformed southern schools after many generations of absolute segregation and a decade of failure by the courts to implement the *Brown* decision. It produced major breakthroughs in bringing black students into public universities in the nineteen states with historically segregated systems. In just a few years' time under the act, the South went from almost complete segregation into being the region with the most integrated schools. That pattern represented deep change that lasted for more than four decades (Orfield and Frankenburg 2014).[5] This happened within five years of the act's passage, with almost no physical coercion. There was a substantial decline in educational achievement gaps in the following years, something not seen in recent decades.

The 1964 Civil Rights Act brought federal education officials and the U.S. Justice Department into the center of policy making for access to schools, created the first legal framework to address Hispanic educational inequality, and produced some of the largest education-related changes in U.S. history. Policies and enforcement actions under the act guided the federal courts as they moved from gradual, token desegregation to a mandate of full and immediate integration by the end of the 1960s. The law powerfully affected the desegregation of southern schools and created the first legal framework for dealing with higher education desegregation. Contrary to widespread beliefs, the desegregation achieved during this period was lasting, and the desegregation of black students continued to rise through the Reagan administration. Serious resegregation began only after a transformed 1990s-era Supreme Court issued three major decisions authorizing a return to neighborhood schools, which produced a steady increase in segregated education (Boger and Orfield 2005; Orfield and Eaton 1996).

The civil rights law came under strong attack in both the executive branch and the courts during the conservative period of the 1970s and 1980s and again under both Bush presidents, but it survived and was reinforced by the Civil Rights Restoration Act of 1987, passed over President Reagan's veto, in which Congress restored and strengthened the reach of the law after a negative Supreme Court interpretation in *Grove City College v. Bell*, 465 U.S. 555 (1984). The 1964 law also led to a decades-long battle over the desegregation and equalization of higher education in the South. It provided the legal basis when the Supreme Court upheld federal authority to protect education rights for non-English-speaking children in *Lau v. Nichols*, 414 U.S. 563 (1974), a decision resting directly on Title VI of the 1964 law. It also provided the lever to force the desegregation of school faculties and to improve equity within schools. It led to research and data collection on race and national-origin issues in the United States that had been largely unavailable; such data, which continues to be collected, helps empower communities to make demands for change.

A law, of course, cannot be better than its enforcement. The Nixon administration virtually ceased administrative enforcement of the act, but the federal courts in *Adams v. Richardson*, 356 F. Supp. 92 (D.D.C. 1973), the first of many decisions on this question, found the Nixon administration to be blatantly violating the law and ordered resumption of enforcement in schools and colleges, a struggle that continued for fifteen years as courts worked to force the executive branch to implement the law. This extraordinary judicial intervention in executive-branch operations was based on the strong mandatory language in the law. Although federal courts usually give agencies great discretion in administering complex laws, in rulings in 1972 and 1973 a federal district court and a circuit court of appeals found the Nixon administration to be violating the law in hundreds of districts and ordered that the enforcement process be restarted. The court of appeals found that the Department of Health, Education and Welfare (HEW) was "actively supplying segregated institutions with federal funds, contrary to the expressed purpose of Congress" (480 F.2d 1159 [156 U.S.App.D.C. 267]), and ordered the department to set strict deadlines for compliance. The court decisions led the Carter administration to issue standards for the desegregation of higher education in the South.

Throughout five Republican administrations, the Justice Department and the Education Department's Office for Civil Rights reversed policies meant for enforcing the Civil Rights Act, but the enforcement authority available to these departments under the act remained largely intact, except for mandatory urban desegregation plans.[6] The White House worked successfully to transform the federal judiciary, which eventually changed the interpretation of the law.

The central provisions of the Civil Rights Act authorized the Department of Justice to file civil rights lawsuits and prohibited discrimination in federal education programs.[7] The act was written to engage the administrative and financial power and expertise of the federal government on behalf of equal opportunity for schooling. Before the act, a handful of private civil rights lawyers, against overwhelming odds, confronted the resources of fiercely resistant state and local governments. The NAACP and African American leaders in Congress proposed denying federal grants to school systems that were defying the constitutional requirements. Such measures were considered so certain to doom even modest education proposals into the early 1960s that President Kennedy successfully appealed to African American leaders to drop the issue.[8] The 1964 law went much further, mandating compliance with civil rights law for all federal programs, and serious mandatory sanctions for violations. Where there has been vigorous enforcement, there has been major, measurable change. When enforcement ended, the momentum of change slowed, and in some cases reversed. The partial revival of enforcement during the Obama administration shows that the law still has power (Blum 2011; U.S. Department of Education 2011).[9]

The Civil Rights Act addressed educational issues from many directions. In addition to enforcement authority, it provided for the following:

- Research, including a national study and report to Congress on school desegregation, and a four-year extension and broadening of the Civil Rights Commission
- Technical assistance and teacher training to ease the transition to deseg-regated schools (Title IV)
- Community conciliation and help in dealing with racial tensions associated with desegregation through establishment of the Community Relations Service (Title X)
- Federal prohibition of job discrimination (Title VII), which did not originally apply to teachers and principals but did after the law was strengthened in 1972.

Data, Research, and Accountability

Many types of data now used routinely to measure the racial composition or racial change of schools and other institutions did not exist before the Civil Rights Act led to the collection of consistent national data on race and ethnicity. Before the act, few school districts reported racial composition or other related data at the school level. A limited amount of southern segregation data was collected by a private association of southern journalists, the Race Relations Reporting Service. It was not until 1967 that basic school racial data, including data on Hispanic students, was collected nationwide. Without this information, it is impossible to know how the nation's schools and colleges are dealing with racial matters or to systematically monitor school district behavior or racial achievement gaps. Though severely challenged at times, this framework of racial information has survived and was actually expanded in the NCLB.

Broader Impacts

In addition to the direct effects of the Civil Rights Act, there have also been a number of indirect and spinoff effects likely related to it. School desegregation plans, for instance, can have effects on the educational gap between white and minority students, residential choice and the stability of integrated neighborhoods, the college careers of students, and adult attitudes toward students attending integrated schools (Hawley et al. 1983). College desegregation may also have a number of strong impacts (Thomas, McPartland, and Gottfredson 1981, 336–356).[10] There are also strong assertions and complex research findings on the impact of bilingual education, the misassignment of minority students to classes for the developmentally disabled, unequal expulsion practices, and other issues subject to regulation under the Civil Rights Act (Arias and Casanova 1993; Losen and Orfield 2002; Meier and England 1989; Meier and Stewart 1991). In other words, many long-term economic and social consequences of educational policies may ultimately derive from the implementation of the 1964 law. Experiences growing out of Title IV technical assistance for desegregation and out of the Community Relations Service conflict resolution provisions set the stage for the policies on human-relations training for school staffs and on multiethnic curricula that became widespread under the Emergency School Aid Act of 1972. That federal desegregation aid program demonstrated significant benefits both in race relations and academic achievement before it was repealed in the early months of the Reagan administration (Wellish et al. 1976).

School Desegregation

Desegregation merits close attention because, despite skepticism, it is perhaps the clearest documented example of a major Great Society policy with a serious long-term impact on educational equity. This outcome may be attributable to the fact that it provided students with access to better teachers and courses and higher-achieving classmates, factors that appear to influence school outcomes more than financial resources or the accountability reforms in place since 1980. When the civil rights bill went to Congress in 1963, schools in the South remained extremely segregated, and problems associated with school segregation outside the South had barely been explored. In the eleven states of the former Confederacy, less than 1 percent of black students were in desegregated schools (U.S. Civil Rights Commission 1964, 291). Gains were already apparent in the fall of 1964 (*Southern Education Report* 1966).

After the Johnson administration issued guidelines and the federal government began funding-cutoff proceedings against scores of districts that refused to comply with orders to desegregate, virtually all southern districts began desegregation by 1965. That fall, 6 percent of black southern students were in integrated schools, and the rate of change was accelerating both in the South and in the border states (Orfield 1969). Most southern school districts complied with what the strictest federal courts were requiring.

Federal officials defined the goal of the *Brown* decision in a way that was ultimately adopted by the Supreme Court, namely, by requiring actual integration, not small transfer programs. From the spring of 1964 to the fall of 1966, the percentage of southern black students attending other than all-black schools had increased almost 1,400 percent, and most schools in the South had begun faculty integration, then considered a radical change (Orfield 1969). Although the courts had failed for a decade, the administration produced tough standards that they embraced and continued to enforce as constitutional minimums for decades. In May 1968, a unanimous Supreme Court adopted this approach: "The burden on a school board today is to come forward with a plan which promises realistically to work and promises realistically to work *now*."[11] Segregated systems had to be changed "root and branch" and the schools integrated along a number of dimensions with no further delay. That decision remains in effect to this day as a remedy for illegal segregation, though later decisions encouraged courts to end desegregation plans after a period of years. The Civil Rights Act of 1964 changed the South, in many ways irreversibly. As late as 2004, the South had the nation's most integrated schools—and though integration was far below its peak, the region is very far from returning to the kind of absolute segregation that existed before the Civil Rights Act. Many researchers have pointed to black access to better-integrated schools as a basic reason for the dramatic closing of the achievement gap for a generation between whites and blacks in the region where most blacks live (Grissmer and Flanagan 2000, 55–56).

Enforcement of the act varied drastically over time. Nixon tried to shut down administrative enforcement. The Carter administration modestly revived enforcement. Its Justice Department changed the position of the government substantially in some of the old cases on the Justice docket, and some of the cases represented important new initiatives. The government filed its first city-suburban desegregation cases. But the Reagan administration launched a determined governmental attack on urban school-desegregation standards, supporting local school districts wishing to return to neighborhood schools. The Reagan administration's solicitor general, the conservative Harvard Law professor Charles Fried, noted that some of his administration's positions were so extreme that he could not support them (Fried 1991). The Reagan administration and both Bush administrations appointed federal civil rights officials who fought school desegregation, the integration of higher education, and affirmative action. Though the Civil Rights Act was still on the books, its implementation was closely linked to politics, particularly after the GOP adopted the Southern Strategy and the white South became the most important base of a party that often controlled the executive branch and broke the long Democratic lock on the House majority.[12]

Enduring School Desegregation

Statistics from the South show the powerful impact of the period of active enforcement of civil rights laws in the southern and border states. That impact reached its high point more than a quarter century ago. Since that time, there has been no additional progress and there has been significant resegregation (see table 7.1). During this period, the population of Hispanics in the nation's schools has increased rapidly, and their segregation has become significantly more severe in all regions as the *barrios* grew and there was no desegregation policy. The Supreme Court belatedly recognized the right of Hispanic students to attend desegregated schools in *Keyes v. School District No. 1*, 413 U.S. 189 (1973), but neither the Nixon administration nor its successors made any serious effect to enforce the decision, whose reach was gravely limited the next year by a Supreme Court decision protecting the suburbs of metropolitan areas from desegregation. Two Supreme Court decisions in the 1990s authorizing a return to segregated neighborhood schools, and one in 2007 strictly limiting many common forms of voluntary integration and magnet school plans, came during this period of continuous resegregation.

The most dramatic change in segregation levels for any region occurred in the South between 1965 and 1970. It had a clear and obvious relationship to federal policy. This was the impact of the Civil Rights Act and the Johnson administration's enforcement. There was no Supreme Court ruling on Hispanic segregation until after this era. Latino segregation increased steadily in all portions of the country with substantial Hispanic populations, except Colorado and Nevada (probably a result of court orders in Denver and Las Vegas). The Nixon administration's Office for Civil Rights explicitly decided to pursue bilingual education rather than desegregation. By the late 1980s, Latinos were significantly more segregated than African Americans.

It is very likely that without the federal push for desegregation of black

Table 7.1. Southern black students in majority-white schools, selected years, 1954–2005 (%)

Year	%	Year	%
1954	0.0	1988	43.5
1960	0.1	1991[a]	39.2
1964	2.3	1998	32.7
1968	23.4	2000	31.0
1970	33.1	2005	27.0
1980	37.1	2011	23.3

Source: Southern Education Reporting Service (Sarratt 1966, 362); HEW press release, May 27, 1968; OCR data tapes; NCES CommonCore of Data statistics, 1991–2005; Orfield and Frankenburg 2014.
[a]The Supreme Court accepted resegregation.

students and without the litigation following the busing decisions, as well as the enactment of President Johnson's fair housing bill in 1968, the general pattern of growing segregation that affected Hispanics would have been present in the black community as well. The substantial increase in the number of predominantly minority central-city school systems and the outward expansion of ghettos during the period were forces working in that direction. When the courts ended desegregation plans in the 1990s, school segregation in the South grew rapidly (Boger and Orfield 2005).

The gains were large and long-lasting, even in the face of strong opposition from several administrations, and levels of segregation today are far lower than those that existed before LBJ's reforms. His administration made the totally segregated region of the country better than the rest for generations. When he acted on civil rights, virtually no whites in the South had gone to school with black classmates. When Barack Obama ran for president and carried several southern states, millions of whites had grown up in integrated schools.

Before the Johnson administration, no serious federal research had been conducted on race relations, and little on poverty in schools, and no programs helped schools deal with race relations and effective integration. The Civil Rights Act and the funding decisions made by research offices of the Johnson administration provided help for planning desegregation and training teachers and staff. It also helped create university-based centers to advise school systems.

College Desegregation

Though the 1964 Civil Rights Act applied to colleges, the distinctive nature of colleges and college-enrollment decisions created special problems in the nineteen states with black colleges, which clearly violated the constitutional prohibition against de jure segregation. Despite the overwhelmingly white student bodies at the flagship campuses of state university systems, very little was done. The impetus for a serious enforcement effort came when a federal court found HEW guilty of nonenforcement of the Civil Rights Act in higher education and set deadlines for the development of statewide college desegregation plans. In 1964, at least 97 percent of the black students in five southern states were attending black colleges. More than three-fourths of all southern black collegians were in segregated institutions in every southern state. A federal district court ruled in November 1972 that the Nixon administration had failed to enforce the law in ten states, and the judge set deadlines for new state desegregation plans or initiation of funding-cutoff proceedings.[13] The court ordered stronger standards in 1977 (*Fairfax* 1978, 36). The Reagan administration abandoned this approach (U.S. Department of Justice 1981), but the court rejected the Reagan policies and required plans showing substantial desegregation progress.[14] But an increasingly conservative Supreme Court decided *Allen v. Wright*, 468 U.S. 737 (1984), to limit the right to sue federal agencies over the nonenforcement of antidiscrimination policies, which led the lower courts to drop the case. The Reagan plan went forward.

Before the Civil Rights Act, higher education systems in a number of southern states were almost completely segregated. On a standard measure of segregation—the dissimilarity index or desegregation index, a measure in which 100 means absolute segregation among the various campuses and 0 would mean no segregation—a random distribution of students in which each campus would reflect the statewide percentages of students of different races, the indices for southern systems were near 100. By 1980, they were about as segregated as those in the rest of the country, even through the South had considerably higher percentages of black students. Their levels of integration continued to rise until about 2000, when significant resegregation began to occur (Litolff 2007). It seems likely that these results reflect the impact of the Civil Rights Act and the court orders and administrative enforcement that led to desegregation plans in all states with a history of segregation by law. In spite of a complex and inconsistent history, the law created significant progress. By 1976, for example, black students in community colleges in the South were less segregated than any other region (Thomas, McPartland, and Gottfredson 1981, 339–340). Between the 1975–1976 academic year and the 1980–1981 academic year, the percentage of southern black graduates receiving BA degrees from predominantly white institutions climbed from 32.1 to 41.2 percent, and the number receiving degrees at these institutions grew by almost a third, much more rapidly than the growth in white colleges outside the South. As the years passed, these trends continued, and the leading public universities, the institutions that trained most of the leadership in most states, became substantially integrated. Since most African Americans have always lived in the South, these were very important changes.

Latino Education

Right out of college, Lyndon Johnson taught poor Mexican American children, and he often talked about this experience and the conditions in which the children lived. Though their numbers were still small outside the Southwest, and the U.S. Census did not undertake a national count of Hispanics until 1980, the Civil Rights Act and an amendment to the Elementary and Secondary Education Act became important forces in Latino education.[15] The Civil Rights Act created the legal basis for bilingual education, which remains a continuing issue in Latino education. Some early bilingual efforts received funds from the antipoverty program and from Title I of the ESEA. The modest Bilingual Education Act was added to the ESEA in 1968, and its limited funds spurred interest in the field and helped initiate the training of professionals and the recruitment of Hispanic teachers and school staff members. The Nixon administration used the Civil Rights Act prohibition on national-origin discrimination as the basis for a 1970 memorandum requiring districts to provide education that met the needs of Spanish-speaking children, emphasizing bilingual approaches. In 1974 the Supreme Court recognized and upheld HEW's authority to regulate in this area under Title VI of the Civil Rights Act in *Lau v. Nichols*. In 1975, the Office for Civil Rights published the "Lau Remedies," which spelled out the standards that districts were supposed to meet in bilingual programs; it became the dominant enforcement tool for the remainder of the decade. The regulations led to programs across the country, a large demand for teachers trained in bilingual education, state laws and policies supporting the goal, and a change in the educational experience of many hundreds of thousands of children (U.S. Department of Health, Education and Welfare 1975). The Nixon, Ford, and Carter administrations encouraged this approach; but it faced strong opposition during the Reagan administration, which cut funding and encouraged other approaches.

Bilingual education was eliminated from the Elementary and Secondary Education Act when it became NCLB in 2001. Nonetheless, important ideas had been developed, a new profession fostered, and attention focused on an urgent problem. Although some critical states, including California, repealed their laws on bilingual education during this period, and three states adopted referenda banning bilingual education, the basic idea of bilingual education policy survived in a diminished form, and there is increasing evidence that it offered a better chance for non-English-speaking students in a country where a tenth of students now fall into that category and experience severe difficulties in school (Gándara and Hopkins 2010).

Creating a New Federal Role: The Legislative Triumphs of 1965

After his great electoral victory, LBJ, who had won passage of the Civil Rights Act and the antipoverty program in 1964, appointed a secret task force with broad authority to propose whatever was necessary to institute major federal aid to the public schools. Congress was likewise working on issues that had been stalemated since World War II. Eager to make large changes, Johnson wanted fast action. He eschewed ideological positions in favor of pragmatic policies that would equalize educational opportunity—changes that education experts believed would work and could be made into law. Nothing like Johnson's task-force approach to major education policy changes would happen during the next half century—the Reagan and George W. Bush initiatives were far more ideological and much less connected with the education profession. Johnson saw his job as breaking the barriers, making political judgments, getting things going, trying to maintain successes, and acting quickly on many fronts. As a former legislator, he knew that once a program became established, it developed a constituency that would fight to maintain and expand it.

For the education bill there was a prestigious task force headed by John Gardner, a leading foundation executive whom Johnson would later appoint secretary of the Department of Health, Education and Welfare, and an administration task force. The recommendations, which included strong congressional input, were taken seriously. This is in striking contrast to the other genuinely influential initiatives that were pursued in the succeeding decades. The Reagan report *A Nation at Risk*, which launched the massive focus on standards and testing that prevailed for the next three decades, was a dramatic, short public report full of major errors and inaccurate conclusions.[16] The NCLB, negotiated between congressional leaders and the George W. Bush White House, almost totally ignored education research and the advice of leaders in the field, rejecting analyses (which proved accurate) that the central accountability mechanism was so flawed that it would brand the vast majority of U.S. schools as failures by 2013 (Berliner and Biddle 1995; DeBray 2006).

Johnson wasted no time after his election. In his state of the union address on January 4, 1965, Johnson said, "We do not intend to live in the midst of abundance, isolated from neighbors, confined in blighted cities and bleak suburbs, stunted by a poverty of learning and an emptiness of leisure." He promised "a program in education to ensure every American child the fullest development of his mind and skills." While there was a great deal to do, he said, "We begin with learning," and he wanted to begin immediately, at all levels. He called for preschool education, aid to "public schools serving low-income families," and scholarships and loans to make college possible for students without money to pay. He knew schools by themselves were not enough; he already had the War on Poverty and civil rights enforcement in motion, and Medicaid was on the front burner. He had urban policy plans for the improved development of "entire metropolitan areas" (Johnson 1965, 4–7). But education was at the center.

A week after the address, Congress received his education message, "Toward Full Educational Opportunity." Recognizing that education "is primarily a state function," he said that the federal role was to see to it that there was a "basic floor under these essential services for all adults and children" (Johnson 1965, 26). At that time, he said, "almost half of our school districts conduct no kindergarten classes," and out of 26,000 school districts, only about 100 had any kind of preschool education. So the president proposed expanding Head Start, which had began in his first year in office. His central proposal was "a major program of assistance to . . . schools servicing children of low-income families" (27). This was to be the first major program of federal aid to schools across the country in American history.

Johnson called for more education at all levels and for expanded opportunities for those excluded by race or poverty. The legislation came fast and on many fronts. It wasn't all fully thought-through, and policies were shaped, in part, by strategies for overcoming barriers in Congress.

The president was injecting government into many areas where there were obvious needs but little knowledge about what would work. He tried to do it through a flawed system of state and local institutions that ran the schools and employed almost all the educators. Not long after his triumphs, he faced bitter opposition. Knowing that that always happened to presidents, he was intensely focused on getting everything he could enacted into law. Despite the incredible speed of his legislative operation—even as he was getting Medicare and Medicaid enacted, the war in Vietnam was taking shape, and Martin Luther King's Selma-to-Montgomery voting rights march led him to successfully push for the epic Voting Rights Act—the education legislation was his first priority and central to his vision. Much of what his administration and Congress built so quickly turned out to be durable, shaping important parts of the nation's educational policy for the next half century.

Johnson often talked about his experience as a teacher, a principal, an education lobbyist in the state capital, and a director of a youth program for poor young people during the Great Depression. In contrast to the long-held conservative idea that the federal government had no role in education, or to the "blame the schools and teachers" policies that would come along in the Reagan era, he had a positive view of schools, the teaching profession, and the families who were struggling to improve their kids' chances in life. In addition, he had a practical sense about the kind of people who ran schools and districts and about the limits of the federal role. Acutely aware of the race and class dimensions of unequal educational opportunity, he strongly supported a wide variety of strategies—educational, antipoverty, and civil rights—to improve opportunities for poor and minority children. He knew that good ideas counted for nothing if he couldn't get the votes he needed in Congress, and no president had more experience in that line of work. Knowing how Congress members thought, he was willing to meet their political needs, encourage and pressure them, and win their support.

A quarter century of watching division and committee barriers make it impossible for Congress to respond to urgent educational needs made Johnson eager to forge a decisive breakthrough while he had a huge congressional majority and public support. The system works well to create large new policies only when one party with the same goals has dominant control of both elected branches of government and when the judicial system will, at a minimum, not undermine its efforts. Johnson enjoyed the most favorable conditions for progressive legislation between the New Deal and the present. With strong liberals in charge of the education committees in both the House and the Senate, along with the votes to override the House Rules Committee, he had a unique chance if he could overcome the deep division between parochial-school advocates and defenders of separation of church and state within the Democratic Party (Fenno 1963, 195–235).

The school bill was a masterpiece of balance. Aid was concentrated not on schools but on very poor children (with family incomes under $2,000). The law was drawn, however, so that all congressional districts and a great many schools would get some money, though schools of concentrated poverty would get more. The law was intended to strengthen the receiving schools, not regulate them. It required no specific educational approaches or assessments, but included a long and broad list of eligible expenditures. It provided significant aid in the form of services, books, and the like for poor children in religious schools, but not so much that public school advocates could not accept it in return for the much larger funds they were to receive. Rather than running over the tradition-bound state departments of education, it provided money to strengthen and professionalize them. The book and library forces were cheered by substantial new funds for educational resources. And there was Title III, which provided unprecedented funds for federal officials to initiate major educational experiments. Since the law's funding favored poor kids, it sent a great deal of money into core inner-city and rural southern districts, many of them Democratic Party strongholds. LBJ and his staff negotiated acceptance from the forces that had blocked previous efforts (Jeffrey 1978, 59–91).

Winning Federal Aid

Because President Johnson's telephone calls were secretly recorded, we can listen in to his conversations on the education bill, which show his consistent intensity for education reform. He saw his education bill as the centerpiece of his legislative agenda and believed that the entire Great Society program was at risk if he didn't win quickly. The principal threat was the matter of aid to Catholic schools, an issue that deeply split the Democratic Party's northern urban and conservative southern Protestant constituencies as well as advocacy groups representing public and Catholic schools. Johnson's drive was to provide enough aid to satisfy the Catholic hierarchy and to move the bill quickly enough to prevent mobilization of the demands of urban Democrats for more direct aid, which would be unacceptable to other groups and perhaps unconstitutional. The parochial schools, for example, would get books, but they would be owned by the public schools and "lent" to the religious schools. Johnson insisted, "We're going to give it to kids," he said, "whether they are black or Mexican or Catholic or Protestant."[17] This political problem shaped important aspects of the legislation that have lasted almost a half century. Rather than aiding schools directly, the theory was to provide aid for poor children so that it would not look like aid to religious institutions.

LBJ believed that he had to achieve political momentum in Congress with the education bill. "We got to pass it, that's number one." If he got education, then he was more likely to get his big Medicare bill. "The first thing I want is legislation."[18] "If they beat that education bill we've had it." This is the bill, he repeated; "everything else is secondary."[19] LBJ put constant pressure on the House, where the Democratic divisions were most serious, to enact the bill at what amounted to congressional light speed in early 1965. Under intense White House pressure on the House Education Committee chair, the bill was rushed through that committee and the Rules Committee and then sped to the House floor, where it had a resounding victory. In the Senate, the Democratic majority passed the Elementary and Secondary Education Act without changing a word, avoiding the endless possibilities of delay and division in a chamber where delay and obfuscation were typical. Since there was such a fierce rush to get the law through, and since the administration was orchestrating a hurricane of legislative activity involving health care, voting rights, and immigration reform, it is not surprising that the senators were willing to sacrifice their traditional role on this measure in order to achieve a historic breakthrough.

By the end of 1965, an enduring framework of education policy from prekindergarten through college was in place. Johnson loved to talk about the number of new education bills he had passed. The number was huge, twenty by one count, and many of them would have been seen as substantial accomplishments in other administrations. In the Great Society, however, attention on education-specific measures focused on the two game-changing laws, the ESEA and the Higher Education Act of 1965, laws that deeply altered the role of the federal government in education for generations. The ESEA was an elemental change in American education; it attracted a great deal of attention as it moved through Congress and has remained significant. The Higher Education Act, much less controversial, moved the federal government into an even deeper role, since it tried to separate income and wealth from college opportunity and to make higher education far more dependent on federal aid than the public schools for the portion of the total cost that was federally funded. These education bills were seen by the president and his staff as closely related to the civil rights and antipoverty laws and programs. Johnson did not share the assumption of the Reagan reforms and the NCLB that school policy by itself could dramatically change outcomes. It was no accident that both the public school and higher education reforms were built around alleviating the effects of family and community poverty on educational opportunity.

A New Federal Role in Higher Education

The Higher Education Act faced less public scrutiny than the ESEA, and its road to enactment was less direct. Substantial congressional input allowed compromises to be worked out with higher education constituencies. The draft bill and the president's message went to Congress in January 1965, followed by extensive hearings. A conference committee met to resolve differences between the House and Senate versions. The bill was finally enacted with a variety of modifications in late October 1965.

As with the ESEA, the central focus was on students, not institutions. The basic goal was to help students go to college who otherwise would be unable to do so. The major problems in passing the bill largely concerned battles between public and private colleges (the private sector is much larger in higher education) about how the formulas would work and how much money would go to institutions rather than students. An important 1961 study by Alice Rivlin, *The Role of the Federal Government in Financing Higher Education*, concluded that although there were many important reasons to expand the role of the federal government in supporting higher education, there was no agreement on the basic guidelines of what a good policy would be. Should the aid go to the institutions or the students? If to institutions, for what purpose and how should private institutions be supported? If to students—to how many, chosen by what means, with what choice of colleges they could attend, for how much of their costs, and so on. Rivlin noted many arguments for and against various solutions, and her analysis recommended only a modest scholarship program with relatively low awards to students with high scores and high need (Rivlin 1961, ch. 8). The act, however, set higher-education policy on a different course.

The 1965 act provided temporary institutional funding, but its core and enduring features focused primarily on need-based grants and guaranteed loans. In addition, it set up special assistance for historically black colleges and universities. These three features have endured, despite being modified substantially and subjected to fluctuations in budgetary resources according to the ideology and fiscal constraints of succeeding administrations. Though the aid went to individual students, it was extremely important to their institutions, since it made it possible for more qualified low-income students to attend without compelling colleges to provide full scholarships, thereby increasing their market and tuition revenue and lowering their costs. The Higher Education Act had a number of provisions directing aid to colleges, but those were minor and did not become part of the backbone of long-term federal aid policy. The significant policies were those that provided need-based scholarships to students whose families could not afford to send them to college, as well as subsidized and guaranteed students loans to families with higher incomes who needed help paying for college.

Republicans had historically opposed direct federal scholarships in favor of tuition tax credits that would offset families' college expenses by cutting their federal taxes. Tuition tax credits or deductions favor families with enough income and wealth to file long-form tax returns (a relatively small minority of taxpayers), because they allow those families to be reimbursed for some of their tuition costs. For those who owe no taxes because their income is low, or who file short-form returns, there is no subsidy—and for those low-income families who cannot afford to front the money for college, their children cannot go.

The Higher Education Act set two essential pieces of the compromise that have lasted for nearly a half century. The federal government would support students through a combination of grants to poor students and guaranteed loans for those from more favorable circumstances still needing money. The loan programs offered private banks the ability to receive a risk-free return on the loans at a tidy profit. From the Johnson administration's standpoint, it was invaluable to have the support of the bankers and to lower the immediate federal budget cost to almost nothing before the loans were made, and then to include only the annual-interest subsidies. The costs eventually ballooned as public funding for colleges declined sharply, which has caused college costs to rise much faster than family income since 1980.

The Higher Education Act was strengthened, and its basic purposes were institutionalized, by the 1972 amendments, whose principal author was Senator Claiborne Pell (D-RI). That legislation built on the 1965 law and set clear guidelines for an expanding system of student aid. That rapid expansion of student aid, along with persisting low tuition, the rapid growth of campuses, and affirmative action for college admissions, created what may have been the best opportunities ever for going to college regardless of a student's income or wealth. At their peak, Pell Grants paid about 60 percent of recipients' average cost of college. The Pell Grant, which runs through the regular appropriations cycle, does not automatically increase with the cost of college, so its real value has dropped dramatically, starting with severe cuts in the Reagan years, even as college tuition soared (Johnstone 1986, 126–142). In contrast, the tax subsidies for tuition were increased substantially during the Clinton administration as the Democratic Party shifted from trying to alleviate poverty to addressing the concerns of the middle class, which became much more severe as college costs rose too rapidly for families to manage them (Morris 1999, 223–225, 627).[20] The continuing vitality of these issues was apparent very early in the Obama administration, which increased the maximum amount of the Pell Grant and lowered the cost of federal student aid by bypassing bankers and providing direct federal loans, thus eliminating expensive middlemen. On the student aid front, the Obama administration won a large temporary growth of need-based aid, which, unfortunately, coincided with large increases in college costs caused by sharp cutbacks in state funding for public colleges during and after the Great Recession that began in 2008. President Obama's agreement with Congress to forestall a government shutdown in 2011 included some cuts to Pell Grant funding.

The Johnson initiatives are important because they created the basic formula for university–federal government relations and the aid that has helped millions of students attend college. The idea that federal aid should be centered on students rather than institutions has been maintained. These increasingly costly programs, however, have been strongly battered and reshaped periodically by the political winds of federal and state politics as the financial barriers to college have risen—and as federal aid has fallen far short of creating equal access to college, though it did make major gains for a decade and more. The rapid actions of the Obama administration show that it is still possible to recapture parts of the Great Society vision. The fact that the federal government has been paying up to a fourth of the total cost of higher education relates directly to LBJ's initiatives. The shortfalls of these programs relate strongly to the most important conservative successes—long-lasting cuts in federal and state tax revenue and major increases in incarceration costs, which have resulted in lower public support for higher education and soaring tuition. The other massive burden on state governments results from another Johnson initiative, Medicaid, which provides medical care to the poor without effective cost-control measures.

From the perspective of the 1960s, current college costs are unimaginable, as is the share of the costs being borne by students and their families. The Higher Education Act ushered in a period of remarkable increase in college opportunities and resources for colleges and universities, but its ongoing power was limited by massive policy and tax changes beginning in the 1980s and large continuous tuition increases as states cut higher education funding. As the costs soared, Pell Grants and guaranteed loans were often insufficient to pay for four-year colleges, but covered the tuition in mushrooming community colleges. The basic ideas raised in 1965, however, are still at the center of the policy debate.

The 1960s saw the baby boomers enter college. Students born during the first postwar year, 1946, were going to college in 1964, with millions following. During the 1960s, enrollment grew an astonishing 120 percent, reflecting not only the population boom but also an increase from 24 to 35 percent in college attendance. About three-fourths of students (74 percent) were in public colleges, and only a fourth attended community colleges (Snyder 1993, 66). The federal government was a minor source of funding for higher education until World War II, when there were massive outlays for research, war-related training, and the GI Bill. The federal share then fell to 14 percent in the mid-1950s. It rose sharply in the 1960s as the higher-education enterprise was mushrooming, reaching a high point of about a fourth of the total. During the conservative 1980s, however, it fell to about a tenth (71–72). Johnson-sponsored legislation helped the system grow dramatically. During this period, the United States led the world in access to higher education. It has declined dramatically in the OECD ratings as other nations have boosted their completion rates much higher than those in the United States.[21]

It would take a long and complex book to give even general descriptions of all the educational and education-related reforms enacted in the Great Society's legislative flood, to say nothing of tracing their lasting impact, so this analysis touches on only a few great landmarks of those laws. The greatest of the education laws was the Elementary and Secondary Education Act, but important and lasting education programs were also created by the War on Poverty legislation in 1964. The Higher Education Act deeply altered the relationship between the federal government, the nation's students, and the colleges and universities. The 1964 Civil Rights Act brought about the most important expansion of minority education rights since the adoption of the Thirteenth and Fourteenth Amendments following the Civil War, and its impact has lasted for a far longer period. Though the overall poverty program ended in the 1980s, its key educational innovations live on. Each of these laws, which were passed in an amazing two-year period, has had long-lasting impacts on American education and society.

After the Political Tide Turned

President Johnson's education agenda was enacted with a huge congressional majority, and there was money to spend in a prosperous time. By 1966, the costs of the Vietnam War were exploding; taxes were going up as a result; anger about urban riots was growing; white resistance to desegregation efforts in the cities stiffened; the black power movement was splitting up the civil rights constituency and alienating the public with talk of violence; and the budget was threatening to go out of balance. Johnson continued to have an ambitious program of reforms, but nothing in education that could compare to what was accomplished in 1964 and 1965.

After a severe loss of congressional Democrats in the 1966 midterm elections, there were no more massive educational reforms. Johnson's goal was "to get . . . the programs we have already passed funded, and try to get them organized and executed in the proper manner" (Johnson 1966, 1378). There were many skirmishes to keep his programs intact and create roots around the country to sustain them for the future. Each year there were bitter fights over congressional efforts to cut back the Civil Rights Act and to try to limit the Supreme Court's efforts on school desegregation, but they were defeated until Nixon took office. Even in his last year, Johnson managed to enact the third of his great civil rights acts, the Fair Housing Act, which, if seriously enforced, might have opened good schools across the country to black and Latino children. He signed the largest subsidized-housing law in U.S. history, ending the construction of high-rise projects and providing vouchers for poor families to move into decent private-sector housing. The Nixon administration turned back these reforms.

Did the Johnson Education Reforms Work?

Lyndon Johnson hoped he was setting in motion a train of social and educational reforms that could end poverty and create more equal opportunity in American society. Instead, his was the last activist liberal administration for generations. On some fronts, particularly in civil rights, a serious counterattack began even before he left office. The only Democratic presidents during the next half century were moderates with limited education agendas and no serious civil rights or urban reform proposals. In the 1980s, the aspirations of government and its commitment to domestic reform shrank dramatically, tax cuts slashed public funds, and education reform turned away from issues of equity across race and class lines even in the Clinton and Obama administrations. Democratic presidents talked about the middle class, rarely about the poor, and tried to avoid the issue of race. The classic claim of the conservative movement was that government had tried to do too much in the 1960s, that the programs had failed, that government could do little to change inequality, and that too much government was counter-productive. What was needed were higher standards, more accountability for schools and teachers, and more competition from charter schools.

To a certain extent, the Johnson reforms were moves into unknown territory. Knowledge about the effects of educational reforms in the Johnson era was limited, and the government was trying to do things it had never done before. An unprecedented and highly influential national study commissioned by Congress as part of the 1964 Civil Rights Act surprised the nation by showing that, in general, schools had much more limited impacts on test scores than had been widely assumed and that there was little relationship between per-student spending and educational outcomes. This 1966 report, *Equality of Educational Opportunity*, widely known as the Coleman Report, found that students' social background was more powerful than the schools in affecting test scores, and that the major influence from schools came from the social background of the other students and the test scores of the teachers—two factors much more likely to be changed for nonwhite students by desegregation than by compensatory education. It and many subsequent studies showed that the impact of schools was stronger on students from poor families than on those from the middle class. When the first major evaluations of Title I, Head Start, and other programs were undertaken, the results tended to confirm the findings of the Coleman Report, showing no significant difference in test scores directly linked to the programs.

By the time of the Nixon administration, the disappointing results were being used to argue against funding for the programs, or to argue in favor of cuts to them. Some historians, including Hugh Davis Graham, in his widely cited *The Uncertain Triumph: Federal Education Policy in the Kennedy and Johnson Years* (1984), reach the same conclusion based on such data. But the long-term comparison of outcomes of the Great Society reforms with those of the conservative reforms shows a very different story, as does a focus on nontest outcomes, such as rates of high school graduation and college entrance.

A first step in evaluating the Johnson administration's education reforms is to think about what they were designed to accomplish. It is not fair to judge a reform a failure for not doing what it was not intended to do. Many evaluations assumed that the ESEA was a federal reform program for poor kids, an educational treatment operated by or through the federal government. It is very clear, however, in both the official documents concerning the ESEA and in the words of the law, that it was not about implementing any coherent, measurable program. In fact, such an approach would have been anathema in that period of profound opposition to federal control of education. All the documents recognize that explicitly. The law specifically authorizes use of funds for a wide variety of programs to be chosen by state and local recipients. There was no significant accountability system. The law was designed to find a legal and political formula for transferring resources from the federal government to thousands of American schools, making more money available to areas and schools with greater concentrations of poor families. It was designed to increase the capacity of the educational institutions and to focus their attention especially on poor schools and children. Though it never amounted to more than a small percentage of the nation's education spending, it contributed a much larger percentage to poor schools in very poor states and cities. Many supporters of the law saw it as an indirect way to achieve the longtime liberal goal of general aid to education.

The purpose of the law was described in broad and sweeping terms in a Senate committee report on the bill. (Committee reports on enacted bills are taken very seriously by administrators and courts in defining the purposes of legislation, and this was especially true in the Senate, since the Senate passed the House bill rapidly, with relatively little record). The Senate report said that school districts could use the money for "programs and projects which will meet the educational needs of educationally deprived children in those public schools in the district having high concentrations of children from low-income families." Congress did not "prescribe the specific types of programs' projects," because "such matters are left to the discretion and judgment of the local public educational agencies" (U.S. Senate 1965, 5). The committee concluded: "To the maximum extent possible, this legislation gives encouragement to local school districts to employ imaginative thinking and new approaches to meet the educational needs of poor children" (6). Possible approaches listed as examples in the report included classroom reduction, preschool, teacher training programs, remedial programs, construction to upgrade school buildings, media centers, programs for non-English-speaking children, counselors, social workers, summer camps, and provision of food and clothes for poor children (6). An extraordinary variety of school expenditures were authorized. In fact, the Republican minority on the committee charged that "this bill is a thinly veiled attempt to launch a general Federal aid to education program by means of a spurious appeal to purposes which it would not adequately serve" (66).

U.S. commissioner of education Francis Keppel said that the law did not establish a "federal educational policy" but was "designed to help support State and local programs." As a measure of accountability, the ESEA would require reports showing that the federal dollars were used for "reasonable effective programs for disadvantaged children with the type of program as well as the administration of such programs remaining under the control of State and local authorities."[22] The political background of the bill was a combination of the long-term desire for general aid and the need to key it to individual children's needs in order to circumvent the opponents of direct aid to parochial schools.

Since the funding was aimed at schools with concentrations of poor children, the law raised powerful expectations. But since the funding had no specific educational content or requirements, and was turned over to state and local school officials to administer, there was wide variation in what happened. In evaluating its results, it is important to consider the underlying theory of action in the law: to get much more federal money to help schools, particularly schools serving the poor, with the hope that reporting requirements and research studies would help target the effort more specifically in the future.

A leading national expert, Ralph Tyler, observed: "In the first two years of operation of this program, it became apparent that most local schools had not analyzed the complex problems involved in improving the education of disadvantaged children. The plans of many schools in the first year or two were simple ones, such as adding teachers or teacher aides to the school staff, or using more audio-visual materials" (1974, 169). Such efforts were not likely to bring rapid changes.

Attacks soon came over the expenditures of Title I money. The advisory group appointed under the law, the National Advisory Council on the Education of Disadvantaged Children, reported that about a fourth of the money was being spent on summer programs but that there had not been effective efforts in many places to recruit genuinely disadvantaged students (National Advisory Council on the Education of Disadvantaged Children 1967). Marian Wright Edelman's Washington Research Project and the NAACP Legal Defense Fund published a harsh report in 1969, *Title I of ESEA: Is it Helping Poor Children?*, charging that the funds were often being used for general expenditures in school districts, not for educating poor children. This was a damning critique from the heart of the civil rights movement. Obviously, simply handing out money for the general purpose of helping disadvantaged children often did not effectively direct funds to the children that needed the most help. Instead, the allocations functioned as a kind of general aid that went to school officials who had not made a high priority of aiding relatively powerless groups of poor students and families in their districts. The program came under increasing pressure to regulate its expenditures.

Judged by its basic political goal of creating a viable framework for transferring resources, the ESEA was a brilliant and enduring success. Within five years, the results were apparent: "By fiscal 1970 total federal funds for preschool, elementary and secondary, vocational, and higher education were . . . 2.4 times those in 1965. . . . The proportion of aid specifically for the disadvantaged rose from nothing before the Great Society to $3.1 billion in fiscal 1972, a fourth of all federal educational expenditures" (Levitan and Taggart 1976, 121). That was the first goal of the legislation, and it had been accomplished. It also created momentum for continuing increases in educational funds, even though President Nixon vetoed three of the first four education funding measures of his administration (Orfield 1975, 133–150). The programs quickly developed a constituency, and all efforts to simply turn the money over to the states to do with as they wished were defeated in the coming decades. The federal role had been established, and it was tied directly to schools of poor children. It survived major political and ideological changes.

Judged by whether it changed the average educational outcomes for students in schools receiving the funds, the ESEA has produced results that were not unusual, given the structure of the program. There were no significant short-term test score gains directly linked to the funds. Other outcomes, such as graduation, improvement of teachers, and the like, were not systematically measured. Since much research was documenting the strong influence of out-of-school inequalities on test scores, this result was hardly surprising.

But this may be a fundamentally wrong way to look at the impact of the Johnson reforms. The education reforms were part of a much larger set of social policy reforms. The Great Society, unlike the present, far more conservative era, did not see educational opportunity as separate from the rest of a child's life and his or her family's condition. So a much better way to evaluate the impact of Johnson-era reforms on educational attainment is to look at the long-term success, measured broadly, of students who began, or experienced a significant part of, their education under the Johnson policies, compared with those educated under the major policy alternatives enacted in the succeeding decades. When one looks from this perspective, the answer is very different. Students from the Great Society period made significant gains in test scores, high school completion rates, and access to college, and the shrinking of the racial and ethnic achievement gaps were notable. Such changes have been strikingly absent under succeeding education policies, which often attacked rather than supported public schools and teachers. The administrations supporting those reforms implemented broader policy changes that produced extreme economic polarization in American society (Bartels 2008; Johnston 2003).

Although the Johnson administration initiated the largest program of aid to poor schools in American history, it was aware that money by itself was not enough and that racial change had to be part of the solution. The president directed the Civil Rights Commission to prepare a 1967 report, *Racial Isolation in the Public Schools*, which found that segregated schools were persistently unequal (U.S. Civil Rights Commission 1967). Commissioner of Education Harold Howe II spoke to a 1967 national conference about what it would take to make a real difference in a segregated and impoverished school: "We are talking about massive per-pupil expenditures, about providing a great variety of special services ranging from health and psychological care to remedial education efforts. We are talking about remaking the relationship between the school and the home, and between the school and employment opportunity." Such an effort, to have a real chance at success, would have to bring exceptional principals and teachers to the schools that usually got the weakest and least experienced ones, and to find some way to provide educational continuity in communities where there was massive turnover from one year to the next. The institutions that would have to do this—the urban school districts, Howe said—were "ill-supported by the State in which they exist" and "beset by self-appointed critics with every conceivable viewpoint" (Howe 1967). Howe saw desegregation as an essential part of a path to education equity. After centuries of systemic inequality, only in the mid-1960s did the three branches of government commit themselves to serious support of the rights of African Americans, and only then were we seeing "some fruits" of those changes (Howe 1967). The federal government never made the kind of comprehensive commitment Howe suggested.

When the formal evaluations of the Great Society programs began to come in, they showed what any reader of the Coleman Report (1966) might have expected—that there was no significant short-term relationship between the money spent and the test scores of the students. Since there was neither a specific program prescribed by the law nor any serious accountability measures, this should not have been very surprising. Because, in the early years of the ESEA, Congress did not approve the appropriations until after the school year began, there was no way to integrate the program effectively with instruction. (Congress later adopted "forward funding" of education programs so that educators could plan ahead.) It was not surprising that many observers visiting Title I schools found closets full of equipment and materials that had not yet been put into effective educational use.

The discouraging evaluations provided ammunition for continuing conservative attacks on the effort. Early reports by General Electric researchers on the ESEA's first two years showed enormous difficulties in figuring out what was going on in even a very small group of districts among the 20,000 existing programs. Instead of focusing on outcomes of the multiple goals of the program, including improved attendance, graduation, college going, and so on, the study—like most of those that came later—focused on test scores only and found that the test data, in a period in which every district had its own testing, timing, and method of reporting data, was chaotic. The study found no discernible impact of the program (Jeffrey 1978, 160–162). Other reports, including a large HEW study of Title I reading programs and a Westinghouse–Ohio State University study of Head Start, reached similar conclusions in the early 1970s (162–167). It was clear by this point that a modest addition to the budget of most schools was unlikely to substantially increase test scores, at least in the short run. Clearly, as the Coleman Report had concluded, school programs were much less powerful than optimists had concluded, and the segregation of children in schools of concentrated poverty was more harmful.

There have been endless disputes over the evaluation of the preschool and the Title I programs. Reviewers of Head Start, for example, have pointed out the health and family benefits of the program, along with the need for further programs to sustain early gains—or for a better, deeper, more professional form of high-quality preschool to produce lifelong gains. A major 2010 federal report of a sophisticated random-assignment study of Head Start by several of the nation's leading research organizations showed clear learning, social, and health benefits during the program, but few lasting effects of a program that was unevenly implemented (Puma et al. 2010). Congress has never been able to fully fund Head Start for eligible students, to say nothing of raising its quality or continuing its programs for older students. Probably what is needed is something more like the costly preschool programs that show long-term benefits, such as the High Scope and Abecedarian projects. The last major evaluation of Title I, the *Prospects* study, provided another round of disappointment in the early 1990s. Summarizing all of the major studies of the program's first three decades, researchers concluded, using the best meta-analysis techniques, that the program generated small test-score gains that appeared to grow as it matured, and that the nature of the benefit depended upon the quality of program implementation (Borman and D'Agostino 1996, 309–326). What was clear from all of these evaluations was that the test-score gains were modest at best and that the other gains had still not been seriously evaluated.

It is fundamentally unfair to judge the Johnson programs by test scores, because they were not specific educational treatments. In spite of the optimistic rhetoric, they were policies to provide state and local educators with federal resources to do with as they thought best, within the wide latitude allowed by the law in the case of Title I. This decentralized approach was consistent with the traditions of American education, despite modest efforts at stimulating parental involvement and influence—and decentralization helped both the enactment and survival of the programs.

The education reforms were a subset of a much broader and interrelated social agenda. Head Start was part of the poverty program, as were the first college-access and assistance programs. They were interrelated with other efforts to help students and their families. The prohibition against job discrimination in the Civil Rights Act and the affirmative action in federal hiring and contracting greatly expanded middle-class jobs for black and Latino adults, and thus improved the situation of their children. Desegregation was rapidly increasing, and millions of black children, especially in the South, were getting access to better schools with better teachers and higher levels of competition, though often with difficulty.

The Great Society program tried to bring down barriers, build bridges, and provide opportunities for families. In many ways, its remarkable changes provided momentum for increased educational opportunity and attainment for several decades until the policies were explicitly reversed in the 1980s and 1990s during the Reagan-Bush era, and by the Supreme Court headed by Chief Justice William Rehnquist.[23] Although it was impossible to show any substantial short-term gains in individual programs, the aggregate change in circumstances of nonwhite families in the United States that grew out of this period of multidimensional change was substantial.

Three positive changes beginning in the 1960s and not repeated since deserve special attention. Beginning in the 1960s there was a substantial decline in the racial gap in academic achievement as measured by test scores, which continued into the early 1980s. Access to preschool increased dramatically and, according to a National Academy of Sciences report, during the 1968–1985 period "rates of participation in early schooling have not only grown dramatically among black and white students, but they have often been greater among blacks" (Janes and Williams 1989, 333). School desegregation for black students continued to increase until 1988 despite the opposition of the Nixon and Reagan administrations, showing that this remained a deep and durable reform until the Supreme Court changed the law in 1991 (Orfield and Eaton 1996).

Fifty years of research on the impact of desegregation on student achievement, graduation rates, and college success indicates that desegregation produces significant benefits on multiple dimensions for nonwhite students (Reardon and Rhodes 2011), and it may actually have been the most successful educational innovation of the Great Society. The largest declines in the white-black and the white-Hispanic gaps on the National Assessment of Educational Progress, the "Nation's Report Card," took place between the first test data in 1971 and the 1986–1988 period, after which the gaps began to grow again for a generation (Rampey, Dion, and Donahue 2009). Although the systematic national test was not implemented until after the 1960s, careful analysis of existing test data shows that these trends clearly began in that decade (Koretz 1986). High school completion rates rose dramatically by 13 percent from 1960 to 1970, and college attendance by high school graduates rose from 52 to 62 percent of a much larger cohort (Tyler 1974). College access rates rose steeply during this period for black and Latino high school graduates, whose numbers were also growing rapidly. For a brief period in the mid-1970s, when college costs were still low, affirmative action had not yet been constrained by the Supreme Court's decision in *Regents of University of California v. Bakke*, 438 U. S. 265 (1978) (which limited a race-conscious admissions policy at the UC–Davis medical school), and financial aid had not been undermined by the cuts in the Reagan budgets, nonwhite students had as good a chance of starting college as white students, though not nearly as high a likelihood of completion. The peak for black college access came in 1977 (Janes and Williams 1989, 338–339). This was a remarkable story: these students were getting access to the best public universities in the South, from which previously they had been almost totally excluded. These major gains were limited or reversed in the 1980s.

During the Reagan administration, the three preconditions for increasingly equitable college access were reversed. Civil rights enforcement virtually ceased as the government changed sides on civil rights issues (Amaker 1984). Tuition rose rapidly as state and federal funds were cut; the Pell Grant program was slashed in the face of rising costs, exacerbating the problem. The racial gap in college access, which had declined dramatically, now rapidly widened (Koretz 1990, 76–77). While there is no consensus that the Pell Grant by itself changed college attendance substantially for the poor, in part because of its complexity and the rapid rise in tuitions (Bowen, Kurzweil, and Tobin 2005, 200), college going expanded rapidly and there was a dramatic but temporary closing of the racial gap in college access as well as a rapid increase in access of nonwhite students to elite institutions. These changes were related to a number of impetuses, certainly including civil rights law.

Johnson's leadership overcame seemingly impossible barriers to allow the federal government to play a substantial role in education, bringing dramatically increased funding to educational institutions from preschool to graduate school. The policies were sufficiently well thought out and congruent with the forces in the political and educational structures of the country that each one has endured, with intervening modifications, for nearly a half century. They fostered a trend of increasingly equitable education in American society that lasted until the Reagan and Bush administrations, and the Supreme Court they put in place, created a decisive shift in politics, ideology, and, eventually, constitutional law. The policies that challenged Johnson's programs and replaced or altered some of them have not been associated with the kinds of gains that began in the Great Society period.

In evaluating the Great Society's impact on education, it is important to compare it with what came before and after. The reforms permanently changed the capacity of the federal government to act on educational matters. No conservative president skeptical of those changes could reverse or eliminate the major programs or end the expectation of federal leadership created by the Johnson innovations. No other administration so clearly saw the powerful links between race, poverty, and education or enacted a program of similar range. By those standards, its accomplishments were all the more remarkable.

These reforms, even at their peak, did not, of course, end educational inequality, but they surely strengthened American education. Johnson administration efforts at all levels of education have reshaped the role of the federal government in education and had a deep impact on American society. Education and civil rights policies enacted as part of Johnson's Great Society remain formative today, and the other major federal initiatives tried since that time have produced little (Darling-Hammond 2010; Fuller et al. 2006; Lee 2006; Lee 2008, ch. 5; Sunderman 2008). If one looks at the most important programs of the current federal government, one would point to the ESEA (temporarily renamed NCLB); in higher education, one would point to Pell Grants and guaranteed student loans, both originating in the 1965 Higher Education Act. In preschool education, it would be Head Start; in college access, the Trio programs, also derived from the War on Poverty. For troubled adolescents, the Job Corps, from the same source. In the education of the one-tenth of students who come from non-English-speaking homes, the 1964 Civil Rights Act and the 1968 Bilingual Education Act. The most visible presidential initiatives since the Johnson years either failed to be enacted, such as the various proposals for education block grants or vouchers, or very visibly failed in operation, such as the Goals 2000 legislation, which grew out of the support of George H. W. Bush and

Bill Clinton, and the NCLB, which grew out of the initiative of President George W. Bush to impose on the country a set of policies modeled on educational policy in Texas.

Johnson's educational vision was, in some central ways, an extremely optimistic one. Education was a good thing; educators were dedicated people; and many excluded students could be given real educational opportunity. Money, supported by civil rights policy, would bring down barriers, open doors, strengthen the capabilities of institutions, and quickly change the country. It was deeply disappointing when most of the research conducted in the 1960s showed that the problems were much deeper than had been assumed and that the short-term impact of any given program, even a dramatic expansion of previous efforts, was small. The disappointments were particularly severe in education. Test scores became the only metric used to evaluate educational outcomes, and test scores proved to be the indicator most tightly linked to family socioeconomic status and the most difficult to change significantly at the school level. As a result, many programs were described as failures, and proposals for radical alternatives were put forward. We now have reasonable ways of looking more broadly at the impact of a wide array of interventions, including the radically different approaches that became dominant from Reagan to the present.

Since the Reagan era, it has become commonplace to think about education policy separate from social policies, to blame educational inequalities on the teachers and their unions and school bureaucracies, and to try to solve these problems by accountability and sanctions meant to produce more equal outcomes. This was not the approach taken by Lyndon Johnson or the policies of the Great Society. Johnson and his administration saw educational inequality as inherently connected with race and poverty, and education policy was integrally linked with the War on Poverty and the great civil rights laws of the administration. The administration was engaged in struggles to create healthier families in improved communities, and workplaces that were far fairer than ever before in U.S. history.

A half century of sophisticated research on educational opportunity, in the United States and across the world, has shown that Johnson's approach was much more responsive to the real dimensions of educational inequality than the programs of subsequent administrations, and was thus more likely to have an impact (Rothstein 2004; Rumberger 2011). Since LBJ's approach was not just an educational intervention; since there was a simultaneous impact on many dimensions; since one of the fundamental outcomes was on racial and ethnic inequality; and since serious change takes time to show its consequences, the best way to think about the impact of the Great Society's educational reforms may be to take a broader look at trends in attainment and racial gaps in opportunity and achievement in the period following the Johnson reforms.

As mentioned above, the 1966 Coleman Report found that the most important influences on student achievement were family background and a student's peer group. In other words, social class mattered seriously, and many of the benefits of integration were related, in good measure, to giving lower-class students access to middle-class schools and peers. Schools were less influential than Americans had assumed; poverty and inequality were critically important in determining school outcomes. It was discouraging for those who believed that schooling by itself could solve problems of inequality in American society, and that we could simply leave the schools segregated by race and class and expect big changes.

There was a great burst of research evaluating components of the Great Society, beginning with the poverty program in 1964. Most of this research was looking for quick and unambiguous gains from programs. It didn't find them. It showed that inequalities were much more deeply rooted and multidimensional, and that real change was harder to accomplish, than the optimists had hoped (Aaron 1978; Haveman 1987, 191–218; Rivlin 1971). This conclusion was disheartening to those who had fought for the new programs, and it provided powerful ammunition for those attacking them and wanting to cut back on federal initiatives or send the money back to the states in block grants. Change was difficult, and it was easy to say the education policy failed.

The present analysis, however, employs another set of criteria. The first one is persistence. No one, certainly not President Johnson or the leaders of his administration, thought that they had reached the final best policies in a few weeks of frenetic activity spent putting together an astonishing legislative program between the end of the 1964 election and the new congressional session. Since that time there have been eleven presidential elections, six shifts of party control of the executive branch, dramatic shifts in Congress, and major ideological changes as well as massive research on educational and social policy. The first test of the Great Society program is how well the policy compromises proposed by Johnson and, in most cases, enacted by large bipartisan majorities have survived and remained the framework for policy. The second is how they compare with alternatives that were enacted into policy or experimented with in significant ways in the following decades.

The Great Society policies were designed so that they could be enacted by Congress. Although it is useful to compare them with the best policies that advocates could imagine, it is more meaningful to compare them with alternatives that history has shown to be feasible in the last half century, especially given the reality of policy making. By this standard, the work of the Great Society looks stunningly successful. Most of the basic framework that was so quickly created has survived in education and in related civil rights policies. The few alternatives that have been seriously pursued have either failed in enactment or implementation. Much about the framework of U.S. educational policy today would be easy for someone from 1965 to understand, because the laws still exist.

A second test is to look less at test scores and more closely at the expansion of opportunity and access in American education, the end of state-imposed segregation, the increase in high school and college completion, and substantial declines in the enormous gaps in access and completion for minority students, who were central to the thought of the Great Society planners and President Johnson. Since the Great Society brought a wide array of social changes, it is reasonable to ask a much broader question: how did the young people growing up under that array of comprehensive social reforms fare compared with those who came along later, under the reform model growing out of the conservative movement in the 1980s and embraced, to varying degrees, by all administrations for three decades? The Reagan reforms were isolated from broader social reforms, were much more exclusively focused on schools and a narrow range of test scores, and directly specified the particular goals they wanted to achieve as well as the sanctions that would be used to pursue them. In other words, these later, narrower reforms set out limited, specific goals and used much more directive federal and state policies to pursue them. The Great Society reforms, by contrast, strictly adhered to the tradition of noninterference in decision making on curriculum, educational requirements, and assessment, which had always belonged to state and local officials, so long as the funds were used by schools serving the poorest children. The goal was to strengthen the system, the poor schools, and even the state education offices, which were given federal funds for expansion and professionalization of their often politicized and inadequate staffs.

The best research shows educational attainment growing, access to college soaring, segregation dropping dramatically, and a tremendous narrowing of the gap in access to college for young people beginning education during and immediately following the Great Society period. The momentum created by these wide-ranging reforms kept these dimensions of progress alive through the 1970s and, in some ways, into the 1980s. The basic premise of the Reagan reforms—the claim that there had been a decline in standards and educational achievement—was false. The National Assessment of Educational Progress, the only continual national tests since the early 1970s, showed no such decline. (It was true that average SAT scores had declined, but that was because of a huge increase in high school completion and college going, which meant that a substantially larger portion of high school juniors and seniors were taking the SAT, lowering average scores but not the scores of the more privileged students, like those who had been almost the only test takers in earlier years. Thus, a good trend was interpreted by the Reagan administration and the public as a failure.) By the late 1980s, under the new conservative policy framework, progress had stalled, and none of the major equity goals of the reforms, including those of Goals 2000 and the NCLB, have yet been realized.

Title VI as a Model for Expanding Educational Opportunity

The Great Society expanded access and strengthened institutions. In addition, it greatly expanded the demand for remedies to end other limits on educational opportunity. Creating new federal rights, defining new legal categories of nondiscrimination and connecting them to funding-cutoff remedies, and compiling new data on previously ignored issues proved to be a powerful model, especially in expanding the educational rights of handicapped children and girls. Modest funding to help handicapped children was written into the 1965 ESEA and its amendments, but when the movement was spurred by favorable court decisions, the advocates succeeded in creating a right and defining its denial as discrimination by enshrining these ideas in the Education for All Handicapped Children Act (1975). Similarly, when the women's movement exploded in U.S. society in 1970, it soon focused on a similar remedy, which was written into Title IX of the Education Amendments of 1972. Both these laws soon developed strong constituencies and had large impacts on U.S. education. Civil rights law created new ways of thinking about fundamental problems of rights and equity in American schools.

Education Policy in the Decades after LBJ

After Lyndon Johnson's administration, the federal government remained a force in education; it could not pull away, even when presidents like Nixon and Reagan wanted to turn the money and authority back to the states. The idea that the federal government was supposed to be the source of special support for poor and excluded students was embedded in the law and expectations, and in the basic formulas of grants, which persist today. It is not overstating the case to say that after the extraordinary outbursts of new policy and new leadership in 1964 and 1965, the role of the federal government in U.S. education was permanently expanded and eventually embraced by conservatives as well as liberals.

Following LBJ were years of deadlocks and battles between Congress and the White House, but few significant policy initiatives until the administration of President Reagan. Reagan offered the country a vision that considered efforts to fight discrimination and poverty to be futile distractions. His administration reduced the federal resources available for education and insisted that state and local officials raise standards and accountability and engage the forces of competition in schooling—ideas supported by Presidents Bill Clinton, George W. Bush, and Barack Obama. This movement, however, created few new federal programs or institutions, except for the bipartisan political bargain in 2001 that became the NCLB. The NCLB produced few results despite sanctioning thousands of schools and vastly expanding testing requirements (Fuller et al. 2006; Lee 2006). It has now been substantially rejected by both parties. Responding to a congressional deadlock over education legislation that had lasted for more than a decade, and to the collapse of the NCLB, the Obama administration gave states waivers from being branded total failures under the NCLB. Obama's "Race to the Top" policy required states to lift their limits on charter schools and to further increase assessments and sanctions for teachers, continuing the post-Reagan policy direction. The style since Reagan has been to attack and put pressure on the schools and teachers serving disadvantaged children, without doing anything to address the underlying disadvantages. This stance is deeply at odds with the Johnson approach, which saw American public education as a good thing, a crucial set of opportunities that needed not management by the government but resources and support to strengthen the institutions and expand their services. The Johnson administration's conflict with American education, and it was sometimes serious, was about giving previously excluded students access to mainstream opportunities and ending the apartheid system that had dominated education in seventeen states throughout their history. It was not about taking control of any educational processes within the schools.

The Supreme Court and Educational Rights

Lyndon Johnson's reforms swept in a wave of new education laws and the most important civil rights laws in the nation's history, and they were supported for a brief time by all three branches of government. In the U.S. system, however, the courts have the ultimate responsibility for interpreting laws and the Constitution. Johnson had the good fortune to take office at the high point of the Warren Court, the most progressive in U.S. history, especially on issues of racial justice. Johnson took a hugely significant step with the appointment of Thurgood Marshall, the great civil rights advocate, as the first black member of the high court. His other successful appointment, Abe Fortas, was a strong liberal committed to social change, an eminent Washington lawyer, and LBJ's longtime legal and political advisor. When Chief Justice Earl Warren resigned in 1968, Johnson nominated Fortas to become chief justice, ignoring the advice of his close counselor Clark Clifford, his attorney general, and the White House special counsel that the appointment would seem far too political (Yalof 1999, 90–94).

But Johnson left office with a critical vacancy unfilled. Justice Fortas's nomination as chief justice was defeated in an ugly battle, turning in part on Johnson's continuing use of a Supreme Court justice as a personal political advisor. Fortas was driven from the court by scandal within months; Nixon's attorney general took the issue directly to the chief justice (Newton 2006, 503–504). At a time when an eminent lawyer or senator might have been readily confirmed, Johnson chose his old friend and nominated as associate justice another friend, a former fellow member of the Texas congressional delegation, federal judge Homer Thornberry (Johnson 1971, 544–547). The nominations produced the first defeat of a high-court nominee in four decades (Murphy 1988). With the chief justice spot unfilled there was no vacancy for an associate justice. Incoming president Richard Nixon, whose Southern Strategy included attacks on the court's civil rights decisions, was thus given a rare opportunity to make a massive, immediate impact on the basic definition of rights in America. Nixon made four appointments in his five years, and had a much greater and longer-lasting impact on the court than LBJ. Nixon's appointments definitively ended the progressive period of the Warren Court (Murphy 1988), an impact that soon changed the direction of major educational equity issues.

The conservative presidents who made all the appointments to the court for the next quarter century had far fewer legislative goals but were intensely focused on controlling the courts and reversing the Warren Court's expansion of rights. They made ten appointments before a Democratic president got one, in 1993. The court soon began to limit and reverse civil rights. By the time of President George H. W. Bush, the appointments consolidated the most conservative court in more than a half century.

The consequences for national educational policy were quick in coming. Within five years, the Supreme Court decided two giant turning points in

U.S. education law. In *San Antonio Independent School District v. Rodriguez*, 411 U.S. 1 (1973), a case about equalizing funding for a poor, heavily Mexican American area of San Antonio, the high court held 5–4 that there was no federal right to an education and, therefore, no federal right to equal resources for education—a decision directly in conflict with the deepest values of the Johnson era. The decision ended the possibility of schools winning financial equalization in federal courts. Four of the five negative votes were Nixon appointees, two of them seats that Johnson had failed to fill successfully. The next year, in *Milliken v. Bradley*, 418 U.S. 717 (1974), another 5–4 decision rejected school desegregation across city-suburban lines. The lower courts had held that such a decision would deny unconstitutionally segregated students any remedy in cities with few white or middle-class students, and Justice Thurgood Marshall noted in his dissent that millions of segregated minority students in large metropolitan areas would continue to be confined to weak and declining ghetto schools. This was the end of the search for a remedy in many of the largest metropolitan areas. It was the first Supreme Court decision limiting desegregation in the two decades since *Brown*, and marked the end of the expansion of desegregation law.

These two significant decisions, which left millions of students in persistently separate and unequal schools without any constitutional remedy, had extraordinary impacts on the future of American education, severely damaging the pursuit of educational equity. As James MacGregor Burns, the eminent presidential historian concluded, the way Johnson had handled the final Supreme Court appointments "did sharp and enduring damage to . . . liberal causes" (Burns 2009, 199). The political scientist David Yalof concluded: "Only Johnson's refusal to heed dispassionate advice prevented this liberal tide from extending well into the future with a more sympathetic chief justice in place. And the Republican presidents that followed him thus received a golden opportunity to steer the court in a decidedly more conservative direction" (Yalof 1999, 96). It was a case from a poor Mexican American district in San Antonio, not far from the president's home, where the right to an equal education was defeated—and the burning dissent of Johnson's one appointee, Thurgood Marshall, in the desegregation case showed that national policy had been profoundly limited.

A Reckoning

In President Johnson's farewell address, made while his power and popularity were shattered by war and division in the country, he noted: "In the sweep of things, a President has only so much time . . . to do the things that he really believes in and he thinks must be done. Within those limits, he can only give it the best he has . . . We leave the plow in the furrow, and actually the field is only half tilled" (quoted in Fields 1996, 311).

In federal education policy, no other president has ever plowed with more energy and success, particularly in his first years, and none has opened so many fields of action or planted so many fruitful seeds. In the nature of doing so much so fast, and with so little time to finish the work or repair the mistakes before he lost the initiative and was forced to give up his plow, the work was incomplete. In many ways, the field was indeed "only half tilled."

Lyndon Johnson wanted to change America, and American education has never been the same since the transformations in 1964 and 1965. But the Great Society included far more than major educational reforms. Since there was a simultaneous impact on many dimensions, since one of the most fundamental was on racial and ethnic inequality, and since serious change takes time to show its consequences, the best way to think about the Great Society's impact may be to take a broad look at trends in attainment and racial gaps in opportunity and achievement in the period following the Johnson reforms. Those impacts were very substantial and have not been repeated since.

Johnson's legacy has been clouded by the domestic upheavals and national division over the Vietnam War at the end of his presidency. Since 1980 there has been little discussion about the links between education, support for teachers, enforcing civil rights, and fighting poverty. LBJ's achievements in educational opportunity, broadly defined, should be recognized as a unique tour de force of a true legislative genius with a profound vision. In just two years of incredible accomplishment, Johnson and the Congress he helped elect built many of the structures that still shape the country's schools nearly a half century later. We can compare the gains triggered by the Great Society with the failures of the following decades. Perhaps one day the country will turn once again to Johnson's half-plowed fields, build upon what was planted there, and revive dreams that have been long neglected. No one has equaled his enduring impact on educational opportunity for all.

Notes

1. Vice President Hubert Humphrey emphasized this point in 1964 (140): "I know of no one associated with the federal government, directly or indirectly, who has the slightest desire to control the curricula of the various school systems or who

believes that federal control is desirable public policy. This was a constant theme for LBJ and his administration."

2. Johnson brought in radical reform in immigration policy in 1965 as another civil rights measure, ending an unambiguously racist policy and stirring major demographic change in U.S. schools and communities; see chapter 5 of this volume for a discussion of LBJ's immigration policies.

3. Earlier versions of discussion of issues in this section can be found in Grofman (2000) and Orfield (1969).

4. Though it will not be discussed further here, it is important to note that the Voting Rights Act of 1965 also had dramatic impacts on schools. Many districts that had never had minority representation changed from at-large to district elections under the act, and the first nonwhite members were elected. The battles over districting continue today (Foster 1984, 25–34; *Leadership Insider* 2008).

5. Statistics calculated from the National Center for Educational Statistics, U.S. Department of Education.

6. Senators Joseph Biden (D-DE) and Thomas Eagleton (D-MO) sponsored an amendment to weaken the government's power to combat urban desegregation; perhaps not surprisingly, the biggest cities in their states were facing desegregation orders.

7. Federal courts had rejected efforts by the Kennedy administration to intervene in civil rights matters until the law was passed (Sarratt 1966, 69–71). Kennedy had proposed permitting enforcement actions to counteract discrimination in federal education programs; the bill President Johnson supported and signed *mandated* such action (Parmet 1984, 264–273).

8. The revival of enforcement efforts has been apparent in a series of investigations and settlements with the state of Arizona and the Los Angeles school district, among others.

9. The Obama administration has, for example, obtained major policy changes from the Arizona State Department of Education, a resegregating school system in Mississippi, and the Los Angeles Unified School District, among other successes. It issued new guidance to all school districts and colleges on desegregation and affirmative action in December 2011.

10. Research evidence on the nature of these impacts was accepted by the Supreme Court in 2003 as a major basis for authoring the continuation of affirmative action in *Grutter v. Bollinger*, 539 U.S. 306 (2003).

11. *Green v. New Kent Co.*, 391 U.S. 430 (1968).

12. LBJ had predicted that there would be a large political cost in the South from the civil rights laws, but the change was larger and more lasting than could have been predicted. Three decades after the Voting Rights Act, the Republican Congress was led by Newt Gingrich of Georgia and Trent Lott of Mississippi (Sack 1996). Lott eventually had to step down for publicly speaking in favor of the segregationist policies of Senator Strom Thurmond (R-SC), a fierce segregationist (Halbfinger 2002). On Nixon's Southern Strategy, see Dent (1978).

13. *Adams v. Richardson*, 356 F. Supp. 92 (D.D.C. 1973).

14. *Washington Post*, May 24, 1983.

15. Large Hispanic populations were present in Greater New York, Chicago, and Miami.

16. The George H. W. Bush administration suppressed a report it had commissioned from the Sandia National Lab, which found serious errors in the administration's education policy assertions (Berliner and Biddle 1995, 166–167).

17. LBJ, conversation with John McCormack, May 14, 1964. Citation 3452, LBJ Library.

18. LBJ, conversation with Vice President Humphrey, March 6, 1965, citation 7024.

19. Ibid.

20. Though Clinton's advisors believed tax subsidies to be a poor way to aid students, the issue was one of the most popular in his election campaign polling, and he adopted it.

21. In 2007, the United States lagged behind thirteen other nations in higher-education completion rates according to the *OECD Factbook 2010*, "Tertiary education graduation rates" (www.oecd-ilibrary.org/education/tertiary-education-graduation-rates_20755120-table1).

22. Francis Keppel to Douglass Cater, memorandum, Mar. 3, 1965, containing responses from Keppel to Senator Jacob Javits (R-NY); in Papers of Lyndon Baines Johnson, President, 1963–1968, files of S. Douglass Cater, box 25, p. 5, LBJ Library.

23. Supreme Court cases involving consideration of federal education policies include *Board of Education of Oklahoma City v. Dowell*, 498 U.S. 237 (1991), and *Freeman v. Pitts*, 503 U.S. 467 (1992).

References

Aaron, Henry J. 1978. *Politics and the professors: The Great Society in perspective.* Washington, D.C.: Brookings Institution.

Amaker, Norman C. 1984. *Civil rights and the Reagan administration.* Washington, D.C.: Urban Institute Press.

Arias, M. Beatriz, and Ursula Casanova, eds. 1993. *Bilingual education: Politics, practice, and research.* Chicago: University of Chicago Press.

Bartels, Larry M. 2008. *Unequal democracy: The political economy of the new gilded age.* Princeton, N.J.: Princeton University Press.

Bennett, Michael J. 1996. *When dreams came true: The GI Bill and the making of modern America.* Washington, D.C.: Brassey's.

Berliner, David C., and Bruce J. Biddle. 1995. *The manufactured crisis: Myths, fraud, and the attack on America's public schools.* Reading, Mass.: Addison-Wesley.

Blum, Howard. 2011. LAUSD agrees to revise how English learners, blacks are taught. *Los Angeles Times*, Oct. 11.

Boger, John Charles, and Gary Orfield, eds. 2005. *School resegregation: Must the South turn back?* Chapel Hill: University of North Carolina Press.

Borman, Geoffrey D., and Jerome V. D'Agostino. 1996. Title I and student achievement: A meta-analysis of federal evaluation results. *Educational Evaluation and Policy Analysis* 18, no. 4 (Winter).

Bowen, William G., Martin A. Kurzweil, and Eugene M. Tobin. 2005. *Equity and excellence in American higher education.* Charlottesville: University of Virginia Press.

Brady, David W., and Craig Volden. 1998. *Revolving gridlock: Politics and policy from Carter to Clinton.* Boulder, Colo.: Westview.

Burns, James MacGregor. 2009. *Packing the court: The rise of judicial power and the coming crisis of the Supreme Court.* New York: Penguin.

Coleman, James S. 1966. *Equality of Educational Opportunity study.* Report prepared for the U.S. Department of Health, Education and Welfare, Washington, D.C.

Darling-Hammond, Linda. 2010. *The flat world and education.* New York: Teachers College Press.

DeBray, Elizabeth. 2006. *Politics, ideology, and education: Federal policy during the Clinton and Bush administrations.* New York: Teachers College Press.

Dent, Harry S. 1978. *The prodigal South returns to power.* New York: Wiley.

Fairfax, Jean. 1978. Current status of the *Adams* case: Implications for blacks and other minorities. In *Beyond desegregation: Urgent issues in the education of minorities*, 36–46. New York: College Board.

Fenno, Richard, Jr. 1963. The House of Representatives and federal aid to education. In Robert L. Peabody and Nelson W. Polsby, eds., *New perspectives on the House of Representatives.* Chicago: Rand McNally.

Fields, Wayne. 1996. *Union of words: A history of presidential eloquence.* New York: Free Press.

Foster, Lorn S. 1984. Section 5 of the Voting Rights Act and its effects upon southern school boards. *National Educational Review* 35, no. 1 (Jan.).

Fried, Charles. 1991. *Order and the law: Arguing the Reagan revolution.* New York: Simon and Shuster.

Fuller, B., K. Gesicki, E. Kang, and J. Wright. 2006. *Is the No Child Left Behind Act working? The reliability of how states track achievement.* Berkeley: Policy Analysis for California Education.

Gándara, Patricia, and Megan Hopkins, eds. 2010. *Forbidden language: English learners and restrictive language policies.* New York: Teachers College Press.

Graham, Hugh Davis. 1984. *The uncertain triumph: Federal education policy in the Kennedy and Johnson years.* Chapel Hill: University of North Carolina Press.

Grissmer, David W., and Ann Flanagan. 2000. Moving educational research toward scientific consensus. In David W. Grissmer and J. Michael Ross, eds., *Analytic issues in the assessment of student achievement.* Washington, D.C.: National Center for Education Statistics.

Grofman, Bernard, ed. 2000. The 1964 Civil Rights Act and American education. In *Legacies of the 1964 Civil Rights Act.* Charlottesville: University of Virginia Press.

Halbfinger, David M. 2002. In Lott's life, long shadows of segregation. *New York Times*, Dec. 15.

Haveman, Robert H. 1987. Policy analysis and evaluation research after 20 years. *Policy Studies Journal* 16.

Hawley, Willis, Robert L. Crain, Christine H. Rossell, R. Fernandez, Janet W. Schofield, and W. P. Trent. 1983. *Strategies for effective desegregation: Lessons from research.* Lexington, Mass.: Lexington Books, D. C. Heath.

Heckman, James J. 2011. The economics of inequality: The value of early childhood education. *American Educator* (Spring): 31–36.

Howe, Harold, II. 1967. National ideals and educational policy. Address to the National Conference on Race and Education, U.S. Commission on Civil Rights, Washington D.C., Nov. 17.

Humphrey, Hubert H. 1964. *War on poverty*. New York: McGraw Hill.

Janes, Gerald David, and Robin M. Williams Jr. 1989. *A common destiny: Blacks in American society*. Washington, D.C.: National Academies Press.

Jeffrey, Julie Roy. 1978. Education for children of the poor: A study of the origins and implementation of the Elementary and Secondary Education Act of 1965. Columbus: Ohio State University Press.

Johnson, Lyndon B. 1965. State of the union address (Jan. 4). In *Public papers of presidents of the United States* (LBJ Papers, vol. 1, 1965). Washington, D.C.: Government Printing Office.

———. 1966. *Public papers of the presidents*. Nov. 3.

———. 1971. *The vantage point: Perspectives of the presidency, 1963–1969*. Austin: Holt, Rinehart and Winston.

Johnston, David Cay. 2003. *Perfectly legal: The covert campaign to rig our tax system to benefit the super rich—and cheat everybody else*. New York: Portfolio.

Johnstone, D. Bruce. 1986. *Sharing the costs of higher education*. New York: College Board.

Koretz, Daniel. 1986. Trends in Educational Achievement. Washington, D.C.: Congressional Budget Office.

———. 1990. *Trends in postsecondary enrollment of minorities*. Santa Monica: Rand.

Koretz, Daniel, Elizabeth Lewis, and Lenore Desilets. 1990. *Trends in the postsecondary enrollment of minorities*. Santa Monica, Calif.: Rand.

Leadership Insider: Practical Perspectives on School Law and Policy. 2008. Oct. Published by the National School Boards Association.

Lee, Jaekyung. 2006. Tracking achievement gaps and assessing the impact of NCLB on the gaps: An in-depth look into national and state reading and math outcome trends. Cambridge, Mass.: Civil Rights Project, Harvard University. www.civilrightsproject.ucla.edu.

———. 2008. Two takes on the impact of NCLB on academic improvement: Tracking state proficiency trends through NAEP versus state assessments. In Gail Sunderman, ed., *Holding NCLB accountable: Achieving accountability, equity, and school reform*. Thousand Oaks, Calif.: Corwin.

Levitan, Sar A., and Robert Taggart. 1976. *The promise of greatness*. Cambridge, Mass.: Harvard University Press.

Litolff, Edwin H., III. 2007. Higher education desegregation: An analysis of state efforts in systems formerly operating segregated systems of higher education. PhD diss., Louisiana State University.

Losen, D.J., and Gary Orfield, eds. 2002. *Racial inequality in special education*. Cambridge, Mass.: Harvard Education Press.

Meier, Kenneth J., and Robert E. England. 1989. *Race, class, and education: The politics of second-generation discrimination*. Madison: University of Wisconsin Press.

Meier, Kenneth J., and Joseph Stewart Jr. 1991. *The politics of Hispanic education*. Albany: State University of New York Press.

Morris, Dick. 1999. *Behind the Oval Office*. Los Angeles: Renaissance.

Murphy, Bruce Allen. 1988. *Fortas: The rise and ruin of a Supreme Court justice*. New York: Morrow.

National Advisory Council on the Education of Disadvantaged Children. 1967. *Report of the Advisory Council on the Education of Disadvantaged Children*.

Newton, Jim. 2006. *Justice for all: Earl Warren and the nation he made*. New York: Riverhead.

Orfield, Gary. 1969. *The reconstruction of southern education: The schools and the 1964 Civil Rights Act*. New York: Wiley.

————. 1975. *Congressional power: Congress and social change*. New York: Harcourt Brace Jovanovich.

————. 1978. *Must we bus? Segregated schools and national policy*. Washington, D.C.: Brookings Institution.

Orfield, Gary, and Susan E. Eaton. 1996. *Dismantling desegregation: The quiet reversal of "Brown v. Board of Education."* New York: New Press.

Orfield, Gary, and E. Frankenburg. 2014. *Brown at 60: Great progress, a long retreat, and an uncertain future*. Los Angeles: Civil Rights Project.

Parmet, Herbert S. 1984. *JFK: The presidency of John F. Kennedy*. New York: Penguin.

Price, Hugh Douglas. 1962. Race, religion and the Rules Committee: The Kennedy education bills. In Alan F. Westin, ed., *The uses of power*. New York: Harcourt, Brace and World.

Puma, Michael, Stephen Bell, Ronna Cook, Camilla Heid, and others. 2010. *Head Start impact study: Final report*. Report prepared for the U.S. Department of Health and Human Services, Administration for Children and Families. Washington, D.C.

Rampey, Bobby D., Gloria S. Dion, and Patricia L. Donahue. 2009. *The nation's report card: Trends in academic progress in reading and mathematics 2008*. Report prepared for the U.S. Department of Education.

Reardon, Sean F., and T. . 2011. The effects of socioeconomic school integration plans on racial school desegregation. In Erica Frankenberg and Elizabeth DeBray, eds., *Integrating schools in a changing society: New policies and legal options for a multiracial generation*. Chapel Hill: University of North Carolina Press.

Rivlin, Alice M. 1961. *The role of the federal government in financing higher education*. Washington, D.C.: Brookings Institution.

————. 1971. *Systematic thinking for social action*. Washington, D.C.: Brookings Institution.

Rothstein, Richard. 2004. *Class and schools: Using social, economic, and educational reform to close the black-white achievement gap*. New York: Teachers College Press.

Rumberger, Russell W. 2011. *Dropping out: Why students drop out of high school and what can be done about it*. Cambridge, Mass.: Harvard University Press.

Sack, Kevin. 1996. Congress reflecting southern shift to the GOP. *New York Times*, May 2.

Sarratt, Reed. 1966. *The ordeal of desegregation*. New York: Harper and Row.

Snyder, Thomas, ed. 1993. *120 years of American education: A statistical portrait*. Washington, D.C.: U.S. Department of Education.

Southern Education Report. 1966. Jan.–Feb.

Sunderman, Gail, ed. 2008. Holding NCLB accountable: Achieving accountability, equity, and school reform. Thousand Oaks, Calif.: Corwin.

Thomas, Gail E., James M. McPartland, and Denise C. Gottfredson. 1981. Desegregation and black student higher educational access. In Gail E. Thomas, ed., *Black students in higher education.* Westport, Conn.: Greenwood.

Tyler, Ralph. 1974. The federal role in education. In Eli Ginzberg and Robert M. Solow, eds. *The Great Society: Lessons for the future.* New York: Basic Books.

U.S. Civil Rights Commission. 1964. *Public education: 1964 staff report.* Washington, D.C.: Government Printing Office.

———. 1967. *Racial isolation in the public schools.* Washington, D.C.: Government Printing Office.

U.S. Department of Education. 2011. Press Release: U.S. Departments of Education and Justice reach settlement with Arizona Department of Education to ensure that potential ELL students are properly identified. Mar. 25.

U.S. Department of Health, Education and Welfare. 1975. Office for Civil Rights. Task force findings specifying remedies available for eliminating past educational practices ruled unlawful under *Lau v. Nichols.* [Lau Remedies]. Aug. 11. Washington, D.C.: Government Printing Office.

U.S. Department of Justice. 1981. Press Release. Aug. 26.

U.S. Senate. 1965. Committee on Labor and Public Welfare. *Elementary and Secondary Education Act of 1965: Report to accompany H.R. 2362.* 89th Cong., 1st sess. S. Rep. 146.

Wellish, Jean B., Alfred C. Marcus, Anne H. MacQueen, and Gary A. Duck. 1976. *An in-depth study of the Emergency School Aid Act (ESAA) Schools.* Santa Monica, Calif.: System Development.

Whalen, Charles, and Barbara Whalen. 1985. *The longest debate: A legislative history of the 1964 Civil Rights Act.* Cabin John, Md.: Seven Locks Press.

Yalof, David Alistair. 1999. *Pursuit of justices: Presidential politics and the selection of Supreme Court nominees.* Chicago: University of Chicago Press.

CHAPTER 8

The Health Care Legacy of the Great Society

PAUL STARR

The Medicare and Medicaid programs enacted in 1965—the largest and most durable health care initiatives of the 1960s—exemplify the greatest and the worst aspects of Lyndon B. Johnson's leadership and legacy. Johnson was instrumental in passing the legislation, and the programs it established have undoubtedly improved the financial security and access to medical care of the elderly and the groups among the poor eligible for coverage.

But Medicare and Medicaid have also created severe and lasting problems for both health care and government in the United States. So eager were Johnson and other Democratic leaders to placate health care interest groups that the financing provisions, particularly for Medicare, sharply inflated medical costs, sowed doubt that a universal program was feasible, and distorted the allocation of public spending for decades to come. The legislation institutionalized two tiers of public health care finance. Singling out seniors for special treatment encouraged them to regard themselves as a distinct interest group, more deserving than others in need. Establishing Medicaid as a separate program, to be run by the states, relegated the poor to a variable, lower tier of protection, with sharply restricted eligibility in the South and Southwest. The link between Medicaid and welfare eligibility increased the work disincentives of welfare. The complicated structure created by the 1965 legislation added to the complexity and administrative burden of the health care system. In these and other ways, what some regard as high achievements of the Johnson years contributed to the gravest failings of America's health care and social welfare systems.

In sheer cost, Medicare and Medicaid came to outstrip by a wide margin all other domestic programs dating from the Johnson years. While many other initiatives of that era were later ended or substantially altered, Medicare and Medicaid became all too entrenched in more or less their original form. Congress later changed some critical aspects of the programs, such as Medicare's payment methods, but most of the central, structural features of the two programs remain intact.

The policy experts who originally conceived Medicare hoped that it would develop through incremental expansion, as Social Security did, ultimately leading to a system of universal health coverage. Partly because of decisions made at its inception, however, Medicare proved difficult to extend to other groups. Instead of leading to a universal system, Medicare generated political forces that obstructed reform. When Democrats in 2010 finally passed a program for near-universal coverage, they did so over the resistance of the elderly, and they did not build on Medicare; rather, they extended Medicaid and private insurance. On taking control of the House of Representatives the next year, Republicans voted not only to repeal the 2010 legislation but also to replace the traditional Medicare program with a "premium support" for private insurance and to turn Medicaid into a block grant to the states. Progressives would still like to make the traditional Medicare program the basis for universal coverage, but "Medicare for all" faces political obstacles that, if anything, have grown with time. Half a century after they were enacted, the health care programs of the Johnson years continue to have an uncertain and contested legacy.

The Origins of Medicare and Medicaid

The origins of Medicare and Medicaid lie in the peculiar sequence of development of social policy in the United States. The major European nations enacted health insurance programs for industrial workers in the late nineteenth and early twentieth centuries, typically in the same period when they established related programs for industrial-accident insurance, unemployment compensation, and old-age pensions. In the United States, however, a series of efforts to establish publicly financed health insurance met defeat. Between 1915 and 1919, after a successful campaign for industrial-accident insurance, Progressive reformers failed to secure passage of compulsory health insurance at the state level. In 1935, when Congress passed the Social Security Act, it provided for income protection during unemployment and in old age, but not for protection against the costs of illness. Those choices reflected the urgent priorities and political pressures of the time: the Depression focused attention on unemployment, and the Townsend movement pressed for income relief for seniors. But the American Medical Association opposed publicly financed health insurance and threatened to sink the entire Social Security bill if it covered health care. In 1938, when some members of Franklin Roosevelt's administration sought to revive health insurance, he retreated again in the face of opposition from the AMA and conservatives in Congress. The failure to enact a health insurance program early in the twentieth century then opened the way for the rise of employment-based private health coverage. That system was gaining a firm foothold by the late 1940s when Harry Truman became the first president to call for national health insurance. But a coalition organized by the AMA and backed by business attacked the proposal as "socialized medicine" and exploited the rising ideological tensions of the Cold War; Truman was decisively defeated (Starr 1983).

As a result of these developments, the United States, unlike other advanced societies, introduced old-age insurance before health insurance and created a corps of policy experts and federal program executives whose vision for health care reflected their experience in initiating and building Social Security. Some members of this bureaucratic elite—such as Wilbur Cohen, the go-to expert in the field during the middle decades of the twentieth century—served almost continuously in the federal government from the New Deal through the 1960s (Derthick 1979; Berkowitz 1995). After Truman's defeat on national health insurance, it was the Social Security policy experts who in 1951 proposed adding a limited hospital-insurance benefit for the elderly on Social Security. By the time the political winds had shifted in a more liberal direction in the 1960s, the idea of a limited program of hospital insurance for seniors had taken on a life of its own.

No other country has created a separate health insurance system for the elderly; it is a peculiar American invention, established without a full appreciation of its political implications. To be sure, once employer-based insurance had taken root, a separate program for seniors had a definite rationale. The elderly didn't fit into an employer-based model, and most couldn't afford to buy coverage, especially as Blue Cross moved away from community rating in the face of competitive pressures from commercial insurers in the early post–World War II decades. In that period, seniors continued to be a relatively needy group, with a higher poverty rate than was true for the working-age population. The supporters of a hospital-insurance program for seniors believed that integrating it into Social Security would give it immediate legitimacy. Just as the elderly had a right to Social Security benefits earned by contributions during their working years, so they could now be understood to have earned a right to hospital insurance. All these considerations lent persuasiveness to the idea of introducing national health insurance for the elderly alone.

While Medicare grew out of the social-insurance tradition, Medicaid grew out of systems of public assistance for the poor. Before the 1930s, charity hospitals and clinics for the poor were established and financed at the state and local level, often as private, voluntary institutions. During the New Deal, however, the federal government began providing support for relief, and local welfare agencies began recognizing medical care as an "essential relief need." Some voluntary hospitals and clinics then billed welfare agencies for services previously provided for free, so localities were able to shift some of the cost to the federal government. Gradually, a function that had been mostly private and entirely local became increasingly public and partly federal. In 1950, Congress enacted a small program of federal aid to the states for the medical costs of welfare recipients. This federal assistance was the direct antecedent of Medicaid.

In Congress, the first effort to pass a health insurance program for seniors began in 1957 with the introduction of a bill by a Rhode Island representative, Aime Forand. Recognizing the appeal of adding hospital insurance to Social Security, congressional opponents tried to preempt the idea in 1960 by enacting a program targeted to the elderly poor and run by the states. Known as Kerr-Mills for its two sponsors, both Democrats—Senator Robert Kerr of Oklahoma and Representative Wilbur Mills of Arkansas, the chairman of the House Ways and Means Committee—the program extended to the medically indigent elderly the earlier federal aid to the states for welfare recipients' medical care. Under the program, the federal government paid 50 percent to 80 percent of a state's costs for medically impoverished seniors. The lower a state's per capita income, the higher the share of its spending the federal government reimbursed.

Kerr-Mills, however, did not stop the political movement for what became popularly known as Medicare. John F. Kennedy made it a prominent issue in his 1960 presidential campaign, and public opinion polls indicated wide support for the measure. But despite the limited scope of the proposed coverage, the opposition from organized medicine and conservative Republicans was just as fierce as it had been to national health insurance. While President Kennedy was alive, a coalition of Republicans and southern Democrats blocked Medicare and many other liberal initiatives. As chairman of Ways and Means, Mills was the single most formidable congressional obstacle to the hospital-insurance measure, though support for it was growing in his committee as Democrats were added in the early 1960s (Marmor 1973).

Mills's objections to the Medicare proposal concerned its fiscal ramifications. He was worried that increases in payroll taxes would eventually lead

to a revolt against the whole Social Security system. In addition, while Social Security used wage-related contributions to pay for wage-related benefits, there would be no such relationship between contributions and benefits
in the coverage of hospital costs. Once a federal program paid the hospital
bills of the elderly, there would also inevitably be demands to cover doctors'
bills and other health care expenses. In short, while not opposed to Medicare in principle, Mills wanted to prevent it from setting in motion a chain
of consequences that he thought could ultimately destroy Social Security.
He also did not want to support a bill until he was sure he would have the
votes to pass it (Mills 1971, 1987; Zelizer 1998).

The Shaping of the Legislation

After becoming president, Johnson used his mastery of Congress to push
Kennedy's priorities, including Medicare. In 1964, the administration's allies added the hospital-insurance proposal to a Social Security bill in the
Senate, which passed it 49–44 (filibusters were rare in those days, except
on civil rights). The House remained the obstacle. As taped White House
telephone conversations show, President Johnson talked with Mills in June
about expanding Medicare in the House to cover physicians' services, which
the president referred to as an addition with "sex appeal." Although Johnson courted Mills relentlessly, insisting the congressman would get all the
credit and the glory ("It will be the biggest thing you have ever done for
your country"), Mills backed off and blocked the hospital-insurance program from becoming law (Zelizer 1998; Blumenthal and Morone 2009).
But the huge Democratic congressional majorities elected in 1964 shifted
the odds in favor of Medicare, and Mills as well as some other prominent
southern Democrats moved to support the legislation in the wake of the
Democratic landslide.

In 1965, the great surprise lay in how broad a bill Congress adopted,
covering not only the hospital costs of the elderly but also their physicians'
bills (as Johnson had urged the previous year), as well as expanded services
to the poor on welfare. The expansion, however, came about in a surprising
way that made it appear to be a concession to conservatives, which in some
ways it was.

As 1965 began, the AMA and Republicans were criticizing the Democrats' Medicare proposal not only because it established a form of compulsory insurance, but also on the grounds that a program limited to hospital
coverage was too meager. In addition, many Democrats, including Mills,

were worried that Medicare would disappoint the elderly if it failed to cover doctors' bills. In February 1965, the ranking Republican on Ways and Means, John Byrnes of Wisconsin, offered a plan called Bettercare: a voluntary insurance program for the elderly, partly subsidized out of general revenue, that would cover bills from physicians, hospitals, and nursing homes. Byrnes's model was the Federal Employees Health Benefit Plan (the original model for what are now called insurance exchanges). In what came off as a grand synthesis, Mills combined three elements: the Democrats' compulsory hospital-insurance program, which became Part A of Medicare; the Republican voluntary program, which would cover physicians' bills and become Medicare Part B (though without private insurers); and an expansion of the Kerr-Mills program (no longer restricted to the elderly poor), the approach favored by the AMA, which became Medicaid. This "three-layered cake" was the basis of the legislation—the Social Security Amendments of 1965—passed by both houses of Congress and signed into law by President Johnson on July 30 in a ceremony at Independence, Missouri, in honor of eighty-one-year-old former president Truman.

Who was responsible for the final shape of the 1965 legislation? Although some historical accounts focus entirely on Mills, the most influential analysis has emphasized what Martha Derthick (1979) calls "the dynamic of the two Wilburs"—not just Mills but also Wilbur Cohen, who, as undersecretary of Health, Education and Welfare, represented the Johnson administration in shepherding the bill through Congress. But in a 2009 book, *The Heart of Power: Health and Politics in the Oval Office*, David Blumenthal and James A. Morone claim that Johnson himself played a coequal role with Mills: "We now know—through extensive White House telephone tapes and memos—that LBJ was in on the legislative coup. He cooked up the entire business with Mills—always promising that Wilbur Mills would reap all the credit. Mills later acknowledged as much: 'We planned that, yes. Oh, yes'" (Blumenthal and Morone 2009, 164).

But Blumenthal and Morone overstate their case. Consider the quotation from Mills—'We planned that, yes. Oh, yes"—which Blumenthal and Morone quote twice, as if it proved their argument. The quotation comes from a series of oral-history interviews that Mills gave the LBJ Presidential Library, but the full transcript does not bear out the claim that Mills was talking about Johnson when he said, "We planned that." Asked "where the idea of combining . . . three different proposals" had come from, Mills said: "I think it came from us on the committee. . . . Oh, I developed the whole thing in the committee. I mean, we did, with the help of the staff people, by my questions and other questions of other members we developed the idea and the program." After noting that Cohen had reacted with "amazement" to the idea of combining the three proposals, the interviewer asked whether the bill had been "pieced together," and Mills replied, "No, it was planned. . . . We planned that, yes. Oh, yes" (Mills 1987). Contrary to what Blumenthal and Morone say, there is no indication that the "we" in that sentence included Johnson. "We" plainly refers to the members of the committee. When Mills elsewhere gives credit to Johnson, he credits Johnson's general efforts in pushing the legislation.

The telephone conversations cited by Blumenthal and Morone date from the spring of 1964, a year before the law passed Congress, and show only that Johnson encouraged Mills to add coverage of physicians' services, not that Johnson had anything to do with the idea of co-opting the Republican and AMA proposals and adding them to the Democrats' hospital-insurance bill. Since Byrnes introduced his proposal in February 1965, the conversations in 1964 could not have anticipated how shrewd it would be politically to add physicians' services on the basis of a subsidized, voluntary program. If Johnson "cooked up the entire business with Mills," Blumenthal and Morone do not have the evidence to prove it.

Moreover, the three "layers" of the 1965 legislation, each with its own separate financing, make sense from the standpoint of concerns that Mills, not Johnson, had raised from the beginning of the Medicare debate. Mills wanted to prevent overreliance on payroll taxes, and that is what his final bill achieved; the federal share of Medicare Part B and Medicaid would come out of general revenues. By enacting those parts of the legislation at the same time, Mills also walled in Medicare Part A, limiting future demands to expand the program as part of a social-insurance scheme. In that respect, Mills was successful, and the liberals who thought Medicare would lead to national health insurance were outflanked and beaten. Just as Mills wanted, the United States has not extended Medicare into a universal health system paralleling Social Security. But in a larger sense, Mills failed. While he limited the scope of the health insurance financed by payroll taxes, he approved payment methods and other policies that produced the long-term fiscal damage that he was trying to avoid.

From a short-term political perspective, Mills's synthesis was a success. The incorporation of the Republican and AMA proposals gave the legislation a bipartisan air. Although only ten Republicans in the House voted for the bill on the critical motion, many more joined in on the final roll call, and it passed 313–115. A year later, on July 1, 1966, the start-up went off without a hitch: doctors and hospitals cooperated, and there were no waiting lines for care, as some had feared. Moreover, the ideological as well as interest group resistance disappeared, partly because once doctors discovered how much money they could make from Medicare, they no longer had any interest in rousing popular opposition to "socialized medicine."

The Costs of Political Accommodation

Mills's maneuver has generally been regarded as a brilliant legislative coup and a liberal victory. It was a brilliant coup, but not exactly a liberal one.

By establishing separate and unequal programs for the elderly and the poor—one piggybacked on the shoulders of Social Security, the other shackled to public assistance ("welfare")—the 1965 legislation created two moral frameworks for the public financing of health care. The benefits for the elderly in the upper tier have been understood as an earned right, even though seniors have never paid enough in payroll taxes to earn their insurance coverage (in fact, the first wave of beneficiaries didn't pay anything). That moral claim has nonetheless given Medicare political security, making it unthinkable—at least until recently—to rescind the program, cap it, or cut it in a recession. In contrast, recipients of Medicaid or welfare are not regarded as having earned a right to coverage, and that lack of a moral claim has made Medicaid politically insecure and more vulnerable to cutbacks.

The legal provisions for the two programs reflect this difference in their moral underpinnings. While Congress established Medicare nationally, it left Medicaid to the vagaries of the states; Medicare provided the same benefits to the elderly wherever they lived, but Medicaid did not do the same for the poor. States did not have to participate in Medicaid (Arizona did not establish a Medicaid program until 1982), and they had wide discretion about eligibility criteria, the scope of covered services, and payments to health care providers. According to a formula favoring the poorer states, the federal government paid between 50 percent and 77 percent of a state's Medicaid expenditures, but the states in the South and Southwest, although bearing the smallest share of their own costs, nonetheless restricted eligibility the most severely. The federal law originally linked eligibility for Medicaid to eligibility for welfare, thereby limiting the program to the poor who fit into the eligible categories: the aged, the blind, the disabled, and families with dependent children. Single, able-bodied adults couldn't get Medicaid coverage no matter how poor they were. If a state agreed to run a Medicaid program, it had to cover all welfare recipients (and after 1972, all recipients of Supplemental Security Income), though it could also receive federal funds for covering the poor with incomes up to 133 percent of the state's cutoff for welfare as long as recipients fell into the eligible categories. But because states varied in their criteria for welfare and their willingness to cover others among the poor, many of the poor who could qualify for Medicaid in, say, New York could not qualify in Mississippi. As a result, the proportion of the population without health coverage remained far greater in the more conservative states, typically those in the South and Southwest; nationally, 60 percent of Americans living below the poverty level remained ineligible for Medicaid nearly two decades after it was enacted (Davis and Rowland 1983). The more liberal states were also more liberal in the range of services they covered. Even in those states, however, the lesser moral standing of Medicaid was reflected in payment rates to doctors so low that many refused to take Medicaid patients.

In a universal system, people do not have to be poor enough to qualify for health care. But because eligibility for Medicaid was tied to welfare, it created a problem analogous to job lock. Just as many people found themselves unable to quit a job to start a business of their own because they would lose health benefits, so many welfare beneficiaries faced the loss of health coverage if they took the kind of job typically available to them—low-wage work without health insurance. Consequently, Medicaid recipients who suffered from chronic health problems or had a sick child had a strong incentive not to take a job. The Medicaid-welfare link, according to one study, increased the welfare rolls by about one-fourth (Moffitt and Wolfe 1992).

Although Medicare was universal among the elderly, its benefit package was not generous. To pass the legislation in the Senate, the Johnson administration and party leaders fought off efforts by liberals to add coverage of prescription drugs and catastrophic medical costs. Seniors who could afford supplemental insurance would buy it. But the limited benefit package in Medicare would inevitably leave many lower-income elderly exposed to substantial financial burdens from illness, and the limitations would prove exceedingly difficult to correct in future years.

While the scope of Medicare's benefits was limited, its financing provisions for the services it did cover were all too generous. Spooked by the long opposition of the AMA to a federal program and anxious to have the full cooperation of doctors and other health care interests, the Johnson administration and Congress failed to impose any cost restraints on health care providers. The Medicare legislation explicitly denied the government any power to set rates: "Nothing in this title shall be construed to authorize any federal officer . . . to exercise any supervision or control over the . . . compensation of any institution . . . or person providing health services" (sec. 102A). Following the practice of Blue Cross (which the hospitals had originally established), Medicare Part A and Medicaid paid hospitals according to their costs. The higher a hospital's costs, the more it would be paid—a surer way of promoting health care inflation could not have been devised. Any hospital that cut its costs would be reimbursed less. Medicare Part B paid doctors their "customary" fees, assuming them to be in line with "prevailing" rates in their area or to be "reasonable." But the legislation set no standard for reasonableness, and it required the government to outsource claims payments to the insurance industry. Since private insurers acted as "carriers," merely passing along the costs to the government, they had no incentive to exert any control.

As the administration's representative in the negotiations over Medicare, Cohen bears primary responsibility for the legislation's abject concessions to the health care industry. Why did the legislation pay hospitals according to their costs? Because, Cohen later explained, that is what the American Hospital Association wanted (Cohen 1984). Taped White House conversations during the congressional proceedings show that Cohen kept Johnson informed about important financing provisions. When Cohen updated the president about decisions in Ways and Means on March 23, 1965, Johnson asked whether the bill would allow a doctor to "charge what he wants":

> *Cohen*: No, he can't quite charge what he wants to. . . . What the Secretary of HEW would have to do is make some kind of agreement with somebody like Blue Shield, let's say, and it would be their responsibility . . . [to] regulate the fees . . . of the doctor . . . What he [Mills] tried to do is be sure the government wasn't regulating the fees directly, that you deal with the individual doctor. . . . This intermediary, the Blue Shield, would have to do all the policing so that the government would have its long hand—
> *LBJ*: All right, that's good. (Beschloss 2001, 241)

But it wasn't good to turn over responsibility for the fees to private insurers and give them no incentive to rein in those charges. Like hospital costs, doctors' fees surged immediately after Medicare went into effect in 1966. In the final decisions on the bill, the Johnson administration lost on only one issue related to the cost of the program. Fulfilling a promise to the AMA, Mills insisted that hospital-based specialists such as pathologists, radiologists, and anesthesiologists, who were typically paid by salary at the time, instead be paid fee-for-service under Medicare Part B—a provision that led to the vast enrichment of those specialties in years to come.

Ingenious as it was as a political compromise, Mills's three-layered cake and related provisions added a tremendous amount of complexity to health care finance. The law resulted in four systems for financing health care for the elderly. Medicare itself was divided into two parts that worked on different principles. Its limited benefit package led many of the elderly to buy private supplemental insurance. And if they were poor enough or spent down their assets and ended up in a nursing home, seniors would be covered by Medicaid. To be sure, Medicare's administrative costs were lower than those of private insurers because the government didn't do any marketing, medical underwriting, or even much questioning of claims—it just paid them. But like the multiplicity of private insurance plans, the multiplicity of government payment systems created under the 1965 legislation inflicted an enormous paperwork burden on patients and families and required providers to hire legions of administrative personnel. Critics of a single system of national health insurance had said it would be top-heavy with bureaucracy, but the more unified or standardized systems in other advanced countries have much less administrative complexity than the U.S. programs. It was political compromise that turned health care in the United States into a bureaucratic nightmare.

From the start, the costs of Medicare and Medicaid proved to be much higher than the Johnson administration projected (Derthick 1979). In his oral history interviews in 1987, Mills said the biggest mistake had been underestimating the cost, and he cited what happened with Medicaid: "We were told by Bob [Myers], the actuary, that the cost of Medicaid over Kerr-Mills in the first year would be $250 million, nationwide. It was $250 million in New York State alone" (Mills 1987).

Over the next several decades, Medicare and Medicaid skewed public spending *toward* health care and *within* health care. The programs resulted in the medicalization of social welfare expenditures. Medicaid, which accounted for less than 5 percent of means-tested program outlays in 1966, represented 30 percent by 1972 and 40 percent by 1985 (Burtless 1986). Together, Medicare and Medicaid soaked up so much of the public budget at both the federal and state levels that other social programs were starved for funds. Within health care, both programs heavily favored technologically intensive, hospital-based services over public health and preventive care and promoted procedurally oriented medical and surgical specialties over primary practice. Medicare, as Rick Mayes and Robert A. Berenson (2006) put it, became "the leading vehicle for the federal government's subsidization and massive expansion of the U.S. healthcare system." For example, Medicare reimbursement of hospitals included the costs of capital expenditures, and because Medicare beneficiaries represented roughly 40 percent of hospital revenue, the program defrayed 40 percent of the cost of any new hospital investment. The federal government did not cover 40 percent of a new school building that a local district wanted to build, but it did pay for 40 percent of a new wing built by the local hospital, no questions asked. The contrast in the physical plant and technological resources of hospitals and schools in the United States is partly the result of this difference in policy.

The 1965 legislation produced these effects on governmental spending and public investment not only because of its financing provisions, but also because of the political forces the program generated. Although there had not been much of a senior lobby before 1965, Medicare encouraged its development; the American Association of Retired Persons (AARP) built its membership through the sale of Medigap insurance. For-profit hospitals had been of minor importance before 1965, but Medicare's payment provisions encouraged the conversion of nonprofit hospitals into for-profit institutions, along with the growth of the commercial health care industry (Starr 1983). Medical schools became the centers of sprawling networks of high-technology health care. Together with seniors, the hospitals, medical schools, doctors, and others who profited from Medicare represented an overwhelming force favoring the persistence of the program's original structure.

Policy Change and Structural Persistence

The legacy of any law, program, or policy depends on how deeply it becomes entrenched. By "entrenchment," I don't mean only institutionalization—that is, the adoption of formal regulations, administrative routines, and other practices and norms concerned with implementing a policy. Entrenchment also depends on whether a policy generates effects on politics and society that feed back positively or negatively on the policy itself (Pierson 2004; Hacker 2002). A policy or program becomes deeply entrenched when it develops self-reinforcing support from well-organized stakeholders; when it becomes embedded in social relationships and expectations; when private organizations create complementary arrangements and enterprises (for example, supplemental insurance); and when additional layers of law and policy are built on top of the original program and become interdependent with it. On all these dimensions, Medicare and Medicaid became strongly entrenched—so strongly that most of their central features remain intact nearly a half century later, despite important changes to the programs.

Consider the legacies left by five aspects of the original legislation: the basic duality between Medicare and Medicaid; the complexity of financing arrangements; the fee-for-service insurance model and methods of payment; covered benefits; and eligibility rules.

The Basic Duality

The two programs continue to be separate, and no significant effort has been made to consolidate them. Medicare remains a universal federal program, Medicaid a means-tested, federal-state program. The former still falls within a social-insurance framework; the latter within a public-assistance framework. The financing of Medicare Part A continues to come from payroll taxes, which flow into a dedicated trust fund, while the money for Medicare Part B comes from general revenues and premiums paid by the beneficiaries. Although the exact provisions have changed since the law was first enacted, Congress continues to set a floor of requirements for Medicaid and to share some of the cost if states provide wider coverage and additional benefits above that floor. Depending on political ideology and partisan control, states vary sharply in the share of their population they cover, and thanks to the Supreme Court decision on the Medicaid provisions of the Affordable Care Act (ACA), those state-to-state variations have become even more extreme as some states have fully expanded Medicaid and others have refused to do so.

Program Complexity

Subsequent legislation has, if anything, made the system even more complex than it was at the start. In addition to the four separate arrangements for paying for seniors' health care created as a result of the 1965 law, Congress created a fifth in 2003 when it added a prescription drug plan (Medicare Part D) on a different basis from Parts A and B. The establishment of the State Children's Health Insurance Program (SCHIP) in 1997—which states could run as a separate program, an expansion of Medicaid, or a combination of the two—added one more layer to governmental financing of health care. The insurance exchanges and affordability subsidies under the ACA represent another financing layer. This is not to say that Medicare's prescription drug coverage, the children's program, or the new subsidies are ill conceived. The pattern, however, has thus far been not to consolidate but to add layer upon layer to the financing system, partly to avoid disturbing the interests in established programs. Health policy in the United States is a case of path-dependent policy development run wild.

Fee-for-Service Insurance and Methods of Payment

Congress modeled Medicare and Medicaid on the private, fee-for-service insurance system prevailing at the time the legislation was enacted. Medicare's payment provisions—retrospective reimbursement of hospital costs and payment of reasonable charges to doctors—followed the practices that Blue Cross and Blue Shield had established at the behest of the providers. In the language of institutional analysis, the structures of Medicare and the dominant form of insurance were "isomorphic." In the 1980s, however, in seeking to control expenditures, Congress changed Medicare's payment methods, and because the changes held down federal spending, Congress continued to maintain Medicare in its traditional form—that is, fee-for-service coverage by any willing provider—even as that system virtually disappeared from private insurance. In this respect, a change in policy has contributed to structural persistence in Medicare and a growing divergence between Medicare and private insurance.

Originally, Medicare had no provision for making prospective, monthly payments for enrollees in prepaid group practice plans, the forerunners of "health maintenance organizations" (a term introduced in 1971). HMOs were an anomaly in Medicare's fee-for-service universe, in which hospital and doctors' services were paid separately and no organization had any incentive to limit hospital use. Even when Congress provided for Medicare to pay HMOs on a capitation basis in the 1970s, the plans continued to enroll only a small share of Medicare beneficiaries. Although some state Medicaid programs began shifting the poor into HMOs, scandals in California and elsewhere initially set back that movement as well.

The biggest change in Medicare's payment system came in 1983, when in the midst of a Social Security financing crisis, the Reagan administration proposed, and Congress approved, a shift to paying hospitals prospectively per hospital stay according to the patient's diagnosis, instead of retrospectively on the basis of their costs. Yet even then, Medicare continued to pay hospitals retrospectively for the costs of capital investments and graduate medical education. Initially, the new system was a boon to hospitals, which made huge profits from it. Those high returns then led Congress to cut payment rates, slowing Medicare's expenditure growth (Mayes and Berenson 2006). In the belief that prospective hospital payments had been a success, Congress went on to introduce a parallel reform in payments made to physicians. Adopted in 1989 and carried out three years later, the new method replaced the payment of "reasonable" charges with a fee schedule based on an analysis of the resources required for different services (a "resource-based relative value scale," or RBRVS).

This sequence of developments opened up a gap between Medicare and private insurance in two respects. First, Medicare payment rates, to hospitals and to doctors, began to be significantly lower than those paid by private insurers. Second, partly because hospitals were able to charge more for privately insured patients, driving up premiums, employers and insurers sought ways to reduce their own costs and began promoting HMOs as well as a wider range of alternatives to traditional insurance, which together came to be called "managed care." By the mid-1990s, the managed-care revolution was in full swing in the private sector.

In response to fiscal pressures, some states moved toward greater use of managed care in their Medicaid programs. The Clinton administration encouraged that change, offering states waivers from federal requirements if they used the savings from managed care to extend Medicaid eligibility to people previously excluded from the program (Smith and Moore 2008). Managed-care plans made some inroads in Medicare as well in the early 1990s, and when Republicans took control of Congress in 1995, they argued that the traditional Medicare program was a "dinosaur" that needed to be "modernized" by turning it into a voucher system for private insurance. A voucher worth a fixed amount of money, however, would no longer ensure access to the full benefits that Medicare had previously provided. Similarly, Republicans wanted to turn Medicaid into a block grant to the states, which would effectively end the entitlement of the eligible poor to specific benefits under federal law. In a historic confrontation with the Republican Congress, President Clinton defeated those efforts. But in 2003, Republicans in control of both Congress and the White House passed the Medicare Modernization Act, creating a prescription drug benefit to be provided entirely through private insurers. The same legislation sharply increased Medicare payments to private managed-care plans; in fact, in 2008 Medicare paid private plans $1,100 more per beneficiary than it would have cost the federal government if those beneficiaries had remained in traditional, fee-for-service Medicare (Medicare Payment Advisory Commission 2008). Private insurers used some of the extra money to provide extra benefits in order to entice seniors to enroll, and about 25 percent of Medicare beneficiaries made the shift. Nonetheless, with three-quarters of the elderly in the traditional program, the policy legacy of Medicare's original structure remained strong.

Covered Benefits

Like the reliance on fee-for-service payment, the original limits of the Medicare benefit package—particularly the omission of prescription drug and catastrophic coverage—reflected patterns of private insurance that were common in the 1960s. But while the scope of private, employer-based coverage expanded in the ensuing decades, it proved difficult to make corresponding changes to Medicare. Many of the affluent elderly purchased supplemental coverage or received retiree health benefits from companies they had worked for. Consequently, they had little interest in broader Medicare benefits, especially if they had to pay more for them.

The difficulties of expanding the Medicare benefit package were nowhere better illustrated than in the passage of the Medicare Catastrophic Coverage Act of 1988 and its repeal the following year. The chief source of hostility to the law, which provided coverage for prescription drugs as well as catastrophic medical bills, lay in its financing provisions. President Reagan had insisted that he would not sign the legislation if it included a tax increase, and to comply with that demand and avoid adding to the deficit, Congress required seniors to pay the entire cost of the added coverage through two kinds of premiums. A flat monthly premium of $4 to be paid by all seniors would pay for one-third of the program's cost, while the remainder would be covered by an additional, income-related premium due from seniors who paid income taxes of at least $150. These premiums would take the form of a surtax of 15 percent on their tax liability in 1989, up to a maximum of $800 for individuals and $1,600 for couples; in 1993, the surtax would rise to 28 percent, capped at $1,050 for individuals and $2,100 for couples. At the time the law passed, the media gave little attention to the financing provisions. But once the more affluent elderly realized that they would have to pay a surtax for a program that many of them did not need, there was a sharp political backlash, and Congress repealed the program (Himelfarb 1995).

During the 1990s, proposals to expand Medicare benefits focused primarily on the costs of prescription drugs, which were rising sharply. In 1993, as part of his comprehensive reform plan, President Bill Clinton proposed adding prescription drug coverage to Medicare, and he introduced a new proposal for prescription drugs during his second term, again without success. After Al Gore took up the issue in his 2000 presidential campaign, George W. Bush also committed himself to adding prescription drug coverage to Medicare, insisting that he would succeed where the Democrats had failed. For Bush, prescription drug coverage served as a way to revive what had all along been the Republican alternative to Medicare—subsidized private insurance—and to build political support among the elderly, a crucial constituency for his political fortunes given the pivotal role of Florida in the 2000 election and its potential importance in 2004. But the initial reaction of seniors to the program passed by Congress in 2003 was not favorable. Under the original provisions, seniors would pay $35 in monthly premiums, an annual deductible of $250, one-fourth of the cost of drugs between $250 and $2,250, *all* of the cost from $2,250 to $5,100 (the so-called "donut hole"), and 5 percent of the cost above that level. In other words, out of the first $5,100 in yearly drug costs, they would have to pay $4,020 (79 percent) out of pocket. The legislation also barred them from purchasing supplemental "wraparound" coverage to reduce any of this amount (Oliver, Lee, and Lipton 2004). At the time Bush signed the bill, polls showed only 26 percent of seniors approved of the program, with 47 percent against and the rest undecided. Among the public as a whole, opinion ran against the legislation 56 percent to 39 percent (Oliver, Lee, and Lipton 2004). In a poll in January 2006, when the program went into effect, 77 percent of seniors said it was "too complicated" (Hamel, Deane, and Brodie 2011). But unfavorable polls did not dissuade the Republicans from going through with the program, and the prescription drug benefit has since been provided entirely by private insurers.

Nursing-home care was another area where Medicare benefits were originally limited, and that limitation has remained. As a result, instead of being protected against the financial risks of long-term care on a social-insurance basis, the elderly must spend down their assets to qualify for coverage under Medicaid. (The ACA originally included a voluntary governmental program for long-term care insurance, but Congress repealed it in 2012 after the Obama administration declared that it could not carry it out.) Leaving long-term care to Medicaid has had political consequences. At the state level, nursing-home interests often have more influence in the budgetary process than do the low-income young families on Medicaid or the community health centers and other providers that serve them. Nonetheless, Medicaid has in one respect been more generous than Medicare. The benefit package has generally been broader, particularly in the more liberal states, though other factors, such as low payment rates, often impede poor people's effective access to medical care.

Eligibility Rules

In 1972 Congress extended eligibility for Medicare to two groups below age sixty-five: end-stage renal disease patients (who faced a life-or-death need for kidney dialysis), and people with disabilities who had qualified for Social Security disability insurance for two years. At that time, these steps were generally thought to be interim measures because both President Nixon and congressional Democrats were offering proposals for national health insurance. But the moment for bipartisan agreement on universal coverage was lost when the two parties failed to settle their differences before Nixon's fall from power.

Since 1972, no major changes have been made in Medicare eligibility. In the late 1990s, Clinton proposed allowing those fifty-five to sixty-four to buy into the Medicare program if they had no other coverage, and a national commission on Medicare in 1997 called for an increase in the Medicare eligibility age to sixty-seven. But nothing was done either to lower or to raise the age of eligibility.

In recent decades, the growth in public coverage has come through Medicaid and SCHIP. In 1984, largely through the work of Representative Henry Waxman, chairman of the health subcommittee on the House Energy and Commerce Committee, Congress began extending Medicaid coverage for low-income children and pregnant women. Year by year, Congress extended coverage a little further, typically first as an option for the states and then as a mandate. The biggest steps came in 1989 and 1990 when Congress mandated that states phase in Medicaid coverage for all children in families with incomes beneath the federal poverty level and all children up to age five in families with incomes up to 33 percent above the poverty level (Smith and Moore 2008). These requirements reduced some of the state-to-state variation in Medicaid eligibility and weakened the Medicaid-welfare link. That link was further reduced with welfare reform legislation in 1996, which enabled those cut off from cash benefits to retain eligibility for Medicaid. In 1997, the enactment of SCHIP, another means-tested expansion focused on the young, provided access to health coverage for children in families who earned too much to qualify for Medicaid but not enough to afford private insurance. Unlike Medicaid, SCHIP was set up not as an entitlement but rather as a program with a fixed budget.

The introduction of prospective payment in Medicare and the expansion of eligibility for Medicaid are the most important changes in those programs since 1965. But on the whole, the institutional structure of Medicare and Medicaid has been remarkably stable. The full range of mechanisms of entrenchment mentioned earlier have been at work: the creation of strong stakeholder interests in the status quo; socially embedded expectations, as individuals and institutions have come to rely on the programs; complementary businesses, such as supplemental insurance, which have helped support and wall in the programs; and layers of additional law and policy.

I am not arguing that change is impossible. On the contrary, change is inevitable because of the underlying problems of cost and coverage that the programs have aggravated or failed to correct. From 1970 to 2009, health care expenditures jumped from 7 percent to 17.7 percent of gross domestic product in the United States—an increase out of line with the experience of the other rich democracies, where costs rose but still averaged only 9.3 percent of GDP (OECD 2013). Over the same four decades, the proportion of Americans without health coverage increased from about 10 or 12 percent to 16.7 percent (Starr 2011a; U.S. Bureau of the Census 2010). Rising costs contributed to the growth of the uninsured population; as health care costs increased while median income stagnated, the number of Americans unable to afford coverage went up. That, in turn, increased the demand for governmental intervention. Medicare and Medicaid have actually been cheaper than private insurance; still, Americans pay more in taxes for their limited public programs than the citizens of all other nations pay for national health insurance. As two critics of the American health care system point out, Americans have been "paying for national health insurance—and not getting it" (Woolhandler and Himmelstein 2002).

Thanks to slower than anticipated cost increases since the passage of the ACA, the projections of future spending on Medicare and Medicaid have dropped sharply. If the rate of spending growth since 2010 continues over the long term, the fiscal pressures created by the two programs will dissipate. But spending slowed in the 1990s only to grow again, and it is a brave forecaster who will take the slow growth from 2009 to 2013 as proof that the health-cost beast has been tamed. More likely, with institutions thus far little changed, the long-run patterns will return, and with them the sharp divisions between Republicans and Democrats over how to respond. In the face of Republican efforts to turn the programs from defined-benefit to defined-contribution systems, Democrats will face hard choices. To defend the programs, they will have to change them, imposing stricter controls on payment, perhaps extending them to the system as a whole in order to avoid widening the disparities between public and private payers (see Starr 2011b).

The Living Political Legacy

In the early 1970s under President Nixon, Democrats and Republicans came close to agreeing on a plan for universal health insurance. But in the following two decades, the divisions between the two parties on health care reform widened until they took positions in sharp contradiction to each other. In 1993, Clinton proposed a system that would have made health insurance a right of all Americans. Two years later, led by Newt Gingrich, Republicans proposed turning Medicare into a voucher system and Medicaid into a block grant, which would effectively have ended the rights to health benefits that at least some Americans had enjoyed under federal law.

Much the same pattern unfolded under President Barack Obama. In 2010 Democrats passed the ACA, which at the time was expected to extend coverage to about thirty-two million people without insurance—half of them through an expansion of Medicaid, half through subsidized private insurance coverage to be provided through new state-based insurance exchanges. But after taking control of the House of Representatives in 2011, Republicans voted to repeal the ACA and to end the earlier federal health entitlements. As in 1995, they sought to replace Medicare with a "premium support" for private insurance, and Medicaid with a block grant to the states—policies that would allow the federal government to wash its hands of the problem of health-care cost containment. Though blocked from achieving their goals at the federal level, Republicans were nonetheless able in many of the states to prevent Medicaid from being expanded and to enact laws interfering with enrollment in the insurance exchanges.

Although the two parties' positions are antithetical, they do have one thing in common: neither party has recently proposed to expand Medicare or to create a system for the under-sixty-five population on a social-insurance basis. In that respect, the legacy of Medicare has fallen short. In the 1960s, many Democrats hoped that they would be able to achieve with Medicare what they had achieved with Social Security: start out with a program that offered limited benefits and didn't cover everyone, and then gradually raise the standards and expand the coverage until the program provided a decent floor of protection for everyone. But the Social Security analogy proved to be wrong.

From its establishment in 1935, Social Security was well suited to incremental expansion. The generation that initially entered the program—many of whom had lost their savings during the Depression—received an especially good deal in retirement income, and every time Congress extended the program to cover additional workers, contributors increased faster than recipients, improving the program's finances. Social Security was also entirely compatible with private employer pensions; the program provided a base retirement income, which pensions and individual savings could supplement. This experience suggested that health insurance could also follow an incremental path.

Yet the 1965 legislation establishing Medicare did not create the same favorable conditions for program expansion. The failure to build in cost controls at the inception of the program led many people to conclude that a universal program built on Medicare's principles would be fiscally irresponsible. Medicare encouraged seniors to see themselves as a separate group with interests morally superior to those of the poor on Medicaid. The growth of supplemental insurance led the more affluent elderly to resist broader benefits, at least if they had to pay for them on a progressive basis. Together with the federal tax expenditures for employer-provided insurance, Medicare helped create a large bloc of voters who were unaware how much of a public subsidy they received and who believed that other people shouldn't expect government to pay for their health care. In short, federal policy toward health insurance exhibited a pattern that was the reverse of Social Security. Instead of leading step by step to a universal system, incrementalism worked against it.

Paradoxically, although seniors like Medicare—in fact, they are the age group most satisfied with their health insurance (Hamel, Deane, and Brodie 2011)—they are also the most resistant to a universal, public program. In 2008, a national survey by the Harvard School of Public Health and Harris Interactive asked whether the health care system would be better, worse, or about the same if the United States had "socialized medicine." Among those who said they understood the term, there was a striking difference in responses by age. Fifty-five percent of the youngest group—eighteen to thirty-four years old—said socialized medicine would be better, while 30 percent said it would be worse. Among those thirty-five to sixty-four years old, 45 percent said it would be better, while 38 percent said it would be worse. Just one age group had a majority against socialized medicine—the one age group that, according to conservatives' definition of the term, has socialized medicine: 57 percent of people over age sixty-five said it would be worse, while only 30 percent thought it would be better (Blendon and Benson 2011).

The ACA was not socialized medicine; it was an effort to fill in the holes of the existing insurance system with a minimum of disruption to established institutions and the protected public. But much of the protected public could never be won over to a program that they perceived as primarily benefiting the poor and minorities. No age group was more opposed to the ACA than the elderly. Indeed, in some polls, they were the only age group opposed to the law; a Gallup poll in June 2010 found 60 percent of seniors saying the adoption of reform was a "bad thing," while 57 percent of those eighteen to twenty-nine years old, along with a plurality of other age groups, said it was a "good thing" (Saad 2010). Beginning with Sarah Palin's "death panel" scare in 2009, Republicans and conservative organizations played on the fears of the elderly that health care reform would hurt them, and during the campaigns for the midterm elections, they ran ads accusing the Democrats of cutting Medicare. After winning large gains in the 2010 election—thanks in part to a twenty-one-point swing toward the GOP among elderly voters—Republicans in the House of Representatives turned around and voted to end the traditional Medicare program altogether, beginning with people turning sixty-five in 2022. Under the 2011 House Republican premium-support plan, according to the Congressional Budget Office, the typical sixty-five-year-old in 2022 would pay twice as much a year out of pocket as under current Medicare—$12,500 compared with $6,150 (CBO 2011). Subsequent iterations of the Republican proposals backed away from eliminating the traditional public Medicare program, but continued to call for gradually raising the age of eligibility for Medicare to sixty-seven without any measure to replace coverage for sixty-five- and sixty-six-year-olds.

For thirty years after the adoption of Medicare and Medicaid, Republicans and Democrats cooperated in sustaining the programs (Oberlander 2003). Although that politics of consensus broke down in 1995, Clinton's success in defending the programs from Gingrich's attacks seemed to reassert the earlier view that the basic policies were too popular to be overturned. But the Republicans' revival of efforts to eliminate health care entitlements in 2011 suggests that at some point when their party controls both Congress and the presidency, they may well end the commitments that the United States made in 1965.

Those commitments were an extraordinary step in a country that had so long resisted making the cost of health care a public responsibility. But that does not excuse the mistakes made by Johnson, Mills, and other Democrats when they passed Medicare and Medicaid. Assessing Johnson's role, Blumenthal and Morone write, "He stands alone as the most effective healthcare president in American history" (2009, 205). If the standard of judgment is only the ability to pass legislation, Johnson deserves that praise. But if the standard is whether the legislation adopted serves the nation's long-run interest, the historical judgment cannot be so generous. The Medicare and Medicaid programs helped give the United States the most costly and inequitable health care system in the advanced democracies. There can be no exempting Johnson or his administration from responsibility for the resulting damage to the public welfare and the national interest.

Note

This article draws on arguments and evidence developed at greater length in Starr 2011a.

References

Berkowitz, Edward D. 1995. *Mr. Social Security: The life of Wilbur Cohen.* Lawrence: University Press of Kansas.

Beschloss, Michael, ed. 2001. *Reaching for glory: Lyndon Johnson's secret White House tapes, 1964–1965.* New York: Simon and Schuster.

Blendon, Robert J., and John M. Benson. 2011. Attitudes about the U.S. health system and priorities for government action. In Robert J. Blendon, Mollyann Brodie, John Benson, and Drew E. Altman, *American public opinion and health care*, 39–59. Washington, D.C.: CQ Press.

Blumenthal, David, and James A. Morone. 2009. *The heart of power: Health and politics in the Oval Office.* Berkeley: University of California Press.

Burtless, Gary. 1986. Public spending for the poor: Trends, prospects, and economic limits. In Sheldon H. Danziger and Daniel H. Weinberg, eds., *Fighting poverty: What works, what doesn't.* Cambridge, Mass.: Harvard University Press.

Cohen, Wilbur H. 1984. Medicare, 1965–1985–2000. Speech at conference "Medicare: Reaffirming the vision, retooling the instrument," Woodrow Wilson School of Public and International Affairs, Princeton University. Nov.

Congressional Budget Office. 2011. Long-term analysis of a budget proposal by Chairman Ryan. Apr. 5.

Davis, Karen, and Diana Rowland. 1983. Uninsured and underserved: Inequities in health care in the United States. *Milbank Memorial Fund Quarterly/Health and Society* 61:149–176.

Derthick, Martha. 1979. *Policymaking for Social Security.* Washington, D.C.: Brookings Institution.

Hacker, Jacob. 2002. *The divided welfare state: The battle over public and private social benefits in the United States.* New York: Cambridge University Press.

Hamel, Elizabeth C., Claudia Deane, and Mollyann Brodie. 2011. Medicare and Medicaid. In Robert J. Blendon, Mollyann Brodie, John Benson, and Drew E. Altman, *American public opinion and health care*, 151–188. Washington, D.C.: CQ Press.

Himelfarb, Richard. 1995. *Catastrophic politics: The rise and fall of the Medicare Catastrophic Coverage Act of 1988.* University Park: Pennsylvania State University Press.

Marmor, Theodore R. 1973. *The politics of Medicare.* Chicago: Aldine.

Mayes, Rick, and Robert A. Berenson. 2006. *Medicare prospective payment and the shaping of U.S. health care.* Baltimore: Johns Hopkins University Press.

Medicare Payment Advisory Commission. 2008. *Report to the Congress: Medicare payment policy.* Washington, D.C.

Mills, Wilbur. 1971. Oral history interview I, by Joe B. Frantz. Internet copy, LBJ Library. www.ssa.gov/history/pdf/mills1.pdf.

————. 1987. Oral history interview II, by Michael L. Gillette. Internet copy, LBJ Library. www.ssa.gov/history/pdf/mills2.pdf.

Moffitt, Robert, and Barbara Wolfe. 1992. The effect of the Medicaid program on welfare participation and labor supply. *Review of Economics and Statistics* 74:615–626.

Oberlander, Jonathan. 2003. *The political life of Medicare.* Chicago: University of Chicago Press.

Oliver, Thomas R., Phillip R. Lee, and Helene L. Lipton. 2004. A political history of Medicare and prescription drug coverage. *Milbank Quarterly* 82:283–254.

Organization for Economic Cooperation and Development. 2013. OECD health data 2013: Frequently requested data indicators. www.oecd.org/els/health -systems/oecdhealthdata2013-frequentlyrequesteddata.htm.

Pierson, Paul. 2004. *Politics in time: History, institutions, and social analysis.* Princeton, N.J.: Princeton University Press.

Saad, Lydia. 2010. Verdict on healthcare reform bill still divided. Gallup, June 22. www.gallup.com/poll/140981/verdict-healthcare-reform-bill-divided.aspx.

Smith, David G., and Judith D. Moore. 2008. *Medicaid politics and policy, 1965–2007.* New Brunswick, N.J.: Transaction.

Starr, Paul. 1983. *The social transformation of American medicine.* New York: Basic Books.

————. 2011a. *Remedy and reaction: The peculiar American struggle over healthcare reform.* New Haven, Conn.: Yale University Press.

————. 2011b. The Medicare bind. *American Prospect,* Nov. 24–35.

U.S. Bureau of the Census. 2010. Current Population Reports, P60-238, *Income, poverty, and health insurance coverage in the United States: 2009.* Report prepared by Carmen DeNavas-Walt, Bernadette D. Proctor, and Jessica C. Smith. Washington, D.C.: Government Printing Office.

U.S. Department of Health and Human Services. 2009. National health expenditures: 2009 highlights. Available at McKnights.com, http://media.mcknights .com/documents/20/national_health_expenditures_4937.pdf.

Woolhandler, Steffie, and David U. Himmelstein. 2002. Paying for national health insurance—and not getting it. *Health Affairs* 21:88–98.

Zelizer, Julian E. 1998. *Taxing America: Wilbur D. Mills, Congress, and the state, 1945–1975.* New York: Cambridge University Press.

CHAPTER 9

LBJ's Legacy in Contemporary Social Welfare Policy: Have We Come Full Circle?

CYNTHIA OSBORNE

This chapter reflects on today's social welfare policies and the extent to which they have been influenced by LBJ's vision of a Great Society that helps "more Americans, especially young Americans, escape from squalor and misery, and unemployment rolls where other citizens help to carry them" (Johnson 1964a). LBJ's original vision for a War on Poverty is arguably quite different from the one that was eventually fought (and, some would argue, lost). But it is his vision of what could have been, indeed what should have been, that is his legacy.

Today's social policy priorities are heavily influenced by the initial ones of the War on Poverty, although this has not always been the case. U.S. social policy has come full circle in many respects. Today's policies emphasize job creation, work supports, and human capital development—all original tenets of the War on Poverty. In the 1970s and 1980s, social welfare policy focused almost exclusively on cash assistance, or "welfare," which was not a centerpiece of LBJ's vision. Significant changes in the social, political, economic, and demographic climate over the past fifty years pose new challenges for today and call for a renewed strategy to fight poverty and disadvantage and ensure that the United States is poised to be economically competitive in an increasingly global economy.

This chapter begins with a discussion of the scope of today's poverty problem and compares it with those that LBJ highlighted in the mid-1960s. Unfortunately, poverty remains pervasive, and it is increasingly concentrated among single mothers and their children, and less educated minorities. Additionally, many families who do not fall below the official poverty threshold are struggling to make ends meet, and for too many reaching the middle class remains an elusive dream.

The chapter then highlights today's social policy priorities and discusses which elements have been influenced by LBJ's legacy and which have been designed to meet contemporary challenges. For example, today's work-support policies focus on allowing single mothers to move from welfare to work, rather than on providing income maintenance for low-wage male breadwinners. Additionally, because of the dramatic demographic changes that have taken place since the 1960s, there is now an emphasis on strengthening families and keeping fathers connected to their children.

Next, the chapter discusses the federal government's approach to fighting poverty, the structures in place to accomplish its antipoverty goals, and the changes in these areas over the past fifty years. In his inaugural state of the union address in 1964, LBJ stated, "Our aim is not only to relieve the symptoms of poverty, but to cure it, and above all, to prevent it" (Johnson 1964a). His vision was premised on a comprehensive, coordinated approach that included efforts at the federal, state, and local levels. Regrettably, today's approach toward fighting poverty is more segmented, and funding streams are siloed, which makes the coordination of services difficult. In addition, preventive efforts have largely been replaced by temporary services attempting to remedy systemic problems.

The chapter concludes by discussing the legacies of LBJ's policies and the lessons we should heed in order to meet the social challenges of today and the next fifty years. No longer are we fighting poverty simply because it is the just thing to do. Today, our challenges are greater. We live in an increasingly global and competitive world; our families are more fragmented and less able to support their children; and many of our schools continue to fail to educate our young people. The growth in our population is fueled only by those who are relatively disadvantaged, and our next generation of workers and parents is simply not prepared for the coming challenges. To remain economically competitive and to keep the promise of the American dream alive, we must adopt a comprehensive new commitment to invest in the nation's children and provide the supports necessary for our citizens to be self-reliant.

The Poverty Problem

Ironically, the War on Poverty was waged at a time when poverty rates had fallen substantially, driven by a huge post–World War II economic expansion. Not all groups shared in this prosperity, however, because of racial discrimination and geographic isolation, which prompted the call to action. Unfortunately, the proportion of Americans living in poverty has remained persistently high since 1964, when the War on Poverty was begun. In 2009, over 43.6 million people, or approximately 14.3 percent of the population, were officially poor (U.S. Bureau of the Census 2012, table 2). This figure is slightly higher than the poverty rate in 1967, when 14.2 percent of the population was poor. Although the rate has fluctuated somewhat with changes in the economic cycle, since 1967 the poverty rate has not exceeded 15.2 percent (in 1983) and has not been less than 11.1 percent (in 1973). This lack of progress leaves many asserting that we waged a war on poverty, and poverty won (Katz 1989, 79).

Our poverty measure, however, is increasingly inadequate to identify those who are in need. On one hand, the poverty measure may overstate the number of Americans who are poor because it does not reflect in-kind transfers and other resources designed to help the poor (Blank 2008a, 237–238). On the other hand, our poverty measure may underestimate those truly in need. The poverty measure is a derivative of the frugal food budget from 1963, when the average family spent one-third of its income on food. To determine who was poor, Mollie Orshansky, a researcher in the Social Security Administration, multiplied the frugal food budget by three to set the initial threshold, and subsequently Congress has made few changes to the threshold beyond indexing that number to inflation and adjusting for family size (Fisher 1992). The threshold may have overstated the number of poor in 1963, because poor families spent more of their household income on food than the average family. Today, however, food constitutes far less than one-third of family budgets because it has become relatively cheap, while costs for housing, health care, education, and energy have risen faster than inflation (Blank and Greenberg 2008, 6). Thus, the official poverty measure does not adequately account for what a typical family needs in order to be self-sufficient.

Families with incomes up to twice the official poverty measure are generally considered low income; these families are at high risk of falling into poverty and have a difficult time affording their basic needs (Waldron, Roberts, and Reamer 2004, 12). More than one-third of Americans are low income, and fully 41 percent of children live in low-income families (National Center for Children in Poverty 2009, 8). Therefore, although the poverty challenge is large, the problem of ensuring that families can provide for themselves without the risk of falling into poverty is even greater.

Composition of the Poor

While the poverty rate has remained relatively stable over the past fifty years, the composition of the poor has shifted significantly, which means that the target of social welfare policies has also changed. Today, those in poverty are more likely than in years past to be racial and ethnic minorities or to be single mothers and their children and are less likely to be elderly or to live in families.

Children are increasingly overrepresented among the poor (see table 9.1). Today, although children constitute only 24.5 percent of the population, they make up 35.5 percent of those in poverty. By contrast, the elderly are significantly underrepresented among the poor, which was not the case in the 1960s. Elderly poverty was quite high fifty years ago; approximately 30 percent of those sixty-five years of age and older were poor, yet today, since Social Security payments are reflected in family income, less than 9 percent of senior citizens live in poverty.

Child poverty is higher today than it was when Johnson waged the War on Poverty; in 2009, more than 20 percent of children were poor, compared with less than 17 percent of children in 1967. Poverty is particularly high, however, for children who are racial and ethnic minorities. Whereas more than 20 percent of children live in poverty today, the rate is 39 percent for African American children and 35 percent for Hispanic children, compared with only 12 percent for white children (U.S. Bureau of the Census 2011b, 70–73). As the number of Hispanic children increases in the population, we can expect to see child poverty increase as well unless there is a significant change of course. The Hispanic population is expected to triple in size from 2005 through 2050 and to account for most of the nation's population growth during that period (Passel and Cohn 2008, i). If these projections are correct, Hispanics will make up 29 percent of the U.S. population in 2050, compared with 14 percent in 2000 (i).

Whites have always been underrepresented among the poor, but in 1967 they constituted a majority of the poor. This is no longer the case. In 2009, 42.5 percent of the poor were non-Hispanic whites, and there was no clear racial or ethnic majority group of poor individuals. Poverty *rates* are also considerably lower for whites than for other racial and ethnic groups. The poverty rate for non-Hispanic whites is approximately 9 percent, compared with roughly 25 percent for African Americans and Hispanics.

More than 70 percent of the poor live in families, meaning that they share a household with a person to whom they are related by blood or marriage (U.S. Bureau of the Census 2011b, 15). In 2009, almost two-thirds of poor families were headed by a single parent (most commonly a single mother), which is in sharp contrast to the situation 1967, when most poor families were headed by two parents. This change is cause for concern because of the much higher rate of poverty among single-parent families. Ap-

Table 9.1. U.S. poverty composition and rates, 1967 and 2009 (%)

	1967			2009		
	Population	*Poor*	*Poverty rate*	*Population*	*Poor*	*Poverty rate*
Overall		14.2			14.3	
Age						
Younger than 18	35.9	41.9	16.6	24.5	35.5	20.1
18–64	54.7	38.6	10.0	62.7	56.7	12.9
65 and older	9.3	19.4	29.5	12.7	7.9	8.9
Race/ethnicity						
White[a]	87.9	68.4	11.0	64.9	42.5	9.4
Black	11.0	30.6	39.3	12.7	22.8	25.9
Asian	NA	NA	NA	4.6	4.0	12.5
Hispanic	NA	NA	NA	16.1	28.4	25.3
Other	1.0	1.1	14.7	1.7	—	—
Family type[b]						
Married	90.3	69.7	9.6	74.1	37.8	5.8
Single	9.7	30.3	38.8	18.8	50.5	29.9
Work experience[c]						
Full-time	NA	NA	NA	41.7	8.9	2.7
Part-time	NA	NA	NA	23.3	27.1	14.5
Not working	NA	NA	NA	35.0	64.0	22.7

Source: U.S. Census.
Note: All figures are percentages.
[a]Hispanic and non-Hispanic whites are combined in 1967 only.
[b]Includes only the population living in family households in which there are at least two people related through either blood or marriage.
[c]Includes only the population over age sixteen.

proximately 6 percent of married-couple families are officially poor, whereas the poverty rate for families with a female householder is over five times as high (18). As families become more complex and less stable, and as more children are born and raised in single-parent families, poverty will remain high (McLanahan 2009, 128).

Changes in Family Structure

The dramatic changes in the family over the past fifty years pose perhaps the biggest challenge for fighting poverty and promoting self-sufficiency. More children live in single-parent families than at any time in the past, and this is especially true for racial or ethnic minority children and children whose parents have lower levels of education (Child Trends Data Bank 2013). These children are at an increased risk of negative social, emotional, and academic outcomes relative to their peers who live with both of their continuously married parents (Amato 2005, 86, 89).

In 1965, Daniel P. Moynihan predicted that if not addressed, nonmarital childbearing and family instability would become a major problem in our country and hinder social policy efforts. His report, which focused on African Americans, lamented the high unemployment rate among African American males and the destruction that lack of employment had on the black family (Moynihan 1965). At that time, close to 25 percent of black children were born outside of marriage, and approximately one-quarter lived in single-parent homes (8–9).

Today, more than 40 percent of all children are born to an unmarried mother, yet this number differs considerably by race or ethnicity (Child Trends Data Bank 2013). Indeed, over 72 percent of African American children are born outside of marriage, half of Hispanic children, and slightly over one-quarter of non-Hispanic white children (Martin et al. 2011). Additionally, approximately half of all children will spend some part of their childhood without both of their biological, married parents, but again this is much more common for racial and ethnic minorities and for children with less educated parents (Brown 2010, 1060).

Persistently high rates of male unemployment and a decline in returns to skills among less educated males have certainly contributed to the increase in the share of children living in unmarried-parent households (Blank 2008b, 3–4); however, this is not the only story (Edin and Reed 2005, 126). Marriage has become an unobtainable goal for many; indeed, marriage is now a proxy for success within each socioeconomic group (117, 121). Non-marriage often reflects significant personal barriers, including substance abuse, depression, and incarceration (McLanahan 2009, 116), all characteristics that make a successful marriage difficult and that negatively influence children's well-being. These factors also limit adults' ability to find and hold stable employment, and low earnings often translate into low marriage rates.

Population Growth

Another important demographic change is that U.S. population growth is being fueled by those who are relatively disadvantaged. Latinas and women with lower levels of education have birth rates that are significantly higher than other women (Matthews and Ventura 1997, 6). In fact, the birth rate of college-educated women is below replacement level (6). At current rates, the U.S. population will likely expand to 438 million people by 2050, up from approximately 300 million today, and approximately 82 percent of this growth will be driven by immigrants and their descendants (Passel and Cohn 2008, i). Without new efforts, this population growth will pose challenges to social policy and to U.S. prosperity. Currently, as many as 30 percent of Hispanics do not graduate from high school (Fry 2011, 5), and their median household incomes are significantly less than their non-Hispanic white peers (U.S. Bureau of the Census 2010, 5).

The Changing Labor Market

Changes in the labor market over the past fifty years, which have led to an increase in income inequality, pose a significant challenge for today's battle against poverty. The emergence of a technology- and service-based economy has led to a bifurcation in necessary skills sets, so that today's jobs are now either high skilled and high wage or low skilled and low wage (Iceland 2003, 76). No longer can a high school graduate expect to earn enough and garner sufficient benefits from his company to support a family, as was often possible in the 1970s and early 1980s.

Indeed, work does not guarantee an escape from poverty; in 2004, 61 percent of families with incomes below the poverty level contained at least one worker, and 28 percent of poor families contained at least one person who worked full-time, year-round (Blank, Danziger, and Schoeni 2006, 1). Thus, social policy cannot rely solely on creating jobs, because many low-skilled jobs simply do not pay enough to lift a family out of poverty, especially if there is only one earner.

Two incomes are now necessary to support a low-skilled household. Among the very low-skilled, however, two-parent families are increasingly rare, and most less educated households are represented by a single mother struggling to support her children through a combination of her earnings, social support (e.g., Temporary Assistance for Needy Families, Supplemental Nutrition Assistance Program/food stamps), and sometimes support from the father of her children or other family members.

Women have entered the labor market at high rates over the past fifty years. Today, approximately 60 percent of women work (U.S. Bureau of the Census 2011a), and the fastest entrants into the labor market are women with young children (Shealy et al. 2005, 7). Thus, there is a growing need for child care and other work supports that allow families with two earners as well as single-parent families to fulfill their dual obligations of employment and child rearing.

Summary of the Poverty Problem

The proportion of Americans in poverty or at risk of falling into poverty will continue to rise in the absence of intervention. The population is growing fastest among the poorest; children are increasingly likely to live in a single-mother household, which significantly increases their odds of being poor; jobs for less skilled workers do not pay enough to ensure self-sufficiency; and parents increasingly have to balance competing demands of family and work. These contemporary problems were not considerations of LBJ's War on Poverty; his emphasis was on employment and human capital development, primarily among breadwinning males. Today's social policies, however, must address these demographic and social issues, in addition to creating jobs and increasing educational outcomes, in order to be effective at helping American families, reducing inequality, and ensuring that the United States remains economically competitive.

LBJ's War on Poverty

The shifting priorities of U.S. poverty policy reflect changing beliefs about both the sources of poverty and the role of government in the lives of the poor. During the nineteenth century, poverty was viewed as an individual problem attributable to a lack of motivation. Strategies to prevent poverty focused on improving the individual person. During the early twentieth century, poverty came to be viewed more as a social problem that resulted from the broader economic context of the Great Depression (Quadango 1999, 76; Iceland 2003, 11–12). Consequently, FDR's antipoverty policies focused on job creation.

LBJ viewed poverty as the result of both the economic context and individual human response to a lack of opportunity (Johnson 1964a). The bold objective of the War on Poverty was to eliminate poverty through job creation and human capital development. This policy priority corresponded to LBJ's belief that poverty in a prosperous society was perpetuated by a lack of access to stable employment at a sufficient wage. Strategies to promote job creation focused on federal investment in community economic development (Russell 2004, 113; Johnson 1964b). Strategies to develop human capital included skills training and placement opportunities for adults, along with early-childhood interventions to improve the educational prospects of the next generation.

LBJ considered employment the most important factor in breaking the cycle of poverty (Johnson 1968). The administration considered other strategies, particularly cash and in-kind assistance, to be short-term, low-priority solutions (Plotnick and Skidmore 1975, 5). Strategies that focused on individual motivation were also developed, but always in conjunction with human capital development, such as the parenting components of Head Start (Clark 2002, 7, 160).

The War on Poverty began in 1964 with the establishment of the Office of Economic Opportunity (OEO). The OEO was designed to address both individual and social causes of poverty by improving individuals' job skills as well as entire communities, from the bottom up. One set of OEO programs—including VISTA, the Job Corps, work-study, and the Neighborhood Youth Corps—sought to teach job skills and provide work experience to individuals. A second set of programs sought to improve neighborhoods through Community Action Programs, which included organizing nongovernmental organizations at the local level. The Head Start program sought to address the cycle of poverty through early intervention. Cash-transfer programs remained outside the OEO because LBJ believed that such programs would not be necessary once individuals could access jobs (Plotnick and Skidmore 1975, 57).

The social and economic context of the time was reflected in the populations prioritized by the Great Society programs. The targets of job training were young men perceived to be the primary breadwinners for families (Johnson 1964b). A second target was the next generation of workers. Head Start and the programs of the Elementary and Secondary Education Act combined to provide federal support for children's education from pre-kindergarten through high school. In addition, LBJ extended opportunities for college through federal loan and work-study programs (Plotnick and Skidmore 1975, 21–22). Importantly, the War on Poverty initiatives strongly supported racial integration because LBJ believed racial injustice was a root cause of poverty and lack of opportunity for African Americans (Orleck and Hazirjian 2011).

Much of LBJ's policy agenda was focused on gains that could be made only in the long run. It takes time for economic planning and investment to develop new industries that will respond to job training. New opportunities for early childhood education and college would take a full generation to bear fruit. The short-term priorities of the Johnson administration—job training and work opportunities—were unlikely to have a long-term impact if new jobs were not created to absorb the newly trained workers. Many critics argue that the failure of the War on Poverty is attributable to the public focus on short-term results for policies that required long-run implementation (Bailey and Duquette 2014).

Contemporary Social Welfare Policy

The failure of the War on Poverty to quickly reduce poverty levels and allow families to be self-sufficient led to a revised set of policy priorities in the 1970s and 1980s that focused on increasing cash assistance. The new social policy priority was to provide cash support in order to prevent children from growing up poor. Cash support became an entitlement as activists launched a campaign for "welfare rights" (Piven and Cloward 1971).

Aid to Families with Dependent Children (AFDC) entitlements grew, and the welfare rolls quadrupled from 1960 to 1973 (Piven and Cloward 1971, tables 2, 2.1). By 1973, 11 million Americans were receiving cash welfare (AFDC), and over the next generation, nearly one-third of the nation's children experienced being on welfare (Burke and Burke 1974, 9; Moynihan 1991, 134–135). Food stamps, housing subsidies, and other in-kind programs also grew (Murray 1994, 63). The demographics of families were also changing (as noted above); rates of single-motherhood increased, and women entered the workforce in greater numbers.

By the mid-1990s, many welfare reformers had a new set of policy priorities, whose primary goal was to reduce welfare dependence. And like

LBJ, President Clinton prioritized employment (with supports) as the central strategy for combating poverty and government reliance. The policies of welfare reform in 1996 echoed LBJ's focus on employment. Welfare was no longer an entitlement designed to allow single mothers to stay at home with their children; as part of the Personal Responsibility and Work Opportunity Reconciliation Act (PRWORA), employment became a necessary condition for cash assistance eligibility (U.S. Department of Health and Human Services 1996).

Additionally, in response to demographic changes, PRWORA aimed to encourage two-parent families, discourage out-of-wedlock births, and enhance the collection and enforcement of child support. Policies such as assistance with transportation and child care responded to demographic changes and gave women greater access to employment during the 1990s.

Unlike the War on Poverty, however, welfare reform did not prioritize the creation of new jobs, and the success of employment policies was mostly dependent on macroeconomic conditions that determined whether jobs were available for the target population. In addition, welfare reform did not focus on employment among men or on human capital development (education and job training), which were central tenets of the War on Poverty. The 1996 welfare reforms led to significant decreases in the welfare rolls and increases in mothers working, but did not lead to significant and sustained declines in poverty, particularly child poverty. The wages of the many new working mothers were not sufficient to lift a family out of poverty, and when employment opportunities contracted, the new system could not fully support families in need.

Today, education policy, particularly for improving elementary and secondary schools, is stated as a major policy effort by the Obama administration. There has likewise been a growing interest in supporting programs with an emphasis on early education or prekindergarten (Carnero and Heckman 2003, 50). Head Start is one of the few lasting policy legacies of the War on Poverty, and its central premise was to ensure that disadvantaged children showed up to school ready to learn. The results of Head Start have not been as positive as the longevity of the policy may suggest (52). But since research shows clearly that gaps in educational and socio-emotional outcomes at school entry persist throughout school and into adulthood (50), policies today should renew their focus on ensuring that all children show up to school ready to learn. The costs of early care and education are high, and the returns are not immediate; thus, a public that demands quick results often supports these policies only reluctantly.

Family-strengthening programs were largely ignored by the War on

Poverty; however, today social policy must address the changing nature of families. As noted earlier, when LBJ waged the War on Poverty, most poor individuals lived in married-parent households, and families were largely stable. Teen pregnancy rates were high, but nearly all children were born inside of marriage.

In the previous decade, under the George W. Bush administration, social policy emphasized marriage promotion (more in rhetoric than in policy, since only $150 million a year was allocated for marriage promotion or fatherhood initiatives) (U.S. Department of Health and Human Services 2012). The goal was to get unmarried parents to marry, in the hope that their children would not be poor (U.S. Department of Health and Human Services 2010, xi). These programs have been largely unsuccessful at increasing marriage, reducing poverty, or improving children's outcomes, primarily because the parents' economic and social characteristics did not improve (27–28). The Obama administration has continued a focus on family strengthening, particularly emphasizing responsible fatherhood and ensuring that nonresident fathers emotionally and financially support their children.

LBJ's Legacies

When LBJ declared a national War on Poverty, he ended a debate on whether the federal government should contribute to the social safety net and began a debate on how the federal safety net should be structured. LBJ's vision to eliminate poverty required a new approach to the governance of antipoverty programs. From an administrative perspective, the War on Poverty represented an innovative expansion and restructuring of federal social policy, which continues to influence welfare policy today. The governance structure of the War on Poverty was characterized by central coordination of federal antipoverty programs, expansion of federally funded entitlements and mandates to the states, a new relationship between the federal government and nongovernmental organizations, and news ways of measuring the effectiveness of policies.

The Federal Governance of Antipoverty Programs and Mandates for States

LBJ's first important contribution was to centralize the governance of antipoverty programs. He inherited a fractured system of governmental antipoverty programs that housed food, housing, jobs, and cash assistance programs in different administrative agencies. A major part of the plan for the War on Poverty was to centralize the command of all relevant programs in a single administrative office (Gillette 1996, xiv, xviii). The OEO was designed to address both individual and social causes of poverty by increasing individual job skills while improving communities from the bottom up.

Although the OEO itself was short-lived, the vision for coordinated antipoverty programs was revived in the 1996 welfare reform legislation. Under welfare reform, states were supposed to design programs to coordinate services that help individuals enter the job market and maintain stable employment, although the extent to which this occurred varied considerably.

Before the War on Poverty, the federal government's role in welfare policy was limited. Cash-assistance programs were small. FDR's federal employment programs set a precedent for the federal government's involvement, which LBJ built on through the work of the OEO (Handler and Hasenfeld 1991, 84; Russell 2004, 164). The OEO structure fundamentally changed the role of the federal government by providing a combination of federal job-training programs and local community programs to promote job growth (Plotnick and Skidmore 1975, 3). These community programs not only bypassed state governments, but also in many cases were established in an adversarial relationship to the states (Katz 1989, 100). For example, grassroots groups received legal assistance from the OEO to sue states for welfare entitlements (Handler and Hasenfeld 1991, 118). At the time, it was common for states to deny eligibility or benefits to groups of families entitled to assistance under federal regulations. A new role for the federal government in the War on Poverty included ensuring that states met their welfare obligations through the courts (Piven and Cloward 2005, 261–262), and the federal government used the War on Poverty initiatives to enforce racial integration (Hamilton and Hamilton 1997).

During the War on Poverty, the federal government took on poverty and community building as national issues, whereas previously they had been issues for the states (Clark 2002, 54–55). One strategy in the War on Poverty was the expansion of federal entitlement programs and mandates for the states. LBJ used federal mandates to force states to increase welfare benefits and extend eligibility to excluded groups. This strategy included providing legal assistance to local community groups to sue states for benefits (Handler and Hasenfeld 2005, 262). Some argue that while the OEO did not intend to increase entitlements, the precedents of the Great Society quickly led to the routine use of entitlements and unfunded federal mandates in the 1970s (Piven and Cloward 2005, 262; Melnick 2005, 396–397).

The legacy of this implementation structure was an incrementally expanded role of federal mandates and judicial involvement in policy making. The practice was expanded from welfare to environmental policy and workers rights, and today a great deal of public policy has been litigated and negotiated through court processes, with an increasing impact on governmental budgets at all levels (Melnick 2005, 395–403).

Welfare reform responded to the problem of growing entitlements and unfunded mandates by removing the AFDC entitlement. States are now permitted to determine eligibility locally, and time limits are placed on individual recipients. States are funded via block grants rather than open-ended entitlements, and thus the states assume the costs or reap the financial benefits of changes in caseloads. Other social programs of the Great Society, such as Medicare and Medicaid, remain as entitlements, and debates continue about strategies to contain their growing costs.

The key difference between the current system and LBJ's vision is that coordination is now the responsibility of the states. The federal government encourages coordination at the state level through incentives to blend and braid federal funding streams for TANF, child care, and job training and placement. Additionally, while LBJ failed to anticipate the importance of cash-assistance programs as a component of a coordinated antipoverty strategy, welfare reform explicitly integrates work promotion and supports with cash assistance via TANF. Thus, welfare reform restructured LBJ's vision for a coordinated attack on poverty by using incentives to states to coordinate cash assistance and job promotion.

Collaboration with Community-Based Organizations

The Great Society altered the structure of federalism through its use of private community groups to implement federal social policy. The OEO bypassed state governments in its efforts to develop local abilities to provide antipoverty services (Piven and Cloward 2005, 353). LBJ called for the federal government's "maximum feasible participation" in local communities, including partnerships with local nonprofit service providers and advocacy groups to create locally relevant responses to cyclical poverty (Clark 2002, 43–44). OEO programs worked to develop local nonprofits as service providers and advocacy organizations and even helped local legal aid organizations sue states for welfare benefits (Piven and Cloward 2005, 261–262). The impact of maximum feasible participation on public administration in the United States has been profound. This strategy of building local capability was the basis for the rise in participatory democracy in the 1970s and spurred the growth of political and intellectual movements focused on participation in public administration (Melnick 2005, 390–393).

Much of today's social policy continues to depend on private service providers. But the practice has spread its roots of cultivating locally grown service and advocacy organizations to a culture of outsourcing to both nonprofit and for-profit organizations. Welfare reform, for example, encourages the use of private, for-profit educational institutions, including corporate for-profit universities and job training centers. The No Child Left Behind Act encourages the use of for-profit corporations to provide tutoring and even school management. This shift from local nonprofit to national for-profit subcontracting reflects a new focus on privatization as an efficiency-enhancing governance strategy. Meanwhile, some programs, such as Head Start, continue to support local child care organizations, which is in line with LBJ's vision of community building through nonprofit provision of government-supported services.

Measurement of Performance Outcomes

The OEO began the practice of systematically measuring the impact of antipoverty programs. All social programs in the War on Poverty were required to demonstrate an impact on the number of families living in poverty. This requirement led to the development of better counts of poverty and a coordinated approach to analysis of the social safety net. Although many programs remain uncoordinated, it is common for researchers today to examine the holistic effect of federal and state programs on families and the poverty rate.

Welfare reform fundamentally changed the way governmental planners approach social policy, although the idea of measuring the effectiveness of social programs is still in place. Since the goal of welfare reform was to reduce welfare dependency (in contrast to reducing poverty), states are no longer held accountable for lifting families out of poverty. Instead, they are held accountable for reducing the number of families on the welfare rolls through mechanisms such as work requirements, time limits, and stringent eligibility requirements.

LBJ's influence on the governance of current social policy is complex. Many of his strategies are being applied to new goals. The vision of a coordinated attack on poverty remains in welfare reform's coordinated approach to supporting work. But since the new goal is to reduce dependency, this strategy is no longer designed to eliminate poverty. The strategy of decentralization to nongovernmental service providers also remains, but again the goal has shifted from grassroots community development to reducing costs and improving efficiency through the use of for-profit contractors. States have been freed from many of the requirements for entitlement funding. This approach has allowed for local experimentation and innovation that can either promote or subvert LBJ's vision, depending on local preferences.

Lessons Learned from the War on Poverty

The lessons learned from the War on Poverty and the legacies of Lyndon Johnson should continue to inform future public policy priorities in order to reduce poverty and maintain economic competiveness. Several lessons should be heeded in contemporary social policy.

First, conversations about poverty and inequality are more effective if they emphasize investment rather than only social justice. Social justice and equal opportunity are ideals to be strived for, but they no longer seem to motivate the American public to act. The notion that our country will not be as strong or economically competitive if we continue to permit more than 50 percent of low-income children to drop out of high school, over 40 percent of low-income boys to go to jail, close to 40 percent of young girls to get pregnant before age twenty, and more than 50 percent of our kids to grow up in unstable home environments is more likely to motivate the public to make investing in children and families a top priority.

Second, investing in young children and sustaining that investment through their transition to adulthood is necessary to eliminate poverty. This investment includes prekindergarten, a topic surrounded by much discussion, as well as earlier essential investments and interventions. If we wait until children are age four to try to intervene, we will continually need to close a gap, and the results will be no different from what they are when we intervene at kindergarten or beyond. Prenatal investments and early parenting interventions such as home visitation have proven to be effective, and high-quality child care has lasting, positive effects on low-income children. These interventions are costly, but so are the costs of challenges that result from failing to invest in children when they are young, such as school dropout, teen pregnancy, and incarceration. In addition to early-childhood interventions, investments for youth such as after-school, summer, and service-learning programs have proved effective at closing the achievement gap and keeping teens on the path to become healthy, productive adults.

Third, job creation is the signature of social policy. It is not just good economic policy to have a strong economy; it is also great social policy. But a rising tide no longer seems to lift all boats in the same way that it did in the past. In the late 1990s, a tsunami of economic growth made an impact on people's lives, but other periods of prosperity have not resulted in significantly better lives for those at the bottom. We have to be more targeted about job-creation strategies and take into consideration local markets and unemployment rates.

We also must remember, however, that employment does not guarantee that a person will not be poor, much less middle class. Work supports that allow dual-earning couples and single-parent families to balance providing for their children and caring for them are important. For example, early child care is a support that serves dual roles. Additionally, wage subsidies like the earned income tax credit (EITC) should be available to all workers, not just parents.

Fourth, family-strengthening programs should be prioritized, in addition to work supports. LBJ's policies did not heed Moynihan's concerns about changing family structures, and now the family is both a cause and effect of persistent poverty. Current policies emphasize increasing marriage rates by providing relationship-skills training. The skills, which are necessary, can be used with other relationships in people's lives, but this approach is insufficient. The multiple barriers to marriage among low-income parents need a multidimensional approach to amelioration. The emphasis should be on relationship stability and the stability of resources, which are crucial for healthy child development. A renewed emphasis on limiting unprepared pregnancies should be a central tenet of our social policy agenda; waiting to focus on the parents' marriage until after a child arrives is too little too late.

Additionally, family-strengthening programs need to renew a focus on men. Our social policies have largely focused on women and their children for the past forty years. For men, we have provided only limited job training programs, child support enforcement, and prison. Expanding the EITC to fathers so that it is on par with what is offered to their female counterparts is a step in the right direction. So is recognizing and addressing the reasons that men abandon their families, yet still holding them accountable for meeting their responsibilities. If we continue to neglect men, families will continue to disintegrate and be dependent on governmental support.

Finally, all poverty alleviation strategies should be integrated into a coordinated, comprehensive approach. Although the War on Poverty addressed education, employment, and health, all its programs were framed as antipoverty programs. Participation in one program led to inclusion in others, so each participant benefited from an array of services, resources, and supports (Clark 2002, 85). As programs were relocated from the OEO after LBJ's presidency, they increasingly took on the characteristics of their new host agencies, resulting in the siloed system we have today. Many of the programs once considered antipoverty programs are now isolated, even though all serve our most vulnerable populations, who typically have overlapping needs. Governmental agencies at the federal, state, and local levels must better coordinate with one another and with community-based organizations in order to work together to serve poor children and families. Luckily, advances in information technology have the promise to help facilitate this change.

The precise degree to which the War on Poverty was successful is not completely clear. On one hand, the poverty rate in America has hardly changed. On the other hand, LBJ's vision behind the initiative was too complex to be measured merely by the poverty rate. If his goal had been simply to push families up above the poverty level, he could have focused his efforts on cash and other financial supports. Instead, his efforts were grounded in the belief that the poor should attain self-sufficiency through their own hard work, with their government and communities working in partnership in the background to facilitate their success. The programs he initiated—such as the Job Corps, Head Start, and VISTA—were created to serve as a means to that end, and most have withstood the test of time. Although the War on Poverty did not end poverty as LBJ envisioned, it is still a great legacy.

References

Amato, Paul R. 2005. The impact of family formation change on the cognitive, social, and emotional well-being of the next generation. *Future of Children* 15, no. 2. Available at the website of the Education Resources Information Center: www.eric.ed.gov/PDFS/EJ795852.pdf.

Bailey, Martha, and Nicolas Duquette. 2014. *How Johnson fought the War on Poverty: The economics and politics of funding at the Office of Economic Opportunity.* Population Studies Center Research Report 14-813. Ann Arbor: Institute for Social Research, University of Michigan. www.psc.isr.umich.edu/pubs/pdf/rr14-813.pdf.

Blank, Rebecca M. 2008a. How to improve poverty measurement in the United States. *Journal of Policy Analysis and Management* 27, no. 2: 233–254. Available at the website of the Brookings Institution: www.brookings.edu/~/media/research/files/papers/2008/6/poverty%20blank/06_poverty_blank.pdf.

———. 2008b. *High priority poverty reduction strategies for the next decade.* Report prepared for the Charles Stewart Mott Foundation's "Defining Poverty Reduction Strategies" Project. Washington D.C.: Brookings Institution. www

.brookings.edu/~/media/Files/rc/papers/2008/08_poverty_strategies_blank/08 _poverty_strategies_blank.pdf.

Blank, Rebecca M., Sheldon H. Danziger, and Robert F. Schoeni, eds. 2006. *Working and poor.* New York: Sage Foundation.

Blank, Rebecca M., and Mark H. Greenberg. 2008. *Improving the measurement of poverty.* Hamilton Project, discussion paper 2008-17. Washington, D.C.: Brookings Institution. www.brookings.edu/~/media/Files/rc/papers/2008/12 _poverty_measurement_blank/12_poverty_measurement_blank.pdf.

Brown, Susan L. 2010. Marriage and child well-being: Research and policy. *Journal of Marriage and Family* 72, no. 5 (Sept.).

Burke, Vincent J., and Vee Burke. 1974. *Nixon's good deed: Welfare reform.* New York: Columbia University Press.

Carnero, Pedro, and James J. Heckman. 2003. Human capital policy. IZA Discussion Paper 821.

Child Trends Data Bank. 2013. Births to unmarried women. www.childtrends.org /?indicators=births-to-unmarried-women.

Clark, Robert F. 2002. *The War on Poverty: History, selected programs and ongoing impact.* Lanham, Md.: Rowman and Littlefield/University Press of America.

Edin, Kathryn, and Joanna M. Reed. 2005. Why don't they just get married? Barriers to marriage among the disadvantaged. *Future of Children* 15, no. 2 (Fall). http://futureofchildren.org/futureofchildren/publications/journals/article/index .xml?journalid=37&articleid=109).

Fisher, Gordon M. 1992. The development of the Orshansky Poverty Thresholds and their subsequent history as the official U.S. poverty measure. Available from the U.S. Bureau of the Census: www.census.gov/hhes/povmeas/publications /orshansky.html.

Fry, Richard. 2011. *Hispanic college enrollment spikes, narrowing gaps with other groups.* Washington D.C.: Pew Hispanic Center. www.pewhispanic.org/files /2011/08/146.pdf.

Gillette, Michael L. 1996. *Launching the War on Poverty: An oral history.* New York: Twayne.

Hamilton, Dona Cooper, and Charles V. Hamilton. 1997. *The dual agenda: The African American struggle for civil and economic equality.* New York: Columbia University Press.

Handler, Joel F., and Yeheskel Hasenfeld. 1991. *The moral construction of poverty: Welfare reform in America.* Newbury Park, Calif.: Sage.

Iceland, John. 2003. *Poverty in America.* Berkeley: University of California Press.

Johnson, Lyndon B. 1964a. State of the union address (Jan. 8). Available at American Rhetoric: Online Speech Bank, www.americanrhetoric.com/speeches /lbj1964stateoftheunion.htm.

———. 1964b. Special message to Congress (Mar. 16). Available at the Internet Modern History Sourcebook: www.fordham.edu/halsall/mod/1964johnson -warpoverty.html.

———. 1968. Annual message to the Congress on the state of the union (Jan. 17). Available at the website of the LBJ Library, www.lbjlib.utexas.edu/johnson /archives.hom/speeches.hom/680117.asp.

Katz, Michael B. 1989. *The undeserving poor.* New York: Pantheon.

Martin, Joyce, Brady E. Hamilton, Stephanie J. Ventura, Michelle J. K. Osterman, Sharon Kimeyer, T. J. Matthews, and Elizabeth C. Wilson. 2011. Births: final data for 2009. *National Vital Statistics Report* 60, no. 1. Available from the Centers for Disease Control and Prevention: www.cdc.gov/nchs/data/nvsr/nvsr60 /nvsr60_01.pdf.

Matthews, T. J., and Stephanie J. Ventura. 1997. Birth and fertility rates by educational attainment: United States, 1994. *Monthly Vital Statistics Report* 45, no. 10. Available from the Centers for Disease Control and Prevention: www.cdc.gov /nchs/data/mvsr/supp/mv45_10s.pdf.

McLanahan, Sara. 2009. Fragile families and the reproduction of poverty. *Annals of the American Academy of Political and Social Science* 621, no. 1.

Melnick, Shep. 2005. From tax and spend to mandate and sue: Liberalism after the Great Society. In Sidney M. Milkis and Jerome M. Mileur, eds., *The Great Society and the high tide of liberalism*, 395–403. Amherst: University of Massachusetts Press.

Moynihan, Daniel Patrick. 1965. *The Negro family: The case for national action.* U.S. Department of Labor, Office of Policy Planning and Research.

———. 1991. Social justice in the next century. *America* (Sept. 14).

Murray, Charles. 1994. *Losing ground.* New York: Basic Books.

National Center for Children in Poverty. 2009. *Low income children in the United States: National and state trend data, 1998–2008.* New York: National Center for Children in Poverty. www.nccp.org/publications/pdf/text_907.pdf.

Orleck, Annelise, and Lisa Gayle Hazirjian, eds. 2011. *The War on Poverty: A new grassroots history, 1964–1980.* Athens: University of Georgia Press.

Passel, Jeffrey S., and D'Vera Cohn. 2008. *U.S. population projections, 2005–2050.* Washington D.C.: Pew Research Center. http://pewhispanic.org/reports/report .php?ReportID=85.

Piven, Frances Fox, and Richard A. Cloward. 1971. *Regulating the poor.* New York: Pantheon.

———. 2005. The politics of the Great Society. In Sidney M. Milkis and Jerome M. Mileur, eds., *The Great Society and the high tide of liberalism.* Amherst: University of Massachusetts Press.

Plotnick, Robert D., and Felicity Skidmore. 1975. *Progress against poverty: A review of the 1964–1974 decade.* New York: Academic Press.

Quadango, Jill. 2003. Unfinished democracy. In Louis Kushnick and James Jennings, eds., *A new introduction to poverty: The role of race, power, and politics.* New York: New York University Press.

Russell, Judith. 2004. *Economics, bureaucracy, and race: How Keynesians misguided the War on Poverty.* New York: Columbia University Press.

Shealy, Katherine R., Ruowei Li, Sandra Benton-Davis, and Laurence M. Grummer-Strawn. 2005. *The CDC guide to breastfeeding interventions.* Atlanta: U.S. Department of Health and Human Services, Centers for Disease Control and Prevention. www.cdc.gov/breastfeeding/pdf/breastfeeding_interventions .pdf

U.S. Bureau of the Census. 2010. Current Population Reports, P60-238, *Income, poverty, and health insurance coverage in the United States: 2009.* Report prepared by Carmen DeNavas-Walt, Bernadette D. Proctor, and Jessica C. Smith. Washington, D.C.: Government Printing Office.

————. 2011a. Newsroom: Facts for features, women's history month (Jan.). www .census.gov/newsroom/releases/archives/facts_for_features_special_editions /cb11-ff04.html.

————. 2011b. Current Population Reports, P60-239, *Income, poverty, and health insurance coverage in the United States.* Report prepared by Carmen DeNavas-Walt, Bernadette D. Proctor, and Jessica C. Smith. Washington D.C.: Government Printing Office. www.census.gov/prod/2011pubs/p60-239.pdf.

————. 2012. Poverty: Historical poverty tables—people. Table 2: Poverty status of people by family relationship, race, and Hispanic origin: 1959 to 2012. www .census.gov/hhes/www/poverty/data/historical/people.html.

————. 2013. Poverty: Highlights. www.census.gov/hhes/www/poverty/about /overview/index.html.

U.S. Department of Health and Human Services. 1996. Administration for Children and Families, Office of Child Support Enforcement. The personal responsibility and work opportunity reconciliation act of 1996. www.acf.hhs.gov/programs/css /resource/the-personal-responsibility-and-work-opportunity-reconcilliation-act.

————. 2010. Administration for Children and Families, Office of Planning, Research and Evaluation. The Building Strong Families Project: Strengthening unmarried parents' relationships; The early impacts of building strong families. Report by Robert G. Wood, Sheena McConnell, Quinn Moore, Andrew Clarkwest, and JoAnn Hseuh. www.acf.hhs.gov/sites/default/files/opre/15_impact _main_rpt.pdf.

————. 2012. Office of Family Assistance. About healthy marriage and responsible fatherhood. www.acf.hhs.gov/programs/ofa/programs/healthy-marriage/about.

Waldron, Tom, Brandon Roberts, and Andrew Reamer. 2004. *Working hard, falling short: America's working families and the pursuit of economic security.* Baltimore: Annie Casey Foundation. Available from the Working Poor Families Project, www.workingpoorfamilies.org/pdfs/Working_Hard.pdf.

PART IV

CITIES, THE ENVIRONMENT, AND SCIENCE POLICY

CHAPTER 10

Lyndon Johnson and the Cities

NORMAN J. GLICKMAN AND ROBERT H. WILSON

Lyndon Baines Johnson brought a dedication to eradicating poverty, particularly urban poverty, to his presidency.[1] With pressure from much of his political base—including civil rights leaders, labor unions, and big-city mayors—and with a large Democratic majority, Johnson passed a breathtaking array of social programs soon after his election. With the mission of creating the Great Society, Johnson and Congress enacted programs to reduce poverty and hunger, build better housing and urban infrastructure, improve education, and create jobs. Many of these programs had an explicit big-city focus, while others targeted poor people wherever they lived. Johnson built on New Deal approaches to cities and expanded the social safety net, but also engaged new political actors, especially minorities.

Although most of the resources for these initiatives originated in the federal budget, Johnson wisely recognized the importance of enlisting the energies of state and local governments and community organizations. In August 1967, he said: "This job cannot be done in Washington alone. Every housing official, every mayor and every governor must vigorously enforce their building, health, and safety codes to the limit of the law. . . . Not even local officials, however, can change these conditions themselves. Unless private citizens become indignant at the treatment of their neighbors, unless individual citizens make justice for others a personal concern, poverty will profit those who exploit the poor" (Johnson 1967). Besides being concerned about the poor who lived in cities, Johnson believed cities were engines of economic prosperity. In 1967, he formed the Task Force on Cities and directed it to provide suggestions to reduce segregation and poverty in cities. The president wrote, "No one can doubt that much of the future of America hinges upon how we deal with the problems of our cities. Not only are our cities home for most Americans, they are also the nerve centers for our communications, transportation, and commerce" (Johnson 1967).

Conflict abounded in this era. A growing sense of urban decay—high levels of concentrated unemployment, poverty, and the like—and urban rioting became all too common. The pressure on Johnson from minorities clashed with the views of southern Democrats, the conservative wing of the party, which opposed help for minorities and the poor. To succeed, Johnson had to marshal his considerable political skills to put together majorities in both houses for his legislative agenda.

Despite the overarching successes, few of the urban initiatives had much longevity or impact. LBJ altered or terminated some while still in office. Others were changed or dropped by subsequent administrations as a result of major conservative political shifts.

Nonetheless, many of LBJ's urban initiatives deserve note. Obviously, the launching of the Department of Housing and Urban Development (HUD), in 1965, stands out. Part of the Great Society effort, it was designated to help create affordable housing and give voice to the aspirations of often-forgotten urban poor. In 1968, the Government National Mortgage Association (Ginnie Mae) helped expand several existing housing programs and spawned new ones that came after LBJ's term. It increased the flow of capital to the housing sector, insuring private mortgage lenders against default. Other urban-focused legislation followed.[2] HUD's influence waned considerably because of its often-weak leadership and the political winds that buffeted urban development.

As a preliminary indicator of impact, 13.7 percent of the U.S. population was in poverty in 1969, a figure that declined slightly a decade later. In 2008, the figure stood at 13.2 percent, largely unchanged over the previous four decades (U.S. Bureau of the Census 2012). More than forty years later, the promise of the Great Society to reduce poverty remains unfulfilled, a topic more thoroughly discussed in chapter 9 of this volume. Or more broadly, scholars across the ideological spectrum have argued that urban policy—some urban renewal and infrastructure projects, economic and community development programs, and the like—has been a failure (Katz 2010).[3]

LBJ's urban policies were the last link with New Deal liberalism. The politics that he embraced and the people who supported him—urban liberals, big-city mayors, minorities, and trade unionists—were quickly losing power. Others, both analysts and politicians, considered some of the Great Society programs inefficient and poorly targeted. In many ways, 1968 was a political watershed, the year the New Deal/Great Society era ended. Even if Johnson had stayed in power, the political forces around him were changing; he could not have continued Great Society–type programs even if he had wanted to do so. Richard Nixon and other politicians who came to power owed nothing to Johnson's backers. Conservative political forces reduced federal resources for cities and especially for fighting poverty.

We address three sets of questions in this chapter:

1. What were Johnson's primary urban policies and what outcomes did they produce? How did LBJ define urban problems, and what was the justification for the federal government's involvement? What policy instruments did the administration adopt? Did these build on past experience or represent new roles for the federal government?
2. What factors explain the sustainability or disappearance of the urban policies in subsequent administrations, including challenges rising from the changing nature of cities? What policies did subsequent presidents adopt?
3. What legacies and lessons related to policy design, assessment, and sustainability are relevant to contemporary policy analysis?

We find that few of Johnson's policies survived the conservative counterrevolution intact. Yet, despite attempts to tear down the Great Society, Johnson's legacy—like LBJ himself—looms large. We provide some important lessons for urban policy makers from the experience of the Johnson years and find that some federal roles in cities established during the Johnson era continue. But today we are at a quite different juncture in history: though the economy has rebounded from the Great Recession, it is growing less rapidly than the economy of the Johnson era. Yet many of the problems that Johnson faced continue to plague the nation.

The Johnson Administration and Cities

We recognize the difficulties in defining a satisfactory framework for examining urban policy. There are two types of policy. First are the explicitly urban policies aimed at cities, including inner-city affordable housing and community development. Additionally, some federal policies not principally concerned with cities also have substantial urban impacts (Glickman 1980). For instance, the nation's largest housing program, tax subsidies to homeowners, is an implicit, or "stealth," policy that, by helping finance suburban development, has had far larger impacts on cities than any of HUD's programs. The tax expenditures of roughly $300 billion annually of these benefits from the home-interest deductions from federal income taxes and related housing subsidies are far more than what HUD and other urban programs spend. Most of these tax expenditures go to upper-income and suburban families and encourage sprawl (Hanson, Brannon, and Hawley 2014). Similarly, policies to improve metropolitan transportation through highway construction led to suburban sprawl and the decline of central cities. Defense expenditures had substantial spatial effects by moving important manufacturing to the South and West, known as the "Gun Belt" (Markusen et al. 1991). At the same time, income-support programs such as the earned income tax credit have significant positive urban impacts because the poor reside disproportionately in cities (Kneebone and Berube 2008). These critically significant policy arenas are beyond the scope of this chapter.[4]

Urban policy debates occurred in the context of a powerful anti-urban bias dating from the American Revolution. Thomas Jefferson famously spoke of the virtues of a rural society, and the U.S. Constitution makes no mention of cities or local governments. The emergence of the industrial city in the early twentieth century, which brought with it many European newcomers, contributed to anti-immigration legislation. Another source of opposition to urban policy is a belief that free markets produce the best social outcomes—that intervention to change land uses and spatial change is counterproductive, and that decisions on local service provision should be entirely the responsibility of local government (Dreier, Mollenkopf, and Swanstrom 2004). Despite significant opposition to federal involvement in cities, such actions that affect cities are common, although, as we will show, often weak.

Given the difficulties of defining and sorting out the effects of direct urban programs, those that indirectly affect cities, and the wide range of LBJ's policy initiatives, we aggregate urban-oriented policies and programs into two broad categories: urban aid and infrastructure, and housing and community development.[5] Policies and programs in each category involve substantial federal funding, and the changing nature of federalism and intergovernmental relations in each of these policy arenas is an important backdrop to this study. After Johnson, urban policy was largely devolved to states and localities.

Federal Policies and Cities before Johnson

Johnson's initiatives extended and amplified an activist federal role in urban affairs established during the Franklin D. Roosevelt administration. The Great Depression created a context in which a substantially larger federal role could receive congressional approval, but the specific approach reflected the fact that the United States was well on its way to becoming an urban, industrial society. The wide range of social-policy initiatives—social welfare (especially Aid to Families with Dependent Children [AFDC]), education and training programs for youth, Social Security, assistance to the working-age poor, public health, and labor laws, among others—had become elements of the country's national public agenda and social safety net.

Many FDR initiatives attempted to revive the economy by building infrastructure and creating labor-intensive public works—new roles for the federal government. Given their urban impacts, we observe the emergence of new urban policy systems and new sets of intergovernmental relations involving federal, state, and local governments (Kleinberg 1995). The Public Works Administration (PWA 1933) funded highways, bridges, buildings, and other infrastructure with theretofore rarely observed cooperation between federal, state, and local governments in program implementation. The Works Progress Administration (1935) utilized direct-employment programs, including labor-intensive urban projects, employing about 2.3 million people each year (101). FDR pursued an aggressive approach to housing. The reform of the banking system encouraged the creation of home-loan banks (savings and loans, or S&L institutions) to mobilize capital for affordable home mortgage loans, thereby encouraging homeownership (Hays 1995; Kleinberg 1995, 101–110; Dreier, Mollenkopf, and Swanstrom 2004). His administration initiated subsidized public housing, involving initially the PWA and later the Federal Housing Administration (FHA 1934) and United States Housing Authority (1937). A significant expansion of public housing and a revitalization of declining inner cities continued in the Truman administration with the Housing Act of 1949. Urban renewal funds were transferred to localities for slum clearance, housing construction, and economic development. In these efforts, there appeared two policy objectives that would become a continuing source of political conflict in the following decades: assisting low-income urban populations, and promoting economic development through infrastructure investment and commercial redevelopment.

Policies adopted during the Dwight D. Eisenhower administration represented a significant reorientation of federal policy toward cities: a shift from redistributive policies and a focus on low-income urban populations to urban renewal and commercial redevelopment. The aversion to governmental intervention, along with a preference for market solutions, reflected Eisenhower's policy agenda; it also fueled congressional resistance to the New Deal from both southern Democrats and Republicans (Hays 1995; Mollenkopf 1983). Criticism from residents and small businesses displaced by urban renewal resulted in a provision in the Housing Act of 1954

that encouraged citizen participation in urban renewal projects, a practice
that would become institutionalized in the urban legislation of the 1960s
and later. The federal government's investments in infrastructure and housing policy became tilted heavily toward suburban development. Intervention in housing markets was weighted toward homeownership, through the
Veterans Administration and the FHA; a preexisting federal tax deduction
for interest payments on home mortgage loans facilitated new housing construction. Also, the FHA and other federal agencies redlined many neighborhoods in order to prevent integration and to placate homebuilders, who
had lobbied heavily with the agency. Finally, revisions to urban renewal, observed in the 1954 creation of the Urban Renewal Administration, emphasized commercial development and resulted in less focus on public housing
(Dreier, Swanstrom, and Mollenkopf 2004).

The National Interstate and Defense Highways Act of 1956 created a
joint federal- and state-funded program, reshaping the New Deal highway program into one administered through state governments and providing increased benefits to rural states (Kleinberg 1995; Mollenkopf 1983). It
played a major role in decentralizing jobs and families. First, it helped cities
outside the Northeast-Midwest core—in the South and West—gain better access to major markets and attract new migrants. Second, the National
Highway System helped decentralize metropolitan regions and aided suburban development. These multilane highways made commuting from the
suburbs easier and cheaper than before. In essence, the new roads both encouraged and, through the gasoline tax, subsidized suburban development,
facilitating white flight.

At the start of the Franklin Roosevelt administration, the United States
was well on its way to becoming an urban, industrial society. Three decades
later, at the conclusion of the Eisenhower presidency, a new pattern of urban geography had emerged, that of suburbanization and declining central cities. The prosperity of the post–World War II era and rising family incomes led to changing patterns of housing consumption; widespread
use of the automobile and an array of federal policies further encouraged
suburbanization (Dreier, Mollenkopf, and Swanstrom 2004). This pattern
was reinforced by public school desegregation following the 1954 *Brown
v. Board of Education* decision, which increased white flight, and redlining
practices in the real estate industry (Hays 1995; Jackson 1985). The ability
of suburban areas to form separate local-government jurisdictions, including independent school districts, permitted the formation of a new variety
of educational segregation, one that reinforced the effects of metropolitan-
level racial housing segregation.

The Johnson Administration (and the Kennedy Legacy)

John F. Kennedy devoted significant attention to urban issues during his presidential campaign in 1960, in part to distinguish his priorities from the neglect of such matters by Eisenhower. Elected with substantial support in cities, Kennedy paid attention to urban issues (Biles 2011). His New Frontier addressed urban poverty through proposals for job creation and manpower training for the unemployed. He attacked the problems of housing in the inner city through the expansion of public housing programs and a new subsidy program targeted to rental housing for low-income families (Hays 1995; Biles 2011). After assuming the presidency, Johnson moved quickly and ambitiously to expand Kennedy's initiatives and incorporate them into his own social agenda (Dallek 1998). LBJ led a transformation of the federal government, including reforming the federal bureaucracy to align it with the needs of an urban society and to implement the Great Society programs. His view of the federal government's role was clear. He stated in a 1966 message to HUD:

> The only legitimate function of government is to help people. Your job is not just to run an efficient office. Your real job is to enrich the lives of the two out of three Americans who now live in our overcrowded cities. You know that you are the people who must carry our cities from the dark ages of stagnation and neglect into the bright sunshine of the twenty-first century. . . . You have not only to plan for the future, but also to make up for the neglect and the failures of more than 50 years. (Johnson 1966)

Relying heavily on external and interagency task forces, Johnson placed the issues of cities on the national policy agenda and produced an extraordinary array of federal legislation.[6]

Before turning to the two primary components of Johnson's urban policies (urban aid and infrastructure, and community development and housing; see table 10.1), it is important to note that the Great Society initiative included other elements with urban impacts.[7] In Johnson's view, the government had the obligation to help lift individuals from poverty by providing the education and skills needed to attain good jobs and self-sufficiency. Several War on Poverty initiatives—including Head Start (for preschool children, addressed in chapter 6 of this book); the Neighborhood Youth Corps, Job Corps (teenagers), and Upward Bound (college preparation); and the Elementary and Secondary Education Act of 1965 (addressed in chapter 7)—were designed to enhance human capital through basic education, job train-

Table 10.1. Urban policies and programs: Johnson administration

Overview and policy approach	Urban aid and infrastructure	Community development and housing
Focus on distressed cities and neighborhoods	Creation of the following agencies and departments:	Office of Economic Opportunity
Bringing jobs to people	Urban Mass Transit	Community Action Program
Comprehensive efforts in infrastructure, education and training, housing finance and construction, and community development	Administration	Model Cities
	Dept. of Transportation	Special Impact Program (CDC Funding)
	Dept. of Housing and Urban Development	FHA to support lower income families
Reform of governmental structure and intergovernmental relations to achieve policy objectives	Economic Development Administration	Government National Mortgage Association (Ginnie Mae)
	Additional programs:	Federal National Mortgage Association (FNMA, or Fannie Mae) for low-income housing
	Water and wastewater grants	Expansion of public housing
		Housing rental support
		Fair Housing Act
		National Housing Act
		VISTA

ing, and work experience. The beneficiaries tended to be low-income urban residents. But these programs also provided greater mobility for job seekers: they were able to take their new skills and search for jobs beyond their home cities—a "people to jobs" strategy. They were important components of Johnson's urban strategy.

Urban Aid and Infrastructure

Federal government funding of urban infrastructure began with the New Deal, as noted above. The Interstate Highway System (envisioned in 1938, becoming reality under Eisenhower as the National System of Interstate and Defense Highways) was effective in moving traffic into and out of cities and on loops around cities; it was less successful in moving people within relatively dense central-city areas. Under Johnson, the Urban Mass Transportation Act of 1964 provided $375 million for large-scale urban public or private rail projects, and the administration created the Urban Mass Transit Administration. The program adopted the financing model of the Interstate Highway System, in which federal funds had to be matched by cities and states. At LBJ's request, Congress created the Department of Transportation in 1966, reflecting the importance of transportation to the national economy. Although the funding of urban transit programs did not gain the sustained support enjoyed by highway programs in the decades to follow, urban transit programs became permanent features of federal efforts in the nation's cities. The administration further expanded infrastructure investment through the Public Works and Economic Development Act of 1965, creating the Economic Development Administration (EDA) to fund projects in economically distressed communities, many of them rural. The mission of the agency was to generate employment, retain existing jobs, and stimulate industrial and commercial growth.

The Johnson administration expanded another federal role when it resolved a congressional stalemate on water policy. Water pollution resulting from both industrial waste and urban water issues (waste treatment and runoff) had grown substantially in preceding decades. Industrialists, public health specialists, conservationists, and municipal authorities had different interests and brought different perspectives to bear on the problem (Rohrer et al. 1970). Attempts to encourage federal involvement in the 1950s, through grants to localities for water systems and water quality standards, were largely unsuccessful because of congressional resistance. The Water Quality Act (1965) and Clean Water Restoration Act (1966) helped fund urban water systems through matching grants tied to national water standards. This federal role in metropolitan areas was particularly important given the challenges of multijurisdictional collaboration in water supply and river systems (see chapter 11 for more on water policy).

Housing and Community Development

To address urban poverty, a critical element of the War on Poverty, the Johnson administration adopted multiple strategies. Some programs were targeted to individuals, including a major expansion of income security and social services programs, such as food stamps, supplemental social security, the indexing of social security, and Medicaid and Medicare (Katz 1989). Great Society programs introduced new approaches as the federal government became directly involved in neighborhood social service provision. Further, low-income inner-city residents participated in the design and governance of these programs. Though this represented new federal roles and innovation in policy implementation, important elements of the programs were drawn from experiences of nongovernmental community-based organizations. By the 1960s, initiatives such as the Gray Areas Program and Mobilization for Youth (addressing problems of youth gangs in New York City's Lower East Side) provided innovative neighborhood-based models (Weismann 1969; Halpern 1995).

Based on earlier experimentation with development strategies in poor communities (Halpern 1995; Kleinberg 1995), the Community Action Program (CAP) adopted an innovative form of policy implementation. It sought partnerships with disadvantaged communities so that neighborhood groups could act on their own behalf. Under the "maximum feasible participation" provision of the Economic Opportunity Act of 1964, along with changes in local political processes resulting from the Voting Rights Act of 1965, low-income inner-city residents had the opportunity to become actively involved in the design and implementation of services (Howard, Lipsky, and Marshall 1994). Importantly, the Voting Rights Act led to increased minority participation and the election of ethnic and racial-minority mayors, council members, and state officials (Sampson 2004).

Substantial resistance to CAP, especially from mayors who feared the loss of political power, forced a reformulation of program design for federal assistance to disadvantaged communities. The Demonstration Cities and Metropolitan Development Act of 1966 (commonly referred to as the Model Cities Act) restructured federal assistance; it gave local governments more control over program implementation, including the extension of program focus to urban redevelopment and the weakening of citizen-participation requirements (Howard, Lipsky, and Marshall 1994). Politically, Model Cities reflected the practical accommodation to local-government resistance to political mobilization of disadvantaged communities, as well as the largely unsuccessful intergovernmental framework of CAP.

The Johnson administration adopted another set of initiatives—community economic development—that previously was centered outside governmental purview (Halpern 1995). The concept dates to rural cooperatives and African American economic strategies adopted to cope with racial segregation, especially those based on the ideas of Booker T. Washington. Community economic development attempts to mobilize capital and markets in local low-income communities. In contrast to the social assistance and human capital efforts of the Great Society, community development corporations (CDCs) attempt to nurture economic activity with multiplier effects to be realized in poor neighborhoods. Emerging in the late 1950s without governmental support, CDCs were formed in Chicago, Philadelphia, Newark, and Cleveland. The federal government extended support to this emerging field in the Special Impact Program (SIP), under Title 1-D of the Economic Opportunity Act, and administered it through the Office of Economic Opportunity (OEO). The SIP was of modest size, and its expenditures were focused on relatively few CDCs (Vidal and Keating 2004).

Johnson took aggressive action on the housing needs of low-income families. Following reports from several task forces, he proposed (and Congress approved in 1965) the Department of Housing and Urban Development Act. Building upon some Kennedy administration initiatives (Hays 1995), he expanded the provision of public housing, encouraged the FHA to expand support for homeownership to lower-income individuals, and substantially expanded rental-assistance programs for low-income housing. To complement the federal institutional support structure for middle-class housing created in the 1930s, the Federal National Mortgage Association (Fannie Mae) was privatized. Its functions were transferred to the newly created Government National Mortgage Association in 1968, thereby expanding the availability of mortgage funds for moderate-income families through government-guaranteed mortgage-backed securities. Early on, it became evident that the focus would be on housing and not on broader issues of urban development (Dreier, Mollenkopf, and Swanstrom 2001).

The Housing Act of 1968 called for "a decent home and living environment for every American family," capturing one of Johnson's most ambitious goals (Hays 1995, 107). The act called for the rehabilitation or construction of twenty-six million housing units, including six million for low- and moderate-income families. In addition, the act prohibited racial discrimination in housing markets and required that equal numbers of any low- and moderate-income units demolished had to be replaced, thereby overturning the highly criticized practice of displacing low-income residents from so-called blighted areas for purposes of commercial revitalization (Hays 1995). The many efforts of the Johnson administration to expand support for housing to low-income populations met substantial resistance on several fronts: the housing industry voiced concern about housing-market disruptions; others feared that undeserving families would gain access to housing services subsidized by the public sector.

Urban Policy after LBJ

What appeared to be an age of unlimited opportunity for social and urban power in 1964 had been transformed into an age of limits by the time Johnson's presidency ended. A variety of economic forces, including increased foreign competition and the rise of OPEC, generated new challenges for the U.S. economy. The auto and steel industries, long the pillars of large cities, began extended declines. Deindustrialization began to take its toll on the urban system (Bluestone and Harrison 1982).

As the economy restructured, so did American cities: suburbanization increased, and interregional shifts to the Sun Belt accelerated. Technological change reshaped the business environment: electronic and telecommunication advances allowed firms to disperse worldwide; at the same time, there were immense increases in international trade and direct foreign investment. The United States lost considerable manufacturing employment overseas, which hurt many Rust Belt cities. These economic changes were exacerbated by trade policies such as the North American Free Trade Agreement (NAFTA), which liberalized international trade, often at the expense of workers and cities in the Rust Belt. At the same time, migration to the Sun Belt and the growth of regional financial services helped cities in that region grow. Another facet of America's deindustrialization was the substantial increase in retail trade and service jobs—many of which do not pay good wages or carry benefits.

Central cities continued to hollow out as highway construction, mortgage subsidies, and many other factors propelled households and jobs from central cities to the suburbs and, later, the exurbs (Sugrue 2005; Glickman, Lahr, and Wyly 1996; Wyly, Glickman, and Lahr 1998; Dreier, Mollenkopf, and Swanstrom 2004).[8] Unemployment became more concentrated in blue-collar inner-city neighborhoods, and job growth in cities trailed that in the suburbs (Glaeser, Kahn, and Chu 2001). William Julius Wilson (1996) accurately pinpoints the "new poverty" in inner-city neighborhoods in his *When Work Disappears*. Sprawl meant a spatial mismatch of jobs for many low-income, low-education workers, especially minorities (Kain 1968). The spatial reconfiguration of cities that continued and reinforced longstanding patterns exacerbated problems of poverty and unemployment. Urban poverty, which had declined in the 1960s and 1970s, increased significantly in the 1980s, declined again in the 1990s, but has increased again in this century (Jargowsky 2003). Further, central-city poverty rates remain more than twice those in the suburbs.

In the 1980s and later, many inner suburbs began to see higher rates of poverty, deteriorating housing, and increasing crime (Berube and Kneebone 2006). Although still a larger problem in central cities than in the suburbs, these historically urban indicators of decline became a broader problem outside metropolitan cores. The notion of "distressed cities" changed: no longer could policy makers refer to poverty as solely a central-city issue.[9]

Presidents and Urban Policy after LBJ

Between Johnson's administration and 2014, five Republicans and three Democrats have held the presidency. Each president adopted distinctive approaches to urban affairs (table 10.2), influenced in part by partisan and electoral considerations as well as by economic conditions (Mollenkopf 1983). Democratic presidential candidates had typically drawn higher support from urban areas, while suburban voters favored Republicans. Patterns of spatial benefits consistent with traditional partisan voting can be identified in federal policies incorporating the priorities and interests of both the president and Congress (Caraley 1976). In this section, we discuss the major initiatives and policy approaches toward cities adopted by the eight presidents who served from 1969 through 2014.

The end of the Great Society and the age of devolution of social policy began in earnest with the election of Richard Nixon. Sharing little of Johnson's interest in cities and the poor, he began to undo much of what he inherited. Nixon substantially dismantled Johnson's community development efforts: he closed the Office of Economic Opportunity and downgraded the citizen-participation requirements of Model Cities. He did away with categorical grants and replaced them with his New Federalism—which largely substituted block grants for categorical programs and expanded the roles of state and local governments. Federal funding for metropolitan projects increased under Nixon (see tables 10.1 and 10.2), but the shift in spatial impact was beneficial to Nixon's suburban, Republican political base and detrimental to large cities dominated by Democrats. He placed a moratorium on public housing construction and downgraded efforts to address metropolitan desegregation (Biles 2011).

But Nixon did not completely abandon cities. The National Urban Policy and New Community Development Act of 1970 created a loan fund for infrastructure investments in new towns, although it resulted in few investments (Biles 2011). Nixon also adopted important environmental policies, including the establishment of the Environmental Protection Agency in 1970.

Gerald Ford, who had an antipathy to cities, agreed with Nixon's actions

Table 10.2. Urban policies and programs: Nixon through G. W. Bush

Overview and policy approach	Urban aid and infrastructure	Community development and housing
	Nixon/Ford	
• Less targeting of urban grants • Decentralization of decision making and regional approaches through revenue sharing (New Federalism) • Less funding for the poor • Greater preference for market-based solutions to spatial restructuring, i.e., greater emphasis on people to jobs, rather than jobs to people • Less attention paid to racial desegregation	• General revenue sharing (increased aid to suburban jurisdictions) • New Community Development Corporation • Aid to NYC (Ford) • Environmental Impact Statements • Water and air quality	• Community Development Block Grants (CDBG) • Reform of Model Cities (consolidation of categorical grants and less targeting of the poor) • Housing assistance plans • Black entrepreneurship • Earned Income Tax Credit (EITC) • Section 8 housing vouchers
	Carter	
• Last link to the New Deal policies • Pledged aid to cities, but backtracked after issuing National Urban Policy statement • Reduced funding to cities • Emphasis on urban effects of nonurban policies • Supported faith-based initiatives • Proposed national development bank (not approved by Congress) • Public-private partnerships • Emphasis on people to jobs • Initiated decline in support for urban priorities	• Aid to distressed cities • Urban Development Action Grants (UDAG)	• Extended CDBG • Targeted Jobs Tax Credit • Expansion of public service employment • Community Reinvestment Act

Table 10.2. (*continued*)

Overview and policy approach	Urban aid and infrastructure	Community development and housing
	Reagan	
• Believing that urban policies had failed, ended serious federal support for cities and reversed previous policies • Slashed funding for distressed cities, believing that cities would succeed if national economy grew rapidly via tax cuts and supply side economics • Ignored previous debate about jobs-to-people versus people-to-jobs • Arguing that "government is the problem," created an urban policy vacuum that later presidents continued	• Ended general revenue sharing • Reduced funding for UDAG and mass transit • Superfund	• Economic Recovery Program (expected to reduce urban poverty) • Reductions in funding for CDBG and housing • Enterprise zones
	George H. W. Bush	
• Revival of public-private partnerships and housing vouchers, especially for public housing projects • HOPE VI • Supported community self-reliance with the Thousand Points of Light program	• Reform of metropolitan planning organizations via the Intermodal Surface Transportation Efficiency Act	• Expanded housing vouchers • HOPE VI for public housing reform • Comprehensive housing affordability strategies • Community policing
	Clinton	
• Emphasized people to jobs, metropolitan solutions • Ended traditional welfare policy and required work for low-income people	• Reform of metropolitan planning organizations via the Transportation Equity Act	• Increased HOPE VI vouchers and Moving to Opportunity public housing reform • TANF welfare reform replaced sixty-year approach with work requirements

(*continued*)

Table 10.2. (continued)

Overview and policy approach	Urban aid and infrastructure	Community development and housing
	Clinton (continued)	
		• Enterprise zones and enterprise communities, tied to training and community services
	George W. Bush	
• Steep funding reductions for urban programs • Emphasis on community self-reliance	• Further reform of metropolitan planning organizations via the Safe, Accountable, Flexible, Efficient Transportation Equity Act	• Further reductions in HOPE VI • Faith-based initiatives for community services • No Child Left Behind Act

to roll back Johnson's programs. Upon assuming the presidency, Ford faced a serious national recession and a financial crisis in New York City. Despite the apocryphal *New York Daily News* headline "Ford to City: Drop Dead," the federal government extended loans (at above-market rates) to resolve the crisis (Biles 2011). Biles (2011, 220) characterizes the Nixon-Ford years as going beyond budget cutting and instead representing "a change in culture of the executive branch that represented an abandonment of Great Society efforts to nurture the cities." Although concern with urban affairs had substantially faded by the time Jimmy Carter came to office, Nixon and Ford began the movement of reducing funding for big cities and putting more responsibility in the hands of the states. That generally decentralized urban policy system continued for three more decades.

When Jimmy Carter came to the Oval Office in 1977, there was deep pessimism about America's cities (Sugrue 2008). Many of the large industrial cities had lost population and were facing high unemployment and poverty. Carter campaigned for the presidency as a supporter of cities and as a reformer of federal–local relations. But despite his rhetoric, he did not believe in a strong federal role: he wanted to see more power devolved to the states. His New Partnership to Preserve America's Communities argued that state and local governments should be full partners in the federal government's initiatives in cities. In addition, he felt that community organizations—especially faith-based groups—should have a strong voice in urban affairs, a reflection of his Christian communitarianism.

Carter proposed giving aid to distressed cities through Urban Development Action Grants and EDA loan guarantees, as well as an expanded Community Development Block Grant program. He required that all federal agencies take account of the impacts of their nonurban policies on cities (Glickman 1980). Midway in his administration, facing a declining economy, Carter put forward an austerity program that largely abandoned cities as a focus of policy. The post-Johnson decline in urban policy's importance continued (Sugrue 2008). Biles (2011, 352) argues that Carter's New Partnership "was cut from the same cloth as the New Federalisms of the Republican administrations bracketing his own."

Ronald Reagan put an end to urban policy. His 1982 *Urban Policy Report* stated that targeted urban programs were ineffective and that, as a matter of principle, urban matters were the responsibility of state and local governments (Eisinger 1985; Orlebeke 1990; Wolman 1986). He believed that the growth of the national economy and a vibrant private sector would do all that could be done for cities. He cut HUD's budget in half and funds for mass transit by one-third (Biles 2011). The private sector, he and his conservative allies maintained, could solve problems of poverty and poor housing without governmental intervention: urban poverty could best be remedied by promoting a healthy national economy. This notion was encapsulated in the expression "a rising tide will lift all boats."

While Reagan aggressively slashed urban programs, George H. W. Bush promised a "kinder, gentler nation." Yet, once in office, his version of New Federalism was accompanied by a sharp cut in federal funding (Rich 1993).[10] Rather than furnishing money to create more jobs and housing, Bush called for greater volunteerism from community groups and others—what he called a "thousand points of light." His main urban initiative, championed by his HUD secretary, Jack Kemp, was the creation of enterprise zones. EZs called for regulatory and tax incentives to attract businesses to inner-city neighborhoods; the program emphasized free-market capitalism to encourage urban development. Bush also put forward the Homeownership and Opportunity for People Everywhere (HOPE) program, which was aimed at increasing the role of private developers in affordable housing development. But Bush's funding for HOPE and EZs was limited. As a result, cities saw very little difference between the policies of Bush and Reagan (Biles 2011).[11]

Bill Clinton continued the devolution process. For the most part, his "Third Way" philosophy marked a continuation of policies from the previous two administrations, although he withstood attempts by Republicans to dismantle HUD. He put forward a modest enterprise zones/enterprise communities effort, which added some social supports to the Reagan-era program. Little funding accompanied these programs. Clinton's most dramatic urban policy move came when he ended the traditional welfare system (AFDC), which was an entitlement, and replaced it with Temporary Assistance to Needy Families (TANF)—which required work and training and was time limited. Clinton thus continued the abandonment of Great Society programs.

Reaffirming the position that the federal government should have no formal role in urban policy, George W. Bush's administration proceeded to cut urban programs further. He made some weak attempts at creating faith-based policies to play to his evangelical base, but abandoned them early in his administration (DiIulio 2007). He took little interest in the devastation visited upon New Orleans by Hurricane Katrina. He sought to improve urban schools through the No Child Left Behind (NCLB) program, which emphasized substantial testing and placed most of the funding responsibilities on cash-strapped school systems. The NCLB received considerable criticism, even from former proponents of school choice (Ravitch 2010).

Federal Funding of Urban Policy

We now move to an empirical assessment of federal spending on urban policies over a fifty-year period. First, all federal transfers to state and local government are disaggregated into three types in order to establish funding priorities (see figure 10.1; all figures are in natural logarithms of constant 2000 dollars). Federal grants to state and local governments increased significantly through the 1970s; the declines during the 1980s, noted above, were replaced by modest growth in overall funding during the following two decades. The composition of this federal funding changed dramatically in the 1980s as transfers to individuals became the primary source of growth in federal transfers to state and local governments. Federal transfers for capital investments never returned to the types of increases observed during the Johnson administration, although funding trended slightly upward in the 1990s. The category of "other transfers," including all place-based and

Fig. 10.1. Federal grants to state and local governments, 1962–2008

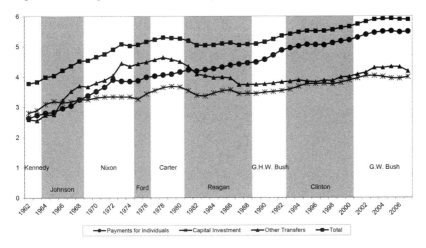

Source: Office of Management and Budget, "Fiscal Year 2015 Historial Tables" (Executive Office of the President of the United States, 2014), Table 12.1—Summary Comparison of Total Outlays for Grants to State and Local Governments: 1940–2019 (in Current Dollars, as Percentages of Total Outlays, as Percentages of GDP, and in Constant [FY 2009] Dollars).

general aid to cities, declined precipitously after Carter. In other words, the relatively rapid rise in federal transfers to state and local governments ended in the mid-1970s, but the overall level of funding was sustained until the early 1990s, when a moderate upward trend began. But these federal transfers are today more heavily oriented to people based expenditures (that is, transfers to individuals) than place-based expenditures.

We observe that the stagnation of federal transfers for capital investments was even more dramatic for urban infrastructure (see figure 10.2). The rapid increases in federal funding for mass transit and water and wastewater systems initiated by Johnson were continued in the Nixon administration. But following that period of robust growth in federal expenditures, the national consensus around this federal role faded. Initiatives to provide aid to cities have come and gone, such as general revenue sharing (introduced during the Nixon administration). Later presidents tested many approaches to urban development, including urban revitalization, brownfield remediation, and enterprise zones. Today, local governments are increasingly responsible for raising the capital they need for urban investments. Even when federal funding is available, as for urban transportation or water systems, matching local funds are usually required. Many governments are

Fig. 10.2. Urban infrastructure spending, 1962–2008

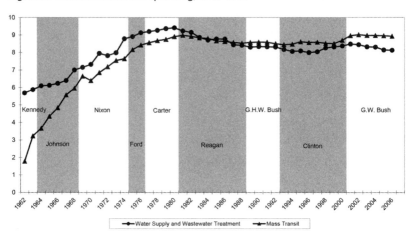

Source: Congressional Budget Office, "Supplemental Tables," n.d., Table W-8. Total Federal Spending for Infrastructure, 1956–2009 (in Millions of 2009 Dollars).

turning to private-public partnerships for the provision of infrastructure. But many believe that the level of investments in the nation's infrastructure has been inadequate for decades (Choate and Walter 1983; American Society of Civil Engineers 2008).

Although the level of funding for urban infrastructure has not substantially changed since the Reagan administration, other federal policy initiatives have proved sustainable and effective for infrastructure planning in cities and metropolitan areas. Extensive collaboration among local policy actors through metropolitan planning organizations organized around transportation planning emerged under federal requirements. The consolidation of funding for highway and mass-transit systems gave local decision makers discretion over the types of intermodal transportation investments.

The pattern of federal funding for housing and community development confirms the preference for people-based over place-based policies discussed above (see figure 10.3). First, despite criticism around program design, along with reductions for most of the LBJ housing initiatives, figure 10.3 indicates that federal transfers for housing assistance have actually grown through the fifty-year period, although certainly at a slower rate of increase in the 1980s and later. Housing assistance has increasingly taken the form of housing vouchers for low-income families and tax credits for affordable-housing construction. Today, the market-based strategy for low-income housing relies on production by the private and nonprofit sectors, and the

Fig. 10.3. Federal funding for community development and housing, 1962–2008

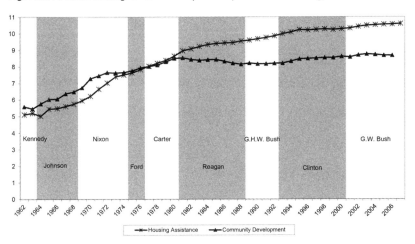

Source: Office of Management and Budget, "Fiscal Year 2015 Historical Tables," Table 3.2—
Outlays by Function and Subfunction: 1962–2019.

federal government provides vouchers to families to obtain housing in the
market. Despite a broad political consensus at the national level around this
approach, demand for low-income housing greatly exceeds supply.

The rapid increase for community development funding initiated by
Johnson continued through the Carter years (see figure 10.3). Even though
some of the cuts in funding during the 1980s were restored later, federal
funding for community development has essentially stagnated since the
early 1980s, further reflecting the lack of support for federal place-based
policy. It can be argued, however, that despite numerous presidential and
congressional attempts to terminate federal funding for community development, sustaining even this level of funding suggests a measure of effective political support. It is also interesting to note that most presidents have
supported the nongovernmental sector, of which community development
is one segment. Faith-based organizations, for example, garnered support
from several presidents. Despite the relatively modest and diminished role
of the federal government in community development, the nongovernmental sector has evolved into a critical service provider for state and local governments. While some critics view the reliance on nongovernmental actors
as a means of rationalizing the lack of public-sector commitment for social
services, there is little doubt that the proliferation of such groups represents
a measurable improvement in social capital among these populations (Rich
1993; Halpern 1995; Vidal and Keating 2004).

The Johnson Legacies

Our discussion of post-Johnson urban policy showed that relatively little remains today in a form that Johnson would recognize. The transformation, and in some cases, abandonment, of Johnson-era urban policy was initiated even before the end of his term in 1968, the year that marked the end of the liberal New Deal/Great Society era. Later presidents were less interested in and less committed to solving urban problems, and the nature of cities and their regions evolved, making LBJ's approach difficult to sustain.

Politically, there was a rightward shift, meaning that the actions of markets, not public officials—especially not federal civil servants—were increasingly emphasized. There was going to be less growth in federal funds for older cities, and the spending that remained was going to be used in different ways. Vouchers and other "market mechanisms" substantially replaced direct grants, from HUD or other agencies, to provide affordable housing and other services. Additionally, the focus shifted to state and local governments; private-sector and nonprofit organizations were used to implement policies. At the local level, this meant increasing fiscal pressure on governments, which undertook an array of projects that they could not always afford. Given the highly fragmented local-government system, with thousands of municipalities, they not only lacked resources, but also had limited ability and incentive to act on important infrastructure projects that crossed borders. Administrations after LBJ's did less to confront these problems.

The practice of the federal government using its resources to mobilize capital for national objectives, including aid and infrastructure investments in cities, was established by FDR. The model was evident in Eisenhower's strategy for building a national highway system. LBJ brought an even more ambitious level of intergovernmental integration in a broader range of collective goods important to urban dwellers, including water and wastewater systems, and at higher levels of funding than previously. LBJ's efforts particularly benefited the many rapidly growing cities in the 1960s. The primary governmental agency involved in this practice, the U.S. Department of Transportation (which was created by LBJ), gained powerful constituencies over the decades. The practice of embedding national objectives, whether environmental standards or incentives to encourage local-government cooperation, has also come to be firmly established, albeit contested, in the federal system.

President Johnson believed that it was a moral imperative to provide affordable housing, but the policies he adopted were not particularly innovative; they built largely on approaches introduced by FDR. For LBJ, the spatial distribution of poverty meant that housing policy, and the Great Society broadly, had a significant big-city orientation. The inability of HUD to move beyond a fairly narrow range of constituencies meant that it would never gain a solid institutional foundation, unlike other elements of LBJ's administrative reform. Johnson introduced a rapid increase in federal funding for housing, and though the rate of increase slowed later, real funding has indeed grown since that time. But Johnson's policy of direct spending on public housing has been almost entirely abandoned. It was replaced by privatization, demolition, the use of housing vouchers, and the private provision of rental properties—an approach followed by every president since Carter. Thus, federal funding for low-income families has been sustained for several decades, albeit at modest levels of funding compared with existing needs. The mechanisms Johnson advocated have been cast aside.

In contrast to housing policy, the LBJ efforts in mobilizing poor urban communities were truly innovative. The Civil Rights Act and Voting Rights Act provided mechanisms to protect minority-group interests in their interaction with local government. In community development, two forms of innovation are noteworthy. First, the identification of alternative means of implementing policy reflected a critique of local-government delivery and political systems that were, at worst, racially discriminatory or, at best, insensitive to the cultural dimensions of communities—and therefore ineffective in delivering services. Second, local political systems were incapable of incorporating the interests of excluded communities. By providing these groups standing as service providers, the federal government attempted to encourage community groups to develop the capacity to serve their neighborhoods. As described above, the policy quickly encountered stiff resistance from state and local governmental officials.

Johnson's policies, nevertheless, helped establish a community economic development architecture that later spawned the work of nonprofit intermediaries like the Local Initiatives Support Corporation, the Enterprise Foundation, and NeighborWorks America, and these organizations are still to some extent underwritten by federal policies and funding. Several large national foundations—Ford, Rockefeller, and others—also funded and played substantial roles in the support of community organizations.

In addition, LBJ's efforts to combat racial discrimination and secure voting rights for minority populations have had lasting effects on urban minority communities. Thousands of community-based organizations (some faith-based, others secular) play important roles in the lives of citizens today. The Bush presidents, Clinton, and Obama have all embraced the importance of nongovernmental organization and volunteerism. In sum, Johnson's policies dealing with poor minority communities were important in a historical sense, but the growth and diversification in this sector could not have been predicted in the 1960s.

Johnson believed that to accomplish his goals in urban America, a restructuring of federalism was important. Johnson reconfigured the machinery of the federal government to align with what he saw as the needs of an urban, industrial, and racially divided society. States and localities—what Justice Louis Brandeis labeled the "laboratories of democracy"—were frequently implementers of his programs. But for constitutional (dual sovereignty under federalism) and political reasons, federal leadership in urban policy was quickly curtailed. After LBJ, the federal role in urban policy was largely devolved to the states, which had the authority to determine the responsibilities and resource capacities of local governments. In addition, the hollowing-out of the federal government during the conservative age meant that federal capacity to address the problems of urban America was further diminished. Johnson's attempt to reshape the intergovernmental system to address urban issues largely failed, but the new forms of intergovernmental relations consolidated by Nixon and further modified thereafter provide a visible, but less prominent, federal presence in urban matters even today (Advisory Commission on Intergovernmental Relations 1980).

LBJ made unparalleled attempts to help big cities; local officials who had much to gain from the large influx of federal funds, especially for infrastructure, were jubilant in most cases. But opposition formed when funding bypassed city hall and went directly to community organizations. Compared with policies from the administrations that followed, the Johnson initiatives stand out as the most ambitious federal attempts to address problems of the inner city. The scale and breadth of LBJ's efforts were truly impressive. Johnson believed that a Great Society required vibrant and just cities.[12] Given the inability or unwillingness of state and local governments to address urban problems, Johnson found that the federal government had an important role to play in the everyday lives of all people, especially the poor. His vision was for a broader and more activist role than that of his predecessors and, as it turned, than those of his successors. In addition, the record suggests that his policy ambitions for urban America remain unfulfilled.

Notes

The authors thank Eric Thronson and Lindsey Foster for their very able research assistance, Cheryl McVay and Arlene Pashman for editorial assistance, and Leah Brooks (University of Toronto) for comments on an earlier draft of the paper. We are grateful for helpful suggestions from James DeFilippis and Roland V. Anglin of Rutgers University. We also thank the Lyndon Baines Johnson Foundation, the Mike Hogg Professorship of Urban Policy, and Rutgers University for resources used to undertake this project.

1. Importantly, Johnson's goal of fighting poverty was not widely shared by the American public. According to public opinion polls at the time, only 9 percent wanted to end poverty (Newman and Jacobs 2010).

2. These included the community development block grants (1974), urban development action grants (1977), antihomelessness legislation (1988), HOPE VI to revitalize and privatize public housing (1992), and other laws and regulations. Many of these later efforts weakened Johnson's goal of federal leadership in urban housing.

3. There are many reasons why poverty has remained stubbornly high, including the much slower rate of economic growth after the Johnson years. Policy failures are but one part of the situation.

4. Similarly, we do not discuss landmark civil rights and voting rights legislation in detail, even though these had significant impacts on urban residents.

5. Other policies that affect cities (e.g., health care, education, labor markets, and immigration) are examined in other chapters in this volume.

6. Johnson made extensive use of external (eight between 1964 and 1967) and interagency (seventeen between 1965 and 1968) task forces to analyze issues and to develop policy recommendations on urban matters.

7. Another important initiative, the Immigration and Nationality Act of 1965, had important effects on demographic diversity of U.S. cities (Singer 2004; Katz 2010); see chapter 4 of this book.

8. Leichenko (2001) shows that the population ratio of central cities to suburbs declined from 0.43 (1970) to 0.35 (1997). That ratio has declined further in the twenty-first century. Suburban employment growth brought forth population shifts as people followed jobs outwardly within metropolitan areas.

9. We recognize that rural areas had higher rates of poverty than metropolitan areas; our discussion here is limited to nonrural areas.

10. Presidents Nixon, Ford, Reagan, and George H. W. Bush each proclaimed their own versions of the New Federalism.

11. In addition, the Intermodal Surface Transportation Efficiency Act of 1991, adopted after intense negotiation between Congress and the George H. W. Bush administration, substantially enhanced transportation planning and coordination, which was particularly important in metropolitan areas (Biles 2011). This piece of legislation led to important reforms in metropolitan planning.

12. LBJ's efforts to combat racial discrimination, a topic not fully addressed in this chapter, undoubtedly improved the lives of many minorities. Despite some variation in the level of active support to eliminate racial discrimination after Johnson, no subsequent administration has directly questioned the rightfulness of this position.

References

Advisory Commission on Intergovernmental Relations. 1980. *Citizen participation in the American federal system.* Washington, D.C.: Advisory Commission on Intergovernmental Relations.

American Society of Civil Engineers. 2008. Report card for America's infrastructure 2005 (updated for 2008). www.asce.org/reportcard/2005/index.cfm.

Berube, Alan, and Elizabeth Kneebone. 2006. Two steps back: City and suburban poverty trends 1999–2005. Washington D.C.: Brookings Institution. www .brookings.edu/reports/2006/12poverty_berube.aspx.

Biles, Roger. 2011. *The fate of cities: Urban America and the federal government, 1945–2000*. Lawrence: University Press of Kansas.

Bluestone, Barry, and Bennett Harrison. 1982. *The deindustrialization of America: Plant closings, community abandonment, and the dismantling of basic industry*. New York: Basic Books.

Caraley, Demetrio. 1976. Congressional politics and urban aid. *Political Science Quarterly* 91 (Spring): 19–45; also in *Publius* 16 (Winter 1980): 49–79.

Choate, Pat, and Susan Walter. 1983. *America in ruins*. Durham, N.C.: Duke Press Policy Studies.

Dallek, Robert. 1998. *Flawed giant: Lyndon Johnson and his times, 1961–1973*. New York: Oxford University Press.

Dilulio, John J., Jr. 2007. *Godly republic: A centrist blueprint for America's faith-based future*. Berkeley: University of California Press.

Dreier, Peter, John Mollenkopf, and Todd Swanstrom. 2004. *Place matters: Metropolitics for the twenty-first century*. 2nd ed. Lawrence: University Press of Kansas.

Eisinger, Peter K. 1985. The search for a national urban policy, 1968–1980. *Journal of Urban History* 12 (Nov.): 3–23.

Glaeser, Edward, Matthew Kahn, and Chenghuan Chu. 2001. Job sprawl: Employment location in U.S. metropolitan areas. Washington, D.C.: Brookings Institution. www.brookings.edu/reports/2001/07metropolitanpolicy_edward-glaeser —matthew-kahn—and-chenghuan-chu.aspx.

Glickman, Norman J., ed. 1980. *The urban impacts of federal policies*. Baltimore: Johns Hopkins University Press.

Glickman, Norman J., Michael L. Lahr, and Elvin K. Wyly. 1996. *State of the nation's cities*. Report prepared for the U.S. Department of Housing and Urban Development and the United Nations Habitat II Conference. New Brunswick, N.J.: Center for Urban Policy Research, Rutgers University.

Halpern, Robert. 1995. *Rebuilding the inner city: A history of initiatives to address poverty in the United States*. New York: Columbia University Press.

Hanson, Andrew, Ike Brannon, and Zackary Hawley. 2014. Rethinking tax benefits for home owners. *National Affairs* 19:40–54.

Hays, R. Allen. 1995. *The federal government and urban housing: Ideology and change in public policy*. 2nd ed. Albany: State University of New York Press.

Howard, Christopher, Michael Lipsky, and Dale Roger Marshall. 1994. Citizen participation in urban politics: Rise and routinization. In George Peterson, ed., *Big-city politics*, 153–178. Lanham, Md.: Urban Institute Press.

Jackson, Kenneth T. 1985. *Crabgrass frontier: The suburbanization of the United States*. New York: Oxford University Press.

Jargowsky, Paul A. 2003. *Stunning progress, hidden problems: The dramatic decline of concentrated poverty in the 1990s*. Washington, D.C.: Brookings Institution.

Johnson, Lyndon B. 1966. Telephone message to the employees of HUD on the occasion of the department's first anniversary (Nov. 10). Available at the American Presidency Project, www.presidency.ucsb.edu/ws/?pid=28021.

———. 1967. Letter to the Task Force on the Cities. July 22.

Kain, John F. 1968. Housing segregation, Negro employment, and metropolitan decentralization. *Quarterly Journal of Economics* 82, no. 2: 175–197.

Katz, Michael. 1989. *The undeserving poor: From the war on poverty to the war on welfare.* New York: Pantheon.

———. 2010. Narratives of failure? Historical interpretations of federal urban policy. *City and Community* 9:13–22.

Kleinberg, Benjamin. 1995. *Urban America in transformation: Perspectives on urban policy and development.* Thousand Oaks, Calif.: Sage.

Kneebone, Elizabeth, and Alan Berube. 2008. *Reversal of fortune: A new look at concentrated poverty in the 2000s.* Washington, D.C.: Brookings Institution.

Leichenko, Robin M. 2001. Growth and change in U.S. cities and suburbs. *Growth and Change* 32:326–354.

Markusen, Ann R., Peter Hall, Scott Campbell, and Sabina Deitrick. 1991. *The rise of the gunbelt: The military remapping of industrial America.* New York: Oxford University Press.

Mollenkopf, John H. 1983. *The contested city.* Princeton, N.J.: Princeton University Press.

Newman, Katherine, and Elisabeth S. Jacobs. 2010. *Who cares? Public ambivalence and government activism from the New Deal to the Second Gilded Age.* Princeton, N.J.: Princeton University Press.

Orlebeke, Charles J. 1990. Chasing urban policy: A critical retrospect. In Marshall Kaplan and Franklin James, eds., *The future of national urban policy*, 185–201. Durham, N.C.: Duke University Press.

Ravitch, Diane. 2010. Why I changed my mind about school reform. *Wall Street Journal.* Mar. 9.

Rich, Michael. 1993. Riot and reason: Crafting an urban policy response. *Publius* 23 (Summer): 115–134.

Rohrer, Daniel M., David C. Montgomery, Mary E. Montgomery, David J. Eaton, and Mark G. Arnold. 1970. *The environmental crisis: A basic overview of the problem of pollution.* Skokie, Ill.: National Textbook.

Sampson, Charles. 2004. Identifying and understanding the effects of mayoral change in minority governed municipalities. Paper presented at the annual meeting of the Midwest Political Science Association, Palmer House Hilton, Chicago, Illinois, Apr. 15.

Singer, Audrey. 2004. *The rise of new immigrant gateways.* Washington, D.C.: Brookings Institution.

Sugrue, Thomas J. 2005. *The origins of the urban crisis and inequality in postwar Detroit.* Princeton, N.J.: Princeton University Press.

———. 2008. Carter's urban policy crisis. In Gary M. Fink, ed., *The Carter presidency: Policy choices in the post–New Deal era*, 137–157. Lawrence: University of Kansas Press.

U.S. Bureau of the Census. 2012. Poverty: Historical poverty tables—people. Table 2: Poverty status of people by family relationship, race, and Hispanic origin: 1959 to 2012. www.census.gov/hhes/www/poverty/data/historical/people.html.

Vidal, A., and W. Dennis Keating. 2004. Community development: Current issues and emerging challenges. *Journal of Urban Affairs* 26, no. 2: 125–137.

Weissman, Harold, ed. 1969. *Employment and educational services in the mobilization for youth experience.* New York: Association Press.

Wilson, William J. 1996. *When work disappears: The world of the new urban poor.* New York: Knopf.

Wolman, Harold. 1986. The Reagan urban policy and its impacts. *Urban Affairs Quarterly* 21, no. 3: 311–335.

Wyly, Elvin K., Norman J. Glickman, and Michael L. Lahr. 1998. A top 10 list of things to know about American cities. *Cityscape* 3:7–32.

CHAPTER 11

The Past and Future of the Johnson
Administration's Water Quality Policies

DAVID J. EATON

Before the administration of President Lyndon Johnson, the U.S. Congress had not resolved whether water pollution represented a local or regional problem to be managed by the cities or states themselves, or whether the federal government should lead water-pollution control initiatives. During the Johnson administration, Congress and the White House cooperated on a series of legislative and appropriation initiatives establishing the legitimacy of a federal role in regulating and partnering to support state and local water quality management.

This chapter includes sections about water quality programs before, during, and after the Johnson administration, including future directions in which U.S. water quality policy may evolve. In addition, the chapter argues that Lyndon Johnson's administration transformed the process of managing water quality within the United States by creating the first modern national program for assurance of water quality. The innovations included ambient water quality standards; funds for wastewater infrastructure; legal, regulatory, and administrative programs; and research. Over the more than four decades since Johnson left office, public preferences for water quality may have changed, but the water quality goals and institutional relationships developed under the Johnson administration to protect water quality have continued.

Water Quality Standards before
the Lyndon B. Johnson Administration

Many religious traditions and premodern societies had oral and written water quality expectations or prohibitions. For example, as early as the era of

Augustus Caesar (reigned 27 BC–AD 14), Vitruvius suggested the elimination of lead pipes because "water . . . conducted through lead pipes . . . is found to be harmful for the reason that white lead is derived from it, and this is said to be hurtful to the human system" (Vitruvius 1960, bk. 8, ch. 6). Such a proposal for regulation was unusual at the time, since the Roman aqueducts had been used "safely" for centuries and water was already extensively treated at settling basins at the terminus of each aqueduct before entering the distribution system. Vitruvius did not seek to show a cause-and-effect relationship between lead pipes and health, but rather extrapolated from epidemiological (community use of lead paint) and occupational health (lead fumes) experiences. He did not demonstrate that health benefits would exceed the costs of replacing lead with earthenware pipes. It should be noted that his suggestions for the replacement of lead pipes were never implemented. His failure might have reflected a lack of consensus among Roman water-supply professionals that a problem existed or that his solution would be best. Another reason for inaction could have been that the magistrates, rather than the Roman Senate, held the purse strings for public works (DeCamp 1963, 211).

Any modern national water quality program can draw upon lessons from the Vitruvius story, which indicates six elements for a successful set of national water quality standards.

- There must be a legitimate basis for a central government to seek to impose water quality expectations and a financing mechanism to help pay for water and wastewater infrastructure improvements.
- There should be a rationale for water quality management based on health evidence.
- To enforce a standard, there should be performance measures indicating success or failure.
- To ensure consent of the regulated, they should perceive the standard to be reasonable in its engineering, administrative, and financial implications.
- The federal government should provide funds to support water and wastewater infrastructure improvements.
- There should be some certainty of enforcement consequences, lest the standard become an empty exhortation.

It can be argued that an initial step toward national water quality standards began with the Magna Carta's clause 33, which has been interpreted as establishing the monarch's right to manage navigable rivers and the limits to such controls, since it demands the removal of all fish weirs in order to ensure navigation rights. Article I, section 8 of the U.S. Constitution has been interpreted to mean that the powers of the British sovereign over navigable water were passed to Congress: "The Congress shall have the power . . . to regulate commerce . . . among the several states." These principles provide a legal basis for regulating water quality within navigable rivers in the United States.

The second element, evidence regarding a water quality health risk, also was imported. In 1854, John Snow documented how cholera was associated with water consumed from the Broad Street Pump in London (Snow 1855). Louis Pasteur provided evidence for the germ theory of disease during the 1860s and 1870s (Pasteur and Lister [1878/1867] 1996). Soon afterward, the U.S. government took initial steps to regulate water quality. During the period between 1886 and 1948, more than ninety bills were introduced in Congress for asserting federal control over water pollution programs; for encouraging research related to water pollution; or for financing state, local, or industrial antipollution measures (U.S. House 1969, 340). Although a number of important laws were enacted, many more proposals stalled in congressional committees or ended in a presidential veto.

The first water pollution control act was an 1886 law that prohibited the dumping of impediments to navigation in New York harbor (Congressional Quarterly 1966, 636). That law was followed in 1899 by the Rivers and Harbors Act, which forbade such dumping in all navigable waters (Carpenter 1968, 519). The Oil Pollution Act of 1924 was designed to prevent oil discharges that might disrupt commerce into navigable waters (519). Congress's rationale for these laws was that water pollution should be abated if it interfered with navigation.

The United States established the first modern water quality requirement for the purity of drinking water supplied by common carriers in interstate commerce (primarily trains), the Interstate Quarantine Regulations in 1914 (*Public Health Reports* 1914, 2957–2967), adopted by the Treasury Department on October 21, 1914, on the recommendation of the U.S. surgeon general (Rohlich, Eaton, and Lovelace 1978, 10–11). These regulations had four attributes that set them apart as a modern environmental standard: a health rationale; a test of feasibility; a defined scope for ease of implementation; and a performance measure to indicate whether a regulated institution was in compliance with the standard. The preface to the surgeon general's report stressed a distinction between "standards of purity," which cannot exist, because purity is an absolute, and "limits of permissible impurity," and articulated three concepts that since then have guided U.S. environmental quality standards (*Public Health Reports* 1914). Recommendations were made for limits of permissible impurity based on the following requirements:

- Water supplies be free from injurious effects upon the human body and free from offensiveness to the sense of sight, taste, or smell
- Supplies be attainable by common carriers without prohibitive expense
- Water examinations necessary to determine whether a given water supply meets the requirements be as few and as simple as is consistent with the end in view

(*Public Health Reports* 1914)

In keeping with the state of knowledge of water supply practice, the Treasury Department promulgated only a bacteriological standard to ensure a quality of water equal to that of municipal supplies that had been demonstrated by experience to be safe and affordable (*Public Health Reports* 1914). The potential health effects of other physical and chemical properties of water were left to further study.

In 1936, Senator Alben Barkley (D-KY) and Representative Carl Vinson (D-GA) introduced a bill to control water pollution in U.S. surface waters, which died in committee. A similar bill was passed by Congress in 1938 but vetoed by President Franklin Roosevelt (U.S. House 1969, 340). After a report in 1939 by the Special Advisory Committee on Water Pollution, part of the National Resources Committee, a new bill was introduced in 1940, but it died in a House-Senate conference committee (340–341). After this failure, no significant water pollution control legislation was considered until the end of World War II. The House of Representatives held hearings on water pollution in November 1945, and in November 1947 the Conference of State Sanitary Engineers sponsored a national meeting that provided some impetus to a water pollution bill from Senator Barkley and Senator Robert Taft (R-OH), the 1948 Water Pollution Control Act (341–342). That bill called for the U.S. surgeon general to initiate federal research, technical assistance, and federal loans to states and interstate agencies for the investigation of water pollution and the planning of pollution abatement works; authorize loans to municipalities and industries for water pollution abatement works; promote interstate water quality compacts; and enforce pollution abatement on interstate waters (341–342).

The House and the Senate Public Works Committees held extensive hearings on the bill. Representatives of states, local governments, and conservation organizations testified in support of the bill, providing material on the health effects of poor water quality, the ineffectiveness of state laws, and the long-term costs of polluted waters to industry (U.S. House 1969, 344–350). The surgeon general, who would be responsible for implementing the provisions of the Barkley-Taft bill if it passed, testified in favor of it. Industrial representatives opposed the bill as unnecessary, believing that state regulation was adequate. They argued that federal preemption of water quality standards would be unjustified (as they argued that some pollutants were harmless and others beneficial), harmful to property rights, and detrimental to the nation's economic health and productivity (346). Some state and local government representatives were "somewhat ambivalent" about federal water pollution legislation on the grounds that states had sufficient statutory responsibility to handle such "local concerns" (349). Philip B. Fleming, administrator of the Federal Works Agency (FWA), termed water pollution control "primarily an engineering problem" and recommended that responsibility for water pollution be shared by the FWA and the U.S. Public Health Service (PHS) (349–350). When the final version of the bill was reported by the House and Senate committees, it represented "a compromise between a number of views" (346) and reflected numerous committee meetings held during the drafting and hearing stages of the legislative process. Although the law was self-described as "experimental" and subject to change on the "basis of experience with its operation" (346), it did set a precedent for shared federal responsibility in water pollution control.

After different versions of the bill were resolved by a Senate-House conference committee, the bill passed both houses, and President Truman signed it as Public Law 80-845, the Federal Water Pollution Control Act, on June 30, 1948 (Congressional Quarterly 1965, 740). The act directed the surgeon general to request the Justice Department to institute federal court action to stop water pollution in interstate waters with the consent of the state in which pollution originated. The law authorized $27.8 million in federal loans for the construction of local sewage treatment plants, administration of state and municipal water pollution control programs, and research (U.S. House 1969, 351, 500).

The federal government moved cautiously in implementing the law. For ten years before 1957, the federal government never convened a single conference or a hearing on interstate water pollution; as late as December 1959, only eleven initial hearings or conferences had occurred (U.S. Department of the Interior 1970). Of those eleven hearings, enforcement actions had begun on seven (Task Force on Enforcement Procedures n.d.), and the PHS's first water quality enforcement suit was not filed until September 29, 1960 (U.S. Department of the Interior 1970). Of the $22.5 million in loans authorized for annual grants under the Federal Water Pollution Control Act, only in 1950 and 1951 were the full amounts appropriated and spent (352–353). Congress took no action when (in 1950) the president's Water Resources Policy Commission recommended a six-point program of legislative action on stream pollution (352–353).

The Federal Water Pollution Control Act was extended for three additional years in 1953 without a change in terms. In 1954, the U.S. Department of Health, Education and Welfare (HEW, which included the Public Health Service) sought to revise the law in cooperation with industry, conservation interests, and representatives of state and local governments (Jennings 1969, 74; U.S. House 1969, 353). As a result, in 1955 the Senate passed Senate Bill 890, which authorized matching grants (not only loans) for states and interstate agencies for pollution control activities; eliminated state consent before federal abatement court proceedings could be instituted; and allowed states to establish water quality standards. The PHS proposed amendments in a related House bill (H.R. 9540), which would set water quality standards for interstate streams if the states did not do so; initiate federal court action without the consent of a state in which pollution originates; and authorize $100 million in annual state or city grants-in-aid and provide up to $500,000 per municipal sewage treatment plant (Sundquist 1968, 325). Industry and state opposition to federal water quality standards was so instantaneous and intense that Speaker Sam Rayburn (D-TX) decided to postpone consideration of the bill until the following session rather than risk its defeat (324). John A. Blatnik (D-MN), chair of the House Subcommittee on Rivers and Harbors of the House Public Works Committee, reacted to the postponement of H.R. 9540 by saying, "If the polluters don't like S. 890, let's give them a bill they really won't like" (quoted in Sundquist 1968, 325).

After rounds of hearings and compromises, a revised H.R. 9540 was eventually passed by the House and Senate. Despite reservations over the grants section, President Eisenhower signed the bill into law as the Water Pollution Control Act of 1956, Public Law 84–660, on July 9, 1956 (Jennings 1969, 77). These amendments to the 1948 Water Pollution Control Act created enforcement procedures for abating interstate pollution, established a nine-member Water Pollution Control Advisory Board, awarded $100,000 for research fellowships, authorized annual grants of $3 million to assist states in developing comprehensive water pollution control programs, and authorized $50 million in grants a year over a ten-year period to cover 30 percent or $250,000 (whichever was less) of the costs of municipal sewage treatment plants (Congressional Quarterly 1956, 570–571).

Passage of the law did not lead to rapid action regarding water pollution control. President Eisenhower, who continued to characterize pollution as "a uniquely local blight" (Sundquist 1968, 333), opposed further federal intervention in water pollution control. In 1957, he proposed a Joint Federal-State Action Committee to determine which federal functions could be discontinued and handed over to the states (327); that committee recommended that the grants for local sewage treatment plants be discontinued and that the federal tax on local telephone service be rebated to the states as a potential funding source for antipollution measures (Jennings 1969, 79). In 1958, Eisenhower requested that Congress discontinue the grants provided for in the 1956 legislation (80).

Representative Blatnik proposed H.R. 3610 to amend the law by increasing the total authorization for sewage treatment plants and the ceiling for individual grants (Sundquist 1968, 328). During hearings in May 1958, conservation groups and the American Municipal Association favored the legislation, while industry and the administration opposed it. State pollution control agencies changed their position and supported treatment plant grants because, as one opponent from two years earlier confessed: "Apparently we were wrong and you were right." Another wrote that the grant program was "quite effective in accelerating sewage treatment works construction . . . and in many instances such projects could not have been undertaken [without federal aid]" (329). Although the House Public Works Committee supported Blatnik's bill by a vote of 21–7, no attempt was made to pass it in the full House (328–329). Senator Robert S. Kerr (D-OK), chairman of the Senate Public Works Committee, supported H.R. 3610, and his compromise bill passed the Senate (Congressional Quarterly 1959, 267). As Congress was nearing adjournment, House and Senate supporters postponed final action on H.R. 3610 until 1960 in order to avoid a pocket veto (Congressional Quarterly 1960, 250). A compromise bill then passed both houses easily; President Eisenhower vetoed it, saying water pollution was still "a uniquely local blight," and the House failed to override his veto (250–251).

Despite the stalemate between Eisenhower and the Democratic Congress before the 1960 election, at least some parts of the federal government had enunciated each of the six principles that could become the basis for national water quality programs: a rationale for federal action; a health basis for standards; performance measures for success; a reasonableness test of administrative feasibility; federal support for wastewater infrastructure; and enforcement of water quality violations.

After his election, President Kennedy cooperated with Congress on water quality, but did not propose his own agenda. The Kennedy administration endorsed Blatnik's efforts to establish through H.R. 4036 a federal water quality role that would extend federal authority to all navigable interstate waters; create a Federal Water Pollution Control Administration in the Department of Health, Education and Welfare; and authorize up to $100 million in 1964 for sewage treatment plant construction (Jennings 1969, 93–101; Sundquist 1968, 330–331). Despite continued industry opposition to extending federal authority over navigable rivers, the bill passed. In 1961, President Kennedy signed the Federal Water Pollution Control Act Amendment, Public Law 87-881, "with great pleasure" (Sundquist 1968, 348).

Senator Edmund Muskie (D-ME) introduced legislation in 1963 to establish a "positive" national policy of "keeping waters as clean as possible" and to raise the ceiling on individual sewage treatment construction grants (Sundquist 1968, 349). For the bill to pass the Senate in 1963, Muskie had to compromise on standards and grants. Federal grant authorizations were lowered. Water quality standards became an "option" a state could adopt. The Senate passed the bill 60–11 (Congressional Quarterly 1963, 240). Since no parallel bill had passed the House, a conference committee could not be impaneled before the 1964 elections.

The Eisenhower administration's implicit approach to water quality was to defer federal action and leave water quality a state matter. The Kennedy administration followed Congress's lead and crafted incremental improvements for a nascent federal water quality role. Lyndon Johnson's approach to water quality was different in kind from that of any previous U.S. president: he embraced and supported an effort to codify a federal role in protecting the nation's water quality, as discussed below, through proclamations, legislation, appropriations, administrative orders, enforcement, and the development of skilled professionals willing to work toward water quality.

The Johnson Administration's Approach to Water Quality Standards

Lyndon Johnson from the start of his administration was committed to enhancing the nation's water quality by using all the government's legal, financial, and regulatory resources. He promulgated priorities for water quality as part of separate messages to Congress; sought congressional support; and passed and then implemented his priority legislation. Johnson specified in writing his priorities, found common cause within Congress to achieve them, pushed the bills to passage, implemented the laws, and focused on enforcement to achieve outcomes. While many American presidents have given lip service to environmental quality, President Johnson established his priorities and delivered on them.

Water Quality Proclamations to Congress

Each year at the beginning of 1965, 1966, 1967, and 1968, Johnson sent a special message to Congress on his administration's priorities for conserving and restoring the natural beauty of the United States (see table 11.1 for a list of Johnson's water quality priorities).

In his message to Congress on February 28, 1965, entitled "Conservation and Restoration of Natural Beauty," Johnson went to the heart of the challenge for managing water quality nationally: "Every major river system is now polluted. Waterways that were the sources of pleasure and beauty and recreation are forbidden to human contact and objectionable to sight and smell. Furthermore this pollution is costly, requiring expensive treatment of the drinking water and inhibiting the operation of growth on industry . . . The longer we wait to act, the greater the dangers and the larger the problem" (Johnson 1965). Johnson sought to prevent water pollution by setting effective national water quality standards; correcting pollution through enforcement activity; paying for water quality improvements through increased federal grant ceilings for wastewater treatment plant construction; encouraging effective state participation through substantial grants to state pollution control programs; and preventing future pollution by promoting research and demonstration projects on hard-to-solve problems such as controlling polluted water discharges via combined storm and sanitary sewers as well as nonpoint source control (Johnson 1965; Congressional Quarterly 1965, 748).

In his February 23, 1966, message to Congress, which dealt with pollution, natural beautification, and recreation, Johnson proposed "the right to clean water—and the duty not to pollute it." He stated that the United States would go beyond water standards "to clean and preserve entire river basins from their sources to their mouths." To implement that objective, Johnson's draft legislation sought to extend the system of national water quality standards to intrastate waters; enhance federal funding of wastewater treatment; support the regulatory efforts of states, local communities, and interstate river basin organizations; develop funding partnerships for constructing wastewater infrastructure; establish a National Water Commission to advise on the full range of water problems; and invest in research

Table 11.1. Johnson administration's water quality priorities

A. Message to Congress on conservation and restoration of natural beauty (Feb. 8, 1965)

- Provide, through the setting of effective water quality standards, combined with a swift and effective enforcement procedure, . . . a national program to prevent water pollution at its source rather than attempt to cure pollution after it occurs . . . and . . . provide positive controls for the discharge of pollutants into our interstate or navigable waters.
- With the cooperation of States and cities—using the tools of regulations, grants, and incentives—we can bring the most serious problem of river pollution under control.
- Increase project grant ceilings and provide additional incentive for multi-municipal projects under the waste treatment facility construction program. . . Increase the ceilings for grants to State water pollution control programs. . . Provide a new research and demonstration construction program leading to the solution of problems caused by the mixing of storm water runoff and sanitary waste.
- Abate pollution caused by direct [federal] agency operation, contracts and cooperative agreements.
- Clean up the [Potomac] river and keep it clean, so it can be used for boating, swimming and fishing.

B. Message to Congress on pollution, beautification and recreation (Feb. 23, 1966)

- [We] must combine all the means at our disposal—Federal, state, local and private—progressively to reduce the pollution of our rivers . . . to achieve high standards of water quality throughout the basin . . . to clean all of America's rivers . . . *to clean and preserve entire river basins from their sources to their mouths.* (emphasis in the original)
- I propose a new kind of partnership—built upon our creative federal system . . . Appropriate water quality standards . . . must be adopted for every part of the basin . . . States and local communities must develop long-range plans to achieve those standards and preserve them . . . A permanent river basin organization . . . [must be formed] to carry out the plans . . . Communities must be willing . . . to contribute funds necessary for constructing facilities [or] to levy charges for use.
- I propose the establishment of a National Water Commission to review and advise on the entire range of water resource problems.

C. Message to Congress on protecting our national heritage (Jan. 30, 1967)

- I am renewing my recommendation for the enactment of legislation to establish a National Water Commission.

Table 11.1. (*continued*)

D. Message to Congress: "To Renew a Nation" (Mar. 8, 1968)

- I have asked the Secretary of the Interior to speed the review of the remaining standards and plan so the Federal Grants can . . . help the states and communities.
- We need a comprehensive system to control all pollution in American waters . . . I propose . . . the Oil Pollution and Hazardous Substances Control Act of 1968.
- To help cities and communities of America to assure citizens that the water they drink is safe, I propose the Safe Drinking Water Act of 1968.
- The heart of a water pollution control program is the community water treatment plant which prevents refuse, debris and filth from fouling the waters. . . . I recommend an appropriation of $225 million for grants. . . . I recommend legislation to allow annual installment payments, . . . [to] generate a total of about $1 to $1.4 billion in construction.
- Last year when I asked Congress to establish a National Water Commission. . . . I urged Congress to complete its action and authorize the Commission.
- To help cities and communities of America assure citizens that the water they drink is safe, I propose the Safe Drinking Water Act of 1968.

Source: Lyndon B. Johnson Presidential Library.

on integrated waste disposal systems, improved water treatment technology, and the measurement and monitoring of pollution (Johnson 1966a).

In his message to Congress on January 30, 1967, Johnson stressed environmental issues other than water quality. His 1967 water quality management target of opportunity was to create a National Water Commission to advise on the full range of national water issues (Johnson 1967).

In his final conservation message to Congress, delivered on March 8, 1968, Johnson renewed his call for "conservation" to be "a moral imperative" (Congressional Quarterly 1968, 61-A–67-A). He repeated his four steps for improving water quality: a standard for each body of water; enforcement of discharge controls that apply to the public and private sectors; construction of wastewater treatment plants; and cooperation among cities, counties, and states, and among the states, to clean "water bodies . . . in their entirety" (62-A–67-A). Johnson informed Congress that he had directed the interior secretary to speed the review of all state standards. He encouraged municipalities to levy user charges to pay for wastewater treatment. Johnson again asked Congress to authorize a National Water Commission and proposed a new Safe Drinking Water Act that would set national standards for potable drinking water (62-A–63-A). Johnson recognized that U.S. communities would require many billions of dollars of investment in sewers and waste-water treatment plants in order to clean up U.S. rivers.[1] Congress had previously authorized $760 million for fiscal year 1969. Johnson asked Congress for an additional $225 million in grants and $475 million in supplemental construction commitments for that budgetary year (62-A–63-A). Throughout 1968, the House and Senate could not agree on these bills. As a result, all these issues were left to the Nixon administration.

Johnson's Water Quality Legislation

President Johnson's water quality legislative agenda was expansive yet careful. His legislation created the federal government's capacity to help states improve water quality. He sought feasible appropriations and avoided battles in the courts or in Congress in which he might not prevail. From 1965 through 1966, he signed three major bills addressing water quality policy: the Water Resource Planning Act of 1965, the Water Quality Act of 1965, and the Clean Water Restoration Act of 1966.

The section below does not describe or evaluate Johnson administration water-resource legislation passed during the period 1963–1968 but not directly relevant to water quality. That legislation includes the Water Resource Research Act of 1964 (Pub. L. 80-379, which created water research centers at land-grant colleges) (Congressional Quarterly 1964, 507–510); the Salt Water Conversion Act of 1965 (Pub. L. 89-118); the Fish-Wildlife Preservation Act of 1966 (Pub. L. 89-669); the Water for Peace Conference of 1966 (Pub. L. 89-799); and the Scenic Rivers Act of 1968 (Pub. L. 90-542), as well as bills authorizing specific water infrastructure construction projects through the U.S. Army Corps of Engineers or the Bureau of Reclamation within the Interior Department.

On July 22, 1965, Johnson signed into law the Water Resources Planning Act, Public Law 89-80 (Congressional Quarterly 1965, 759–761). The law provided statutory authority for the federal Water Resources Council and authorized creation of federal-state river basin planning commissions. The law delivered on a priority that had been a target of opportunity since the New Deal and the Kennedy administration, namely, to create institutions that could coordinate federal, state, interstate, regional, rural, and private water development plans for river basins. The law authorized funds for the council and for federal matching grants to state water resource planning programs. Some of Johnson's contributions to this legislation were his support of language enabling the state appointment of members to commissions as well as assurances against federal encroachment on state water rights (Congressional Quarterly 1965, 759).

Johnson's proposal for a water quality bill in 1965 required that each state adopt a set of water quality standards for navigable interstate waters, and that these state standards would become part of national standards (Johnson 1965). While the concept of "standards" had been part of a bill (introduced in 1963 by Senator Muskie) that had passed the Senate, Johnson's proposed standards were considerably tougher; the draft bill authorized the federal government to set standards if a state chose not to do so (Congressional Quarterly 1965, 743). The issue of "water quality standards" required almost four months to resolve in the House-Senate conference. The final compromise left the primary responsibility for setting standards for interstate waters with the states. If, by June 30, 1967, any state had failed to establish standards or to file a declaration of intent to establish standards, or if the standards were unacceptable to the secretary of HEW, the federal government retained the authority to impose its own standards (Sundquist 1968, 363; Congressional Quarterly 1965, 748). The final Water Quality Act of 1965 (Pub. L. 89-234) followed the recommendations of President Johnson on the points contained in his message to Congress on natural beauty. The law authorized $150 million a year for ten years for grants to support construction of sewer systems and wastewater treatment, and $20 million annually for four years for equal matching grants for municipalities to construct separate storm and sanitary sewers (Sundquist 1968, 364–367; Congressional Quarterly 1965, 748). To receive sewage treatment construction grants, a state would have to file an intention to set water quality standards.

From the perspective of U.S. environmental history, the Water Quality Act represents a remarkable accomplishment. Before its passage, the United States did not have a single national environmental standard that applied to water, air, or land. President Eisenhower was correct in asserting that pollution was a local issue, since environmental quality policy had remained a states'-rights issue, subject to local and state regulation and management.

The Water Quality Act required each state to set ambient water quality standards for all navigable interstate surface waters by 1967, or else the federal government could preempt state inactivity. Although the standards were only limits on permissible impurity against which streams could be evaluated, any enforcement would require limits on pollutant discharge, in effect setting a precedent for effluent limits upon individual dischargers. The law set a precedent for states to voluntarily extend water quality standards to intrastate, nonnavigable surface waters, and even ground waters.

During 1965, Muskie's Senate Subcommittee on Air and Water Pollution held a series of regional hearings on water pollution that led to a draft bill for increasing federal financial involvement in water quality management (Sundquist 1968, 365). The Johnson administration's 1966 version of that water quality bill raised expenditure levels and provided for the transfer of the Federal Water Pollution Control Administration (FWPCA) to the Department of the Interior; established a comprehensive river basin approach to water resource planning; and articulated a citizen's right to clean water (Congressional Quarterly 1966, 632). After haggling over the sums of money necessary to prevent and abate water pollution, both houses passed unanimously the Clean Water Restoration Act of 1966, Public Law 89-753 (Sundquist 1968, 367). The bill authorized appropriations totaling $3.55 billion during fiscal years 1967–1971 for grants for construction of sewage treatment plants and eliminated existing dollar ceilings on the amount of a single grant.

The Clean Water Restoration Act of 1966 provided that a federal grant could pay for as much as 50 percent of a community's construction costs for developing sewers and wastewater treatment plants. The federal contribution (40 or 50 percent) was conditional on state participation in the financing of treatment plants and on the state establishing quality standards for intrastate bodies of water (to qualify for a 50 percent federal share). The law established a grant program for research on industrial water pollution control and on advanced waste treatment and water purification methods; in addition, it increased general water pollution research ($313 million during fiscal years 1967–1969) (Congressional Quarterly 1966, 632). It authorized federal grants to assist river basin planning organizations and increased grant authorizations to assist state and interstate water pollution control agencies. The law also gave the interior secretary new investigative powers to use at pollution abatement conferences or hearings, and extended pollution abatement procedures to cases of international water pollution. The Clean Water Restoration Act provided incentives for states to adopt ambient water quality standards for intrastate surface waters. The annual funds it authorized for the construction of sewage treatment plants were fourteen times the allocations made under Eisenhower's administration and seven times those that had been approved under Kennedy. Also in 1966, Congress approved Johnson's transfer of the authority for water pollution control from HEW to the Department of the Interior.

Although the Johnson administration passed no other major water quality laws after 1966, it was not for lack of trying. The 1965 Water Quality Act and 1966 Clean Water Restoration Act established national ambient water quality standards among the states, provided funds for wastewater infrastructure, and codified enforcement procedures to clean up pollution from municipal and industrial wastes. The unsuccessful bills of 1967–1968 attempted to enlarge the scope and financial support of federal water pollution control activities, efforts that eventually culminated under President Nixon in the passage of the Water Quality Improvement Act of 1970 and the 1972 Clean Water Act.

During 1967 both the Senate and the House held hearings to investigate water pollution control programs and consider the results of two presidential studies on water pollution. One study evaluated methods to "minimize the threat of oil spillage disasters at sea which endangered public health, safety and the nation's natural resources" (Congressional Quarterly 1967, 1008). The other study proposed a national program for regulating surface-mining operations. The Senate's oversight hearings on the operation of the FWPCA reported that a state could degrade surface water quality under existing law if the Department of the Interior did not object. That controversy was not resolved for four months, and then only by Secretary of the Interior Stewart Udall's assertion that all state standards would have to conform to a nondegradation policy (Carter 1968, 49).

In 1967 the Senate passed an omnibus water pollution control bill, but Congress was unable to complete action before the session ended (Congressional Quarterly 1967, 1006–1009). That bill reflected priorities in Lyndon Johnson's message to Congress, including provisions that would have authorized the secretary of the interior to initiate research and demonstration projects to prevent, control, or abate pollution caused by oil spills or acid drainage from mines. It contained a one-time appropriation of $15 million for watershed or drainage area projects to control or eliminate acid drainage, and it repealed the Oil Pollution Act of 1924, placing oil pollution under the FWPCA and toughening the enforcement provisions (Congressional Quarterly 1967, 1006–1009).

In 1968, both houses approved different versions of an omnibus water pollution control bill but were unable to reconcile the differences in committee before Congress adjourned. The bill contained provisions for oil pollution controls, pollution from marine vessels, and the compliance of federal licensees with water quality standards. It also authorized the federal government to pay its share of sewage treatment plant funds on an installment basis (Congressional Quarterly 1969, 514). The 1968 hearings on water quality identified a number of issues that eventually were addressed by subsequent, Nixon-era legislation. The hearings addressed such issues as linking a particular discharge to violations of ambient water quality standards; the slow pace of construction of sewage and wastewater treatment

Table 11.2. Johnson administration's federal water pollution enforcement

Date of enforcement conference	Body of water	States
Dec. 2, 1963; Sept. 27, 1967	Lower Connecticut River	MA, CT
Dec. 17, 1963	Monongahela River	WV, PA, MD
Jan. 15, 1964	Snake River	ID, WA
Feb. 7–8, 1964; Feb. 28, 1967; Mar. 1, 1967; Mar. 22, 1967	Upper Mississippi River	MN, WI
Feb. 11, 1964; Dec. 18, 1968	Merrimack and Nashua Rivers	NH, MA
May 5–6, 1964	Lower Mississippi River	AR, TN, MS, LA
May 26, 1964; July 26, 1967	Colorado River	CO, UT, AZ, NV, CA, NM, WY
July 21, 1964	Missouri River/Omaha	NE, KS, MO, IA
Jan. 26, 1965; May 28, 1968	Blackstone and Ten Mile Rivers	MA, RI
Feb. 2, 1965	Lower Savannah River	SC, GA
Feb. 2–9, 1965; Jan. 4–5, 1966; Jan. 31, 1966; Dec. 11–12, 1968	Calumet Rivers and tributaries	IL, IN
	Wolf Lake and Lake Michigan	
Feb. 16–17, 1965	Mahoning River	OH, PA
June 15–18, 1965	Detroit River	MI
Aug. 3–5, 1965; Oct. 10–12, 1965; Mar. 22, 1967; Oct. 4, 1968	Lake Erie	MI, IN, OH, PA, NY
Sept. 8–9, 1965	Lower Columbia River	WA, OR
Sept. 14–15, 1965; Jan. 18, 1966; Mar. 4, 1966	Red River (North)	MN, ND
Sept. 28–30, 1965; Sept. 20–21, 1967	Hudson River	NJ, NY
Apr. 27–28, 1966; Nov. 10, 1966	South Platte River	CO
July 14–15, 1966	Chattahoochee River and tributaries	AL, GA
July 18–20, 1966	Lake Tahoe	CA, NV
Sept. 20–21, 1966; June 21, 1967	Moriches Bay, South Bay	NY
Apr. 20, 1967	Penobscot River and Bay	MA
June 13–14, 1967	Raritan Bay	NJ, NY
Sept. 6, 1967; Oct. 6, 1967	Puget Sound	WA

Table 11.2. (*continued*)

Date of enforcement conference	Body of water	States
Nov. 11–12, 1967	Eastern New Jersey Shore	NJ
Jan. 31, 1968; Feb. 1–7, 1968; Mar. 7–12, 1968	Lake Michigan	MI, IN, IL, WI
Apr. 11, 1968	Coosa River	GA, AL
May 20, 1968	Boston Harbor	MA
Nov. 7, 1968	Pearl River	MS, LA
Nov. 13, 1968; Dec. 19–20, 1968	Lake Champlain	NY, VT

Source: U.S. Department of the Interior 1970.

infrastructure; and the potential of technology to improve the quality of surface waters.

Water Quality Enforcement

Johnson's reputation as a political operator must have made a difference when it came to interstate and intrastate water quality enforcement actions, because after he stated his expectations for water quality results, the states acceded to his priorities. Under four presidents between 1950 and 1970, the U.S. government initiated a total of fifty water quality enforcement actions (U.S. Department of the Interior 1970). In Lyndon Johnson's five years in office alone, the U.S. government initiated twenty-two new federal enforcement actions against water pollution in navigable waters and continued pressure to resolve ten enforcement actions begun under Eisenhower or Kennedy (table 11.2) (U.S. Department of the Interior 1970). Enforcement was so successful that within eighteen months of Johnson's becoming president, without having to go to court even once, his administration convinced thirty-six states, as well as their communities and businesses, to invest $1.78 billion to resolve water pollution enforcement issues identified at water pollution conferences (Task Force on Enforcement Procedures n.d., 3).

Johnson's administration was prepared to move forward on requiring municipalities and industries to obtain permits or licenses to discharge wastes into navigable waters under the authority of the Water Quality Act (Task Force on Enforcement Procedures n.d., 5–6). While the responsible federal agency (first HEW and later the Department of the Interior) did not

Table 11.3. Authorizations for water pollution control, 1948–1966

Statute	Sewage treatment authorization	Other provisions and their authorizations
Pub. L. 845: Water Pollution Control Act (1948)	$22.5 M/y (loans)	—
Pub. L. 845: Extension of Pub. L. 845 (1953)	$22.5 M/y (loans)	—
Pub. L. 660: Amendments to Water Pollution Control Act (1956)	$50 M/y (grants) 30% or $0.25 M/plant (lesser)	Research; $0.1 M State administration programs; $3 M
Pub. L. 88: Amendments to Water Pollution Control Act (1961)	$80 M/y ('62) $90 M/y ('63) 30% or $0.6 M/plant (lesser)	Research; — State administration programs; $5 M/y New treatment methods; $5 M/y
Pub. L. 234: Water Quality Control Act (1965)	$150 M/y 30% or $1.2 M/plant (lesser)	Up to 50% to separate storm and sanitary sewers; $20 M/y
Pub. L. 753: Clean Water Restoration Act (1966)	$3.55 B/5 years No ceiling on projects (limits from state activity)	New treatment methods; $20 M/y Industry treatment projects; $20 M/y Control of storm vs. sanitary sewers; $20 M/y State administration programs; $10 M/y

Source: Rohrer et al. 1970, 101–103.
Note: M = million; B = billion; y = year.

choose to extend enforcement to an emission permit system, the idea would surface later and be enacted as part of the Federal Water Pollution Control Act Amendments of 1972, more commonly known as the Clean Water Act (Pub. L. 92-500).

Appropriations

For five years Lyndon Johnson fought to increase the federal funds spent for construction of sewers and wastewater treatment plants (see tables 11.3

and 11.4). In 1966, the Clean Water Restoration Act provided incentives for states to adopt ambient water quality standards for intrastate surface waters. As mentioned earlier, in 1969 the law authorized spending for the construction of sewage treatment plants that was fourteen times the largest amount authorized under Eisenhower's administration and at least seven times the largest amount approved under Kennedy (table 11.4) (Controller General of the United States 1970, 9).

Table 11.4 lists federal authorizations, appropriations, and expenditures for construction of sewage treatment plants during the fiscal years from 1957 through 1969, Lyndon Johnson's last fiscal year in office. Although authorizations rose, congressional appropriations increased more slowly. Under the U.S. system, an authorization allows Congress to fund a program up to a specified level. Congress separately can appropriate a smaller sum or none at all. The executive branch retains flexibility regarding how much appropriated money to spend. For example, in fiscal year 1969 (which began on October 1, 1968), Johnson's last year in office, Congress appropriated only $214 million for sewage treatment facility construction out of an authorization of $700 million. Even after Congress authorizes and then appropriates a grant, there is no assurance that the funds will be spent. Pres-

Table 11.4. Spending on construction of sewage treatment plants, 1957–1969 (millions of dollars)

Fiscal year	Authorization	Appropriation	Expenditure
1957	50	50	37.942
1958	50	45.7	47.380
1959	50	46.8	
1960	50	46.1	
1961	50	45.6	45.161
1962	80	80	64.510
1963	90	90	92.228
1964	100	90	85.427
1965	100	90	85.523
1966	130	121	
1967	150	150	
1968	450	203	
1969	700	214	
Total	2,050	1,272.2	458.171

Source: Controller General of the United States 1970, 9.

idents Eisenhower and Nixon made a point of withholding sewage treatment plant construction funds (*Business Week* 1970, 11). President Johnson tried his best to spend what Congress had appropriated (U.S. Department of Health, Education and Welfare 1966, 41).

Between 1965 and 1969, Congress may have made headlines through its large wastewater treatment authorizations, but its appropriations did not come close to President Johnson's understanding of wastewater infrastructure needs, which are shown in table 11.5. An internal Johnson administration memorandum estimated that it would take at least a $20 billion construction program to build waste treatment plants that would treat the urban wastewater of 80 percent of the U.S. population in 1973 (based on an assumption that the cost of sewage collection would be $100 per person added to the cost of construction of new secondary wastewater treatment plants) (Task Group on Water Pollution 1965). In 1965, the Johnson administration actually had in place plans to request and spend, much faster, a larger appropriation of funds through the "expected" second term of the Johnson presidency (Task Group on Water Pollution 1965).

When Congress did not appropriate as much as Johnson requested, he was not a leader to give in easily. He considered creative accounting that would speed more money to states and cities to build wastewater treatment plants. In 1965, his administration conducted a study to observe how federal support for construction of sewage collection and treatment would leverage contract awards (construction) for collection and treatment facilities.

Table 11.5. Needed expenditures on waste facilities, 1966–1973 (millions of dollars)

Year	Collection	Treatment	Total
1966	500	800	1,300
1967	600	1,000	1,600
1968	900	1,200	2,100
1969	1,300	1,300	2,600
1970	1,500	1,500	3,000
1971	1,650	1,650	3,300
1972	1,650	1,650	3,300
1973	1,650	1,650	3,300
Total	9,750	10,750	20,500

Source: Task Group on Water Pollution 1965.

Table 11.6. Federal expenditures for construction of wastewater collection and treatment facilities, 1956–1964 (millions of dollars)

Year	Collection	Treatment	Total	Loan amounts included in total
1956	1	6	7	1
1957	3	55	59	3
1958	5	47	52	5
1959	4	47	51	4
1960	5	47	51	5
1961	17	55	72	17
1962	63	95	158	37
1963	130	173	303	31
1964	34	98	132	25

Source: Task Group on Water Pollution 1965.

In 1967 and 1968 Johnson sought congressional approval to allow the federal government to make annual installment payments in addition to lump-sum grants (Johnson 1968), in order to prepay state contributions to speed up construction. Based on internal studies, the Johnson administration expected to leverage federal construction grants so that each dollar of federal grants would generate a minimum of $3 in new wastewater infrastructure construction (table 11.6) (Task Group on Water Pollution 1965).

Administrative Orders

President Johnson used executive orders and reorganization to mobilize national water quality management. On November 13, 1965, he signed Executive Order 11258, which dealt with the "prevention, control, and abatement of water pollution by federal activities" and required all federal agencies to "step up the efforts in the nationwide battle against water pollution" (White House 1965). The order outlined steps that federal agencies must take to prevent, control, and treat water pollution by all federal installations and operations, including any borrowers, grantees, or contractors under programs financed by the U.S. government and conducted by other organizations, in order to "ensure that the Federal Government will provide the leadership in preventing and abating water pollution in the United States by setting its own house in order." (The order was a Johnson administration innovation to mobilize federal agencies to act to prevent and control water pollution. It required federal agencies to evaluate their water effluents, treat their water pollution, and comply with water quality criteria, as well as to use municipal wastewater treatment systems whenever possible.

On February 28, 1966, President Johnson authorized the Reorganization Plan of 1966, which moved all water pollution activities other than health-related aspects of pollution (such as section 3[b] of the Water Quality Act) from HEW to the U.S. Department of the Interior (Johnson 1966b). This reorganization created internal accountability for water quality programs within the U.S. government. The Nixon administration reorganized further by moving all environmental quality programs when it created the U.S. Environmental Protection Agency (EPA).

Human Resources for Water Quality Management

In each of the bills indicated above, the Johnson administration included funds for fellowships, scholarships, training, and internships to develop new human resources to help manage the cause for clean water. Much of the staff recruited during the Johnson administration remained as civil servants through the Nixon administration and beyond, with continuing interest in water quality. I served on the staff of the president's Council on Environmental Quality (CEQ) between 1970 and 1973 and worked, in part, on water issues, giving me a chance to meet federal staff members concerned with water quality management.

Many of Nixon's professionals concerned with water quality standards were alumni of the Johnson administration. One case will illustrate just how long the Johnson reach could be. Alvin (Al) L. Alm spent three decades in water quality. He was a staff member at the Office of Management and Budget responsible for investment in wastewater infrastructure from 1964 to 1968. When President Nixon was elected and wanted his own staff in key posts, he nominated Russell (Russ) Train to be undersecretary of the Department of the Interior to work on water quality and conservation. Train hired Alm as his administrative assistant. When Train was named to head the CEQ in 1970, Alm became his staff director (U.S. Environmental Protection Agency 2001). So Alm, who had been "educated" under Johnson, was thus selected to shepherd through Congress the Nixon administration's bills that Johnson had hoped to pass. Alm was a Johnson-style civil servant, a man who counted votes and tried to avoid any conflict he could not control. Of Alm it was said, and I observed this firsthand: he never sought to call a meeting the outcome of which had not been prearranged.

Alm served as a civil servant dealing with water quality and the environment for over thirty years (not continuously), from the Johnson administration through the Clinton administration. During that period, he continued to influence the trajectory of water quality policy, sometimes directly and sometimes indirectly. As staff director of the newly created CEQ, he supervised the staff that brought forward President Nixon's priority environmental legislation. Each year Alm supervised the development of no fewer than four annual messages to Congress containing the Nixon administration's proposed environmental legislation, in a manner comparable to Johnson's annual environmental messages: excerpts from the state of the union address (CEQ 1970a, 250–253); a separate President's Message on the Environment (254–271); an annual statement of the president's environmental program (CEQ 1970b); and an annual report on the state of the environment that described the Nixon administration's environmental priorities (CEQ 1970a).

From 1973 to 1977, Alm served as assistant administrator for planning and management at the EPA, where he helped develop the water pollution permit system and built EPA's economic analysis capability. Both elements were key components for implementing national water quality standards. In that role, Alm implemented ideas that had been developed within the Johnson administration (Alm 1993). From 1977 to 1980, Alm coordinated President Carter's energy plan and then served as assistant secretary for policy and evaluation at the U.S. Department of Energy (DOE). During the 1980s and 1990s, Alm served as deputy administrator at the EPA under William Ruckelshaus (after 1983). He later served as President Clinton's assistant secretary of energy in charge of cleaning up U.S. nuclear waste sites. Given the flow of personnel such as Al Alm from the Johnson period into subsequent administrations, it may not be surprising how sustainable the water quality policy decisions have been, as discussed below.

Water Quality Standards from Nixon through Bush and into the Future

Water quality standards have continued to evolve over the forty-five years since the end of the Johnson administration. Table 11.7 includes the acts and laws signed during the period from President Nixon to George W. Bush. It is beyond the scope of this article to describe in full the provisions of the contemporary Clean Water Act or to go into detail regarding the legislative, administrative, or judicial progress between 1967 and the present.

Table 11.7. Federal clean water legislation, 1886–2002

Year	Act	Public law
1886	Rivers and Harbors Act	24 Stat 329
1899	Rivers and Harbors Act	30 Stat 1151, 1152
1948	Federal Water Pollution Control Act	P.L. 80-845
1956	Water Pollution Control Act of 1956	P.L. 84-660
1961	Federal Water Pollution Control Act Amendments	P.L. 87-88
1965	Water Quality Act of 1965	P.L. 89-234
1966	Clean Water Restoration Act	P.L. 89-753
1970	Water Quality Improvement Act of 1970	P.L. 91-224, Part I
1972	Federal Water Pollution Control Act Amendments	P.L. 92-500
1977	Clean Water Act of 1977	P.L. 95-217
1981	Municipal Wastewater Treatment Construction Grants Amendments	P.L. 97-117
1987	Water Quality Act of 1987	P.L. 100-4
1990	Coastal Zone Act Reauthorization	P.L. 101-508
2002	Federal Water Pollution Control Acts Amendments	P.L. 107-303

Source: Copeland 2010.
Note: The legislation in this table is codified in part as 33 U.S.C. 1251–1387.

Many of the unresolved water quality issues articulated by Johnson in his messages to Congress or in the actions of his administration were addressed in the Federal Water Pollution Control Act Amendments of 1972 (Pub. L. 92-500). The statute required all municipal and industrial wastewater to be treated before being discharged into waterways, increased federal grants for construction of wastewater treatment plants, and strengthened and stream-lined enforcement. The law made operational Johnson's goals of "cleaning a river from its source to its mouth" by establishing the following goals: by 1977, the best practicable control technology (BPT) for industry or secondary treatment (for municipalities) would be used to limit wastewater discharges; by 1983, navigable waters would be "fishable and swimmable"; by 1985, point sources of pollution should have a goal of "zero discharge" of pollutants; and by 1989, pollutants should be removed from wastewater by the "best available technology" (BAT) (U.S. Environmental Protection Agency 1972). Of course, each of these deadlines came with options for variances, exemptions, and extensions. Subsequently, municipalities were allowed to seek extensions to July 1, 1988, to achieve secondary treatment.

But the EPA reported that by 1988 at least 86 percent of all U.S. cities had failed to meet that deadline (Copeland 2010).

The 1972 Marine Protection and Research Standards Act prohibited unacceptable ocean dumping, making the United States the first nation to seek to prevent ocean pollution. The 1977 Clean Water Act Amendment gave states more autonomy over federal program priorities and strengthened control on toxic pollutants.

By 1981, just fourteen years after states were required to adopt a water quality standard for interstate waters, investments in the prevention and treatment of polluted water had improved a key measure of water quality: bacterial pollution. In 1987, a national evaluation assessed twenty-four measures of water quality from 1974 to 1981 at 300 locations within two water quality networks along major U.S. rivers. That study found widespread decreases in fecal bacteria and lead concentrations, reflecting, according to the authors, widespread wastewater treatment (removal of bacteria) and a major federal initiative to prevent lead air pollution (Smith, Alexander, and Wolman 1987). During the same period there were widespread increases in nitrates, chloride, arsenic, and cadmium concentrations in surface waters, reflecting an increased use of salt on highways, nitrogen fertilizers, and oil and petroleum combustion. That study indicated continuing problems from nonpoint sources (Smith, Alexander, and Wolman 1987).

The 1987 Water Quality Act (Pub. L. 100-4) expanded the scope of water quality standards beyond point sources, the pipes that deliver wastes to a treatment plant or a water body. The law required states to examine all their surface waters and assess which ones had "impaired" water quality, even after point sources had been controlled. After cities and industries construct and operate wastewater treatment plants, water pollution in urban areas can continue through storm flows discharged untreated via pass-through or around wastewater plants. A second source of uncontrolled pollution has been nonpoint sources, such as agricultural runoff, discharges from farmland, animal feedlots, construction sites, or open places where wastewater flows but not through pipes. Section 303(d) of the Water Quality Act requires states to identify pollutant-impaired water segments and develop "total maximum daily loads" that establish a maximum amount of pollution a water body can receive before it violates ambient water quality standards. Section 319 of the law requires states to develop and implement a point-source-pollution management program to protect surface or ground waters (Smith, Alexander, and Wolman 1987).

By 1999, more than 65,000 industrial and municipal sources of discharge were obligated to obtain National Pollutant Discharge Elimination System (NPDES) permits from the states or from the EPA, each of which was in the form of a five-year, technology-based effluent limit, via a BPT or a BAT (Copeland 2010). The BPT limits regulated discharges to control bacteria or organic wastes that consume oxygen. The BAT limits controlled toxic pollutants, heavy metals, pesticides, and organic and inorganic chemicals. In addition, the EPA promulgated criteria for more than 115 pollutants, including 65 toxic chemicals called "priority pollutants" (Copeland 2010). These standards and criteria are distinct from either the discharge permits required for state standards on surface water segments or U.S. Army Corps of Engineers dredge-and-fill permits.

A state like Texas may have multiple criteria for one stream water quality parameter. For example, Texas has six separate bacteriological standards, two each for *E. coli*, enterococci, and fecal coliform; they apply to two circumstances of surface water segments—contact recreation and noncontact recreation.

As we enter the second decade of the twenty-first century, what has changed and what has remained the same regarding national water quality standards? One element that has changed is that national water quality standards are the status quo. States regulate the quality of the surface waters, interstate and intrastate, both navigable and not navigable; many states regulate the quality of their groundwater as well.

Johnson would recognize three policy ambiguities that have yet to be resolved, even after forty years: the issue of "national" water quality standards; the need for funds to prevent, control, and treat wastewater; and the challenge of controlling nonpoint sources of pollution.

Water Quality Standards

The United States has yet to come to a "final answer" to the question of "permissible impurities" in water, a "standard" representing a value judgment that evolves over time. Johnson chose to define national standards of water quality in 1965 based on state standards for each water body. He sought to create national standards, discussed above, that could meet operational definitions of the limits on acceptable impurities as initially defined by the Interstate Quarantine Regulations in 1914.

The tension continues today between an "ideal limit of water impurities" and the costs and complexity of pollution prohibition. For example, during 2009–2010, the Texas Commission on Environmental Quality (TCEQ) considered a staff draft of proposed revision for Texas water quality standards (TCEQ 2008; see table 11.8). The historical bacteriological standard in Texas was a geometric mean of 126 colonies of *E. coli* per 100 ml. from any surface water segment with the potential for contact recreation, which in effect included any flowing river or stream or modest lake, except those segments excluded by legislation. The surface water segments classified as noncontact recreation sites were those such as the Houston Ship Channel, an area fenced and bounded by private property, and the Rio Grande/Rio Bravo, which is fenced and patrolled as an international border. The proposed standard for *E. coli* was to be about two-thirds higher, a geometric mean of 206 colonies per 100 ml. The noncontact recreation standard was proposed to increase from a geometric mean of 605 colonies per 100 ml. to 2,060 colonies, an increase of more than 300 percent (TCEQ 2008).

The TCEQ commissioners in the end decided not to go along with their own staff proposal to relax the state's bacteria standards. There was intensive national-level pressure from environmental organizations, along with a risk of legal challenge from the EPA, which must consent to state standards if they differ from federal standards. After eighteen months of evaluation, the TCEQ rejected the proposed standards by a 2–1 vote of its commissioners (Dulay 2010). What would it have meant for Texas to relax its *E. coli* and enterococci standards while retaining unchanged limits to fecal coliform with a geometric mean of 200 colonies per 100 ml. for contact recreation and 2,000 colonies noncontact recreation? The revisions shown in table 11.8 did not become a standard, so the matter is moot at present in Texas.

For *E. coli*, the TCEQ in effect continues to use the 126 colonies per 100 ml. standard for almost all surface water segments. A segment can be classified as "partial contact" (with a new standard of 206 colonies per 100 ml.), but such a change must be documented through a Use Attainability Analysis, which is a historical review with a conclusion that there are no persons who have direct contact with the surface water. This may mean in effect that the stream may be ephemeral with no flow except during flood events. If there is no flow, there is no contact (while assuming that contact recreation is not a likely event during a flood). The standard of 605 colonies per 100 ml. continues for any surface water segments established under law when there are demonstrated physical barriers or patrols to prevent contact recreation (Dulay 2010).

The eighteen-month Texas exercise to revise its water quality standards indicates how the Johnson administration's concept of state standards subject to federal oversight had become both flexible and conservative. A state may seek changes, but pressure from federal regulators, for-profit businesses,

Table 11.8. Proposed revisions of Texas's water quality standards

A. Revision of segment criteria

Current segments and criteria
  As of 2008 there are only two recreational categories of surface waters, contact and noncontact.
  Almost all water bodies are assigned contact recreation standards.
Future segments and criteria
  Primary contact recreation (PCR) applies to all classified fresh waters and tidal waters and to most unclassified fresh waters of tidal waters.
  Secondary contact 1 (SCR1) applies to segments where primary contact is unlikely to occur, a channel is less than 0.5 meters deep, and substantial pools of more than 1 meter deep do not occur.
  Secondary contact 2 (SCR2)—not defined.
  Noncontact recreation (NCR)—segments where no contact can occur.

B. Revised bacteriological criteria

| | Geometric Mean Criteria (colonies/100 ml.) | | | |
Uses	E. coli (FW)	Enterococci (salty inland FW)	Enterococci (SW)	Fecal coliform (FW and SW)
Existing standards				
Contact recreation	126	—	35	200
Noncontact recreation	605	—	168	2,000
Proposed standards				
Primary contact	206	54	35	200[a]
Secondary contact 1	630	165	—	1,000
Secondary contact 2	1,030	270	—	1,000
Noncontact recreation	2,060	540	350	2,000

Source: TCEQ 2008.
[a]Fecal coliform will be gradually phased out as a criterion for salty inland waters, but will continue to be used for oyster waters (14/100 ml. median).
Note: These revisions were proposed for consideration on Jan. 6, 2009. FW = freshwater; SW = saltwater.

or nongovernmental organizations can encourage a transparent standards-setting process with public disclosure, and any changes must be justified by risk assessment.

When Johnson asked Congress to clean entire river basins "from their sources to their mouths" (Johnson 1966a), his approach—reliance on a collection of state standards to become national standards—was inherently ambiguous. Indeed, there is no escape from uncertainty about what constitutes an acceptable contaminant level for any particular water use or any water segment.

Wastewater Treatment

For any person not in the water quality field, it may be hard to understand how Congress could spend more than $69 billion on sewers and wastewater treatment plants over fifty years, and communities could invest many more billions in matching funds, and yet the task is not complete. One estimate is that there remains a need for at least $140 billion more to build or upgrade wastewater treatment plants in order to achieve Johnson's goals (Copeland 2010). If sewage collection and treatment have occurred, why does there need to be a never-ending stream of investments?

There is a one-word answer: growth. A wastewater collection and treatment system is like a baby's excretory system. As a baby develops, its systems grow; likewise, a community's waste collection and treatment system must be operated, maintained, and enlarged in scale as the community grows. When a baby becomes an adult and moves from mother's milk to single-malt scotch, the excretory system needs to become more sophisticated in order to handle diverse chemical challenges. As our communities grow and their economic activities become more complex, new treatment processes must be developed and applied to treat water pollution from biological waste, chemical wastes, neutraceuticals and pharmaceuticals. Not only is there no end to the needed investment to treat wastewater, but today's water quality challenges are more likely to come from water pollution that flows off lands rather than within pipes, otherwise known as "nonpoint" sources, as discussed below.

Nonpoint Sources

In Johnson's conservation messages, he referred to the technical challenge of runoff from farms and storm water, which is not collected and is so hard to treat. Johnson sought funds to support research to address nonpoint pollution. While much progress has been made on land management practices and infrastructure that can prevent or reduce pollution from nonpoint sources, there remain issues of technological feasibility, costs, and social equity. Indeed, the major restatement of the Clean Water Act in 1987 (the Water Quality Act of 1987) sought to address those contaminants in surface waters that had increased rather than decreased after investments in wastewater treatment plants: nutrients (nitrates and phosphates), chlorides, and heavy metals associated with fertilizers, animal wastes, fuel combustion, and salt application to highways (Smith, Alexander, and Wolman 1987).

The 1987 Water Quality Act (Federal Water Pollution Control Act, as amended through Pub. L. 107-303, section 303) requires states to assess each surface water segment to see whether ambient surface water quality would fall below standards despite the application of best available treatment technology in wastewater treatment plants. As of November 20, 2008, Texas had examined 925 water bodies within the state to see whether they met standards or were "impaired" (TCEQ 2008). Of those 925 water bodies, nearly 30 percent (234 water bodies) were listed as "impaired for recreation."

What does "impaired" mean when the best-available technology is in use? It means that natural processes may on their own lead to an ambient water quality that exceeds the limits of impurity within a surface-water segment. Or it may mean that natural processes, in combination with the land management practices of farmers, ranchers, and others in rural areas, contribute to a circumstance where ambient water quality standards are exceeded.

In one recent hearing on a stream segment on Texas's 303(d) list of impaired water bodies, a dairy farmer whose herd produces the highest quality of milk complained that the adjacent stream segment was impaired even though he uses the "best-available technology" to prevent pollution from his herd (Dulay 2010). Should the United States demand of the State of Texas that a farmer spend more money—beyond even the best-available technology—because the sum of all nonpoint pollution sources in a particular water body leaves biological or nutrient levels above state standards?

One of the reasons that Texas sought to restate its standards is the burden of conducting so-called 303(d) studies on all 274 water bodies in Texas now classified as impaired. Such studies require a great deal of money and time and might not yield commensurate improvements to water quality. At what point does a level of scrutiny diverge from standards "without prohibitive expense"? For example, the proposed 2009 changes in Texas's water quality standards would have removed 26 of 64 river segments now termed "impaired" (on the 303[d] list) from the noncompliant segments, along with both 303(d) classified reservoirs (TCEQ 2008; source for all figures in this paragraph). Changes in the segment criteria to exclude perennial non-flowing streams would lead to a delisting of 16 of 20 intermittent streams (without ponds) and 32 of 144 permanent streams that meet the revised primary contact standard. If the TCEQ were to have adopted (and the EPA accepted) Texas's proposed 2009 revisions to its water quality standards, the TCEQ estimated that 79 of the 274 water bodies now listed as "impaired for recreation" (28 percent) would have met the revised standards.

Comments

Perhaps only Lyndon Johnson and his family know why he sought to improve the nation's water quality during his administration. Perhaps growing up in Johnson City, where clean water was not easy to come by, may have influenced him. Perhaps his experiences as a young congressman advocating for the Highland Lakes system gave him a sense of accomplishment for ensuring that people would have clean water. Lady Bird's lifetime commitment to environmental quality no doubt motivated his zeal for water quality results. Whatever the origin of Johnson's focus, the outcomes were summarized by one of the Johnson family's friends, Laurence Rockefeller, chairman of the Citizen's Advisory Committee on Recreation and Natural Beauty:

> By example and dedication, President Johnson and his inspired, most able partner, Lady Bird Johnson, have instilled a new spirit and faith that we can build a better and more beautiful America. During their stewardship, concern for the quality of the environment has become a major goal of the American people. Through their leadership, our aspirations as a people have been raised to reach for new, non-material objectives. They have shown us that healthy land, water and air cannot only add to the health and welfare of man, but the dignity of the human spirit as well. There is still much to be done, but I believe that it will be recorded that it was in this time of Lyndon and Lady Bird Johnson that the American people made the decision that the quality of their environment is a major component of their dignity as a people—a decision that will bring a new sense of purpose, progress in productivity and greater joy of life for future generations of Americans. (Rockefeller 1969)

When Lyndon Johnson became president, water quality was not a national issue. When he left office, five years later, his vision and force of will "to clean all of America's rivers" had put in place a long-term national commitment that has remained a consistent U.S. policy under both political parties. Johnson's proclamations, legislation, appropriations, administrative orders, and enforcement actions represent a remarkable legacy of accomplishment. A mere fourteen years after Lyndon Johnson left the presidency, a national study concluded that the bacteriological water quality in the nation's surface waters had improved. Despite the continuing need for investment, water quality continues to improve.

The United States provided global leadership on this issue, seeking to ensure water quality nationwide not only as a right but also as a moving target of continual improvement. Johnson's commitments to construct sewers and to treat wastewater to a minimum of a secondary quality set a performance standard that the rest of the world has yet to emulate or achieve. His concern about nonpoint sources created a continuing challenge, since natural processes alone or in combination with revised land management can lead to circumstances where water bodies can be classified as impaired even though the people who live and work in the region use best-available technologies to prevent, control, and treat water pollution.

While there remain plenty of venues within the United States where the water quality can and should be improved, there is no question that the United States has developed a system to prevent, control, and treat water pollution. The United States has Lyndon Johnson, among many others, to thank for it.

Notes

Many of the original references cited in this chapter were obtained from documents within the Lyndon Baines Johnson Presidential Library (the LBJ Library). Two graduate students, Desiree M. Ledet and Elizabeth Long, gathered materials from the LBJ Library and the UT-Austin libraries. Three sources (the Bess Harris Jones Centennial Professorship of Natural Resource Policy Studies, the Jack S. Blanton Endowed Research Fellowship, and the George A. Roberts Endowed Research Fellowship, the last two at the Institute for Innovation, Creativity and Capital at UT-Austin) provided financial support for the research and writing of this chapter. Jayashree Vijalapurum, Martha Harrison, and Carrie Williams revised the manuscript. Marcel Dulay and Stephen Niemeyer contributed facts and details to the story of Texas's efforts to revise its surface-water quality standards. The author acknowledges the support of two grants from the Centennial Symposium, one that supported this research and a second that subsidized research assistance.

1. For estimates of costs to provide wastewater treatment to the U.S. urban population, see Task Group on Water Pollution 1956, 4–20.

References

Alm, Alvin. 1993. Oral history interview conducted by Dennis Williams in McLean, Virginia, Apr. 12 and June 23. EPA website, www2.epa.gov/aboutepa /alvin-l-alm-oral-history-interview.

Business Week. 1970. Feb. 6, 11.

Carpenter, Richard A. 1968. Federal policy and environmental chemistry. *Environmental Science and Technology* (July).

Carter, Luther J. 1968. Water pollution: Officials graded into raising quality standards. *Science* 160 (Apr. 5).

CEQ [Council on Environmental Quality]. 1970a. *Environmental quality: The first annual report of the Council on Environmental Quality.* Washington, D.C.: Government Printing Office.

———. 1970b. *The president's 1970 environmental programs.* Washington, D.C.: Government Printing Office.

Congressional Quarterly. 1956. *Congressional Quarterly Almanac* 12.

———. 1959. *Congressional Quarterly Almanac* 15.

———. 1960. *Congressional Quarterly Almanac* 16.

———. 1963. *Congressional Quarterly Almanac* 19.

———. 1964. *Congressional Quarterly Almanac* 20.

———. 1965. *Congressional Quarterly Almanac* 21.

———. 1966. *Congressional Quarterly Almanac* 22.

———. 1967. *Congressional Quarterly Almanac* 23.

———. 1968. *Congressional Quarterly Almanac* 24.

———. 1969. *Congressional Quarterly Almanac* 25.

Controller General of the United States. 1970. *Report to Congress: Examination into the effectiveness of the construction grant program for abating, controlling, and preventing water pollution.* Washington, D.C.: General Accounting Office.

Copeland, Claudia. 2010. *Clean Water Act: A summary of the law.* Congressional Research Service Report for Congress. Available at the website of the National Council for Science and the Environment: www.cnie.org/nle/crsreports/10May /RL30030.pdf.

DeCamp, L. Sprague. 1963. *The ancient engineers.* New York: Ballantine.

Dulay, Marcel. 2010. Unpublished advice provided by Marcel Dulay, P.E., of Parsons Engineering, Inc. (Aug. 8).

Jennings, M. Kent. 1969. Legislative politics and water pollution control, 1956–61. In Frederic N. Cleaveland, Royce Hanson, M. Kent Jennings, John E. Moore, Judith Heimlich Parris, and Randall B. Ripley, *Congress and urban problems: A casebook on the legislative process.* Washington, D.C.: Brookings Institution.

Johnson, Lyndon B. 1965. Special message to Congress: Conservation and restoration of natural beauty. Feb. 8. Accessible at the website of the LBJ Library: www.lbjlib.utexas.edu/johnson/archives.hom/speeches.hom/650208.asp.

————. 1966a. Special message to Congress: Proposing measures to preserve America's natural heritage. Feb. 23. Lyndon B. Johnson Presidential Library.

————. 1966b. Message to Congress: Reorganization plan no. 2 of 1966. Feb. 28. Lyndon B. Johnson Presidential Library.

————. 1967. Message to Congress: Protecting our natural heritage. Jan. 30. Lyndon B. Johnson Presidential Library.

————. 1968. Message to Congress: To renew a nation. Mar. 8. Lyndon B. Johnson Presidential Library.

Pasteur, Louis, and Joseph Lister. (1878/1867) 1996. *Germ theory and its applications to medicine and On the antiseptic principle of the practice of surgery.* New York: Prometheus.

Public Health Reports. 1914. Nov. 6: 2957–2967.

Rockefeller, Laurence S. 1969. Comments in a privately published book entitled *Quality of the environment,* given to patrons of a dinner for President Johnson, Jan. 13. Lyndon B. Johnson Presidential Library.

Rohlich, Gerald H., David Eaton, and R. Barry Lovelace, eds. 1978. *Impact of the Safe Drinking Water Act in Texas.* Policy Research Project 21. Austin: Lyndon B. Johnson School of Public Affairs, University of Texas at Austin.

Rohrer, Daniel M., David C. Montgomery, Mary E. Montgomery, David J. Eaton, and Mark G. Arnold. 1970. *The environmental crisis: A basic overview of the problem of pollution.* Skokie, Ill.: National Textbook.

Smith, Richard A., Richard Alexander, and M. Gordon Wolman. 1987. Water quality trends in the nation's rivers. *Science* 235 (Mar. 27): 1607–1615.

Snow, John. 1855. *On the mode of communication of cholera.* London: Churchill. Available on the website of the Fielding School of Public Health, UCLA: www.ph.ucla.edu/EPI/snow/snowbook_a2.html.

Sundquist, James L. 1968. *Politics and policy: The Eisenhower, Kennedy, and Johnson years.* Washington, D.C.: Brookings Institution.

Task Force on Enforcement Procedures. N.d. Memorandum (#13) to the Committee on Economic Incentives for Pollution Abatement. Attachment II: Enforcement actions, January 1957–May 1965. Lyndon B. Johnson Library.

Task Group on Water Pollution. 1965. Memorandum to the members of the Committee on Economic Incentives for Pollution Abatement. (Sept. 21). Lyndon B. Johnson Presidential Library.

TCEQ [Texas Commission on Environmental Quality]. 2008. Unpublished proposed water quality standard revision from the Water Quality Standards Workgroup. Nov. 11.

U.S. Department of Health, Education and Welfare. 1966. *Grants in aid and other financial assistance programs administered by the United States Department of Health, Education and Welfare.* Washington, D.C.: Government Printing Office.

U.S. Department of the Interior. 1970. Federal Water Pollution Control Administration. *Federal water pollution enforcement actions.* Washington, D.C.: Government Printing Office.

U.S. Environmental Protection Agency. 1972. *The challenge of the environment: A primer on EPA's statutory authority.* www2.epa.gov/aboutepa/water-challenge -environment-primer-epas-statutory-authority.

———. 2001. "In Memoriam: Former Deputy Administrator Alvin L. Alm." EPA website, www2.epa.gov/aboutepa/memoriam-former-deputy-administrator-alvin-l-alm.

U.S. House. 1969. Subcommittee on Science, Research, and Development of the Committee on Science and Astronautics, *Technical information for Congress*. Washington, D.C.: Government Printing Office.

Vitruvius, Marco Pollio. 1960. *The ten books on architecture*. Translated by Morris Hicky Morgan. New York: Dover.

White House. 1965. Office of the White House Press Secretary. News release: Prevention, control and abatement of water pollution by federal activities (Nov. 17). Lyndon B. Johnson Presidential Library.

CHAPTER 12

LBJ, Science, Technology Policy, and Lessons for the Future

GARY CHAPMAN

President Lyndon Baines Johnson is not commonly remembered for his contributions to U.S. science and technology policy. The Johnson presidency is typically praised for historic legislation on civil rights, health care, and education, and criticized for the war in Vietnam. But Johnson's political career coincided and was deeply intertwined with the biggest expansion of scientific and technical knowledge in the history of the world, as well as with the United State's rise to unchallenged preeminence in science and technology, the two signature features of the twentieth century.

LBJ came to power on the issue of rural electrification of Central Texas, which he addressed in his first week in Congress, in 1937 (Woods 2006, 133). Having grown up without electricity, Johnson was highly motivated to bring the benefits of electric power to his constituents in Texas's Tenth Congressional District. He made public power his number one issue. And when electricity came to the Central Texas region, radio soon followed, a technology that would become the Johnson family business in 1942 when Lady Bird Johnson bought radio station KTBC in Austin (172).

Johnson also witnessed, from a powerful position as a congressional ally of President Roosevelt, the birth of the vast American science-based arsenal that won World War II. The war started a new partnership between the federal government and universities, as well as a new form of private-sector research and development, each a piece of the foundation for a scientific and technical infrastructure that would dramatically change the world in the postwar years. When Johnson was elected to the Senate in 1948, the United States was just beginning to build this foundation of new relationships and institutions, which would form the base of American power during the Cold War. Johnson's experiences with rural electrification, radio, and the success of American science and technology during the war gave him a strong faith in large state-sponsored technological initiatives meant to improve the lives of Americans. This was a faith that most Americans shared during LBJ's political career. Millions of men who left the military after World War II took advantage of the GI Bill to go to college, and then streamed into the new plants of the postwar defense and aerospace industries. American universities rapidly expanded their research facilities and programs. The era encompassed the aftereffects of the Manhattan Project and the atomic bomb, the discovery of the structure of DNA, and, shortly after LBJ left the White House, the first men on the moon and the first digital bits passed on a communications network that would eventually span and reshape the world, a system that would come to be called the Internet.

LBJ's political career was thus an integral part of what has come to be called a "golden age" of science in the United States, when government funding for science and technology was strong and rising, when scientists and engineers enjoyed a long period of influence and prestige, and when there was a consensus among Americans about the value and benefit of scientific and technological progress. Although there is some disagreement about the length of the "golden age," several historians date the end to the late 1960s (Greenberg 2001, 60), a time that roughly coincides with LBJ's replacement in the White House by Richard Nixon in January 1969.

Under Nixon, the "golden age" of U.S. science policy quickly came to an end. Nixon disliked and distrusted scientists—he blamed elite scientists for Republican defeats, including his own in 1960—and as campus unrest over the war in Vietnam intensified and opposition to the war spread to academic science departments, Nixon and his aides became even less inclined to support scientists and engineers (Greenberg 2001, 164–165). Prominent scientists who had believed they were serving the nation with apolitical scientific advice were now plunged into a rancorous political fight with the White House; at the same time, the consensus view of science and technology as unalloyed benefits to society was being challenged by the new youth counterculture. Daniel S. Greenberg writes, "After Nixon, the scientists who served in the White House harbored no noble delusions about loyalty to values that transcend politics and presidents" (164).

All presidents since Roosevelt have believed that they have a science policy, although this phrase has been used to describe very different relationships, programs, and priorities, and there has been little consistency between administrations. Presidents have been highly selective about what scientific advice they heed or how they manage the politics of scientific controversies. Successive presidents after Eisenhower ignored the scientific community's skepticism about the value of manned space exploration, for example. Presidents have also imposed political calculations on the scientific community, such as distributing research money based on geographic and political considerations instead of solely on scientific merit. Presidents have pushed programs that have little support in the scientific community, including expensive weapons programs, expensive space programs, and programs that threaten the autonomy of scientific institutions. A chasm between the White House and the scientific community deeper than anyone alive can remember developed under President George W. Bush. While federal research and development funding grew under his administration, there were multiple sources of friction between the Bush White House and the scientific and technical communities, and extreme partisanship plagued discussions of scientific and technical subjects in Congress and within the executive branch. In short, the relationship between the White House and scientists has often been a delicate dance of political power and principle.

Many scientists and engineers hope that this relationship between the White House and the scientific and technical communities will improve in the near future. For a variety of reasons—primarily global climate change and the related challenge of finding new sources of energy—many people believe that scientific research is more important now than ever. But the United States is also facing global competition in scientific and technical research and education in ways that are new and alarming. The chronic apathy and underperformance of American students in math and science classes is routinely described as a national crisis, especially in light of the superior performance of students in China, India, and other nations. But many scientists and leaders in related fields worry that partisan political conflict over scientific issues has contributed to public doubt and confusion over science. The National Science Foundation's report *Science and Engineering Indicators, 2008* says that while public support of science remains high—scientists enjoy public esteem second only to the military's—Americans "perceive a significant lack of consensus among scientists" on controversial issues, including global climate change and stem cell research (National Science Foundation 2008). Because most scientists agree on climate change and stem cell research, there is concern that politicians are exaggerating the significance of dissent, and that this could have a side effect, in the minds of some Americans, of devaluing scientific advice at a time when the nation urgently needs scientific solutions to problems.

For all these reasons, attention to the relations between scientists and policy makers, and between scientists and the public, appears needed. The experience of President Johnson may be illuminating because the roots of many conflicts over science began during his administration. LBJ's was the last White House administration of science's "golden age," and the last one before latent conflict over science's role in society exploded into decades of political conflict. A reexamination of LBJ's science and technology policy could therefore be helpful in understanding how we got to where we are today, and also help frame the big issues the country confronts.

Vannevar Bush and the Emergence of U.S. Science and Technology Policy

In the field of science policy, the foundational role of Vannevar Bush, President Franklin Roosevelt's wartime science adviser, is a familiar one. Bush, an engineer from MIT who cofounded what became the Raytheon Corporation, persuaded Roosevelt to launch the National Defense Research Committee in 1940, which Bush then chaired. The committee of scientists was absorbed a year later by the Office of Scientific Research and Development (OSRD), with Bush as its director. Bush oversaw the mobilization of scientists throughout the United States to help the war effort, and dozens of technologies emerged out of OSRD programs. Bush created the Manhattan Project under the OSRD and managed the atomic weapon program until 1943, when it was taken over by the army.

In November 1944, Roosevelt asked Bush to draft a plan for postwar science policy. FDR died in April 1945; Bush's report was delivered to President Truman that July. *Science: The Endless Frontier* became the "blueprint" for postwar American science policy, an explanation for why the U.S. government should continue to invest in scientific and technical research, basic and applied, for both national security and national prosperity. Bush also called for the formation of the National Research Foundation, to be controlled by a small board of members appointed by the president and directed by someone chosen by the foundation members. Truman objected to this arrangement, preferring a director chosen by the president. After five years of debate and political bargaining, Truman signed the National Science Foundation Act of 1950; the foundation was to have a director and board appointed by the president. Bush and other scientists believed that the national research agenda should be controlled by scientists themselves. Truman and the Senate were persuaded by the director of the Bureau of the Budget, Harold Smith, that the federal government should not relinquish its constitutional authority to determine how federal funds were spent (Blanpied 1998).

A key player in the five-year debate over the national research institution was Senator Harvey Kilgore (D-WV). He sponsored a bill to create the National Research Foundation, but he advocated for the federal government to play a much larger role in setting the research agenda, and he envisioned a program that looked more like the Department of Agriculture's Extension Service, with a focus on practical applications of research and a wide geographic distribution of research opportunities (Brooks 1996, 1618). The National Science Foundation took on a character more like Bush's vision, and the counterargument of Kilgore would lay dormant for another fifteen years.

The mythical narrative of the birth of the U.S. science establishment, which developed over the decades after the publication of *Science: The Endless Frontier* and took on aspects of Prometheus's creation of man from clay, has been challenged by a number of historians and critics of the Vannevar Bush blueprint. David Hart traced the complex relations that emerged from World War II in *Forged Consensus: Science, Technology, and Economic Policy in the United States, 1921-1953* (1998). Bush, writes Hart, "was brilliant and effective in mobilizing the nation's scientific and technological resources for World War II, but *Science, The Endless Frontier,* is better seen as a political tactic than as an original blueprint" (206). Daniel S. Greenberg calls the "hagiography" of Bush's plan "a creation myth" (2001, 41). Dan Sarewitz, a former staff member of the House Science Committee, criticizes Bush's "linear" model of benefits from basic research to applied development, and the implicit claim that the larger the research apparatus for the nation, the larger the benefits (1996, 17–21).

In retrospect, Bush's report can be seen both as a visionary justification for federal spending on scientific and technological research in U.S. universities and research laboratories, and as a political tactic meant to protect the autonomy of scientists from the vagaries of political wrangling and influence. Isolating scientists from politics while also building a massive and expensive scientific and technical research infrastructure proved to be an impossible goal, although the success of American science during World War II created a consensus among scientists from elite institutions that lasted a long time. Also, in retrospect, it was Bush's call to bond the federal government to science and technology research that created the conditions for U.S. scientists and engineers to become entangled with political controversies thereafter.

The difficulties of the relationship between scientists and policy makers became evident immediately after the end of World War II, when Bush, Leo Szilard, Albert Einstein, Niels Bohr, and other prominent physicists called for the international control of atomic energy. The scientists who had developed the first atomic bomb—or who, like Einstein, had made it possible—were tormented by regrets. President Truman, who had ordered the bombs dropped on Nagasaki and Hiroshima, did not share these regrets—he called Robert Oppenheimer, after a personal meeting with the famous physicist, a "crybaby" (Herken 2000, 31). Truman was focused on retaining the power of the White House and competing with the Soviet Union, so he either ignored or rejected the advice of scientists with more idealistic and expansive goals, including Vannevar Bush (37–38). Thus, Truman not only retained the (brief) "atomic monopoly" of the United States, but also ordered the development of the hydrogen bomb, which Bush and other science advisers opposed.

But the clearly vital importance of science and technology to national security embedded science and technology policy into governmental affairs in the early postwar years. Throughout the 1950s, the competition between the Soviet Union and the United States was manifested primarily through scientific and technological developments such as the H-bomb, long-range jet bombers, and, eventually, intercontinental rockets. The historian Stuart Leslie of Johns Hopkins University observed: "The military-driven technologies of the Cold War defined the critical problems for the postwar generation of American scientists and engineers. Indeed, those technologies virtually redefined what it meant to be a scientist or engineer. . . . The new challenges defined what scientists and engineers studied, what they designed and built, where they went to work, and what they did when they got there" (1993, 9).

Because of this context, in the 1950s nearly 100 percent of the research funding supported by the federal government was for military-related activities. This limitation constrained the kind of advice that the president received from science advisers, and created a national security cadre of influential scientists, nearly all of whom came from a handful of elite universities, particularly from institutions in the Cambridge, Massachusetts, area. Throughout the 1950s, bridges were built between Washington and universities such as MIT, Harvard, Stanford, and the University of California. The universities sent prominent scientists and engineers to assist the federal government, and received in return the large defense-related research contracts that characterized the Cold War era. Federal spending on research and development grew 14 percent annually, on a dollar-adjusted basis, between 1953 and 1961, an explosive rate of growth for any spending program over such a period of time (Smith 1990, 39).

It was this blurring of the lines between military agencies and university research labs that would create many flash points in the future. As more scientists were drawn into the politics of the Cold War, more of them began to express their reservations about U.S. policies, especially those who were at academic institutions.

At the same time, however, a growing number of defense-related research institutes were employing scientists for pure research. The national laboratories, largely holdovers from World War II, continued to grow, and organizations such as the RAND Corporation, Lincoln Laboratories at MIT, the Stanford Research Institute, the MITRE Corporation, and others were set up to do research for the federal government. These institutions began to develop their own cultural identities, which were more in tune with their Pentagon sponsors and with the booming defense and aerospace industries than with the academy. Within a short time, there were two camps in science policy: the "peace" scientists, who favored arms control and international solutions to nuclear stalemate, and the "war" scientists, who believed in U.S. technological and military supremacy. In the former group were Einstein, Szilard, George Kistiakowsky (Eisenhower's science adviser), and Jerome Wiesner (Kennedy's science adviser). The "war" scientists were symbolized for decades by Edward Teller, known as the "father of the hydrogen bomb" and a cofounder and leader of the Lawrence Livermore National Laboratory in California. Teller alienated his fellow physicists by testifying against Robert Oppenheimer during the latter's appearance before the House Un-American Activities Committee in 1954, and later by vigorously opposing a comprehensive test ban treaty. But Teller was an unusually prominent and outspoken symbol of an immense new number of defense scientists and engineers employed by the defense industry, the Pentagon, and the new research labs and think tanks created by Cold War spending.

When President Eisenhower officially created the post of "special assistant to the president for science and technology" in 1957, along with a new President's Science Advisory Committee (PSAC), he appointed James Killian, the president of MIT, someone familiar with what came to be called "the Cambridge crowd" of advisers that shuttled between the Boston area and the White House. The creation of PSAC came quickly after the Russian launch of the *Sputnik* satellite, on October 4, 1957, an event that famously shocked the United States, both because of the threat of a Soviet nuclear-armed missile reaching the country and because the Russians had beaten Americans into space. On October 15, Eisenhower convened a meeting of scientific advisers, including Isidor Rabi, an MIT physicist who had worked on the Manhattan Project, won the Nobel Prize, and served as Truman's science adviser. Rabi recommended that the president appoint a permanent science adviser, a suggestion that Eisenhower heeded with some ambivalence (Herken 2000, 102, 104). Eisenhower offered the job of science adviser to Killian, and the new committee and position were announced on November 7, 1957.

The *Sputnik* shock created reverberations throughout the U.S. government, and the Soviet Union jolted Americans a month later, on November 3, 1957, with *Sputnik II*, a second satellite that carried a half-ton payload and a live dog (Wang 2008, 71). Americans had simply assumed, and scientists and political leaders had often affirmed this assumption, that U.S. superiority in science and technology was unquestionable. *Sputnik* unleashed a burst of American soul-searching, as well as a fear of nuclear war, that surprised and perplexed Eisenhower (Wang 2008, 73).

Sputnik opened an opportunity for the opposition party, the Democrats, both to pound the White House on the "missile gap" and to rush to propose new programs and legislation that would position the Democrats to take back the White House in the 1960 election. And leading the Democrats in the U.S. Senate was Majority Leader Lyndon Baines Johnson.

Johnson, *Sputnik*, and the Missile Gap

LBJ had been part of the debates about U.S. military policy since his days in the House, when he served on the Naval Affairs Committee, and also as a reserve officer in the navy. Roosevelt sent Johnson to the South Pacific during World War II as part of a three-man investigation of the theater. In 1948, Johnson was elected to the Senate and appointed to the Senate Armed Services Committee. In that role, he created and then chaired an influential Preparedness Investigating Subcommittee, created in 1949 and highly visible during the Korean War. After that war ended, the subcommittee faded in importance, but *Sputnik* offered an opportunity to revive both it and Johnson's national role. LBJ was a protégé of Senator Richard Russell, the powerful southern Democrat who chaired the Senate Armed Services Committee. Russell was keen to let Johnson run with the agenda of U.S. control of space. George Reedy, Johnson's close aide, said, "The issue is one which, if properly handled, would blast the Republicans out of the water, unify the Democratic Party, and elect you president" (quoted in Johnson 2006, 80).

Johnson was not the only Democratic senator to see the political potential in *Sputnik*. Senator John F. Kennedy blasted the Eisenhower administration for "complacent miscalculations, penny-pinching, budget cutbacks, incredibly confused mismanagement and wasteful rivalries and jealousies" (quoted in Wang 2008, 72). Both Kennedy and Johnson viewed Americans' concern about *Sputnik* and Russian science as a way to craft a broad agenda of legislation and political opposition in areas covering science, space exploration, defense policy, and education. Out of this came the National Aeronautics and Space Administration (NASA), the Pentagon's Advanced Research Projects Agency (ARPA), and the National Defense Education Act, which was meant to stimulate math and science education in U.S. public schools.

Johnson called hearings on the missile gap and space before his long-dormant Preparedness Investigating Subcommittee in November 1957, and he asked prominent scientists to testify first in order to frame the issues around space and not just military squabbles over funding. The big names from science were Edward Teller, Vannevar Bush, and the rocket scientist Werner von Braun. LBJ added university scientists to the subcommittee staff from Harvard, Rice University, and Cal Tech (Woods 2006, 333). Johnson, who dominated the hearings, turned the discussion away from arcane and mind-numbing debates about military technology to a broad reformulation of U.S. society from top to bottom. LBJ saw the space issue as a political winner.

The missile gap issue was kept alive into the presidential election of 1960, after which it disappeared. In February 1961, just weeks after President John F. Kennedy's inauguration, Secretary of Defense Robert McNamara told reporters that there was no missile gap between the United States and the Soviet Union (Raymond 1961). But the "space race" was still on, and Kennedy asked LBJ to chair the new Space Council in April 1961 (Woods 2006, 392). A few days later, the Soviet Union sent the first man into space, Yuri Gagarin. The U.S. astronaut Alan Shepard then became the first American in space in May of that year. Johnson, McNamara, and von Braun all advised Kennedy that the emphasis of science policy should be "manned exploration of the moon" (393). Just two weeks after Shepard's orbital flight of about fifteen minutes, President Kennedy told a joint session of Congress that he pledged the nation to put a man on the moon by the end of the decade.

Johnson's key leadership role in the space program put him in routine contact with scientific leaders, especially Kennedy's science adviser, Jerome Wiesner, an MIT engineer. Wiesner was part of the Cambridge scientific establishment that had settled in as advisers on science-related policy since the end of World War II. While Wiesner and Johnson are both on record as having pleasant things to say about each other, Wiesner was far more comfortable with Kennedy than Johnson was with Wiesner. Kennedy and Wiesner came from similar university backgrounds, and Johnson thought of Kennedy's Cambridge aides as "the Harvards." Johnson was occasionally annoyed by scientists' general skepticism about manned space exploration, which many scientists thought cost too much for too little scientific value (a skepticism that remains today). Wiesner's rapport with Kennedy earned him the nickname the "czar of science," particularly important in an administration that was ramping up science spending. Johnson was often oriented more to his allies in Congress, where Texans helped secure the new federal space facility for Houston.

Wiesner discovered quickly that Johnson was not interested in the details of scientific controversy. Following the Kennedy assassination in 1963 and Johnson's inauguration as President, concern was voiced that perhaps Johnson was not as familiar with PSAC's agenda as the scientists would have preferred, and that Wiesner might have to put effort into the "educational process" of making Johnson a president comfortable with, and supportive of, scientists (Wang 2008, 236). Wiesner stayed in place after the assassination, but Kennedy had already picked his successor, Donald Hornig, chairman of the chemistry department at Princeton and a member of PSAC. Wiesner intended to return to MIT to become dean of science. Hornig sat in Princeton waiting for LBJ to decide whether to move along his appointment. Finally, LBJ accepted the appointment and brought Hornig to Washington as his new special assistant on science and technology in January 1964. The relationship would not be an easy one.

President Lyndon Johnson and Science

The Kennedys and Johnson had been joined by a shotgun wedding in 1960, and the friction between Kennedy's smooth northeastern urbaneness and Johnson's Texas populism was a constant irritant to LBJ. He distrusted Kennedy's brain trust of intellectuals, including the elite scientists who were part of the establishment embedded in PSAC and other influential government committees. McGeorge Bundy, Johnson's national security adviser, felt compelled to tell Johnson that "the prima donnas of science will be glad to work with and for" Hornig (quoted in Wang 2008, 237). Johnson himself never really warmed to Hornig. (Hornig is not mentioned in LBJ's autobiography, *The Vantage Point: Perspectives of the Presidency 1963-1969*.) A distinguished scientist, Hornig was nevertheless confronted by an outsize political personality unfamiliar to him: "I had little feeling for the strong, dominant personality who saw everything in political terms, and President Johnson had little feeling for academicians and scientists, although he always held them in great respect" (quoted in Wang 2008, 238). Wiesner later said that Hornig "had to carry the burden of Johnson's alienation from scientists" (Herken 2000, 147).

Nevertheless, Johnson owed some gratitude to scientists in the 1964 presidential election, when several prominent scientists concerned about Barry Goldwater started Scientists and Engineers for Johnson-Humphrey, a rare venture into partisan politics. Among those leading the group were George Kistiakowsky, Eisenhower's science adviser, and Detlev Bronk, former president of the National Academy of Sciences (Harsha 2004, 12). The organization quickly grew to 50,000 members and, using donations, published a booklet titled *The Alternative Is Frightening*. Particularly damaging to Goldwater was a radio broadcast sponsored by the group that featured members of the Manhattan Project declaring that Goldwater could not be trusted with the "power that could destroy mankind" (Greenberg 2001, 155). Goldwater never recovered from his "bomb-dropper" image, and Johnson's victory was a landslide.

Johnson thus had the backing of the scientific establishment when he was elected president in November 1964. Hornig was not an imposing or commanding figure in the Johnson White House, but scientists gave him credit for hard work, a low-key strength that helped resolve some complicated issues, and navigation of the difficult relationship between the scientific community and the White House, which became increasingly strained because of the war in Vietnam (Boffey 1969, 453).

Johnson was very interested in the space program, although he was not always in agreement with scientists about what the space program was all about. Johnson was less interested in pure science, and he felt that for all the money that was being spent on research, there should be political benefits comprehensible to ordinary Americans. Hornig said that Johnson said to him, "For $18 billion per year, there ought to be something to say at least once a week." Johnson said he wanted to know "what science could do for grandma" (Herken 2000, 149). There was a shift in presidential priorities toward applied research with political payoffs. LBJ was often deaf to the scientific adviser's arguments about the importance of basic research. In 1966 and 1967, when Johnson met with directors of the National Institutes of Health to discuss biomedical research, Hornig was not invited (Boffey 1969, 454).

LBJ's interest in the practical applications of science and technology and in their political benefits led federal science and technology in some new directions. Before the Kennedy administration, nearly all federal spending on research and development (R&D) had some relationship to national security or nuclear technology. That began to change during the Kennedy years as Kennedy and his advisers started to think about how to use science and technology policy to improve the economy. This trend accelerated under Johnson. Hornig was asked, for example, how scientists could contribute to the War on Poverty, and so the science adviser tried to develop programs for research on improving low-income housing (Hornig 1968, 22).

In addition, scientists were engaged in assessing the risk to the environment from pesticides, following the publication of Rachel Carson's landmark book *Silent Spring* (1962). PSAC created an Environmental Pollution Panel in 1964 and released the first comprehensive look at the environment by a federal commission, *Restoring the Quality of Our Environment*, which confirmed Carson's claims about pesticides (President's Science Advisory Council 1965). Johnson wrote in the foreword to the report, "Ours is a nation of affluence. But the technology that has permitted our affluence spews out vast quantities of wastes and spent products that pollute our air, poison our waters, and even impair our ability to feed ourselves." Johnson's commitment to environmental issues led Congress to introduce over 200 bills on environmental quality, more than under any other president, and the issue became a lifelong passion of LBJ's wife, Lady Bird. Johnson also set up, in 1965, the prototype for the Environmental Protection Agency, the Environmental Science Services within the Department of Commerce.

This expansion of the portfolio of science and technology policy in the White House led to a growing staff and budget in the Office of Science and Technology. Hornig's budget doubled in his five years in the White House, to $1.8 million, and the full-time staff grew from fifteen to twenty-one (Boffey 1969, 457). PSAC was diversified to include new fields and people from different parts of the country.

But the science establishment was incubating a growing resistance to what would become LBJ's chief problem, the war in Vietnam. In late 1965, Wiesner and Kistiakowsky—both leaders of Scientists and Engineers for Johnson-Humphrey—wrote Johnson a letter asking him to reconsider the military escalation in Vietnam. Johnson did not reply, nor did anyone from the White House. Wiesner tried again, through Vice President Hubert Humphrey, in early 1966, and the result was the same (Herken 2000, 150). This was the beginning of a widening rift between scientists and the Johnson White House, which would strain personal relations and eventually lead to a complete breakdown of the link between the White House and elite American science.

In January 1966, twenty-nine prominent scientists from Cambridge-area universities signed a letter of protest over the use of chemical defoliants in Vietnam (Herken 2000). Within a short time, Johnson stopped talking to his scientific advisers, and even threatened to skip the annual award ceremony bestowing the National Medal of Science (Herken 2000). The scientific and engineering communities began to split into two camps: those looking for a technical solution to the war, and those developing a growing passion for resisting the war altogether. By the end of the Johnson presidency, lamented George Kistiakowsky in a letter to the *New York Times*, the science advisory role had been "largely taken over by professional military scientists and those in the aerospace industry and think tanks" (quoted in Herken 2000, 164).

The alienation of academic scientists from the Pentagon and the White House extended to the issue of the proposed antiballistic missile (ABM) system, which was opposed by the pro-disarmament scientists on PSAC and supported by Pentagon managers and the aerospace industry. James Killian, Kistiakowsky, Wiesner, Hornig, Herbert York, and other current and former members of PSAC all opposed the ABM. But Johnson was being taunted in 1967 by Richard Nixon, who suggested that not deploying ABMs would mean that a new missile gap accusation could be used against Johnson (Primack and von Hippel 1974, 63).

The weight of Vietnam brought down LBJ; on March 31, 1968, he announced that he was dropping out of the race for reelection. The Democratic Party split lost the White House to Richard Nixon. The "golden age" of science was over.

After LBJ: The Partisan Wars

After the Johnson presidency, relations between the federal government and the scientific community seesawed between collaboration and conflict. While funding continued to flow, and there were major breakthroughs made possible by government support, the deep divisions caused by the war in Vietnam and controversies over strategic nuclear weapons ended the postwar consensus and began years of mutual suspicion. In the Nixon White House, writes the science policy historian Gregg Herken, "Distrust and the effects of partisan politics were increasingly evident in White House relations with PSAC" (2000, 176). Nixon ignored PSAC when preparing for the Strategic Arms Limitation Talks (SALT). Nixon fumed at scientists on campus who were writing letters and joining campus protests over the war.

When Nixon was reelected in 1972, he dissolved PSAC and the Office of Science and Technology, and turned science advising over to the director of the National Science Foundation.

Similar struggles over science policy continued through the Carter and Reagan years in the White House. Disputes raged over strategic weapons systems such as the MX missile and the Strategic Defense Initiative (SDI) regarding how to achieve a comprehensive test ban treaty, and over environmental controversies. President Reagan deliberately kept secret his plans for a giant antimissile system, the SDI, so that the scientific community could not sabotage it before its birth. George Keyworth, Reagan's science adviser, did not even learn of Reagan's speech announcing the SDI until four days before it was delivered, a development that "stunned" Keyworth (Herken 2000, 211). Reagan's plan was greeted with harsh criticism from scientists and engineers, who questioned its feasibility. One of the chief critics was Richard Garwin, one of the most familiar public scientists, who had angered Nixon when he testified against the supersonic transport (SST), and Carter when he tried to push the White House on a comprehensive test ban.

Garwin had broken with the traditional White House model of science adviser when he decided to go public with his criticisms of the SST program after heading the "ad hoc SST Review Committee" within Nixon's Office of Science and Technology. The White House withheld the Garwin committee's report, and the White House and industry lobbyists were pushing for funds to build the SST. Garwin felt he had to act "no longer as adviser but as citizen" (Herken 2000, 179).

The cultural upheavals of the 1960s and 1970s did not leave the scientific community unaffected. There was a new attention to, and new thinking about, the social responsibility of scientists and engineers. At MIT there was a strike of the faculty in January 1969 to promote "a public discussion of problems and dangers related to the present role of science and technology in the life of our nation" (Leslie 1993, 233). A student-faculty study group on this issue quickly evolved into a public-interest organization called the Union of Concerned Scientists. Other organizations of scientists had already developed, particularly the Council for a Livable World, founded by Leo Szilard, and the Federation of American Scientists, which was founded by members of the Manhattan Project, including Hans Bethe. At the same time, pockets of conservative scientists were found at the national laboratories—especially at Lawrence Livermore National Laboratory, under the tutelage of Edward Teller—and at defense-related think tanks such as the RAND Corporation and the Marshall Institute, which was founded in 1984 as a home to outspoken champions of the SDI.

Government leaders of various political leanings could thus mobilize scientists against each other, by favoring one group of scientists or another. Reagan had a high regard for Teller and his "O Group" at Livermore. The Democratic Congress found its scientific advice from the Congressional Office of Technology Assessment and the Congressional Research Service, as well as by calling on scientists and engineers to testify in hearings.

George Keyworth, Reagan's science adviser, succumbed to the pressure within the Reagan White House to support the president's programs, particularly the SDI, which had been derisively labeled "Star Wars." Keyworth admitted that he became a "cheerleader" for the program, which was held in low esteem by most scientists and academic engineers, and especially by the prestigious physicists of the Cold War generation who had long fought Teller. "By the second anniversary of Reagan's SDI announcement," writes Herken, "relations between the science adviser and the scientific community were under more strain than at any time since their nadir in the closing days of the Nixon administration" (2000, 215).

These disputes damaged the prestige of the science adviser position. The scientific community was struggling with a conundrum: how to revive the respect and influence that science enjoyed during the "golden age" after World War II, but also how to adapt to an increasingly partisan political environment that made most decisions involving science and technology subservient to partisan political ends. The Vietnam War and the bitter fights over strategic weapons ended the framework of consensus that existed well into the Johnson presidency. Once that consensus had been cracked, there were no obvious ways to put it back together again.

When the Soviet Union collapsed in August 1991, the science policy community was not prepared. There had been some talk in the previous years about a "post–Vannevar Bush science and technology policy," but there was little substantive thinking about what would hold U.S. science policy together after the end of the Cold War. In the later years of the first Bush presidency, a downturn in the economy and the rise of Japan and other economies fostered more talk about a U.S. technology policy that might help America compete. But Bush's economic advisers were free-market loyalists who objected to any governmental intervention in the economy. These advisers were at odds with Bush's science adviser, Alan Bromley, whose office produced a document in 1990 titled *U.S. Science and Technology Policy* (Bromley 1990). Scientists and engineers within the Bush White House battled economists and budget managers over how much the government should do to help U.S. technology. The result was a confusing hodgepodge of programs and ideas. Lewis Branscomb, a veteran technology policy expert at Harvard University, said "all the elements of an adequate technology policy are already part of the Bush administration—except coordination, a clear rationale, sufficient funding and political will" (quoted in Chapman 1992, 45).

It was not until the Clinton administration came to the White House in 1993 that the idea of a "post–Cold War" science and technology policy began to sink in. Bill Clinton and Al Gore released a white paper on technology policy as one of the first documents to come out of their administration, in February 1993, just weeks after the inauguration. The paper, titled *Technology for America's Growth: A New Direction to Build Economic Strength*, attempted a distinct break with the past: "The traditional federal role in technology development has been limited to support of basic science and mission-oriented research in the Defense Department, NASA, and other agencies. This strategy was appropriate for a previous generation but not for today's profound challenges. We cannot rely on the serendipitous application of defense technology to the private sector. We must aim directly at these new challenges and focus our efforts on the new opportunities before us, recognizing that government can play a key role helping private firms develop and profit from innovations" (Clinton and Gore 1993, 7). The president and vice president proposed a dramatic and expensive R&D program aimed at improving America's economic competitiveness. But these ambitions ran into the economic realities of large federal budget deficits, and Clinton's own economic advisers advocated policies to balance the federal budget. Clinton was also distracted by an even bigger issue, reforming U.S. health care, which absorbed the attention of most of the people in the White House working with congressional leaders.

In 1994, the midterm elections put the Republicans in control of Congress. The new Speaker of the House, Representative Newt Gingrich, who had his own ideas about the role of science and technology in the United States. Gingrich put one of his chief allies, Representative Robert Walker of Pennsylvania, in charge of the newly renamed House Science Committee. Walker set about dismantling all the Clinton-Gore proposals for science and technology, and he cut the federal R&D budget by 34 percent over five years. The professional staff of the House Science Committee was turned over to political appointees, and a highly partisan and rancorous atmosphere descended on the committee.

In 2000, Walker became the technology adviser to presidential candidate George W. Bush. When the Bush-Gore race unfolded, the partisan divisions in the science and engineering communities deepened, and plummeted even further when the election became essentially a statisti-

cal stalemate, resolved by a Supreme Court decision. After the inauguration of President George W. Bush, in 2001, a new science adviser was not
appointed for nine months. Even then, the new appointee, John H. Marburger III, was stripped of the title "special assistant to the president," an
effective demotion of the job.

George W. Bush and his staff brought the partisan conflict that had sim-
mered in science policy to a rolling boil. Bush's publicly expressed skepticism about global climate change, his opposition to stem cell research, and
his ambivalence about the theory of evolution alienated scientists in the
United States and around the world. But it was the Bush administration's
penchant for distorting scientific evidence for political purposes that set off
a firestorm of anger and accusations from scientists and brought relations
between the White House and scientists to their lowest point in a generation. Democratic opponents of the White House accused Republicans of a
"war on science" (Dean 2004; Mooney 2006).

Accusations and evidence piled up about political distortions of scientific information in governmental reports. Both academic and government
scientists deplored the political manipulation of scientific data and conclusions. "Science and facts are not a factor in decisions, and ideology dominates," said Kevin Trenberth, a climate scientist at the National Center
for Atmospheric Research on the website Live Science (Britt 2008). David Baltimore, a Nobel laureate, president of Cal Tech until 2006, and president of the American Association for the Advancement of Science in 2007,
called the intrusion of White House politics into scientific reports "unprecedented" (Baltimore 2004). Baltimore joined nineteen other Nobel laureates—including Leon Lederman, Harold Varmus, Steven Weinberg, and
Norman F. Ramsey—in signing a letter created by the Union of Concerned
Scientists in February 2004 that asserted that the Bush administration had
deliberately distorted scientific evidence in reports and programs on health,
biomedical research, and nuclear weapons (Union of Concerned Scientists 2004).

A dramatic case of the bitter partisan fights unfolded when Susan F.
Wood, assistant commissioner for women's health and director of the Office
of Women's Health at the Food and Drug Administration, resigned in protest, in September 2005, over delays imposed on an approved women's con-
traceptive known as the "morning after pill." Wood charged that political
interference was keeping the FDA from a final ruling that would move the
drug to market. "I can no longer serve as staff when scientific and clinical
evidence, fully evaluated and recommended for approval by the professional
staff here, has been overruled," she wrote in the e-mail announcement of

her resignation (quoted in Kauffman 2005). In July 2007, former surgeon general Richard H. Carmona testified before a congressional panel that his office was routinely deterred by administration officials from reporting correct information on birth control, sex education, and global health issues (Harris 2007).

Scientists chafed at the persistent pressure of conservative religious activists to introduce "creationism" into public school science curricula. When President Bush said in August 2005 that "intelligent design," a variation of "creationism," should be taught alongside evolution in public schools, his science adviser, John Marburger, had to insist that "intelligent design is not a scientific concept." Marburger, reported the *New York Times*, "said it would be 'over-interpreting' Mr. Bush's remarks to say that the president believed that intelligent design and evolution should be given equal treatment in schools," but the *Times* then noted that conservative religious activists interpreted the president's remarks in exactly this way (Bumiller 2005).

Finally, medical scientists and the Bush administration clashed over stem cell research. Stem cells are widely regarded as a key tool in future medical discoveries in gene therapy. Congress passed a bill lifting restrictions on stem cell research in 2007, but President Bush vetoed the bill—only his second veto—in June of that year. Three Harvard University stem cell researchers, Kevin Eggan, Chad Cowan, and Douglas Melton, were surprised to learn that their work was being used in a White House report opposing embryonic stem cell research. The three wrote to members of Congress: "We are surprised to see our work on reprogramming adult stem cells used to support arguments that research involving human embryonic stem cells is unnecessary. Our work directly involves the use of human embryonic stem cells . . . [and] is precisely the type of research that is currently being harmed by the President's arbitrary limitation on federal funding for human embryonic stem cell research"; they went on to accuse the White House of "a clear misrepresentation of our work" (Eggan, Cowan, and Melton 2007).

Many scientists believed that President Bush pushed away the scientific community—in one sense quite literally, by demoting the White House science adviser and moving the Office of Science and Technology Policy out of the White House (Thompson 2003). A February 2004 report from the Union of Concerned Scientists claimed: "There is significant evidence that the scope and scale of the manipulation, suppression, and misrepresentation of science by the Bush administration are unprecedented." An accompanying statement, titled "Restoring Scientific Integrity in Policymaking," was signed by more than 15,000 scientists, and the 62 original signers included winners of the Nobel Prize and two former White House Science Advisers, John H. Gibbons and Neal Lane (Union of Concerned Scientists 2004).

In the last two years of his presidency, George W. Bush attempted to reach out to scientists with a new burst of funding for the physical sciences, and a new American Competitiveness Initiative (ACI), which focused on improving math and science education and the "pipeline" of skilled workers. In his 2006 state of the union speech, Bush promised to double the budgets, over ten years, of the National Science Foundation, the Department of Energy's Office of Science, and the National Institute for Standards and Technology (Bush 2006). Congress refused to fully fund the president's funding request for science agencies for fiscal year 2007. But for the fiscal year 2009 budget under consideration in 2008, Bush reiterated his support for the ACI and for doubling funding for the physical sciences (Jones 2008). The ACI bill passed by Congress required an annual "National Science and Technology Summit" of national leaders, and the first one was held at Oak Ridge National Laboratory in Tennessee in August 2008.

The ACI agenda happened to dovetail with a major report from the National Academies of Science, released in 2005, titled *Rising above the Gathering Storm: Energizing and Employing America for a Brighter Economic Future*. The committee that produced the report was chaired by Norman Augustine, a former CEO of Lockheed Martin and a longtime White House science adviser, and the members included a distinguished list of national leaders, such as Craig Barrett, chairman of Intel Corporation; Robert Gates, who became secretary of defense; Charles Vest, president emeritus of MIT; and Nobel laureates Steven Chu and Joshua Lederberg, among others (National Academies of Science 2007). The report called for, among other things, large increases in funding for K–12 math and science education, a long-term commitment to funding basic research, a new ARPA-like technology office within the Department of Energy, and a new Presidential Innovation Award. The committee also recommended reform of the U.S. intellectual property system, assuring broadband Internet access for all Americans, and tax incentives for R&D and innovation.

After many years of federal science budgets that were basically flat in inflation-adjusted dollars, Bush's commitment to the ACI goals gave hope to some scientists and disappointed others. Robert Berdahl, president of the Association of American Universities, said, "Question: Is the President's budget good or bad for the vital research and education that is performed by America's research universities? Answer: Yes" (quoted in *Science* 2008). The National Institutes of Health and NASA budgets stayed flat, while there were large increases for the National Science Foundation and scientific research work at the Department of Energy. Science projects at the National Institute of Standards and Technology received a 22 percent increase (*Science* 2008).

While these funding requests encouraged scientists in fields that were favored, anxiety, wariness, and discouragement were still strong in the science policy community. Some scientists believed that the "war on science" during the Bush administration had eroded the stature of science in the minds of Americans, although the National Science Foundation's report *Science and Engineering Indicators, 2008* showed that the public trusts scientists more than members of any other profession except the military (National Science Foundation 2008). There was still a sense among many prominent scientists that the U.S. system of funding research and development was broken. The glory days of large research and development labs such as Bell Labs appeared to be gone for good. The financial success of companies like Google and Facebook, emblematic of the Internet age and largely decoupled from science-based innovation, raised the question whether the long relationship between privately funded R&D and government-steered R&D will flourish again, the way it did in LBJ's era.

Throughout the postwar history of science and technology policy there has been an underlying debate about whether federal funding for research is, or should be, tied to "national goals." And the corollary questions about national goals include "What should they be?" and "Who gets to choose?"

A framework of trust between government policy makers and scientists and engineers, and between policy makers, scientists, and the public, must be restored. This framework should be built around several important elements. The scientific integrity of governmental information is paramount, something that was damaged during the George W. Bush administration. The role of science adviser should be one of honest broker, in contrast to a role as "cheerleader" or advocate for the administration's policies. The adviser needs to be both an "insider" and an honest broker who may disagree with the president—a significant challenge. It is a relationship that takes skill and mutual understanding, but one essential to rebuilding the trust relationships between government, the scientific and technical communities, and the general public.

In the White House administrations since 1980, the line between politics and governing has blurred as top leaders in the White House have played strongly political roles in what has come to be called a "permanent campaign." The people damaged the most by this trend have been governmental officials responsible for scientific and technical information and maintaining trust with the public. A regrettable by-product of this deterioration of trust is that it has become more difficult to attract top scientific talent to government service. While there are still talented people in federal government positions, scientists with the stature of Killian, Wiesner, Kistiakowsky, Rabi, and Hornig are more often on the outside today rather than in public service. It will likely take a long time to reconstitute a trust relationship in the midst of what can be expected to be uninterrupted hyperpartisan politics. Nevertheless, both the scientific and engineering communities and the White House leadership should focus on the task of rebuilding trust.

The Lessons of the LBJ Era for Science and Technology Policy

The problems that ended the golden era of science were becoming evident during the Johnson presidency, particularly the deep divisions over the war in Vietnam. Lyndon Johnson was increasingly angry at academics over their opposition to the war, and Nixon intensified the White House's alienation from the academy, to the point of including Jerome Wiesner, a former White House science adviser, on his famous enemies list. Since then, scientists and engineers, especially those in universities, have been buffeted by partisan politics. This turmoil contrasts sharply with a period of remarkable consensus that produced numerous transformations of American society, including the use of space and the development of the information age.

Thus, one lesson of the Johnson era is that political consensus can harness the abilities of scientists and engineers to achieve national goals and move the country forward. Leaders have been searching for the "moral equivalent of war" to replace the motivation that the Soviet threat inspired in Americans. But the ability of political leaders and prestigious scientists and engineers to work together, under a framework of broad national goals, is clearly a product of leadership itself, as Lyndon Johnson so grandly demonstrated.

The features of the Cold War consensus should not be exaggerated, of course—there were plenty of disagreements and even the early signs of cultural upheaval. But Johnson's faith in change—in civil rights, health care, and education—made everyone else ambitious. While LBJ is often criticized today for being too ambitious and trying to do too much all at once, Johnson-sized ambition seems far more suited to the challenges we face today. The country urgently needs new sources of energy, ways to address global climate change, and a better system of health care. The current fractured and fractious array of scientific programs seems ill suited to these tasks.

Johnson understood that government-funded scientists and engineers need to be part of something that the public supports. Johnson was an instinctive critic of the argument that unfettered basic research is a national goal in itself; science policy experts have since come around to the more complex view that the model of a linear connection between basic research and new social goods is flawed, and that there needs to be attention paid to how we solve pressing problems through science and technology. Restarting the country's innovation engine will take broad and open minds, not simply repeating patterns that scientists and engineers believe in.

Johnson's biggest legacy was to open American civic life to more participants by expanding civil rights and educational opportunities. The U.S. scientific and engineering communities have not yet figured out how to embrace this way of thinking by becoming full participants in American democracy without being trapped and diverted by partisan politics. Prominent scientists and engineers have not yet developed a way to communicate the role of science and engineering in U.S. society that speaks to the concerns of ordinary Americans. Johnson had an undeniable gift in this respect, of being able to translate complex policy goals into straightforward appeals whose legitimacy was contained in the way these appeals were expressed. After years of squabbling over White House science policies, scientists and engineers need to rediscover how to communicate the national consensus that the country needs.

The United States is entering what may be its most difficult period of fiscal challenge ever. The country's capacity for innovation is flagging at just the time we need it most, when we need to push through economic difficulties to a new ascent to economic prosperity. The contributions of science and technology are more important than ever, but our national assets have been weakened by neglect and a loss of scientific integrity. A new golden age for U.S. science and engineering needs to be established—an era of integrity, leadership, public purpose, and national will.

References

Baltimore, David. 2004. A forum on the Bush administration's use and abuse of science in policymaking. Wheeler Auditorium, University of California at Berkeley Graduate School of Journalism, Oct. 12.

Blanpied, William A. 1998. Inventing U.S. science policy. *Physics Today* 51, no. 2 (Feb.): 34-40.

Boffey, Philip. 1969. The Hornig years: Did LBJ neglect his science advisor? *Science* 163, no. 1 (Jan. 31): 453–458.

Britt, Robert Roy. 2008. Scientists say Bush stifles science and lets global leadership slip. *Live Science*, Jan. 30. www.livescience.com/technology/080130-bush-legacy.html.

Bromley, D. Allan. 1990. *U.S. science and technology policy*. Washington D.C.: Executive Office of the President.

Brooks, Harvey. 1996. The evolution of U.S. science policy. In Bruce L. R. Smith and Claude E. Barfield, eds., *Technology, R&D, and the economy*. Proceedings of a conference undertaken jointly by the Brookings Institution and American Enterprise Institute for Public Policy Research, Oct. 1994. Washington, D.C.: Brookings Institution Press.

Bumiller, Elizabeth. 2005. Bush remarks roil debate over teaching of evolution. *New York Times*, Aug. 3.

Bush, George W. 2006. State of the union address. Executive Office of the President. http://georgewbush-whitehouse.archives.gov/news/releases/2006/01/20060131-10.html.

Chapman, Gary. 1992. Push comes to shove on technology policy. *Technology Review* 95, no. 8 (Nov.–Dec.): 42–49.

Clinton, William J., and Albert Gore Jr. 1993. *Technology for America's growth: A new direction to build economic strength*. Washington, D.C.: White House.

Dean, Howard. 2004. Bush's war on science. June 29. Available at Stories in the News, www.sitnews.us/HowardDean/062904_dean.html.

Eggan, Kevin, Chad Cowan, and Douglas Melton. 2007. Letter to Representatives Diana DeGette and Mike Castle (Jan. 10).

Greenberg, Daniel S. 2001. *Science, money, and politics: Political triumph and ethical erosion*. Chicago: University of Chicago Press.

Harris, Gardiner. 2007. Surgeon General sees 4-year term as compromised. *New York Times*, July 11.

Harsha, Peter. 2004. IT research and development funding. In William Aspray, ed., *Chasing Moore's law: Information technology policy in the United States*. Raleigh, N.C.: SciTech.

Hart, David M. 1998. *Forged consensus: Science, technology, and economic policy in the United States, 1921–1953*. Princeton, N.J.: Princeton University Press.

Herken, Greg. 2000. *Cardinal choices: Presidential science advising from the atomic bomb to SDI*. Stanford, Calif.: Stanford University Press.

Hornig, Donald F. 1968. Oral history interview conducted by David G. McComb. Dec 4. Lyndon Baines Johnson Library Oral History Collection, www.lbjlib.utexas.edu/johnson/archives.hom/oralhistory.hom/Hornig-D/hornig1.PDF.

Johnson, Robert David. 2006. *Congress and the Cold War*. New York: Cambridge University Press.

Jones, Richard M. 2008. President Bush signals his intention for American competitiveness initiative. *American Institute of Physics Bulletin of Science Policy News*, Jan. 30. www.aip.org/fyi/2008/013.html.

Kauffmann, Marc. 2005. FDA official quits over delay on Plan B. *Washington Post*, Sept. 1.

Leslie, Stuart. 1993. *The Cold War and American science: The military-industrial academic complex at MIT and Stanford*. New York: Columbia University Press.

Mooney, Chris. 2006. *The Republican war on science*. New York: Basic Books.

National Academies of Science. 2007. *Rising above the gathering storm: Energizing and employing America for a brighter economic future.* Washington, D.C.: National Academies Press.

National Science Foundation. 2008. *Science and engineering indicators, 2008.* Chapter 7: Science and Technology; Public Attitudes and Understanding. www.nsf .gov/statistics/seind08/c7/c7h.htm.

President's Science Advisory Council. 1965. *Report of the Environmental Pollution Panel.* Washington, D.C.: U.S. Government Printing Office.

Primack, Joel, and Frank von Hippel. 1974. *Advice and dissent: Scientists in the political arena.* New York: Basic Books.

Raymond, Jack. 1961. Kennedy defense study finds no evidence of "missile gap." *New York Times,* Feb. 7.

Sarewitz, Dan 1996. *Frontiers of illusion: Science, technology and the politics of progress.* Philadelphia: Temple University Press.

Science. 2008. Physical sciences win out over biomedicine in 2009 budget proposal. *Science Daily News,* Feb. 4. http://news.sciencemag.org/2008/02/physical -sciences-win-out-over-biomedicine-2009-budget-proposal.

Smith, Bruce L.R. 1990. *American science policy since WWII.* Washington, D.C.: Brookings Institution Press.

Stokes, Donald E. 1997. *Pasteur's quadrant: Basic science and technological innovation.* Washington, D.C.: Brookings Institution Press.

Thompson, Nicholas. 2003. Science friction: The growing—and dangerous—divide between scientists and the GOP. *Washington Monthly,* July–Aug. www .washingtonmonthly.com/features/2003/0307.thompson.html.

Union of Concerned Scientists. 2004. Restoring scientific integrity in policymaking. www.ucsusa.org/scientific_integrity/abuses_of_science/reports-scientific -integrity.html.

Wang, Zuoyue. 2008. *In Sputnik's shadow: The president's Science Advisory Committee and Cold War America.* New Brunswick, N.J.: Rutgers University Press.

Woods, Randall Bennett. 2006. *LBJ: Architect of American ambition.* New York: Simon and Schuster.

PART V

IMPROVING PUBLIC MANAGEMENT

CHAPTER 13

Reform of the Federal Government: Lessons for Change Agents

LAURENCE E. LYNN JR.

On August 25, 1965, President Lyndon B. Johnson asked members of his cabinet and other agency heads to implement a new planning and budgeting system. "The objective of this program is simple," he said: "to use the most modern management tools so that the full promise of a finer life can be brought to every American at the least possible cost" (Johnson 1965).

As discussed below, the introduction of what was known in the Department of Defense (DoD) as the Planning-Programming-Budgeting System (PPBS) to all federal departments and agencies was immediately controversial. Five years later, following its highly uneven implementation across the government, President Richard M. Nixon's newly created Office of Management and Budget (OMB), which had replaced the old Bureau of the Budget, quietly rescinded Johnson's mandate. Although still alive and well in the DoD, PPBS is often regarded as just another in a series of federal government reform initiatives that almost inevitably proceed, in George Downs and Patrick Larkey's phrase, "from hubris to helplessness" because of unrealistic ambitions, conceptual ambiguity, bureaucratic resistance, and partisan politics (Downs and Larkey 1986).

This chapter was drafted as president-elect Barack Obama was preparing to assume office in 2009. During his campaign, he said, "We cannot meet twenty-first century challenges with a twentieth century bureaucracy" (quoted in Shoop, Brodsky, and Rosenberg 2008), and he supposedly had a government reform advisory committee in place even before his election. Among those eager to help the new president was the IBM Center for the Business of Government; its *Operators Manual for the Next Administration* and *Getting It Done: A Guide for Government Executives* (Abramson et al. 2008) were written in hopeful anticipation that President Obama would launch his own government-reform initiatives. Apart from a frisson when Obama created the position of chief performance officer, however, administration management initiatives amounted only to low-profile efforts to improve functional, not policy, management—procurement, information technology, personnel administration, performance monitoring—drawing on best practices from the corporate sector.

The focus of this chapter is neither the techniques nor the merits of PPBS per se. The focus, rather, is the processes of its implementation and the long-term consequences for public administration. This chapter draws on the archival resources of the Lyndon B. Johnson Presidential Library; the large contemporaneous and postmortem literature of analysis, praise, criticism, and lessons learned concerning PPBS; my personal experience in policy making and budgeting at the DoD and the former Department of Health, Education and Welfare (HEW) in the 1960s and 1970s; and continuing reflection on subsequent presidential reform initiatives, including those of Bill Clinton, George W. Bush, and Barack Obama. It concludes with some lessons for those who would attempt to make major changes in the way the federal government plans for the allocation of budgetary resources.

The next section reviews the PPBS reform process. The following ones consider the legacies of PPBS, both those that were intended and those that emerged as by-products of the reform effort. The concluding section distills lessons for change agents from the PPBS record and more recent experiences with federal government reform.

LBJ'S PPB Initiative

Throughout 1965, the Johnson administration had been preparing the president's budget for fiscal year 1967. Confronting the rising and projected costs of the war in Vietnam, the budgetary implications of pursuing Great Society policy goals, and growing political pressures from LBJ's allies and opponents in Congress and elsewhere, administration officials needed to communicate discipline and restraint in the budget if they wanted to accomplish their highest priorities without a tax increase. By mid-June, cabinet officers and agency heads were coming under increasing presidential pressure to identify potential savings in their budgets in order to make room for higher-priority policies and programs.

The Politics of Budget Reform

On June 22, 1965, the recently appointed director of the Bureau of the Budget (BoB), Charles L. Schultze, wrote to cabinet officers asking each to establish a task force "to identify those activities in which savings might be made to accommodate a significant part of the new or expanded programs contained in your budget preview submissions."[1] Each was to identify a "*band of lower priority* activities," along with the legislation or executive orders needed to eliminate or restructure them, and "a three-tiered priority ranking of proposed program *increases*." Only two months later, on August 25, the president directed his cabinet officers and agency heads to adopt PPBS, which Robert McNamara had implemented as a framework for military force structure planning and budget making.

PPBS was an innovation in federal budgeting. Beginning in 1921, American presidents were required by law to submit an "executive budget" proposal to Congress for the ensuing fiscal year. To prepare it, BoB issued limits, or "ceilings," on the amount that each department and agency was allowed to request. Following a process of give-and-take between BoB and agency officials, approved budget requests were compiled and submitted to Congress as the president's annual budget request. Then, following further give-and-take between administration officials and legislators, funds would be authorized and appropriated to the executive branch for execution.

All federal budget requests and appropriations were in the form of inputs, or "objects of expenditure"—salaries, operating expenses, and construction—not of outputs, or what these expenditures were supposed to accomplish in policy terms. This process had long been criticized for obscuring the real purposes of the executive budget: achieving public policy goals. Following blueprints created at the RAND Corporation, a U.S. Air Force think tank, McNamara, immediately after assuming office, overlaid but did not replace the traditional budget process and categories with a process of "planning" and "programming." Specialized staffs analyzed proposed expenditures for what they were expected to accomplish in maintaining or increasing military capabilities and what they would cost, that is, their cost-effectiveness in performing military missions, such as strategic nuclear deterrence, close tactical air support of troops in combat, and airlift and sealift of military forces to theaters of conflict.

McNamara's use of PPBS had been both praised and criticized by lawmakers, senior military leaders, and professors of political science, among others. LBJ's mandate to all departments and agencies to use a similar cost-effectiveness approach in their budgeting was destined to draw even more intense political and academic criticism, including from those who conceded the value of PPBS for national security planning but doubted that the diverse goals of domestic policies and programs were equally appropriate for economic analysis, which might distort rather than clarify how Great Society policy goals might best be achieved. Costs and effectiveness in these areas were very difficult to measure.

What accounts for the relatively abrupt launching of such a controversial initiative by Schultze and LBJ? A conjecture based on oral history interviews in the archives of the Lyndon B. Johnson Presidential Library is that the August directive was a clever bit of bureaucratic politics by Schultze and LBJ's aide (and McNamara's former assistant) Joseph A. Califano.[2] Their purpose was to head off what they considered an unwise move by other presidential aides: committing LBJ to promulgating a comprehensive set of long-term policy goals for the United States. Abandoning their previous plan to introduce program budgeting in domestic agencies selectively and on a pilot basis, Schultze and others of like mind decided to implement PPBS immediately and across the board, even though there had been virtually no preparation for such a bold, potentially disruptive move.

In a memorandum to the president dated August 13, 1965, Schultze struck the notes that would appeal to the president in the initial, emphasized paragraph: "*To be really useful and to avoid making costly mistakes, the establishment of goals towards which domestic policy will be directed must be part of a much broader programming and budgetary system, a la McNamara.*"[3] Schultze's memo was relayed to the president by Califano on August 16, covered by his own memorandum outlining the hows and whys of a system that "pays off handsomely in Defense," and recommending that LBJ lead a cabinet meeting to introduce it. The president was evidently happy to go "all in" with PPBS because, although knowing little of its techniques, he was deeply impressed with whatever accounted for the former head of the Ford Motor Company's apparent brilliance as a policy and budget maker at the DoD.[4] The cabinet meeting that launched the initiative was held on August 25, and the president announced it to the public at a press conference later in the day.

The politics were clear. House Ways and Means Committee chairman Wilbur Mills warned administration officials against tax increases in 1966 and advised excluding projected increases in spending for Vietnam from the regular budget submission. The overriding political goal was to communicate forcefully that the federal domestic budget was under firm control and that the projected surpluses of 1964 would not turn into large deficits. The president's mandate to implement PPBS across the board was an unmistakable symbol of his commitment to fiscal discipline. *Time* magazine, at least, was impressed: in his budget for fiscal year 1967, LBJ had "set out right away to cut the budget back as much as he could, both because he thought it was in the nation's interest and because he realized that it would be a dramatic indication to businessmen that he was going to run a tight ship—and that they were all welcome aboard" (*Time* 1966).

Evolution Becomes Revolution

The operating model for PPBS was the program budgeting system implemented by McNamara at the Pentagon in 1961 (Hitch 1967; Schultze 1968). Developed by the RAND Corporation (Novick 1966), its purpose was to unify and integrate the strategies, forces, programs, and budgets of the DoD. The tool to accomplish this purpose was a mission-oriented program structure for the department as a whole that conceptually eliminated the distinctions among the three services. The costs and mission benefits or effectiveness of alternative programs, or combinations of program elements, were estimated and compared. Ultimate decisions regarding program authorizations and appropriations, reached after intensive deliberations within DoD, between the secretary and the president and his staff, and between the administration and Congress, were incorporated in the annually updated Five-Year Defense Program, which became the baseline for the next annual round of analyses and deliberations.

Following this model, the foundations of PPBS in each agency were to be output-oriented program structures. The formalities of the system were three types of documents organized around the program structure: program memoranda, which succinctly presented agency program recommendations, alternatives considered in the course of deliberations, and the rationale for the agency's choice; a program and financial plan, a complete and authoritative summary of the outputs and costs of agency programs presented on a multiyear basis; and special studies, the analytic basis for the recommendations in the program memoranda. The purpose was to integrate planning, programming, and budgeting across the multiple bureaus of domestic departments and agencies and to provide for outcome- or output-oriented deliberations and choices based on analyses of alternative ways of accomplishing a given objective.

As important as any of the documents associated with PPBS in the DoD and in the domestic agencies was the principle that the heads of departments and agencies should have access to an independent source of analysis, information, and ideas, thus liberating them from total dependence on the program bureaus for policy advice. How these analytic staffs were incorporated into deliberation and decision making on policy and the budget could vary widely across agencies: McNamara used his analysts to define the issue and decision agendas, forcing the services and the Joint Chiefs of Staff to work with "whiz kids" they might otherwise ignore. Officials in domestic agencies might use these specialized staff resources as an in-house think tank to address high-priority or crosscutting issues offline. The notion that experts in policy analysis and program development and planning should henceforth have "a place at the table" during deliberations and decision making was a break from the past that transcended in importance any of the new documents required by PPBS (Lynn 1999; Rivlin 1971).

Perhaps the most significant aspect of PPBS implementation was what did *not* happen: agencies were not expected to change the format of their detailed budget requests, and the president's budget was submitted to Congress in the old, objects-of-expenditure format. Moreover, BoB insisted that PPBS and regular budget staffs be separate, with the PPBS offices staffed with new, analytically trained people. Within BoB itself, responsibility for PPBS implementation was assigned to the recently created Office of Program Evaluation, headed by a former RAND official, who had no defined role in the regular budget process (Williams 1971). On March 15, 1966, LBJ exhorted his heads of departments and agencies to "recruit as many of the best, analytically trained people as you can find," as McNamara had done, although he also urged them "to train the most able and promising people now on your staff in modern techniques of program analysis and management" (Johnson 1966).

The result was a two-track budget preparation process within the executive branch: one track used the program structures and analyses required by PPBS, the other track prepared budgets in the familiar appropriations structures. Not surprisingly, internal communications on preparation of the budget for fiscal year 1967 over the next few months made virtually no reference to the new system; the June 22 procedures were evidently still operative in preparing the "real budget." Agency heads were chided for "excessive budget requests," and pressures to achieve additional budgetary savings and to restrain current year spending intensified.

While the serious political business of budget preparation was taking place, however, BoB concurrently pressed federal departments and agencies to move forward with the new system. On October 12, 1965, BoB issued Bulletin 66-3, which provided detailed guidance and instructions, as well as tight deadlines, on implementing PPBS. An official responsible for PPBS implementation was to be designated within ten days, and an approved agency program structure was to be in place by February 1, 1966 (U.S. General Accounting Office 1997). Concurrently with regular budget preparation, ordinarily a time of peak workloads, agencies were expected to create the foundation for an entirely new way of making policy and budget decisions.

Advocates for program budgeting at the DoD and across the government often portrayed the system as a new or even revolutionary approach to budget making. Many of its advocates emphasized how PPBS represented a significant break from past practice, as it assuredly had in the DoD. Schultze's statement on PPBS in August 1967 before a subcommittee of the Senate Committee on Government Operations, for example, was a historical case for PPBS (U.S. Senate 1967a, 28–32). Many outside experts were similarly enthusiastic. The movement to link social science research and methods with policy making in assessing "costs" and "effectiveness" were described as "a new orientation in American government" (Gross and Springer 1967). PPBS was described as "potentially the most significant management improvement in the history of American government" because of its orientation toward linking inputs with the outputs and outcomes thereby produced (9).

Such claims were overblown. PPBS had numerous antecedents at the federal level, enumerated by Comptroller General Elmer Staats in 1968: a long history of BoB review of the cost-benefit analysis of water resource programs required by Congress; long-range budget projections featuring high, low, and most likely estimates for use in policy making; a systematic budget preview process conducted by BoB; a mission-related functional framework for budget preview and special analyses of selected programs; lawfully sanctioned performance- and cost-based budgeting; and selective development of formal agency program planning (Staats 1968). As Staats put it: "[PPBS was] not an 'entirely new' or 'revolutionary' system of budgeting as has been frequently stated: nor did it have its entire base in the Department of Defense as has been stated also. Rather, it was an outgrowth of a number of developments that took place over a long period of time, although it was not developed in as highly formalized a fashion as embraced in the President's announcement of 1965" (7).

The idea that government executives needed specialized staff resources in their own offices had a similar history. From 1933 to 1943, when it was abolished by Congress, the National Resources Planning Board (NRPB), located in the Executive Office of the President, conducted an ambitious policy planning program. The Department of the Interior had a tradition of policy planning and analysis dating back to the New Deal and the long tenure of Harold Ickes as secretary. An Office of Policy Planning had been a fixture in the Office of the Secretary of State since George F. Kennan directed it, beginning in 1947. Within the Johnson administration, the Office of Systems Analysis in the DoD, with its staff of well-trained civilian and military "whiz kids," was the keystone of program budgeting. The Office of Research, Plans, Programs and Evaluation with a similar role had been created at the Office of Economic Opportunity.

The president's reform initiative, in other words, could have been viewed more as evolution than as revolution and might have elicited less skepticism had that been emphasized. Senator Henry Jackson (D-WA) noted during the hearing that overstating and overplaying what PPBS could do created uneasiness both in Congress and in the agencies (U.S. Senate 1967a). A roster of academic critics from outside government sounded a similar theme: PPBS advocates were making claims that could not be fulfilled. Said Elmer Staats in 1968, "There is a significant body of opinion that PPB has been oversold. Perhaps the proponents of PPB have not been careful enough to delineate what it can do best from the areas of decision making in which it may flounder" (12).

It was the revolution, not the evolution, that captured the attention of government reformers, however. Over the next few years, ideas and practices associated with PPBS in one form or another spread widely and rapidly to Staats's Government Accounting Office (GAO), to state and local governments, and to other countries (Gross 1969). According to Selma Mushkin (1969, 167), by 1969 "as many as 50 or 60 cities and counties have begun to group expenditures in terms of objective-oriented program structures, to view public services in terms of products provided to the public, to take account of the longer-range implications of program decisions in regard to both costs and outputs, and to step back from administrative pressures and ask about alternative ways of meeting public demands." The transformation of the federal government across the board, however, was a struggle.

Slouching Toward PPBS

Despite the Johnson administration's efforts to defend PPBS against criticisms that were occasionally well taken but often distinctly wrongheaded, the bureaucratic response to Johnson's mandate was relatively tepid. In November 1966, LBJ found it necessary to excoriate his cabinet and agency heads for moving too slowly and failing to use the new system to make management decisions. Confusion was palpable as officials tried to figure out just what PPBS required of them. It did not help matters that BoB itself seemed confused (Gross 1969). It did not help, either, that career officials associated with preparing the regular budget were still mired in the confusion associated with efforts to create "performance budgets" and "program budgets" as urged by the two Hoover Commissions nearly a decade earlier (Gross 1969). Temptations were strong to put PPBS implementation on a back burner or to comply with its requirements symbolically rather substantively.

According to a retrospective GAO assessment, "PPBS implementation proceeded slowly—even after several years of effort" (U.S. General Accounting Office 1997, 37). A 1969 study of PPBS in sixteen agencies revealed substantial variation in how effectively it was implemented and concluded: "Observers of the budgeting process agree that PPB has had limited influence on the major resource allocation decisions in domestic agencies of the federal government. This limited impact is generally attributed to PPBS's lack of attention to political bargaining, a major feature of traditional budgeting" (Harper, Kramer, and Rouse 1969, 632). Wrote Elizabeth Drew (1967, 9) at the time, "How well PPB has worked, agency by agency, has depended more than anything on how seriously the man at the top has taken it, how hard he worked to attract good people to do the job, how much he lent his authority to the adoption of a system of hard analysis." "An analysis of the results of recent studies, discussions with Budget Bureau and other officials, and testimony before congressional subcommittees," said a 1970 study, "leads one to conclude that PPBS has thus far been rather ineffectual as a presidential staff tool" (Botner 1970, 423).

Some, however, saw the glass as half full. "The only fair way to judge the planning-programming-budgeting process at this point," said Drew (1967, 28), "is in its historical context. There is no question that it is primitive, and this is due in some part to the fact that it is new. Defense Secretary McNamara is said to believe that the process itself did not yield great payoffs for him until it had been under way for at least four years; the more thoughtful observers have always believed that in such areas as health and education it might take still longer." She continued: "The Art of systems analysis is in about the same stage now as medicine during the last half of the 19th century." Alain C. Enthoven (1966, 138), who led PPBS implementation for McNamara, wrote: "It has reached the point at which it can do more good than harm on the average."

HEW generally received the highest marks for PPBS implementation from observers. The advent of PPBS was linked to efforts to improve the quality of the social data and statistics available to policy planners, and to the production of social indicators and social accounts. "No conscientious budget-examiner could rely uncritically on the data presented on education, mental illness, crime, delinquency, transportation, and urban problems by scores of competing bureaus anxious to justify budget proposals by magnifying their past record or their future contributions to the 'public interest'" (Gross and Springer 1967, 10). William Gorham, a former McNamara adviser who was named the first assistant secretary for planning and evaluation at HEW, put it this way: "The very process of analysis is valuable in itself, for it forces people to think about the objectives of Government programs and how they can be measured. It forces people to think about choices in an explicit way" (1967, 7).

In support of these ideas, the president, on March 17, 1967, sent a remarkable message to Congress, titled "The Quality of American Government" (Johnson 1967). Johnson focused, in particular, on "the institutional machinery which enables law to work in response to the will of the Congress and the people. It is a condition of any law," he continued, "that its effectiveness must be judged by its administration. . . . There are substantial improvements to be made." He identified areas of potential improvement, including government reorganization, increased efficiency, the public service, and the federal system. Governmental efficiency referred to full value for every tax dollar. PPBS, which "is forcing us to ask the fundamental questions that illuminate our choices," was the instrument for accomplishing this goal: "This new system cannot make decisions. But it improves the process of decision making by revealing the alternatives—for decisions are only as good as the information on which they are based." But, supporters noted, PPBS "will not be able to function fully until more trained men and women, more data, better cost accounting and new methods of evaluation are available." The last sentence was arguably the seed of Johnson's most significant public administration reform legacy, discussed below.

"A Death in the Bureaucracy"

Government reform initiatives closely identified with a particular administration seldom survive other than in institutional memory or in vestigial remnants. On June 21, 1971, in a memorandum accompanying Circular A-11, its regular communication to agencies concerning budget preparation, Richard Nixon's OMB instructed agencies as follows: "Agencies are no longer required to submit with their budget submissions the multi-year program and financing plans, program memoranda and special analytical studies . . . or the schedules . . . that reconcile information classified according to their program and appropriation structures" (Schick 1973, 146). Memorably labeled "a death in the bureaucracy" by Allen Schick, the reason put forward by the OMB for abandoning the PPBS management tools was "to simplify budget submission requirements."

In amplification, William A. Niskanen, OMB's assistant director for evaluation at the time of PPBS's demise (and, ironically, a former RAND defense analyst and an original McNamara whiz kid), said, "At this time . . . these methods are no longer new. More importantly, the U.S. experience with these methods suggests that, as yet, they have neither substantially changed nor significantly improved the process of making budgetary choices" (1972, 155). Concluded one veteran observer of PPBS, "Certainly the closely linked proponents of the status quo—the congressional subcommittees, the bureaus, and the interest groups—recognized the threat posed by analysis of the costs and benefits of their favorite programs and alternatives thereto. One might also suggest that, however ineffective, PPBS was *too* effective for the groups presently dominating the budgetary bargaining process" (Botner 1972, 255). The birth of PPBS was economic common sense. Its death was political common sense.

LBJ'S Legacies as an Agent of Administrative Reform

The significance of Lyndon Johnson's efforts to reform the federal government as an institution can be viewed from many perspectives. In one view, PPBS reflected America's cultural inclination toward the "scientific management" of business and government and the substitution of rational analysis for hunch, guesswork, and ideology (Lynn 2006). A second perspective casts PPBS as one of a long series of vain efforts to achieve a level of government efficiency approaching that of business. From a more specialized perspective, PPBS has been viewed as a stage in a federal budget reform process that had its first significant expression in the Budget and Accounting Act of 1921; next in the recommendations of two Hoover Commissions; then in the Budget and Impoundment Control Act of 1974, which created the Congressional Budget Office, a principal source of analytic support to the Congress, and a legislative budget process that still prevails; and, in 1993, in the Government Performance and Results Act, which undergirded the administrative reforms of Presidents Clinton, Bush, and Obama.

PPBS is all those things: scientific management, a flawed move toward efficiency, and a budget reform. The interesting question, however, is not whether PPBS succeeded or failed as any or all these things, but how LBJ's PPB mandate, along with his other efforts on behalf of strengthening the institutions of the executive branch, affected a trajectory of change in the administration of the federal government that was already well under way and that continues to this day. If President Johnson had rejected what Schultze and Califano proposed to him, would anything be different now?

The answer to this counterfactual is yes—and the differences would not have been positive.

What PPB Wrought

In a literal sense, PPBS was soon forgotten, but not gone. Today, it is a basic planning process used in its birthplace, the DoD, and overseen by the director of program analysis and evaluation, who reports to the deputy secretary of defense. But PPBS's legacies are much broader and more significant than that rocky life and the near-total demise of its most visible manifestations suggest. LBJ's bold initiative produced three legacies of enduring importance:

- The institutionalization of policy analysis, an administrative technology employed by departments and agencies at all levels of American government
- Policy analysis as a distinct component of public affairs education in American universities (well represented by the Lyndon B. Johnson School of Public Affairs at the University of Texas at Austin) (Lynn 1996, 1999)
- A robust interest in public policy in traditional academic disciplines and fields and in new fields and subfields, including policy analysis, program evaluation, program development, and public management, concerned with achieving and sustaining democratic governance

A Place at the Table

"PPB failed because it did not penetrate the vital routines of putting together and justifying a budget," concluded the public budgeting scholar Allen Schick (1973, 147). "Always separate but never equal, the analysts had little influence over the form or content of the budget." What Schick failed to mention in his PPBS obituary, however, was the language in the OMB circular that ostensibly killed PPBS: "However, the substance of multiyear program planning, analysis and evaluation will continue to be stressed. Agencies should be prepared to furnish future-year estimates when requested, and should provide memoranda and analyses in support of program proposals and related issues" (quoted in Botner 1972, 254). The idea of an organized analytic capability to support policy and budget making was to remain very much alive.

I cannot help seeing Schick's elegy as personally ironic. Having spent more than three years in the PPBS machine in the DoD, I found myself, the year after its alleged death, at the head of the busy and vital Planning and Evaluation office at Secretary Elliot Richardson's HEW. With OMB's blessing, we soon created a process that tightly linked the work of that office with budget making and, as well, linked up with policy shops then thriving in the Department of Housing and Urban Development and the Department of Labor on a number of policy initiatives. Later in the Nixon administration, I directed the office at the Department of the Interior that combined the policy analysis and budget functions and reported directly to the secretary and undersecretary of the department. Both offices are still in existence.

The premise of PPBS was that the form in which information is presented to policy makers will govern decision making and that with the availability of output-oriented program analyses, the emphasis in deliberation and decision making would shift from justification to analysis (Schick 1966). In the Executive Office of the President, the National Resources Planning Board, as noted above, reflected this premise during the New Deal. The aim of PPBS was to institutionalize this premise at the level of individual departments and agencies, and the effort can generally be regarded as having been successful well beyond the scope originally envisioned. Downs and Larkey (1986) note that PPBS contributed to institutionalizing the role of economists, policy analysts, and accountants in budget and policy making, perhaps especially at state and local levels of government, where studies and evaluations have become virtually routine. They also note that the effort to implement such an ambitious decision-making system revealed more clearly than heretofore the politics of the budgetary process.

In short, policy analysis and research, program evaluation, and related analytic activities have been represented "at the table" at all levels of government far more often since PPBS made this idea seem like common sense to executives who sought active leadership roles in government.

Education for Public Policy and Management

In his March 15, 1966, memorandum to department and agency heads, LBJ had directed the chairman of the Civil Service Commission and the director of BoB "to organize an education program in these techniques at several universities. "I want you," the president said, "to nominate some of your most able people for this intensive training in modern, analytic methods" (Johnson 1966). Just as the great expansion of positive government during the New Deal had stimulated a similar expansion of universities' commitment to providing education for public service, so too did PPBS and LBJ's exhortations to expand the talent pool of individuals trained in analysis and management stimulate the expansion of university programs in public policy (Mushkin 1969).

Sensing opportunity in the policy-analysis movement, an entrepreneurial group of public officials, foundation executives, and university faculty members and administrators gathered resources and institutional support for the creation, beginning in 1968, of graduate professional schools offering degrees in policy-related fields (Yates 1977). Substantial financial support was provided by the Ford Foundation for the creation of such schools at Harvard University, Duke University, the University of California at Berkeley, the University of Texas at Austin, Carnegie-Mellon University, and elsewhere. The master's in public policy (MPP) degree was soon a popular option for idealistic undergraduates who preferred high-level public service to careers in law or business. Courses and concentrations in public policy analysis, policy-making processes, program evaluation, and related topics are now common in traditional schools of public administration and public affairs. The National Association for Schools of Public Affairs and Administration now accredits not only public policy schools but also programs with substantial public-policy-oriented content.

Although the focal mission of the new public policy schools was training in policy analysis, a concern for the implementation of public policies soon led to a curricular emphasis on public policy implementation and management. By the late 1970s, with the early onset of the global economic slowdown and the political imperative of controlling the costs of government, the place of public management not only in public policy schools but also in public administration and public affairs programs grew rapidly in importance.

Intellectual Capital for Governance

President Johnson's decision to require a sound analytic basis for the policy and budget recommendations of all domestic agencies was immediately criticized, especially by social scientists, for its apparent assumption that theories, data, and methods were available for the analysis of domestic policy issues and alternatives. The government-ready intellectual foundations for defense policy analysis had been under development since the creation of Project RAND by the U.S. Air Force in 1946 and could draw on even earlier traditions of military operations research. The availability of such foundations for domestic policy analysis was limited primarily to the use of cost-benefit analysis in federal infrastructure projects and to research traditions spawned by the Progressive era's bureaus of municipal research.

Because of the accelerated expansion of financial support for social research and development by the federal government and philanthropic foundations that was stimulated by the expansion of Great Society social safety net programs—an expansion that continued throughout the Nixon administration—existing academic disciplines, fields, and subfields, as well as new fields such as program evaluation (discussed in chapter 14) and social indicators, contributed to a significant expansion of policy and policy-oriented research and analysis. The current popularity of evidence-based policy making and performance measurement and management—the latest manifestations of scientific management in the public sector—can trace their lineage to the accelerated academic interest in the content and formulation of public policy stimulated by PPBS and the policy analysis movement.

Lessons for Change Agents

For all its positive legacies, LBJ's PPBS initiative might be judged a failure in one important respect: its implementation by officials in his administration. The tendency to create expectations that PPBS could not fulfill, the failure to link PPBS to relevant antecedents and precedents in the executive branch, and the decision, no doubt politically compelling, to preserve the existing format for presenting and administering the president's budget to Congress were seen by many at the time as undermining PPBS's prospects for transforming federal policy and budget making. While many in and out of government were attracted to and motivated by the ideals of program budgeting as well as by its anecdotal successes, the apparent hubris also elicited criticism and opposition not only by those whose interests were threatened but also by idealists and realists who believed that American democracy operated, or ought to operate, according to principles different from "cost-effectiveness" (Lynn 1999).

That said, though traditional object-of-expenditure accounting remains a foundation of federal budgeting, a steady evolution toward output-oriented policy making is evident in the federal planning and budgeting process.

Table 13.1. Six essential tasks for incoming government executives

1. Before confirmation, be careful.
2. Learn how things work.
3. Act quickly on what can't wait.
4. Develop a vision and a focused agenda.
5. Assemble your leadership team.
6. Manage your environment.

Source: Abramson et al. 2008, 2.

This evidence can be found in the president's annual budget submission, which includes a variety of analytical perspectives; in the documents produced by agencies in compliance with the Government Performance and Results Act; and in the reports of the CBO and the Government Accountability Office. This evidence is the cumulative result of efforts over the years to reform federal budget administration.

Against this background, the discussion that follows suggests ten lessons from the PPBS implementation experience. Lessons learned and principles and prescriptions for best practice typically come in two flavors: unexceptionable bromides that sound more useful than they are—for examples, see table 13.1 (also see Breul and Kamensky 2008)—and analytically derived "factors that affect" success—for examples, see the list of factors affecting the implementation of PPBS in table 13.2. The lessons offered here will not be altogether free of a certain proverbial quality. Many, although not all, will be familiar to students of administrative reform and organizational change. Their justification, as with all proverbs and words of wisdom, is that they will produce good results if followed.

While I aspire to academic objectivity—or, more accurately, while I disavow any material interest in what I am about to recommend (I disavow any interest in consulting fees)—it is also the case that these lessons have been filtered through my own experience in government, specifically with PPBS. I joined the systems analysis staff of the Office of the Secretary of Defense in 1965, when PPBS had been operational for four years, and remained there for nearly four years. I became assistant secretary of HEW for planning and evaluation in 1971 and assistant secretary of the interior for program development and budget in 1973, two positions that had their origins in PPBS and continue to reflect its spirit.

1. Before launching a government reform initiative, find out where the gov-

ernment has been and where it is now—and why. Before embarking on re-forms that will require cooperation and support from career officials, leg-islators, and other stakeholders, take the trouble to gather two kinds of information: the background of the status quo—its political and institu-tional origins, its constituencies, and impartial professional assessments of how well it is working; and any antecedents to features of the proposed re-form initiative to which reference might be made.

Reform initiatives usually elicit three types of responses: it can't be done; it shouldn't be done; and we are already doing it. Elicit these types of re-sponses *before* going forward in order to craft implementation plans that have a better chance of succeeding, to widen the potential base of support,

Table 13.2. Factors affecting the implementation of PPBS

1. The extent of the participation in system and process design by officials most concerned with the effects that the system may have on programs.
2. Identification of common areas of interest and a process that focuses on these areas.
3. Performance of studies that demonstrate the usefulness of analysis and the publicizing of such studies.
4. The attitude of the congressional committees responsible for an agency's substantive activity and its appropriations.
5. The attitude of the major clientele groups affected by the agency's programs.
6. The attitude of the examining group within the Bureau of the Budget respon-sible for reviewing and evaluating the agency's program.
7. The age of the agency or its programs.
8. The extent to which the agency has an already-developed analytic capability and the nature of the process through which those activities are incorporated into decision making.
9. The susceptibility of the agency mission to analytic effort, notably the difficulty in designing benefit measures for the evaluation of programs.
10. The difficulty of, or the extent to which, appropriate data and accounting systems have been developed.
11. The degree of congruity between the analytic program structure and the agency's organization structure.
12. As an outgrowth of the previous two factors, the difficulty associated with translating cost and other information from the basic appropriations accounts in which the budget is prepared to the program structure in which it is examined and in which programs are evaluated.

Source: Harper, Kramer, and Rouse 1969, 631–632.

and to disarm potential critics who want to claim nothing is new. Reforms based primarily on a normative ideal of how government *ought* to work leave their proponents needlessly vulnerable to criticism and opposition.

2. Real change agents go "all in." Numerous qualms were expressed concerning the wisdom of across-the-board implementation of PPBS; "careful and incremental" was better, experienced officials insisted. The official responsible for McNamara's sweeping reform of DoD planning and budgeting had expected change to be introduced over several years, but McNamara insisted on immediate and full implementation (Held 1966). At least one doubtful official later praised LBJ's instincts, noting that reforming a large bureaucracy requires immediate and total commitment and pressure from the top (Gross 1969; Botner 1970).

Many disagree with the wisdom of an "all in" approach to reform. Academic literature on managing change often recommends the accumulation of "small wins" and early successes to establish the credibility of ambitious reform concepts. In the public sector, however, when reforms often cut against the grain of traditional political processes, bureaucratic routines, and habits of thought, an immediate and bold commitment and determined follow-up are probably essential to gaining the attention necessary to carry new ideas forward. If preparation has been thorough and the implementation strategy is sound, boldness will be rewarded.

3. Work through existing institutions, not ad hoc arrangements. Reform initiatives often attempt to bypass existing offices and procedures on the mistaken assumption that doing so will ensure the visibility of the reform effort and preclude the delay associated with overcoming resistance and the need to compromise with the status quo. Even if it takes time and resources, it is far better to engage existing institutions—statutory authorization, overhead agencies (budget, personnel, audit, and financial management), existing channels of action and information, and other standard operating routines—and either co-opt or alter them to further the goals of reform.

The two-track budget process created to accommodate PPBS and, for that matter, the ad hoc arrangements created to further the Clinton administration's Reinventing Government reforms were expedient, but unhelpful for the ultimate objectives of the reforms. In contrast, the Nixon administration's promotion of New Federalism and the Bush administration's performance-oriented program evaluation had more impact because they astutely engaged the budget examiners at OMB and, through them, department and agency staffs. If reorganizations are used to further reform, in other words, the success of the reforms should become everybody's responsibility.

4. Change agents must be absolutely clear about the concept, its rationale, and the steps needed to implement it. Vagueness, ambiguity, and confusion are the nemeses of reform, especially when exhibited by its principal sponsors. Every reform initiative that aspires to change the status quo should be accompanied by a user's guide, a "government reform for dummies," that leaves no one in doubt about what terms mean and what behaviors and actions are expected, when, and why. Without clarity about what is to change and how, the tens of thousands of officials whose cooperation is needed will focus on tasks that are mandatory, that they know how to do, and that enjoy political and stakeholder support. The tendency to "wait out" the change agents must be overcome both by clear assignments of responsibility and by minimizing any ambiguity concerning what officials are responsible for doing or accomplishing.

5. Craft a sound argument for any reform initiative that is easily comprehended by supporters and critics alike. Those who speak for the reforms in public, whether agency heads, public information officials, or program officials, should be provided with talking points and fact sheets that enable the administration to be seen as being on the same page. The more controversial the reforms, the more essential it is to present unity concerning their purpose, rationale, approach, and prospects.

6. Reform needs champions; fill key subcabinet positions with people who care about it. Identifying candidates for senior executive positions and for other Plum Book positions is an intensely political process.[5] Though appointments are the first step in the transition from campaigning to governing, the two are often so interrelated during the creation and vetting of candidate lists that it may be difficult to establish qualifications for governing without passing through political filters associated with campaigning. Thus, positions vital to the success of government reform initiatives may well be filled by those with little commitment to, or aptitude for, reform.

Few will disagree that durable reform needs champions, officials who accord it a high priority, not only in traditional management positions or in specially created roles but also in policy making and other staff positions as well. If lessons 3 and 4 have been heeded, championing reform will more likely be seen as part of the mandate, of course, but even with adequate preparation, aptitude and interest in government reform should be part of the vetting process.

7. Remember: government is politics, not economics. Administrative reform, especially of domestic agencies, has few if any politically powerful stakeholders, and in a showdown, political rationality trumps technical rationality. Reform of domestic government "has the potential for directly affecting the electorate and is therefore likely to be surrounded by a well-entrenched structure of interests" (Dirsmith, Jablonsky, and Luzi 1980, 321). A contrast can be seen in foreign policy, which "is not nearly as laden with political overtones." But even in foreign policy, partisan politics often rules. As a memorandum prepared by the staff of a national security subcommittee of the Senate Government Operations Committee in 1967 put it, "If PPBS develops into a contest between experts and politicians . . . the winners . . . will be the politicians" (U.S. Senate 1967b, 18).

McNamara used to instruct his analytical staff, "You do the analysis, I'll do the politics." In today's leakier, more transparent government, there is greater political risk in unleashing analytic staffs to "think the unthinkable" and assess the merits of ideas that incite important internal and external opposition. Senior officials whose careers have been in politics rather than in business or academia may be reluctant to do so. Analytic staffs are nonetheless in a far better position than they were in the 1960s to assemble ideas, information, and analysis from a wide variety of external sources: think tanks, universities, consultancies, professional associations, published literature, and the media—for example, on the managerial implications of approaches to health care reform. They need to be protected in this work; but, on the other side of the coin, policy and management analysts must exhibit political awareness appropriate to their exposed roles.

8. Reforms that are oversold invite skepticism and will eventually be perceived to have failed. As already noted, PPBS was launched with inflated expectations. As they were intended to do, these expectations attracted considerable favorable attention from advocates, critics, and impartial observers. As the postmortems accumulated in the late 1960s, however, the predominant judgment was disappointment, which was often attributed to unrealistic initial expectations (Botner 1970). Protests by supporters that progress had nevertheless been made had little or no political traction, especially if that progress was at the expense of politically important interests. And it virtually guaranteed that the search for "the next big thing" was already under way.

As with lesson 6, heeding this lesson entails conundrums: How can agency deliberations be both political and analytical? How can reform initiatives be promoted both with boldness and with modesty and nuance? Such challenges are why senior federal executives earn the big bucks.

9. Reform takes time; it will begin to become meaningful in a second term at the earliest. Even if aspirations are bold and realistic, preparation is thorough, the change to be implemented is clear, and the right people are in charge, successfully implementing a reform strategy will take time. Virtually every governmental organization and program is procedurally and substantively complex. Sorting through them to identify the implications of a change strategy and working to overcome the obstacles to moving forward requires patience, steady leadership, and a human face rather than brute-force insistence on getting it done—now! The No Child Left Behind Act reforms of public education of the George W. Bush administration were still very much a work in progress over a decade later, hampered in the early stages by insensitive leadership by its champions in the Department of Education but facilitated by more adaptive leadership later on. You learn by doing.

10. To survive transitions, reforms must be institutionalized. The goals and instruments of government reform should be woven into the fabric of agency operations by being made part of the routines of existing institutions, thus establishing an internal constituency for their continuation. If lesson 3 has been heeded, much of the institutionalization will already have been accomplished. For example, if a statutory basis for the reforms has been established, it will be harder for successor administrations to undo them. Executive orders and departmental directives may also be used for this purpose, although these are more easily undone. If reforms can be undone simply by abolishing an office temporarily established to implement them, then they are probably doomed. The formalities of PPBS were doomed because all it took to undo them was the revising of OMB instructions concerning the preparation of agency budget requests. Clinton-era reforms were abruptly terminated on the day George W. Bush took office because they lacked a permanent institutional home; websites were taken down, and information was no longer available.

The compulsive government reinventer David Osborne, author with Ted Gaebler of *Reinventing Government* (1992) and other guides to government reform, offered president-elect Obama this advice early in the transition:

> Obama should define the outcomes most important to Americans—improved healthcare, better education, a cleaner environment and so on—and around each organize a team made up of strategic thinkers from OMB and the various policy councils and czars' offices. Their job would be to analyze what drives the desired outcome, to define the most effective strategies, and to rank all programs—existing and proposed—from most cost-effective to least. The President would set a spending target for each outcome and strategy and "purchase" from the top of the list. When the money ran out, he would draw a line and, with necessary adjustments for political realities, propose to eliminate programs below the line. (Osborne 2008)

It is hard to miss the same heady tone of hubris in this injunction that animated early advocates of PPBS and the same faith in rational means to set goals, analyze alternative ways to achieve them, choose the most appropriate ones, and budget for them.

Before following this or any other agenda for government reform, change agents should test them against the Lessons for Change Agents listed above. Government reformers need to be more than blossoming idealists. As well, they need to be shrewd, canny, and politically sophisticated if they are to avoid being carried off the battlefield on their shields. Doing it the right way takes more time and preparation, and people with the right skills and temperaments, but patience and forbearance have a much greater likelihood than eagerness and arrogance of being rewarded with enduring success.

Notes

1. Charles L. Schultze to the Cabinet, memorandum, June 22, 1965, box 21, LBJ Library.
2. Joseph A. Califano Jr. and Charles L. Schultze, interviews for Oral History Archives, LBJ Library.
3. Charles L. Schultze to the president, memorandum ("National Goals"), Aug. 13, 1965, box 22, LBJ Library.
4. Joe Califano to the president, memorandum, Aug. 16, 1965, box 22, LBJ Library.
5. The Plum Book (the cover is plum-colored) is a document titled *United States Government Policy and Supporting Positions*. Published after each presidential election, it lists the 7,000 or so federal government jobs not subject to competitive civil service rules.

References

Abramson, Mark A., Jonathan D. Breul, Daniel J. Chenok, John M. Kamensky, and G. Martin Wagner, eds. 2008. *Getting it done: A guide for government executives.* Lanham, Md.: Rowman and Littlefield. Published for the IBM Center for the Business of Government.

Botner, Stanley B. 1970. Four years of PPBS: An appraisal. *Public Administration Review* 30, no. 4: 423–431.

———. 1972. PPB under Nixon. *Public Administration Review* 32, no. 3: 254–255.

Breul, Jonathan D., and John M. Kamensky. 2008. Federal government reform: Lessons from Clinton's "Reinventing Government" and Bush's "Management Agenda" initiatives. *Public Administration Review* 68, no. 6: 1009–1026.

Dirsmith, Mark W., Stephen F. Jablonsky, and Andrew D. Luzi. 1980. Planning and control in the U.S. federal government: A critical analysis of PPB, MBO and ZBB. *Strategic Management Journal* 1:303–329.

Downs, George W., and Patrick D. Larkey. 1986. *The search for government efficiency: From hubris to helplessness.* New York: Random House.

Drew, Elizabeth B. 1967. HEW grapples with PPBS. *Public Interest* 8:9–29.

Enthoven, Alain C. 1966. Choosing strategies and selecting weapon systems. In Samuel A. Tucker, ed., *A modern design for defense decision: A McNamara-Hitch-Enthoven anthology.* Washington, D.C.: Industrial College of the Armed Forces.

Gorham, William. 1967. Notes of a practitioner. *Public Interest* 8:4–8.

Gross, Bertram M. 1969. The new systems budgeting. *Public Administration Review* 29, no. 2: 113–137.

Gross, Bertram M., and Michael Springer. 1967. A new orientation in American government. *Annals of the American Academy of Political and Social Science* 371, no. 1: 1–19.

Harper, Edwin L., Fred A. Kramer, and Andrew M. Rouse. 1969. Implementation and use of PPB in sixteen federal agencies. *Public Administration Review* 29, no. 6: 623–632.

Held, Virginia. 1966. PPBS comes to Washington. *Public Interest* 4 (Summer): 102–115.

Hitch, Charles J. 1967. *Decision-making for defense.* Berkeley: University of California Press.

Johnson, Lyndon B. 1965. Statement by the President to cabinet members and agency heads on the new government-wide planning and budgeting system. Aug. 25. Available at the American Presidency Project, www.presidency.ucsb .edu/ws/?pid=27182.

———. 1966. Memorandum on the need for training in modern management methods. Mar. 15. Available at the American Presidency Project, www .presidency.ucsb.edu/ws/?pid=27492.

———. 1967. Special message to the Congress: The quality of American government. Mar. 17. Available at the American Presidency Project, www.presidency .ucsb.edu/ws/?pid=28141.

Lynn, Laurence E., Jr. 1996. *Public management as art, science, and profession.* Chatham, N.J.: Chatham House.

———. 1999. A place at the table: Policy analysis, its postpositivist critics, and the future of practice. *Journal of Policy Analysis and Management* 18, no. 3: 411–425.

———. 2006. *Public management: Old and new.* New York: Routledge.

Mushkin, Selma J. 1969. PPB in cities. *Public Administration Review* 29, no. 2: 167–178.

Niskanen, William A. 1972. Why new methods of budgetary choices? Administrative aspects. *Public Administration Review* 32, no. 2: 155–161.

Novick, David. 1966. Origin and history of program budgeting. RAND Corporation Paper P-3427.

Osborne, David. 2008. Weeding the federal garden. GovernmentExecutive.com., Nov. 12. www.govexec.com/excellence/management-matters/2008/11/weeding -the-federal-garden/28025.

Rivlin, Alice M. 1971. *Systematic thinking for social action.* Washington, D.C.: The Brookings Institution.

Schick, Allen. 1966. The road to PPB: The stages of budget reform. *Public Administration Review* 26, no. 4: 243–258.

————. 1973. A death in the bureaucracy: The demise of federal PPB. *Public Administration Review* 33, no. 2 (Mar.–Apr.): 146–156.

Schultze, Charles L. 1968. *The politics and economics of public spending.* Washington, D.C.: Brookings Institution.

Shoop, Tom, Robert Brodsky, and Alyssa Rosenberg. 2008. Obama calls for an end of 20th century bureaucracy. GovernmentExecutive.com, Aug. 29. www.govexec.com/oversight/2008/08/obama-calls-for-end-of-20th-century -bureaucracy/27561.

Staats, E. B. 1968. Perspective on Planning-Programming-Budgeting. *GAO Review* (Summer): 3–12.

Time. 1966. Reading the budget for fun and profit. Feb. 18. Available by subscription at www.time.com/time/magazine/article/0,9171,899013,00.html.

U.S. General Accounting Office (USGAO). 1997. *Performance budgeting: Past initiatives offer insights for GPRA implementation.* GAO/AIMD-97-46. Washington, D.C.: Government Printing Office.

U.S. Senate. 1967a. *Planning-Programming-Budgeting: Hearings before the Subcommittee on National Security and International Operations of the Committee on Government Operations,* part 1. 90th Cong., 1st sess.

————. 1967b. *Planning-Programming-Budgeting: Initial Memorandum; Hearings before the Subcommittee on National Security and International Operations of the Committee on Government Operations, part 1.* 90th Cong., 1st sess., Aug. 23.

Williams, Walter. 1971. *Social policy research and analysis: The experience in the federal social agencies.* New York: American Elsevier.

Yates, Douglas T., Jr. 1977. The mission of public policy programs: A report on recent experience. *Policy Sciences* 8:363–373.

CHAPTER 14

Constructing Effectiveness: The Emergence of the Evaluation Research Industry

PETER FRUMKIN AND KIMBERLY FRANCIS

Today, evaluation research is a multibillion-dollar industry focused on answering some variation on the seemingly simple question: "Did the program work?" Over more than four decades, owing to the impetus provided by the administration of Lyndon Johnson, efforts to address this enormously complex question have led to a limited set of large and successful firms—and a massive array of smaller and specialized firms—that collectively employ a large number of trained experts who spend entire careers searching for evidence of impact and effectiveness. This chapter sketches a brief interpretive history of the evaluation industry, tracking the emergence and expansion of the largest and most visible organizational manifestations of the drive to track effectiveness. The intent is not to create a historical narrative that encompasses all the many actors in this long and intricate story line, but rather to pull out selected moments in the emergence of an increasingly unified and organized field.

Government Programs and the Creation of a New Industry

On the fiftieth anniversary of the Brookings Institution, President Johnson made the following statement:

> So we have seen, in our time, two aspects of intellectual power brought to bear on our Nation's problems: the power to create, to discover and propose new remedies for what ails us; and the power then to administer complex programs in a rational way. But there is a third aspect of intellectual power that our country urgently needs tonight, and in my judgment it is being supplied sparingly. It is less glamorous . . . It is less visible and less publicized. . . . But it is not a bit less critical to the success or to the failure that

we may make in the years that are ahead of us. This is the power to evaluate. (Johnson 1966)

At the time, program evaluation was in its infancy as a professional field. New legislation authorizing evaluation set-asides and policies within the executive branch mandating policy and program analyses led to a surge in demand for evaluation research during the latter half of the 1960s and throughout the 1970s. Answering the call were hundreds of contract research and evaluation organizations that had either diversified into a new market or had just recently been formed.

The most important public policy pressure was the dramatic increase in social spending associated with Johnson's Great Society initiatives, exemplified by the Economic Opportunity Act in 1964, as well as the Elementary and Secondary Education Act (ESEA) and the Social Security Amendments, both in 1965. Social welfare spending totaled just over $77 billion in 1965, increasing to almost $146 billion by 1970, $290 billion by 1975, and $493 billion by 1980 (Haveman 1987). In another example, for a period of time in 1973, the $110 billion budget of the Department of Health, Education and Welfare (HEW) was larger than that of the Department of Defense (Staats 1973). Along with these unprecedented increases in public spending on social programs came a keen interest, motivated in part by the administration's need to demonstrate budgetary discipline and avoid the need for tax increases, in determining which innovative programs were the most effective, sparking a "gold rush" of large-scale quantitative evaluations (House 1990; M. Rossi and Wright 1984). Over time, as federal budget resources became scarce and disillusionment with the effectiveness of social programs grew, accountability, cost-effectiveness, and evaluation became even more critical to the social policy enterprise (Schick 1971; Shadish, Cook, and Leviton 1991).

Several important events occurring in the federal government in 1965 and 1966 signaled the birth of modern program evaluation: President Johnson issued an executive order to implement the Planning-Programming-Budgeting-System (PPBS), then in use at the Department of Defense, throughout the agencies of the executive branch (see chapter 13 this volume); the Office of Economic Opportunity (OEO) launched several national antipoverty programs, funded thirteen evaluations of Head Start, and sponsored the creation of the Institute for Research on Poverty at the University of Wisconsin; and the Office of the Assistant Secretary for Planning and Evaluation (ASPE) was established within HEW, and Title 1 of the ESEA included an evaluation reporting requirement, the first major social legislation to do so. While there doubtless have been many other signal moments in government's embrace of evaluation, we focus on these three events because they contributed in ways that almost all the early leaders of the program evaluation field we interviewed argued were critical to the creation of a new evaluation industry.

PPBS

A keystone of the "analytic revolution" in government (O'Connor 2001), PPBS gave President Johnson a way to centralize control of the major nationwide antipoverty programs, which were receiving weak political support at the local level (Jardini 1996). It brought a rational decision-making model to the agencies administering these programs, especially the OEO and HEW, and primed agency staffs and legislators to begin thinking in evaluative terms. Rooted in military operations research and the systems analysis framework developed by RAND in the 1950s, PPBS was a management tool that required all agencies to define their program objectives, project the costs of alternative ways to attain these objectives, and improve performance by achieving the highest benefit for the lowest cost (Staats 1968; Held 1966).

While PPBS helped move the federal government toward a more analytical approach to program planning and resource allocation, its inherent complexity eventually became too cumbersome for practical implementation across the agencies (Weiss 1972). Moreover, the system was designed primarily to improve efficiency in the military—cost and benefit projections of alternative courses of action toward defined military strategies and capabilities (for example, which weapons system is the most cost-effective at destroying a particular target). Newly minted social policy analysts struggled to define criteria by which to measure the effectiveness of social programs (Staats 1970; O'Connor 2001; Wholey et al. 1970), and suffered from a lack of available data on which to draw (Gorham 1967; Weiss 1972).

Interest in PPBS eventually flagged, and Johnson's management innovation was abandoned in 1971. But the government-wide mandate had two important by-products. First, it boosted demand for systematic data and skilled analysts to perform program evaluations, who at the time were principally found in the Department of Defense and RAND (O'Connor 2001). Second, it set in motion the idea that evaluation and analysis are necessary components of any legitimate social policy design and implementation process.

Office of Economic Opportunity

As PPBS was spreading, albeit fitfully, throughout the executive branch, the OEO was breaking new evaluation ground with its antipoverty programs. The original Economic Opportunity Act of 1964 did not specifically mandate program evaluation, but was sufficiently broad to allow for evaluation funding at about 1 percent of program funds (Wholey et al. 1970). In large part because of its financial resources and staff designated for evaluation, the Office of Research, Plans, Programs and Evaluation (ORPPE) was an early leader in federal program evaluation. An Urban Institute review of the evaluation practices of four federal agencies described the OEO as having a more highly developed evaluation system than HEW or HUD. Not surprisingly, the other agencies were considered to be "grossly underfunded" for evaluation (Wholey et al. 1970). In the late 1960s and early 1970s, the ORPPE engaged in ambitious evaluations of Head Start, Follow Through, Upward Bound, VISTA, the Job Corps, and Neighborhood Health Centers, as well as the first large-scale social experiment of the era, the negative income tax experiments. The unfavorable results of the Westinghouse national evaluation of Head Start served as a controversial introduction to assessment for the OEO, but did not quell the executive branch's interest in expanding its evaluation capacity (O'Connor 2001).

By the close of the 1960s most federal agencies had planning and evaluation departments to coordinate the evaluations that were required by most social policy legislation. One estimate found that 800 policy analysts were working across sixteen domestic policy research agencies within the government at this time (J. Smith 1991). Nonetheless, staffing was sparse because of remaining funding barriers and the challenge of recruiting skilled researchers to federal evaluation positions at the time (Shadish, Cook, and Leviton 1991; Wholey et al. 1970). Facing an enormous demand for evaluation research connected to new public programs, coupled with limited in-house capacity, federal evaluation offices looked outside of government to contract research firms as a way of quickly augmenting their operational capacity. An estimated 500 percent increase in federal expenditures on evaluation occurred between 1969 and 1974, with about 60 percent of the 1974 expenditures going toward contract research alone (Rein and White 1977).

Among the beneficiaries of these new federal dollars were the entrepreneurs who developed research organizations to serve the growing appetite for social research and evaluation. In 1970, there were an estimated 300 firms (both for-profit and nonprofit) qualified to receive requests for proposals from the OEO (Wholey et al. 1970). Some of these firms predated the advent of modern program evaluation in the mid-1960s, such as RAND, Westat, and the American Institutes for Research (AIR), and some were initiated in response to or anticipation of the new market. For existing government contractors working in allied research fields, the increased demand for program evaluation in the federal sphere provided an opportunity to diversify and strengthen their industry.

A couple of years before President Johnson's 1966 address to the Brookings Institution, Clark Abt assembled an interdisciplinary collaborative of social scientists and engineers in Cambridge, Massachusetts, to begin offering planning, research, and evaluation services to federal government programs. Abt's training and experience were rooted in the defense research industry and the tools of systems analysis and cost-benefit analysis—indeed, Abt Associates' first contract was to design a game for the Department of Defense to teach counterinsurgency strategy to military trainees—but during his years at the defense contractor Raytheon, he had seen the opportunity to apply those analytical skills to examining and solving problems in education, housing, and social welfare. Abt's interest in instructional game design led to further contracts for elementary school educational games, and the eventual publication of *Serious Games* (Abt 1970), which argued that simulations could be used to guide decision making in the business, government, and education sectors.

In the late 1960s, the OEO asked Abt Associates to evaluate several of its War on Poverty programs, and in 1972 the company began its first large-scale social experiment for HUD—the Housing Allowance Demand Experiment. Also in 1972, Abt Associates took over from the Stanford Research Institute the responsibility for the national evaluation of Follow Through, a massive educational experiment aimed at finding ways to break the cycle of poverty through better education. Follow Through started in 1967 as part of President Johnson's War on Poverty and lasted almost two decades, costing hundreds of millions of dollars.

The intent of agencies administering antipoverty programs was to break the cycle of poverty through better education. Poor academic performance was known to correlate directly with poverty. Poor education then led to less economic opportunity for children of poverty when they became adults, thus maintaining the cycle of poverty for another generation. Follow Through planned to evaluate whether the poorest schools in America, both economically and academically impoverished, could be brought up to a level comparable with those in mainstream America. The actual achievement of the children would be used to determine success. By this time, Abt Associates was well on its way to becoming one of the top-performing contract re-

Fig. 14.1. Abt Associates, annual revenue, 1966–2004

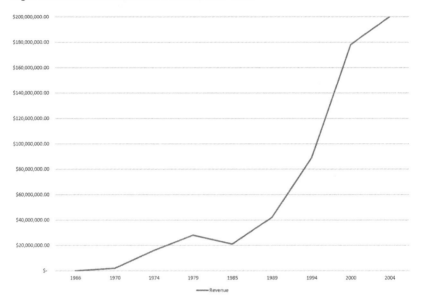

Source: Abt Associates (2006), http.//abtassociates.com, but data no longer available online.

search firms for the federal government, specializing in social and economic programs (see figure 14.1). Its early work on these education programs allowed it to build its practice on the national scene and develop the capacity to carry out very large projects.

While several of the large-scale early evaluations were taking place under the direction of the executive branch for the purposes of finding out what worked and how program implementation might be improved, conservatives were interested in using evaluation to find out which programs did not work and could be terminated. As a senior executive at Abt Associates put it: "Conservatives like Nixon after his 1968 victory wanted to save money on social programs by evaluating their ineffectiveness and cutting away what they felt was liberal waste, and liberals wanted to do just the opposite, to prove that the social programs were having some productive effect" (personal communication with the author). Evaluation research—while in principle operating independently of politics—was thus seen by some early on as a potentially powerful instrument of policy change. As a way to drive the behavior of policy makers, evidence of program failure could prove to be as potent as, or even more potent than, evidence of impact.

The performance of Johnson's antipoverty programs came under congressional scrutiny in 1967, and the hearings surrounding the reauthorization of the Economic Opportunity Act resulted in the passage of the so-called Prouty Amendment, named for Senator Winston Prouty (R-VT). This legislation required the General Accounting Office (GAO) to review the effectiveness of several antipoverty programs and the rigor of the evaluations administered by the OEO (Sperry et al. 1981). The subsequent favorable review of the OEO's evaluation practices in 1969 further legitimated and justified expanded funding for program evaluation (O'Connor 2001), and this requirement became an essential element in most social program legislation of the period.

Aside from spurring the development of evaluation start-up firms, new evaluation legislation bolstered the organizations in existence well before the drastic increase in domestic spending on them. Once such firm was Westat, a statistical and survey research consulting firm that became involved in a national evaluation of day care for the OEO in 1970. Westat emerged in 1961 as a partnership between three statisticians from the University of Wyoming: Edward C. Bryant, who was chair of the statistics department at the time, and Donald W. King and James Daley, both of whom had graduated from Wyoming with master's degrees in statistics in 1960. In 1961, both King and Daley were looking for jobs, and Bryant was leaving his academic post for health reasons. Daley, aware of Bryant's health constraints, suggested forming a consulting company to serve the statistical needs of government, business, and industry. The idea appealed to Bryant, and with the addition of King, the three formed the partnership that became Westat (Bryant 1981). Morris Hansen, a Wyoming graduate and survey statistics pioneer from the U.S. Census Bureau, later joined as senior vice president in 1968.

Primarily a statistical consulting firm (rather than a social science or defense consulting firm), Westat's first projects included expert testimony in a lawsuit about the value of a uranium mine, quality control of crushed rock for a construction company, an assessment of the efficiency of the use of live animals in research for the Humane Society of the United States, and the first Westat survey, which focused on eighty customers of a bank in Golden, Colorado. In 1962, Westat was awarded its first major contract, which helped establish the firm as a major federal contractor: a five-year project to help the U.S. Patent Office improve information retrieval processes. In the late 1960s, Westat's leadership decided that adding survey research expertise to its statistical capabilities would increase the firm's marketability (Bryant 1981), since by then more large-scale social program

Fig. 14.2. Westat, annual revenue, 1961–1980

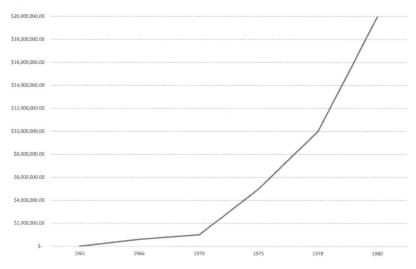

Source: Bryant 1981.

evaluations were taking shape across the federal landscape. Westat's early survey work included the national survey of day care for the Westinghouse Learning Corporation (under an OEO contract) and a two-year longitudinal evaluation of the Public Employment Program for the Department of Labor (DOL). From 1970 to 1980, Westat grew from $1 million in revenue to $20 million (see figure 14.2). Westat now provides a wide range of research and evaluation services in the areas of health, clinical trials, social services, employment/national service, housing, education, substance use, energy and environment, science and technology, transportation, military human resources, and marketing research. Revenue in 2006 was in excess of $425 million.

The Department of Health, Education and Welfare and Title I of the ESEA

HEW progressively became involved in evaluation. The Office of the Assistant Secretary for Planning and Evaluation (ASPE) was created in 1965, primarily to coordinate the implementation of PPBS throughout the agency, and William Gorham, a former RAND and Defense Department analyst, was brought in to head the effort (two years later he became the founding president of the Urban Institute). He soon found that the areas of health, education, and welfare suffered from a profound lack of data suitable for evaluation and the cost-benefit analyses of PPBS. That same year, Gorham recommended to Charles Schultze, Bureau of the Budget director, that 1 percent of all appropriations to HEW be designated for program evaluation (Gorham, personal communication, 2007). This suggestion eventually became law in 1967 and 1968 through eleven pieces of legislation, though in practice evaluation funding in the DOL, HEW, the OEO, and HUD averaged about 0.4 percent of program funds in 1969 (Wholey et al. 1970). One of the ASPE's tasks was to oversee the landmark evaluation mandate of Title I of the ESEA. Originally pushed by Senator Robert Kennedy as a way for local schools to be accountable to parents and communities for how the money was used, the ASPE saw the evaluation requirement as an opportunity to test different education strategies targeted to disadvantaged children by using the input-output model of the PPBS (McLaughlin 1975). Either way, this was an example of direct institutional pressure helping create an industry. HEW enlisted the services of AIR to write case studies of effective Title I programs and to review the evaluation reporting practices over the seven-year period 1965–1972.

AIR was a product of the post–World War II research boom that also produced RAND and the Stanford Research Institute. After John C. Flanagan, an industrial psychologist for the U.S. Army Air Corps in World War II, joined the psychology department at the University of Pittsburgh, he started AIR to focus on workforce, personnel, and education research, which are still emphasized by the firm today. Previously, Flanagan had developed aptitude tests for the Aviation Psychology Program by using the "critical incident technique" to evaluate Army Air Corps candidates (*University Times* 1996).

AIR's first major educational research effort came in 1957 with Project TALENT, a longitudinal survey of high school students that measured the aptitudes and interests of a national sample of 440,000 students. The database became a national resource for improving education through vocational guidance and curriculum development (*AIR News* 2007). In the 1970s, AIR leveraged its expertise in educational evaluation and began conducting evaluations of domestic social programs, including delinquency prevention programs for the Office of Juvenile Justice and Delinquency Prevention in 1976. Currently, one of AIR's high-profile contracts is to support the National Center for Education Statistics for the U.S. Department of Education.

The initial attempt to mandate evaluation reporting from the school districts receiving Title I funding was unsuccessful, for reasons chronicled in other studies (McLaughlin 1975). These included the incompatibility of the cost-benefit evaluation design with the messy reality of school systems, the guarded resistance of school administrators to collecting the data needed by the ASPE, and the resultant lack of usable information for management or accountability. Despite the dismal implementation of the ESEA's evaluation activities, federal agencies proceeded to engage in even more evaluation: "Information gathering has become a necessary activity (qua activity) in the policy system, and faith in the science of systems analysis remains undiminished at the higher echelons of the federal government" (118). An almost ritualistic and unreflective embrace of the idea of evaluation (later identified by Carol Weiss [1972] as "symbolic" evaluation) seems to have helped perpetuate the early diffusion of a culture of evaluation, no matter whether the state of practice remained imperfect (Meyer and Rowan 1991). The culture of evaluation, which had been present in Washington for years, related easily to the early needs of HEW.

The Urban Institute is an example of an industry stalwart that did not emerge to meet government contracting trends or to seize a new market. Rather it was formed directly and consciously by government interests. The idea for an urban research institute started with President Johnson's 1964 Task Force on Cities, which recommended a "national Institute of Urban Development" to be part of a cabinet-level Department of Housing and Urban Development (Bassett 1969). Three years later, in the context of the proliferation of somewhat uncoordinated Great Society programs and a tightening domestic budget, President Johnson's White House staff began to plan the new institute, but as an entity separate from any federal agency (J. Smith 1991). Special assistant to the president Joseph Califano cited two problems that jump-started the planning process for the new research institute: a severe lack of data appropriate for policy decision making, and the lack of objective program analysis and evaluation. In one example, Califano found that no one within HEW could tell him who was receiving welfare benefits except that it was approximately 7.3 percent of the population (Bassett 1969).

The plan was to create a nonprofit research institution that could provide nonpartisan analysis of the nation's urban problems and use these data to advise the government on appropriate programs and policies. Initial start-up funds were provided primarily by HUD and the Ford Foundation, with additional contributions from the DOL, Department of Transportation, HEW, and the OEO. The model for this institute was RAND, a think tank designed to serve the exclusive research needs of the Defense Department until it started to diversify into domestic research in the late 1960s (Bassett 1969; Hayes and Japha 1978; J. Smith 1991). In fact, RAND tried for a year to land the federal contract to locate the Urban Institute within its purview (Jardini 1996). The Urban Institute was organized differently from the RAND model, which had started off focused on the needs of the air force. The Urban Institute would serve any federal agency involved in urban programs—not just HUD. Its first major project was to examine how four government agencies (HUD, the OEO, HEW, and the DOL) evaluated the social programs they sponsored, culminating in the classic study by Wholey (1970) and his associates, *Federal Evaluation Policy: Analyzing the Effects of Public Programs.* Other milestones included the design of a major social experiment, the Experimental Housing Allowance Program, and the development of computer models to simulate how changes in food stamp and welfare programs would affect family incomes.

The environment in Washington was not stable. With the Nixon administration in 1969 came greater control over the research activities of contractors. The funding relationship with HUD survived in part because the contract was amended to give HUD the authority to determine the research projects to be included under it. The unrestricted funds that were briefly enjoyed by the Urban Institute were no more, though staff members were still able to propose research ideas to HUD (Hayes and Japha 1978). Overall, this move to add controls to the nascent evaluation field further consolidated the industry. Research organizations soon conformed to and mirrored the standards and practices of governmental funders at HEW, HUD, and the DOL   on whom all the early players were dependent for financial support. The power to control funding and to define projects was crucial to the establishment of a new industry that would be independent of government but responsive to its needs.

By the 1980s, funding for the Urban Institute shifted away from an exclusive focus on federal grants and contracts and began to include more foundation funding (J. Smith 1991). Over time, the Urban Institute turned into a multidimensional policy research institute working on a wide array of projects and funded by an equally diverse array of clients. The institute was obliged to find a way to enhance its viability and diversify its revenue mix in the face of declining federal resources in the 1980s. This move also reduced the level of government influence on its organizational focus, structure, and activities. Figure 14.3 shows revenue growth during this period of diversification and expansion, from $10 million in the 1980s to $80 million twenty years later.

Fig. 14.3. Urban Institute, annual revenue/expenditures, 1968–2006

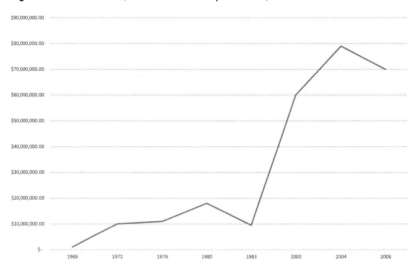

Sources: Bovberg 1983 and Hayes and Japha 1978. Data from 1983 to 1996 are missing.

The Urban Institute's chosen path aside, in the nascent stages of the evaluation field, and for several firms and institutes, contract research and evaluation firms were heavily dependent on the same sources of federal government evaluation dollars, mainly from HEW, the OEO, and HUD. What we know about organizational fields (DiMaggio and Powell 1991) suggests that this placed pressure on competing firms to offer similar services and to structure themselves in similar ways in order to respond to industry standards expected by federal funders. As one CEO of a leading federal evaluation firm confirmed: "The dominant clients of most of the key players . . . are either federal government, state and local governments . . . Those clients have requirements, have modes of doing business, have expectations that all of the players have to be responsive to. And so you get lots of similarities [among firms] driven primarily by client requirements, client behaviors, client characteristics" (personal communication with the author). In this way, the state can consciously or unconsciously shape industry standards by asking for certain approaches and methods of evaluation, as well as determining what is to be evaluated.

The Nixon administration eventually dismantled the OEO, and most of its programs were absorbed into existing bureaucracies at HEW, HUD, and the DOL. Social spending, including program evaluation and applied social research, continued to increase until 1981, when the Reagan administration drastically cut many of the programs built over the preceding twenty years. The evaluation industry, as illustrated by the emergence of several contract research firms and the Urban Institute, matured in the context of governmental pressures and constraints in the form of funding mandates and the expectations of a new federal evaluation culture. We argue that these "coercive" pressures acted on the industry to create a loosely consolidated field.

Diffusion of Existing Evaluation Models

Rapidly unfolding legislative change in the 1960s led to a period of uncertainty surrounding the new evaluation mandates. The uncertainty reflected the growing expectations for data-driven decision making throughout government, coupled with a social policy arena that had little or no capacity to carry this out.

One response to institutional conditions marked by ambiguous goals and a lack of specific technical expertise is to look at what had been successful in neighboring organizational sectors, and to adopt or adapt those models in the new setting (DiMaggio and Powell 1991). President Johnson's executive order for widespread implementation of PPBS is an example of this sort of response; a tried and tested management system that had worked well for the DoD was a logical next step for HEW and other agencies. Soon, analysts who had been trained to evaluate the efficiency and effectiveness of military programs were being asked to apply evaluation and cost-benefit analysis to social programs, whose outcomes were more difficult to operationalize. RAND made its first overture into nondefense research in 1958 with a $35,000 Ford Foundation study to assess the applicability of systems analysis to elementary and secondary education. Two years later, Ford paid RAND $500,000 for a three-year analysis of urban transportation systems. Then, with the widespread implementation of PPBS throughout the executive branch in 1965, RAND analysts were in high demand in the social policy arena.

Though RAND lost a yearlong battle to house the Urban Institute, the New York City–based RAND Institute was established in 1968 with help from the Ford Foundation. It became a springboard for RAND's diversification into social policy research (Jardini 1996). Throughout the 1970s, RAND's income from the domestic policy arena grew to equal its income from defense concerns; but the political climate of the 1980s reversed this

Fig. 14.4. RAND, annual revenue, 1970–2006

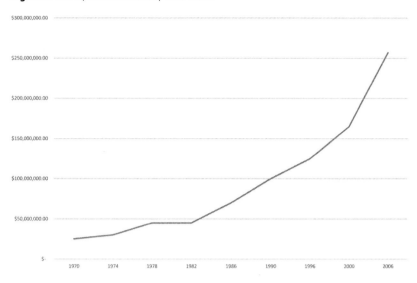

Source: RAND Annual Reports, 1970–2006.

trend, and social policy research shrank to about 20 percent of RAND's to-tal revenue (RAND annual reports, 1970–1990). Overall, RAND's income grew to over $250 million in 2006 (see figure 14.4).

The story of RAND's diversification into social research underscores the influence of a changing policy environment on the evolution of the evaluation industry. In response both to the government's need for management tools and RAND's need to generate income and remain competitive, RAND replicated its innovative systems-analysis approach to management in the uncharted waters of health, education, and welfare administration. In this way, diversifying into new policy sectors was at once an innovative and a mimetic response to an uncertain contracting environment, where sole dependence on defense resources was no longer viable.

The Research Triangle Institute (RTI), a contract research and development institute founded in 1959, had a similar experience. The institute was grounded in chemistry, physics, statistics, engineering, semiconductors, and civil defense research, but the late 1960s brought a profound shift in its research docket. From 1966 to 1969, RTI's revenue from the health, education, population, environment, and transportation sectors rose from 21 percent to 65 percent of the total (Larrabee 1991). This growth coincided with RTI's desire to double the size of the institute in five years (Larrabee 1991) and reflected the changing research priorities of the federal government and private industry.

Another example of diffusion within the industry is the practice of modeling new research institutes, firms, and departments after existing prototypes. As mentioned above, RAND was offered as a prototype for the Urban Institute, though the latter's founders were quite clear about how the two differed (Hayes and Japha 1978). Before that, the Stanford Research Institute (now known as SRI International), one of the first research and development institutes founded after World War II, was a model for RTI. SRI was explicitly mentioned in a 1959 memorandum from the vice president of Duke University announcing the establishment of RTI: "It will be similar to Stanford Research Institute in California, Southern Research Institute in Birmingham, Armour Research Institute Foundation in Chicago and several others" (quoted in Larrabee 1991).

Incidentally, SRI's eventual diversification of its research activities followed a similar course to the one taken by RTI and RAND, starting with a six-year national evaluation of Follow Through for the OEO. While the majority of SRI's current revenue still comes from the Department of Defense (data from www.sri.com), it is also known for its contributions to education research and evaluation.

The ASPE office and the OEO's ORPPE were conceived as replicas of the offices within the DoD that had parallel functions (Haveman 1987). "McNamarism" was not just a new way of planning and assessing programs, but also affected the way new departments were envisioned and organized. The ORPPE attracted early champions of systems analysis, including the economist Joseph Kershaw, who coauthored a RAND publication on systems analysis in 1959, became provost at Williams College in 1962, and then the first director of the ORPPE. Robert Levine, also of RAND, succeeded Kershaw at the OEO. And Sargent Shriver, director of the OEO, reportedly wanted the ORPPE to mimic the Systems Analysis Office at McNamara's Department of Defense: "Systems analysis had the reputation at the time of being *the* solution to all planning and some administrative ills, and Shriver wanted some of that" (Levine 1970, 59).

So far we have seen two examples of how existing cost-benefit management techniques and organizational forms were diffused throughout the emerging evaluation landscape. But the Department of Defense and its attendant contracting industry were not the only exemplars; the field also adopted the social experiment, at the time a leading-edge methodology practiced in several social science disciplines.

The Age of Social Experiments

The use of random assignment and control groups dates back to the early 1900s, when psychologists such as Edward Thorndike conducted educational experiments and the sociologist F. Stuart Chapin studied issues like the effect of public housing and programs for delinquent boys (Oakley 1998). The watershed moment linking this established social science tradition with the evaluation field was the publication of D. T. Campbell and J. C. Stanley's *Experimental and Quasi-experimental Designs for Research* (1963). Campbell and Stanley provided a framework that explicitly linked social research with applied settings at a time when social policy makers were uncertain about how to effectively design interventions for social problems (Haveman 1987). Campbell's vision of the "experimenting society" converged with this uncertain context and produced the golden age of social experiments (Campbell 1969; Oakley 1998; M. Rossi and Wright 1984).

Though scattered social experiments were conducted before the 1960s, social policy evaluators in the late 1960s adopted the experimental design during a period of uncertainty surrounding how best to conduct an evaluation. According to the CEO of a large evaluation firm: "I think very clearly, obviously there was a point in time in which the experience base was not very deep, and so it had to evolve. And I think that firms like Abt and Mathematica and a few of the others that place a lot of emphasis on sophisticated applications of these analytical tools and data collection tools . . . helped to develop the field" (personal communication with the author). The founder of a large evaluation firm echoed these sentiments: "There were few existing research models to draw upon for evaluation designs, but a few of us were widely read and accessed social scientists and learned about the applications of experimental designs in agricultural field experiments and medical drug clinical trials and testing" (personal communication with the author).

In this environment of intense political interest (both liberal and conservative) in the outcomes of the War on Poverty, key antipoverty programs were repeatedly evaluated, though the assessments were not able to provide conclusive evidence of their effectiveness or ineffectiveness. The impetus for experimental evaluations of social policy came from the social sciences, specifically economics, and they were adopted first by the OEO and later by HUD and the DOL. The first large-scale social experiment in the Great Society era usually is taken to be the negative income tax (NIT) experiments (Greenberg, Shroder, and Onstott 1999; M. Rossi and Wright 1984). These experiments began as a dissertation-funding proposal by Heather

Ross, an MIT graduate student, who wanted to know whether guaranteed income payments to low-income families would result in a work disincentive (Greenberg, Shroder, and Onstott 1999). The OEO accepted the idea and turned it into four large experiments spanning six years.[1]

About two years before the first income-maintenance experiment, the OEO had seen an immediate need for a pool of researchers that would focus exclusively on poverty (Haveman 1987). The Institute for Research on Poverty at the University of Wisconsin was established in 1966, and one of its first projects was the design and analysis of the first two NIT experiments (Haveman 1987). Mathematica Policy Research, at the time a fledgling department within a mathematical consulting firm in Princeton, New Jersey, was chosen to collect and analyze data from the NIT experiments.

Mathematica, Inc. was founded in 1959 as a division of the Market Research Corporation of America by the Princeton economist Oskar Morgenstern and several of his university colleagues, including Tibor Fabian, who joined in 1961. Mathematica, Inc. specialized in constructing mathematical models, performing cost-benefit analyses, and using computers to help solve economic problems. Its initial projects were wide ranging, including several for the Department of Defense, development of the lottery system for the State of New Jersey, and cost-benefit analyses of a transportation corridor, the performing arts, and the space shuttle program.

The Institute for Research on Poverty decided on New Jersey as the site of the first NIT experiment because the welfare laws in that state were conducive to a control-group design. That led to the need for an organization in New Jersey to manage the random assignment, data collection, and income payments. The subcontract was given to a newly formed division of Mathematica, called the Urban Opinion Surveys Group. In 1975, the division was incorporated as Mathematica Policy Research, becoming an independent company in 1986. MPR was involved in several seminal social experiments from the late 1960s through the 1970s; it is one of the "big three" evaluation firms that dominate the social experiment market today (Greenberg, Shroder, and Onstott 1999).

Another landmark social experiment, the National Supported Work Demonstration, was launched in 1974 by the newly formed Manpower Demonstration Research Corporation (MDRC). Supported Work was a demonstration project aimed at increasing the employability of former offenders, out-of-school youth, substance abusers, and longtime public assistance recipients. MDRC was formed in New York City for the express purpose of centralizing management of the experiment; it was a collaborative nonprofit venture of the Ford Foundation and the U.S. Departments of Labor (Manpower Administration), HEW, Justice, HUD, and the Special Action Office for Drug Abuse Prevention. Some of MDRC's founders envisioned that if successful at this first task, the organization could manage future demonstrations as well and ultimately build a body of evidence on the effectiveness of antipoverty programs (Brecher 1978). The Ford Foundation prompted the idea for the national demonstration as an extension of a New York City–supported work program that had been operated by the Vera Institute of Justice since 1969.

In 1973, Mitchell Sviridoff, the Ford Foundation's vice president for national affairs, sought advice about the potential project from Eli Ginzberg, a manpower expert at Columbia University's Graduate School of Business. Ginzberg was supportive and agreed to provide research advice. By framing the project as a research-and-development effort, Sviridoff hoped to avoid the mistakes of Head Start, widely seen as having expanded prematurely (Brecher 1978). With $6 million for the first year of a five-year effort, MDRC contracted with Mathematica Policy Research and the Institute for Research on Poverty to design, collect, and analyze the evaluation data. The other bidders were an Urban Institute/Westat team and a RAND/National Opinion Research Center team (Brecher 1978).

Shortly after launching the Supported Work project, MDRC began the National Tenant Management Demonstration Program at the request of the Ford Foundation and HUD. Brecher (1978) recounts that after some initial concern that the new project would interfere with the Supported Work demonstration, the MDRC board agreed to take it on by expanding staff and promising that it would be separated from MDRC if it interfered. This action marked the evolution of MDRC into a "general purpose research and development corporation, likely to prove long-lived and likely . . . to tackle other social issues . . . arising along the borders between the governmental and the private nonprofit sectors of the American economy" (Brecher 1978, 83).

The above examples, while illustrating the application of the social science model of randomized experiments to evaluation questions, also reveal how evaluation firms and institutes were both competitors and collaborators from very early on in the life of the industry. Collaboration among research and evaluation firms and institutes is routine. Other high-profile joint projects from the early years include the Westinghouse and Westat day care study of 1970, and the RAND/Mathematica health insurance experiment of 1972. A preliminary scan of the websites of some of today's largest evaluation organizations reveals many more examples of recent collaborations:

Westat subcontracted to Abt Associates for the design of a web survey for mental health outpatient program staff; the Urban Institute hired Abt Associates to implement a survey of public housing residents; Mathematica Policy Research subcontracted with the Urban Institute to help evaluate children's health insurance programs, and with MDRC to assist with the evaluation of disability programs for youth; and Abt Associates and MDRC are leading the evaluation of the Reading First Program for the U.S. Department of Education. Firms embark on joint projects neither one alone has the capacity needed to win a particular contract. Thus, the need to partner with other firms is determined by the scope of a project, which is in turn controlled by the client (in this case, federal government). In this way, government clients further consolidate the evaluation industry by creating requests for proposals and scopes of work that require the collaboration of competing firms. Collaborative projects between competing firms help generate the context in which professional network ties are forged, cementing an interdependence within the industry. Collectively, these network ties provide the backdrop for the development of professional norms.

Professional Networks and the Search for Legitimacy

The interdependence born out of the experience with collaboration on joint projects reinforces growing peer networks in the field, which contribute to the overall professionalization of the industry. Peer networks no doubt influence hiring practices, as seen in the common strategy of firms hiring personnel from each other's ranks. The CEO of a major evaluation firm explained the rationale for the practice: "You've got a thriving private-sector research community but with a limited number of firms. And if you need to develop additional senior people and more rapidly than you can grow them yourself, you've got to get them from somewhere . . . If you need particular talents, your competitors are the most fertile place to get them" (personal communication with the author). From the firm's perspective, the motivation for hiring from a competitor is the simple need for expertise not found in-house. Many organizations within an industry collectively engaging in this practice, which results in the filtering of personnel (DiMaggio and Powell 1991). Filtering happens when firms look for similar attributes in hiring and promoting staff, and then hire from within the same industry and handful of graduate programs in economics, public policy, and sociology. This practice results in senior staff members who "tend to view problems in a similar fashion . . . and approach decisions in much the same way" (DiMaggio and Powell 1991, 72), and at the field level, an industry made up of organizations that are more similar than they are different.

A cursory review of recent announcements at Abt Associates provides several examples. At the senior level, Abt Associates hired a vice president with ten years of experience at RAND, a senior associate whose career moves included RAND and the COSMOS Corporation, a principal associate who left Abt in 1996 to work at the Urban Institute and was rehired in 2005, a principal associate who had been at RTI for twenty-nine years, and a senior vice president with twenty-six years of experience at RTI and the National Opinion Research Center (NORC). Similarly, the Urban Institute in 2002 hired a former Abt Associates vice president and RAND researcher to direct its Justice Policy Center.

For these personnel transitions to work, it helps for firms to be organizationally and technically similar. If unique firms tend to converge as a result of pursuing similar projects from a handful of federal funders, this also facilitates the flow of personnel across the industry. The tendency for larger firms to resemble one another structurally (for example, for staff members to follow similar career paths and have similar job titles) reinforces their ability to network and collaborate on joint projects.

Professional Associations and the Maturation of a Field

The professionalization of evaluation has been a perennial topic for evaluators (Bickman 1997; Conner and Dickman 1979; Flaherty and Morell 1978; Freeman and Solomon 1979; Morell and Flaherty 1978; Morell 1990; M. Smith 2001). Peer networks support the development of professional associations and the subsequent development of standards, norms, and ethical codes. The establishment of professional associations is a key marker in the professionalization process. In the evaluation field, three associations began about ten years after the evaluation "boom": the Evaluation Network (E-Net), the Council for Applied Social Research, and the Evaluation Research Society (ERS).

E-Net was founded in 1974 "to bring together individuals dedicated to improving theories, practices, programs, and education in evaluation" (*Evaluation News* 1981). Of the two or three associations at the time, E-Net catered more to evaluators who worked on local school and health systems evaluation (Datta 2004). Clark Abt organized the Council for Applied Social Research in the early 1970s, with the intent to connect top quantitative social scientists and the most competitive research organizations, such as Mathematica Policy Research, RAND, RTI, Westat, SRI, and NORC, with officials from the Office of Management and Budget, the Office of Education, the DOL, HUD, and HEW. These evaluators were involved in large-scale evaluations of federal programs, but most federal programs were not being evaluated at the time. The hope was to take stock of what had been learned from evaluation studies thus far and to promote more widespread use of sophisticated quantitative evaluation techniques (Abt 1976).

According to an oral history interview with Lois-ellin Datta, Marcia Guttentag organized the ERS in 1976 as an alternative to the Council for Applied Research that would pay more attention to developing a diverse membership (Datta 2004). In 1981, a merger between the ERS and the Council for Applied Social Research was approved (*Evaluation News* 1981). ERS and E-Net merged in 1986 under the name American Evaluation Association (AEA).

The consolidation of the professional associations occurred during a time of slow growth in the federal evaluation industry, when the Reagan administration cut back many social programs and their attendant evaluation efforts. So as the federal funding forces that had jump-started the industry weakened, normative and professional forces continued to develop as the field sought its identity. Despite the convergence of professional associations and the organizational similarities within the federal evaluation industry, the evaluation field remains highly varied with regard to what evaluation is, what training is required to practice as an evaluator, and what methods and techniques constitute competent practice (Flaherty and Morell 1978; M. Smith 1999; Worthen 1999). Indeed, in 1996, facing declining membership (figure 14.5), the board of the AEA agreed that the association was "not a strong and unified organization" (Bickman 1997). That same year, the association began to explore the possibility of certifying evaluators as one way to strengthen the field.

The subsequent debate over certification illustrates how the evaluation field struggles with professionalization. One characteristic of a fully developed profession is that its members exercise strict control over who is allowed to practice and the competencies required to do so (Morell and Flaherty, 1978). Thus, attempting to certify evaluators is an effort to control and shape the field to a particular set of norms and expectations. While certification programs have surfaced, such as the Evaluator's Institute and the Certificate of Advanced Study in Evaluation at the Claremont Graduate School, formal credentialing has not transpired. The main reason is best summarized by Worthen (1999): "Evaluation is at present so splintered,

Fig. 14.5. American Evaluation Association membership, 1986–2006

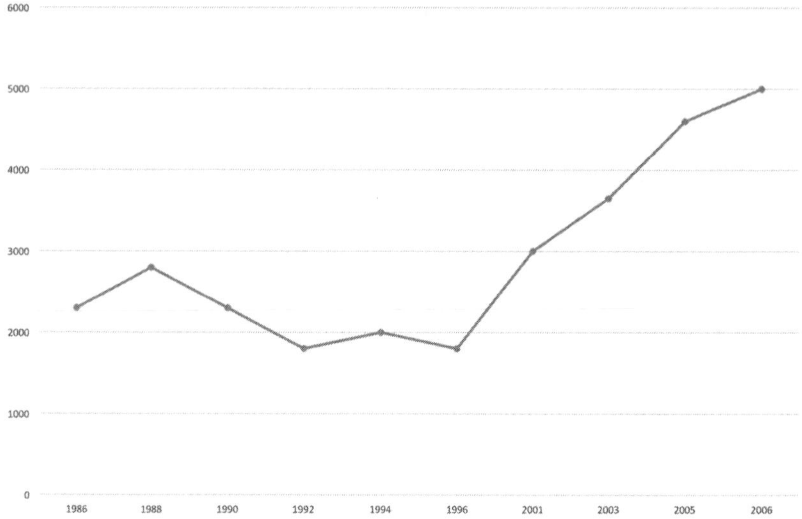

Sources: AEA Newsletter 2007; Summary of AEA Membership 1988; and Bickman 1997.

rooted as it is in so many disciplines, with today's evaluators trained in so many diverse specializations and through such diverse means, that it seems rather optimistic to presume that any agreement can be forged within AEA about what constitutes essential evaluation competencies. Indeed, we evaluators no longer even agree on what evaluation is."

The development of professional standards and guidelines is another way an emerging field tries to consolidate its base and create an identity among its practitioners (Wilensky 1964). The AEA's *Guiding Principles for Evaluators*, first published in 1994, is a code of ethics; the statements are intentionally general in order to encompass the wide range of methods and epistemologies gathered under the umbrella of evaluation. Indeed, its function is more to socialize evaluators around the identity of being an evaluator than to provide regulations and standards for how to do evaluation (Bustelo 2006). The preface to the guiding principles illustrates this intent: "Based on differences in training, experience, and work settings, the profession of evaluation encompasses diverse perceptions about the primary purpose of evaluation . . . Despite that diversity, the common ground is that evaluators aspire to construct and provide the best possible information that might bear on the value of whatever is being evaluated. The principles are intended to foster that primary aim" (AEA 2004). Nonetheless, critics such as P. H. Rossi (1995) observed that the vagueness of the guidelines, while indicating a diversity of perspectives, weakens the field. Indeed, if the base of knowledge for a field is too general or vague, the achievement of professional status is less likely to occur (Wilensky 1964). This is distinct from the purpose of one of the earlier professional associations, the CASR (Center for Applied Social Research), which expressly promoted the use of experimental designs for evaluation.

A major characteristic of the evaluation field is thus its heterogeneity, approximating what Morell (1990) called a "loose coalition" of evaluation. But conflicts over such areas as mission, priorities, and methodology often characterize the development of a profession (Bucher and Strauss 1961) and can be a sign of healthy growth (Conner and Dickman 1979). Contested areas within the field have varied over time (M. Smith 2001), but one issue, concerning whether randomized controlled trials should be the "gold standard" for evaluation, persists. The realization that these designs did not provide timely information to decision makers; did not apply realistically to smaller, localized programs or programs with shifting strategies; and produced uncertain results coupled with high cost, led to the resurgence of alternative evaluation methodologies (House 1990; Maynard 2000; M. Rossi and Wright 1984). While experimental designs were still used for some federally sponsored evaluations, the focus for many evaluators turned toward how to increase use of evaluation findings, which in turn led to the popularity of participatory and collaborative evaluation practices (M. Smith 2001). Consequences of this debate include Peter Rossi resigning his membership from the AEA when it took a position against the U.S. Department of Education's preference for randomized experiments in educational evaluations in 2003 (Lipsey 2007), and perhaps the migration of evaluators to associations like the American Economics Association, the American Public Health Association, and the Association for Public Policy Analysis and Management, which more readily accept experimental designs as the gold standard. The AEA, on the other hand, has purposefully decided not to prioritize particular methodologies, in recognition of the diversity of perspectives and purposes of evaluation—and its membership has increased steadily from 3,000 to 5,000 between 2001 and 2006. Intrafield differences were seen as a necessary sign of progress in the professionalization of evaluation by its practitioners in the late 1970s, and such debates continue today.

The number of professional associations in which evaluators take part exemplifies the breadth and diversity of the field: in addition to the organizations mentioned above, one could add the American Psychological Association and the American Educational Research Association as well. The fact that the primary disciplines of evaluators include psychology, public administration, sociology, economics, public health, and many others (Morell 1990) makes evaluation inherently interdisciplinary and thus loosely consolidated. Indeed, evaluation has been called a "transdiscipline" (Scriven 1993) because it provides a set of tools and methods for use by the primary disciplines—in this way, it has taken root across disciplinary boundaries. Others have classified evaluation as a "metadiscipline," one that encompasses most social science research (Picciotto 1999), and still others lament the lack of professional identity and the failure to develop core practices and methods (Sechrest 1994).

In sum, the evaluation industry was distinguished early on by its interdependence, which set the stage for networking and professionalization. That interdependence, in turn, gave rise to a diversity of perspectives in the broader field of evaluation, as discontentment with large-scale, experimentally designed evaluations grew. Professional associations that began in the mid-1970s represented divergent approaches to evaluation, and were consolidated until the profession eventually had a single organization, the AEA, by 1986. Nonetheless, the way the field evolved, originating in a diverse range of "home" disciplines, offering a variety of avenues to become an evaluator, and maintaining contested areas within the field, signify its status as a "loose coalition" (Morell 1990).

Conclusion

The idea of program evaluation can be traced back far into the history of American public life. Here, we have focused on its emergence and expansion over the half century following Lyndon Johnson's Great Society initiatives. During this time, the field witnessed the growth of a sophisticated industry and the emergence of a profession aimed at discerning effectiveness. While the field of program evaluation took major strides in the 1960s and 1970s to define its agenda and ambitions, it took decades for practices and systems to be built to support the goal of measuring the impact of social programs. The explosive growth of evaluation-firm revenues from the 1970s through the 1990s is evidence not only that the demand for evidence of program impact has been great, but also that the supply of evaluation services has risen to meet this demand.

While we have focused here on the early history of government's move toward measurement, it is important to note that the quest for good evaluation research now extends deeply into the nonprofit sector. Long funded by governments and exposed to their mandates and regulations, nonprofit service providers have also contributed to the growth of the evaluation industry by contracting out to research firms in order to meet their assessment needs. The move to evaluate social programs may have started in government, but today it has been fully absorbed into the practices and priorities of the nonprofit sector, whose role in social service delivery has expanded through the trend toward contracting out and the resulting hollowing-out of the state (Milward and Provan 1993).

The field still faces many obstacles. There remains a significant difference of opinion on the validity of program evaluation for cases in which experimental designs are not possible. Perhaps the most prominent challenges lie in discovering and communicating the limits of evaluation to its consumers. While the work of the major evaluation firms is typically communicated with certitude and scientific heft, the field of program evaluation remains more an art than a science.

The rise of an entire multibillion-dollar industry in evaluation research is testament to the power of the question, made urgent during the Great Society era, "Did the program work?" This simple question lies at the origin of many of the largest and most complex publicly funded evaluations. As government has sought to become more effective and to maximize the impact of its spending programs, evaluation has been a critical means to that end. It not only leads to information about operational effectiveness, but also can have powerful uses for both securing and terminating future funding. Critical to the wise use of evaluation data are an industry and a profession that are both technically sophisticated and ethical. When it comes to evaluation research, the last half century's experience demonstrates that knowledge is indeed power.

Note

1. The exception was the Denver-Seattle experiment, which lasted from 1970 until 1991.

References

Abt, Clark C. 1970. *Serious games.* Lanham, Md.: University Press of America.
———, ed. 1976. *The evaluation of social programs.* Beverly Hills, Calif.: Sage.
AEA [American Evaluation Association]. 2004. *American Evaluation Association Guiding Principles for Evaluators.* Available on the AEA website: www.eval.org /p/cm/ld/fid=51.

AEA Newsletter. 2007. December 21.

AIR News. 2007. AIR celebrates six decades of success. Winter.

Bassett, G. 1969. *The Urban Institute: A history of its organization.* Washington, D.C.: Urban Institute.

Bickman L. 1997. Evaluating evaluation: Where do we go from here? *Evaluation Practice* 18, no. 1: 1–16.

Bovberg, R. 1983. A brief history of the Urban Institute. Sept. Urban Institute Archives, Washington, D.C.

Brecher, E. M. 1978. *MDRC: Origin and early operations.* New York: Ford Foundation.

Bryant, E. C. 1981. *Twenty years and counting: A personal history of Westat.* Rockville, Md.: Westat.

Bucher, R., and A. Strauss. 1961. Professions in process. *American Journal of Sociology* 66, no. 4: 325–334.

Bustelo, M. 2006. The potential role of standards and guidelines in the development of an evaluation culture in Spain. *Evaluation* 12, no. 4: 437–453.

Campbell, D. T. 1969. Reforms as experiments. *American Psychologist* 24:409–429.

Campbell, D. T., and J. C. Stanley. 1963. *Experimental and quasi-experimental designs for research.* Chicago: Rand McNally.

Conner, R. F., and F. B. Dickman. 1979. Professionalization of evaluative research: Conflict as a sign of health. *Evaluation and Program Planning* 2:103–109.

Datta, Lois-ellin. 2004. The oral history of evaluation, part 2: An interview with Lois-ellin Datta, by J. King, M. Mark, and R. Miller. *American Journal of Evaluation* 25, no. 5: 243–253.

DiMaggio, P. J., and W. W. Powell. 1991. The iron cage revisited: Institutional isomorphism and collective rationality. In W. W. Powell and P. J. DiMaggio, eds., *The new institutionalism in organizational analysis.* Chicago: University of Chicago Press.

Evaluation News. 1981. News of the network. Feb.

Flaherty, E. W., and J. A. Morell. 1978. Evaluation: Manifestations of a new field. *Evaluation and Program Planning* 1, no. 1: 1-10.

Freeman, H. E., and M. A. Solomon. 1979. The next decade in evaluation research. *Evaluation and Program Planning* 2:255–262.

Gorham, W. 1967. Notes of a practitioner. *The Public Interest* 8 (Summer): 4–8.

Greenberg, D. H., M. Shroder, and M. Onstott. 1999. The social experiment market. *Journal of Economic Perspectives* 13, no. 3: 157–172.

Guiding Principles for Evaluators. 2004. Fairhaven, Mass.: American Evaluation Association.

Haveman, Robert H. 1987. *Poverty policy and poverty research: The Great Society and the social sciences.* Madison: University of Wisconsin Press.

Hayes, F., and A. Japha. 1978. *The Urban Institute, 1968–1978: An evaluation of its performance, prospects, and financial problems.* New York: Ford Foundation.

Held, V. 1966. PPBS comes to Washington. *Public Interest* 4 (Summer): 102–115.

House, E. R. 1990. Trends in evaluation. *Educational Researcher* 1, no. 3: 24–28.

Jardini, D. R. 1996. *Out of the blue yonder: The RAND Corporation's diversification into social welfare research, 1946–1968.* Pittsburgh: Carnegie Mellon University Press.

Johnson, Lyndon Baines. 1966. Remarks on the 50th anniversary of the Brookings Institution, Washington, D.C. Sept. 29.

Larrabee, C. X. 1991. *Many missions: Research Triangle Institute's first 31 years*. Research Triangle Park, N.C.: Research Triangle Institute.

Levine, R. A. 1970. *The poor ye need not have with you: Lessons from the War on Poverty*. Cambridge, Mass.: MIT Press.

Lipsey, M. W. 2007. Peter H. Rossi: Formative for program evaluation. *American Journal of Evaluation* 28, no. 2: 199–202.

Maynard, R. A. 2000. Whether a sociologist, economist, psychologist or simply a skilled evaluator. *Evaluation* 6, no. 4: 471–480.

McLaughlin, M. W. 1975. *Evaluation and reform: The Elementary and Secondary Education Act of 1965 / Title I*. Cambridge, Mass.: Ballinger.

Meyer, John W., and Brian Rowan. 1991. Institutionalized organizations: Formal structure as myth and ceremony. In Paul J. DiMaggio and Walter W. Powell, eds., *The new institutionalism in organizational analysis*. Chicago: University of Chicago Press.

Milward, H. Brinton, and Keith Provan. 1993. The hollow state: Private provision of public services. In Helen Ingram and Steven Rathgeb Smith, eds., *Public Policy for Democracy*. Washington, D.C.: Brookings Institution Press.

Morell, J. A. 1990. Evaluation: Status of a loose coalition. *Evaluation Practice* 11, no. 3: 213–219.

Morell, J. A., and E. W. Flaherty. 1978. The development of evaluation as a profession: Current status and some predictions. *Evaluation and Program Planning* 1, no. 1: 11–17.

Oakley, A. 1998. Experimentation and social interventions: A forgotten but important history. *BMJ (British Medical Journal)* 317:1239–1242.

O'Connor, A. 2001. *Poverty knowledge: Social science, social policy, and the poor in twentieth-century history*. Princeton, N.J.: Princeton University Press.

Picciotto, R. 1999. Towards an economics of evaluation. *Evaluation* 5, no. 1: 7–22.

Rein, M., and S. H. White. 1977. Can policy research help policy? *Public Interest* 49:119–136.

Rossi, M., and James D. Wright. 1984. Evaluation research: An assessment. *Annual Review of Sociology* 10:331–352.

Rossi, P. H. 1995. Doing good and getting it right. *New Directions for Program Evaluation*, no. 66: 55–60.

Schick, Allen. 1971. From analysis to evaluation. *Annals of the American Academy of Political and Social Science* 394:57–71.

Scriven, M. 1993. Hard-won lessons in program evaluation. Special issue, *New Directions for Program Evaluation*, no. 58.

Sechrest, L. 1994. Program evaluation: Oh what it seemed to be! *Evaluation Practice* 15, no. 3: 359–365.

Shadish, W. R., T. D. Cook, and L. C. Leviton. 1991. *Foundations of program evaluation*. Newbury Park, Calif.: Sage.

Smith, J. A. 1991. *The idea brokers: Think tanks and the rise of the new policy elite*. New York: Free Press.

Smith, M. F. 1999. Should AEA begin a process for restricting membership in the profession of evaluation? *American Journal of Evaluation* 20, no. 3: 521–532.

————. 2001. Evaluation: preview of the future #2. *American Journal of Evaluation* 22, no. 3: 281–300.

Sperry, R. L., T. D. Desmond, K. F. McGraw, and B. Schmidt. 1981. *GAO, 1966–1981: An administrative history*. Washington, D.C.: Government Printing Office.

Staats, E. B. 1968. Perspective on planning-programming-budgeting. *GAO Review* (Summer): 3–2.

————. 1970. The relationship of budgeting, program planning, and evaluation. *GAO Review* (Winter): 3–10.

————. 1973. Challenges and problems in the evaluation of governmental programs. Unpublished manuscript. Pittsburgh.

Summary of AEA Membership. 1988. *Evaluation Practice*, vol. 9, 84–86.

University Times. 1996. John C. Flanagan obituary. May 9.

Weiss, C. H. 1972. *Evaluation research: Methods of assessing program effectiveness*. Englewood Cliffs, N.J.: Prentice-Hall.

Wholey, J. S., J. W. Scanlon, H. G. Duffy, J. S. Fukumoto, and L. M. Vogt. 1970. *Federal evaluation policy: Analyzing the effects of public programs*. Washington, D.C.: Urban Institute.

Wilensky, H. L. 1964 The professionalization of everyone? *American Journal of Sociology* 70, no. 2: 137-158.

Worthen, B. R. 1999. Critical challenges confronting the certification of evaluators. *American Journal of Evaluation* 20, no. 3: 533–555.

PART VI

CONCLUSIONS

CHAPTER 15

Fifty Years Later: Legacies and Lessons of LBJ's Domestic Policies

NORMAN J. GLICKMAN, LAURENCE E. LYNN JR.,
AND ROBERT H. WILSON

The case studies in this book demonstrate that President Johnson produced extraordinary domestic policy successes. He broadly expanded the federal presence in many policy areas and broke new ground in others. Johnson's pragmatic, highly varied approaches to policy design and implementation had one consistent characteristic: his urgency to pass legislation as quickly as possible. He expected future Congresses to change the laws he championed, and those modifications, inevitable in the nation's constitutional scheme of governance, have shaped what is regarded as his enduring legacy.

Despite his achievements, the case studies reveal a mixed or ambiguous record of institutionalized policy change over the long term. In the case of the War on Poverty, for example, poverty rates are now standard social indicators published by the Bureau of the Census, and even in the politically polarized years following the 2010 midterm elections, the reduction of poverty remained on the public policy agendas of both Democrats and Republicans, although characterized by dramatically different means and ends. But because the connection between economic growth and poverty has weakened—the main poverty indicator is virtually unchanged from when Johnson left office—Johnson's centralized and coordinated strategy for eliminating poverty has given way to regarding means-tested income maintenance and jobs programs, or "social welfare," as a safety net for individuals and families unable to prosper in the workforce.

More broadly, later presidents, Democrat and Republican alike, and much of the public came to question a bipartisan consensus that the federal government could or should be the guarantor of social well-being and equity. This was true not only with respect to the elimination of poverty and hunger, but also for policies directed at, for example, access to affordable health care, human-rights-oriented immigration policies, and voting rights.

Yet despite the dramatic shift of American politics to the right of the New Deal and the Great Society, the case studies in this book provide abundant evidence that today's national public policy agenda ranges over the same policy spaces created and shaped by Johnson, even if the scope, purposes, and forms of federal action have changed substantially.

Assessing the accomplishments of this ambitious president has received attention from scholars, particularly historians and political scientists, and journalists (see the discussion of the extensive literature on the Johnson presidency in chapter 1). Schools of presidential studies disagree on the appropriate analytical framework and the different weights to be placed on personality and institutional context and formal processes. Drawing on the analysis presented in this volume, the editors of *LBJ's Neglected Legacy* cast this chapter in an institutional perspective that examines not only a president's capacity to reach goals while working *within* the existing federal system, but also a president's impact *on* the system (Skowronek 2009). Institutional thinking is infused with value that "stretch[es] the time horizon backward and forward [and] senses the shadows of both past and future lengthening into the present" (Helco 2006, 737).

The extended historical and longitudinal perspective adopted here demonstrates not only that negotiations across multiple institutions and actors at the time of policy initiation are important—the position adopted by those using an institutional framework—but also that a fuller understanding of the effectiveness of those policies emerges once the factors determining the longevity of policies, or lack thereof, have been determined. The analyses in this book do not just concern the effectiveness of Johnson as an advocate of legislation but also appraise the institutionalization and enduring nature of his policies. This chapter considers whether these policies achieved their intended effects as the political, social, and economic context of the country evolved. In other words, did initiatives adopted during LBJ's presidency define the path of subsequent legislative, regulatory, and administrative processes?

Assessing Lyndon Johnson's Legacies

Answers to the three research questions posed in chapter 1 are addressed in this chapter:

- First, what was the policy and institutional status quo at the time that the LBJ administration adopted a particular initiative, what can be called the "inherited status quo"? What were the antecedents for LBJ's initiatives, and were federal resources devoted to the issue?

- Second, what were the features of the "new status quo," that is, the changes brought about by federal legislation or executive action, at the conclusion of the Johnson administration? Concerned with patterns in policy design, this chapter identifies the structures and processes used in Johnson's policies as well as the funding mechanisms and delivery systems employed to implement the policy. Did the administration create mechanisms to support the policies?
- Finally, was the policy sustained, altered, or terminated after LBJ left office? Here, the chapter seeks to identify the subsequent trajectory of Johnson's creations and the factors shaping that trajectory, relying both on characteristics of the American bureaucratic system as well as politics and public attitudes and values, and their status—that is, Johnson's legacy—in the second decade of the twenty-first century.

Each of these questions was explored in the preceding chapters on the particular policies. These findings are now placed in an institutionalist and comparative perspective to understand, more broadly, how Johnson's domestic agenda has affected today's federal government.

The Inherited Status Quo

For purposes of this analysis, the concept of the inherited status quo has two dimensions. First, as Johnson assumed the presidency, what was the nature or status of a policy issue, and what factors shaped his understanding and approach to the issue? Second, what role, if any, did the federal government play in these areas at that time? As argued in chapter 1 and documented in other chapters in this volume, Johnson fervently believed that the federal government had an obligation to improve the public's well-being. Cast in this perspective, the inherited status quo frames the remarkable breadth and progressiveness of his agenda.

In civil and political rights, the status quo that Johnson inherited featured racial discrimination in public schooling, higher education, voting, housing markets, public accommodations, and public-service provision. Southern Democrats had effectively exercised their power in Congress to resist federal action (Katznelson 2013), but the civil rights movement had been gaining strength. The late 1950s and early 1960s saw tensions and conflicts escalating rapidly. The federal government had taken action to desegregate the armed services and had intervened to force compliance with racial desegregation of public schools in the mid-1950s. Johnson, as leader of the Senate, had been instrumental in the passage of the 1957 Civil Rights Act. To secure passage, Johnson retreated from a relatively strong bill and retained a relatively weak voting-rights provision in the final version. The weaknesses of this legislation became apparent as the civil rights movement grew in strength. The Kennedy administration developed legislation, the Civil Rights Act, but it languished in Congress. As Johnson became president, federal involvement in ending racial discrimination had been, on net, tentative, and pressure around civil rights was mounting.

In immigration policy, nativist laws adopted in the 1920s allowed immigration primarily from northern European countries and imposed strict national quotas on immigration from southern Europe, Latin America, and Asia. The southern congressional leadership had prevented reform of this policy for decades. Even though immigration reform was not a prominent issue when Johnson moved into the White House, he was sensitive to world opinion, motivated in part by U.S. competition with the Soviet Union in the developing world.

Several of Johnson's proposals furthered the agenda of previous presidential administrations, especially the New Deal, as is highlighted in various chapters. In these areas, the inherited status quo included significant federal resources devoted to the policy, including organizational capacity. But in Johnson's view, existing federal policy provided inadequate coverage for many social and economic challenges. For instance, FDR constructed public housing partly to increase employment in the construction industry. The 1949 Housing Act provided subsidies to build housing for poor families. Eisenhower and Kennedy, too, made modest efforts to provide support, but these efforts did not come close to meeting the unfilled demand for housing among low-income families. In fact, the large-scale demolition of public housing during the 1950s and early 1960s decimated housing markets in many neighborhoods for poor families in large cities. It should be noted that an important element of the inherited status quo was a broad consensus that regulation of housing markets was a state and local government responsibility under the reserved-powers provisions of the Constitution.

The federal government's involvement in building infrastructure dates to the early days of the republic. Most relevant here, however, was FDR's deep commitment to building roads and other public facilities to provide work for the unemployed. He created the Public Works Administration and other agencies with a similar mission. In the mid-1950s, Eisenhower's Interstate Highway System consolidated a long-held ambition for the construction of a national road system. But the quicker access from central cities to the suburbs that these systems generated contributed to loss of population in cities and facilitated the relocation of urban residents and businesses to the suburbs. The 1960s urban riots contributed to "white flight," too. This depopulation and economic decline of central cities had been subject to development efforts in previous administrations, but the transportation and housing needs were apparent.

The inherited status quo in several policy areas reflected political disagreement, even stalemate, over the role of the federal government in American society. For instance, Presidents Theodore Roosevelt, Franklin Roosevelt, and Harry Truman failed to pass national health care legislation, largely because of opposition from the American Medical Association. Before LBJ's presidency, efforts by states and Congress had failed to address deteriorating water quality in the country. In fact, Congress had not resolved whether water pollution was a state or local matter or one that the federal government had authority to address.

In other domains, the inherited status quo was in flux when Johnson took office. The United States had a long history of excellence in science and technology, and the federal government assumed important roles in those areas during World War II and later. Dwight Eisenhower created the position of special assistant to the president for Science and Technology Policy and the President's Science Advisory Committee (PSAC). As a leader in the Senate, Johnson understood the importance of science. In addition, President Kennedy promised to put a man on the moon by the end of the 1960s. Thus, momentum for federal science policy had been gaining before the Johnson presidency. Changes were also evident in efforts to develop national policy and planning capabilities. Only remnants of FDR's efforts to create such capabilities remained in a handful of federal agencies in 1963. Beginning in 1961, JFK's defense secretary, Robert McNamara, implemented a system for the efficient planning and management of military forces that had been developed at the air force's consulting firm, the RAND Corporation. By 1964, experts in the field and congressional authorities recognized the system as a potential model for other domestic agencies.

The federal government's involvement in several policies examined in this book was relatively limited at the time LBJ became president. Education policy, for example, had historically been the domain of state and local governments. Other than federally enforced school desegregation, there was no broad-based federal K–12 education policy, a result both of provisions of the U.S. Constitution (the reserved-powers clause) and a political predisposition for localism; thus, responsibility for service provision fell exclusively to state and local governments. This made it particularly difficult to bring educational change to southern schools locked in segregationist structures.

In the field of higher education, the federal government participated in the nineteenth century in the creation of state land grant colleges.[1] Since that time, beyond supporting research conducted in universities, the role had been somewhat limited. The GI bill subsidized higher education for returning World War II veterans, and its success provided a justification for expanding the federal role under Johnson. The Soviet Union's advances in space and threats through missile technology made the need for better-trained scientists and engineers a national priority. Higher-education opportunities were extensive and growing, but policies to expand access to college for the great majority of potential students had not been a concern of the federal government.

The antecedents for the Head Start program date from the Progressive era; the U.S. Children's Bureau, created in 1912, focused on the needs of children and their mothers. When Johnson took office, the bureau, associated with the Social Security program in Eisenhower's Department of Health, Education and Welfare (HEW), was a potential source of support for early-childhood education inspired by psychologists and other social scientists who were finding positive benefits for child development from early-intervention programs. Here, one sees a relatively modest federal role, but academic research provided the foundation for the Johnson initiative.

Other than in public housing, there was very little federal involvement in urban-based community development before 1964. Some funding and ideas for community development in poor urban neighborhoods was provided by community-based organizations, such as rural cooperatives, which had existed for decades but had little federal government support; by the Ford Foundation; and by other national philanthropies, but local groups were left to grapple with often adversarial mayors and council members. With few exceptions, there was no community development "industry" enabling local nonprofits and churches to help their neighborhoods.

This section has briefly described the inherited status quo LBJ faced as he began to formulate his domestic policy agenda for the issues discussed in this volume. Given the scope of the inherited status quo, it is not surprising to see, as the chapters in this book have documented, that Johnson's initiatives had diverse origins. He adopted ideas from task forces, executive branch staff members, scientists, private-sector interests, military personnel, community-based organizations, state and local governments, and others. In several policy areas there was a significant federal presence, and Johnson's own understanding of some policy issues had developed through his congressional experience. Thus, the LBJ administration built upon a wide range of administrative capabilities and experiences when developing initiatives. These efforts are examined next.

What LBJ Achieved—and How

The longer-term implications of policy design for implementation, performance, and institutionalization were, as seen in several case studies, subordinated to the demands of political bargaining with interest groups and Congress. Congressional opposition to tax increases became an additional constraint, and further budget reductions occurred during the congressional appropriations process, particularly after the 1966 midterm elections, which weakened the Democratic Party's dominance of Congress. Johnson, like all presidents, had to contend with furthering his agenda and creating a new policy and administrative status quo in the face of contentious politics, including conflicts within his own party, and while under significant resource constraints.

At the conclusion of the Johnson presidency, the new status quo generated by the set of policies examined in this book could be observed in concrete form through structures, processes, service-delivery systems, funding, and managerial directives. These tangible expressions of policy create dependencies, interdependencies, and expectations; at times, conflict takes place among units of government and their agents, stakeholders, and other public bodies. These relationships may lead to changing values and attitudes and thereby contribute to the institutionalization of an initiative. This section identifies the types of implementation structures used and assesses their ability to expand governmental capacity and generate interdependencies that could lead to changing values and attitudes, thus setting the stage for the long-term sustainability of the policies, a topic addressed in the next section.

Structures and Processes

To initiate this discussion, a few observations on the policy design of the LBJ initiatives examined in this book are offered. A striking feature of the design of several of them was the complex, multidimensional implementation approach. For example, to achieve the specific objective of racial equality, Johnson incorporated a range of programs and mechanisms to address

discrimination in public accommodations, housing markets, public institutions, elections, immigration reform, and public and higher education. Similarly, to end poverty and promote community development, LBJ and his
staff developed programs in nutrition, health, job training, and housing.
In public education, improvement in outcomes for disadvantaged—especially urban—children incorporated compensatory funding to schools, free
lunches, day care services, and early-childhood education. Enforcement of
nondiscriminatory hiring practices and minority representation on school
boards, through the enforcement of the Voting Rights Act (VRA), were
also important elements of school reform. Finally, Johnson's federalization
of water quality management employed a comprehensive toolbox of administrative technologies, including national water quality standards, federal
funding of wastewater treatment, new partnerships in service delivery collaboration, and research for the monitoring and development of new technologies. The comprehensive nature of policy design matched the complex
nature of the policy problems.

Compromise with Congress helped alter policy design. Johnson's health
initiative, following legislative bargaining, was enacted in two programs.
Medicare administration was associated with HEW's administration of
other social insurance programs insofar as it was financed by a social insurance mechanism, the payroll tax. In sharp contrast, Medicaid administration was associated with HEW's other means-tested public assistance
programs, since it was financed by a matching grant administered by the
states. This philosophical bifurcation effectively eliminated any chance for
national health insurance. The Elementary and Secondary Education Act
was also a product of compromise over administrative details, including involvement of the Catholic hierarchy, in order to secure swift passage of this
pathbreaking act. A Johnson deal to secure passage of the Higher Education Act provided college financial aid for poor students but also for students from modest-income families. These examples remind us that a range
of actors helped shape the Johnson legislation.

Mobilizing Organizational Capacity

New financial and programmatic resources for his ambitious health and education initiatives were assigned to the secretary of HEW, a department
created under Eisenhower. In the area of civil rights, voting rights, and immigration, the power and authority of the Department of Justice (DOJ)

were crucial enforcement elements. In these cases, the legislation expanded the authority of existing bureaucracies, and Johnson's leadership encouraged aggressive enforcement.

Other initiatives led to a remarkable proliferation of new governmental organizations. The creation of a new department, agency, or office, even when it represented the consolidation of existing programs, had various effects, including sharpening the political and administrative focus on specific policy areas or objectives as well as the president's control over the new agency's agendas. Johnson's strategy included the consolidation of existing programs into new cabinet-level departments. The creation of the Department of Transportation (DOT) and the Department of Housing and Urban Development (HUD) enabled Johnson to expand the magnitude and scope of federal roles in highway development and public housing. In the case of DOT, evolutionary processes brought about organizational changes as Johnson expanded Eisenhower's National Interstate and Defense Highways Act of 1956.[2] Recognizing the larger challenge of multimodal transportation for the nation's development agenda, DOT consolidated and coordinated all federal programs related to the broad transportation challenge.

Large administrative units can provide political cover for more controversial programs, rendering them less vulnerable to hostile political oversight. At the same time, they become more vulnerable to internal bureaucratic competition for scarce budgetary resources. Departments and officials created to attract political attention and support, which Johnson tended to favor, may, however, become lightning rods for political opposition and interparty competition. An instructive example of both phenomena is the Office of Economic Opportunity (OEO), created as an independent federal agency to administer and coordinate several new, experimental programs to fight the War on Poverty. Many OEO programs became a focus for opposition by governors and mayors who were aggrieved at being bypassed by LBJ's community-oriented "maximum feasible participation" approach to social policy and urban renewal.[3] The OEO was, as a consequence, eliminated as a bureaucratic entity by Richard Nixon. But most of its programs, including Head Start, were retained and transferred to administrative conglomerates such as HEW, where their missions survived, although their new bureaucratic contexts transformed them. The goals and means of achieving Johnson-era policies typically have changed over the years, as Johnson fully expected, even if policy structures such as the OEO have not. This outcome is more likely for policies with weaker or more controversial constituencies.

Innovation in Implementation Processes

Johnson's programs inevitably incorporated familiar implementation mechanisms, including bureaucratic service-delivery administration, enforcement through sanctions and incentives, and regulatory and funding mechanisms. But we also find innovative implementation strategies. While there may be disagreement whether Johnson himself should be credited with originating these strategies, it is in the expansive and innovative use of implementation processes that the new status quo found at the conclusion of Johnson's administration is visible.

Funding mechanisms, and their sustainability, are crucial to effective implementation. Johnson used traditional federal mechanisms for funding but also introduced new processes. Federal expenditures on social policy grew dramatically. Much of the funding occurred through grants-in-aid and involved the targeting of specific, eligible populations, thereby closely aligning expenditures with programmatic goals. Economically and educationally disadvantaged groups often benefited from this new spending. In community development and housing programs, Medicaid, Head Start, elementary and secondary education, and university scholarships, funding was means-tested, that is, targeted at those with low incomes. These expenditure mechanisms did not necessarily represent innovation in federal policy making, but their use expanded considerably in LBJ's goals.

Intergovernmental financing mechanisms, involving federal matching funds, induced state and local governments to assume major responsibilities for funding investments in, for example, urban infrastructure, water-quality improvement, and public education. Federal funding also leveraged private outlays. In the case of higher education, commercial banks provided loans in exchange for federal guarantees of repayment. Medicare and Medicaid recipients received services through the private health-care system.

The mobilization of subnational governments and nongovernmental organizations in Johnson's initiatives led to an often overlooked expansion of functional capabilities of these organizations. Existing public-service systems in state and local government—such as primary, secondary, and higher education or infrastructure provision—were called upon to expand services and, thereby, capability. In addition, these organizations were required to open their doors to underrepresented groups and new missions. As a result, nonprofit organizations, community groups, banks, insurance companies, colleges and universities, hospitals, and medical practices became agents for implementing Johnson's policies.

Through these implementation processes, the U.S. administrative state, including all levels of government, became larger and more encompassing, even if it lacked the capabilities of more unitary, state-centered democracies. The appropriate calibration of federal incentives (sometimes with sanctions) to secure collaboration with non-federal-government actors and to achieve political support for programmatic goals was a source of conflict during the Johnson presidency. The expansion of this capability and public-sector expenditures not only affected service providers, but also caused the recipient communities to become constituencies and a source of support for programs. Low-income communities in community development, families involved with Head Start, or college students with bank-financed loans, as well as the elderly and low-income families in Medicare and Medicaid, became constituents. Congressional districts throughout the nation that benefited from K–12 education funding became a source of support.

Regulatory and enforcement processes were crucial elements in several of Johnson's policy initiatives, and some represented an expansion into new or heretofore limited federal government interests, such as national standards for environmental quality. The implementation process for civil rights and voting rights involved the new powers of enforcement assigned to the DOJ and represented a significant new status quo. The preclearance provision of the VRA for changes in election systems in covered jurisdictions was particularly controversial. Rather than continuing the traditional practice of federal government presumption that actions by subnational governments were legitimate and legal, the preclearance provisions required covered jurisdictions to demonstrate that changes were not discriminatory. In another case of expanded regulatory authority, in 1964 the secretary of HEW prohibited applications for construction funding for medical facilities unless there was nondiscrimination in service provision. Here the federal government used the power of the purse to prevent discrimination by private-sector actors contracting with the federal government, and hospitals were quick to comply with this requirement.

The complex implementation strategies found in the Johnson initiatives led to challenges in coordination across federal agencies and with subnational governments. The administration developed new mechanisms, such as councils of governments, designed to coordinate federal agencies with overlapping missions. Several plans combined a regulatory or enforcement role with increased funding. Federal funding for water-related projects was contingent on state governments' agreement to enforce national water quality standards. In higher education, enforcement of desegregation accompanied the expansion of federal support for loans and grants to college students, thus easing the burden of meeting desegregation mandates.

Intrabureaucratic and intergovernmental conflict appeared before the conclusion of LBJ's presidency, but in broader perspective, many new structures and processes created sources of support, and administrative interdependencies emerged. State and local governments became partners in the implementation of federal policies by agreeing to support national priorities in return for federal funding. This observation by no means suggests that intergovernmental relations were without conflict. Intense state and local opposition to some Johnson initiatives emerged during his presidency. Rather, the ambitious policy agenda and complex implementation strategies helped create a new status quo with multiple sources of interdependencies but also subject to administrative and political tensions.

Managing the Bureaucracy

Improving the quality and efficiency of public administration through training in, and use of, modern management techniques was a persistent concern of Johnson's Bureau of the Budget (BOB) and of Johnson himself. Management and accountability measures were incorporated in antipoverty programs and water quality improvement, although in some areas, such as Head Start, there was little initial concern for management and control. Johnson's strategies for project and program management, however, recognized the challenge of bureaucratic politics.

The Planning-Program-Budgeting System (PPBS) was a key feature of the public-management functionality. The president and his budget advisers believed that the success of mission-oriented planning and programming in the DOD under the dynamic businessman Robert S. McNamara warranted an executive order directing all federal agencies and departments to adopt it. The Johnson administration's determination to ensure cost-effective management of LBJ's Great Society and other initiatives (thus reassuring conservatives in his own party, among others) required evidence that appropriated funds would not be wasted.

This mandate led to the creation of offices of policy planning and program development in many federal departments, notably in social policy agencies such as the DOL, HUD, and HEW. These offices both sponsored and undertook policy analysis and program evaluation and urged the inclusion of evaluation "set-asides" in appropriations legislation. A network of private research organizations (such as the Urban Institute) evolved to expand the research community's capacity to undertake such policy-oriented activities for the federal government. Enthusiasm for the new administrative technologies varied widely among agencies. The administration promoted program evaluation through conventional federal grants and contracts for research. For this reason, as well as for the face validity of its premise—that policies and programs should be evaluated to determine whether they were efficient and effective—an evaluation constituency quickly formed both inside and outside government, and there was little political controversy concerning the appropriateness of this mechanism, at least until negative evaluations were reported.

There was another side of the PPBS and program evaluation story, however. It required rigorous analysis of budget proposals by using unfamiliar, outcome-oriented terms. In addition, agency professionals were also to conduct the long-required budget formulation by using input-oriented budget formats. This dual requirement, reflecting two distinct budgeting principles, proved immediately unpopular with budget professionals and policy makers, ensuring uneven, even hostile implementation of the new and unfamiliar cost-effectiveness information.

Changing Values

Beyond structures and processes, institutionalization of new policies can be affected, positively or negatively, by beliefs, norms, and standards held by the public. Several examples of value conflict with significant political implications emerged by the end of Johnson's presidency. Johnson's reform of civil rights, voting rights, immigration, and public education were rife with conflict. For example, the public-accommodations provisions of the Civil Rights Act conflicted with a long-held cultural value about the right to conduct private business independent of federal government oversight. Desegregation of public institutions, initiated before Johnson's presidency but expanded under his administration, and the prohibition against racial discrimination in employment and housing markets were imbued with broad and deep value conflicts. Johnson's immigration reform replaced the nativist policy and values dating from the 1920s with a system of quotas reflecting the values of a nation committed to being an open society. Under LBJ's domestic policy agenda, the federal government forced change in commonly accepted social practices. Some practices were quickly accepted by the broader society, thus providing further support for the institutionalization of elements of LBJ's agenda, as in the desegregation of public accommodations and public institutions. Value conflicts in other elements of the agenda were not resolved during the LBJ administration, and some would remain controversial in the decades that followed.

Johnson's Neglected Legacy

A comparison of the inherited status quo with the set of federal policies and administrative capabilities found at the conclusion of Johnson's presidential administration, the topics addressed in the last two sections, reaffirms the breadth and ambition of LBJ's legislative goals and his impact on the administrative state. He left a federal government that was more capable than before, albeit more complex, and that oversaw a broader domestic policy agenda. This discussion now turns to an examination of the extent to which the Johnson initiatives were sustained. The reader should note that the selection of policies included here encompasses only a small number of his legislative accomplishments. Nevertheless, this set of policies provides, we believe, an empirically rich foundation for reflecting on his legacies.

An assessment of the ultimate legacies of Johnson's presidency must include four landmark enactments that addressed the rights of citizenship: the Civil Rights Act of 1964, the Immigration and Nationality Act of 1965, the Voting Rights Act of 1965, and the Civil Rights Act of 1968 (known as the Fair Housing Act). While the civil rights and voting rights acts were contentious and drew significant opposition, the administration expected immediate effects. Not so in the case of immigration reform, which was regarded as of no major significance at the time. These acts, moreover, were steadily liberalized, and their enforcement was strengthened in the decades that followed. They produced long-term demographic effects, some unforeseen, and their indirect social and programmatic effects have profoundly, often controversially affected virtually every aspect of U.S. social, cultural, and political life—even the socially decisive aspects of American jurisprudence.

Less well understood is how Lyndon Johnson's policy and program initiatives—their structures and processes, funding, and management—expanded and reshaped the federal government's ability to provide for the general welfare and altered Americans' points of view about appropriate federal responsibilities. LBJ's heavy footprints in American political, social, and economic life remained highly visible in subsequent decades. This added capability was institutionalized in contemporary federal roles, departments, agencies, and programs that trace their origins to his domestic policy initiatives.

The concept of "legacy" in public affairs is difficult to conceptualize and even more difficult to measure, as discussed in chapter 1. First, even to imagine what contemporary governance would have been had Johnson not become president—the counterfactual to his presidency—is barely possible. True, John F. Kennedy's New Frontier might well have led to similar policies and legislative successes. Had LBJ avoided a large-scale war in Vietnam, the era of liberal government might have been longer and more robust. All this is speculation, of course. Second, identifying aspects of contemporary American government that can be reasonably attributed to Johnson's policy choices requires numerous fraught judgments concerning which later developments are and are not due to his policies. Finally, both data and methods to measure, much less to evaluate, long-term program effects are of uncertain accuracy and, in any event, would require assumptions that would inevitably be controversial.

These difficulties notwithstanding, *LBJ's Neglected Legacy* attempts to assess, in a general way, how Johnson's initiatives have reshaped the institutions and practices of American government. Such appraisals can be justified based on the analyses by this volume's authors and on the concept that institutional historians call "path dependence." As discussed in the preceding section, policies take concrete forms that generate dependencies, interdependencies, and expectations among, potentially, many stakeholders. If sufficiently robust, these mechanisms become institutionalized, creating political and fiscal obstacles to their elimination. These implementation features are referred to here as "sustainability mechanisms." They allow a political regime such as Johnson's to cast long shadows over future political developments.

Because of the sustainability mechanisms associated with Johnson's policies, crediting him with creating and strengthening political institutions that effected lasting changes in politics, public policy, and public administration is appropriate. Through sustained institutional evolution, Johnson's policies can be credited with having influenced American life in profound ways. Indeed, the intensity of conservative opposition to "big government" and the American "welfare state" during the presidency of Barack Obama is an indicator of just how profound these changes have been.

Sustainability and its Consequences

Whether for political reasons or by design, supportive feedback mechanisms played significant, although varying, roles in sustaining Johnson's policies in subsequent decades. The semipermanence of these aspects of Johnson's new status quo reflects the political importance of key relationships between the federal government and state and local governments, as well as between policy makers and constituencies including service providers, administrators and administering organizations, and beneficiaries of Johnson's programs.

Not all feedback mechanisms had an equal influence on federal policy, either during the Johnson years or later. Variation in the influence of these mechanisms across policies helps explain the differences in sustainability of LBJ's initiatives. In education policy, federal funding reached virtually every school district in the country and generated a great breadth of support. The extension of the VRA to address language minorities in 1975 greatly expanded the constituencies affected by the law. By contrast, the nongovernmental constituencies engaged in community development were relatively weak compared with those mechanisms that supported federal funding of infrastructure investments. That is, some constituencies and interdependencies could produce deep commitment, but had less influence in sustaining levels of federal commitment in subsequent decades.

Health and Education: Sustaining the Federal Reach

The most far-reaching of Johnson-initiated federal roles, those concerned with providing resources and standards for education and health care, are dramatic examples of the importance of sustainability mechanisms to his legacy. Today, the Centers for Medicare and Medicaid Services (within the Department of Health and Human Services [HHS]) provide access to health care for tens of millions of Americans. Johnson's health policies continue, in their original structural and procedural forms, to support access to health care for low-income adults and children: matching grants to the states and, for older Americans, an entitlement to health care financed through a federal payroll tax.

Similarly, Johnson's education initiatives provided federal funds to expand the resources available to public schools for educating poor children. In addition, they offered loans and grants to financially needy students for postsecondary education. Head Start provides comprehensive education, health, nutrition, and parent-involvement services to low-income children and their families.

Mechanisms that Sustain Federal Leadership

Many Johnson initiatives did not establish altogether new federal roles, as discussed in the preceding section. Federal involvement in housing, infrastructure improvement, and social welfare had been initiated by previous administrations, but Johnson broadened and refocused these functions and placed them on a more politically and administratively sustainable footing. Such initiatives have enjoyed considerable political support among state and local governments and affected policy communities. Even though intergovernmental disagreements emerged over the extent of nonfederal discretion in regulatory and expenditure decisions, the flow of funds generated sustained support for the new and expanded federal roles and programs by enlarging their constituencies through centrally administered feedback mechanisms.

To fulfill these expanded roles, the administration created mission-driven federal programs, agencies, and cabinet-level departments. DOT and HUD firmly institutionalized this capacity. Successful institutionalization of the federal role in environmental protection took place. Although relatively unheralded at the time and later overshadowed by the creation of the U.S. Environmental Protection Agency during the Nixon administration, the political popularity of Johnson's initiation of federal support for water quality improvement was a precedent for further expansion of the federal role in environmental protection in subsequent decades. The creation of the Department of Education by Jimmy Carter had antecedents in Johnson's education policy.

Because of the administrative technologies employed in grant programs, negotiated changes born of experience and of shifts in political priorities were bound to occur. Most of these led to a relaxation of federal controls over subnational governments and to variability in funding levels and mechanisms. In general, services supported by federal grants are now produced and delivered, to a greatly expanded extent, by nonprofit and for-profit private organizations, often with a more market-oriented, vouchers approach replacing the public-sector provision of services.

New Constituencies

Civil society and nongovernmental actors provided significant support for several of Johnson's domestic programs. Associations of beneficiaries, service providers, and, in some cases, new advocacy organizations for specific groups of beneficiaries, such as the poor and elderly, emerged in the 1960s in response to Johnson's initiatives. Nongovernmental organizations that engaged in direct service delivery, funded by the federal government, also provided positive feedback in support of federal initiatives. Other private, for-profit organizations benefiting from the interdependencies created by

LBJ's initiatives include the construction industry involved in building infrastructure; banks that provided student loans; hospitals (some having converted from nonprofit to for-profit status); insurance companies; and physicians and other health care providers.

Two instances of inadequate supportive feedback mechanisms demonstrate how weak support creates political vulnerability. Despite the increasing use of scientific information throughout the federal government, a priority encouraged by Johnson himself, the science-advisory capacity that LBJ established failed to mobilize the support of the scientific community. In fact, the national scientific community was divided, and opposition to the war in Vietnam contributed to Johnson's downgrading of this advisory function because of its susceptibility to the antiwar sentiments of the scientific community. After Johnson, federal scientific agencies have found only tepid support for their missions from the science-advisory capacity of the Executive Office of the President. Nor was the broader scientific community, outside government, supportive of those missions.

In the second case—the implementation of PPBS—the initiative relied largely on voluntary compliance by agencies, despite the coordinating role attempted by the OMB. Without associated changes in congressional appropriations structures, or sanctions applicable to noncompliant agencies, there were no reinforcing mechanisms to support the goal of PPBS making federal policy making more cost-effective. Even though the federal bureaucracy appreciated the introduction of planning and evaluation through PPBS, the Nixon administration terminated the effort even though the role of analysis and evaluation would eventually become institutionalized.

Public Attitudes and Values

The implementation of Johnson's legacies led, both immediately and over time, to changes in public attitudes and values concerning appropriate ways to promote the general welfare of Americans. At least until the political swing to the right that began in earnest in the 1980s, and the eventual shift to the right of the U.S. Supreme Court following a sequence of conservative appointments after 2001, Americans were more egalitarian and more disposed to support civil and human rights for both themselves and oppressed groups around the globe.

Among the most important of these changed values are those that sustain public policies for racial and gender equality, educational opportunities for low-income and early-childhood students, poverty alleviation for those who are poor for reasons beyond their control, and health care access for older Americans as well as those who cannot afford private health insurance. Placing issues of environmental quality on the public agenda gave momentum to the environmental movement that ensued, which, though weakened in later decades, still provides a broad base of political support renewed by subsequent generations of young activists.

Some of the consequential changes in America's political ethos are indirect, however. Though the OEO and federal support of community action disappeared almost immediately following the end of Johnson's presidency, contemporary grassroots activism, now supported by local governments, community foundations, and nonprofit entities (including faith institutions), undoubtedly derives its energy from Johnson-era efforts to promote community organization and leadership development. In a similar vein, even though Johnson's executive order directing the creation of a government-wide budgeting-system program was repealed by his successor, the catalyzing idea that policy makers should have access to expert knowledge and ideas took root in political culture at all levels of American government. It is now manifest in state and local planning and program-development offices, the Congressional Budget Office, the Government Accountability Office, the proliferation of new and expanded think tanks and consultancies devoted to policy issues, and university degree programs that train policy professionals for public service.

Even as they advanced and modernized American liberalism, many Johnson policies were, or became, ideologically polarizing. For example, a deep ideological cleavage now dominates immigration politics as the nation moves toward the majority-minority demographic status that already exists in some states and in local jurisdictions in most large cities. Attempts by states to satisfy the standards of the VRA have produced implausible electoral maps and political controversy around election systems. A larger, more influential, more centralized, and more expensive federal government is now vigorously opposed by a Republican Party complaining of federal overreach, dangerous levels of government debt, tax burdens thought to stifle economic growth, and unconscionable duplication and waste.

In other policy areas, commitment to values that Johnson promoted has faded. Public support for a social safety net of the dimensions that LBJ advocated has declined. No clearer direction of this movement can be seen than in the welfare reform of the 1990s, under the leadership of a Democratic president, which ended an entitlement to income support for those in poverty. U.S. society rejected the complete abandonment of the social safety net, but it surely was shredded. Similarly, later administrations sustained compensatory funding for the education of poor children, but de facto segregation of schools (by race, ethnicity, and socioeconomic status) has become common once again. Americans have become skeptical of or ambivalent toward once broadly shared values concerning the expansion of access to health care and the need to confront and eliminate poverty through public sector programs.

LBJ's Ultimate Legacy: Politics of Change

Johnson was a political man, a product of the liberal democratic politics of his time. He changed American public policy and institutions in the direction charted by FDR. In the institutionalized values rooted in New Deal, Fair Deal, New Frontier, and Great Society, LBJ's legacies live on.

The effects of Johnson's efforts are, as seen above, evident in contemporary American politics. For some of the more controversial measures, Johnson himself anticipated continual reshaping of those initiatives. Some current political conflicts are consequences of political compromises that subordinated foreseeable problems of implementation, an inevitable result of Johnson's "laws on the books" strategy and its short-run focus. Still other effects were unanticipated when the original laws were put on the books and have emerged only over time.

The shift to the political right that began with the Nixon presidency became pronounced under Reagan. President Johnson, who was trying to complete the New Deal, could not have foreseen the level of polarization that would surface at the time of the Obama administration. The phenomenon that has enabled much of Johnson's legacy to survive that shift is the political sustainability of many of his policies, especially in civil rights, voting rights, education, health, environmental protection, transportation, and modern public management. The dark side of that sustainability, however—the sustainability of New Deal/Great Society liberalism—is that badly needed changes in programs such as Medicare, Medicaid, and Social Security have been thwarted by the politics of sustainability: the resistance to change of "entitlement" constituencies and "interest group" liberalism are also Johnsonian legacies.

Johnson understood the political consequences of the Civil Rights Act and the Voting Rights Act. He understood that the passage of those bills meant the end of dominance for the Democratic Party in the South. Although desegregation and the enforcement of equal protection of the law for women, racial and ethnic minorities, and, later, handicapped children and the disabled are no longer as volatile as they once were, the extension and enforcement of rights for protected groups remain litigious and, as in the case of equal rights for gays, have been highly divisive. Issues associated with race, ethnicity, gender, and other forms of discrimination, many of which originated during the Johnson era, are now, arguably even more than then, at the center of American politics. The establishment and enforcement of those rights is a big idea that endures.

Unforeseen, however, were the long-term consequences of the Immigration Act's elimination of discriminatory visa categories. The resulting growth in Hispanic immigration has led to major demographic shifts that have had transformative social, cultural, political, legal, and programmatic effects. With the U.S. Bureau of Citizenship and Immigration Services continuing to follow Johnson-era visa policies, changing demographic patterns and associated population growth will continue to alter the American political landscape toward a minorities-as-majority politics. In another example of the unforeseen, tensions between the scientific community and the presidency might have been inevitable, but Johnson's imposing of political priorities on federal support for science and technology, and his downgrading of the role of science advisers, which Eisenhower had elevated, were immediately sustained by the Nixon administration and continued by many successors, for many of the same political reasons.

Medicare might well serve as a cautionary tale for those designing complex legislation such as the Patient Protection and Affordable Care Act of 2010. The Medicare program combines structural defects traceable to Johnson's indifference to downstream implementation problems. It enjoys a political invulnerability due to the entitlement to cost-reimbursed health care it provides to all older Americans. Financed by a permanent appropriation, the program's continuing cost growth has become the major contributor to federal budget deficits and rising national debt. Entitlement reform has become an increasingly divisive and partisan issue in American politics. Democrats favor increases in progressive income tax rates, and Republicans favor benefit reductions, privatization, and other structural changes. Controversies have also marred the popularity of student loan programs as controversies over borrowers' debt burdens, repayment rates, and appropriate interest rates occurred.

Like the twentieth century's other progressive presidents, Johnson further centralized policy-making authority and institutional capability in the federal government. It has not been a zero-sum game, however, in which subnational governments lost what the federal government gained. As discussed earlier, many Johnson-era initiatives stimulated growth in the capability, enforcement obligations, and regulatory authority of state and local governments as well. For example, all states and many localities now have departments of transportation or equivalent agencies. Urban- and community-planning agencies have proliferated to administer and coordinate disparate programs. Enforcing federal Medicaid eligibility and coverage rules has become increasingly controversial as state Medicaid budgets have grown.

The reins of authority, especially over financial flows and the court-recognized enforceability of federal rules, continue to be firmly, even if less visibly, held in Washington; state and local dependence on federal financial grants, transfer payments, permanent appropriations, and the like ensures continuing accountability to Congress. Thus, the interdependence that promotes policy sustainability has both good and bad political consequences. Pushback from Republican and centrist administrations began with Johnson's successor, Richard Nixon, who emphasized the New Federalism: devolution of authority, services integration, and an increased role for civil society and market forces. In recent years, a serious political effort has been mounted to reverse New Deal/Great Society federal growth under the banners of ending federal overreach, achieving sustainable fiscal balance, and restoring states' rights.

As Robert Dallek points out in chapter 2, Lyndon Johnson is unfailingly remembered for the manifold effects of the war in Vietnam. By studying the institutional changes that LBJ initiated in domestic government and their consequences, this volume has documented his neglected legacy: the transformation of American governing institutions, public values, and politics, which has furthered the progressive governance initiated by Theodore Roosevelt and Franklin D. Roosevelt, and nurtured and protected by Harry S. Truman and John F. Kennedy. LBJ—the master legislator—was also an agent of social and political change. Farsighted policy makers have much to learn from the legacy of Lyndon Johnson.

Notes

1. Abraham Lincoln signed the Morrill Act to fund state land grant colleges in 1862.

2. The Bureau of Public Roads had originally been located in the Department of Agriculture, and then transferred to the Public Works Agency in the 1930s and to the Department of Commerce in 1949.

3. See chapters 9 (Osborne) and 10 (Glickman and Wilson) for discussions of maximum feasible participation.

References

Katznelson, Ira. 2013. *Fear itself: The New Deal and the origins of our time.* New York: Liveright.

Heclo, Hugh. 2006. Thinking institutionally. In R. A. W. Rhodes, Sarah A. Binder, and Bert A. Rockman, eds., *The Oxford handbook of political institutions.* New York: Oxford University Press.

Skowronek, Stephen. 2009. Mission accomplished. *Political Studies Quarterly* 39, no. 4: 795–804.

Acknowledgments

LBJ's Neglected Legacy: How Lyndon Johnson Reshaped Domestic Policy and Government is the outcome of a broad enterprise that owes much to a variety of people and institutions. The effort began in December 2008 when the LBJ School of Public Affairs at the University of Texas at Austin sponsored a symposium to commemorate the centennial of Lyndon Johnson's birth by reflecting on some of the groundbreaking domestic policies passed during his administration. The Lyndon Baines Johnson Foundation provided the resources needed for that conference and the subsequent research leading to this book. Betty Sue Flowers, then director of the LBJ Library, and James Steinberg, the former dean of the LBJ School of Public Affairs, provided organizational and intellectual leadership for that venture. In the second phase of the project that led to this publication, Robert Hutchings, the current dean of the LBJ School, and members of his staff offered important backing.

The Mike Hogg Professorship for Urban Policy, at the University of Texas at Austin, a position held by Robert Wilson, and the Distinguished University Professorship at Rutgers University, a position held by Norman Glickman, provided funding for the project. Finally, the Woodrow Wilson International Center for Scholars in Washington, D.C., provided in-kind research support during Robert Wilson's appointment as a Public Policy Scholar in 2011.

We thank Arlene Pashman and Cheryl McVay for excellent and careful editing of the manuscript. They helped make the text more readable and interesting. Beth Rutter provided critical logistical support during the last phases of the project. The LBJ Library and Museum was an important resource for the research conducted for several of the chapters in this volume. We are indebted to the expertise and helpfulness of its staff. Robert

Devens, editor in chief of the University of Texas Press, was instrumental in bringing the manuscript to production. We also thank our external reviewers for comments and critical assessments of a draft of the book. In sum, we are grateful to the many that have made concrete contributions to enhancing this piece of work.

Finally, we thank our wives, Elyse Pivnick, Pat Lynn, and Rita Wilson, for their support and patience while we toiled over this manuscript.

Norman J. Glickman, Princeton, New Jersey
Laurence E. Lynn Jr., Austin, Texas
Robert H. Wilson, Austin, Texas
May 2014

Contributors

Editors

NORMAN J. GLICKMAN is Distinguished University Professor at Rutgers University. He has written and edited more than ten books and monographs and one hundred articles, including, as coauthor, both *The New Competitors: How Foreign Investors are Changing the U.S. Economy* and *The State of the Nation's Cities: America's Changing Urban Life.*

LAURENCE E. LYNN JR., formerly Sid Richardson Research Professor at the Lyndon B. Johnson School of Public Affairs, University of Texas at Austin, is the Sydney Stein, Jr. Professor of Public Management Emeritus at the University of Chicago. Recent publications include *Public Management: A Three-Dimensional Approach* (with Carolyn J. Hill), *Public Management: Old and New,* and *Madison's Managers: Public Administration and the Constitution* (with Anthony M. Bertelli).

ROBERT H. WILSON is the Mike Hogg Professor of Urban Policy at the Lyndon B. Johnson School of Public Affairs, the University of Texas at Austin. His publications include, as coeditor, *Metropolitan Governance in the Federalist Americas: Case Studies and Strategies for Equitable and Integrated Development; Urban Segregation and Governance in the Americas;* and *Governance in the Americas.*

Contributors

FRANK D. BEAN is Chancellor's Professor of Sociology and the director of the Center for Research on Immigration, Population and Public Policy at the University of California, Irvine. His most recent book (winner of the American Sociological Association Population Section's Otis Dudley Duncan Award) is *The Diversity Paradox: Immigration and the Color Line in 21st Century America* (with Jennifer Lee).

SUSAN K. BROWN is an associate professor of sociology and the director of the Program for Demographic and Social Analysis at the University of California, Irvine. She coauthored "The Dimensions and Degree of Second-Generation Incorporation in U.S. and European Cities" (*International Journal of Comparative Sociology*).

ESTHER CASTILLO is a lecturer in the Department of Sociology, University of California, Fullerton. She is coauthor of a chapter in *Members-Only Assimilation? Unauthorized Migration and Mexican American Mobility* (forthcoming).

JORGE CHAPA is a professor at the Institute of Government and Public Affairs and in the Departments of Sociology and Latina/o Studies at the University of Illinois in Urbana-Champaign. He is coeditor of *Implementing Diversity: Contemporary Challenges and Best Practices at Predominantly White Universities* (2010) and coauthor of *Apple Pie and Enchiladas: Latino Newcomers in the Rural Midwest* (2004).

GARY CHAPMAN was a senior lecturer at the LBJ School of Public Affairs at the University of Texas at Austin, which he joined in 1994, until his untimely death in 2011. He published on technology and society in a wide variety of venues, including the *New York Times, New Republic, Washington Post, Technology Review, Communications of the ACM*, and many others.

ROBERT DALLEK is a professor of history emeritus at the University of California, Los Angeles. In addition to a two-volume biography of Lyndon Johnson, his recent work includes *An Unfinished Life: John F. Kennedy, 1917–1963, Nixon and Kissinger: Partners in Power*, and *Camelot's Court: Inside the Kennedy White House*.

DAVID J. EATON is the Bess Harris Jones Centennial Professor in Natural Resource Policy Studies at the LBJ School of Public Affairs, University of Texas at Austin. Among his recent publications are *The American Title Insurance Industry* and *A Comprehensive Transboundary Water Quality Management Agreement: ASCEI EWRI Standard 33-09*.

KIMBERLY FRANCIS is a senior research associate in social and economic policy at Abt Associates, Inc.

PETER FRUMKIN is a professor of social policy, faculty director of the Center for Social Impact Strategy and director of the Master's in Nonprofit Leadership program, all at the University of Pennsylvania. His recent publications include *Building for the Arts* and *The Strategic Management of Charter Schools*.

GARY ORFIELD is a professor of education, law, political science, and urban planning at the University of California, Los Angeles. He recently coedited *The Resegregation of Suburban Schools: A Hidden Crisis in American Education* and *Educational Delusions? Why Choice Can Deepen Inequality and How to Make Schools Fair*.

CYNTHIA OSBORNE is an associate professor and the director of the Child and Family Research Partnership at the LBJ School of Public Affairs at the University of Texas at Austin. She has published numerous articles highlighting the changing nature of the American family and its implications for children living in poverty. Her articles have appeared in journals such as *Demography*, the *Journal of Marriage and Family*, and *Social Science Review*.

ELIZABETH ROSE is library director at the Fairfield Museum and History Center in Fairfield, Connecticut; she previously taught American history at Vanderbilt University and Trinity College. She is the author of *The Promise of Preschool: From Head Start to Universal Pre-kindergarten* and A *Mother's Job: The History of Day Care, 1890–1960*.

PAUL STARR is professor of sociology and public affairs and Stuart Professor of Communications and Public Affairs at Princeton University. His work includes *The Social Transformation of American Medicine* (1983), *Freedom's Power: The History and Promise of Liberalism* (2008), and *Remedy and Reaction: The Peculiar American Struggle over Health-Care Reform* (2011).

Index